Best Places to Raise Your Family

The Top 100 Affordable Communities in the U.S.

1st Edition

Bert Sperling and Peter Sander

WILEY

Wiley Publishing, Inc.

Acknowledgments

The list of folks who helped along the way is long. First, there are the dozens upon dozens of interviewees who took the time to tell us more about where they live and why it's a good place—or not—for families. In alphabetical order by last name, notables include Susan Aser, Laurel Ballou, Milly Banta, Jonathan Bowen, Mike Casale, Richard Casiello, Lee Colarossi, Pat Conard, René Gabrielle, Mercedes Hendriksson, John Hernandez, Carol Hess, Don Kilander, Gerry King, Connie Kuntzman, Ann Latta, Rudy Meyer, Carolyn Parks, Dale Reel, Kathy Russell, Phyllis Schmidt, Sherry St. John, Kathy Stephens, Pam Stevens, Rhonda Thomas, and Kathy Tucker, among many, many others. The deadline was tight and it wouldn't have been met without the help of J. Scott Bobo of San Jose, California, and ShaNeena Hunter of Sacramento, California. And none of this research would have turned into a book without the excellent professional work of Jenny Anmuth and the rest of the editorial and production team at Wiley. Finally, the book wouldn't have happened at all without the motivation and support rendered by my family: wife Jennifer, and boys Julian and Jonathan who largely inspired it in the first place.

—Peter Sander

For over twenty years, my work has been to evaluate and compare different cities and towns. I'd like to thank all the people who have shared their experiences and feelings about their hometown, so I could tell others about the special place they've found. I'd also like to thank my associates, Adam DuVander and Al Olsen, whose work has enabled our studies and information to reach millions of people. I was very fortunate that my sons, Ted Sperling and Bert Sperling, were able to take some time from their busy lives to help with this book's research and analysis, and contribute their opinions. Finally and most importantly, I want to thank my wife, Gretchen, for her insights and unwavering support of our mission. Much of my work is the result of our long discussions about livability and the sense of place that is so important to any community.

—Bert Sperling

Editor: Jenny Anmuth
Production Editor: M. Faunette Johnston
Cartographer: Andrew Dolan
Photo Editor: Richard Fox
Interior Designer: Melissa Auciello-Brogan
Production by Wiley Indianapolis Composition Services

Contents

Contents

Contents

List of Tables & Maps

Tables

List of Tables & Maps

Maps

Icons Used in this Book

BEST OF THE BEST   The "top ten" best places to raise your family.

BEST   A "top ten" place in a specific category, such as Education, Standard of Living, Lifestyle, and/or Health & Safety.

TIPS   Insider tips on how to find your best place.

★   Important information you should know.

About the Authors

Peter Sander is a professional author, researcher, and consultant in the fields of business and personal finance. He has written 13 books including *Cities Ranked & Rated*, *Value Investing For Dummies*, *The 250 Personal Finance Questions Everyone Should Ask*, *The Pocket Idiot's Guide to Living on a Budget*, and *Niche and Grow Rich*. His educational background includes an MBA in Logistics Management from Indiana University, a BA in Urban Affairs and Administration from Miami University of Ohio, and professional training and examination as a Certified Financial Planner (CFP™). His career includes 20 years as a marketing and logistics program manager at a major high tech firm. Among numerous national and local television and radio appearances, Sander's credits include NBC *Today*, CNBC, CNNfn, Fox News, and Business Talk Radio. Originally from Cincinnati, OH, and now living with his wife and family in Granite Bay, CA, he has traveled in all 50 U.S. states.

For twenty years, **Bert Sperling** has been helping people find their own Best Place to live, work, play, and retire. His work continues to appear in the national media nearly every month. His 2004 book, *Cities Ranked and Rated* (also co-authored with Peter Sander) profiles metro areas in the United States and Canada, and was introduced on the *Today* show.

Sperling's studies and comparisons of cities cover a broad range, including such topics as best places to Live, Best Places for Seniors, Best Places to Retire, Most Stressful Cities, Best Cities for Dating, Most Fiscally Fit Cities, America's Healthiest Cities, Most Drivable Cities, Best and Worst Cities for Fleas, Most Romantic Cities, Most Photogenic Cities, Best Places to Buy a Second Home, Best Cities for Teens, Most Unwired Cities (Wi-Fi), Best Cities for Sleep, and Most Fun Cities. His firm's website, **www.bestplaces.net**, provides insight and guidance to millions of visitors each month, and its content is found on such websites as MSN, eBay, Yahoo!, and the *Wall Street Journal*.

Bert was born in Brooklyn, New York, and has lived in such diverse places as Kodiak, Alaska; Carmel Valley, California; Key West, Florida; Oslo, Norway; and Long Island, New York. He currently makes his home in Portland and Depoe Bay, Oregon, with his wife Gretchen, and their faithful English Bull Terriers, Ruthie and Molly.

An Invitation to the Reader

Throughout this book, we identified many important facts related to living in a place, and added elements of each place's livability and character. But there's always more to know. We'd appreciate your "across the back fence" comments about living in a place, and we also encourage your feedback on the other topics of interest—facts or analysis—you would like to see covered in future books. Please post your responses at **www.bestplaces.net/rankedandrated** or **rankedandrated.blogspot.com,** or write to:

Best Places to Raise Your Family, 1st Edition
Wiley Publishing, Inc.
111 River St., 5th Floor
Hoboken, NJ 07030-5774

100 Best Places: Ranked & Rated by Category

Drumroll please . . . here are the 100 top affordable communities in the United States in which to raise your family, listed alphabetically. *Note:* To review the 100 places organized in more comprehensive tables (grouped alphabetically and by region), with more information (such as state, size, and nearest metro area), please flip to p. 10 and p. 12 at the end of this section.

The 100 Best Places to Raise Your Family

Abilene, TX

Albuquerque (Sandia Heights), NM

Anchorage, AK

Appleton, WI

Arden-Brandywine, DE

Arlington, TX

Austin (West), TX

Bellingham, WA

Bethlehem, PA

Broken Arrow, OK

Cary, NC

Castle Rock, CO

Charlottesville, VA

Chelmsford, MA

Columbia, MD

Columbia, MO

Coralville, IA

Coraopolis–Moon Township, PA

DeForest, WI

Denver (Park Hill), CO

Eagle, ID

East Islip, NY

Elkhorn, NE

Eugene, OR

Evendale, OH

Fargo, ND

Farragut, TN

Flower Mound, TX

Folsom, CA

Fort Collins, CO

Franklin, TN

Gainesville, FL

Gaithersburg, MD

Getzville, NY

Grants Pass, OR

Green Bay, WI

Greer, SC

Herndon, VA

Hilliard, OH

Hixson, TN

Hollywood Park, TX

Hudsonville, MI

Irmo, SC

Kaysville, UT

continued

1

100 Best Places: Ranked & Rated by Category

Kendall Park, NJ

Lake Zurich, IL

Lakeville, MN

Lancaster, PA

Lawrence, KS

Lexington, KY

Livingston, NJ

Logan, UT

Loma Linda, CA

Louisville, CO

Madison, AL

Matthews, NC

Maumee, OH

Minden, NV

Mobile West, AL

Mount Vernon, WA

Mukilteo, WA

Nashua, NH

Newtown, CT

Noblesville, IN

North Attleboro, MA

Norwood, NJ

Oak Park, IL

Olympia, WA

Orange Park, FL

Pittsford, NY

Rancho Santa Margarita, CA

Rapid City, SD

Reno, NV

Richmond, VA

Roanoke, VA

Rochester, MN

Rogers, AR

Roswell, GA

Santa Clarita, CA

Sharon, MA

Shawnee, KS

Sheboygan, WI

Spokane, OR

St. Charles, MO

Sugar Land, TX

Tyler, TX

Valrico, FL

Vancouver-Camas, WA

Virginia Beach, VA

Waukesha, WI

Wausau, WI

West Chester, PA

West Des Moines–Clive, IA

West Lafayette, IN

West Nyack, NY

Weston, FL

Wichita (West), KS

Winchester, VA

Winters, CA

York, PA

While researching and writing this book, we examined thousands of facts and figures (which you'll see in our many data tables), but we also spent hours pondering statistics that don't fit into those tables, conversations that don't get quoted, and gut feelings that aren't easily put into words. For most great places, it's the *combination* of hard facts and intangibles that makes each one great. In other words, what's most important is how everything works together. We wanted to present what "bubbled up" to the top for us in a fun and informative way; hence, the following rankings of best places in various categories.

Remember, of course, that these are our own personal, subjective assessments based largely on individual perceptions and experience. Hopefully, they'll help you sort through the longer list of places and take notice of neighborhoods you might not have otherwise read about. But take them for what they are: recommendations based on our expert opinions.

Because we consider all 100 places in this book to be the best, it was hard to rank them from 1 to 100, but we can certainly tell you what we think are the top 10, or in other words: the overall "Best of the Best." Each of these top 10 places is denoted here, as well as with a Best-of-the-Best icon in chapter 5.

Best of the Best

1. Louisville, CO
2. Gaithersburg MD
3. Roswell, GA
4. Lakeville, MN
5. Flower Mound, TX

6. Fort Collins, CO
7. Cary, NC
8. Sugar Land, TX
9. Columbia, MD
10. Noblesville, IN

The following lists are our "Best Bets" in the book's five major categories, along with additional "runners-up" presented to give you a bigger picture. Each of the places listed in these five "Best for" categories is denoted with a [BEST] icon in its neighborhood highlights table in chapter 5.

Note: The places in the following lists are listed alphabetically, and are not ranked in any particular order.

Best for Standard of Living

Austin (West), TX
Elkhorn, NE
Farragut, TN
Flower Mound, TX
Hollywood Park, TX

Madison, AL
Pittsford, NY
Roswell, GA
Shawnee, KS
Sugar Land, TX

Best for Standard of Living Runners-up

Arlington, TX
Cary, NC
Evendale, OH
Green Bay, WI
Irmo, SC

Noblesville, IN
Richmond-Tuckahoe, VA
Rogers, AR
Sheboygan, WI
St. Charles, MO

Best for Education

Cary, NC
Charlottesville, VA
Gainesville, FL
Gaithersburg, MD
Louisville, CO

Roswell, GA
Sharon, MA
Sugar Land, TX
West Lafayette, IN
West Nyack, NY

Best for Education Runners-up

Flower Mound, TX
Lake Zurich, IL
Lakeville, MN
Livingston, NJ
Newtown, CT

Noblesville, IN
Pittsford, NY
Rancho Santa Margarita, CA
Richmond-Tuckahoe, VA
West Des Moines–Clive, IA

Best for Lifestyle

Albuquerque (Sandia Heights), NM
Columbia, MD
Fort Collins, CO
Louisville, CO
Mukilteo, WA

Newtown, CT
Oak Park, IL
Rancho Santa Margarita, CA
Reno, NV
Winchester, VA

Best for Lifestyle Runners-up

Austin (West), TX
Bellingham, WA
Castle Rock, CO
Charlottesville, VA
Denver (Park Hill), CO
Eagle, ID
Eugene, OR
Folsom, CA
Gaithersburg, MD
Kaysville, UT

Lakeville, MN
Logan, UT
Minden, NV
Roanoke, VA
Sharon, MA
Spokane, WA
Vancouver, WA
Virginia Beach, VA
West Chester, PA
Weston, FL

Best for Health & Safety

Appleton, WI
Columbia, MO
Coralville, IA
DeForest, WI
Fargo, ND

Nashua, NH
Roanoke, VA
Rochester, MN
West Des Moines–Clive, IA
Winchester, VA

Best for Health & Safety Runners-up

Cary, NC
Charlottesville, VA
Elkhorn, NE
Farragut, TN
Green Bay, WI

Lexington, KY
Rapid City, SD
Richmond-Tuckahoe, VA
Sheboygan, WI
Wausau, WI

Author's Choice Awards

The following categories and lists are just for fun, and to help give you an overview of what stood out for us among the 100 best places to raise your family.

Note: The places in the following lists are listed alphabetically, and are not ranked in any particular order.

In the Standard of Living Category
Best Blue-Collar Bets
Appleton, WI

Bellingham, WA

Green Bay, WI

Hilliard, OH

Lancaster, PA

Roanoke, VA

Tyler, TX

Sheboygan, WI

West Mobile, AL

York, PA

Best Places for Big Houses on a Budget
Broken Arrow, OK

Elkhorn, NE

Flower Mound, TX

Irmo, SC

Madison, AL

Matthews, NC

Noblesville, IN

Pittsford, NY

West Mobile, AL

Wichita (West), KS

Best Places for the New Economy
Albuquerque (Sandia Heights), NM

Austin (West), TX

Cary, NC

Chelmsford, MA

Eagle, ID

Fort Collins, CO

Gainesville, FL

Louisville, CO

Madison, AL

Mukilteo, WA

Best Where-the-Puck-Is-Going Places
Bellingham, WA

Coraopolis–Moon Township, PA

Madison, AL

Matthews, NC

Minden, NV

Mount Vernon, WA

Richmond, VA

Shawnee, KS

Sheboygan, WI

Winters, CA

Best Work-at-Home Neighborhoods
Bellingham, WA

Bethlehem, PA

Charlottesville, VA

Fort Collins, CO

Lexington, KY

Mount Vernon, WA

Sheboygan, WI

Winchester, VA

Winters, CA

York, PA

In the Education Category
Best-in-Class Schools
Austin (West), TX

Coraopolis–Moon Township, PA

Flower Mound, TX

Folsom, CA

Gaithersburg, MD

Herndon, VA

Lake Zurich, IL

Noblesville, IN

Rancho Santa Margarita, CA

West Nyack, NY

Best College-Town Scenes

Austin (West), TX
Charlottesville, VA
Columbia, MO
Coralville, IA
DeForest, WI
Eugene, OR

Fort Collins, CO
Gainesville, FL
Lawrence, KS
Lexington, KY
Logan, UT
West Lafayette, IN

In the Lifestyle Category

Best Cul-de-Sac Suburbia

Arlington, TX
Coraopolis–Moon Township, PA
Folsom, CA
Hilliard, OH
Lakeville, MN

Louisville, CO
Orange Park, FL
Rancho Santa Margarita, CA
Santa Clarita, CA
Shawnee, KS

Best City Neighborhoods

Appleton, WI
Denver (Park Hill), CO
Maumee, OH

Oak Park, IL
Sheboygan, WI

Best Small-Town Feel

Abilene, TX
Fargo, ND
Fort Collins, CO
Grants Pass, OR
Greer, SC
Logan, UT

Mount Vernon, WA
Noblesville, IN
Sheboygan, WI
Winchester, VA
York, PA

Best for Outdoorsy Types

Camas, WA
Charlottesville, VA
Eagle, ID
Fort Collins, CO
Grants Pass, OR

Irmo, SC
Minden, NV
Rapid City, SD
Spokane, WA
Wausau, WI

Best Picture-Postcard Settings

Anchorage, AK
Charlottesville, VA
Eagle, ID
Fort Collins, CO
Hixson, TN

Minden, NV
Mount Vernon, WA
Mukilteo, WA
Newtown, CT
Olympia, WA

Best for Just Plain Fun
Arlington, TX
East Islip, NY
Farragut, TN
Folsom, CA
Grants Pass, OR

Minden, NV
Orange Park, FL
Richmond-Tuckahoe, VA
Santa Clarita, CA
Virginia Beach, VA

Best Capitol Ideas
Austin (West), TX
Cary, NC
DeForest, WI
Denver (Park Hill), CO
Folsom, CA

Hilliard, OH
Noblesville, IN
Olympia, WA
Richmond, VA
West Des Moines–Clive, IA

Best for a Country (& Western) Feel
Abilene, TX
Broken Arrow, OK
Castle Rock, CO
Eagle, ID
Kaysville, UT

Logan, UT
Minden, NV
Rapid City, SD
Rogers, AR
Tyler, TX

Best for Water Sports
Bellingham, WA
Farragut, TN
Flower Mound, TX
Folsom, CA
Grants Pass, OR

Irmo, SC
Orange Park, FL
Rancho Santa Margarita, CA
Virginia Beach, VA
Weston, FL

Best for Beach Lovers
Arden-Brandywine, DE
East Islip, NY
Orange Park, FL
Rancho Santa Margarita, CA
Santa Clarita, CA

Sugar Land, TX
Valrico, FL
Virginia Beach, VA
West Mobile, AL
Weston, FL

Best Small-Town Downtowns
Bellingham, WA
DeForest, WI
Eugene, OR
Fort Collins, CO
Lexington, KY

Noblesville, IN
Roanoke, VA
Sharon, MA
Sheboygan, WI
West Chester, PA

100 Best Places: Ranked & Rated by Category

Best Big-City Downtowns

Chelmsford, MA

Denver (Park Hill), CO

Kaysville, UT

Lakeville, MN

Mukilteo, WA

Norwood, NJ

Oak Park, IL

Sharon, MA

Vancouver-Camas, WA

West Nyack, NY

Best for the Art(s) Minded

Coraopolis–Moon Township, PA

Evendale, OH

Gaithersburg, MD

Getzville, NY

Hudsonville, MI

Mukilteo, WA

Oak Park, IL

Pittsford, NY

Roanoke, VA

Vancouver-Camas, WA

Best for Professional Sports Lovers

Coraopolis–Moon Township, PA

Evendale, OH

Flower Mound, TX

Getzville, NY

Lake Zurich, IL

Noblesville, IN

North Attleboro, MA

Roswell, GA

Shawnee, KS

St. Charles, MO

Best Power 'Burbs

Coraopolis–Moon Township, PA

Eagle, ID

Flower Mound, TX

Herndon, VA

Lake Zurich, IL

Lakeville, MN

Rancho Santa Margarita, CA

Roswell, GA

Santa Clarita, CA

Sugar Land, TX

Best for Nature Lovers

Bellingham, WA

Eugene, OR

Farragut, TN

Gainesville, FL

Mount Vernon, WA

Norwood, NJ

Olympia, WA

Sharon, MA

Vancouver-Camas, WA

Waukesha, WI

Best Warm-All-Winter Places

Gainesville, FL

Hollywood Park, TX

Loma Linda, CA

Orange Park, FL

Rancho Santa Margarita, CA

Santa Clarita, CA

Sugar Land, TX

Valrico, FL

West Mobile, AL

Weston, FL

Best Winter Sports Wonderlands
Appleton, WI
Fargo, ND
Fort Collins, CO

Reno, NV
Wausau, WI

Best for History Buffs
Arden-Brandywine, DE
Charlottesville, VA
Chelmsford, MA
Franklin, TN
Hixson, TN

Oak Park, IL
Richmond-Tuckahoe, VA
St. Charles, MO
Winchester, VA
York, PA

Best for Sun Gods & Goddesses
Abilene, TX
Albuquerque (Sandia Heights), NM
Folsom, CA
Loma Linda, CA
Minden, NV

Rancho Santa Margarita, CA
Reno, NV
Santa Clarita, CA
Weston, FL
Winters, CA

In the Health & Safety Category

Best If Health Is Your Care
Fargo, ND
Loma Linda, CA
Roanoke, VA

Rochester, MN
Tyler, TX

Best Places to Keep Your Door Unlocked
Castle Rock, CO
Elkhorn, NE
Hilliard, OH
Kendall Park, NJ
Lake Zurich, IL

Lakeville, MN
Nashua, NH
Newtown, CT
Pittsford, NY
Roswell, GA

THE 100 BEST PLACES TO RAISE YOUR FAMILY
GROUPED ALPHABETICALLY

	NEIGHBORHOOD NAME	ZIP CODE	NEIGBORHOOD TYPE	APPROXIMATE LOCATION	METRO AREA NAME	METRO AREA CATEGORY
1	Abilene, TX	79606	Small city	North central TX	Abilene, TX	SMALLER
2	Albuquerque (Sandia Heights), NM	87122	Outer suburb	Albuquerque northeast	Albuquerque, NM	MID-SIZED
3	Anchorage, AK	99516	Small city	South central AK	Anchorage, AK	SMALLER
4	Appleton, WI	54911	Small city	East central WI	Appleton-Oshkosh-Neenah, WI	SMALLER
5	Arden-Brandywine, DE	19810	Inner suburb	Wilmington northeast	Wilmington-Newark, DE-MD	MID-SIZED
6	Arlington, TX	76002	Outer suburb	Fort Worth southeast	Fort Worth–Arlington, TX	LARGEST
7	Austin (West), TX	78732	Outer suburb	Austin west	Austin–San Marcos, TX	MID-SIZED
8	Bellingham, WA	98226	Small city	Northern WA	Bellingham, WA	SMALLER
9	Bethlehem, PA	18018	Small city	Southeastern PA	Allentown-Bethlehem-Easton, PA	MID-SIZED
10	Broken Arrow, OK	74012	Outer suburb	Tulsa east	Tulsa, OK	MID-SIZED
11	Cary, NC	27513	Outer suburb	Research Triangle cities area	Raleigh-Durham–Chapel Hill, NC	MID-SIZED
12	Castle Rock, CO	80104	Suburban town	Denver south	Denver, CO	LARGE
13	Charlottesville, VA	22901	Small college town	West central VA	Charlottesville, VA	SMALLER
14	Chelmsford, MA	01824	Outer suburb/ suburban town	Boston north	Lowell, MA-NH	LARGEST
15	Columbia, MD	21045	Outer suburb/exurb	Central MD	Baltimore, MD	LARGE
16	Columbia, MO	65203	Small college town	East central MO	Columbia, MO	SMALLER
17	Coralville, IA	52241	College-town suburb	Iowa City west	Iowa City, IA	SMALLER
18	Coraopolis–Moon Township, PA	15108	Outer suburb/ suburban town	Pittsburgh west	Pittsburgh, PA	LARGE
19	DeForest, WI	53532	College-town suburb	Madison northeast	Madison, WI	MID-SIZED
20	Denver (Park Hill), CO	80220	City neighborhood	Denver east	Denver, CO	LARGE
21	Eagle, ID	83616	Outer suburb/ suburban town	Boise west	Boise City, ID	MID-SIZED
22	East Islip, NY	11730	Outer suburb	Central Long Island	Nassau-Suffolk, NY	LARGEST
23	Elkhorn, NE	68022	Outer suburb/ suburban town	Omaha west	Omaha, NE-IA	MID-SIZED
24	Eugene, OR	97405	Small college town	Central OR	Eugene, OR	SMALLER
25	Evendale, OH	45241	Inner suburb	Cincinnati north	Cincinnati, OH-KY-IN	LARGE
26	Fargo, ND	58104	Small city	Eastern ND	Fargo, ND	SMALLER
27	Farragut, TN	37922	Outer suburb	Knoxville west	Knoxville, TN	MID-SIZED
28	Flower Mound, TX	75028	Outer suburb	Dallas north	Dallas, TX	MEGA
29	Folsom, CA	95630	Outer suburb	Sacramento east	Sacramento, CA	LARGE
30	Fort Collins, CO	80526	Small city	Northern CO	Fort Collins–Loveland, CO	SMALLER
31	Franklin, TN	37064	Satellite city	Nashville south	Nashville, TN	MID-SIZED
32	Gainesville, FL	32605	Small college town	North central FL	Gainesville, FL	SMALLER
33	Gaithersburg, MD	20878	Outer suburn/exurb	DC suburbs	Washington, DC-MD-VA-WV	LARGEST
34	Getzville, NY	14068	Outer suburb	Buffalo northeast	Buffalo–Niagara Falls, NY	MID-SIZED
35	Grants Pass, OR	97526	Small town	Southern OR	Josephine County	SMALLEST
36	Green Bay, WI	54313	Small city	East Central WI	Green Bay, WI	SMALLER
37	Greer, SC	29650	Small town	Northwest SC	Greenville-Spartanburg-Anderson, SC	MID-SIZED
38	Herndon, VA	20170	Outer suburb/exurb	Northern VA	Washington, DC-MD-VA-WV	LARGEST
39	Hilliard, OH	43026	Outer suburb	Columbus west	Columbus, OH	MID-SIZED
40	Hixson, TN	37343	Inner suburb	Chattanooga north	Chattanooga, TN-GA	SMALLER
41	Hollywood Park, TX	78232	Outer suburb	San Antonio north	San Antonio, TX	MID-SIZED
42	Hudsonville, MI	49426	Outer suburb/ suburban town	Grand Rapids southwest	Grand Rapids–Muskegon-Holland, MI	MID-SIZED
43	Irmo, SC	29212	Outer suburb	Columbia northwest	Columbia, SC	MID-SIZED
44	Kaysville, UT	84037	Outer suburb/ suburban town	Ogden south/ Salt Lake City north	Salt Lake City-Ogden, UT	SMALLER
45	Kendall Park, NJ	08824	Outer suburb	Newark/New York City southwest	Middlesex-Somerset-Hunterdon, NJ	LARGEST
46	Lake Zurich, IL	60047	Outer suburb/exurb	Chicago NW	Chicago, IL	LARGEST
47	Lakeville, MN	55044	Outer suburb	Minneapolis–St Paul south	Minneapolis–St. Paul, MN-WI	LARGE
48	Lancaster, PA	17601	Small city	Southeastern PA	Lancaster, PA	SMALLER
49	Lawrence, KS	66049	Small college town	East central KS	Lawrence, KS	SMALLER
50	Lexington, KY	40503	Inner suburb	Lesington south	Lexington, KY	SMALLER
51	Livingston, NJ	07039	Inner suburb	East central New Jersey	Newark, NJ	LARGEST
52	Logan, UT	84321	Small college town	Northern UT	Logan, UT	SMALLEST

NEIGHBORHOOD NAME	ZIP CODE	NEIGBORHOOD TYPE	APPROXIMATE LOCATION	METRO AREA NAME	METRO AREA CATEGORY
53 Loma Linda, CA	92354	Exurb	Inland Empire–Los Angeles east	Riverside–San Bernardino, CA	LARGEST
54 Louisville, CO	80027	Outer suburb/suburban town	Denver NW/Boulder SE	Boulder-Longmont, CO	LARGE
55 Madison, AL	35758	Small town/outer suburb	Huntsville west	Huntsville, AL	SMALLER
56 Matthews, NC	28105	Inner suburb	Charlotte south	Charlotte-Gastonia–Rock Hill, NC-SC	MID-SIZED
57 Maumee, OH	43537	Inner suburb	Toledo west	Toledo, OH	MID-SIZED
58 Minden, NV	89423	Small town	Western NV	Douglas County	SMALLEST
59 Mount Vernon, WA	98273	Small town	Northern WA	Mount Vernon–Anacortes, WA	SMALLEST
60 Mukilteo, WA	98275	Suburban town	Seattle north	Seattle-Bellevue-Everett, WA	LARGEST
61 Nashua, NH	03062	Satellite city	Southern NH/Boston north	Nashua, NH	SMALLER
62 Newtown, CT	06470	Small town	Danbury east/Bridgeport north	Danbury, CT	SMALLER
63 Noblesville, IN	46060	Suburban town	Indianapolis north	Indianapolis, IN	MID-SIZED
64 North Attleboro, MA	02760	Outer suburb/suburban town	Between Boston, Providence	Providence–Fall River–Warwick, RI-MA	LARGE
65 Norwood, NJ	07648	Suburban town	Northern New Jersey	Bergen-Passaic, NJ	LARGEST
66 Oak Park, IL	60302	City neighborhood	Chicago W	Chicago, IL	LARGEST
67 Olympia, WA	98501	Small capital city	West central WA	Olympia, WA	SMALLER
68 Orange Park, FL	32073	Outer suburb	Jacksonville south	Jacksonville, FL	MID-SIZED
69 Pittsford, NY	14534	Inner suburb/suburban town	Rochester southeast	Rochester, NY	MID-SIZED
70 Rancho Santa Margarita, CA	92688	Exurb	Orange Co./Los Angeles southeast	Orange County, CA	LARGEST
71 Rapid City, SD	57702	Small city	Southwestern SD	Rapid City, SD	SMALLEST
72 Reno, NV	89523	Outer suburb	Reno west	Reno, NV	SMALLER
73 Richmond, VA	23233	Small capital city	East central VA	Richmond-Petersburg, VA	MID-SIZED
74 Roanoke-Tuckahoe, VA	24018	Small city	Southwest VA	Roanoke, VA	SMALLER
75 Rochester, MN	55902	Small city	Southeast MN	Rochester, MN	SMALLER
76 Rogers, AR	72758	Small town	Northwest AR	Fayetteville-Springdale-Rogers, AR	SMALLER
77 Roswell, GA	30075	Outer suburb/exurb	Atlanta north	Atlanta, GA	LARGEST
78 St. Charles, MO	63304	Outer suburb/suburban town	St Louis NW	St. Louis, MO-IL	LARGE
79 Santa Clarita, CA	91354	Outer suburb/exurb	Los Angeles northeast	Los Angeles–Long Beach, CA	LARGEST
80 Sharon, MA	02067	Inner suburb/suburban town	Boston south	Boston, MA-NH-ME	LARGEST
81 Shawnee, KS	66216	Outer suburb	Kansas City KS west	Kansas City, MO-KS	LARGE
82 Sheboygan, WI	53044	Small town	Wisconsin Lake Michigan shore	Sheboygan, WI	SMALLEST
83 Spokane, OR	99223	Inner suburb	Spokane south	Spokane, WA	SMALLER
84 Sugar Land, TX	77479	Outer suburb/exurb	Houston southwest	Houston, TX	LARGE
85 Tyler, TX	75791	Small city	East Texas	Tyler, TX	SMALLER
86 Valrico, FL	33594	Outer suburb	Tampa east	Tampa–St. Petersburg-Clearwater, FL	LARGE
87 Vancouver-Camas, WA	98607	Outer suburb/suburban town	Portland northeast	Portland-Vancouver, OR-WA	LARGE
88 Virginia Beach, VA	23456	Satellite city	Southeast VA shore	Norfolk–Virginia Beach–Newport News, VA-NC	LARGE
89 Waukesha, WI	53186	Suburban town	Milwaukee southwest	Milwaukee-Waukesha, WI	MID-SIZED
90 Wausau, WI	54403	Small town	North central, WI	Wausau, WI	SMALLEST
91 West Chester, PA	19382	Satellite city	Philadelphia west	Philadelphia, PA-NJ	LARGEST
92 West Des Moines–Clive, IA	50325	Outer suburb	Des Moines west	Des Moines, IA	MID-SIZED
93 West Lafayette, IN	47906	Small college town	Northwest IN	Lafayette, IN	SMALLER
94 West Mobile, AL	36695	Outer suburb	Mobile west	Mobile, AL	MID-SIZED
95 West Nyack, NY	10994	Outer suburb	Hudson Valley/New York City north	New York, NY	LARGEST
96 Weston, FL	33326	Outer suburb	Fort Lauderdale west	Fort Lauderdale, FL	LARGEST
97 Wichita (West), KS	67212	Inner suburb	Wichita west	Wichita, KS	MID-SIZED
98 Winchester, VA	22602	Small town	Northern VA Shendandoah Valley	Winchester, VA-WV	SMALLEST
99 Winters, CA	95694	Small town	Yolo County–Sacramento west	Yolo, CA	SMALLER
100 York, PA	17402	Small city	Southeastern PA	York, PA	SMALLER

100 Best Places: Ranked & Rated by Category

NEIGHBORHOOD NAME	ZIP CODE	NEIGBORHOOD TYPE	APPROXIMATE LOCATION	METRO AREA NAME	METRO AREA CATEGORY	REGION
46 Noblesville, IN	46060	Suburban town	Indianapolis north	Indianapolis, IN	MID-SIZED	Midwest
47 West Lafayette, IN	47906	Small college town	Northwest IN	Lafayette, IN	SMALLER	Midwest
48 Hudsonville, MI	49426	Outer suburb/ suburban town	Grand Rapids southwest	Grand Rapids–Muskegon–Holland, MI	MID-SIZED	Midwest
49 West Des Moines–Clive, IA	50325	Outer suburb	Des Moines west	Des Moines, IA	MID-SIZED	Midwest
50 Coralville, IA	52241	College town suburb	Iowa City west	Iowa City, IA	SMALLER	Midwest
51 Sheboygan, WI	53044	Small town	Wisconsin Lake Michigan shore	Sheboygan, WI	SMALLEST	Midwest
52 Waukesha, WI	53186	Suburban town	Milwaukee southwest	Milwaukee-Waukesha, WI	MID-SIZED	Midwest
53 De Forest, WI	53532	College town suburb	Madison northeast	Madison, WI	MID-SIZED	Midwest
54 Green Bay, WI	54313	Small city	East Central WI	Green Bay, WI	SMALLER	Midwest
55 Wausau, WI	54403	Small town	North central, WI	Wausau, WI	SMALLEST	Midwest
56 Appleton, WI	54911	Small city	East central WI	Appleton-Oshkosh-Neenah, WI	SMALLER	Midwest
57 Lakeville, MN	55044	Outer suburb	Minneapolis–St Paul south	Minneapolis–St. Paul, MN-WI	LARGE	Midwest
58 Rochester, MN	55902	Small city	Southeast MN	Rochester, MN	SMALLER	Midwest
59 Lake Zurich, IL	60047	Outer suburb	Chicago NW	Chicago, IL	LARGEST	Midwest
60 Oak Park, IL	60302	City neighborhood	Chicago W	Chicago, IL	LARGEST	Midwest
61 Saint Charles, MO	63304	Outer suburb/ suburban town	St Louis NW	St. Louis, MO-IL	LARGE	Midwest
62 Columbia, MO	65203	Small college town	East central MO	Columbia, MO	SMALLER	Midwest
63 Rapid City, SD	57702	Small city	Soutwestern SD	Rapid City, SD	SMALLEST	Great Plains
64 Fargo, ND	58104	Small city	Eastern ND	Fargo, ND	SMALLER	Great Plains
65 Lawrence, KS	66049	Small college town	East central KS	Lawrence, KS	SMALLER	Great Plains
66 Shawnee, KS	66216	Outer suburb	Kansas City KS west	Kansas City, MO-KS	LARGE	Great Plains
67 Wichita (West), KS	67212	Inner suburb	Wichita west	Wichita, KS	MID-SIZED	Great Plains
68 Elkhorn, NE	68022	Outer suburb/ suburban town	Omaha west	Omaha, NE-IA	MID-SIZED	Great Plains
69 Broken Arrow, OK	74012	Outer suburb	Tulsa east	Tulsa, OK	NEW TO LIST	Great Plains
70 Flower Mound, TX	75028	Outer suburb	Dallas north	Dallas, TX	MEGA	Texas
71 Tyler, TX	75791	Small city	East Texas	Tyler, TX	SMALLER	Texas
72 Arlington, TX	76002	Outer suburb	Fort Worth southeast	Fort Worth–Arlington, TX	LARGEST	Texas
73 Sugar Land, TX	77479	Outer suburb/exurb	Houston southwest	Houston, TX	LARGE	Texas
74 Hollywood Park, TX	78232	Outer suburb	San Antonio north	San Antonio, TX	MID-SIZED	Texas
75 Austin (West), TX	78732	Outer suburb	Austin west	Austin–San Marcos, TX	MID-SIZED	Texas
76 Abilene, TX	79606	Small city	North central TX	Abilene, TX	SMALLER	Texas
77 Louisville, CO	80027	Outer suburb/ suburban town	Denver NW/ Boulder SE	Boulder-Longmont, CO	LARGE	Intermountain
78 Castle Rock, CO	80104	Suburban town	Denver south	Denver, CO	LARGE	Intermountain
79 Denver (Park Hill), CO	80220	City neighborhood	Denver east	Denver, CO	LARGE	Intermountain
80 Fort Collins, CO	80526	Small city	Northern CO	Fort Collins–Loveland, CO	SMALLER	Intermountain
81 Eagle, ID	83616	Outer suburb/ suburban town	Boise west	Boise City, ID	MID-SIZED	Intermountain
82 Kaysville, UT	84037	Outer suburb/ suburban town	Ogden south/ Salt Lake City north	Salt Lake City–Ogden, UT	SMALLER	Intermountain
83 Logan, UT	84321	Small college town	Northern UT	new MSA - Logan, UT	SMALLEST	Intermountain
84 Albuquerque (Sandia Heights), NM	87122	Outer suburb	Albuquerque northeast	Albuquerque, NM	MID-SIZED	Intermountain
85 Minden, NV	89423	Small town	Western NV	Douglas County	SMALLEST	Intermountain
86 Reno, NV	89523	Outer suburb	Reno west	Reno, NV	SMALLER	Intermountain
87 Santa Clarita, CA	91354	Outer suburb/exurb	Los Angeles northeast	Los Angeles–Long Beach, CA	LARGEST	California
88 Loma Linda, CA	92354	Exurb	Inland Empire–Los Angeles east	Riverside–San Bernardino, CA	LARGEST	California
89 Rancho Santa Margarita, CA	92688	Exurb	Orange Co./Los Angeles southeast	Orange County, CA	LARGEST	California
90 Folsom, CA	95630	Outer suburb	Sacramento east	Sacramento, CA	LARGE	California
91 Winters, CA	95694	Small town	Yolo County–Sacramento west	Yolo, CA	SMALLER	California
92 Eugene, OR	97405	Small college town	Central OR	Eugene, OR	SMALLER	Pacific NW
93 Grants Pass, OR	97526	Small town	Southern OR	Josephine County	SMALLEST	Pacific NW

continues

NEIGHBORHOOD NAME	ZIP CODE	NEIGBORHOOD TYPE	APPROXIMATE LOCATION	METRO AREA NAME	METRO AREA CATEGORY	REGION
94 Bellingham, WA	98226	Small city	Northern WA	Bellingham, WA	SMALLER	Pacific NW
95 Mount Vernon, WA	98273	Small town	Northern WA	Mount Vernon–Anacortes, WA	SMALLEST	Pacific NW
96 Mukilteo, WA	98275	Suburban town	Seattle north	Seattle-Bellevue-Everett, WA	LARGEST	Pacific NW
97 Olympia, WA	98501	Small capital city	West central WA	Olympia, WA	SMALLER	Pacific NW
98 Vancouver-Camas, WA	98607	Outer suburb/ suburban town	Portland northeast	Portland-Vancouver, OR-WA	LARGE	Pacific NW
99 Spokane, OR	99223	Inner suburb	Spokane south	Spokane, WA	SMALLER	Pacific NW
100 Anchorage, AK	99516	Small city	South central AK	Anchorage, AK	SMALLER	Pacific NW

METRO AREA CATEGORIES			
Based on Total Population			
> 5 million	LARGEST	200,000 to 500,000	SMALLER
2 to 5 million	LARGE	< 200,000	SMALLEST
500,000 to 2 million	MID-SIZED		

part

I

Introduction

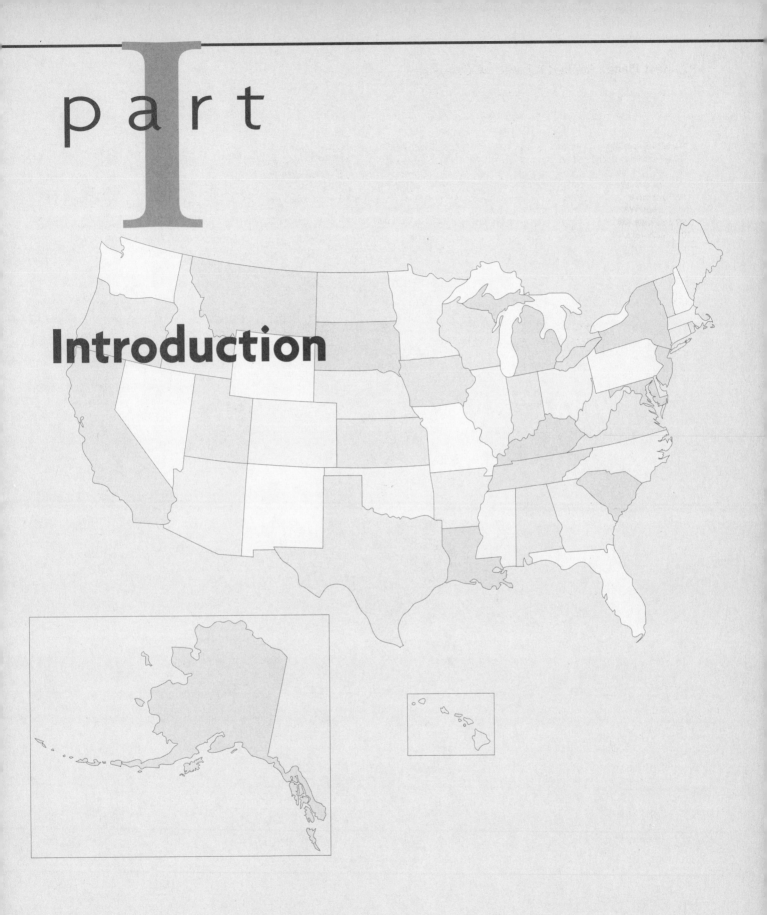

1

Finding Your Best Place

Where you live affects your financial welfare, happiness, and overall quality of life. The good news is that in today's mobile, networked, knowledge-based economy, it's easier than ever before to relocate. As a family, if you choose the right place, you can achieve a balance between standard of living and the quality-of-life factors—such as education, lifestyle, health, and safety—most aligned to your family's interests. Yes, you may have to give some things up, like 250 days of sunshine a year or easy access to Broadway theater. But if there were a "perfect" place, we'd all be there. This book will help you, as a family, choose *your* best place—the best city, the best suburb, or the best small town—by presenting and analyzing factors relevant to your idea of an attractive and affordable lifestyle.

In many ways, life in the 1950s seemed simpler. Families tended to stay put, and typically worked in the same place for life. They had smaller homes, smaller living spaces, and fewer gadgets. "Big-ticket" items like college and healthcare weren't so "big ticket," and family breadwinners could do quite well in the working world without a college degree. One income supplied most if not all of what a family needed. But now, those things that seemed so accessible in the post-WWII consumer prosperity have become considerably more difficult to obtain.

Today, even defining the word "family" is a challenge. A family used to consist of two parents and one or more children. That convention now seems narrow. But, despite the sweeping social and technological changes that have shifted our definition of family, some things have remained, and will continue to remain, the same through the years. Families want prosperity, harmony, and health. They want to achieve personal growth, realize dreams, and create a better life for the next generation. They also want safety and security.

Where you live can make a difference in *how* you live. Although your home can be wherever your family gathers, some places are better suited for families than others. In the following pages, we examine 100 best places in the United States for families and explain why we selected each one. All of this information will help you as you make one of life's most important decisions: where to raise your family.

Getting Started

If you're thinking about moving, perusing this book is a great way to get started. It acquaints you with 100 of the best neighborhoods in the United States that we think are excellent places to raise your family. In these pages, you'll find comparative facts and analysis, augmented with our own experience and judgment as well as that of the residents we interviewed in each community. You'll have a base of knowledge from which to further research (and hopefully visit) the places that interest you.

We don't expect that our list of 100 will fit every family's needs. You may not agree with the choices, or you may have other important criteria not sufficiently weighed into the selection process for this book. The places may not be practical for you because of your employment or because you need to stay close to other family members. But our *thought process* for choosing the places in this book will inform you about how to look at other places and what questions to ask. With this book, you'll learn how to appraise a place and decide whether a particular neighborhood fits your family's long-term needs and criteria.

We looked at various places according to five major categories of data: People, Standard of Living, Education, Lifestyle, and Health & Safety. These categories, and the subcategories within them, make a good checklist as you consider where to raise your family.

Who this Book Is For and Why

This book is for families who have, or intend to have, children. According to the U.S. Census, there are some 75 million families in the United States today, and some 36 million families with children. The facts and thoughts in this book are particularly valuable to those 36 million families, but also, if not more so, to mobile couples and single adults who plan to raise kids in the future.

If you're considering a move—before or while raising children—and aspire for a more comfortable, enjoyable life, this book is for you.

People Planning a Move— or Planning a Family

- *Planning an immediate move.* Whether voluntarily or involuntarily (as in a job transfer, a dislocation, or a specific family need), you're moving soon. You're trying to decide where to go. The choice may be among metropolitan areas, or among several neighborhoods within a given metropolitan area.

- *Planning a move in the near future.* Perhaps you're planning a series of career steps or deciding among several choices for career location or advancement. Or, instead of pursuing opportunities, you're looking to improve your educational environment or to reduce living or housing costs. Your move is likely to happen in the next few years.

- *Planning for the long term.* Especially for newlyweds, singles, or couples planning to one day raise a family, and families with young children, now's a good time to start figuring out where you want to be. It can make a huge difference.

Families with Aspirations

We suspect, and assume, that most of you reading this book—regardless of demographic, social, or economic background—strive for a better standard of living, to build family wealth, to achieve in education and in the workplace, to grow intellectually, to grow physically, and to make better lives for yourselves and your children. You want your children to grow into socially adept, economically independent, balanced citizens. We believe that all of these things are possible, and are affected by where you choose to live. Through choosing your best place, this book aims to help you, and your family, fulfill such aspirations.

The Quest for Value

When selecting places to include in this book, we sought areas of *value,* not just outright excellence. For every attribute used in our determination of best places, you probably know a place that has something better—better schools, lower crime, more beautiful streets, better housing, more interesting architecture, better restaurants, or better public services. But how much does it cost to live there? Surely the quality of life is excellent in Jupiter, Florida; Lake Forest, Illinois; Shaker Heights, Ohio; Beverly Hills, California; or Greenwich, Connecticut. But these high-end neighborhoods are too expensive for many families.

Believe it or not, as recently as 1970, the median national home selling price was $23,000, while the median national household income was $33,181. If you take the ratio of these two figures and compare it over time, or between places, you get a good idea of the relative *affordability* of homes. We call this measure the "Home Price Ratio" and use it throughout this book. In 1970, the national ratio was about 0.70 ($23,000/$33,181). The comparable numbers for 2005 are $208,500 (for the home) and $44,684 (for the income), giving a ratio of about 4.7. One interpretation: Homes are ⅐ as affordable as they were just 35 years ago. A real wake-up call.

Until recently, prices of housing, college education, and healthcare (not to mention gas prices) were increasing at three times the normal inflation rate. Household incomes, on the other hand, have trailed inflation slightly, resulting in steady decreases in savings rates as families struggle to maintain spending habits and their standard of living. With these facts in mind, *Best Places to Raise Your Family* strives to strike a balance between the features of a community that influence family lifestyle and the community's affordability. We tried to find the best neighborhood "for the buck" in an area.

The Importance of Context

We believe that many factors of family success, such as educational achievement, are contextual. If the population of a given area is highly educated, that leads to better school performance and educational quality for its students. Why? Because parents demand it—and support it by volunteering and participating in the schools, voting for necessary financing initiatives, and promoting their own children's achievement at home.

These kinds of inferences—which are supported by research—are used throughout the book. In many ways,

⭐ What Is an "MSA"?

In this book, we discuss individual neighborhoods and towns, as well as the "metro areas" in which these neighborhoods and towns lie. Our definition for a Metropolitan Statistical Area, or "MSA," comes directly from the federal Office of Management and Budget (OMB) and is defined as a place that has "at least one urbanized area of 50,000 or more population, plus adjacent territory that has a high degree of social integration with the core as measured by commuting ties."

MSAs are typically defined as one, and sometimes more than one, urban core and their county or counties. An MSA can cross state lines, and many do. The relationship between urban cores and counties can be one-to-one, one-to-many, many-to-one, or many-to-many, as the following examples illustrate:

- One core to one county (Tyler, Texas–Smith County)
- One core to many counties (Des Moines, Iowa–Polk, Dallas, and Warren counties)
- Many cores to one county (Fort Collins-Loveland, Colorado–Larimer County; Davis, Woodland, and Winters, California–Yolo County)
- Many cores to many counties (Appleton-Oshkosh-Neenah, Wisconsin–Outagamie, Winnebago, and Calumet counties)

In all regions except New England, if a county is integrated with an urban core, the *entire* county is included, regardless of size and content. Ordinarily, it's pretty logical, but it produces odd situations in the West, where large, empty areas are classified as part of an MSA. Examples include the Mojave Desert in San Bernardino County (part of the MSA of Riverside–San Bernardino, California) and much of the Grand Canyon in Cococino County (part of the Flagstaff, Arizona MSA).

Going forward, when discussing data, we use the terms "area," "metro area," and "MSA" interchangeably. See p. 10 for a listing of the 100 best places along with their MSAs.

---

this book is about finding the right economic, social, educational, and environmental context. And while some of these characteristics are measured directly, like home prices, others are measured by looking at once-removed indicators like educational attainment.

Place Can Make a Big Difference

To a certain degree, many aspects of American life have become homogenized. Many commercial businesses and services have evolved into nationwide enterprises, driven by improved transportation, communication, economies of scale, and the benefits of national brand recognition. As a natural result, many products and services become more uniform regardless of locale—restaurants, groceries, hotels, shopping malls, realtors, banks, merchandise retailers, and homebuilders, just to name a few examples.

But there are large differences between each and every neighborhood, and this book will give you the tools to appraise them. Some, like physical setting and recreation, must be taken at face value. Others, like educational quality, are devilishly hard to measure. But, thanks to the wide availability of research and national statistics from government and quasi-public agencies and the private sector, it's now possible to measure a great deal about a neighborhood.

In this book, we'll illustrate the stunning differences between places in terms of, for example, home prices, employment, overall cost of living, median incomes, crime rates, and commute times. Across the United States, there are big differences among large composite geographic areas:

- Median home prices range from under $80,000 to well over $550,000.
- The Cost of Living Index (a percentage comparison of a place to the national average) ranges

---

(TIPS) State Codes

The U.S. Postal Service has its own set of "shorthand" two-letter codes representing each state (see Table 1.1, below). In chapter 5 headings, we adopted this method of shorthand. Most are straightforward, but some, for the "A" states (Alaska, Arkansas, Alabama, Arizona) and "M" states (Massachusetts, Maryland, Maine, Michigan, Minnesota, Missouri, Mississippi, Montana), take some getting used to.

---

from under 80 (80% of the national average) to over 200% (twice the national average).

- Violent crime incidents range from under 0.2% to almost 1% of the population rate, while property crime incidents range from under 2% to almost 7% of the base, that is, 7 incidents per 100 people living in the area.

- Average commute times, from a home to a workplace, range from under 18 minutes to almost 40 minutes.

Neighborhood Matters

As large as the differences are between metro areas, it's not too surprising that neighborhoods *within* metro areas also vary substantially. (For the purposes of this book, a "neighborhood" is defined at a zip code level.) Going from affluent suburbs to impoverished inner-city areas, it's easy to see the differences right away, and they show up in the statistics too. In the Los Angeles area, it isn't surprising that the affluent neighborhoods of Beverly Hills and Santa Monica are far different from the inner-city neighborhoods of East L.A. To reinforce the point, here are some sample facts taken from neighborhood zip codes within the Los Angeles–Long Beach metropolitan area that illustrate the wide variation among places to live in a single metropolitan area:

- The percentage of married-with-children households ranges from 5% to 48%.

- Median home price ranges from $217,000 to $1.5 million.

- Median household annual income ($ for entire household) ranges from $21,000 to $118,000.

- Four-year degree attainment (% possessing 4-year degree) ranges from 2% to 44%.

- Violent crime risk (1 to 10 scale, 1 being the low and 10 being the high) ranges from 2 to 8.

Among the defined metro areas, there are some 15,258 neighborhoods, or zip codes, and while the differences between most are subtle, they are present. Each neighborhood across the United States has a unique mix of factors that creates a particular lifestyle and standard of living. Each neighborhood has intangible features, like appearance, history, convenience, and location, that influence its residents as well. All attributes of an area—tangible, measurable, intangible, abstract—fit together to define a place's character.

There Is No Perfect Place

Of course, there is no perfect place to live. If such a place existed, we'd *all* be there. You and your family must seek a place with the right balance or set of

TABLE 1.1 U.S. STATES & POSTAL CODES			
Alaska	AK	Montana	MT
Alabama	AL	North Carolina	NC
Arkansas	AR	North Dakota	ND
Arizona	AZ	Nebraska	NE
California	CA	New Hampshire	NH
Colorado	CO	New Jersey	NJ
Connecticut	CT	New Mexico	NM
Delaware	DE	Nevada	NV
Florida	FL	New York	NY
Georgia	GA	Ohio	OH
Hawaii	HI	Oklahoma	OK
Iowa	IA	Oregon	OR
Idaho	ID	Pennsylvania	PA
Illinois	IL	Rhode Island	RI
Indiana	IN	South Carolina	SC
Kansas	KS	South Dakota	SD
Kentucky	KY	Tennessee	TN
Louisiana	LA	Texas	TX
Massachusetts	MA	Utah	UT
Maryland	MD	Virginia	VA
Maine	ME	Vermont	VT
Michigan	MI	Washington	WA
Minnesota	MN	Wisconsin	WI
Missouri	MO	West Virginia	WV
Mississippi	MS	Wyoming	WY

tradeoffs between different features and attributes *for you*. California has a great climate and a good economy for certain professions, but the cost of living and stress factors are extreme. New York has a great economy and outstanding cultural assets, but it also has a high cost of living and stress. Kansas and Texas have excellent cost profiles, but they also have harsh climates, isolation, and a relative lack of cultural assets.

Throughout our search through 32,000 zip codes, we admittedly never found the perfect place. But by weighing a number of factors—including standard of living, education, health, safety, and lifestyle—we found 100 of the best places in the United States to raise families. And by carefully considering our recommendations, and our analyses of the major characteristics in each area, you can find the place that's right for you and your family.

Today's Families and Family Trends

Raising a family has never been a simple task, but today, life's demands can feel faster, costlier, and more stressful than ever before. This chapter explores some current family trends—and relevant statistics pertaining to family life—in greater depth.

By Way of Definition

Many of today's families aren't easily defined. Due to divorce, separation, waiting longer to have children, adoption, live-in but not married couples, same-sex couples, unusual employment requirements, and countless other varied lifestyle choices, a family is hard to categorize.

As you read on, the following U.S. Census definitions are important to understand in order to accurately interpret the data. But keep in mind that these definitions were used solely for data-collection purposes and to compare one place to another statistically. This book is intended for all kinds of families.

- According to the U.S. Census, a *household* consists of all people who occupy a housing unit as their usual place of residence regardless of relationship. A household may consist of a person living alone or multiple unrelated individuals or families living together.

- According to the U.S. Census, a *family* consists of two or more people, one of whom is the householder, related by birth, marriage, or adoption and residing in the same housing unit.

- According to the U.S. Census, a *married-with-children* or a *single-with-children* family has one or more naturally related or adopted children under the age of 19 living with them in their household.

In this book, we gathered much of our family data from the U.S. Census through their extensive Decennial Census and ongoing population research obtained through their annual American Community Surveys.

Households, Families & Family Composition

The next several pages provide a brief statistical sketch of today's families, where they are moving, and why. Special focus is placed on families with children—their makeup, history, and major trends observed over the past 50 years.

In Table 2.1 it's worth noting that:

- The number of families (75.6M) and families with children (36M) have increased 90%, almost

in lock step with the population as a whole since 1950.

- The number of households (111.3M) has, however, increased by almost 150%. More people are living in smaller groups or alone in separate housing units, which may, at least in part, explain the surge in housing demand over the past few years.

- The rate of household formation slowed a bit in the 1991 to 2000 period from the 2 decades

23

	HOUSEHOLDS AND FAMILIES			FAMILIES WITH CHILDREN UNDER 18						
				ALL FAMILIES W/CHILDREN		TWO-PARENT FAMILIES		ONE-PARENT FAMILIES		
YEAR	ALL HOUSE-HOLDS	ALL FAMILIES	FAMILIES AS A % OF TOTAL HOUSEHOLDS	# OF FAMILIES WITH CHILDREN UNDER 18	% FAMILIES WITH CHILDREN UNDER 18	MARRIED-COUPLE FAMILIES	% MARRIED-COUPLE FAMILIES W/CHILDREN	TOTAL	MOTHER ONLY	FATHER ONLY
2003	111,278	75,596	67.9%	35,968	47.6%	25,914	72.0%	10,054	8,139	1,915
2000	104,705	72,025	68.8%	34,605	48.0%	25,248	73.0%	9,357	7,571	1,786
1990	93,347	66,090	70.8%	32,289	48.9%	24,537	76.0%	7,752	6,599	1,153
1980	79,108	58,426	73.9%	30,517	52.2%	24,568	80.5%	5,949	5,340	609
1970	63,401	51,237	80.8%	28,665	55.9%	25,406	88.6%	3,260	2,925	335
1960	52,799	45,111	85.4%	25,690	56.9%	23,358	90.9%	2,332	2,099	232
1950	43,554	39,303	90.2%	20,324	51.7%	18,824	92.6%	1,500	1,272	229

TABLE 2.1   FAMILY COMPOSITION HISTORY 1950-2003

Source: U.S. Census Bureau, September 2004

prior, but seems to be on the rise again, with almost seven million new households created since 2000.

- Families as a percent of households declined from 90.2% in 1950 to 67.9% in 2003, a rather dramatic drop, reflecting more people living alone, moving away from home earlier in life, and living longer (and separately) in older age. Stated differently, in the 1950s it was less likely for younger people to form a household until married.

- Having children is still "in style" for families. The percentage of families with children has dropped only modestly, 51.7% to 47.6% since 1950, though it was a bit higher through the 1960s, 1970s, and 1980s. The slight decline in recent years is probably due to aging baby boomers who remain as families but their kids have grown up and gone. The total number of families with children has increased 75% since 1950.

- While the percentage of families with children has stayed relatively constant, the percent involving a married couple has dropped significantly, from 92.6% to 72% over the years. The number of one-parent families has grown almost seven-fold since 1950 and now comprises 28% of all families with children. There has also been a dramatic increase in the number of men heading up such families.

Two-Earner Families: The Trends

U.S. Census data reveal some interesting facts and trends about family earner status. Unfortunately, these figures are only available since 1986. But the trends over the previous 3 decades show a dramatic increase in two-earner status across all categories and particularly for families with children.

On Table 2.2, these interesting trends stand out:

- The percentage of married-with-children families with double earners is *higher* than that of married couples without children, and the gap has stayed consistent over time. The 2003 figures show that 65% of married-with-children couples have dual incomes, and a quick calculation, based on removing the married-with-children figure from the total, shows that 47% of married-without-children households are dual earner couples. This runs somewhat against intuition, with couples waiting longer to have children and the growing number of so-called "DINKs" (Double Income No Kids). Interestingly, it underscores the need to work to balance the family budget when kids are involved. The lower two-earner percentage for families without children may be explained by married-without-children families including older couples who (1) may not need the extra income or (2) have continued to observe a more traditional single-earner way of life.

- Married-with-children two-earner families rose steadily, peaking in 1997 at a high of 68.4%, dropping to 65.7% today. This is still a high number—two in three families with children have two earners. The retrenchment to single-earner families comes despite higher housing prices. It likely results from the end of the 1990s economic boom and the 2001 terrorist attacks

	ALL MARRIED COUPLES			MARRIED W/CHILDREN UNDER 18			MARRIED W/CHILDREN UNDER 6		
YEAR	**TOTAL MARRIED COUPLES**	**HUSBAND AND WIFE WORKING**	**% HUSBAND AND WIFE WORKING**	**TOTAL W/CHILDREN UNDER 18**	**HUSBAND AND WIFE WORKING**	**% HUSBAND AND WIFE WORKING**	**TOTAL W/CHILDREN UNDER 6**	**HUSBAND AND WIFE WORKING**	**% HUSBAND AND WIFE WORKING**
2003	58,586	32,585	55.6%	26,445	17,383	65.7%	12,014	6,884	57.3%
2002	56,747	31,637	55.8%	25,792	17,233	66.8%	11,531	6,796	58.9%
2001	56,592	31,794	56.2%	25,980	17,563	67.6%	11,732	7,054	60.1%
2000	55,311	31,095	56.2%	25,248	17,116	67.8%	11,393	6,984	61.3%
1999	54,770	30,635	55.9%	25,066	16,887	67.4%	11,461	6,878	60.0%
1998	54,317	30,591	56.3%	25,269	17,168	67.9%	11,773	7,310	62.1%
1997	53,604	30,466	56.8%	25,083	17,160	68.4%	11,584	7,142	61.7%
1996	53,567	29,952	55.9%	24,920	16,769	67.3%	11,782	7,189	61.0%
1995	53,858	29,999	55.7%	25,241	17,024	67.4%	11,951	7,406	62.0%
1994	53,171	29,279	55.1%	25,058	16,635	66.4%	12,118	7,283	60.1%
1993	53,171	28,898	54.3%	24,707	16,064	65.0%	11,942	6,934	58.1%
1992	52,457	28,592	54.5%	24,420	16,054	65.7%	11,925	6,972	58.5%
1991	52,147	28,167	54.0%	24,397	15,778	64.7%	12,100	7,061	58.4%
1990	52,317	28,056	53.6%	24,537	15,768	64.3%	12,051	6,932	57.5%
1989	52,100	27,731	53.2%	24,735	15,757	63.7%	12,011	6,772	56.4%
1988	51,809	27,016	52.1%	24,600	15,489	63.0%	11,915	6,651	55.8%
1987	51,537	26,466	51.4%	24,645	15,238	61.8%	11,966	6,618	55.3%
1986	50,933	25,428	49.9%	24,630	14,606	59.3%	11,924	6,271	52.6%

Source: U.S. Census Bureau, September 2004

and their resulting refocus on home life and safety of children.

- Married-with-children families with children under 6 have experienced the same trends, with a peak in 1998, as married-with-children families in general. Fully 57% of these couples are dual earners.

Working from Home

The greater tendency to work from home is a strong trend driving, among other things, a family's flexibility to choose places. According to U.S. Census figures, 23% more people worked at home in 2000 than 1990. We haven't seen any official statistics since, but this figure has likely increased dramatically since then as more companies have downsized and spun off small niche businesses or contracting arrangements. Companies have been more flexible, too: Fully 31% of work-at-home employees still work for companies. The trend has also been facilitated by technology, and the desire of more people to get out of big cities in favor of lifestyle improvements.

The work-from-home phenomenon gives more flexibility to location decisions, and it brings a lot of choices into this book that might not have come into play otherwise. But working from home, particularly in

Single- Versus Double-Income Families

Families with two adults often cope with growing home prices and other big-ticket items by producing two incomes. In more than half of married families, both a husband and a wife work. While helping lighten financial loads, the two-earner phenomenon has hardly put most families on "easy street," as evidenced by median income statistics, which, while incorporating the growth of two-earner families since 1970, still haven't kept up with big-ticket items such as housing. Add to that the necessity of daycare, in its own right a major expense, and the stresses and expenses of getting everybody where they have to go, and it's not hard to see that two earners, while raising the standard of living, fall well short of removing all the pressure. One of the objectives of this book is to identify places that could be affordable for families with a single income, and still offer much-needed opportunities for fun and leisure.

	TABLE 2.3 FAMILIES WITH CHILDREN BY STATE — Sorted by State — 2003		
		FAMILIES	
STATE	**TOTAL**	**WITH OWN CHILDREN UNDER 18**	**% WITH OWN CHILDREN UNDER 18**
U.S. Avg.	71,787,347	34,588,368	48.2%
AK	152,337	88,484	58.1%
AL	1,215,968	561,458	46.2%
AR	732,261	334,604	45.7%
AZ	1,287,367	608,218	47.2%
CA	7,920,049	4,117,036	52.0%
CO	1,084,461	543,588	50.1%
CT	881,170	419,285	47.6%
DC	114,166	49,104	43.0%
DE	204,590	95,175	46.5%
FL	4,210,760	1,779,586	42.3%
GA	2,111,647	1,051,302	49.8%
HI	287,068	129,322	45.0%
IA	769,684	361,153	46.9%
ID	335,588	170,463	50.8%
IL	3,105,513	1,514,561	48.8%
IN	1,602,501	767,836	47.9%
KS	701,547	345,091	49.2%
KY	1,104,398	516,344	46.8%
LA	1,156,438	572,053	49.5%
MA	1,576,696	748,865	47.5%
MD	1,359,318	662,172	48.7%
ME	340,685	157,325	46.2%
MI	2,575,699	1,236,713	48.0%
MN	1,255,141	626,291	49.9%
MO	1,476,516	699,779	47.4%
MS	747,159	363,416	48.6%
MT	237,407	111,807	47.1%
NC	2,158,869	995,648	46.1%
ND	166,150	80,453	48.4%
NE	443,411	217,636	49.1%
NH	323,651	158,410	48.9%
NJ	2,154,539	1,025,556	47.6%
NM	466,515	235,030	50.4%
NV	498,333	238,846	47.9%
NY	4,639,387	2,231,381	48.1%
OH	2,993,023	1,409,912	47.1%
OK	921,750	434,793	47.2%
OR	877,671	410,803	46.8%
PA	3,208,388	1,430,808	44.6%
RI	265,398	124,867	47.0%
SC	1,072,822	495,276	46.2%
SD	194,330	95,180	49.0%
TN	1,547,835	707,305	45.7%
TX	5,247,794	2,723,330	51.9%
UT	535,294	299,746	56.0%
VA	157,763	76,409	48.4%
VT	1,847,796	881,893	47.7%
WA	1,499,127	742,481	49.5%
WI	504,055	213,072	42.3%
WV	1,386,815	665,239	48.0%
WY	130,497	63,263	48.5%

Source: U.S. Census Bureau, September 2004

	TABLE 2.4 FAMILIES WITH CHILDREN BY STATE — Sorted by Percentage — 2003		
		FAMILIES	
STATE	**TOTAL**	**WITH OWN CHILDREN UNDER 18**	**% WITH OWN CHILDREN UNDER 18**
U.S. Avg.	71,787,347	34,588,368	48.2%
AK	152,337	88,484	58.1%
UT	535,294	299,746	56.0%
CA	7,920,049	4,117,036	52.0%
TX	5,247,794	2,723,330	51.9%
ID	335,588	170,463	50.8%
NM	466,515	235,030	50.4%
CO	1,084,461	543,588	50.1%
MN	1,255,141	626,291	49.9%
GA	2,111,647	1,051,302	49.8%
WA	1,499,127	742,481	49.5%
LA	1,156,438	572,053	49.5%
KS	701,547	345,091	49.2%
NE	443,411	217,636	49.1%
SD	194,330	95,180	49.0%
NH	323,651	158,410	48.9%
IL	3,105,513	1,514,561	48.8%
MD	1,359,318	662,172	48.7%
MS	747,159	363,416	48.6%
WY	130,497	63,263	48.5%
VA	157,763	76,409	48.4%
ND	166,150	80,453	48.4%
NY	4,639,387	2,231,381	48.1%
MI	2,575,699	1,236,713	48.0%
WV	1,386,815	665,239	48.0%
NV	498,333	238,846	47.9%
IN	1,602,501	767,836	47.9%
VT	1,847,796	881,893	47.7%
NJ	2,154,539	1,025,556	47.6%
CT	881,170	419,285	47.6%
MA	1,576,696	748,865	47.5%
MO	1,476,516	699,779	47.4%
AZ	1,287,367	608,218	47.2%
OK	921,750	434,793	47.2%
OH	2,993,023	1,409,912	47.1%
MT	237,407	111,807	47.1%
RI	265,398	124,867	47.0%
IA	769,684	361,153	46.9%
OR	877,671	410,803	46.8%
KY	1,104,398	516,344	46.8%
DE	204,590	95,175	46.5%
ME	340,685	157,325	46.2%
AL	1,215,968	561,458	46.2%
SC	1,072,822	495,276	46.2%
NC	2,158,869	995,648	46.1%
TN	1,547,835	707,305	45.7%
AR	732,261	334,604	45.7%
HI	287,068	129,322	45.0%
PA	3,208,388	1,430,808	44.6%
DC	114,166	49,104	43.0%
WI	504,055	213,072	42.3%
FL	4,210,760	1,779,586	42.3%

Source: U.S. Census Bureau, September 2004

self-employment, puts more financial demands on most families, with less stability and decline in such safety-net benefits as health insurance and fixed-retirement contributions. Self-employed home workers may even be more locked into one place than before if they own a business in their area, but not necessarily. And working from home usually requires more living space to accommodate offices and so forth. Bottom line: Working from home opens up more possibilities, but still requires solid strategic thinking about the features and value of a place. See p. 5 for our list of the top 10 work-at-home neighborhoods.

Family Composition by State

In general, families seek locations where there are other families for the company of other children and parents, as well as the types of housing, education, infrastructure, and resources that support families. The presence of families with children becomes sort of a self-fulfilling prophecy; families with children attract more families with children. Therefore, it's interesting to note places that have higher or lower concentrations of families with children already. See Tables 2.3 and 2.4.

On average, 48% of U.S. families have children. It varies from a low of 42% in Florida and Wisconsin (due to presence of retirees) to 58% in Alaska and 56% in Utah. California, where the stereotypical couple is con-

sidered youthful and, more cynically, too self-absorbed for children, actually has the third-highest incidence of children in families. It is interesting that Wisconsin, considered by many to be an ideal family place (and home to six best places in this book), is tied for the lowest percentage of families with children. Like Florida, the population tends to be older, with a large number of "empty nesters" in the state.

Data at more specific neighborhood levels is presented in Table 2.9 and later in chapter 5.

Family Composition by Metro Area

At the metro-area level, statistical breakouts between children "haves" and "have nots" are striking. These tables break down the four major categories of families: married, married with children, married without children, and single with children. See Tables 2.5, 2.6, 2.7, and 2.8.

Two of the top three metro areas by percentage are dominated by large military bases and base housing for career military personnel. Most of the others have populations substantially older than national averages (Punta Gorda, Florida; Bismarck, North Dakota; and Grand Forks, North Dakota). Areas with low readings are dominated by college towns (Bryan–College Station, Texas; Gainesville, Florida; and Auburn-Opelika,

TABLE 2.5 PERCENT MARRIED
Metro Area Level Data

METRO AREA	STATE	POPULATION	% MARRIED
% OF POPULATION, WITH OR WITHOUT CHILDREN			
Jacksonville	NC	146,128	67%
Punta Gorda	FL	152,180	67%
Enid	OK	57,199	66%
Rapid City	SD	91,721	65%
Grand Forks	ND-MN	95,846	65%
Fayetteville-Springdale-Rogers	AR	342,730	65%
Bismarck	ND	97,052	65%
Billings	MT	132,977	65%
Wausau	WI	127,047	63%
Fort Smith	AR-OK	213,480	63%
U.S. Average			58.0%
Bryan–College Station	TX	159,477	47%
New York	NY	9,431,308	46%
Jackson	MS	454,102	46%
Los Angeles–Long Beach	CA	9,910,252	46%
Gainesville	FL	223,861	46%
Albany	GA	123,750	45%
Auburn-Opelika	AL	119,714	45%
Jersey City	NJ	608,916	42%
Bloomington	IN	122,758	40%
Tallahassee	FL	290,948	38%

Source: U.S. Census Bureau, September 2004

TABLE 2.6 PERCENT MARRIED WITH CHILDREN			
Metro Area Level Data			
% OF POPULATION WITH 1+ CHILDREN UNDER 19			
METRO AREA	STATE	POPULATION	% MARRIED WITH CHILDREN
Provo-Orem	UT	393,823	46%
Laredo	TX	214,133	45%
McAllen-Edinburg-Mission	TX	636,921	42%
El Paso	TX	707,911	41%
Jacksonville	NC	146,128	40%
Dubuque	IA	89,960	38%
Fayetteville	NC	303,914	38%
Salt Lake City–Ogden	UT	1,388,051	38%
Houma	LA	198,069	38%
Cheyenne	WY	83,942	37%
U.S. Average			29%
Barnstable-Yarmouth	MA	168,351	20%
Fort Lauderdale	FL	1,736,176	20%
Tallahassee	FL	290,948	20%
Tampa–St. Petersburg–Clearwater	FL	2,532,659	20%
Fort Myers–Cape Coral	FL	492,304	19%
Daytona Beach	FL	530,073	19%
West Palm Beach–Boca Raton	FL	1,218,412	19%
Jersey City	NJ	608,916	19%
Sarasota-Bradenton	FL	633,473	16%
Punta Gorda	FL	152,180	15%

Source: U.S. Census Bureau, September 2004

TABLE 2.7 PERCENT MARRIED WITHOUT CHILDREN			
Metro Area Level Data			
% OF POPULATION WITH 1+ CHILDREN UNDER 19			
METRO AREA	STATE	POPULATION	% MARRIED WITHOUT CHILDREN
Punta Gorda	FL	152,180	50%
Sarasota-Bradenton	FL	633,473	43%
Fort Myers–Cape Coral	FL	492,304	42%
Naples	FL	287,458	41%
Fort Pierce–Port St. Lucie	FL	349,172	39%
Ocala	FL	280,525	39%
Daytona Beach	FL	530,073	38%
Redding	CA	175,665	37%
Melbourne-Titusville–Palm Bay	FL	505,260	36%
Fayetteville-Springdale-Rogers	AR	342,730	36%
U.S. Average			31%
Jackson	MS	454,102	23%
Bryan–College Station	TX	159,477	23%
McAllen-Edinburg-Mission	TX	636,921	23%
Los Angeles–Long Beach	CA	9,910,252	22%
Jersey City	NJ	608,916	22%
Anchorage	AK	271,700	22%
Albany	GA	123,750	21%
El Paso	TX	707,911	20%
Tallahassee	FL	290,948	20%
Laredo	TX	214,133	19%

Source: U.S. Census Bureau, September 2004

Alabama) and by singles strongholds like New York and Los Angeles.

At the top of the list are major Utah areas, dominated by the Mormon culture, and Texas border towns, where young immigrant Hispanic families dominate the population. Interestingly, because of other negatives, only one metro area listed, Salt Lake City–Ogden, Utah, has a neighborhood selected as one of the 100 best places to

TABLE 2.8 PERCENT SINGLE WITH CHILDREN Metro Area Level Data			
% OF POPULATION WITH 1+ CHILDREN UNDER 19			
METRO AREA	**STATE**	**POPULATION**	**% SINGLE WITH CHILDREN**
Albany	GA	123,750	22%
Sumter	SC	105,953	17%
Jackson	MS	454,102	17%
New Orleans	LA	1,340,403	16%
Florence	SC	128,459	16%
Flint	MI	443,045	16%
Memphis	TN-AR-MS	1,171,164	16%
Tallahassee	FL	290,948	15%
McAllen-Edinburg-Mission	TX	636,921	15%
El Paso	TX	707,911	15%
U.S. Average			9%
Iowa City	IA	115,490	6%
St. Cloud	MN	173,755	6%
Sarasota-Bradenton	FL	633,473	6%
Danbury	CT	224,806	6%
Sheboygan	WI	112,664	6%
Grand Forks	ND-MN	95,846	6%
Fargo-Moorhead	ND-MN	179,036	6%
Punta Gorda	FL	152,180	5%
Dubuque	IA	89,960	5%
Bismarck	ND	97,052	5%

Source: U.S. Census Bureau, September 2004

raise your family. In other words, the presence of families with children, while a good indicator especially at the neighborhood level, gives a far from complete picture.

Geographically, and socio-economically, the highest percentages of single-with-children families tend to be found in smaller, less economically robust cities in the South, and the lowest occur in the upper Midwest and in retirement areas.

The highest married-without-children percentages—in fact, 8 out of the top 10—occur in the big retirement spots in Florida. There is no clear pattern for low married-without-children percentages, but a few college towns, and border towns where children are more likely to be present, are on the list.

Family Composition by Neighborhood

Because many families want the company of other children and parents as well as the types of housing, education, infrastructure, and other resources that support families, this book mostly identifies neighborhoods that already have concentrations of families with children at least approaching the national average of 29%. That said, 30 of our neighborhoods have concentrations of less than 29%, but are selected because (1) the concentration is still relatively high for the area as a whole and (2) other features, amenities, and services in the area are conducive to raising families. The specific facts and features of our selection process will become clearer later in the book.

★ Fuzzy Math?

If you're wondering why the average percentage of married with children (29%) in Table 2.6 doesn't match the percent with children given by the U.S. Census figures in Table 2.1, it is because the denominator is different. In Table 2.1, the denominator is households; in Table 2.6, it's the population taken as a whole.

TABLE 2.9 FAMILIES WITH CHILDREN, THE 100 BEST NEIGHBORHOODS			
Married with Children as a Percent of Total Households, 2003			
U.S. AVERAGE: 29%			
HIGHER		LOWER	
Flower Mound, TX	53.2%	Eagle, ID	32.4%
Sugar Land, TX	53.2%	Albuquerque (Sandia Heights), NM	32.4%
Kaysville, UT	52.4%	Franklin, TN	32.3%
Anchorage, AK	47.6%	Fort Collins, CO	32.0%
Lakeville, MN	46.6%	Richmond-Tuckahoe, VA	31.4%
Lake Zurich, IL	44.9%	Evendale, OH	31.4%
Virginia Beach, VA	44.5%	Livingston, NJ	31.2%
Arlington, TX	44.2%	Logan, UT	30.9%
Santa Clarita, CA	44.2%	Weston, FL	30.6%
St. Charles, MO	44.0%	West Chester, PA	30.4%
Hudsonville, MI	43.2%	Cary, NC	30.3%
Fargo, ND	42.8%	Winchester, VA	29.9%
Green Bay, WI	42.4%	Folsom, CA	29.8%
West Mobile, AL	42.0%	Minden, NV	29.8%
Broken Arrow, OK	41.2%	Maumee, OH	29.7%
Valrico, FL	39.7%	Vancouver-Camas, WA	29.7%
Tyler, TX	39.6%	Nashua, NH	29.7%
Elkhorn, NE	38.8%	Chelmsford, MA	29.6%
West Nyack, NY	38.5%	Rapid City, SD	29.3%
DeForest, WI	38.5%	Spokane, WA	29.0%
Herndon, VA	38.3%	Waukesha, WI	28.6%
Shawnee, KS	37.9%	Rogers, AR	28.5%
Irmo, SC	37.7%	North Attleboro, MA	28.4%
Sharon, MA	37.6%	Madison, AL	28.2%
Gaithersburg, MD	37.4%	Lancaster, PA	28.1%
Sheboygan, WI	37.1%	Rochester, MN	27.7%
Farragut, TN	36.6%	Lawrence, KS	27.4%
Greer, SC	36.5%	Appleton, WI	27.4%
Mukilteo, WA	36.4%	Gainesville, FL	27.2%
Reno, NV	36.3%	Bellingham, WA	26.9%
Kendall Park, NJ	36.3%	Wausau, WI	26.8%
Pittsford, NY	36.2%	Hollywood Park, TX	26.6%
Castle Rock, CO	35.6%	Arden-Brandywine, DE	26.3%
Winters, CA	35.3%	Loma Linda, CA	25.9%
Matthews, NC	35.2%	Lexington, KY	25.4%
West Des Moines–Clive, IA	34.8%	Mount Vernon, WA	25.0%
Newtown, CT	34.7%	Columbia, MO	24.9%
East Islip, NY	34.4%	Roanoke, VA	24.7%
Getzville, NY	34.2%	Olympia, WA	23.8%
Columbia, MD	34.2%	Eugene, OR	23.5%
Louisville, CO	33.7%	Coraopolis–Moon Township, PA	23.2%
Orange Park, FL	33.4%	York, PA	23.0%
Noblesville, IN	33.4%	West Lafayette, IN	21.2%
Norwood, NJ	33.2%	Grants Pass, OR	21.1%
Hixson, TN	32.6%	Charlottesville, VA	20.9%
Abilene, TX	32.6%	Oak Park, IL	19.3%
Rancho Santa Margarita, CA	32.6%	Austin (West), TX	19.0%
Hilliard, OH	32.5%	Coralville, IA	18.5%
Wichita (West), KS	32.5%	Bethlehem, PA	18.4%
Roswell, GA	32.4%	Denver (Park Hill), CO	16.0%

Source: U.S. Census Bureau, 2004

Mobility

Now we switch gears just a bit to focus not on where families *are*, but where they're *going*. The next few tables examine who's moving in general, how many families are moving, and the reasons *why*.

Overall population mobility, when viewed statistically, tends to surprise most people. The total number of people moving from one place to another, in either the same county or a different county, has been dropping gradually since 1990, with 14.2% having moved during the 2002 to 2003 period compared to 17.0% in 1991. Even at this somewhat diminished rate, one person in seven moves each year. Or, stated differently, every person moves approximately once every 7 years.

While the total number of movers has declined as a percentage of the population, the tendency to make a *large* move has increased. The percentages moving *to a different county* have increased steadily from 34% to 36% to 38% to 39%. While some people are simply moving to another county farther out in the exurban sphere of the same metro area, the percentage moving to a different county in the same state has remained relatively constant. But the percentage of people moving to a different state is the biggest recent increase in long-distance movers: Approximately 15% to 17% of movers were state to state in the early 1990s, and most recently, the percentages range from 19% to 20%.

See Table 2.10 for more specific statistics on U.S. population mobility.

Family Household Mobility

With the overall mobility picture in mind, it's interesting to look at the trends in *family* mobility.

Family households, on the whole, are somewhat less likely to move than the population overall. While

14.2% of the U.S. population moved in 2002 to 2003, only 11.6% of *families* moved during the same period. Parents generally seek stability for themselves and their children, staying in the same schools if possible and staying the course with current employment.

But what's interesting is how much more likely a family with very young children (under 6) is to move (19%) than other family groups and than the population as a whole. Parents contemplating a move are more likely to do so before school patterns are established, and may also find themselves in need of bigger homes during the early years of raising children.

Reasons for Moving

In addition to tracking moving patterns, the U.S. Census also tracks reasons given for moving. Table 2.12 summarizes given reasons for moves from one county to another, which are called *intercounty* moves.

We see a dramatic shift in primary reasons given for moving, especially notable during the short 3-year period from 2001 to 2003. In 2001, as for the last few years of the 1990s, job- and career-related moves topped the list of reasons at 31%. Although it might

TABLE 2.10   U.S. POPULATION MOBILITY, 1990–2003

| YEAR | TOTAL 1 YEAR OLD AND OVER | NON-MOVERS | TOTAL MOVERS | % MOVING | SAME COUNTY | | DIFFERENT COUNTY | | | | | | MOVERS FROM ABROAD |
					NUMBER MOVING	% OF MOVERS	NUMBER MOVING	% OF MOVERS	IN STATE	% OF MOVERS	OUT OF STATE	% OF MOVERS	
2002	282,556	242,463	40,093	14.2%	23,468	58.5%	15,356	38.3%	7,728	19.3%	7,628	19.0%	1,269
2001	278,160	237,049	41,111	14.8%	23,712	57.7%	15,836	38.5%	8,066	19.6%	7,770	18.9%	1,563
2000	275,611	236,605	39,007	14.2%	21,918	56.2%	15,333	39.3%	7,550	19.4%	7,783	20.0%	1,756
1999	270,219	226,831	43,388	16.1%	24,399	56.2%	17,242	39.7%	8,814	20.3%	8,428	19.4%	1,746
1998	267,933	225,297	42,636	15.9%	25,268	59.3%	15,939	37.4%	8,423	19.8%	7,516	17.6%	1,429
1997	265,209	222,702	42,507	16.0%	27,082	63.7%	14,222	33.5%	7,867	18.5%	6,355	15.0%	1,203
1996	262,976	219,585	43,391	16.5%	27,740	63.9%	14,348	33.1%	7,960	18.3%	6,389	14.7%	1,303
1995	260,406	217,868	42,537	16.3%	26,696	62.8%	14,480	34.0%	8,009	18.8%	6,471	15.2%	1,361
1994	258,248	215,931	42,317	16.4%	27,908	65.9%	13,631	32.2%	7,888	18.6%	5,743	13.6%	778
1993	255,774	212,939	42,835	16.7%	26,638	62.2%	14,952	34.9%	8,226	19.2%	6,726	15.7%	1,245
1992	252,799	209,700	43,099	17.0%	26,932	62.5%	14,772	34.3%	7,855	18.2%	6,916	16.0%	1,395
1991	247,380	204,580	42,800	17.3%	26,587	62.1%	14,957	34.9%	7,853	18.3%	7,105	16.6%	1,255
1990	244,884	203,345	41,539	17.0%	25,151	60.5%	15,003	36.1%	7,881	19.0%	7,122	17.1%	1,385

Source: U.S. Census Bureau, 2004

TABLE 2.11   U.S. FAMILY HOUSEHOLD MOBILITY, 2003
TOTAL AND BY AGE OF CHILDREN

ALL FAMILY HOUSEHOLDS	TOTAL IN GROUP	TOTAL IN GROUP MOVING DURING 2003	% OF GROUP MOVING DURING 2003	WITHIN MSA	BETWEEN MSAS	% OF MOVERS MOVING BETWEEN MSAS
Total	52,593	6,088	11.6%	4,521	1,567	25.7%
No own child <18	17,841	1,866	10.5%	1,323	543	29.1%
Under 6 only	8,355	1,591	19.0%	1,207	384	24.1%
Under 6 & 6-17	7,097	900	12.7%	677	223	24.8%
6-17 only	19,301	1,731	9.0%	1,314	417	24.1%

Source: U.S. Census Bureau, 2004

TABLE 2.12 REASONS FOR MOVING, 2001-2003				
PEOPLE MOVING, IN THOUSANDS, BASED ON SURVEY				
REASON	**INTERCOUNTY MOVES 2003 TOTAL MOVES: 15,332**		**INTERCOUNTY MOVES 2001 TOTAL MOVES: 15,356**	
PERSONAL OR FAMILY	**4,369**	**28.5%**	**3,924**	**25.6%**
Change in marital status	1092	7.1%	851	5.6%
To establish own household	697	4.5%	712	4.6%
Other family resaon	2,580	16.8%	2,361	15.4%
JOB OR CAREER RELATED	**4,278**	**27.9%**	**4,747**	**31.0%**
New job or job transfer	2,849	18.6%	3,384	22.1%
To look for work or lost job	466	3.0%	500	3.3%
To be closer to work/easier commute	602	3.9%	631	4.1%
Other job-related reason	361	2.4%	232	1.5%
RETIREMENT	**187**	**1.2%**	**187**	**1.2%**
HOUSING RELATED	**4,724**	**30.8%**	**4,231**	**27.6%**
Wanted own home, not rent	1,095	7.1%	1,182	7.7%
Wanted new or better home/apartment	1,740	11.3%	1,495	9.8%
Wanted cheaper housing	695	4.5%	541	3.5%
Other housing reason	1,194	7.8%	1,013	6.6%
LIFESTYLE RELATED	**1,921**	**12.5%**	**2,244**	**14.6%**
Wanted better neighborhood/less crime	415	2.7%	500	3.3%
To attend or leave college	648	4.2%	758	4.9%
Change of climate	148	1.0%	205	1.3%
Health reasons	302	2.0%	292	1.9%
Other reasons	408	2.7%	489	3.2%

Source: U.S. Census Bureau, 2004

have been reasonable to think that number would stay the same or even grow with job dislocations in a contracting economy, a stronger "life first" mentality emerged, probably in part fostered by the 2001 terrorist attacks. The Personal or Family category absorbed almost all of the loss in job-related moves. Relocation rationale shifted noticeably toward family and personal reasons, including a greater interest in being closer to relatives and children.

Housing-related moves jumped 3% in just 2 years. This is particularly significant in that these are intercounty moves. Housing has always been a big reason for *intra*county moves, as people "move up" into larger homes or try to improve convenience, schools, or overall neighborhood surroundings. The fact that *inter*county housing-related moves are on the rise suggests that recent real estate price activity has spurred more people into action, and that more people are looking at value and living cost as part of the overall lifestyle value proposition.

It's worth noting that climate barely moves the meter in terms of actual move motive. Only 1.3% of intercounty movers cited it as the reason in the most recent survey.

Recommended Reading

To learn more about the big-picture structural, environmental, and societal trends affecting today's families with children, take a look at the following books.

- *On Paradise Drive*, David Brooks. Simon & Schuster (June 2005). In this informative and entertaining analysis, Brooks looks at the evolution of suburban living—past, present, and future—and points out the social and behavioral trends (some obvious, some not so obvious) that are evident in today's family life.

- *The Rise of the Creative Class*, Richard Florida. Basic Books (reprint edition: January 2004). Florida explores the rise of the knowledge economy—and the knowledge worker. He explains what these kinds of workers need and what role their location plays.

- *Bowling Alone*, Robert Putnam. Simon & Schuster (August 2001). Putman examines the decline of "social capital" (voluntary community cohesiveness once ubiquitous in America), the geography of the decline, and the implications.

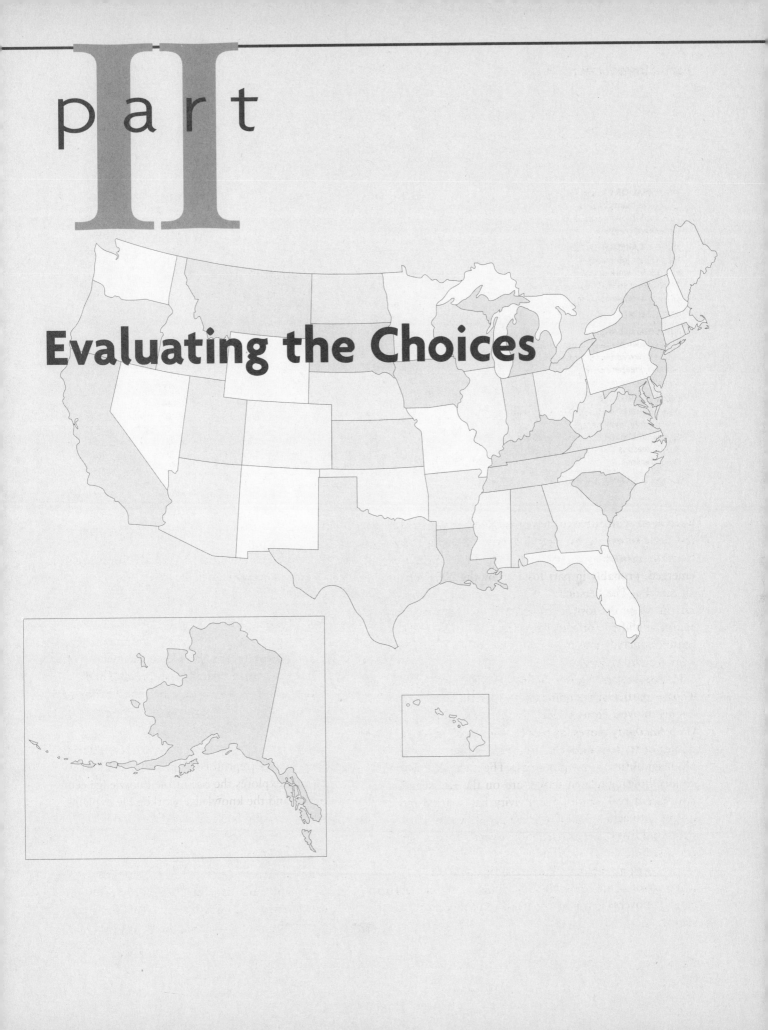

part II

Evaluating the Choices

chapter

What Makes a Best Place Best?

W e're not complaining, but it was hard to choose the 100 best places to raise your family. Why? Because there are so many places to choose from. In fact, using our approach, there are more than 32,000 possibilities. And each one has its standout traits and its not-so-great qualities. Sure, there are utopian enclaves with a great physical setting, desirable lifestyle, top-notch schools, little crime, and high-paying jobs for professionals—but houses cost $750,000 and up. On the flip side, there are plenty of places with excellent new homes on quiet streets costing under $200K, but they're set in towns where there's nothing to do, few places to work, and harsh climates. We set out to examine a mix of characteristics, weigh their strengths and weaknesses, find a good balance, and present the best places to live that are *attainable* and *affordable* for you and your family.

It Isn't Just the Facts

Finding the best place to raise your family means considering what kind of "package" you're looking for. This means weighing a combination of factors, including a neighborhood's location, population, standard of living, education, lifestyle, and health and safety—plus the "feel" or character of a place. As you'll see throughout the book, many of these attributes are measurable, and we've collected a broad assortment of calculated statistics and concrete facts.

But a best place can't be judged solely on its facts and features—what's most important is how they all work together. The "connective tissue"—that immeasurable stuff that makes the whole greater than the sum of its parts—was crucial to us as we examined places for this book.

If you depend too much on numbers, you can quickly find yourself in the weeds. The computer algorithm

capable of finding the "optimal" mix among hundreds of facts has yet to be invented (or has yet to be made available to most of us), and if it were available, we wouldn't understand the result anyway. Further, data isn't perfect, or can be misleading. Does the fact that a college town has low median household incomes, high percentages of "single" households, low median ages, and low rates of home ownership make it a bad place for families? Hardly. But that's what the numbers would indicate on the surface.

Finally, and perhaps most importantly, the extensive database queries and multivariate optimization routines that might earmark a statistician's approach can't model the ambience, the flavor, and the look and feel of a place. It's how the facts work together that counts; it isn't *just* the facts.

The *Best Places* Approach

In researching and writing this book, we used a targeted approach to select 100 places that are all great choices for kids and adults. Specifically, we kept in mind a family focus, a neighborhood-level view, and a significant emphasis on intangibles.

Family Focus

As the title suggests, *Best Places to Raise Your Family* looks at factors inherently important while raising a family. That means that certain features and attributes—such as education, cost of housing, cost of living, and certain "lifestyle" features like amusement parks, children's museums, and commute times—bubble to the top and receive special attention.

"Focus" Categories

As part of creating a "family" point of view, *Best Places* groups all facts in the data tables into five major categories for analysis and presentation:

- *People* illustrates the demographic characteristics of an area. Population size, growth, and mix—with a concentration on family statistics—are closely examined. As an example, the presence of "married with children" households was important in our selection process because it implies that infrastructure and community offerings are already conducive for families in a particular area. Other factors, like religious mix, are presented for interest but were not considered in place selection.

- *Standard of Living* examines the facts that define current, and potential, family prosperity in the area—chiefly income and costs. Income includes job security, the mix of jobs in an area, and future employment. Costs include the overall cost of living, cost of housing, taxes, and daycare. Several less tangible items, like *what kind* of home you can get for your money, are included in this category as well.

- *Education* looks at both specific results and context. Educational *attainment* summarizes the level of education of local residents, while *achievement* conveys the specific academic results of schools in the area. *Resources* include school facilities at all levels, school size, and funding.

- *Lifestyle* is a complex set of factors influencing general family development and the quality of life. Included are "things to do" such as arts and cultural resources, entertainment venues, and recreational activities, as well as "background" factors like commute times, climate, and the physical attractiveness of an area.

- *Health & Safety* evaluates crime rates and health hazards, as well as the healthcare resources available to mitigate them.

In chapter 5, where each place is discussed separately, fact tables are organized and presented according to these five categories. "People" facts are presented as background material, while facts in the other four categories are broken out and discussed separately in each narrative. In other words, you'll see headings in the narrative on each place for Standard of Living, Education, Lifestyle, and Health & Safety, but not for People. The People statistics are mentioned in the narrative's introduction, if noteworthy, and are otherwise self-explanatory in the tables.

For a table of the specific facts included in each category and more information about them—where they come from and what they mean—refer to tables 4.1 through 4.4 in chapter 4.

Selection

Our mission was to select 100 top communities for raising a family, period, and not to compare all of those communities to one another. For fun and easy reference, we highlight the top 10 places—what we call the "Best of the Best" locales—in a list at the front of the book (p. 3), as well as with icons in chapter 5. We also rank and rate neighborhoods based on specific categories in the Author's Choice section on p. 4.

In chapter 5, as we discuss each of the best places for families, we highlight the "pros'" (strengths) and "cons" (weaknesses or concerns), because no matter how good a place is, it still has some issues prospective residents need to watch for. Remember—there's no perfect place.

Neighborhood View

Viewing the United States with a family focus makes it more valuable to look at certain facts for specific *neighborhoods* within metro areas, rather than at entire cities or counties. We chose the best places based on a blend of neighborhood and metro area information.

Metropolitan Statistical Areas (MSAs, or metro areas) are often used as the basis for comparing and choosing places. By definition, MSAs are a composite of incorporated and unincorporated areas, cities, towns, and neighborhoods. As such, characterizing a metro area means looking at many measures as cross sections of the area, composite averages, or summaries.

Best Places to Raise Your Family goes even deeper than MSAs to identify and collect key facts that really matter by neighborhood—for example, home prices, education statistics, and property taxes. We conducted interviews and other research at neighborhood levels to add as much local color as possible. Our overriding objective was to paint a picture of what life is like in each particular locale.

As Part of a Metro Area

All neighborhoods on our 100 Best Places list are part of a metropolitan area (see p. 10), although in some cases a very small one. Metro areas come in different sizes:

- Largest (more than 5 million people)
- Large (between 2 and 5 million)
- Mid-size (between 500,000 and 2 million)
- Smaller (between 200,000 and 500,000)
- Smallest (fewer than 200,000)

Some attributes, and their measures, don't vary much (if at all) across the area, like climate statistics or information on art museums and professional sports teams. Where it makes the most sense, metro area or MSA-level data is presented as part of our neighborhood analysis.

Types of Neighborhoods

To help you grasp the nature of each neighborhood in this book, we developed an informal descriptive classification consisting of 11 different neighborhood types. These "types" have common characteristics like location with respect to a major city or city core, size, age, appearance, physical layout, economic role, and geographic role within the region. The classification isn't precise; some communities have features of more than one "type" of neighborhood. But, in general, these classifications help identify the key characteristics of a place. For a list of all 100 places organized according to this classification system, please refer to the table on p. 41 and to the Index by Neighborhood Type on p. 463.

- *City Neighborhood:* Older areas adjacent to a downtown core; usually rectangular grid-street patterns; mixed housing types with abundant older bungalow-style homes; mixed demographics; public transit; and relatively infrequent use of automobiles. Example: Denver (Park Hill), Colorado.

- *Inner Suburb:* Suburbs up to 15 miles from the city core; inside the beltway (usually a three-digit Interstate highway); mostly built before 1970; mixed housing types; and economically dependent on city core but with some residents who commute farther out into suburbs. Most have a recognizable downtown core. Example: Maumee, Ohio.

- *Outer Suburb:* Usually outside the beltway; mostly built after 1970; mostly single-family homes; little to no public transportation; long commutes to city core inner suburbs, or other outer suburbs; and little to no downtown core unless built up from a base as a "suburban town" (see below). Example: Shawnee, Kansas.

- *Exurb:* A new area usually with large homes built into (or on top of) country settings; many expansive planned subdivisions and communities; economically self-sufficient, as most residents live and work in the area or in a nearby outer suburb; and commutes or other interactions with central portions of the metro area and especially downtown are relatively rare, usually only for entertainment or airport access. Example: Santa Clarita, California.

- *Suburban town:* What was once a small town in the country now, thanks to the automobile, has become a suburban town. Includes a well-used downtown and commercial area with historic buildings, a strong local government, and an assortment of local cultural amenities and services; has a mix of older housing near the old core, surrounded by acres of new suburban homes; and some residents work locally, but more likely to commute to a nearby neighborhood or into the metro area core. Example: Waukesha, Wisconsin.

- *Satellite City:* A full city close to a much larger city; could be, looks like, and functions like its own city but within a larger metro area, and has strong economic ties to the larger city nearby; larger than a suburban town; has a strong downtown core, historic interest, local services, and amenities; often surrounded by newer "bedroom" style suburbs. With a strong identity; residents say they are from that city (the satellite city), not the larger metro area, although many may work in the larger city and commute there using public transit. Example: West Chester, Pennsylvania.

- *Small City:* A city of more than 50,000 residents *not* close to another metropolitan area; economically self-sufficient; has a complete downtown core; includes older and newer suburbs; and offers a complete set of amenities and services. Example: Rapid City, South Dakota.

- *Small Town:* Like a "small city," but smaller, with a population less than 50,000. Example: Wausau, Wisconsin.

- *Small College Town:* Like a "small town" (some also qualify by population as a "small city") except that the economy is dominated by one or more colleges or universities; the student influx may more than double the town's population, and may strongly affect certain statistics like average age, percent married with children, and average incomes; the university provides majority of cultural enrichment, healthcare services, and employment; and downtown areas are clean, lively, and historic. To make our list, the town must have some substantial employment outside the university. Example: Lawrence, Kansas.

- *College-Town Suburb:* In two cases, we chose not the college town itself but a suburb or suburban town close by. Example: DeForest, Wisconsin.
- *Small Capital City:* Similar to a small college town except that state government is the dominant employer and supplies some of the cultural enrichment, notably museums; characterized by strong historic interest, high educational attainment, and very stable economy. Example: Olympia, Washington.

Beyond these 11 groups, we identified three more combination groups: inner suburb/suburban town, outer suburb/suburban town, and outer suburb/exurb. These descriptive "types" are used where the neighborhood has strong elements of both characteristics. Again, these "types" are shown on p. 41 as well as in chapter 5.

Emphasis on Intangibles

Our review of places included everything from specific home prices to how an area looks from the ground and air to what locals say about it. *Best Places* draws heavily from intangible factors and always considers them along with the statistical facts.

The *Best Places* Qualifying School

It could have taken *years* to put this book together.

There are more than 32,000 zip codes in the United States, and many, especially in urban areas, have more than one "neighborhood." To collect the facts and get a strong on-the-ground reading for *all* of these places is clearly impossible. So we had to create a process to quickly narrow down a large list of possibilities into a select—but diverse—set of candidates for further analysis. That process involved a blend of techniques, from standard data queries and quantitative analysis to mapping techniques to satellite photo interpretation to local websites to, last but not least, in-person visits and telephone interviews with residents.

Here's the process in a nutshell. First, we did some high-level filtering to quickly narrow the candidates list to a manageable size. Next, we took a close look at tangible facts and some intangibles to further whittle it down. A couple of rounds of fact testing then served to discard a few more areas or validate our choices. Once down to a manageable list of 100, we started the interview process, and adjusted the list as necessary according to what we found. Here are more specifics about how we made each "cut."

From 32,000 to 15,000

Approximately 15,000 of the more than 32,000 zip codes in the United States are within metropolitan areas. These "metro areas" can either be *macropolitan* areas, defined around a core of 50,000 or more, or so-called *micropolitan* areas, defined around a core of 10,000 (both are U.S. Office of Management and Budget definitions). Our rule: A neighborhood, to qualify, must be near enough to a city large enough to provide some services, jobs, and basic amenities, so at the outset we cut the 17,000 zip codes that *do not* lie within a metro area.

We took only two areas defined by the U.S. Office of Management and Budget (OMB) as "micropolitan"— Grants Pass, Oregon, and Minden-Gardnerville, Nevada. Our preference was clearly to choose places close to a larger area that would, more likely, have a greater number of resources for families. Small towns like Storm Lake, Iowa; Circleville, Ohio; Bellows Falls, Vermont; and Bishop, California, are all fine places to raise a family, but more so for the people who already live there. For movers, they don't offer as much opportunity as the places we selected. As a priority, we looked for neighborhoods—residential enclaves of larger urban areas—rather than small towns, although there are a few small towns with populations below 50,000 on our list.

From 15,000 to 900

In this second cut, candidates from poorly rated metro areas were cut. Most were smaller metro areas like Joplin, Missouri; Baton Rouge, Louisiana; and Merced, California, but some were larger such as Cleveland, Ohio, and Detroit, Michigan. Several thousand zip codes were cut. The metro area candidates list at this point was about 200, organized by large, medium, and small places. Using a software mapping program known as Microsoft MapPoint linked to a file of U.S. Census facts containing married-with-children households as a

(TIPS) Avoiding the Traps

As tempting as it is to depend wholly on data filtering to choose the best places to live, it's easy to be misled. Without looking at the nuances of a local situation, it's easy to fall into traps like these:

- Some high percentages of married-with-children households are actually small zip code areas adjacent to military bases, many of which are designated military off-base housing complexes. While probably good family places, the military-only nature isn't what we sought for this book.
- Some of the highest 4-year educational attainment percentages are found in zip codes defined within a college campus.
- Some of the lowest household income levels, likewise, are found in college towns or near college campuses. When students are removed from the mix, the picture is much different.

percentage of total households, and other facts, we chose one to six neighborhoods in each metro area.

Generally, we sought neighborhoods in which at least 20% of households were married with children (MWC). Of course, we made some exceptions—in college towns, where young singles in the population tend to diminish married-with-children percentages, as well as in some transitioning economies like Bethlehem, Pennsylvania.

We also eliminated zip codes at the far rural periphery of metro areas, as rural areas like small towns tend to be high in MWC but low in housing, resources, and amenities. We also considered median home prices to make sure we weren't choosing the wealthiest part of an area—always a good place to live, but impractical for most. The median home prices for a neighborhood could exceed the metro-area average, but not by a great margin. Any area with a median home price over $500,000 was removed—unless the neighborhood was part of a more expensive area like New York, New Jersey, California, or the Chicago area.

Finally, if an area couldn't be clearly qualified or disqualified by MWC or median home prices, we relied on educational attainment statistics, such as the percentage of a population with 4-year degrees. As a general guiding principle, areas in which less than 10% of residents claimed a 4-year degree were cut.

While the data certainly leads to the right places, it can't be solely depended on to make selection decisions. Context, as in the presence of a large university, influences the facts and must be understood. Add that context to the large body of intangible factors in each area and you can see that selecting best places requires much more than pushing a button on a computer.

From 900 to 175

Now that we had anywhere from one to six neighborhoods in an area, the task at hand was to select the best among multiple neighborhoods in an area, and in some cases, drop some metro areas from the list. A mix of data—including married-with-children percentages, home prices, cost of living indexes, buying power indexes, and educational attainment—was used. (See chapter 4 for an explanation of each of these data.) In the cases where it was a close call, we weighed additional data such as school scores and qualitative observations. Often, we looked at aerial satellite photos, local websites, and street layouts and facilities on MapPoint to help us make our decisions.

From 175 to 100

We took another look at the standards variables—such as percentages of married-with-children households, home prices, and the cost of living—but brought the rest of the facts into the mix. We looked at statistics on commute times, arts and recreational amenities, and crime risk. Special emphasis was placed on local school performance. Using detailed test score data obtained through Greatschools.net, we generally cut neighborhoods with schools not performing up to state averages. On the flip side, neighborhoods that exhibited excellent test scores or even strong parent comments about local schools were selected. We looked at more aerial photos and any other kind of photo we could find. We looked at more local websites. This cut was very deliberate and we spent many hours selecting the final best places to raise your family.

⭐ Cul-de-sacs Aren't for Everyone

We could easily find 100 family places around the country that would look alike to an alien visiting from outer space—or, better yet, to a middle-class suburbanite visiting from Anywhere, USA. Imagine dead-end streets, cul-de-sacs, tract homes, trees, yards, strip malls, grocery stores, modern schools, parks, arterial roads, and freeway interchanges.

But we felt it disingenuous to land on the typical modern family city-fringe "outer suburb" everywhere we looked. We thought it would be more valuable to offer a diverse base of neighborhood types to try to suit different families' tastes, needs, and lifestyles. Similarly, we also tried to achieve geographic diversity—a spread across all geographic regions and as many states as possible. As such, the effort to achieve a diverse mix was part of the qualification process, especially in the 900 to 175 round of elimination.

The List of 100

With the list of 100 in hand, we began a lengthy interview process. In most cases, our first conversation was with a real estate agent, and especially with a relocation specialist in the area if we could find one. Why? Because real estate agents know what's most important to those relocating into an area. The interview was structured around our five major categories—People, Standard of Living, Education, Lifestyle, and Health & Safety. To give you even more choices, we also asked about nearby neighborhoods that could be good alternatives for families. Our goal was to seek out someone who had lived in a particular area for many years, raised a family there, and knew all of the neighborhood's comings and goings. We also found many city and county officials helpful—we even spoke with a former senator along the way.

The interviews largely confirmed our statistical data and the visual looks we had conducted with software programs. But we did eliminate and replace nine neighborhoods during the interview process, due to new information we gathered.

For a complete list of the 100 best places to raise your family, refer to p. 1. See the maps on p. 42–45.

By Region, State & Type

For a regional picture, take a look at the 100 best places plotted on the following maps, as well as the breakdown in the following summary tables.

By Region

Personal preference, employment, or family reasons may motivate families to "shop" for a best place within a given region. To help you look for a place this way, Table 3.1 groups the best places to raise your family by 10 informally defined U.S. regions.

TABLE 3.1 THE 100 BEST PLACES BY REGION		
2006		
REGION	**STATES INCLUDED**	**NO. OF PLACES**
Midwest	IA, IN, IL, MI, MN, MO, OH	20
Northeast	CT, DE, MA, NJ, NY, PA	18
Mid-Atlantic	MD, NC, SC, VA	12
Intermountain	CO, ID, NM, NV, UT	10
Pacific NW	AK, OR, WA	9
South	AL, AR, GA, KY, TN	8
Texas	TX	7
Great Plains	KS, ND, NE, OK, SD	7
California	CA	5
Florida	FL	4

By State

Although it would have been nice to include a place from each of the 50 states, it didn't work out that way. There are 10 states with no identified neighborhoods in this book. Does this mean these states are lousy places to raise a family, or that there are *no* good neighborhoods statewide? Of course not. There *are* good places in all 50 states, but with only 100 slots, we weren't able to fit them in. Some states, like Montana and Wyoming, aren't populous enough to have the kind of breadth and depth in economic and job base we were looking for. Throughout the selection process for this book, we favored places that had sufficient job variety to support large segments of the population, not just a few individuals with specialized skill sets. See Table 3.2.

By Type

Table 3.3 on neighborhood type shows that, indeed, the largest slice of our 100 best places consists of outer suburbs, but small city and small towns also appear near the top of the list.

TABLE 3.2 THE 100 BEST PLACES BY STATE							
2006							
Texas	7	Utah	2	Oregon	3	Oklahoma	1
Virginia	6	Alaska	1	Tennessee	3	South Dakota	1
Wisconsin	6	Arkansas	1	Alabama	2	Arizona	0
California	5	Connecticut	1	Iowa	2	Hawaii	0
Pennsylvania	5	Delaware	1	Illinois	2	Louisiana	0
Washington	5	Georgia	1	Indiana	2	Maine	0
Colorado	4	Idaho	1	Maryland	2	Mississippi	0
Florida	4	Kentucky	1	Minnesota	2	Montana	0
New York	4	Michigan	1	Missouri	2	Rhode Island	0
Kansas	3	North Dakota	1	North Carolina	2	Vermont	0
Massachusetts	3	Nebraska	1	Nevada	2	West Virginia	0
New Jersey	3	New Hampshire	1	South Carolina	2	Wyoming	0
Ohio	3	New Mexico	1				

TABLE 3.3 THE 100 BEST PLACES BY NEIGHBORHOOD TYPE		
2006		
TYPE OF PLACE	EXAMPLE	NO. OF PLACES IDENTIFIED
Outer suburb	Lakeville, MN	22
Small city	Rochester, MN	14
Outer suburb/suburban town	Coraopolis–Moon Township, PA	11
Small town	Grants Pass, OR	11
Inner suburb	Evendale, OH	9
Small college town	Gainesville, FL	7
Outer suburb/exurb	Columbia, MD	6
Suburban town	Noblesville, IN	6
Satellite city	West Chester, PA	4
Small capital city	Olympia, WA	2
Inner suburb/suburban town	Sharon, MA	2
Exurb	Rancho Santa Margarita, CA	2
College-town suburb	Coralville, IA	2
City neighborhood	Oak Park, IL	2

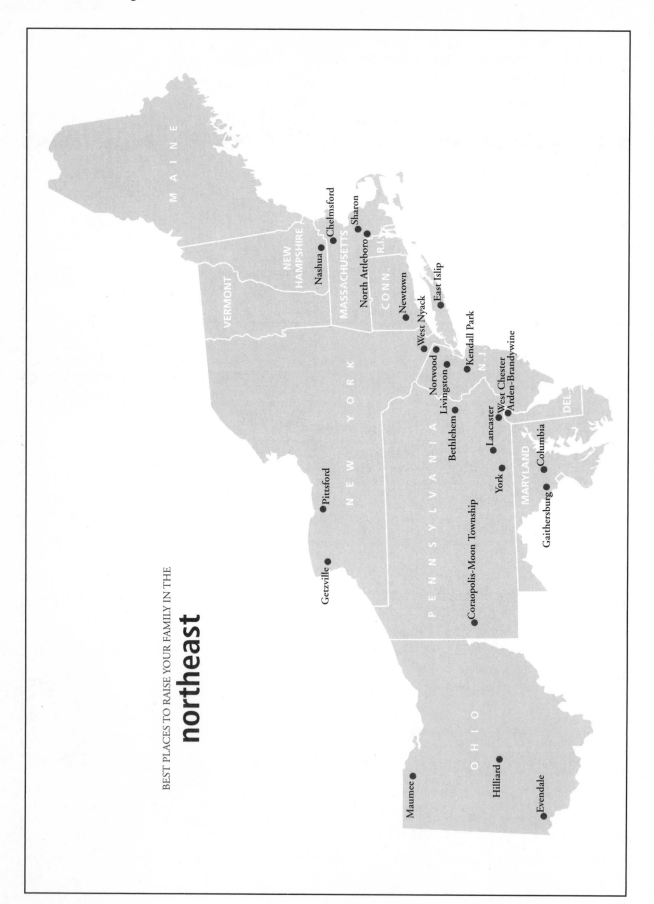

BEST PLACES TO RAISE YOUR FAMILY IN THE
northeast

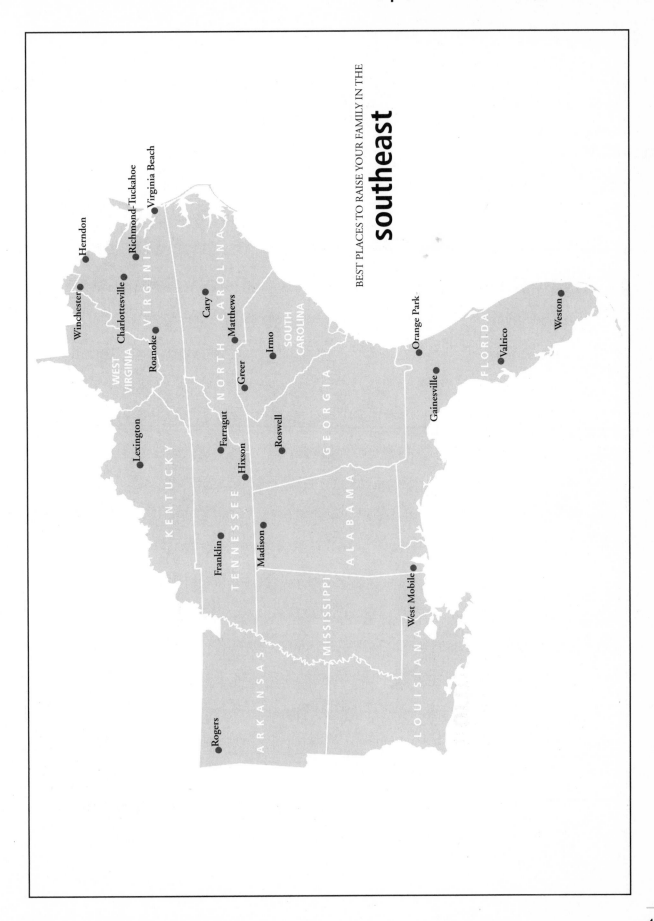

BEST PLACES TO RAISE YOUR FAMILY IN THE

central states

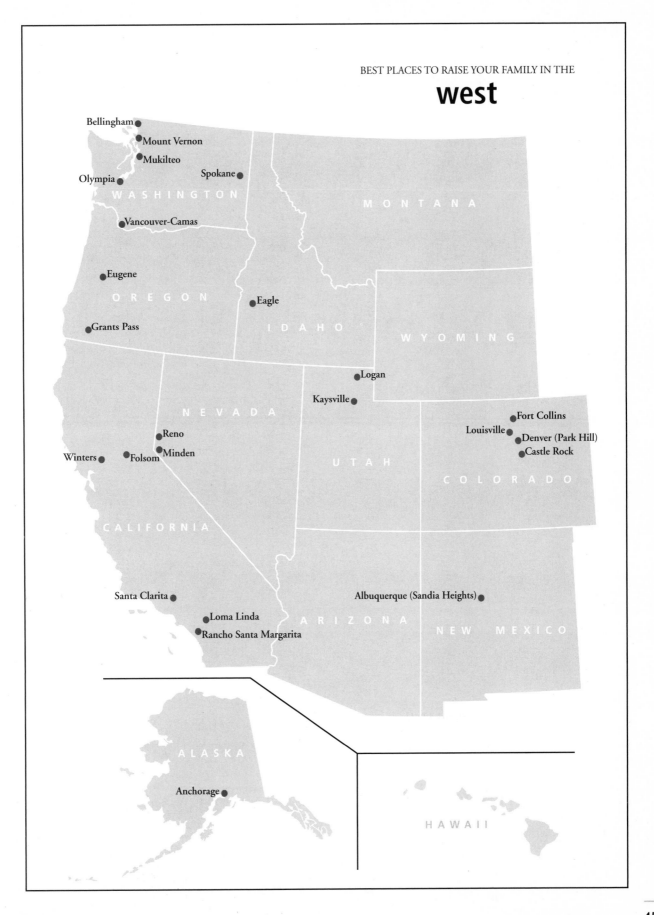

BEST PLACES TO RAISE YOUR FAMILY IN THE

west

A Closer Look at the Facts

This book is filled with facts, often stated as numbers in tables, which may at times feel complex or overwhelming. But this chapter is designed to walk you through our processes and help you understand every piece of information we present.

In this chapter, we give you a sense of how the data is organized, what each number means, and how we came up with it. We also explain factual trends—what's getting better, what's getting worse, and what you should keep track of as you continue your quest for your own best place. We provide important analysis, show you what we mean with examples, and provide more than 80 tables to illustrate, at a glance, what's best in a particular place and what isn't. Finally, we teach you how to find and interpret some of this information for yourselves.

Where Do the Facts Come From?

We've collected hundreds of pieces of information about each place, but for the sake of convenience and clarity, we don't show them all in this book. Everything from the number of cloudy days per year to annual utility costs to the attendance at the local symphony is incorporated somewhere—either presented directly or built into one of the many scores, ratings, and indexes we do show.

Here are some of our major sources.

Sperling's BestPlaces

Co-author Bert Sperling has been collecting data and analyzing livable cities for 25 years, and he maintains a large database with feeds from government and private agencies all over the United States. Bert also uses models and tools to turn raw data into valuable information, and he has developed many scores and ratings for various presentations targeted at different users.

Bert conducts a number of leading studies and analyses, covering topics that range from "The Best Places for Singles" to "America's Most Unwired Cities." You can check out most of Bert's data online at **www.bestplaces.net**.

Original Sources

Nearly all data shown and used in *Best Places to Raise Your Family* are collected and processed through Sperling's BestPlaces. However, it's interesting to look at

some of Bert's original sources, which include major public agencies, trade associations, and private organizations. Here are a few examples and what each one provides:

- U.S. Census Bureau: Provides population and demographics data, commute statistics, and information on certain commercial activities and employment.
- Bureau of Labor Statistics: Provides economy, employment, and cost-of-living information.
- National Climatic Data Center: Provides climate data, including history and averages.
- Department of Education, National Center for Education Statistics: Provides facts on primary and secondary schools and school districts, as well as on higher education.
- Centers for Disease Control and Prevention: Provides facts on disease, health hazards, and healthcare.
- American Medical Association: Provides physician statistics.
- American Museum Association: Provides information on museums, including size, quality, and attendance.
- American Symphony Orchestra League: Provides data on orchestras and attendance.

- American Library Association: Provides statistics on libraries and book volume counts.
- Greatschools.net, a private nonprofit consolidator and portal: Provides local primary and secondary school information, including test scores and parent reviews.

Later in this chapter, as we explain the facts used in this book, we also provide the source and the year the data was obtained.

Other Sources

Besides Sperling's BestPlaces, we tapped into several other information suppliers. Many are websites of local government and quasi-public agencies, like Chamber of Commerce websites. As mentioned in chapter 3, we also made extensive use of interviews and conversations with local residents.

Websites

You might be tempted to use local websites to gather more information about the places mentioned in this book. Be aware that, while many have improved in the last few years, some are still "salesy" and hard to navigate. We found some excellent ones along the way—such as the site for Huntsville's Chamber of Commerce at www.huntsvillealabamausa.com—with clear descriptions of their area's economy, local employers, and things to do. Other sites may merely be portals with listings of local hotels and motels, restaurants, and car-repair outlets—data that tends to be outdated and fails to present a complete picture. Here's a summary of what you might find, but remember to look at local websites with caution:

- *City websites:* Most municipalities today have their own site. These are largely administrative in nature, with information on garbage collection, road closures, and other mostly irrelevant topics, but some of the better ones have sections describing the city, its history, its infrastructure, and awards it may have received in other studies. In some cases, better sites are found at the county level.
- *Chamber of Commerce:* The goal and orientation of these organizations is to attract business and commerce to an area. Some are loaded with sales hype, and others concentrate on industrial parks and other potential business locations in the area; but several give excellent summaries of employers and general economic statistics in an area.

- *Convention and Visitors Bureau:* Most large cities have a website for the area's convention and visitors bureau mainly to attract events and meetings. Many of these sites are filled with information on accommodations, restaurants, and entertainment attractions more suited to a travel guide. We find these of little use.
- *Realtor websites:* Despite the fact that these sites are obviously created to sell property, they often have some good information for potential relocation candidates. Most have pictures of homes, which give a good idea not only of home value but also of the character and appearance of local residences. Unfortunately many ask you to register so that a realtor can contact you. For a quick overview of housing in an area, we recommend visiting the National Association of Realtors' website at www.realtor.com—just enter the zip code to learn more about a particular meighborhood.

Web & Software Tools

As we mentioned in chapter 3, mapping software and satellite imagery tools helped us capture the physical layout of a place and some of its resources. Microsoft MapPoint allowed us to "map" selected data items, such as median home prices, by zip code. MapPoint also shows locations for schools, hospitals, and other resources. "Google Earth" (http://earth.google.com) gave us a visual aerial image of most areas. From these images, we could "see" physical layouts, major parks, and recreation facilities—all of which helped us discover new details and direct our further research.

Interviews

Our interviews were treasure-trove of intangible quality-of-life information. By talking to locals and asking questions—where do people work, what do people do, how's the educational environment—we learned what actual residents thought was good and bad about each neighborhood. We also interviewed realtors to pinpoint specifics like property taxes paid as a percentage of the market value of a home and we spoke to daycare providers to get the latest prices in an area.

Can You Do this Yourself?

The facts used in this book come from an assortment of public and private sources widely used in demographic and market research. Much of the information is available free—the hard part is knowing how to find it and how to assemble it into a practical and usable package. We've done most of that legwork for you, and the Sperling's BestPlaces website (www.bestplaces.net) is the go-to site for answers to any additional questions you might have, as well as a great place to continue to get updated information.

As an example, the National Climatic Data Center, a branch of the National Oceanic and Atmospheric Administration (NOAA) of the U.S. Department of Commerce, publishes vast amounts of climate and weather statistics, all available, and most of it online, free. However, the statistics include up to 70 years of monthly weather observations for 18,000 weather stations around the United States. Our process distills this ocean of detail into what's important for you to know about the 100 places highlighted in this book.

Data Timeliness

The data in *Best Places to Raise Your Family* is as timely as possible, but due to the nature of our sources, some statistics may be 5 years old. Is old data a problem? In most cases, it's not. Large numbers don't normally change quickly. Some do, like home prices and employment figures, and so we've made every attempt to keep up-to-date with such figures in this volume.

U.S. government agencies collect vast amounts of data from the U.S. Census every 10 years. Census 2000 statistics are still shown in this book and are still being used as the base for various published government studies. That said, the U.S. Census and other agencies are quickly moving to bring in more and faster updates through annual surveys. The rapidly expanding annual American Community Survey, which provides general population statistics and trend figures through 2004, is the best example. Other than the U.S. Census statistics, most data used in this book was compiled between 2003 and 2005.

A Few Words about Measures

Throughout the book, you'll see a number of raw data values, medians, and averages. In order to make large amounts of very detailed data on a topic more presentable and easier to grasp, we (with the help of Sperling's BestPlaces) processed it into a single value—an *index, score,* or *rating*. All of these numbers are designed not only to give you a quick read on an area, but also to help you compare it to others. Without going too deep

into the mechanics, here are the basic definitions you should understand:

- An *index* compares values for an area to a national average represented as 100. The best example is the Cost of Living Index (COL). An index of 90 for an area means that overall costs of living are estimated at 90% of the national average, while an index of 120 means costs are 20% *higher* than average.

- A *score* combines several measurable attributes of an area, and expresses it on a 0 to 100 scale— 0 being the worst in the United States; 100 being the best. (The exceptions to this rule are the pollen/allergy score and the stress score; in these cases, 0 is the best and 100 is the worst. See p. 106.) Each factor is weighted and added to a composite figure, which is then converted to a 0 to 100 scale, based on the range of values found across the United States.

- A *rating* is like a score, except that it's based on a mix of quantifiable facts and subjective judgment. To avoid confusing it with a score, we present it on a 1 to 10 scale—1 being the worst as judged against the rest of the United States; 10 being the best. An "arts" rating looks at the quantity, size, and attendance of performing and display arts resources, and also incorporates a subjective evaluation on quality.

Presenting the Facts

We could have simply offered you a list of the 100 Best Places, perhaps ranked from top to bottom, made a few comments about each, and sold you a much thinner book. But that would have cheated you out of crucial, and some of the most interesting, information. No two places are alike, and each has a different set of strengths and weaknesses. You want to see for yourself what those strengths and weaknesses are, because no two families have *exactly* the same needs or interests. To help you decide what's right for *you* and to make sure you fully understand the numbers we print here, we supplement our objective data with considerable subjective analysis.

In chapter 3, we introduced the five categories of factual data that this book is largely based on: People, Standard of Living, Education, Lifestyle, and Health & Safety. In this chapter, we explain each fact within these categories. We explain how it was collected and organized into the presentation tables for each place in chapter 5. We also review the best (and sometimes worst) values we found in the most important categories. Our objective in this chapter is to give you a clear understanding of the data and to highlight the top and bottom of the scale in categories that are most important to you.

"Best Of" Analysis

In the front of the book, the "Ranked and Rated by Category" section (see p. 1) illustrates what we think are the best places according to specific categories. The lists and the neighborhoods on them were chosen based on our own personal judgment.

Later in this chapter, as we discuss the data, we build so-called Fact Highlight tables to bring forth the best-in-class places for each attribute. Want to know the top places on our list with regard to the best Cost of Living profiles? See Table 4.25 on p. 71.

Area & Neighborhood Tables

We tried our best to establish the right mix of detailed "Neighborhood" facts and more generalized "Metro Area" facts. For each place we discuss in the book, a Neighborhood Highlights Table shows detailed facts relevant (and available) at the neighborhood level. An Area Highlights Table is also included to show metro area level detail.

Neighborhood detail (at a zip code level) is presented as such because it's what you as a neighborhood resident will experience, and it will be different from what residents of the neighborhood next door experience. Examples include property tax rates, school data, and daycare costs. Some facts and resources simply make more sense to show at the metro area level, because they aren't neighborhood specific, like hospitals, museum ratings, and climate information. All residents of the Boston metro area have access to the same museums and hospitals, and all experience, with minor variations, the same climate. Finally, some items, like cost of living and housing, educational attainment, and growth rates, are shown at *both* the metro area and neighborhood level, so you can see how the neighborhood compares to the rest of the area.

Both types of tables are organized into the five major categories we introduced earlier: People, Standard of Living, Education, Lifestyle, and Health & Safety. If you're looking for a particular piece of information, say,

Median Home Price, you'll want to first determine what category it's in (Standard of Living) and look for it there. You'll also notice that, for clarity, categories are broken down into subcategories. Don't worry; this is all going to seem much clearer as we show and explain Area and Neighborhood Highlight Table examples throughout this chapter.

Area Highlights Table

Roswell, Georgia, the number-three best place to raise your family, is located in the Atlanta, Georgia, Metropolitan Statistical area. See Table 4.1.

In this table, you should note the five major categories, and the 14 subcategories, which include "Income, Employment & Taxes" (under Standard of Living) and "Crime" (under Health & Safety). Note, too, that we show national averages alongside each data item to give you a benchmark, which should help you compare each number and look at it comparatively on a national scale.

Area Data Descriptions

Table 4.1 shows actual data from the Atlanta metro area. But we expect, as you become more familiar with these tables, that you'll want to refer from time to time to a quick summary of what each field is, what it means, and where it comes from. The Area Highlights Data Descriptions table (Table 4.2) helps you do this, and you may want to bookmark it as a handy reference for later, as you comb through the descriptions of the best places in chapter 5. Each fact is explained in more detail, later in this chapter.

Neighborhood Highlights Table

Roswell, Georgia, is part of the Atlanta metro area, and Table 4.4 shows the data we've selected to present at the neighborhood level. Again to review, you'll note a small amount of overlap, as, for example, median home prices are shown for both the area and the neighborhood to facilitate comparison. For some topics like climate, detailed data is presented at the metro area level, like "days mostly sunny" and "days > 90°F," then summarized as a Climate Rating on the Neighborhood Table for quick reference.

Neighborhood Data Descriptions

The data descriptions, sources, and dates for the neighborhood data are explained in Table 4.3.

TABLE 4.1 ATLANTA, GA
EXAMPLE OF AREA HIGHLIGHTS

PEOPLE

SIZE & DIVERSITY	AREA	U.S. AVG	FAMILY DEMOGRAPHICS	AREA	U.S. AVG
Population	4,559,736		% Married	52.80%	53.80%
15-yr Population Growth	63.80%	4.40%	% Single	47.20%	46.20%
Diversity Measure	54	54	% Divorced	9.80%	10.20%
% Religiously Observant	44%	50%	% Separated	3.60%	2.10%
% Catholic	7%	22%	% Married w/Children	28.50%	27.90%
% Protestant	35%	25%	% Single w/Children	12.10%	9.40%
% Jewish	2%	2%	% Married, No Children	27.10%	31.00%
% Other	1%	1%	% Single, No Children	32.30%	31.70%

STANDARD OF LIVING

INCOME, EMPLOYMENT & TAXES	AREA	U.S. AVG	COST OF LIVING & HOUSING	AREA	U.S. AVG
Median Household Income	$52,051	$44,684	Cost of Living Index	91.3	100
Household Income Growth	4.10%	6.10%	Buying Power Index	128	100
Unemployment Rate	4.10%	5.10%	Median Home Price	$166,500	$208,500
Recent Job Growth	-0.10%	1.30%	Home Price Ratio	3.2	4.7
Projected Future Job Growth	19.60%	10.50%	Home Price Appreciation	4.90%	13.60%
State Income Tax Rate	6%	5.00%	% Homes Owned	62.30%	64.10%
State Sales Tax Rate	6%	6.00%	Median Rent	$928	$792

EDUCATION

ATTAINMENT & ACHIEVEMENT	AREA	U.S. AVG	RESOURCES & INVESTMENT	AREA	U.S. AVG
% High School Graduate	78.70%	83.90%	No. of Highly Ranked Universities	4	1
% 2-yr Graduate	7.30%	7.10%	$ Invested per Pupil	$5,795	$6,058
% 4-yr Graduate	22.90%	17.20%	Student/Teacher Ratio	16.2	15.9
% Graduate or Professional Degree	9.50%	9.90%	State University In-State Tuition	$4,272	$4,917
% Attending Public School	91.90%	84.30%			
75th Percentile State University SAT Score (Verbal)	550	477			
75th Percentile State University SAT Score (Math)	560	478			
75th Percentile State University ACT Score	23	20			

LIFESTYLE

RECREATION, ARTS & CULTURE	AREA	U.S. AVG	INFRASTRUCTURE & FACILITIES	AREA	U.S. AVG
Professional Sports Rating	7	4	No. of Public Libraries	134	28
Zoos & Aquariums Rating	9	3	Library Volumes Per Capita	1.8	2.8
Amusement Park Rating	10	3	No. of Warehouse Clubs	10	4
Professional Theater Rating	10	3	No. of Starbucks	91	5
Overall Museum Rating	10	6	Golf Course Rating	9	4
Science Museum Rating	8	4	National Park Rating	2	3
Children's Museum Rating	9	3	Sq. Mi. Inland Water	4	4

CLIMATE			COMMUTE & TRANSPORTATION		
Days Mostly Sunny	219	212	Avg. Daily Commute Time	31.2	24.7
Annual Days Precipitation	116	111	% Commute by Auto	77%	77.70%
Annual Days > 90°F	19	38	Per Capita Avg. Daily Transit Miles	16.7	7.9
Annual Days < 32°F	59	88	Annual Auto Insurance Premium	$1,500	$1,314
July Relative Humidity	70	69	Gas, Cost per Gallon	3.01	3.05

HEALTH & SAFETY

CRIME & ENVIRNOMENTAL ISSUES	AREA	U.S. AVG	HEALTHCARE & COST	AREA	U.S. AVG
Violent Crime Rate	513	517	Physicians per Capita	217	254.3
Change in Violent Crime	-28.80%	-7.50%	Pediatricians per Capita	20.4	16.9
Property Crime Rate	4320	3783	Hospital Beds per Capita	249.2	239.7
Change in Property Crime	-23.40%	-10.10%	No. of Teaching Hospitals	11	1.9
Air Quality Score	32	44	Healthcare Cost Index	104.4	100
Water Quality Score	51	33	Cost per Doctor Visit	$70	$74
Pollen/Allergy Score	63	61	Cost per Dentist Visit	$66	$67
Stress Score	82	49	Cost per Hospital Room	$677	$702
Cancer Mortality Rate	166.2	168.9			

TABLE 4.2 AREA HIGHLIGHTS DATA DESCRIPTIONS

FIELD NAME	DESCRIPTION
PEOPLE	
Population	Total residents in metropolitan area.
15-yr Population Growth	Growth in metro area population, 1990-2003.
Diversity measure	Probability that next person met is ethnicity other than your own.
% Religiously Observant	Percentage of population regularly attending services, all faiths, largest MSA county.
% Catholic	Percentage Catholic, largest MSA county.
% Protestant	Percentage Protestant, all denominations, largest MSA county.
% Jewish	Percentage Jewish, largest MSA county.
% Other	Percentage following other faiths, largest MSA county.
FAMILY DEMOGRAPHICS	
% Married	Percentage of population surveyed as married.
% Single	Percentage of population surveyed as single.
% Divorced	Percentage of population surveyed as divorced.
% Separated	Percentage of population surveyed as separated.
% Married w/Children	Percent of population surveyed as married with one or more children.
% Single w/Children	Percentage of population surveyed as single with one or more children.
% Married, No Children	Percent of population surveyed as married with no children.
% Single, No Children	Percentage of population surveyed as single no children.
STANDARD OF LIVING	
INCOME, EMPLOYMENT & TAXES	
Median Household Income	Average annual gross income for area households.
Household Income Growth	Percentage of growth in average household income, 1990-2003.
Unemployment Rate	Percentage of active job seekers without a job, August 2003.
Recent Job Growth	Percentage of job growth or decline, August 2002-August 2003.
Projected Future Job Growth	Percentage of projected job growth or decline through 2010.
Income Tax Rate	Highest marginal combined state and local rate.
Sales Tax Rate	Most commonly paid total state and local sales tax rate.
COST OF LIVING & HOUSING	
Cost of Living Index	Total cost of living as an index against national average, first quarter 2003; 100 as average.
Buying Power	Ratio of Area median household income to national average, divided by Area Cost of Living Index.
Median Home Price	Median selling price for the average home type in the area, second quarter 2003.
Home Price Ratio	Ratio of median home price to median household income.
Home Price Appreciation	Annual growth rate in home prices, 2000-2003.
% Homes Owned	Percentage of households owning home.
Median Rent	Median rental price for typical rental unit in the area, first half of 2003.
EDUCATION	
ATTAINMENT & ACHIEVEMENT	
% High School Graduate	Percentage of population surveyed with high school diploma.
% 2-yr Graduate	Percentage of population surveyed with 2-year degree or trade school certificate.
% 4-yr Graduate	Percentage of population surveyed with 4-year college/university degree.
% Graduate or Professional Degree	Percentage of population surveyed with graduate or professional degree.
% Attending Public School	Percentage of total students in area attending public school.
75th Percentile State University SAT Score (Verbal)	Average verbal SAT score for admission to the largest state university.
75th Percentile State State University SAT Score (Math)	Average math SAT score for admission to the largest state university.
75th Percentile State University ACT Score	Average ACT score for admission to the largest state university.
RESOURCES & INVESTMENTS	
No. of Highly Ranked Universities	Number of colleges classified as highly competitive.
$ Invested per Pupil	Dollars spent for public education divided by number of students.
Student/Teacher Ratio	Ratio showing number of students per teacher in public schools.
State Universty In-State Tuition	In-state tuition, largest state university.
LIFESTYLE	
RECREATION, ARTS & CULTURE	
Professional Sports Rating	Availability of professional major- and minor-league spectator sports; 1-10 scale.
Zoos & Aquariums Rating	Availability of zoos, aquariums, and animal parks; 1-10 scale.
Amusement Park Rating	Availability, quality, and proximity of traditional amusement parks; 1-10 scale.
Professional Theater Rating	Availability of theater venues registered with Sterns Theater Directory; 1-10 scale.
Overall Museum Rating	Availability and quality of all museums; 1-10 scale.
Science Museum Rating	Availability and quality of science museums; 1-10 scale.
Children's Museum Rating	Availability and quality of children's museums; 1-10 scale.

SOURCE	DATE
U.S. Census 2000/American Community Survey 2004	2004
U.S. Census 2000/American Community Survey 2004	2004
Sperling's BestPlaces	2003
Glenmary Missioners Study	2000
Glenmary Missioners Study	2000
Glenmary Missioners Study	2000
Glenmary Missioners Study	2000
Glenmary Missioners Study	2000
U.S. Census 2000/American Community Survey 2004	2004
U.S. Census 2000/American Community Survey 2004	2004
U.S. Census 2000/American Community Survey 2004	2004
U.S. Census 2000/American Community Survey 2004	2004
U.S. Census 2000/American Community Survey 2004	2004
U.S. Census 2000/American Community Survey 2004	2004
U.S. Census 2000/American Community Survey 2004	2004
U.S. Census 2000/American Community Survey 2004	2004
Claritas, Inc.	2003
Claritas, Inc.	2003
Bureau of Labor Statistics	2003
Bureau of Labor Statistics	2003
Sperling's BestPlaces	2003
Sperling's BestPlaces	2003
Sperling's BestPlaces	2003
Bureau of Labor Statistics	2003
100 Best Places for Familes calculation	2003
National Association of Realtors	2003
Best Places to Raise Your Family calculation	2003
National Association of Realtors/Sperling's BestPlaces	2003
U.S. Census	2003
U.S. Census	2003
U.S. Census	2001
U.S. Census	2001
U.S. Census	2001
U.S. Census	2001
National Center for Education Statistics	2002
National Center for Education Statistics	2002
National Center for Education Statistics	2002
National Center for Education Statistics	2002
Princeton Review	2002
National Center for Education Statistics	2002
National Center for Education Statistics	2002
National Center for Education Statistics	2002
Sperling's BestPlaces	2003
Sperling's BestPlaces	2003
Sperling's BestPlaces	2003
Sperling's BestPlaces/Sterns Theater Directory	2003
Sperling's BestPlaces/American Association of Museums	2003
Sperling's BestPlaces/American Association of Museums	2003
Sperling's BestPlaces/American Association of Museums	2003

continued

TABLE 4.2 (continued)	
FIELD NAME	**DESCRIPTION**

LIFESTYLE *(CONT.)*

INFRASTRUCTURE & FACILITIES

Public Libraries	Number of library facilities including branches.
Library Volumes Per Capita	Number of volumes per 100,000 residents.
No. of Warehouse Clubs	Number of Costco, Sam's Club, and BJ's stores.
No. of Starbucks	Number of Starbucks retail stores.
Golf Course Rating	Availability, quality, and cost of public and private golf courses; 1–10 scale.
National Park Rating	Availability, quality, and proximity of national parks and forests; 1–10 scale.
Sq. Mi. Inland Water	Square miles of nearby inland freshwater including lakes and streams.

CLIMATE

Days Mostly Sunny	Average days per year with mostly sun or partly cloudy.
Annual Days Precipitation	Average days per year with measurable precipitation.
Days > 90°F	Average days per year where temperature exceeds 90°F.
Days < 32°F	Average days per year where temperature drops below freezing, 32°F.
July Relative Humidity	Average percentage relative humidity recorded during July.

COMMUTE & TRANSPORTATION

Avg. Daily Commute Time	Average number of minutes per one-way commute to work.
% Commute by Auto	Percentage of workers commuting as single driver in vehicle.
Per Capita Avg. Daily Transit Miles	Average daily road miles per person per day.
Annual Auto Insurance Premium	Average insurance premium.
Gas, Cost per Gallon	Average cost per gallon of regular unleaded gas, August 2003.

HEALTH & SAFETY

CRIME & ENVIRONMENTAL ISSUES

Violent Crime Rate	Number of murder, rape, robbery, and assault crimes per 100,000 people.
Change in Violent Crime	Change in violent crime rate, 1996–2001.
Property Crime Rate	Number of burglaries, thefts, and auto thefts per 100,000 people.
Change in Property Crime	Change in property crime rate, 1996–2001.
Air Quality Score	Composite of particulates, ozone, and volatile organic compounds; 1–100 scale.
Water Quality Score	Natural and man-made pollutants in runoff and ground water; 1–100 scale.
Pollen/Allergy Score	Composite of grass, tree, and mold allergens; 1–100 scale.
Stress Score	Composite of eight stress factors shown as 1–100 score.
Cancer Mortality Rate	Death rate attributable from cancer or cancer-related causes; 1–100 scale.

HEALTHCARE & COST

Physicians per Capita	Number of accredited generalists and specialists per 100,000 people.
Pediatricians per Capita	Number of pediatric specialists per 100,000 people.
Hospital Beds per Capita	Number of hospital beds per 100,000 people.
No. of Teaching Hospitals	Number of hospitals accredited to teach or train physicians.
Healthcare Cost Index	Health and health insurance cost against national average, first quarter 2003; 100 as average.
Cost per Doctor Visit	Average dollar cost per doctor visit.
Cost per Dental Visit	Average dollar cost per dentist visit.
Cost per Hospital Room	Average dollar cost, daily, per hospital room.

SOURCE	DATE
Sperling's BestPlaces/National Center for Education Statistics	2002
Sperling's BestPlaces/National Center for Education Statistics	2002
Sperling's BestPlaces/Warehouse club sources	2003
Sperling's BestPlaces/Starbucks, Inc.	2003
Sperling's BestPlaces	2003
Sperling's BestPlaces	2003
Sperling's BestPlaces	2003
NOAA/National Climatic Data Center	2003
NOAA/National Climatic Data Center	2003
NOAA/National Climatic Data Center	2003
NOAA/National Climatic Data Center	2003
NOAA/National Climatic Data Center	2003
U.S. Census Bureau	2000
U.S. Census Bureau	2000
Federal Highway Administration	2002
National Association of Insurance Commissioners	2002
American Automobile Association	2003
FBI Uniform Crime Reports	2002
FBI Uniform Crime Reports	2002
FBI Uniform Crime Reports	2002
FBI Uniform Crime Reports	2002
Sperling's BestPlaces	2003
Sperling's BestPlaces	2003
Sperling's BestPlaces	2003
Sperling's BestPlaces	2003
National Centers for Disease Control and Prevention	2003
American Medical Association	2003
American Medical Association	2003
U.S. Department of Health and Human Services	2001
U.S. Department of Health and Human Services	2001
Bureau of Labor Statistics	2003
American Chamber of Commerce Research Association	2003
American Chamber of Commerce Research Association	2003
American Chamber of Commerce Research Association	2003

TABLE 4.3 NEIGHBORHOOD HIGHLIGHTS DATA DESCRIPTIONS

FIELD NAME	DESCRIPTION
PEOPLE	
Population	Total residents in the zip code.
15-yr Population Growth	Growth in neighborhood population, 1990–2005.
5-yr Population Growth	Growth in neighborhood population, 2000–2005.
No. of Households	Total number of households in zip code.
% Married w/ Children	Percent of population surveyed as married with one or more children.
% Single w/ Children	Percentage of population surveyed as single with one or more children.
Average Household Size	Size of average household greater than one member.
Median Age	Median population age in years.
Diversity Measure	Probability that next person met is ethnicity other than your own.
STANDARD OF LIVING	
Median Household Income	Average annual gross income for every U.S. household.
% Household Income > $100K	Percentage of households with annual gross income over $100,000.
Projected Future Job Growth	Percentage of projected job growth or decline through 2010.
Cost of Living Index	Total cost of living as an index against national average, first quarter 2003; 100 as average.
Buying Power	Ratio of Area median household income to national average, divided by Neighborhood Cost of Living Index.
Weekly Daycare Cost	Cost of weekly day care, 4-year-old child.
Median Home Price	Median selling price for the average home type in the neighborhood, second quarter 2003.
"Sweet Spot" Home Price	Approximate price for "benchmark" family home.
Home Price Ratio	Ratio of median home price to median household income.
Median Age of Homes	Median age of neighborhood homes in years.
% Homes Owned	Percentage of households owning home.
Effective Property Tax Rate	Approximate property taxes paid as a percentage of median home value.
Approximate Property Tax Bill	Estimated total dollars property taxes paid for "sweet spot" home.
EDUCATION	
% High School Graduate	Percentage of adult population with high school diploma.
% 4-yr College Degree	Percentage of adult population with 4-year college/university degree.
% Graduate or Professional Degree	Percent of adult population with graduate or professional degree.
$ Invested per Pupil	Dollars spent for public education divided by number of students.
Student/Teacher Ratio	Ratio showing number of students per teacher in public schools.
Primary Test Score Index	Composite test scores vs. state average, largest primary school in zip code.
Secondary Test Score Index	Composite test scores vs. state average, largest secondary school in zip code.
% Subsidized School Lunch	Percentage of students receiving subsidy for school lunch.
% Attending Public School	Percentage of total students in neighborhood attending public school.
LIFESTYLE	
Leisure Rating (area)	Leisure rating for metro area, 1–10.
Arts & Culture Rating (area)	Arts & Culture rating for metro area, 1–10.
Climate Rating (area)	Climate rating for metro area, 1–10.
Physical Setting Rating	Attractiveness of neighborhood physical setting , rating 1–10.
Downtown Core Rating	Attractiveness of downtown core, rating 1–10.
% Commute < 30 Min.	Percentage of neighborhood commute times less than 30 minutes.
% Commute > 1 Hour	Percentage of neighborhood commute times greater than 1 hour.
HEALTH & SAFETY	
Health Rating (Area)	Health score for metro area, 1–10.
Stress Score (Area)	Composite of eight stress factors shown as 1–100 score, metro area.
Violent Crime Risk	Index estimating the potential of violent crime in the neighborhood.
Property Crime Risk	Index estimating the potential of property (non-violent) crime in the neighborhood.

SOURCE	DATE
U.S. Census 2000/American Community Survey 2004	2004
U.S. Census 2000/American Community Survey 2004	2004
U.S. Census 2000/American Community Survey 2004	2004
U.S. Census 2000/American Community Survey 2004	2004
U.S. Census 2000/American Community Survey 2004	2004
U.S. Census 2000/American Community Survey 2004	2004
U.S. Census 2000/American Community Survey 2004	2004
U.S. Census 2000/American Community Survey 2004	2004
Sperling's BestPlaces	2003
Claritas, Inc.	2003
Claritas, Inc.	2003
Sperling's BestPlaces	2003
Bureau of Labor Statistics	2005
Best Places to Raise Your Family calculation	2005
Best Places to Raise Your Family research	2005
National Association of Realtors	2005
Best Places to Raise Your Family research	2005
Best Places to Raise Your Family calculation	2005
National Association of Realtors	2005
U.S. Census	2003
Best Places to Raise Your Family research	2005
Best Places to Raise Your Family calculation	2005
U.S. Census 2000/American Community Survey 2004	2004
U.S. Census 2000/American Community Survey 2004	2004
U.S. Census 2000/American Community Survey 2004	2004
National Center for Education Statistics	2002
National Center for Education Statistics	2002
Sperling's BestPlaces/Greatschools.net	2002-04
Sperling's BestPlaces/Greatschools.net	2002-04
National Center for Education Statistics	2002
Sperling's BestPlaces	2002
Sperling's BestPlaces	2004
Sperling's BestPlaces	2004
Sperling's BestPlaces	2004
Sperling's BestPlaces	2004
Sperling's BestPlaces	2004
U.S. Census 2000/American Community Survey 2004	2004
U.S. Census 2000/American Community Survey 2004	2004
Sperling's BestPlaces	2004
Sperling's BestPlaces	2004
CAP Index, Inc.	2005
CAP Index, Inc.	2005

4.4 ROSWELL, GA
EXAMPLE OF NEIGHBORHOOD HIGHLIGHTS

PEOPLE

Population	46,244
15-yr Population Growth	25.50%
5-yr Population Growth	-0.20%
% Married w/Children	32.4%
% Single w/Children	10.7%
No. of Households	16,542
Median Age	35.8
Avg. Household Size	2.78
Diversity Measure	27

STANDARD OF LIVING — BEST

Median Household Income	$85,884
% Household Income > $100K	43%
Projected Future Job Growth	11%
Cost of Living Index	127
Buying Power Index	154
Weekly Daycare Cost	$160
Median Home Price	$304,000
"Sweet Spot" Home Price	$300,000
Home Price Ratio	3.5
Median Age of Homes	15.9
% Homes Owned	80%
Effective Property Tax Rate	1.40%
Estimated Property Tax Bill	$4,200

EDUCATION — BEST

% High School Graduates	94%
% 4-yr Degree	38%
% Graduate or Professional Degree	19%
$ Invested per Pupil	$6,141
Student/Teacher Ratio	15.7
Primary Test Score Percentile	114.4
Secondary Test Score Percentile	101.3
% Subsidized School Lunch	10.90%
% Attending Public School	79%

LIFESTYLE

Leisure Rating (Area)	9
Arts & Culture Rating (Area)	9
Climate Rating (Area)	7
Physical Setting Rating	6
Downtown Core Rating	3
% Commute < 30 Min.	42%
% Commute > 1 Hour	9%

HEALTH & SAFETY

Health Rating (Area)	3
Stress Score (Area)	8
Violent Crime Risk	29
Property Crime Risk	32

TABLE 4.5 ATLANTA, GA AREA HIGHLIGHTS SEGMENT PEOPLE						
SIZE & DIVERSITY	**AREA**	**U.S. AVG**	**FAMILY DEMOGRAPHICS**	**AREA**	**U.S. AVG**	
Population	4,559,736		% Married	52.80%	53.80%	
15-yr Population Growth	63.80%	4.40%	% Single	47.20%	46.20%	
Diversity Measure	54	54	% Divorced	9.80%	10.20%	
% Religiously Observant	44%	50%	% Separated	3.60%	2.10%	
% Catholic	7%	22%	% Married w/Children	28.50%	27.90%	
% Protestant	35%	25%	% Single w/Children	12.10%	9.40%	
% Jewish	2%	2%	% Married, No Children	27.10%	31.00%	
% Other	1%	1%	% Single, No Children	32.30%	31.70%	

From here, let's move forward into the individual categories and subcategories.

People

This category aims to tell you a bit about your neighbors—how many people live in the area and how they appear in terms of age, marital status, and diversity. As we move forward through these category-by-category sections, we will use excerpts from the Roswell, Georgia–Atlanta Metro Area Highlight tables to show examples of real data.

Tables 4.5 and 4.6 show the Area Highlights and Neighborhood Highlights for Roswell, Georgia, for People. A few notes about the presentation:

- You can see how the facts for a metro area compare to U.S. averages. We don't show national averages for Neighborhood Highlights items because most would be redundant with the Area Highlights Table.

- "Married with Children" (MWC) and "Single with Children" (SWC) percentages are shown at both the area and the neighborhood levels, showing that Roswell has relatively more MWCs and fewer SWCs than the Atlanta area as a whole.

- Facts on religious observances are included at the metro area level. We did not include them at the neighborhood level because that data wasn't available. Clearly, these are "presentation" facts, not "evaluation" facts.

Size & Diversity

How big is that neighborhood, city, or town you're interested in? How diverse is the area, ethnically and culturally? The first column of the Area Highlights Table and the first part of the Neighborhood Highlights Table help answer these questions.

Population Size & Growth

Our goal in developing a list of the best places to raise your family was to offer a choice of large, medium, and small places, plus a choice of rapidly growing and more static areas. The following facts come from the U.S. Census 2005 American Community Survey with data current through 2004.

Population Size

Metro area population sizes have a wide range. The Los Angeles, California, MSA has almost 10 million residents, while the Minden-Gardnerville, Nevada, area has 45,394. You can gauge metro area population sizes by looking at the Largest, Large, Mid-size, Smaller, and Smallest designations in the neighborhood narratives in chapter 5.

At the neighborhood level, population size has a lot to do with the way the zip code is drawn and may or may not connect directly with the feeling of crowdedness or uncrowdedness in the area. Most of our neighborhoods have populations between 20,000 and 50,000; in fact, 65 out of the 100 Best Places fall in this range. The largest is Virginia Beach, Virginia, with 78,449 residents, and the smallest is the "Kohler" area of Sheboygan, Wisconsin (zip code 53044) with 1,946.

TABLE 4.6 ROSWELL, GA NEIGHBORHOOD HIGHLIGHTS SEGMENT	
PEOPLE	
Population	46,244
15-yr Population Growth	25.50%
5-yr Population Growth	-0.20%
% Married w/Children	32.4%
% Single w/Children	10.7%
No. of Households	16,542
Median Age	35.8
Avg. Household Size	2.78
Diversity Measure	27

Fifteen-Year Population Growth

Size is one thing, growth is quite another. Rapid growth brings some good things—a stronger tax base, more conveniences, and better shopping choices. But it also brings traffic headaches and higher home prices. We chose a mix of fast- and slower growing suburbs, the fastest being Castle Rock, Colorado, and the "slowest" (actually negative) including Coraopolis–Moon Township, Pennsylvania, and Evendale, Ohio. These areas showed decline as older industries moved out and some residents fled farther into the suburbs, but represent good values today and, especially in the case of Coraopolis, Pennsylvania, seem to be on the rise again. Table 4.7 is our first Fact Highlight Table, showing Fifteen-Year Population Growth at the neighborhood level:

Five-Year Population Growth

Not surprisingly, many of the same players are on both the 15- and 5-year population growth lists. See Table 4.8.

Diversity

We believe that diversity makes a place a better place to live, just as it makes a workplace a better place to work. Diversity brings value in differing points of view, different interests, and different cultures to learn from. We measure ethnic diversity using our catchall Diversity Measure, and add to it a breakdown of an area's religious mix.

Diversity Measure

Created by Sperling's BestPlaces, the Diversity Measure is a unique way to get a quick read on an area's ethnic and cultural diversity. Strictly speaking, the measure indicates the probability, as a percentage, that the next person you'll see walking down the street is of an ethnic origin *different* than your own. A high number means the area is more diverse. The U.S. average is about 35, meaning that across the country, you have a 35% chance that the next person you'll meet is of different

TABLE 4.7 FIFTEEN-YEAR POPULATION GROWTH
Neigborhood Level Data, 1990–2004
U.S. AVERAGE: 14.9%

FASTEST GROWING			SLOWEST GROWING		
80104	Castle Rock, CO	294.0%	15108	Coraopolis–Moon Township, PA	-6.4%
46060	Noblesville, IN	112.7%	45241	Evendale, OH	-6.0%
77479	Sugar Land, TX	96.4%	14068	Getzville, NY	-3.3%
75028	Flower Mound, TX	94.0%	43537	Maumee, OH	-2.5%
72758	Rogers, AR	84.4%	07039	Livingston, NJ	2.4%
37064	Franklin, TN	81.4%	14534	Pittsford, NY	3.0%
27513	Cary, NC	68.8%	60302	Oak Park, IL	4.4%
98607	Vancouver-Camas, WA	64.8%	79606	Abilene, TX	4.6%
89423	Minden, NV	64.3%	01824	Chelmsford, MA	4.7%
83616	Eagle, ID	61.6%	36695	West Mobile, AL	5.8%
FASTER GROWING			SLOWER GROWING		
32073	Orange Park, FL	55.1%	02067	Sharon, MA	6.1%
78732	Austin (West), TX	50.9%	02760	North Attleboro, MA	8.3%
28105	Matthews, NC	50.9%	37343	Hixson, TN	8.7%
63304	St. Charles, MO	50.8%	06470	Newtown, CT	9.1%
89523	Reno, NV	49.5%	07648	Norwood, NJ	9.4%
22602	Winchester, VA	45.7%	53044	Sheboygan, WI	9.7%
80526	Fort Collins, CO	44.4%	24018	Roanoke, VA	10.6%
21045	Columbia, MD	42.4%	10994	West Nyack, NY	10.6%
98226	Bellingham, WA	41.0%	54403	Wausau, WI	10.7%
66216	Shawnee, KS	39.9%	11730	East Islip, NY	11.6%
33326	Weston, FL	39.8%	23456	Virginia Beach, VA	12.0%
98273	Mount Vernon, WA	39.6%	18018	Bethlehem, PA	12.0%
98501	Olympia, WA	39.3%	91354	Santa Clarita, CA	12.1%
84037	Kaysville, UT	39.0%	74012	Broken Arrow, OK	13.1%
84321	Logan, UT	38.9%	43026	Hilliard, OH	13.3%
98275	Mukilteo, WA	38.4%	57702	Rapid City, SD	13.9%
29212	Irmo, SC	37.9%	67212	Wichita (West), KS	14.9%
55044	Lakeville, MN	37.7%	17601	Lancaster, PA	15.3%
76002	Arlington, TX	35.7%	68022	Elkhorn, NE	15.8%
92354	Loma Linda, CA	35.4%	47906	West Lafayette, IN	16.4%

Source: U.S. Census 2000/American Community Survey 2004

TABLE 4.8 FIVE-YEAR POPULATION GROWTH		
Neigborhood Level Data, 2000–2004		

U.S. AVERAGE: 4.4%

FASTEST GROWING			SLOWEST GROWING		
80104	Castle Rock, CO	35.4%	80027	Louisville, CO	-4.2%
46060	Noblesville, IN	26.8%	45241	Evendale, OH	-3.6%
77479	Sugar Land, TX	24.9%	15108	Coraopolis–Moon Township, PA	-2.4%
75028	Flower Mound, TX	22.5%	14068	Getzville, NY	-1.5%
72758	Rogers, AR	17.2%	79606	Abilene, TX	-1.1%
32073	Orange Park, FL	16.7%	43537	Maumee, OH	-1.0%
37064	Franklin, TN	16.0%	60302	Oak Park, IL	-0.9%
27513	Cary, NC	14.6%	30075	Roswell, GA	-0.2%
98607	Vancouver-Camas, WA	13.7%	01824	Chelmsford, MA	-0.1%
63304	St. Charles, MO	13.0%	14534	Pittsford, NY	0.0%

FASTER GROWING			SLOWER GROWING		
22602	Winchester, VA	12.5%	36695	West Mobile, AL	0.2%
92354	Loma Linda, CA	12.4%	07039	Livingston, NJ	0.4%
89523	Reno, NV	12.2%	80220	Denver (Park Hill), CO	0.4%
22901	Charlottesville, VA	12.0%	02067	Sharon, MA	0.5%
28105	Matthews, NC	11.0%	37343	Hixson, TN	0.8%
95630	Folsom, CA	10.5%	74012	Broken Arrow, OK	1.0%
83616	Eagle, ID	10.5%	53044	Sheboygan, WI	1.2%
33594	Valrico, FL	10.2%	54403	Wausau, WI	1.5%
66216	Shawnee, KS	10.1%	43026	Hilliard, OH	1.9%
89423	Minden, NV	10.0%	47906	West Lafayette, IN	2.1%
76002	Arlington, TX	9.8%	07648	Norwood, NJ	2.1%
95694	Winters, CA	9.3%	24018	Roanoke, VA	2.2%
84037	Kaysville, UT	9.3%	40503	Lexington, KY	2.2%
98501	Olympia, WA	8.4%	06470	Newtown, CT	2.3%
33326	Weston, FL	8.1%	32605	Gainesville, FL	2.4%
98226	Bellingham, WA	8.0%	10994	West Nyack, NY	2.4%
98273	Mount Vernon, WA	7.9%	67212	Wichita (West), KS	2.4%
21045	Columbia, MD	7.6%	02760	North Attleboro, MA	2.5%
60047	Lake Zurich, IL	7.5%	97405	Eugene, OR	2.7%
19382	West Chester, PA	7.4%	66049	Lawrence, KS	2.8%

Source: U.S. Census 2000/American Community Survey, 2004

origin. Most areas are in the teens or 20s but range up to 72 in the case of Loma Linda, California. Table 4.9 shows the neighborhoods with the highest diversity.

Religious Observance & Mix

We researched variations in religious observance and mix across the United States and found some interesting differences. The Glenmary Home Missioners, a Catholic religious service organization, through its Research Center conducts cross-denominational surveys to assess church attendance across the country. From this data, we compiled *observance*—the percentage of the population that regularly attends services—and the *mix* of denominations, which reflects a summary by major religious division of what kind of church people attend.

Religions are grouped into Catholic, Protestant, Jewish, and Other categories. This data is compiled at the metro area level, tabulated for the largest county in the metro area. See Tables 4.10, 4.11, 4.12, and 4.13.

Median Age

Median Age is the age at which half the population is older and half is younger. Metro areas are large enough that Median Age tends to converge close to national averages. But at the neighborhood level, interesting differences start to appear. We see older median ages, not surprisingly, in growing areas once most attractive to retirees, like Grants Pass, Oregon, and Minden, Nevada, and in more "old economy" areas like Pennsylvania. We see younger ages in rapidly growing areas in Texas, California, and other places mainly in the west. Younger families, particularly those looking for other younger families, might especially want to look at Table 4.14.

TABLE 4.9 DIVERSITY SCORE		
Neighborhood Level Data		
U.S. AVERAGE: 54		
MOST DIVERSE		
92354	Loma Linda, CA	72
95694	Winters, CA	70
20170	Herndon, VA	66
17601	Lancaster, PA	66
76002	Arlington, TX	63
20878	Gaithersburg, MD	61
80220	Denver (Park Hill), CO	61
98273	Mount Vernon, WA	59
77479	Sugar Land, TX	57
21045	Columbia, MD	56
MORE DIVERSE		
33326	Weston, FL	53
23456	Virginia Beach, VA	52
92688	Rancho Santa Margarita, CA	48
60302	Oak Park, IL	47
95630	Folsom, CA	46
78232	Hollywood Park, TX	44
08824	Kendall Park, NJ	43
91354	Santa Clarita, CA	40
35758	Madison, AL	36
27513	Cary, NC	36
07648	Norwood, NJ	36
72758	Rogers, AR	35
32073	Orange Park, FL	35
33594	Valrico, FL	34
87122	Albuquerque (Sandia Heights), NM	34
22901	Charlottesville, VA	33
29212	Irmo, SC	33
07039	Livingston, NJ	32
98275	Mukilteo, WA	32
10994	West Nyack, NY	31

Source: Sperling's BestPlaces, 2004

TABLE 4.10 PERCENT CATHOLIC		
Metro Area (Largest County) Level Data		
U.S. AVERAGE: 22%		
HIGHEST PERCENTAGE		
01824	Chelmsford, MA	54%
14068	Getzville, NY	53%
54313	Green Bay, WI	52%
11730	East Islip, NY	52%
02760	North Attleboro, MA	52%
02067	Sharon, MA	51%
06470	Newtown, CT	47%
07648	Norwood, NJ	46%
03062	Nashua, NH	46%
08824	Kendall Park, NJ	43%
HIGHER PERCENTAGE		
15108	Coraopolis–Moon Township, PA	42%
91354	Santa Clarita, CA	40%
54911	Appleton, WI	40%
10994	West Nyack, NY	39%
78232	Hollywood Park, TX	39%
07039	Livingston, NJ	39%
60047	Lake Zurich, IL	39%
60302	Oak Park, IL	39%
54403	Wausau, WI	37%
19382	West Chester, PA	36%
87122	Albuquerque (Sandia Heights), NM	36%
14534	Pittsford, NY	32%
53186	Waukesha, WI	31%
18018	Bethlehem, PA	31%
53532	DeForest, WI	28%
57702	Rapid City, SD	28%
92688	Rancho Santa Margarita, CA	27%
92354	Loma Linda, CA	27%
53044	Sheboygan, WI	27%
55044	Lakeville, MN	26%

Source: Glenmary Research Center, 2000

Family Facts

Aside from overall population statistics, we also think it's interesting and important to show family statistics for each area. These facts are taken from the U.S. Census American Community Survey and reflect data through 2004.

Marital Status & Presence of Children

We look closely at the married-with-children percentage of households on the assumption that their needs and goals are similar to yours. But we also present area detail on all of the census's marital and family status facts, and go further to show married-with-children and single-with-children percentages for each neighborhood. The definitions for these categories, we think, are mainly self-explanatory. Presence of children means that there are one or more children in the household age 18 or younger.

For fact highlights and analysis, refer to Tables 2.5 to 2.9 in chapter 2. These are the categories we include in chapter 5's Area Highlights data tables:

- % Married
- % Single
- % Divorced
- % Separated
- % Married w/children
- % Single w/children
- % Married no children
- % Single no children

Number of Households

The number of households in a neighborhood is somewhat tied to the population in that neighborhood. Like

TABLE 4.11 PERCENT PROTESTANT		
Metro Area (Largest County) Level Data		
U.S. AVERAGE: 25.4%		
HIGHEST PERCENTAGE		
84321	Logan, UT	82%
84037	Kaysville, UT	64%
79606	Abilene, TX	60%
37922	Farragut, TN	57%
75791	Tyler, TX	56%
29650	Greer, SC	54%
24018	Roanoke, VA	50%
37343	Hixson, TN	49%
35758	Madison, AL	49%
74012	Broken Arrow, OK	46%
HIGHER PERCENTAGE		
72758	Rogers, AR	46%
53044	Sheboygan, WI	46%
28105	Matthews, NC	43%
58104	Fargo, ND	43%
36695	West Mobile, AL	43%
37064	Franklin, TN	42%
76002	Arlington, TX	40%
29212	Irmo, SC	40%
40503	Lexington, KY	40%
55902	Rochester, MN	39%
17601	Lancaster, PA	38%
23233	Richmond-Tuckahoe, VA	36%
30075	Roswell, GA	35%
57702	Rapid City, SD	35%
17402	York, PA	34%
67212	Wichita (West), KS	34%
54403	Wausau, WI	34%
32073	Orange Park, FL	33%
65203	Columbia, MO	33%
49426	Hudsonville, MI	32%

Source: Glenmary Research Center, 2000

TABLE 4.12 PERCENT JEWISH		
Metro Area (Largest County) Level Data		
U.S. AVERAGE: 2.2%		
HIGHEST PERCENTAGE		
10994	West Nyack, NY	13%
33326	Weston, FL	13%
11730	East Islip, NY	11%
01824	Chelmsford, MA	8%
07648	Norwood, NJ	7%
07039	Livingston, NJ	7%
91354	Santa Clarita, CA	6%
02067	Sharon, MA	5%
19382	West Chester, PA	5%
08824	Kendall Park, NJ	5%
HIGHER PERCENTAGE		
80027	Louisville, CO	5%
21045	Columbia, MD	4%
06470	Newtown, CT	4%
20878	Gaithersburg, MD	3%
20170	Herndon, VA	3%
60047	Lake Zurich, IL	3%
60302	Oak Park, IL	3%
80104	Castle Rock, CO	2%
80220	Denver (Park Hill), CO	2%
92688	Rancho Santa Margarita, CA	2%
30075	Roswell, GA	2%
63304	St. Charles, MO	2%
14534	Pittsford, NY	2%
19810	Arden-Brandywine, DE	2%
33594	Valrico, FL	2%
14068	Getzville, NY	2%
15108	Coraopolis–Moon Township, PA	2%
02760	North Attleboro, MA	2%
03062	Nashua, NH	2%
23233	Richmond-Tuckahoe, VA	2%

Source: Glenmary Research Center, 2000

population, some variation is caused by the details of how the zip codes are drawn. We tried to pick neighborhoods with a large enough number of households, again, to have enough convenient infrastructure nearby. Eighty of our 100 best places have between 5,000 and 20,000 households.

Average Household Size

We show data for average household size *for households with more than one member* at the neighborhood level. The largest average household size occurs in Kaysville, Utah, with an average of 3.17 per household (U.S. average is about 2.7). Smaller household sizes occur in older city neighborhoods like Park Hill, Colorado, in Denver, and Oak Park, Illinois, and, not surprisingly, in college towns. The lowest reading is 2.16 residents per household in Denver (Park Hill), Colorado.

Standard of Living

We developed this book on the premise that America's families, as importantly as anything else, need to prosper financially wherever they are. Financial troubles are well-known to be one of the leading causes of divorce. But going further, financial difficulties cause stress leading to countless other problems and deterioration in family harmony, and often compromise educational goals. We're not advocating that families move just to try to "get rich." But we do believe that your choice of where to live profoundly affects incomes and costs and whether you can not only "make ends meet" but accumulate wealth to achieve future goals.

With that in mind, we set out to develop a clear picture of each place's "standard of living"—essentially, the factors having to do with a family's income and expenses. There's no concise definition of standard of living. Clearly it doesn't have as much to do with the

TABLE 4.13 RELIGIOUS OBSERVANCE						
% of Population Indicating Regular Church Attendance Metro Areas (Largest County) Level Data						
U.S. AVERAGE: 50.2%						

MOST OBSERVANT

84321	Logan, UT	85%
54313	Green Bay, WI	73%
01824	Chelmsford, MA	73%
53044	Sheboygan, WI	72%
11730	East Islip, NY	72%
14068	Getzville, NY	71%
54403	Wausau, WI	71%
54911	Appleton, WI	70%
84037	Kaysville, UT	70%
02067	Sharon, MA	68%

LEAST OBSERVANT

97526	Grants Pass, OR	20%
89423	Minden, NV	23%
97405	Eugene, OR	25%
98501	Olympia, WA	27%
89523	Reno, NV	28%
66049	Lawrence, KS	29%
98226	Bellingham, WA	29%
22602	Winchester, VA	31%
95694	Winters, CA	32%
98607	Vancouver-Camas, WA	33%

MORE OBSERVANT

06470	Newtown, CT	67%
79606	Abilene, TX	67%
15108	Coraopolis–Moon Township, PA	66%
07648	Norwood NJ	66%
75791	Tyler, TX	65%
78232	Hollywood Park, TX	63%
02760	North Attleboro, MA	63%
57702	Rapid City, SD	63%
18018	Bethlehem, PA	63%
10994	West Nyack, NY	62%
55902	Rochester, MN	62%
37922	Farragut, TN	61%
58104	Fargo, ND	59%
08824	Kendall Park, NJ	58%
03062	Nashua, NH	58%
91354	Santa Clarita, CA	58%
07039	Livingston, NJ	58%
19382	West Chester, PA	58%
29650	Greer, SC	57%
03062	Nashua, NH	57%

LESS OBSERVANT

98275	Mukilteo, WA	33%
32605	Gainesville, FL	34%
23456	Virginia Beach, VA	35%
22901	Charlottesville, VA	36%
95630	Folsom, CA	36%
99223	Spokane, WA	36%
43026	Hilliard, OH	36%
52241	Coralville, IA	37%
99516	Anchorage, AK	37%
47906	West Lafayette, IN	37%
33594	Valrico, FL	38%
80104	Castle Rock, CO	39%
80220	Denver (Park Hill), CO	39%
80526	Fort Collins, CO	39%
27513	Cary, NC	40%
46060	Noblesville, IN	41%
65203	Columbia, MO	41%
92354	Loma Linda, CA	42%
32073	Orange Park, FL	43%
19810	Arden-Brandywine, DE	43%

Source: Glenmary Research Center, 2000

things you own as it does with your *ability*—not always exercised—to buy the things you want and need. Just because you own a big "McMansion" home doesn't mean you have a high standard of living—if you have to forgo college education for your three children to have it.

Are we looking for the "cheapest" areas or cheapest places in an area? Hardly. As we've emphasized already, we're looking for *value*. Some of our 100 best places are admittedly expensive, but these are places where a family can enjoy a good standard of living *relative* to other neighborhoods in an area. Surely Norwood, New Jersey; Newtown, Connecticut; Rancho Santa Margarita, California; and Lake Zurich, Illinois, look expensive individually, but in the context of their metro areas, they represent relatively good values, especially compared to their peer neighborhoods. Our goal is to offer you a range of inexpensive choices as well as a few more

expensive options that have sufficient local incomes to support their higher costs and help you maintain a positive standard of living.

In this section, we offer many facts and tables, but that shouldn't be taken as evidence that standard of living is more important than other variables. It's just that there are more facts and figures available in this category.

Presentation Tables

Looking at Tables 4.15 and 4.16, which sum up the Standard of Living in the Roswell, Georgia, neighborhood and in the Atlanta metro area, you can see that a number of income and cost factors are shown at both the area and the neighborhood level. Two cost factors—daycare cost and property taxes, are shown *only* at the local level. We also included the "sweet spot" family

	TABLE 4.14 MEDIAN AGE Neighborhood Level Data					
		U.S. AVERAGE: 35.5				
OLDEST				**YOUNGEST**		
97526	Grants Pass, OR	41.4		76002	Arlington, TX	28.4
19810	Arden-Brandywine, DE	41		84321	Logan, UT	28.7
89423	Minden, NV	40.9		92688	Rancho Santa Margarita, CA	29.4
17402	York, PA	40.9		84037	Kaysville, UT	29.5
24018	Roanoke, VA	40.8		47906	West Lafayette, IN	29.5
17601	Lancaster, PA	40.5		75028	Flower Mound, TX	29.6
18018	Bethlehem, PA	40.3		55044	Lakeville, MN	29.9
14534	Pittsford, NY	40.1		23456	Virginia Beach, VA	30.5
45241	Evendale, OH	39.7		91354	Santa Clarita, CA	30.6
07648	Norwood, NJ	39.3		43026	Hilliard, OH	31.2
OLDER				**YOUNGER**		
07039	Livingston, NJ	39.2		27513	Cary, NC	31.3
97405	Eugene, OR	39.1		20170	Herndon, VA	31.3
15108	Coraopolis–Moon Township, PA	39		77479	Sugar Land, TX	31.4
57702	Rapid City, SD	38.8		80027	Louisville, CO	31.7
01824	Chelmsford, MA	38.6		52241	Coralville, IA	31.9
32605	Gainesville, FL	38.6		80526	Fort Collins, CO	32
54403	Wausau, WI	38.5		78732	Austin (West), TX	32.1
22901	Charlottesville, VA	38.3		58104	Fargo, ND	32.1
10994	West Nyack, NY	38.1		35758	Madison, AL	32.5
87122	Albuquerque (Sandia Heights), NM	37.9		49426	Hudsonville, MI	32.6
40503	Lexington, KY	37.9		80104	Castle Rock, CO	32.7
78232	Hollywood Park, TX	37.8		63304	St. Charles, MO	32.8
92354	Loma Linda, CA	37.4		74012	Broken Arrow, OK	32.9
37343	Hixson, TN	37.3		95694	Winters, CA	32.9
43537	Maumee, OH	37.2		60047	Lake Zurich, IL	33.2
60302	Oak Park, IL	37.1		20878	Gaithersburg, MD	33.3
02067	Sharon, MA	37		53532	DeForest, WI	33.5
53044	Sheboygan, WI	36.9		50325	West Des Moines–Clive, IA	33.5
03062	Nashua, NH	36.8		36695	West Mobile, AL	33.5
23233	Richmond-Tuckahoe, VA	36.8		54313	Green Bay, WI	33.6

Source: U.S. Census 2000/American Community Survey, 2004

TABLE 4.15 ATLANTA, GA AREA HIGHLIGHTS SEGMENT						
		STANDARD OF LIVING				
INCOME, EMPLOYMENT & TAXES	**AREA**	**U.S. AVG**		**COST OF LIVING & HOUSING**	**AREA**	**U.S. AVG**
Median Household Income	$52,051	$44,684		Cost of Living Index	91.3	100
Household Income Growth	4.10%	6.10%		Buying Power Index	128	100
Unemployment Rate	4.10%	5.10%		Median Home Price	$166,500	$208,500
Recent Job Growth	-0.10%	1.30%		Home Price Ratio	3.2	4.7
Projected Future Job Growth	19.60%	10.50%		Home Price Appreciation	4.90%	13.60%
State Income Tax Rate	6%	5.00%		% Homes Owned	62.30%	64.10%
State Sales Tax Rate	6%	6.00%		Median Rent	$928	$792

home price and approximate property tax bill for a benchmark family home in the area.

Income, Employment & Taxes

The U.S. Census and U.S. Department of Labor Bureau of Labor Statistics collect a great deal of information on employment and incomes, and are increasingly using surveys to keep their information up-to-date. We also relied on data from Claritas, Inc., a leading private supplier of data for market analysis.

In compiling this data, we were interested in incomes, income stability, and growth. We measured incomes directly and looked closely at current, recent, and future employment trends.

TABLE 4.16 ROSWELL, GA NEIGHBORHOOD HIGHLIGHTS SEGMENT	
STANDARD OF LIVING	**BEST**
Median Household Income	$85,884
% Household Income › $100K	43%
Projected Future Job Growth	11%
Cost of Living Index	127
Buying Power Index	154
Weekly Daycare Cost	$160
Median Home Price	$304,000
"Sweet Spot" Home Price	$300,000
Home Price Ratio	3.5
Median Age of Homes	15.9
% Homes Owned	80%
Effective Property Tax Rate	1.40%
Estimated Property Tax Bill	$4,200

TABLE 4.17 MEDIAN HOUSEHOLD INCOME Neighborhood Level Data		
U.S. AVERAGE: $44,684		
HIGHEST		
10994	West Nyack, NY	$116,191
78732	Austin (West), TX	$109,908
99516	Anchorage, AK	$107,470
60047	Lake Zurich, IL	$106,694
07039	Livingston, NJ	$105,769
02067	Sharon, MA	$104,568
06470	Newtown, CT	$102,105
08824	Kendall Park, NJ	$101,760
77479	Sugar Land, TX	$99,555
87122	Albuquerque (Sandia Heights), NM	$98,844
HIGHER		
07648	Norwood, NJ	$98,779
20878	Gaithersburg, MD	$97,790
75028	Flower Mound, TX	$93,617
91354	Santa Clarita, CA	$92,439
20170	Herndon, VA	$91,379
14534	Pittsford, NY	$90,809
30075	Roswell, GA	$87,206
55044	Lakeville, MN	$86,314
95630	Folsom, CA	$83,829
37922	Farragut, TN	$82,326
01824	Chelmsford, MA	$82,209
92688	Rancho Santa Margarita, CA	$81,230
50325	West Des Moines–Clive, IA	$80,455
80027	Louisville, CO	$78,989
11730	East Islip, NY	$78,859
80104	Castle Rock, CO	$78,438
53044	Sheboygan, WI	$77,541
19382	West Chester, PA	$77,454
21045	Columbia, MD	$76,424
23233	Richmond-Tuckahoe, VA	$76,143

Source: U.S. Census 2000/American Community Survey 2004

It's hard to project whether an individual family will have income growth and stability in an area, but we consider it useful to operate on a "rising tide floats all boats" philosophy. Obviously, each family needs to realistically appraise its chances in an area.

With income and normal spending in daily life come taxes, and the differences among states and local taxes are fascinating. Using Sperling's BestPlaces, we tallied the combined state and local income taxes and sales taxes for each area. Through our direct research, we calculated effective property tax rates as a percent of property values. Because sales and income taxes are driven primarily at the state level, we decided to provide summary tables sourced from facts published by the Federation of Tax Administrators, a nonprofit organization serving the public finance community.

Median Household Income

Median Household Income (MHI) is the statistical median income (half are higher, half are lower) for all households with more than one member. Household income includes all income from all sources and all earners. The MHI implicitly captures several factors representative of employment and pay scales in the area, including job mix (number of high-paying jobs), number of earners in the household, and cost-of-living adjustments characteristic of the area.

Not surprisingly, income levels vary considerably across the country. Most, but not all, of the selected neighborhoods in this book have household income levels above the U.S. average of $44,684. The ones below these levels tend to be college towns or smaller towns away from major national and regional economic centers.

Table 4.17 shows neighborhoods with the highest median household incomes. Many are in expensive coastal locations, but a few, like Farragut, Tennessee, are more reflective of the skill level and quality of jobs in the area than the location.

Percent Household Income › $100,000

Median household income tells part of the story, but it's also interesting to note what percentage of households are truly high earners. This fact is presented only at the neighborhood level. The places in this book range from 6% in small towns like Grants Pass, Oregon, and Logan, Utah, to 55% in West Nyack, New York, and in our chosen neighborhood west of Austin, Texas. See Table 4.18.

Household Income Growth

Income growth is at least as important as income levels. Growth indicates improving job quality; that is, more

TABLE 4.18 HOUSEHOLD INCOME > $100,000 Percent of Households with Income > $100K/year, Neighborhood Level Data		
U.S. AVERAGE: $44,684		
HIGHEST		
78732	Austin (West), TX	55%
10994	West Nyack, NY	55%
60047	Lake Zurich, IL	51%
07039	Livingston, NJ	50%
99516	Anchorage, AK	48%
77479	Sugar Land, TX	47%
07648	Norwood, NJ	47%
87122	Albuquerque (Sandia Heights), NM	46%
06470	Newtown, CT	44%
02067	Sharon, MA	44%
HIGHER		
30075	Roswell, GA	43%
14534	Pittsford, NY	43%
75028	Flower Mound, TX	42%
08824	Kendall Park, NJ	42%
20878	Gaithersburg, MD	40%
20170	Herndon, VA	39%
91354	Santa Clarita, CA	38%
50325	West Des Moines–Clive, IA	36%
80104	Castle Rock, CO	34%
37922	Farragut, TN	33%
19382	West Chester, PA	32%
01824	Chelmsford, MA	32%
27513	Cary, NC	31%
55044	Lakeville, MN	31%
95630	Folsom, CA	30%
92688	Rancho Santa Margarita, CA	30%
80027	Louisville, CO	30%
53044	Sheboygan, WI	29%
11730	East Islip, NY	29%
23233	Richmond-Tuckahoe, VA	29%

Source: U.S. Census 2000/American Community Survey 2004

TABLE 4.19 HOUSEHOLD INCOME GROWTH 1990–2004 Metro Area Level Data		
U.S. AVERAGE: 6.1%		
HIGHEST		
02760	North Attleboro, MA	17.6%
02067	Sharon, MA	17.3%
23456	Virginia Beach, VA	14.5%
95630	Folsom, CA	14.5%
08824	Kendall Park, NJ	13.9%
58104	Fargo, ND	13.8%
57702	Rapid City, SD	12.3%
35758	Madison, AL	12.1%
23233	Richmond-Tuckahoe, VA	12.1%
06470	Newtown, CT	12.0%
HIGHER		
92354	Loma Linda, CA	12.0%
55902	Rochester, MN	11.7%
01824	Chelmsford, MA	11.3%
95694	Winters, CA	11.2%
24018	Roanoke, VA	10.9%
55044	Lakeville, MN	10.9%
03062	Nashua, NH	10.9%
99516	Anchorage, AK	10.9%
21045	Columbia, MD	10.6%
17601	Lancaster, PA	10.3%
22901	Charlottesville, VA	10.2%
22602	Winchester, VA	10.1%
37064	Franklin, TN	9.5%
92688	Rancho Santa Margarita, CA	9.5%
11730	East Islip, NY	9.4%
19382	West Chester, PA	9.3%
10994	West Nyack, NY	9.2%
37922	Farragut, TN	9.1%
15108	Coraopolis–Moon Township, PA	9.0%
91354	Santa Clarita, CA	8.9%

Source: U.S. Census 2000/American Community Survey 2004

high-paying jobs are moving in and the mix of jobs is improving. Because job mix is most important at the area level (due to commuting), this fact is presented only at that level. Most people don't live and work in the same neighborhood.

Table 4.19 illustrates that there's strong geographic diversity among places with growing incomes. Many are in the Northeast and Virginia but others are sprinkled throughout the country: Madison, Alabama (near Huntsville); Lakeville, Minnesota, in the Twin Cities area; and Rapid City, South Dakota.

Unemployment Rate

From income levels, let's move on to what creates the income: employment and unemployment. We received the current Unemployment levels and Recent Job Growth from the Bureau of Labor Statistics and present both at the area level.

Table 4.20 shows the lowest employment in college towns (including Charlottesville, Virginia; DeForest, Wisconsin; Columbia, Missouri; and Gainesville, Florida), in cities with strong healthcare (Gainesville again; Rochester, Minnesota; and Roanoke, Virginia), and rapidly rising stars (such as Rogers, Arkansas, and Winchester, Virginia).

Recent Job Growth

Strong job growth in the past year is an excellent indicator of economic strength—whether it's the result of organic growth, recovery from a recession, or a shift in employment to newer industries. All are good news, particularly if unemployment rates are reasonable.

Areas like Rogers, Arkansas, and Reno, Nevada, are on a strong growth track, period. Areas like Wichita, Kansas, and Mount Vernon, Washington are in recovery, while Bellingham, Washington; Spokane, Washington;

TABLE 4.20 UNEMPLOYMENT RATE Metro Area Level Data		
U.S. AVERAGE: 5.1%		
LOWEST		
58104	Fargo, ND	2.0%
22901	Charlottesville, VA	2.0%
32605	Gainesville, FL	2.0%
22602	Winchester, VA	2.0%
53532	DeForest, WI	2.2%
72758	Rogers, AR	2.4%
65203	Columbia, MO	2.4%
24018	Roanoke, VA	2.7%
92688	Rancho Santa Margarita, CA	2.9%
84321	Logan, UT	3.0%
LOWER		
89523	Reno, NV	3.0%
55902	Rochester, MN	3.0%
79606	Abilene, TX	3.1%
20878	Gaithersburg, MD	3.1%
20170	Herndon, VA	3.1%
40503	Lexington, KY	3.2%
54403	Wausau, WI	3.2%
57702	Rapid City, SD	3.3%
08824	Kendall Park, NJ	3.3%
27513	Cary, NC	3.3%
01824	Chelmsford, MA	3.3%
17601	Lancaster, PA	3.4%
89423	Minden, NV	3.4%
37922	Farragut, TN	3.5%
03062	Nashua, NH	3.5%
53044	Sheboygan, WI	3.5%
33594	Valrico, FL	3.5%
37343	Hixson, TN	3.6%
11730	East Islip, NY	3.6%
06470	Newtown, CT	3.6%

Source: Bureau of Labor Statistics, 2005

TABLE 4.21 RECENT JOB GROWTH August 2004–August 2005		
U.S. AVERAGE: 1.3%		
HIGHEST		
72758	Rogers, AR	7.4%
29212	Irmo, SC	6.3%
98273	Mount Vernon, WA	5.7%
98226	Bellingham, WA	5.6%
66049	Lawrence, KS	4.9%
53044	Sheboygan, WI	4.8%
84321	Logan, UT	4.8%
98501	Olympia, WA	4.6%
67212	Wichita (West), KS	4.5%
99223	Spokane, WA	4.4%
HIGHER		
98275	Mukilteo, WA	4.4%
89523	Reno, NV	4.3%
99516	Anchorage, AK	4.3%
40503	Lexington, KY	4.3%
54313	Green Bay, WI	4.2%
33326	Weston, FL	4.1%
32605	Gainesville, FL	4.0%
29650	Greer, SC	3.7%
92354	Loma Linda, CA	3.6%
10994	West Nyack, NY	3.6%
32073	Orange Park, FL	3.6%
33594	Valrico, FL	3.6%
55902	Rochester, MN	3.6%
50325	West Des Moines–Clive, IA	3.5%
80220	Denver (Park Hill), CO	3.4%
80104	Castle Rock, CO	3.4%
83616	Eagle, ID	3.4%
58104	Fargo, ND	3.3%
28105	Matthews, NC	3.1%
95694	Winters, CA	2.9%

Source: Bureau of Labor Statistics, 2005

and Lexington, Kentucky are enjoying favorable transitions (see Table 4.21). We're wary of places where recent job growth is driven in large part by the real estate boom and its related construction, lending, and transaction processing enterprises.

Projected Future Job Growth

Very interesting are the future job-growth projections furnished by Sperling's BestPlaces and derived from long-term economic growth trends in an area. These percentages represent the projected growth for the next 5 years, from 2006 to 2010, and are drawn from a number of economic factors. Data is presented both at the area and neighborhood levels, although in many cases they are similar. To see the places with the highest future job growth, at the neighborhood level, refer to Table 4.22.

The newer "powerhouse" suburbs—like Sugar Land, Texas; Castle Rock, Colorado; Flower Mound, Texas; and Orange Park, Florida—anchor this list, but some notable smaller places also show up, mainly because of attractive locations, excellent work forces, and strong local economic development efforts: Logan, Utah; Rogers, Arkansas; Franklin, Tennessee; and St. Charles, Missouri are a few examples.

State Income Taxes

Comparing income taxes among states is by no means an easy task, but it does reveal interesting differences. All taxes, of course, are a function of *rate* and *basis*; that is, *rate* is the percentage the state or local agency levies on a *basis*, the amount of taxable income. Precise comparisons are elusive, because each state has different rules for calculating the taxable income basis. Further, rates are usually structured into brackets, where the marginal rates on the last taxable earned dollar will

TABLE 4.22 FUTURE JOB GROWTH		
Projected 2005–2010		
U.S. AVERAGE: 10.5%		
HIGHEST		
80104	Castle Rock, CO	52%
77479	Sugar Land, TX	35%
37064	Franklin, TN	30%
72758	Rogers, AR	30%
46060	Noblesville, IN	29%
55044	Lakeville, MN	29%
98607	Vancouver-Camas, WA	27%
75028	Flower Mound, TX	26%
32073	Orange Park, FL	26%
84321	Logan, UT	25%
HIGHER		
80526	Fort Collins, CO	25%
84037	Kaysville, UT	25%
98275	Mukilteo, WA	25%
21045	Columbia, MD	25%
29212	Irmo, SC	22%
83616	Eagle, ID	22%
78732	Austin (West), TX	21%
98226	Bellingham, WA	21%
27513	Cary, NC	21%
98501	Olympia, WA	21%
76002	Arlington, TX	20%
65203	Columbia, MO	20%
63304	St. Charles, MO	20%
58104	Fargo, ND	19%
89423	Minden, NV	19%
78232	Hollywood Park, TX	19%
98273	Mount Vernon, WA	18%
28105	Matthews, NC	18%
49426	Hudsonville, MI	18%
66216	Shawnee, KS	18%

Source: Sperling's BestPlaces, 2005

vary according to an individual's total income level. Add to that the existence of local income taxes (which are outlawed in a few states, like California), and, well, the income taxes you actually pay may be different than what's shown in Table 4.23.

Table 4.23 defines the top tax bracket and shows the rate for that bracket. But for most families the third column is probably the most useful one, showing rates for a typical married-filing-jointly household with a taxable income of $50,000. The table is sorted on that column, and states with tax rates at $50,000 that are *higher* than the U.S. average of 6.0% are shown on the left. But this still doesn't tell the whole story: States have different exemption amounts for children. Several match the federal amount of $3,200, but many more offer less. And some states, like Oregon and Montana, allow you to deduct federal taxes from your income basis, reducing the effective tax rate considerably from the reported 11% and 9%, respectively.

State Sales Taxes

Like income taxes, sales tax policies among states vary considerably, although they don't have quite as much effect on the family "bottom line" as income taxes. As with income taxes, total tax dollars depend on rate and basis. Sales tax basis can vary, and as Table 4.24 shows, some states tax food, as well as prescription and non-prescription drugs, and some don't. Making matters more complicated is the fact that some states have a low base tax rate, allowing substantial local taxes as voted in (or not)—Colorado is a great example. The 2.9% base state sales tax rate is meaningless; in Louisville, Colorado, the total rate exceeds 8%.

There are still five states (Alaska, Delaware, Montana, New Hampshire, and Oregon) with no state sales tax. These states, particularly Oregon and New Hampshire, have become shopping "havens" as residents from nearby high-tax states (Washington, California, and Massachusetts) go on regular shopping expeditions. And while some politicians have dug in hard to resist new taxes, there is increasing pressure, especially in states like Oregon, to begin a sales tax to take care of fiscal woes.

Cost of Living & Housing

The effect of incomes and steady employment on a family's standard of living is quite clear. But regional and local differences in cost of living and especially housing have been dramatic and growing, and make the selection of place a critical factor in determining one's standard of living as a family.

Getting More Expensive—Why?

The best places are, as a rule, getting more expensive. A lot of it has to do with employment and higher expectations for education and lifestyle. Increased mobility and the growth of a "knowledge" or "creative" economy have made it possible to work anywhere, but the reality is that enterprises in the healthiest, most rapidly growing industries—like information technology and media—tend to flock together into intellectually stimulating and climate-friendly centers like the San Francisco Bay Area, New York, Boston, and Seattle, to name a few. In these places, residents can find a community among others with similar needs and interests. These industries have had the strongest employment growth, and while some creative enterprises have sought less-crowded, more cost-friendly environs in

TABLE 4.23 STATE INCOME TAXES

Sorted by marginal rate applied to $50,000 adjusted gross income for married filing jointly
Listing includes top marginal rates, top brackets, and exemption amounts for children

U.S. AVERAGE: 6.0% AT $50,000 BRACKET (AMONG STATES WITH INCOME TAX)

AT OR ABOVE U.S. AVERAGE						BELOW U.S. AVERAGE				
	TOP MARGINAL RATE	TOP MARGINAL BRACKET	MARGINAL RATE AT AGI $50,000	EXEMPTION AMOUNTS FOR CHILDREN	FEDERAL TAXES DEDUCTIBLE?(*)		TOP MARGINAL RATE	TOP MARGINAL BRACKET	MARGINAL RATE AT AGI $50,000	EXEMPTION AMOUNTS FOR CHILDREN	FEDERAL TAXES DEDUCTIBLE?(*)
MT	11.0%	$77,800	10.0%	$1,900	Y	VA	5.75%	$17,001	5.75%	$800	
OR	9.0%	$13,001	9.0%	$154(c)	Y(*)	DE	5.95%	$60,000	5.55%	$110(c)	
ME	8.5%	$34,701	8.5%	$2,850		MA	5.3%	flat rate	5.3%	$1,000	
IA	8.98%	$55,691	7.92%	$80(c)	Y	OH	7.5%	$200,000	5.201%	$1,300	
ID	7.8%	$44,149	7.8%	$3,200		AL	5.0%	$6,000	5.0%	$300	Y
HI	8.25%	$80,001	7.6%	$1,040		MS	5.0%	$10,000	5.0%	$1,500	
VT	9.5%	155,976	7.2%	$3,200		CT	5.0%	$20,001	5.0%	$0	
MN	7.85%	$112,911	7.05%	$3,200		MD	4.75%	$3,000	4.75%	$2,850	
NC	8.25%	$200,000	7.00%	$3,200		CO	4.63%	flat rate	4.63%	$0	
AR	7.0%	$27,900	7.0%	$20(c)		ND	5.5%	$319,101	3.92%	$3,200	
SC	7.0%	$12,500	7.0%	$3,200	Y	MI	3.9%	flat rate	3.9%	$3,100	
UT	7.0%	$8,257	7.0%	$2,400		AZ	5.04%	$300,000	3.74%	$2,300	
NY	7.70%	$500,000	6.85%	$1,000		IN	3.4%	flat rate	3.4%	$1,000	
NE	6.84%	$46,750	6.84%	$101(c)		PA	3.07%	flat rate	3.07%	$0	
NM	6.8%	$40,001	6.8%	$3,200	Y(*)	IL	3.0%	flat rate	3.0%	$2,000	
OK	6.65%	$10,000	6.65%	$1,000		NJ	8.97%	$500,000	2.45%	$1,500	
WI	6.75%	$86,101	6.5%	$2,000							
WV	6.5%	$30,000	6.5%	$2,000							
KS	6.45%	$60,001	6.25%	$2,250							
CA	9.3%	$80,693	6.0%	$265(c)							
GA	6.0%	$10,001	6.0%	$2,700							
KY	6.0%	$8,000	6.0%	$20(c)							
LA	6.0%	$50,000	6.0%	$1,000	Y(*)						
MO	6.0%	$9,000	6.0%	$1,200							

STATES WITH INCOME TAX TIED TO FACTORS OTHER THAN EARNED INCOME

RI	25% of federal income tax
TN	6% on dividends and interest only
NH	5% on dividends and interest only

STATES WITH NO INCOME TAX

AK, FL, NV, SD, TX, WA, WY

(Y) indicates that federal taxes are deductible from state tax basis (adjusted gross income, or AGI). A (*) indicates limitations on this deduction.
(c) denotes tax credit.

Sources: 2005 World Almanac and Book of Facts, Federation of Tax Administrators, CCH Tax Guide

places like Boise, Idaho; Fort Collins, Colorado; Albuquerque, New Mexico; and Richmond, Virginia, the big centers continue to get more expensive. The lack of buildable land is also a factor, especially in the San Francisco Bay and New York areas.

"Second" Destinations

More recently, we've seen rapid growth in population and cost in areas near, but not in, the big coastal centers. Home prices have skyrocketed in places like Las Vegas, Nevada; Phoenix, Arizona; San Diego, California; Sacramento, California, and the DC suburbs of northern Virginia. Why? There are two major factors. The first is spillover growth—high costs in the big centers

and the relative availability of land in these "second" centers. Increasingly, people are settling farther out, while continuing their economic ties to the big center through regular long-distance commutes or some combination of work-at-home and on-site presence. Many companies have set up new offices in these areas to take advantage of the new workforce, effectively creating exurbs around the older urban cores.

Immigration is another factor. For most of U.S. history, immigrants landed in the big centers like New York, Los Angeles, and San Francisco, only to later assimilate and find their "second" destination somewhere else in the United States as jobs and other circumstances dictated. Today, many seek out that "second"

TABLE 4.24 STATE SALES TAXES
January 2005 Base Sales Tax Rate, Before Local Surcharges

U.S. AVERAGE: 5.2% (AMONG STATES WITH SALES TAX)

ABOVE US AVERAGE	STATE RATE	MAX. LOCAL RATE	MAX. TOTAL RATE	BASIS FOOD EXEMPT?	BASIS RX DRUGS EXEMPT?	BASIS NON-RX DRUGS EXEMPT?	BELOW US AVERAGE	STATE RATE	MAX. LOCAL RATE	MAX. LOCAL RATE	BASIS FOOD EXEMPT?	BASIS RX DRUGS EXEMPT?	BASIS NON-RX DRUGS EXEMPT?
TN	7.0%	2.75%	9.75%	6.0%	*		ND	5.0%	2.5%	7.5%	*	*	
MS	7.0%	0.25%	7.25%		*		NM	5.0%	2.25%	7.25%	*	*	
RI	7.0%	na	7.0%	*	*	*	IA	5.0%	2.0%	7.0%	*	*	
WA	6.5%	2.4%	8.9%	*	*		SC	5.0%	2.0%	7.0%		*	
MN	6.5%	1.0%	7.5%	*	*	*	WI	5.0%	0.6%	5.6%	*	*	
NV	6.5%	1.0%	7.5%	*	*		MA	5.0%	na	5.0%	*	*	
IL	6.25%	3.0%	9.25%	1.0%	1.0%	1.0%	MD	5.0%	na	5.0%	*	*	*
CA	6.25%	2.65%	8.9%	*	*		ME	5.0%	na	5.0%	*	*	
TX	6.25%	2.0%	8.25%	*	*	*	UT	4.75%	2.25%	7.0%		*	
AR	6.0%	5.5%	11.5%		*		OK	4.5%	6.0%	10.5%		*	
ID	6.0%	3.0%	9.0%		*		NC	4.5%	3.0%	7.5%	*	*	
OH	6.0%	2.0%	8.0%	*	*		NY	4.25%	4.0%	8.25%	*	*	*
FL	6.0%	1.5%	7.5%	*	*	*	MO	4.225%	4.5%	8.725%	1.225%	*	
PA	6.0%	1.0%	7.0%	*	*	*	AL	4.0%	7.0%	11.0%		*	
VT	6.0%	1.0%	7.0%	*	*	*	LA	4.0%	6.25%	10.25%		*	
CT	6.0%	na	6.0%	*	*	*	GA	4.0%	3.0%	7.0%	*	*	
IN	6.0%	na	6.0%	*	*		SD	4.0%	2.0%	6.0%		*	
KY	6.0%	na	6.0%	*	*		WY	4.0%	2.0%	6.0%		*	
MI	6.0%	na	6.0%	*	*		VA	4.0%	1.0%	5.0%	4.0%	*	*
NJ	6.0%	na	6.0%	*	*	*	HI	4.0%	na	4.0%		*	
WV	6.0%	na	6.0%		*		CO	2.9%	7.0%	9.9%	*	*	
AZ	5.6%	4.5%	10.1%	*	*		AK	0%	7.0%	7.0%			
NE	5.5%	1.5%	7.0%	*	*								
KS	5.3%	3.0%	8.3%		*								

STATES WITH NO STATE SALES TAX

AK	local tax allowed
DE	no local tax
MT	no local tax
NH	no local tax
OR	no local tax

For Basis, (*) means exempted, % rate shown indicates different rate

Source: Federation of Tax Administrators

destination as soon as they enter the country. (The booms in Las Vegas, and in many of the other hot real estate markets, can partially be explained by this factor.) Thus, we expect that while cost profiles in the regional "big" centers will stabilize, growth in these "second" centers should continue for some time with the normal ups and downs that might be seen in any demand and supply–driven market.

Cost Factors

We include an assortment of facts to characterize the cost of living and housing in each area. The Cost of Living Index is a composite barometer of all costs, including housing. Daycare cost figures aren't found in any other book—they were hand- (or telephone-) researched especially for this project.

We look at home prices and housing costs from several angles, including the property taxes paid on homes owned, which, like state income and sales taxes, can vary considerably. Finally, we bring a couple of hand-crafted measures into the mix—such as the Buying Power Index and Home Price Ratio—to give a fast and effective appraisal of the "bottom line" relative Standard of Living in an area.

Most of these measures appear on both the Area and the Neighborhood tables, but some, like daycare cost and property tax rates, appear only on the Neighborhood Table where they're most relevant.

Cost of Living Index

The Cost of Living Index gives one of the quickest "reads" into an area's cost profile—and thus, its

TABLE 4.25 COST OF LIVING INDEX						
Neighborhood Level Data						
U.S. AVERAGE: 100						
LEAST EXPENSIVE				**MOST EXPENSIVE**		
75791	Tyler, TX	82.1		07648	Norwood, NJ	190.7
79606	Abilene, TX	84.0		10994	West Nyack, NY	172.1
72758	Rogers, AR	84.8		02067	Sharon, MA	165.6
74012	Broken Arrow, OK	87.5		06470	Newtown, CT	165.2
17601	Lancaster, PA	87.9		07039	Livingston, NJ	164.4
54403	Wausau, WI	88.1		92688	Rancho Santa Margarita, CA	155.9
67212	Wichita (West), KS	88.4		60047	Lake Zurich, IL	155.8
37343	Hixson,TN	90.1		91354	Santa Clarita, CA	153.9
54911	Appleton, WI	90.2		95630	Folsom, CA	151.2
32605	Gainesville, FL	90.5		11730	East Islip, NY	150.9
LESS EXPENSIVE				**MORE EXPENSIVE**		
84321	Logan, UT	92.1		33326	Weston, FL	148.2
78232	Hollywood Park, TX	92.3		01824	Chelmsford, MA	147.5
18018	Bethlehem, PA	92.5		80027	Louisville, CO	144.7
36695	West Mobile, AL	92.6		98275	Mukilteo, WA	141.1
40503	Lexington, KY	93.0		60302	Oak Park, IL	139.2
76002	Arlington, TX	93.1		80220	Denver (Park Hill), CO	137.3
22602	Winchester, VA	94.1		08824	Kendall Park, NJ	136.6
17402	York, PA	94.1		20170	Herndon, VA	135.3
24018	Roanoke, VA	94.6		99516	Anchorage, AK	134.0
47906	West Lafayette, IN	95.8		02760	North Attleboro, MA	134.0
35758	Madison, AL	96.0		80104	Castle Rock, CO	133.4
65203	Columbia, MO	96.2		55044	Lakeville, MN	132.0
29212	Irmo, SC	96.7		95694	Winters, CA	131.0
52241	Coralville, IA	96.9		87122	Albuquerque (Sandia Heights), NM	130.9
97526	Grants Pass, OR	97.2		19382	West Chester, PA	129.7
46060	Noblesville, IN	97.7		30075	Roswell, GA	126.6
32073	Orange Park, FL	97.7		78732	Austin (West), TX	125.2
57702	Rapid City, SD	97.8		92354	Loma Linda, CA	122.8
68022	Elkhorn, NE	99.2		89423	Minden, NV	120.3
53044	Sheboygan, WI	99.4		03062	Nashua, NH	119.0

Source: Sperling's BestPlaces/Bureau of Labor Statistics, 2005

Standard of Living. The "COL" captures a range of living costs, including housing, food, transportation, utilities, and a catchall "other" category. It's based on research done by the Bureau of Labor Statistics, analyzed further by market research firms, and finally interpreted by Sperling's BestPlaces to generate zip code level figures.

COL is a true index, meaning the national average is 100. In our Roswell, Georgia, example, the COL is 126.6, meaning that costs in Roswell average 26.6% higher than national averages. *Is that good or bad?* It's not only higher than the national average, but it stands out significantly against the Atlanta area average of 91.

Certainly, such a cost premium must be examined in light of what's available in the area, and the *level of income* one can expect to earn in that area. It may be helpful to mention that area COL ranges from a low of 78 in the San Antonio, Texas, area to a high of just over 167 in Orange County, California. It's also useful to note that the 100 best places in this book range from a low of 82.1 (Tyler, Texas) to a high of 190.7 in Norwood, New Jersey, outside of New York City.

We already acknowledged that we're not seeking the cheapest places but rather those that deliver the most *value*. Almost two-thirds of our neighborhoods have a COL above 100, and almost all neighborhood COLs exceed those of their larger metro area.

Table 4.25 shows the lowest and highest COL Indexes among the 100 best places. It's good to be aware of the costs in the expensive places, but in most of those places, income levels and other attractions make them still worth considering. In fact, the next metric, Buying Power Index, puts the COL in perspective by comparing it to local income levels.

Buying Power Index

To assess Cost of Living relative to income levels in an area—perhaps the quickest read of true Standard of

TABLE 4.26 BUYING POWER INDEX (BPI)		
U.S. AVERAGE: 100		
BEST BPI		
78732	Austin (West), TX	196
77479	Sugar Land, TX	194
20878	Gaithersburg, MD	194
75028	Flower Mound, TX	193
14534	Pittsford, NY	181
99516	Anchorage, AK	179
37922	Farragut, TN	179
53044	Sheboygan, WI	175
68022	Elkhorn, NE	171
76002	Arlington, TX	170
RUNNERS UP		
87122	Albuquerque (Sandia Heights), NM	169
08824	Kendall Park, NJ	167
78232	Hollywood Park, TX	164
35758	Madison, AL	163
50325	West Des Moines–Clive, IA	160
63304	St. Charles, MO	158
23233	Richmond-Tuckahoe, VA	155
30075	Roswell, GA	154
60047	Lake Zurich, IL	153
17601	Lancaster, PA	153
14068	Getzville, NY	153
58104	Fargo, ND	152
20170	Herndon, VA	151
10994	West Nyack, NY	151
54313	Green Bay, WI	149
21045	Columbia, MD	149
29212	Irmo, SC	147
55044	Lakeville, MN	146
24018	Roanoke, VA	146
66216	Shawnee, KS	146

Source: *Best Places to Raise Your Family* calculation

Living in an area—we devised the Buying Power Index (BPI). The best way to explain it is by example.

First, we indexed the area's Median Household Income by comparing the neighborhood's MHI to the national average of $44,684. That effectively gives a MHI index that's similar to the COL Index: For Roswell, Georgia, the MHI is $87,206. Divide that by the U.S. average of $44,684, and you get a "Median Household Income Index" of 195; in other words, the Median Household Income is 95% higher than the U.S. average. Sounds great, but remember costs are also higher than national averages, as represented by the COL, and in fact almost 27% higher. The last step in determining the neighborhood's BPI is to divide the "MHI Index," which isn't shown here, by the COL. Dividing 195 by 126.6 gives a Buying Power Index of 154. That, as we'll see, is strong, and indicates a relatively high standard of living in Roswell, Georgia.

The standard of living in the Atlanta area as a whole isn't so bad, either. The MHI is $52,044; divided by the national average of $44,684, that equals an index of 116, which means that it's 16% higher than national averages, against the area's COL of 91, which is 9% below national averages. The resulting BPI of 127 is also healthy if not an outright bargain for a big city.

Table 4.26 shows the neighborhoods with the highest Buying Power Indexes. Note that some places are on the list (Gaithersburg, Maryland, and Anchorage, Alaska, for example) despite their high cost profiles; they ride the coattails of very healthy incomes. Others, like Sugar Land, Texas; Madison, Alabama; and Irmo, South Carolina, have decent incomes for their regions, but their Buying Power is a function of low costs.

Weekly Daycare Cost

The cost of daycare can be a huge financial burden, especially if there are several children to care for. But

(VALUE) Income Tax–Free States

There are still states that have no income tax at all (Alaska, Florida, Nevada, South Dakota, Texas, Washington, and Wyoming) and two states (New Hampshire and Tennessee) that tax investment dividends and interest *only*. Our hats go off to these states, for while some other forms of taxes might be higher than average (such as sales tax in Washington or property tax in Texas), keeping that extra 5% or 6% of an income can be a big help for families.

Moreover, some states just seem to get by on less; we've seen differences as much as 16% in total tax take (income, sales, and property) among states. East Coast states (Connecticut, Rhode Island, and New York) tend to be the highest, approaching 19% of typical incomes, while the intermountain states of Wyoming, New Mexico, and Nevada tend to be lowest, taking less than 5% of a typical income.

TABLE 4.27 WEEKLY DAYCARE COST					
Weekly Cost, 3- to 4-Year-Old Preschooler, Franchised Care Facility					
AVERAGE OF PLACES RESEARCHED: $152/WEEK					
LEAST EXPENSIVE			**MOST EXPENSIVE**		
89423	Minden, NV	$65	10994	West Nyack, NY	$275
29650	Greer, SC	$80	07039	Livingston, NJ	$257
57702	Rapid City, SD	$80	20878	Gaithersburg, MD	$241
84037	Kaysville, UT	$85	01824	Chelmsford, MA	$240
97526	Grants Pass, OR	$85	21045	Columbia, MD	$219
83616	Eagle, ID	$95	19382	West Chester, PA	$218
50325	West Des Moines–Clive, IA	$100	20170	Herndon, VA	$216
78232	Hollywood Park, TX	$104	08824	Kendall Park, NJ	$215
75791	Tyler, TX	$105	11730	East Islip, NY	$215
35758	Madison, AL	$106	03062	Nashua, NH	$210
LESS EXPENSIVE			**MORE EXPENSIVE**		
18018	Bethlehem, PA	$107	19810	Arden-Brandywine, DE	$203
29212	Irmo, SC	$110	55044	Lakeville, MN	$202
54403	Wausau, WI	$110	06470	Newtown, CT	$200
79606	Abilene, TX	$110	92688	Rancho Santa Margarita, CA	$200
24018	Roanoke, VA	$112	02760	North Attleboro, MA	$198
36695	West Mobile, AL	$120	60047	Lake Zurich, IL	$190
53044	Sheboygan, WI	$120	98275	Mukilteo, WA	$188
53532	DeForest, WI	$120	95630	Folsom, CA	$184
95694	Winters, CA	$120	80220	Denver (Park Hill), CO	$181
74012	Broken Arrow, OK	$122	98607	Vancouver-Camas, WA	$175
37922	Farragut, TN	$125	14534	Pittsford, NY	$174
97405	Eugene, OR	$125	43026	Hilliard, OH	$174
98226	Bellingham, WA	$125	45241	Evendale, OH	$174
76002	Arlington, TX	$128	15108	Coraopolis–Moon Township, PA	$172
54313	Green Bay, WI	$130	63304	St. Charles, MO	$171
58104	Fargo, ND	$130	46060	Noblesville, IN	$170
68022	Elkhorn, NE	$130	17601	Lancaster, PA	$162
37343	Hixson, TN	$132	17402	York, PA	$160
89523	Reno, NV	$132	30075	Roswell, GA	$160
22602	Winchester, VA	$135	33326	Weston, FL	$160

Source: *Best Places to Raise Your Family* research

facts on daycare cost are elusive, so we had to resort to our own "by hand" research to collect it. There are no national repositories of research (that are current, anyway), and certainly none that tracks it at the neighborhood level. Further, daycare centers seem reluctant to publish prices online because they change fairly often, and, well, they'd like to tell you about their features first. So we called daycare centers around the country and found an interesting range of prices.

Part of the problem with pricing daycare is that rates vary by type of center and the age and needs of the child. We standardized our quest by specifying daycare for a 3- to 4-year-old (in other words, a preschooler), all day, 5 days per week. We called franchised centers like KinderCare and La Petite Academy wherever we could, but these centers aren't found everywhere. We found a wide range of prices, from $275 per week in West Nyack, New York, to under $100 in several places in the South and West. (The lowest figures we found were $65 in Minden, Nevada, and $80 in Greer, South Carolina, and

Rapid City, South Dakota, but these weren't franchised centers.) Small towns, naturally, were less expensive, but we saw figures in the $130-per-week range in larger Texas cities and in Reno, Nevada. The difference between $275 and $130 per month is $145 per week; taken over a month's time, it is a $600 difference per month or $7,200 per year. That's a significant amount of money.

Table 4.27 shows the areas with the highest and lowest weekly daycare costs.

Median Home Price

The price of a home is a major cost factor for almost everybody, and it can be especially daunting for families. We won't go into detail on the startling rise in the cost of housing over the past several years, particularly between 2001 and 2005, nor the causes because the news media has covered the trends extensively. We won't make any predictions about the future either—you can read about current housing market trends in newspapers and news

TABLE 4.28 MEDIAN HOME PRICE
Neighborhood Level Data

U.S. AVERAGE: $208,500

LEAST EXPENSIVE			MOST EXPENSIVE		
75791	Tyler, TX	$119,700	07648	Norwood, NJ	$631,000
67212	Wichita (West), KS	$121,500	91354	Santa Clarita, CA	$619,000
74012	Broken Arrow, OK	$124,000	10994	West Nyack, NY	$605,700
79606	Abilene, TX	$129,200	92688	Rancho Santa Margarita, CA	$523,800
54911	Appleton, WI	$131,400	07039	Livingston, NJ	$514,400
54403	Wausau, WI	$131,900	95630	Folsom, CA	$500,000
17601	Lancaster, PA	$139,200	06470	Newtown, CT	$499,200
37343	Hixson, TN	$145,400	02067	Sharon, MA	$493,900
76002	Arlington, TX	$150,600	20170	Herndon, VA	$489,700
36695	West Mobile, AL	$151,500	11730	East Islip, NY	$476,000
LESS EXPENSIVE			**MORE EXPENSIVE**		
18018	Bethlehem, PA	$154,300	89523	Reno, NV	$465,500
40503	Lexington, KY	$156,000	89423	Minden, NV	$461,600
84321	Logan, UT	$156,000	33326	Weston, FL	$420,000
72758	Rogers, AR	$157,100	02760	North Attleboro, MA	$413,700
15108	Coraopolis–Moon Township, PA	$160,900	60047	Lake Zurich, IL	$411,000
47906	West Lafayette, IN	$165,500	95694	Winters, CA	$408,800
43537	Maumee, OH	$170,000	08824	Kendall Park, NJ	$408,300
35758	Madison, AL	$171,400	19382	West Chester, PA	$401,300
52241	Coralville, IA	$171,600	01824	Chelmsford, MA	$399,200
78232	Hollywood Park, TX	$173,500	60302	Oak Park, IL	$399,200
17402	York, PA	$174,700	92354	Loma Linda, CA	$363,000
29212	Irmo, SC	$174,800	98275	Mukilteo, WA	$358,800
46060	Noblesville, IN	$176,800	20878	Gaithersburg, MD	$353,400
65203	Columbia, MO	$177,600	21045	Columbia, MD	$350,800
57702	Rapid City, SD	$181,400	99516	Anchorage, AK	$340,000
32605	Gainesville, FL	$183,400	87122	Albuquerque (Sandia Heights), NM	$332,800
29650	Greer, SC	$184,900	19810	Arden-Brandywine, DE	$324,400
68022	Elkhorn, NE	$187,900	98226	Bellingham, WA	$320,100
97526	Grants Pass, OR	$190,000	55044	Lakeville, MN	$310,100
53044	Sheboygan, WI	$192,400	22901	Charlottesville, VA	$304,300

Source: National Association of Realtors/state Realtor associations, 2005

magazines. For our purposes, the important fact is that buying a home is a huge financial undertaking.

And so we bring you the Median Home Price, as furnished to us by the National Association of Realtors, for both areas and neighborhoods. Median Home Price is the level at which half the homes in the area sell for less and half sell for more. Actual prices vary considerably around this figure. More importantly, the median is calculated based on the prevailing type of home sold in an area. The base for calculation will be a lot different in Abilene, Texas (with a three-bedroom, two-bath, 2,000-square-foot home on a ½ acre), than in the heart of Manhattan, where such a residence doesn't even exist. Median home prices for more "urban" areas will necessarily be for smaller single-family residences.

Table 4.28 shows the wide range of prices among the 100 best places in this book.

The next two statistics shed more light on the "reality" of the housing situation as it affects typical families and the affordability of homes in an area.

"Sweet Spot" Home Price

Maybe you're a bit confused. Maybe you're wondering if Median Home Prices are truly representative of what you, a family, can expect to pay in an area. Does the home represented in the "MHP" figure really meet your needs as a family? In some places it does, and in some it doesn't.

For the purpose of this book, we use another representative figure, a "sweet spot" home price for family homes, specifically, to help clarify the housing picture for you.

What is a "sweet spot" home price? It's the estimated price for a four-bedroom, suburban-style home of about 2,200 square feet with a decent-size lot and a reasonable assortment of amenities for the area. How did we decide where the "sweet spot" home price was? By talking to

TABLE 4.29 "SWEET SPOT" HOME PRICES					
APPROXIMATE COST OF TYPICAL FAMILY HOME, NEIGHBORHOOD LEVEL DATA					
LOWEST			**HIGHEST**		
79606	Abilene, TX	$160,000	92688	Rancho Santa Margarita, CA	$650,000
67212	Wichita (West), KS	$160,000	91354	Santa Clarita, CA	$650,000
76002	Arlington, TX	$180,000	07648	Norwood, NJ	$625,000
68022	Elkhorn, NE	$190,000	10994	West Nyack, NY	$550,000
57702	Rapid City, SD	$190,000	20878	Gaithersburg, MD	$550,000
43537	Maumee, OH	$190,000	07039	Livingston, NJ	$550,000
74012	Broken Arrow, OK	$190,000	02067	Sharon, MA	$525,000
29650	Greer, SC	$190,000	95630	Folsom, CA	$525,000
37343	Hixson, TN	$190,000	20170	Herndon, VA	$525,000
29212	Irmo, SC	$190,000	60302	Oak Park, IL	$500,000
LOWER			**HIGHER**		
35758	Madison, AL	$190,000	11730	East Islip, NY	$500,000
54911	Appleton, WI	$200,000	08824	Kendall Park, NJ	$500,000
46060	Noblesville, IN	$200,000	95694	Winters, CA	$500,000
24018	Roanoke, VA	$200,000	06470	Newtown, CT	$475,000
75791	Tyler, TX	$200,000	89523	Reno, NV	$450,000
84321	Logan, UT	$200,000	01824	Chelmsford, MA	$450,000
65203	Columbia, MO	$200,000	89423	Minden, NV	$450,000
78232	Hollywood Park, TX	$210,000	60047	Lake Zurich, IL	$425,000
66049	Lawrence, KS	$210,000	33326	Weston, FL	$425,000
14534	Pittsford, NY	$220,000	19382	West Chester, PA	$425,000
77479	Sugar Land, TX	$220,000	92354	Loma Linda, CA	$425,000
54313	Green Bay, WI	$220,000	99516	Anchorage, AK	$400,000
17601	Lancaster, PA	$220,000	98275	Mukilteo, WA	$400,000
17402	York, PA	$220,000	21045	Columbia, MD	$400,000
18018	Bethlehem, PA	$220,000	02760	North Attleboro, MA	$400,000
28105	Matthews, NC	$220,000	22901	Charlottesville, VA	$375,000
47906	West Lafayette, IN	$220,000	98226	Bellingham, WA	$375,000
36695	West Mobile, AL	$220,000	22602	Winchester, VA	$375,000
75028	Flower Mound, TX	$225,000	33594	Valrico, FL	$360,000
54403	Wausau, WI	$225,000	83616	Eagle, ID	$350,000

Source: *Best Places to Raise Your Family* research

realtors and examining individual listings on the National Association of Realtors website (www.realtor. com). The "sweet spot" home price represents what we think a family would pay for a typical, good-quality family home in each of the 100 best places.

Note that in some neighborhoods, like Roswell, Georgia, the "sweet spot" is almost equivalent to the Median Home price. That suggests that the "typical" home in the area closely matches our "sweet spot" definition—and that there are a lot of them. See Table 4.29.

Home Price Ratio

Like the Buying Power Index, the Home Price Ratio is another of our creations designed to measure the *relative* affordability of an area. A neighborhood with a reported Median Home Price of $350,000 and a Median Household Income of $45,000 is far different from a neighborhood with the same MHP and a MHI of $95,000. Housing is obviously far more affordable for the average family in the latter neighborhood.

The Home Price Ratio is a simple ratio of just these two numbers: Median Home Price divided by Median Household Income. In the first case, dividing $350,000 by $45,000 produces a ratio of almost 7.8; dividing $350,000 by $95,000 yields 3.7.

So what is a "good" Home Price Ratio? Unlike many measures, where there is no clear "good" versus "bad" benchmark, it's possible to determine one here. How? By looking at the implied Home Price Ratio used by lenders to determine whether a buyer qualifies for a conventional loan.

For conventional loans, lenders want buyers to have a certain level of income to qualify for a certain size mortgage. Of course, these rules have been bent in recent years as more aggressive financing entered the picture, but there's still some wisdom in the "old" rules. Specifically, for such a conventional loan, lenders required a 20% down payment. For the remaining 80%, the amount of the loan, the *payment* (principal plus interest) should amount to no more than 28% of the buyer's gross income. Sparing the math details,

TABLE 4.30 HOME PRICE RATIO		
Least Affordable: Ratio Exceeding 5.0		
CONVENTIONAL QUALIFYING STANDARD @6% INTEREST: 4.86		
U.S. AVERAGE: 4.7		
92354	Loma Linda, CA	8.3
89423	Minden, NV	7.9
89523	Reno, NV	7.6
95694	Winters, CA	7.5
98226	Bellingham, WA	7.0
91354	Santa Clarita, CA	6.7
60302	Oak Park, IL	6.6
92688	Rancho Santa Margarita, CA	6.4
07648	Norwood, NJ	6.4
80220	Denver (Park Hill), CO	6.0
11730	East Islip, NY	6.0
95630	Folsom, CA	6.0
02760	North Attleboro, MA	5.9
33326	Weston, FL	5.9
97526	Grants Pass, OR	5.7
22901	Charlottesville, VA	5.6
98273	Mount Vernon, WA	5.6
97405	Eugene, OR	5.5
20170	Herndon, VA	5.4
10994	West Nyack, NY	5.2
98275	Mukilteo, WA	5.2
19382	West Chester, PA	5.2
47906	West Lafayette, IN	5.1

Source: *Best Places to Raise Your Family* calculation

TABLE 4.31 HOME PRICE RATIO (HPR)		
Most Affordable: Ratio Under 3.0		
CONVENTIONAL QUALIFYING STANDARD @6% INTEREST: 4.86		
U.S. AVERAGE: 4.7		
BEST HPR		
76002	Arlington, TX	2.1
75028	Flower Mound, TX	2.3
75791	Tyler, TX	2.3
74012	Broken Arrow, OK	2.3
17601	Lancaster, PA	2.3
67212	Wichita (West), KS	2.4
14534	Pittsford, NY	2.4
35758	Madison, AL	2.4
68022	Elkhorn, NE	2.5
53044	Sheboygan, WI	2.5
RUNNERS UP		
77479	Sugar Land, TX	2.5
78232	Hollywood Park, TX	2.6
79606	Abilene, TX	2.6
78732	Austin (West), TX	2.7
36695	West Mobile, AL	2.7
37922	Farragut, TN	2.7
14068	Getzville, NY	2.7
29212	Irmo, SC	2.8
46060	Noblesville, IN	2.8
54911	Appleton, WI	2.9
37343	Hixson, TN	2.9
15108	Coraopolis–Moon Township, PA	2.9
63304	St. Charles, MO	3.0
54313	Green Bay, WI	3.0
66216	Shawnee, KS	3.0
50325	West Des Moines–Clive, IA	3.1
54403	Wausau, WI	3.1
80104	Castle Rock, CO	3.1
43026	Hilliard, OH	3.1
58104	Fargo, ND	3.1

Source: *Best Places to Raise Your Family* calculation

assuming a 30-year mortgage at 6% interest, a home buyer seeking a conventional loan can afford a home costing 4.86 times his or her annual income.

Thus, 4.86 becomes a benchmark for the Home Price Ratio. Anything less indicates positive affordability in an area; anything more suggests that families will have to "reach" to buy a median-priced home.

In our selection process, we observed HPRs ranging from 2.0 to over 11.0. In fact, the entire state of California had a remarkably high HPR of 9.0, with only Hawaii and the District of Columbia having a statewide average of over 5.0 (and thus higher than our benchmark). We did end up qualifying 23 places (out of 100) with an HPR exceeding the benchmark, so we'll give you the "bad news" first:

Not surprisingly, many of these places are in places known to be difficult to afford: New York, California, and the Washington, DC, area, for example. Some of the places in the above table are college towns, where growth regulation and quality of life coupled with modest student incomes can distort the figures from the perspective of the average working family. We aren't saying these places are impossible to afford, but buyers will need to be selective and, generally speaking, two-earner incomes are likely to help.

Now, for the good news: We found plenty of places with a HPR under 3.0. In such a scenario, housing is quite affordable for the average family; that is, a typical home can be purchased with relatively little financial strain, and a family is more likely to get a nicer home or have the opportunity to "move up" as needs change. Furthermore, these families are more likely to be able to prosper comfortably on one income, and the prospect of job instability is less harrowing. See Table 4.31 for our list of the Home Price Ratio—home affordability—stars.

Home Price Appreciation

Much has been written about the staggering rates of growth in home prices, particularly in certain regions of the country, such as California, Florida, and many East Coast markets. From the National Association of Realtors, we collected the most recent annual statistics available from mid-2004 through mid-2005, and as you

TABLE 4.32 HOME PRICE APPRECIATION Second Quarter 2004–Second Quarter 2005 Metro Area Level Data
U.S. AVERAGE: 13.6%

HIGHEST			LOWEST		
33326	Weston, FL	35%	92688	Rancho Santa Margarita, CA	-6%
89523	Reno, NV	32%	80104	Castle Rock, CO	-6%
89423	Minden, NV	31%	80220	Denver (Park Hill), CO	-3%
95694	Winters, CA	25%	60047	Lake Zurich, IL	-2%
23456	Virginia Beach, VA	22%	47906	West Lafayette, IN	2%
21045	Columbia, MD	21%	74012	Broken Arrow, OK	2%
20878	Gaithersburg, MD	21%	78732	Austin (West), TX	2%
95630	Folsom, CA	20%	67212	Wichita (West), KS	2%
98226	Bellingham, WA	19%	36695	West Mobile, AL	2%
33594	Valrico, FL	19%	75028	Flower Mound, TX	3%
HIGHER			**LOWER**		
22901	Charlottesville, VA	19%	46060	Noblesville, IN	3%
20170	Herndon, VA	19%	76002	Arlington, TX	4%
22602	Winchester, VA	19%	29650	Greer, SC	4%
24018	Roanoke, VA	19%	84037	Kaysville, UT	4%
92354	Loma Linda, CA	18%	43537	Maumee, OH	4%
32605	Gainesville, FL	18%	14534	Pittsford, NY	4%
08824	Kendall Park, NJ	16%	98501	Olympia, WA	4%
11730	East Islip, NY	16%	77479	Sugar Land, TX	4%
07039	Livingston, NJ	16%	28105	Matthews, NC	4%
07648	Norwood, NJ	16%	98607	Vancouver-Camas, WA	5%
10994	West Nyack, NY	16%	80526	Fort Collins, CO	5%
02760	North Attleboro, MA	16%	27513	Cary, NC	5%
19382	West Chester, PA	15%	30075	Roswell, GA	5%
97405	Eugene, OR	15%	40503	Lexington, KY	5%
19810	Arden-Brandywine, DE	15%	43026	Hilliard, OH	5%
32073	Orange Park, FL	15%	68022	Elkhorn, NE	5%
06470	Newtown, CT	14%	35758	Madison, AL	5%
98273	Mount Vernon, WA	14%	78232	Hollywood Park, TX	5%
23233	Richmond-Tuckahoe, VA	14%	29212	Irmo, SC	5%
18018	Bethlehem, PA	13%	49426	Hudsonville, MI	5%

Source: National Association of Realtors/state Realtor associations, 2005

can see in Table 4.32, the gap between the "haves" and "have nots" for home price appreciation is large.

Is strong appreciation good or bad? It depends on your situation and perspective. Strong appreciation goes along with attractive lifestyles, strong employment, and other characteristics that stimulate demand, and thus prices. On the other hand, strong appreciation can also be indicative of limited supply, which correlates strongly with overcrowding. Of course, strong appreciation also makes a place less affordable for a newcomer.

Weaker appreciation sometimes signals overheated markets (as is the story in Rancho Santa Margarita, California), but can, in other instances, signal bargains (as is the case in parts of Colorado, the Midwest, and Texas).

Percent of Homes Owned

Home ownership is a sign of stability, and it suggests that residents will care about their area's appearance and upkeep. We prefer places with percentages of

ownership exceeding 60%, and most of our selections exceed that figure, with the obvious exceptions of college towns, for which scores of 40% or more are good.

Like many of the housing facts, this figure comes from the National Association of Realtors.

Effective Property Tax Rate

Like home prices, property taxes have been in the news lately. Local governments are straining to make ends meet and, particularly with current state and federal fiscal woes, they're depending more than ever on individual and commercial property tax revenues to finance local government, schools, and other infrastructure. The rapid rise in home prices has created strong revenue growth in some areas, particularly those like California and Florida where properties are reassessed upon sale.

Property taxes—like income, sales, and all other taxes—are a function of basis and rate. While most locales have held the line on rates (more precisely, rate

TABLE 4.33 COMPARATIVE RESIDENTIAL PROPERTY TAX BURDENS BY STATE						
LARGEST CITY IN EACH STATE, 2003						
CITY	STATE	NOMINAL RATE PER $100	ASSESSMENT LEVEL	EFFECTIVE RATE PER $100	ESTIMATED HOME VALUE $75K HOUSEHOLD INCOME	ESTIMATED PROPERTY TAX
Providence	RI	$3.88	100%	$3.88	$237,460	$9,213
Bridgeport	CT	$5.52	70%	$3.86	$222,701	$8,596
Newark	NJ	$2.16	137%	$2.96	$289,952	$8,583
Atlanta	GA	$4.47	40%	$1.79	$263,087	$4,709
Los Angeles	CA	$1.08	100%	$1.08	$416,403	$4,497
Manchester	NH	$2.57	100%	$2.57	$171,316	$4,403
Boston	MA	$1.33	100%	$1.33	$323,775	$4,306
New York City	NY	$14.05	8%	$1.12	$379,414	$4,249
Portland	OR	$2.24	80%	$1.79	$231,097	$4,137
Milwaukee	WI	$2.53	100%	$2.53	$159,191	$4,028
Burlington	VT	$2.75	67.6%	$1.86	$213,857	$3,978
Chicago	IL	$7.63	22.1%	$1.69	$232,422	$3,928
Houston	TX	$2.62	100%	$2.62	$147,059	$3,853
Baltimore	MD	$2.46	100%	$2.46	$146,241	$3,598
New Orleans	LA	$17.50	10%	$1.75	$202,471	$3,543
Salt Lake City	UT	$1.37	99%	$1.36	$254,708	$3,464
Indianapolis	IN	$2.17	100%	$2.17	$150,830	$3,273
Portland	ME	$2.57	68%	$1.75	$186,812	$3,269
Philadelphia	PA	$8.26	32%	$2.64	$120,896	$3,192
Fargo	ND	$48.66	4.4%	$2.12	$146,625	$3,108
Seattle	WA	$1.10	90.5%	$0.99	$313,048	$3,099
Anchorage	AK	$1.62	100%	$1.62	$189,261	$3,066
Boise	ID	$1.79	97.8%	$1.75	$174,040	$3,046
Des Moines	IA	$4.48	48.5%	$2.17	$130,554	$2,833
Omaha	NE	$2.16	94%	$2.03	$139,017	$2,822
Jacksonville	FL	$1.94	100%	$1.94	$139,386	$2,704
Billings	MT	$2.03	80%	$1.62	$166,382	$2,695
Columbia	SC	$35.02	4%	$1.40	$186,605	$2,612
U.S. MEDIAN				**$1.50**	**$173,547**	**$2,603**
Albuquerque	NM	$3.82	33.3%	$1.27	$203,708	$2,587
Detroit	MI	$6.73	27.1%	$1.82	$140,903	$2,564
Memphis	TN	$7.27	23.8%	$1.73	$144,571	$2,501
Wilmington	DE	$2.75	53%	$1.45	$166,062	$2,408
Columbus	OH	$4.91	30%	$1.45	$160,474	$2,327
Minneapolis	MN	$1.52	86.4%	$1.32	$175,147	$2,312
Jackson	MS	$16.93	10%	$1.69	$134,155	$2,267
Las Vegas	NV	$3.12	35%	$1.09	$204,052	$2,224
Sioux Falls	SD	$1.77	85%	$1.50	$148,061	$2,221
Phoenix	AZ	$11.65	10%	$1.17	$181,742	$2,126
Louisville	KY	$1.21	100%	$1.21	$168,206	$2,035
Charlotte	NC	$1.16	98%	$1.13	$178,221	$2,014
Honolulu	HI	$0.38	100%	$0.38	$515,041	$1,957
Little Rock	AR	$6.90	20%	$1.38	$141,160	$1,948
Virginia Beach	VA	$1.22	90.6%	$1.11	$173,547	$1,926
Oklahoma City	OK	$10.59	11%	$1.16	$141,078	$1,637
Kansas City	MO	$6.13	19%	$1.16	$136,921	$1,588
Wichita	KS	$11.36	11.5%	$1.31	$120,160	$1,574
Charleston	WV	$1.47	60%	$0.88	$158,520	$1,395
Denver	CO	$6.63	8%	$0.53	$258,014	$1,367
Cheyenne	WY	$7.10	9.5%	$0.67	$164,204	$1,100
Birmingham	AL	$6.95	10%	$0.70	$146,228	$1,024
UNWEIGHTED AVG		$6.05	60.5%	$1.65	$198,997	$3,283

Source: District of Columbia Tax Rates and Tax Burdens Study

changes take difficult-to-attain voting majorities or supermajorities), many have resorted to substantial revisions in basis, or the tax valuation of properties. This has caused uproars, with threats of California Proposition 13–like tax revolts, particularly in many East Coast states and locales where taxes are high already. Of course, the basis changes have some merit, because real estate values have appreciated. But a 20% rise in an $8,000 tax bill is still hard to swallow.

TABLE 4.34 EFFECTIVE PROPERTY TAX RATES
Taxes Paid/Market Value, Neighborhood Level Data

U.S. AVERAGE: 1.5%

LOWEST			HIGHEST		
80220	Denver (Park Hill), CO	0.5%	50325	West Des Moines–Clive, IA	3.5%
35758	Madison, AL	0.6%	14534	Pittsford, NY	3.2%
22602	Winchester, VA	0.7%	76002	Arlington, TX	3.1%
37922	Farragut, TN	0.8%	53044	Sheboygan, WI	3.1%
49426	Hudsonville, MI	0.8%	78732	Austin (West), TX	3.0%
80104	Castle Rock, CO	0.8%	32605	Gainesville, FL	3.0%
19810	Arden-Brandywine, DE	0.8%	60302	Oak Park, IL	3.0%
72758	Rogers, AR	0.8%	77479	Sugar Land, TX	3.0%
36695	West Mobile, AL	0.8%	75028	Flower Mound, TX	2.8%
02760	North Attleboro, MA	0.9%	14068	Getzville, NY	2.6%
LOWER			**HIGHER**		
87122	Albuquerque (Sandia Heights), NM	1.0%	15108	Coraopolis–Moon Township, PA	2.5%
74012	Broken Arrow, OK	1.0%	53532	DeForest, WI	2.5%
27513	Cary, NC	1.0%	68022	Elkhorn, NE	2.5%
65203	Columbia, MO	1.0%	78232	Hollywood Park, TX	2.5%
80526	Fort Collins, CO	1.0%	54403	Wausau, WI	2.5%
29650	Greer, SC	1.0%	33594	Valrico, FL	2.3%
20170	Herndon, VA	1.0%	79606	Abilene, TX	2.2%
37343	Hixson, TN	1.0%	54911	Appleton, WI	2.2%
29212	Irmo, SC	1.0%	63304	St. Charles, MO	2.2%
55044	Lakeville, MN	1.0%	22901	Charlottesville, VA	2.1%
80027	Louisville, CO	1.0%	11730	East Islip, NY	2.0%
89423	Minden, NV	1.0%	58104	Fargo, ND	2.0%
84321	Logan, UT	1.1%	03062	Nashua, NH	2.0%
92354	Loma Linda, CA	1.1%	46060	Noblesville, IN	2.0%
66216	Shawnee, KS	1.1%	92688	Rancho Santa Margarita, CA	2.0%
67212	Wichita (West), KS	1.1%	57702	Rapid City, SD	2.0%
95694	Winters, CA	1.1%	06470	Newtown, CT	1.9%
98226	Bellingham, WA	1.2%	53186	Waukesha, WI	1.9%
18018	Bethlehem, PA	1.2%	83616	Eagle, ID	1.8%
01824	Chelmsford, MA	1.2%	97405	Eugene, OR	1.8%

Source: *Best Places to Raise Your Family* research

Tax rates and basis rules range across the country. In fact, tax rates in most states vary considerably from one *neighborhood* to another, according to what levies have been voted in, and in many cases, how large an industrial or commercial base there is in the area to shift the burden to. Beyond typical appraisal rules and rates, there are a myriad of exemptions or premiums for primary residence, age, and even, in some cases, the presence of children in the household. Because of the complexity and "granularity" of these rates, we decided the best way to approach reporting neighborhood tax rates was to simply find out through examining local tax rolls, with the help of realtors, how much tax is paid on a typical family home in the area. From that, using the home's approximate value, we calculate an *effective property tax rate* for the area. This figure is shown in the neighborhood tables.

To help you better understand current property taxes, bases, and rates, we offer a table constructed by the District of Columbia in their annual "Tax Rates and Tax Burdens" study comparing taxes across the board in 50 states and DC. This oft-quoted study (available online at http://cfo.dc.gov analyzes, among many other things, the different residential property tax assessment rules and rates across the country. Some places have high rates and low assessment values (like North Dakota); others keep the rates relatively low, but assessments are tied rigorously to market value. Table 4.33 shows the DC study's results for the most populous city in each state.

Table 4.34 shows the highest and lowest *effective* property tax rates. Note the wide range—and the tendency for high effective rates to show up in (1) places with lower home values, and (2) places with low or no state income or sales taxes. The state of Texas meets both of these criteria.

TABLE 4.35 APPROXIMATE FAMILY PROPERTY TAX BILLS						
EFFECTIVE PROPERTY TAX RATE "SWEET SPOT" HOME PRICE, NEIGHBORHOOD LEVEL DATA						
LOWEST				**HIGHEST**		
35758	Madison, AL	$1,140		60302	Oak Park, IL	$15,000
37922	Farragut, TN	$1,688		92688	Rancho Santa Margarita, CA	$13,000
80220	Denver (Park Hill), CO	$1,750		07648	Norwood, NJ	$10,000
36695	West Mobile, AL	$1,760		11730	East Islip, NY	$10,000
67212	Wichita (West), KS	$1,760		53044	Sheboygan, WI	$9,300
49426	Hudsonville, MI	$1,763		06470	Newtown, CT	$9,025
72758	Rogers, AR	$1,800		08824	Kendall Park, NJ	$9,000
74012	Broken Arrow, OK	$1,900		10994	West Nyack, NY	$8,800
29650	Greer, SC	$1,900		02067	Sharon, MA	$8,400
37343	Hixson,TN	$1,900		33594	Valrico, FL	$8,280
LOWER				**HIGHER**		
29212	Irmo, SC	$1,900		50325	West Des Moines–Clive, IA	$8,225
65203	Columbia, MO	$2,000		53532	DeForest, WI	$8,125
80104	Castle Rock, CO	$2,002		22901	Charlottesville, VA	$7,875
84321	Logan, UT	$2,200		91354	Santa Clarita, CA	$7,800
80526	Fort Collins, CO	$2,250		60047	Lake Zurich, IL	$7,225
27513	Cary, NC	$2,300		78732	Austin (West), TX	$7,200
24018	Roanoke, VA	$2,400		32605	Gainesville, FL	$7,200
75791	Tyler, TX	$2,400		14534	Pittsford, NY	$7,040
66216	Shawnee, KS	$2,475		03062	Nashua, NH	$6,800
19810	Arden-Brandywine, DE	$2,600		20878	Gaithersburg, MD	$6,600
18018	Bethlehem, PA	$2,640		07039	Livingston, NJ	$6,600
28105	Matthews, NC	$2,640		77479	Sugar Land, TX	$6,600
47906	West Lafayette, IN	$2,640		15108	Coraopolis–Moon Township, PA	$6,500
66049	Lawrence, KS	$2,730		33326	Weston, FL	$6,375
22602	Winchester, VA	$2,738		83616	Eagle, ID	$6,300
40503	Lexington, KY	$3,150		95630	Folsom, CA	$6,300
55044	Lakeville, MN	$3,250		75028	Flower Mound, TX	$6,300
84037	Kaysville, UT	$3,250		14068	Getzville, NY	$6,240
17601	Lancaster, PA	$3,300		19382	West Chester, PA	$5,950
17402	York, PA	$3,300		89523	Reno, NV	$5,850

Source: *Best Places to Raise Your Family* calculation

Approximate Property Tax Bill

One final look at property taxes: What really counts at the end of the day is not the rate, nor the basis, but the property tax bill that has to be paid. We made an attempt to estimate the total annual tax bill, but we must also warn you that detailed local twists and turns, like special exemptions and assessments, may not be included. The "bill" is taken by applying the Effective Property Tax Rate to the "Sweet Spot" Home Price, our measure for value of the typical family home. The results presented in Table 4.35 again show an extremely wide range among areas.

Median Rent

Finally, for those who choose to stay out of the real estate market as buyers, we show, at the area level, the median rent in an area, sourced from the U.S. Census. Due to skyrocketing home prices in some markets, renting has become a more attractive alternative for many families, particularly those requiring more mobility in the near term. Part of the reason that rents are attractive

is high home appreciation itself. This phenomenon has created a class of home investors who are willing to accept below-market rents because their real investment objective is home price appreciation. It's a "buyers market" for home renters, although this may change quickly over the next several years.

Education

When you're raising children, few things are more important than education. It might be oversimplifying a bit, but education is now more than ever the key to long-term financial prosperity for families today and for generations to come.

The Educational Imperative

Perhaps aside from the evolution of information technology and its role in our daily personal and professional lives, few things have changed as much as the role of education in long-term success and prosperity. Today,

⭐ Experts Expect Interest Rate Increases to Drive Home Prices Lower. Are They Right?

Save for minor timing differences, today's national averages for Median Home Price ($208,500) and Median Household Income ($44,684) suggest a Home Price Ratio of 4.67—closely approaching the maximum ratio of 4.86 for a qualifying loan at 6%. Translation: On a national basis, homes *are* still affordable—but not by much.

Now you may wonder what happens if interest rates rise. Again sparing the detailed math, the maximum Home Price Ratio—still based on conventional financing—is 4.38 at 7%, dipping further to 3.97 at 8%. Thus, today's aggregate U.S. median Home Price Ratio of 4.67 clearly signals vulnerability to rising interest rates. Unless incomes rise, home prices must fall—unless people are willing to take on riskier financing (as they already must do in pricier markets).

fully 85% of jobs are classified as "skilled" or "professional," compared to just 40% in 1950—and most of these jobs require proficiency—or at least a basic entry credential—gained through education. On-the-job training is virtually a thing of the past, especially for high-paying jobs. Salaries are almost double for college-educated workers than for those with only a high-school diploma. A college degree, or some form of specialized professional education, has evolved from being an admirable achievement to almost a necessity in today's economy.

Planning for your children's college education means planning ahead, usually somewhere during the primary and secondary education process. College doesn't happen just because parents can afford tuition nor just because Dad or Mom graduated from the same school 20 years earlier. The educational imperative has increased the demand for college education, and the growing number of baby-boomer children coming of age has created still more demand. One result is a well-reported growth in the cost of higher education. But beyond that, as the "supply" of college education has stayed fairly constant, it has become harder—indeed a struggle—to get into the best schools, or sometimes any school at all. So more families, more than ever before, are seeking elementary, middle, and high schools with strong college and/or career preparatory programs.

Evaluating the Schools

An analysis of the best places to raise your family should obviously evaluate the quality of education in each place. Unfortunately, this evaluation is difficult at best. There are so many intangible factors—the personality of a school, its teaching practices, and its administration—that mix together to form the final "product."

We tried our best to sort through many of these intangibles by conducting local interviews, but an opinion given during an interview is just that—an opinion. At the outset of developing this book, we had great ambitions to deliver a complete quantitative evaluation of local schools—the most complete yet—based on the rapidly developing accountability and reporting standards brought by the 2001 Federal No Child Left Behind Act. We planned to present, for the first time, a complete set of statistics and analysis to give you the best and broadest comparative picture of education across the country—based on facts and any intangibles we could add.

We'll admit that we were only partially successful in our quest. Because of NCLB, states are testing more than ever before (and test results just are becoming more visible at the school level). But while the tests have become a bit more standardized, they are still all over the place in terms of what is tested at what grade levels. More frustratingly, there is no consistency in terms of the level, or degree of difficulty, of the standards they test to. Finally, the development of so-called "report cards" is incomplete, particularly from the standpoint of measuring educational progress.

The Role of Context

Particularly in the absence of reliable and definitive measures (such as the kind of data that's available for Standard of Living), we have to depend on certain contextual measures. We believe, and studies have shown, that areas with strong educational attainment—that is, presence of college and advanced degrees—will have good primary and secondary education resources. Why? Because, as mentioned back in chapter 1, families will (1) demand them

★ No Child Left Behind

The details of the landmark No Child Left Behind (NCLB) legislation are well beyond the scope of this book; they fill reams of government documents, reports, and press coverage. But to sum up the main idea: The stated goal is to bring 100% of students up to the "proficient" level on state tests by the 2013–2014 school year, and to hold states accountable for measuring and achieving that result. Schools receiving Federal "Title I" funds must further meet "AYP," or Adequate Yearly Progress, goals for their student populations (and for segments of those populations). If they don't meet those goals, they can face consequences including corrective actions, loss of control over curriculum, and allowing students to transfer to other schools. As U.S. Secretary of Education Margaret Spellings, the original architect of a similar Texas program, explains, the core philosophy is this: "What gets measured gets done."

NCLB requires states to set academic standards, test to them, and create publicly available annual "report cards" so that parents and others can see the results. It also requires teachers to be "highly qualified." In all, there are more than 40 measurable standards for which schools are being held accountable.

The result has been mixed so far. The biggest issues are (1) lack of standardization among states, making interstate comparisons difficult, and (2) lack of funding to achieve these initiatives. Lack of standardization among states leads to much more rigorous standards in some states than others and makes interstate comparisons difficult. The funding issue in particular has resulted in a broad state outcry and has even led to a lawsuit against the Federal Government by the Attorney General of the state of Connecticut.

Further, the Law of Unintended Consequences is hard at work. NCLB is credited with disrupting the teaching process and causing teachers, driven by nervous school boards, to "teach to the test"—a formulaic form of teaching to get students through but skimping on the more memorable and enjoyable aspects of a student's experience. There have also been well-founded outcries that NCLB in effect does just what it is designed to avoid, by leaving incapable children behind as teachers realize there's "no hope" for them and instead focus on the more competent students to keep scores high.

That all said, we believe NCLB is a step in the right direction in respect to measuring school performance, and especially to creating a culture of achieving measurable improvements toward established goals. But the implementation has been difficult. Interpreting the measures right now is like judging a Cabernet after just 1 month in the barrel. Because it's not a "mature" program or process yet, for right now, we have to take what we can get. In the future, we hope that NCLB will increasingly help provide a more dependable standard for school appraisal.

---

(2) support them (by voting for tax increases) and (3) add themselves to the mix by volunteering, participating on school boards, and so forth. Relying on this idea, we used educational attainment as an important qualifier for places, and stand strongly by the notion that a place where 50% or more of the population possesses a 4-year college degree or higher will have good schools.

The other factor shown by studies to have a strong contextual role in education is teacher salaries. Good teachers go where salaries are highest (the metric is most dependable when taken in context of cost of living in the area). They tend to be older and more experienced and stay longer. Reliable data on local teacher salaries wasn't available when we constructed this book, but we hope to add it into future editions. For now, when you're considering a place, this is a good issue to inquire about as you visit individual schools and talk to area parents.

What We Do Measure & How

Study after study has been published on so-called "best places," and in the cases where education is involved, most reports show a standard assortment of metrics published by the U.S. Department of Education's National Center for Education Statistics (NCES). These metrics include enrollment, demographic analysis of that enrollment, student-teacher ratios, school funding, and other important sociological measures like the percentage of students on publicly funded lunch programs, which is basically a measure of economically disadvantaged students in the area. These measures speak to the size of the schools, the mix of students, and public

TABLE 4.36 ATLANTA, GA AREA HIGHLIGHTS SEGMENT						
EDUCATION						
ATTAINMENT & ACHIEVEMENT	**AREA**	**U.S. AVG**		**RESOURCES & INVESTMENT**	**AREA**	**U.S. AVG**
% High School Graduate	78.70%	83.90%		No. of Highly Ranked Universities	4	1
% 2-yr Graduate	7.30%	7.10%		$ Invested per Pupil	$5,795	$6,058
% 4-yr Graduate	22.90%	17.20%		Student/Teacher Ratio	16.2	15.9
% Graduate or Professional Degree	9.50%	9.90%		State University In-State Tuition	$4,272	$4,917
% Attending Public School	91.90%	84.30%				
75th Percentile State University SAT Score (Verbal)	550	477				
75th Percentile State University SAT Score (Math)	560	478				
75th Percentile State University ACT Score	23	20				

investment in these schools—but not their quality. We're continually surprised at how many places are judged to have "great" schools simply because of per-student funding and low student-teacher ratios.

Of course, we do report some of these statistics as "resources and investment" measures, and believe they have some merit. But we don't stop there. Along with those measures, we report "attainment and achievement" measures as we can, including a new composite metric reflecting local primary and secondary academic testing performance against state averages. In most of the narratives on neighborhoods in chapter 5, we offer more highlights of test performance as we see it reported. For examples of area and neighborhood statistics in the category of education, see Tables 4.36 and 4.37.

What about College?

Although we gave the most coverage in this book to primary and secondary education, we also added a few facts and comments about college education. We highlighted places that have top-quality local higher-education facilities and try to give you a few details about admission scores and costs, at least for the major state schools available. College and university choices aren't neighborhood or area driven, but it isn't a bad idea to consider the quality and costs of schools nearby and especially public universities in the state. For those wanting more information on colleges, we recommend The Princeton Review's *The Best 357 Colleges* (Random House, 2005) as an additional reference.

Attainment & Achievement

As with Standard of Living facts, we report some Education facts at the area level, some at the neighborhood level, and a few at both levels. Not surprisingly, facts about specific school performance are presented at the neighborhood level.

The first half of our presentation covers *attainment*, the highest degree level "attained" by the population, and *achievement*, the actual academic testing performance for primary and secondary schools and for college admissions. Be forewarned that there are a lot of statistics out there on graduation rates from particular

(★) Greatschools.net

There are some 65,000 primary and secondary schools in the United States, and to collect facts and comparatively evaluate all of them, or even a tenth of them, is a task well beyond our means. We collaborated with Greatschools.net, a nonprofit organization taking on the ambitious goal of collecting and reporting school information in a format packaged for the public. Their portal (www.greatschools.net) is the best compilation currently available of key school facts. It's worth a visit for anyone looking for an overview of school statistics, testing performance, and parent comments. We looked at test score performances for selected schools, comparisons with state averages, and upward and downward progress. Plans are to increasingly incorporate more and more Greatschools.net data into Sperling's BestPlaces and into future editions of *Best Places to Raise Your Family*.

TABLE 4.37 ROSWELL, GA	
NEIGHBORHOOD HIGHLIGHTS SEGMENT	
EDUCATION	**BEST**
% High School Graduates	94%
% 4-yr Degree	38%
% Graduate or Professional Degree	19%
$ Invested per Pupil	$6,141
Student/Teacher Ratio	15.7
Primary Test Score Percentile	114.4
Secondary Test Score Percentile	101.3
% Subsidized School Lunch	10.90%
% Attending Public School	79%

schools; because there are some pitfalls with these facts, we try to steer clear of them.

Percent High School Graduates

The first stop on our "attainment" tour is the High School Graduation Rate. This fact comes from the U.S. Census, updated through annual surveys, and reflects the percentage of population in a particular place that has graduated from high school *somewhere*. It does *not* reflect the graduation rate from the local high school. Graduation rates from specific schools are notorious for not capturing transfers and other special situations, and generally penalize areas where people are more often moving in and out.

Having said that, high school graduation rates in our selected places are high; in fact, all but four places exceed the national average of 83% and most are in the 90% range. The areas below 83% (namely, Winters, California; Mount Vernon, Washington; and Winchester, Virginia) still have a strong presence of agricultural workers.

Percent 2-Year College Graduates

Presented on the area tables only, this statistic is the percentage of the population that holds a 2-year degree as the *highest* level of education achieved.

Percent 4-Year College Graduates

The next "cut" is 4-year graduates, and both the Area and Neighborhood tables show the percentage of the population that has attained a 4-year college degree as their highest level of education. While there are many excellent 2-year programs, we feel that 4-year degree attainment sends a stronger signal for long-term family prosperity, and is a better contextual indicator for the quality of primary and secondary schools in an area as well. We looked for neighborhoods that had not only a high level of attainment overall, but also high graduation rates in context of the metro area in which they are located.

The national average for 4-year attainment is 17%, and all but 10 of the best places in this book exceed that level, some by as much as 30%. Those that are lower, again, are smaller, more rural communities, and a few have strong heritages in blue-collar professions.

Percent with Graduate or Professional Degree

You might be surprised that 4-year degree figures for prosperous communities, while healthy at 20% to 40%, aren't higher. The reason, in many cases, is that measurable portions of the population have gone beyond to get a graduate or professional degree. In fact, in 27 communities in this book, 20% or more of the population attained a graduate or professional degree as their highest level.

In other words, in 30 of our 100 communities, more than 50% of the residents have achieved either a 4-year or a graduate/professional degree. It makes sense to combine the 4-year and graduate/professional degree attainment into one number to get a true picture of an area, since graduate/professional degree holders also hold a 4-year degree. We didn't do this in the tables—because it's easy enough to "eyeball" and simply add the two scores together—but we did present some totals in Table 4.39.

(TIPS) Understanding the School Data

The 2-year and the 4-year and graduate/professional attainment levels that we present in this book are based on the highest level of degree achieved. In other words, if someone has achieved a 2-year and a 4-year degree, they show up in the reported percentage for 4-year degree attainment. Also, the percentages are taken against the adult population of 25 years and older, not the total population.

TABLE 4.38 PERCENT 4-YEAR COLLEGE DEGREES Four-Year Degree Is HIGHEST Level Attained		
U.S. AVERAGE: 17%		
HIGHEST GRAD RATE		
78732	Austin (West), TX	47%
80027	Louisville, CO	40%
27513	Cary, NC	39%
50325	West Des Moines–Clive, IA	39%
75028	Flower Mound, TX	39%
30075	Roswell, GA	38%
77479	Sugar Land, TX	38%
23233	Richmond-Tuckahoe, VA	37%
53044	Sheboygan, WI	35%
35758	Madison, AL	34%
HIGHER GRAD RATE		
37922	Farragut, TN	34%
20878	Gaithersburg, MD	34%
58104	Fargo, ND	33%
60047	Lake Zurich, IL	33%
19382	West Chester, PA	32%
60302	Oak Park, IL	32%
14534	Pittsford, NY	32%
80104	Castle Rock, CO	32%
43026	Hilliard, OH	31%
92688	Rancho Santa Margarita, CA	31%
29212	Irmo, SC	31%
66049	Lawrence, KS	31%
02067	Sharon, MA	31%
07039	Livingston, NJ	31%
91354	Santa Clarita, CA	31%
06470	Newtown, CT	31%
99516	Anchorage, AK	31%
80526	Fort Collins, CO	30%
20170	Herndon, VA	30%
78232	Hollywood Park, TX	30%

Source: U.S. Census 2000/American Community Survey 2004

TABLE 4.39 COMBINED % 4-YEAR AND GRADUATE/PROFESSIONAL DEGREES Graduate or Professional Degree Is HIGHEST Level Attained		
U.S. AVERAGE: 27%		
HIGHEST		
78732	Austin (West), TX	65%
87122	Albuquerque (Sandia Heights), NM	65%
20878	Gaithersburg, MD	64%
80027	Louisville, CO	63%
27513	Cary, NC	63%
60302	Oak Park, IL	63%
14534	Pittsford, NY	63%
02067	Sharon, MA	62%
77479	Sugar Land, TX	59%
07039	Livingston, NJ	58%
HIGHER		
23233	Richmond-Tuckahoe, VA	58%
30075	Roswell, GA	57%
50325	West Des Moines–Clive, IA	56%
65203	Columbia, MO	56%
21045	Columbia, MD	56%
66049	Lawrence, KS	56%
47906	West Lafayette, IN	55%
37922	Farragut, TN	55%
22901	Charlottesville, VA	54%
19382	West Chester, PA	53%
32605	Gainesville, FL	53%
53044	Sheboygan, WI	53%
55902	Rochester, MN	52%
35758	Madison, AL	51%
52241	Coralville, IA	51%
75028	Flower Mound, TX	51%
80526	Fort Collins, CO	51%
06470	Newtown, CT	51%
10994	West Nyack, NY	50%
60047	Lake Zurich, IL	50%

Source: U.S. Census 2000/American Community Survey 2004

(TIPS) Do Your Homework

Test scores may be a place to start, but we strongly recommend doing more complete research into local schools. Part of the challenge in evaluating schools lies in the fact that many areas are served by more than one school, and often by more than one district. Many school districts give parents options on which school to attend. Our advice is to dig deeper: If you're seriously evaluating a place, go to **www.greatschools.net** to get more detailed testing data, parent comments, and a link to the school website. Look at the school website and find the so-called "report card" (another No Child Left Behind [NCLB] requirement largely implemented to date). But don't stop there—it's worth the time to talk to administrators and teachers, and if possible, talk to parents in the area and visit classrooms. Unfortunately, evaluating schools today is like buying a car—with insufficient comparative facts and no test drive— and the long-term consequences are far more important. Perhaps NCLB will fix the first part, but understanding the school "experience" will always be difficult.

	TABLE 4.40 STATE PRIMARY AND SECONDARY TESTING						
	BEST, WORST, AND AVERAGE STATE SCORES BY SUBJECT AND GRADE						
STATE	NAME OF TESTS OR TESTING PROGRAM	SUBJECTS	WORST GRADE/ SUBJECT	BEST GRADE/ SUBJECT	MINIMUM STATE AVERAGE SCORE (1)	MAXIMUM STATE AVERAGE SCORE (2)	"MEAN" STATE AVERAGE SCORE (3)
AL	Alabama High School Graduation Exam, Stanford 10	R,M,L	3 R	12 R	42.8%	96.3%	63.9%
CA	Standards Test	M, EL	NA	NA	35.3%	40.4%	37.7%
CO	CO Student Assessment Program	R,M,W,S	10 M	3 R	23.7%	73.2%	57.4%
FL	FL Comprehensive Assessment Test	R,M,W	3 R	8 W	66.4%	91.4%	76.7%
GA	Criterion-Referenced Competency Tests, Georgia HS Competency Test	M, EL	8 M	11 EL	54.3%	94.0%	79.5%
IA	Iowa Test of Basic Skills	R,M	4 R	8 R	69.4%	76.2%	73.5%
ID	Idaho Standards Achievement Test	R,M,LA	8 M	4 LA	50.4%	79.0%	72.3%
IA	Illinois Standards Achievement Tests, Prairie State Achievement Exam	R,M,W	11 M	3 M	46.2%	77.4%	58.9%
IN	Indiana Statewide Testing for Educational Progress	M, EL	8 EL	3 EL	62.5%	71.2%	68.1%
KS	Kansas State Assessments	R,M	10 M	4 M	46.6%	74.2%	68.3%
KY	Kentucky Core Content Tests	R,M,W	7 R	4 R	53.7%	83.1%	69.3%
MA	Massachussetts Comprehensive Assessment System	R,M,EL,S	8 S	7 EL	32.1%	65.2%	50.0%
MD	Maryland School Assessment	R,M,W	8 M	5 R	38.2%	64.3%	55.6%
MI	Michigan Educational Assessment Program	R,M,W	12 W	4 R	40.6%	74.1%	52.1%
MN	Minnesota Comprehensive Assessment, Basic Skills Test	R,M,W	3 R	5 W	70.5%	94.3%	77.2%
MO	Missouri Assessment Program	M, CA	10 M	4 M	11.8%	37.3%	28.6%
ND	CAT-Terra Nova	R,M	NA	NA	59.0%	75.0%	71.1%
NH	New Hampshire Educational Improvement	M, LA	10 M	3 M	64.2%	79.6%	74.8%
NJ	New Jersey Assessment of Skills and Knowledge, Grade Eight Proficiency Assessment	M,LA	8 M	11 LA	57.9%	78.3%	70.6%
NV	Iowa Tests of Basic Skills	R,M,LA	7 LA	4 LA	40.7%	52.3%	48.6%
NY	New York Regents Assessments, Regents Exams	M, EL	8 EL	4 M	46.9%	81.0%	66.8%
OH	Ohio Proficiency Test, Ohio Graduation Test	R,M,W	6 R	9 W	63.4%	96.0%	74.0%
OR	State Assessments	R,M	10 M	3 R	42.1%	83.3%	74.9%
PA	Pennsylvania System of State Assessments	R,M,W	11 M	11 W	47.6%	73.2%	62.0%
SC	Palmetto Achivement Challenge Tests	M, EL	6 EL	3 EL	60.8%	85.1%	74.0%
TN	Tennessee Comphrehensive Assessment Program	R,M,LA	7 R	3 M	51.9%	65.1%	57.2%
TX	Texas Assessment of Knowledge and Skills	R,M,W,S	9 M	7 W	55.9%	90.8%	81.4%
UT	Stanford 9	R,M,LA	3 LA	11 M	39.3%	60.9%	48.7%
VA	Standards of Learning	R,M	8 R	11 R	62.0%	91.4%	77.8%
WA	Washington Assessment of Student Learning	R,M,W	10 M	4 R	38.7%	74.3%	59.0%
WI	Wisconsin Knowledge and Concepts Examinations	R,M,LA	8 LA	8 R	64.9%	84.9%	76.7%

Note: States not listed do not compare or report tests against state averages—or are not included in the 100 Best Places list.

SUBJECT KEY:

R: Reading
M: Math
W: Writing
EL: English Language
LA: Language Arts
S: Science
CA: Communication Arts

(1) Lowest state average among all subjects and grades
(2) Highest state average among all subjects and grades
(3) "Mean" state average among all subjects and grades, NOT weighted by number of tests taken

Source: Greatschools.net, 2005

Table 4.38 shows the best places for 4-year attainment, while Table 4.39 shows combined 4-year and graduate/professional attainment. Why are these shown together? Some feel that adding graduate and professional attainment to the mix tilts the list too far toward college towns with their local presence of professors and other academics.

Percent Attending Public School

This statistic helps us show you the amount of participation in the public school system at the area level. This percentage reflects the local acceptance of the public school system, hence it is "achievement" in an indirect sense. It also reflects the availability of private school alternatives.

Among the metro areas we present in this book, we see a range from about 80% to 97% of students attending public schools. The highest percentages tend to be in Western cities and college towns. The lower rates appear to be scattered though the Midwest and parts of the East.

Primary & Secondary School Testing

Now we sail from the safe waters of U.S. Census attainment statistics into the uncharted and stormier seas of evaluating local primary and secondary school achievement. The tools by which to measure school performance are evolving rapidly under No Child Left Behind, state laws, and local initiatives. The challenge remains enormous, as performance testing is still largely left to the states to design and implement as they please.

Table 4.40 summarizes the status of primary and secondary school testing today as reported by Greatschools.net. It shows the status of state testing for states that (1) compare individual school results to state averages (a few still compare to national benchmarks) and (2) have neighborhoods identified as best places in this book. For each state, we list the testing platform—notably, almost all are different. We show the subjects tested. Almost all test for math proficiency, but that's where the consistency ends. States test their own mix of subjects. Some may test language skills quite differently—some testing specifically for reading; a few having specific tests and scores for writing. Some test science curricula. Most states test at different grade levels. Some test at all grade levels; others test at defined intervals, such as 4th, 8th, and 12th grades.

Making comparisons still more difficult, some states apparently have very hard tests; others are easier. If you look at the far-right column of Table 4.40, we've developed a simple average of tested proficiency across all subjects and grade levels in a state. These scores represent the percentage of students taking the tests—across all socioeconomic groups and schools in the state—judged to be "proficient" by state standards. Note the wide range. In Texas, 81% of students are judged "proficient," while in Missouri, only 29% are currently meeting the state benchmark. Clearly, this suggests a difference in testing philosophy—and it makes it hard to compare results using simple mathematics. A school achieving 56% proficiency in Missouri would appear twice as successful as state averages, while such a "2x" level of achievement is statistically impossible in Texas or most other states.

There is also considerable variation among states in terms of which topics are tested most rigorously in which grades. There is a tendency toward lower statewide performance in high-school math (see column

TABLE 4.41 PRIMARY TEST SCORE INDEX Comparison vs. State Averages, All Neighborhood Grade K-8 Schools		
STATE AVERAGE: 100		
HIGHEST		
92688	Rancho Santa Margarita, CA	175
95630	Folsom, CA	173
35758	Madison, AL	151
91354	Santa Clarita, CA	147
99516	Anchorage, AK	143
84321	Logan, UT	139
21045	Columbia, MD	138
60047	Lake Zurich, IL	133
37922	Farragut, TN	131
19382	West Chester, PA	131
HIGHER		
72758	Rogers, AR	130
37064	Franklin, TN	129
89423	Minden, NV	129
14068	Getzville, NY	128
02067	Sharon, MA	127
14534	Pittsford, NY	126
46060	Noblesville, IN	126
80027	Louisville, CO	126
65203	Columbia, MO	124
37343	Hixson, TN	123
97405	Eugene, OR	123
23233	Richmond-Tuckahoe, VA	123
89523	Reno, NV	123
80526	Fort Collins, CO	121
20878	Gaithersburg, MD	121
49426	Hudsonville, MI	121
47906	West Lafayette, IN	120
99223	Spokane, WA	120
10994	West Nyack, NY	119
06470	Newtown, CT	119

Source: Sperling's BestPlaces, from Greatschools.net, 2005

"Worst") but otherwise, the greatest and poorest statewide proficiencies (and implicitly, the difficulty of underlying tests) vary all over the place.

Primary Test Score Index

With testing complexities in mind, we developed a simple composite index taking scores for all subjects at all grade levels tested, kindergarten through 8th grade, for all schools associated with the zip code, and comparing them to state averages. The resulting index indicates composite local scores compared to the state average; an index of 120 means that scores were 20% above the corresponding state averages.

For primary schools, we found the best scores in California (three of the top four scores, in fact). See Table 4.41. But a quick look at state proficiency averages for California reveals a low benchmark—only 37.7% of students statewide across all grades and subjects achieve proficiency, so the bar is relatively low

TABLE 4.42 SECONDARY TEST SCORE INDEX
Comparison vs. State Averages,
All Neighborhood Grade 9-12 Schools

STATE AVERAGE: 100

HIGHEST

65203	Columbia, MO	211
72758	Rogers, AR	151
95630	Folsom, CA	145
21045	Columbia, MD	145
57702	Rapid City, SD	139
19382	West Chester, PA	138
80104	Castle Rock, CO	137
99223	Spokane, WA	135
80526	Fort Collins, CO	135
02067	Sharon, MA	132

HIGHER

89423	Minden, NV	131
63304	St. Charles, MO	127
47906	West Lafayette, IN	126
03062	Nashua, NH	125
15108	Coraopolis–Moon Township, PA	124
89523	Reno, NV	123
20878	Gaithersburg, MD	123
46060	Noblesville, IN	123
14534	Pittsford, NY	122
40503	Lexington, KY	121
80027	Louisville, CO	120
75791	Tyler, TX	120
06470	Newtown, CT	118
43026	Hilliard, OH	118
77479	Sugar Land, TX	117
66049	Lawrence, KS	117
07648	Norwood, NJ	115
45241	Evendale, OH	113
98226	Bellingham, WA	113
27513	Cary, NC	113

Source: Sperling's BestPlaces, from Greatschools.net, 2005

TABLE 4.43 STUDENT-TEACHER RATIO
U.S. AVERAGE: 15.2

LOWEST RATIO

10994	West Nyack, NY	12.9
22901	Charlottesville, VA	13.2
53044	Sheboygan, WI	13.8
63304	St. Charles, MO	14.1
65203	Columbia, MO	14.3
14068	Getzville, NY	14.3
08824	Kendall Park, NJ	14.5
07039	Livingston, NJ	14.6
54403	Wausau, WI	14.6
29212	Irmo, SC	14.8

LOWER RATIO

07648	Norwood, NJ	14.8
55044	Lakeville, MN	14.9
53186	Waukesha, WI	14.9
24018	Roanoke, VA	15
79606	Abilene, TX	15.2
80104	Castle Rock, CO	15.4
53532	DeForest, WI	15.4
68022	Elkhorn, NE	15.4
75028	Flower Mound, TX	15.4
60302	Oak Park, IL	15.4
22602	Winchester, VA	15.4
15108	Coraopolis–Moon Township, PA	15.5
06470	Newtown, CT	15.7
21045	Columbia, MD	15.8
45241	Evendale, OH	15.8
66049	Lawrence, KS	15.8
30075	Roswell, GA	16
29650	Greer, SC	16.1
67212	Wichita (West), KS	16.1
19810	Arden-Brandywine, DE	16.2

Source: National Center for Education Statistics, 2004

(albeit, the tests are probably also hard). The index may be overstating the case a bit for California, but that being said, the case for strong schools in Rancho Santa Margarita, Folsom, and Santa Clarita shouldn't be ignored. We do see some instances, especially in inner-city neighborhoods, where the mix of schools and population drags down composite proficiency. Certain schools in Oak Park, Illinois and the Denver (Park Hill), Colorado neighborhood, for example, test much better than state averages. Again, prospective residents are advised to examine schools on a case-by-case basis.

Secondary Test Score Index

Table 4.42 shows the best composite test score indexes for high schools (more generally, grades 9 to 12). We applaud Columbia, Missouri, for its outstanding performance, but make sure to note the low state average benchmark, part of the reason such a high index is possible.

Resources & Investment

The next set of measures covers public funding investments made in schools at all levels and the resources they buy, with a few figures on college testing and costs sprinkled in.

Expenditures per Pupil

The National Center for Education Statistics collects and publishes figures on public funds spent per student by school district and school. These figures range from $4,000 to $5,000 per student per year in many Western states and smaller towns in the Midwest and South to $10,000-plus in many places in the East. There are some distortions, of course, including how administrative and special-education costs are handled. Some of the differences can be explained by teacher salaries and the overall cost of living in the area, and the fact that many schools in the East have older buildings and infrastructure. Schools in the East are, on the whole, noticeably smaller, with many high schools in the 1,000 to

	TABLE 4.44 SAT SCORES BY STATE Verbal, Math, Composite, 1990–2004, Sorted by Percent Change							
	AVERAGE U.S. % CHANGE 1990-2004: + 2.5%							
STATE	**1990**			**2004**			**CHANGE 1990-2004**	**% GRADS TAKING SAT**
	VERBAL	**MATH**	**COMPOSITE**	**VERBAL**	**MATH**	**COMPOSITE**		
IL	542	547	1089	585	597	1182	8.5%	10%
MO	548	541	1089	587	585	1172	7.6%	8%
MI	529	534	1063	563	573	1136	6.9%	11%
WI	552	559	1111	587	596	1183	6.5%	7%
MN	552	558	1110	587	593	1180	6.3%	10%
NC	478	470	948	499	507	1006	6.1%	70%
SC	475	467	942	491	495	986	4.7%	62%
AR	545	532	1077	569	555	1124	4.4%	60%
MA	503	498	1001	518	523	1041	4.0%	85%
GA	478	473	951	494	493	987	3.8%	73%
CO	533	534	1067	554	553	1107	3.7%	27%
OK	553	542	1095	569	566	1135	3.7%	7%
IN	486	486	972	501	506	1007	3.6%	64%
SD	580	570	1150	594	597	1191	3.6%	5%
KS	566	563	1129	584	585	1169	3.5%	9%
WA	513	511	1024	528	531	1059	3.4%	52%
LA	551	537	1088	564	561	1125	3.4%	8%
AL	545	534	1079	560	553	1113	3.2%	9%
OH	526	522	1048	538	542	1080	3.1%	28%
OR	515	509	1024	527	528	1055	3.0%	56%
VT	507	493	1000	516	512	1028	2.8%	66%
CT	506	496	1002	515	515	1030	2.8%	85%
VA	501	496	997	515	509	1024	2.7%	71%
MS	552	528	1080	562	547	1109	2.7%	5%
U.S. AVG	**500**	**501**	**1001**	**508**	**518**	**1026**	**2.5%**	**48%**
KY	548	541	1089	559	557	1116	2.5%	12%
WY	534	538	1072	551	546	1097	2.3%	12%
ND	579	578	1157	582	601	1183	2.2%	5%
NY	489	496	985	497	510	1007	2.2%	87%
NJ	495	498	993	501	514	1015	2.2%	83%
NE	559	562	1121	569	576	1145	2.1%	8%
TN	558	544	1102	567	557	1124	2.0%	16%
RI	498	488	986	503	502	1005	1.9%	72%

1,500 student range. Comparatively, mega high schools in the West and in places like Texas and Florida often have school populations of more than 2,000, and sometimes more than 2,500, students. There is some merit to the form of smaller, more neighborhood-oriented schools found in the East.

Student-Teacher Ratio

You should know that this ratio, defined as named, reflects some inconsistencies in calculation brought on by special-education programs and/or other local requirements. That said, we favor the lower ratios found in many college towns, smaller cities, and places on the East Coast. The higher figures, again, are found in the West, Texas, and Florida. Table 4.43 shows places with the lowest Student-Teacher Ratio.

State University ACT/SAT Score

For many families, a child's primary and secondary education experiences are thought to be stepping stones toward college, and college entrance exams are an indication of how effective the primary and secondary schools are in preparing students. We don't have data at the school or neighborhood level for college entrance exams; the examination boards do not release such information. But we present the average SAT scores by state in Table 4.44.

It should be noted that some states make more use of the ACT exam, which make their reported SAT score less relevant. To better understand which states use which test, note the column "% grads taking SAT." With that in mind, the most significant improvements in scores appear to be in the South, with North Carolina, South Carolina, Arkansas, and Georgia leading the way.

TABLE 4.45 IN-STATE UNIVERSITY TUITION		
ANNUAL TUITION LESS THAN $5,000		
BASED ON STATE UNIVERSITY WITH LARGEST ENROLLMENT		PRINCETON REVIEW BEST 357?
University of Florida	$2,955	Y
University of Nevada–Las Vegas	$3,270	Y
University of Alaska–Anchorage	$3,517	
Boise State University	$3,520	
University of New Mexico	$3,738	Y
University of Utah	$4,000	Y
University of Georgia	$4,272	Y
North Carolina State University–Raleigh	$4,282	Y
University of Colorado–Boulder	$4,341	Y
University of Oklahoma–Norman	$4,515	Y
University of Alabama	$4,630	Y
University of Kansas	$4,737	Y
University of Tennessee	$4,748	Y
South Dakota State University	$4,802	
University of North Dakota	$4,828	Y

Source: National Center for Education Statistics/Princeton Review

In the area highlight tables, we show three statistics, State University SAT Verbal Score, State University SAT Math Score, and ACT Score, to help readers get an idea of the admissions requirements for the *largest* state university in the state. The scores shown are the reported scores at the 75th percentile; that is, 25% of all admitted students exceed the reported score, and 75% fall below it. The reported scores are for SAT and/or ACT, depending on which test(s) the largest state school uses for admissions. These percentile scores give an idea, but by no means a full assessment, of a state's higher educational resources. Also, remember that these figures refer to a state university, not one necessarily in the area. Our information comes from the National Center for Education Statistics.

State University In-State Tuition

State university in-state tuition is presented, again for the largest state-supported university in the state, and is designed to give you an idea of what a basic good college education in the state will cost. Again, it is a *state* figure, not one for a university in the area. Table 4.45 lists the largest university and denotes if that university was considered one of the "357 best" in 2005 by the Princeton Review.

Percent Subsidized School Lunch

Most primary and secondary schools across the country are eligible for subsidized school lunches, and the National Center for Education Statistics tracks the percentage of student body for each school deemed eligible, based on income levels, for these subsidies. The percentage eligible can be used as a broad and quick guide to the socioeconomic status of families in the area; the higher the figure, the more students come from economically disadvantaged backgrounds. We report this figure at the neighborhood level. As you can see in Table 4.46, the range is broad, and large percentages of subsidized school lunches are found in city neighborhoods like Denver (Park Hill), Colorado, and in many small towns, many with high percentages of agricultural workers, like Mount Vernon, Washington, and Winters, California.

Lifestyle

To most families, financial stability and adequate education are basic necessities. Now we want to show you some of more elusive qualities of a best place to raise your family. We've tried to build an assessment—an image, really—of what life feels like in each of our Best Places. We tell you what each area offers in terms of things to do, and what you can expect the overall experience to be like. Broadly speaking, we examine the amenities, resources, and conveniences of an area against its backdrop—the physical setting, climate, attractiveness, and overall ambience.

Some of the factors are immeasurable or can be measured only indirectly. For instance, the average commute time or the number of Starbucks coffee shops might be used to indirectly "measure" convenience. To supplement our statistics, we discuss "on-the-ground" views of an area's quality of life in chapter 5.

The broad category of Lifestyle is divided into four subcategories: Recreation, Arts & Culture, Infrastructure & Facilities, Climate, and Commute & Transportation. Facts for each of these subcategories occur in either the Area or Neighborhood Highlights tables. Most facts are taken at the area level, because most major arts and recreational amenities serve an entire area, and climate and many aspects of transportation are also characteristic of the area as a whole. We offer summary Leisure, Arts, and Climate Ratings at the neighborhood level, but these ratings are driven by area detail and shown at the neighborhood level mainly for your reading convenience.

See Tables 4.47 and 4.48 for lifestyle statistics.

Recreation, Arts & Culture

The Recreation, Arts & Culture category covers major recreation facilities, performing arts, and museums. These amenities are presented as ratings on a 1 to 10 scale, meaning that a host of qualities and facts like size, attendance, and proximity are considered as facts and

TABLE 4.46 PERCENT SUBSIDIZED SCHOOL LUNCHES
NEIGHBORHOOD LEVEL DATA

LOWEST			HIGHEST		
07039	Livingston, NJ	1%	98273	Mount Vernon, WA	62%
07648	Norwood, NJ	1%	80220	Denver (Park Hill), CO	55%
14534	Pittsford, NY	2%	92354	Loma Linda, CA	55%
91354	Santa Clarita, CA	3%	67212	Wichita (West), KS	50%
78732	Austin (West), TX	3%	32605	Gainesville, FL	48%
60047	Lake Zurich, IL	4%	97526	Grants Pass, OR	48%
02067	Sharon, MA	4%	95694	Winters, CA	46%
01824	Chelmsford, MA	4%	84321	Logan, UT	42%
75028	Flower Mound, TX	4%	53044	Sheboygan, WI	38%
80027	Louisville, CO	5%	18018	Bethlehem, PA	37%
LOWEST			**HIGHEST**		
80104	Castle Rock, CO	5%	98226	Bellingham, WA	37%
10994	West Nyack, NY	5%	36695	West Mobile, AL	36%
08824	Kendall Park, NJ	5%	54403	Wausau, WI	36%
92688	Rancho Santa Margarita, CA	5%	29212	Irmo, SC	34%
11730	East Islip, NY	6%	75791	Tyler, TX	33%
23233	Richmond-Tuckahoe, VA	6%	99223	Spokane, WA	32%
99516	Anchorage, AK	6%	74012	Broken Arrow, OK	30%
19382	West Chester, PA	7%	97405	Eugene, OR	30%
15108	Coraopolis–Moon Township, PA	7%	76002	Arlington, TX	29%
63304	St. Charles, MO	7%	27513	Cary, NC	29%
87122	Albuquerque (Sandia Heights), NM	7%	77479	Sugar Land, TX	29%
02760	North Attleboro, MA	8%	45241	Evendale, OH	28%
95630	Folsom, CA	9%	53186	Waukesha, WI	28%
58104	Fargo, ND	9%	19810	Arden-Brandywine, DE	27%
43026	Hilliard, OH	10%	22901	Charlottesville, VA	27%
24018	Roanoke, VA	10%	84037	Kaysville, UT	27%
55044	Lakeville, MN	10%	40503	Lexington, KY	26%
83616	Eagle, ID	11%	23456	Virginia Beach, VA	26%
30075	Roswell, GA	11%	32073	Orange Park, FL	25%
53532	DeForest, WI	11%	65203	Columbia, MO	25%

Source: National Center for Education Statistics, 2004

then blended with a judgment of quality to arrive at the final rating. Obviously, with many of these ratings, more than one facility is considered. Facts supporting these ratings are typically drawn from the trade associations in which these facilities operate; for instance, Major League Baseball or the American Museum Association.

Area Highlights

The following amenities are rated to give an indication of what's available, but they don't represent everything. Readers interested in specific amenities not shown here, like ballet companies or symphony orchestras, can find them on Sperling's BestPlaces (www.bestplaces.net). We also mention standout amenities and resources in the narratives for each place in chapter 5.

- Professional Sports Rating covers the range of major- and minor-league professional spectator sports in the area.

- Zoos & Aquariums Rating covers the zoos, aquariums, and animal parks. See Table 4.49.

- Amusement Park Rating shows availability, quality, and proximity of amusement parks, with more weight given to nationally prominent facilities like Six Flags and Disney. As a good example of how proximity figures into ratings, highly rated areas may not have such a park within their geographic boundary. Nearby is okay, and a good example is Richmond-Tuckahoe, Virginia, and the Paramount King's Dominion park in Doswell, Virginia, 20 miles north. See Table 4.50.

- Professional Theater Rating shows the availability of registered theater venues.

- Overall Museum Rating is a composite rating drawn from art, science, history, and children's museums in the area. See Table 4.51.

- Science Museum Rating covers museums registered as science museums with the American Museum

TABLE 4.47 ATLANTA, GA AREA HIGHLIGHTS SEGMENT						
LIFESTYLE						
RECREATION, ARTS & CULTURE	**AREA**	**U.S. AVG**		**INFRASTRUCTURE & FACILITIES**	**AREA**	**U.S. AVG**
Professional Sports Rating	7	4		No. of Public Libraries	134	28
Zoos & Aquariums Rating	9	3		Library Volumes Per Capita	1.8	2.8
Amusement Park Rating	10	3		No. of Warehouse Clubs	10	4
Professional Theater Rating	10	3		No. of Starbucks	91	5
Overall Museum Rating	10	6		Golf Course Rating	9	4
Science Museum Rating	8	4		National Park Rating	2	3
Children's Museum Rating	9	3		Sq. Mi. Inland Water	4	4
CLIMATE				**COMMUTE & TRANSPORTATION**		
Days Mostly Sunny	219	212		Avg. Daily Commute Time	31.2	24.7
Annual Days Precipitation	116	111		% Commute by Auto	77%	77.70%
Annual Days > 90°F	19	38		Per Capita Avg. Daily Transit Miles	16.7	7.9
Annual Days < 32°F	59	88		Annual Auto Insurance Premium	$1,500	$1,314
July Relative Humidity	70	69		Gas, Cost per Gallon	3.01	3.05

Association, including natural history and general science museums, as well as planetariums.

- Children's Museum Rating covers the availability and quality of children's museums. See Table 4.52.

Neighborhood Highlights

- Leisure Rating: We thought it might be useful to show a composite rating of all leisure facilities in an area. The Leisure Rating includes ratings shown elsewhere in this table—such as for professional sports, golf, parks, and bodies of water—blended with others not shown but collected by Sperling's BestPlaces, including restaurants, collegiate sports, and skiing. This rating gives the broadest picture of leisure and recreation in the area. It's shown in the neighborhood table (although at the area level) so you can get a quick picture of the place's lifestyle.

- Arts & Culture Rating: Like the Leisure Rating, this composite rating includes displayed categories plus others like classical music, ballet, arts, and arts radio. See Table 4.54.

Infrastructure & Facilities

This category covers items related to the physical environment, either natural or man-made, that provide convenience, setting, and activity.

Area Highlights

- Number of Public Libraries is the number of library facilities in the area, from the National Center for Education Statistics.

- Library Volumes per Capita shows the number of books available per person in the metro area, also from NCES. See Table 4.55.

- Number of Warehouse Clubs is the number of Costcos, Sam's Clubs, and BJ's clubs in an area, compiled by Sperling's BestPlaces from company sources.

- Number of Starbucks is the number of Starbucks coffee shops in an area, presented more than anything as an indicator of the quality and convenience of retail establishments in an area.

- Golf Course Rating reflects the public and private golf courses in an area or nearby—their number, quality, and cost.

- National Park Rating captures the availability and quality of nearby national parks, national forests, and national monuments. Unfortunately we don't have data on local, regional, and county parks, but important local facilities are mentioned in the neighborhood narratives in chapter 5.

- Square Miles Inland Water is a rating compiled from the measured amount of surface water in or near an area, and includes completely enclosed bodies of water, not ocean bays or inlets. See Table 4.56.

TABLE 4.48 ROSWELL, GA
NEIGHBORHOOD HIGHLIGHTS SEGMENT

LIFESTYLE

Leisure Rating (Area)	9
Arts & Culture Rating (Area)	9
Climate Rating (Area)	7
Physical Setting Rating	6
Downtown Core Rating	3
% Commute < 30 Min.	42%
% Commute > 1 Hour	9%

TABLE 4.49 ZOOS & AQUARIUMS
10 Is Best
U.S. AVERAGE: 3

91354	Santa Clarita, CA	10
20170	Herndon, VA	10
20878	Gaithersburg, MD	10
60047	Lake Zurich, IL	10
60302	Oak Park, IL	10
21045	Columbia, MD	10
10994	West Nyack, NY	10
30075	Roswell, GA	9
55044	Lakeville, MN	9
63304	St. Charles, MO	9
23456	Virginia Beach, VA	8
98275	Mukilteo, WA	8
02067	Sharon, MA	8
32073	Orange Park, FL	8
15108	Coraopolis–Moon Township, PA	8
07039	Livingston, NJ	8
22602	Winchester, VA	8
37343	Hixson, TN	8
68022	Elkhorn, NE	8
19382	West Chester, PA	8

Source: Sperling's BestPlaces

TABLE 4.50 AMUSEMENT PARKS
10 Is Best
U.S. AVERAGE: 3

91354	Santa Clarita, CA	10
60047	Lake Zurich, IL	10
60302	Oak Park, IL	10
30075	Roswell, GA	10
55044	Lakeville, MN	10
63304	St. Charles, MO	10
92688	Rancho Santa Margarita, CA	10
23456	Virginia Beach, VA	9
76002	Arlington, TX	9
77479	Sugar Land, TX	9
78232	Hollywood Park, TX	9
45241	Evendale, OH	9
33594	Valrico, FL	9
95630	Folsom, CA	9
98275	Mukilteo, WA	8
98607	Vancouver-Camas, WA	8
37922	Farragut, TN	8
23233	Richmond-Tuckahoe, VA	8

Source: Sperling's BestPlaces

TABLE 4.51 OVERALL MUSEUM RATING
10 Is Best
U.S. AVERAGE: 6

91354	Santa Clarita, CA	10
60047	Lake Zurich, IL	10
60302	Oak Park, IL	10
30075	Roswell, GA	10
55044	Lakeville, MN	10
02067	Sharon, MA	10
10994	West Nyack, NY	10
19382	West Chester, PA	10
11730	East Islip, NY	10
21045	Columbia, MD	10
02760	North Attleboro, MA	10
20170	Herndon, VA	10
20878	Gaithersburg, MD	10
63304	St. Charles, MO	9
23456	Virginia Beach, VA	9
77479	Sugar Land, TX	9
78232	Hollywood Park, TX	9
45241	Evendale, OH	9
33594	Valrico, FL	9
98275	Mukilteo, WA	9
98607	Vancouver-Camas, WA	9
23233	Richmond-Tuckahoe, VA	9
07039	Livingston, NJ	9
80104	Castle Rock, CO	9
80220	Denver (Park Hill), CO	9
92354	Loma Linda, CA	9
18018	Bethlehem, PA	9
15108	Coraopolis–Moon Township, PA	9
14534	Pittsford, NY	9
75028	Flower Mound, TX	9
43026	Hilliard, OH	9
66216	Shawnee, KS	9
46060	Noblesville, IN	9
53186	Waukesha, WI	9
37064	Franklin, TN	9
92688	Rancho Santa Margarita, CA	8
95630	Folsom, CA	8
37922	Farragut, TN	8
49426	Hudsonville, MI	8
07648	Norwood, NJ	8
08824	Kendall Park, NJ	8
28105	Matthews, NC	8
67212	Wichita (West), KS	8
84037	Kaysville, UT	8
22602	Winchester, VA	8
32073	Orange Park, FL	8
14068	Getzville, NY	8
27513	Cary, NC	8
29650	Greer, SC	8
78732	Austin (West), TX	8
40503	Lexington, KY	8

Source: Sperling's BestPlaces

TABLE 4.52 CHILDREN'S MUSEUMS		
10 Is Best		
U.S. AVERAGE: 3		
91354	Santa Clarita, CA	10
60047	Lake Zurich, IL	10
60302	Oak Park, IL	10
02067	Sharon, MA	10
10994	West Nyack, NY	10
20170	Herndon, VA	10
20878	Gaithersburg, MD	10
63304	St. Charles, MO	10
23456	Virginia Beach, VA	10
45241	Evendale, OH	10
98275	Mukilteo, WA	10
46060	Noblesville, IN	10
76002	Arlington, TX	10
30075	Roswell, GA	9
19382	West Chester, PA	9
21045	Columbia, MD	9
07039	Livingston, NJ	9
66216	Shawnee, KS	9
07648	Norwood, NJ	9
55044	Lakeville, MN	8
77479	Sugar Land, TX	8
92354	Loma Linda, CA	8
75028	Flower Mound, TX	8
43026	Hilliard, OH	8
37922	Farragut, TN	8
22602	Winchester, VA	8
87122	Albuquerque (Sandia Heights), NM	8

Source: Sperling's BestPlaces

TABLE 4.53 OVERALL LEISURE RATING		
10 IS BEST		0
10994	West Nyack, NY	10
60302	Oak Park, IL	10
60047	Lake Zurich, IL	10
11730	East Islip, NY	10
91354	Santa Clarita, CA	10
02067	Sharon, MA	10
20878	Gaithersburg, MD	10
20170	Herndon, VA	10
07648	Norwood, NJ	10
92688	Rancho Santa Margarita, CA	10
19382	West Chester, PA	10
92354	Loma Linda, CA	9
07039	Livingston, NJ	9
21045	Columbia, MD	9
55044	Lakeville, MN	9
08824	Kendall Park, NJ	9
80220	Denver (Park Hill), CO	9
30075	Roswell, GA	9
80104	Castle Rock, CO	9
95630	Folsom, CA	9
33594	Valrico, FL	9
77479	Sugar Land, TX	9
75028	Flower Mound, TX	9
80526	Fort Collins, CO	9
84037	Kaysville, UT	9
89423	Minden, NV	9
80027	Louisville, CO	9
15108	Coraopolis–Moon Township, PA	9
02760	North Attleboro, MA	9
53186	Waukesha, WI	9
98501	Olympia, WA	8
14068	Getzville, NY	8
33326	Weston, FL	8
98607	Vancouver-Camas, WA	8
76002	Arlington, TX	8
97405	Eugene, OR	8
45241	Evendale, OH	8
66216	Shawnee, KS	8

Source: Sperling's BestPlaces

Neighborhood Highlights

At the neighborhood level, we devised two catchall ratings designed to capture the quality and overall ambience of physical setting and downtown areas:

- Physical Setting is a 1 to 10 rating of the appearance of the physical surroundings. Mountains, trees, water, cleanliness, and views all figure into our purely subjective judgment. If you look out a window and see a "picture postcard," the place will get a high physical setting rating from us. A setting that is generally attractive if not "picture postcard," such as Roswell, Georgia, will otherwise score well, 6 on our scale. See Table 4.57.

- Downtown Core is our judgment of two things taken together: the local neighborhood downtown and the larger metro area downtown adjacent or nearby. See Table 4.58. Some places, like Vancouver-Camas, Washington, make the list because of the quality of their greater metro area downtown (Portland, Oregon, in this case), while others make it on their own merits, like Sheboygan, Wisconsin, or Roanoke, Virginia. Roswell, Georgia, scores only a "3" in this sub-

category because (1) there is only a small downtown in the area not really taken by locals to be a major "center" in their lifestyles and (2) Atlanta's downtown area is mediocre at best (though improving) and is far away.

Climate

Most families do a lot of things outside, whether in their own yards, in local parks, or on more distant jaunts and expeditions. While climate is known not to be a *primary* factor in deciding where to live (see "Reasons for Moving" in chapter 2), it's safe to say that a better climate fosters more family activities.

Wherever families may be, they tend to learn to adapt to the climate at hand. Families in Michigan or Illinois or upstate New York, for example, learn to enjoy winter

TABLE 4.54 OVERALL ARTS RATING		
10 IS BEST		
10994	West Nyack, NY	10
02067	Sharon, MA	10
20878	Gaithersburg, MD	10
20170	Herndon, VA	10
60302	Oak Park, IL	10
60047	Lake Zurich, IL	10
91354	Santa Clarita, CA	10
55044	Lakeville, MN	10
19382	West Chester, PA	10
15108	Coraopolis–Moon Township, PA	10
55902	Rochester, MN	10
53186	Waukesha, WI	10
14068	Getzville, NY	10
45241	Evendale, OH	10
66216	Shawnee, KS	10
08824	Kendall Park, NJ	10
80220	Denver (Park Hill), CO	10
80104	Castle Rock, CO	10
07039	Livingston, NJ	9
21045	Columbia, MD	9
77479	Sugar Land, TX	9
75028	Flower Mound, TX	9
43026	Hilliard, OH	9
30075	Roswell, GA	9
53532	DeForest, WI	9
23233	Richmond-Tuckahoe, VA	9
84037	Kaysville, UT	9
98607	Vancouver-Camas, WA	9
46060	Noblesville, IN	9
63304	St. Charles, MO	9
43537	Maumee, OH	9
11730	East Islip, NY	9
14534	Pittsford, NY	8
68022	Elkhorn, NE	8
33594	Valrico, FL	8
78732	Austin (West), TX	8
32605	Gainesville, FL	8
24018	Roanoke, VA	8
87122	Albuquerque (Sandia Heights), NM	8
67212	Wichita (West), KS	8

Source: Sperling's BestPlaces

TABLE 4.55 LIBRARY VOLUMES PER CAPITA		
U.S. AVERAGE: 2.8		
MOST BOOKS		
22602	Winchester, VA	20.2
66216	Shawnee, KS	6.9
11730	East Islip, NY	6.3
02067	Sharon, MA	6.0
43537	Maumee, OH	5.5
10994	West Nyack, NY	5.1
45241	Evendale, OH	4.6
63304	St. Charles, MO	4.5
53044	Sheboygan, WI	4.4
43026	Hilliard, OH	4.2
MORE BOOKS		
07648	Norwood, NJ	4.2
06470	Newtown, CT	4.0
53186	Waukesha, WI	4.0
14534	Pittsford, NY	4.0
24018	Roanoke, VA	4.0
47906	West Lafayette, IN	3.9
08824	Kendall Park, NJ	3.9
07039	Livingston, NJ	3.8
60047	Lake Zurich, IL	3.8
60302	Oak Park, IL	3.8
80027	Louisville, CO	3.8
53532	DeForest, WI	3.8
32605	Gainesville, FL	3.7
67212	Wichita (West), KS	3.7
54911	Appleton, WI	3.6
21045	Columbia, MD	3.6
52241	Coralville, IA	3.6
55044	Lakeville, MN	3.5
46060	Noblesville, IN	3.5
03962	Nashua, NH	3.5

Source: National Center for Educational Statistics, 2004

TABLE 4.56 INLAND WATER RATING		
10 Is Best		
U.S. AVERAGE: 3		
10994	West Nyack, NY	10
54911	Appleton, WI	10
55044	Lakeville, MN	10
84321	Logan, UT	10
32073	Orange Park, FL	10
84037	Kaysville, UT	10
89423	Minden, NV	10
89523	Reno, NV	10
11730	East Islip, NY	9
21045	Columbia, MD	9
95630	Folsom, CA	9
22602	Winchester, VA	8
20170	Herndon, VA	8
20878	Gaithersburg, MD	8
98275	Mukilteo, WA	8
23456	Virginia Beach, VA	8
37922	Farragut, TN	8
36695	West Mobile, AL	8

Source: Sperling's BestPlaces

activities. We also know that places with "perfect" climates, like coastal California, tend to be more expensive, and we don't think the average family wants to (or can) pay hundreds of thousands of dollars to have more dry, sunny days.

Point being, we didn't view climate as a major selection factor when choosing our 100 Best Places, but we do want to share with you certain important climate facts. Where the climate is conducive to more outdoor activities—especially in winter—we mention that in chapter 5.

And how do you find out what the climate in an area is really like? Year-round? One approach is to make a daily visit to a weather portal like the Weather Channel (www.weather.com), but we suspect that's not really the most effective approach. Another approach is to talk to

TABLE 4.57 PHYSICAL SETTING 10 Is Best		
U.S. AVERAGE: NM		
99516	Anchorage, AK	10
89423	Minden, NV	10
98273	Mount Vernon, WA	9
98226	Bellingham, WA	9
80526	Fort Collins, CO	9
80027	Louisville, CO	9
98275	Mukilteo, WA	9
87122	Albuquerque (Sandia Heights), NM	8
80104	Castle Rock, CO	8
83616	Eagle, ID	8
84321	Logan, UT	8
98501	Olympia, WA	8

Source: *Best Places to Raise Your Family*

TABLE 4.58 DOWNTOWN CORE 10 Is Best		
U.S. AVERAGE: NM		
22901	Charlottesville, VA	10
80526	Fort Collins, CO	10
24018	Roanoke, VA	10
53532	DeForest, WI	9
80220	Denver (Park Hill), CO	9
97405	Eugene, OR	9
32605	Gainesville, FL	9
20878	Gaithersburg, MD	8
60047	Lake Zurich, IL	8
55044	Lakeville, MN	8
98275	Mukilteo, WA	8
46060	Noblesville, IN	8
60302	Oak Park, IL	8
98501	Olympia, WA	8
53044	Sheboygan, WI	8
99223	Spokane, WA	8
98607	Vancouver-Camas, WA	8

Source: *Best Places to Raise Your Family*

someone in the area, but what if you hit them during a long rainy spell or ice storm or heat wave? As an alternative, we offer summary statistics derived from over 100 years of data collection by the U.S. government.

The facts shown in the next batch of tables give only an overview of key climate characteristics; there are many more aspects of climate data available—including statistics on storm risk, wind, fog, and days below 0°F. You can see a much larger assortment of facts and explanations, in our book, *Cities Ranked & Rated*, or on Sperling's BestPlaces (www.bestplaces.net).

The climate data in this book is sourced from the National Climatic Data Center, an arm of the National Oceanic and Atmospheric Administration, or NOAA, part of the U.S. Department of Commerce. Most readings were taken at the airport serving the metro area.

Area Highlights

The following facts are shown at the area level, and don't vary significantly if at all among neighborhoods within an area.

- Days Mostly Sunny is a fairly self-explanatory statistic: days sunny or partly cloudy and dry. See Table 4.59. The figure ranges from a high of 283 in Albuquerque (Sandia Heights), New Mexico, to a low of 131 in Anchorage, Alaska. Yes, you can subtract this figure from 365 to determine the number of days that NOAA/NCDC considers "cloudy." So 1 in 2 days in places like Albuquerque, much of California, Nevada, Colorado, and parts of Texas are sunny, while 1 in 2 days in places like Anchorage, as well as

Washington, Oregon, Pennsylvania, Michigan, and parts of New York tend to be gloomier.

- Annual Days Precipitation is, again, fairly straightforward, but the nature of rain differs from place to place. In the Pacific Northwest, it is steady and drizzly, and on many rainy days outdoor activities are still possible. Other places have bursts of downpours; still others, particularly in the South, East, and Great Lakes region, have long periods of steady rain (or snow) sufficient to wipe out most outdoor activity. The "wettest" places, not surprisingly, track "cloudy" areas and are in the Pacific Northwest and the Great Lakes areas of Ohio, Michigan, Indiana, Pennsylvania, and upstate New York. See Table 4.60.

- Annual Days > 90 is the number of days, on average, with a daily *high* temperature exceeding 90°F each year. It's a matter of preference, but for most people, warmth is a good thing—unless there's too much of it or it comes with excessive humidity. Not only do we highlight the *warmest* places in Table 4.61, but also the places with the *fewest* days exceeding 90°F—places with relatively cool summers, like Getzville, New York, in the Buffalo area.

- Annual Days < 32 is the number of days, on average, with the daily low temperature below freezing. Places with the most days < 32 have cold winters, or, like areas in Colorado and other parts of the west, have high altitudes and low

TABLE 4.59 DAYS MOSTLY SUNNY		
U.S. AVERAGE: 212		
SUNNIEST		
87122	Albuquerque (Sandia Heights), NM	283
95694	Winters, CA	276
92354	Loma Linda, CA	268
95630	Folsom, CA	265
54403	Wausau, WI	262
91354	Santa Clarita, CA	258
92688	Rancho Santa Margarita, CA	258
89423	Minden, NV	255
89523	Reno, NV	255
33326	Weston, FL	248
SUNNIER		
80027	Louisville, CO	246
80104	Castle Rock, CO	246
80220	Denver (Park Hill), CO	246
80526	Fort Collins, CO	246
79606	Abilene, TX	246
32605	Gainesville, FL	242
33594	Valrico, FL	238
76002	Arlington, TX	234
75028	Flower Mound, TX	233
10994	West Nyack, NY	232
84037	Kaysville, UT	232
84321	Logan, UT	232
78732	Austin (West), TX	231
74012	Broken Arrow, OK	228
78232	Hollywood Park, TX	227
32073	Orange Park, FL	226
67212	Wichita (West), KS	224
29212	Irmo, SC	223
29650	Greer, SC	221
27513	Cary, NC	220

Source: NOAA/National Climatic Data Center

TABLE 4.60 DRIEST CLIMATE		
Annual Days Precipitation		
U.S. AVERAGE: 111		
DRIEST		
92354	Loma Linda, CA	35
91354	Santa Clarita, CA	35
92688	Rancho Santa Margarita, CA	40
89523	Reno, NV	49
89423	Minden, NV	51
95630	Folsom, CA	57
87122	Albuquerque (Sandia Heights), NM	59
95694	Winters, CA	60
79606	Abilene, TX	65
75028	Flower Mound, TX	79
DRIER		
76002	Arlington, TX	79
78232	Hollywood Park, TX	81
78732	Austin (West), TX	82
67212	Wichita (West), KS	84
84037	Kaysville, UT	88
80027	Louisville, CO	88
80104	Castle Rock, CO	88
80220	Denver (Park Hill), CO	88
80526	Fort Collins, CO	88
74012	Broken Arrow, OK	90
83616	Eagle, ID	91
84321	Logan, UT	91
72758	Rogers, AR	96
66049	Lawrence, KS	96
57702	Rapid City, SD	96
75791	Tyler, TX	97
68022	Elkhorn, NE	99
66216	Shawnee, KS	102
58104	Fargo, ND	102
50325	West Des Moines–Clive, IA	106

Source: NOAA/National Climatic Data Center

humidity. Such conditions bring low nighttime temperatures on days otherwise considered pleasant. Places with the fewest days below freezing, not surprisingly, are in the South and in places near considerable water, such as the Pacific Northwest. See Table 4.62.

- July Relative Humidity shows the reading for the hottest month of the year. The highest humidity occurs in the southern parts of the country, dropping gradually as you move farther north. High humidity is also recorded in the Pacific Northwest, but it's more comfortable than the south due to cooler temperatures.

Neighborhood Highlights
Climate phenomena are generally applicable to an area at large. However, we do include a composite climate rating on the Neighborhood Highlights tables in chapter 5.

- Climate Rating compiles a wide assortment of climate facts on temperatures and temperature extremes, precipitation, humidity, cloud cover, storm risk, fog, and wind. For many of these factors, an acceptable range is identified. For example, some precipitation is a good thing, but not too much and not too little. So a range is defined, and if an area falls outside the range (too dry or too wet), it loses points. These range-modified scores are all compiled into the Climate Rating with 10 being best and 1 being worst. The rating is subjective because different people have different views of what ranges are acceptable. Climate ratings are presented on the Neighborhood Highlights tables to give you a quick view of climate as you consider other neighborhood factors.

TABLE 4.61 HOTTEST AND COOLEST SUMMERS						
Annual Days > 90 Degrees						
U.S. AVERAGE: 38						
HOTTEST				**COOLEST**		
78232	Hollywood Park, TX	111		14068	Getzville, NY	2
32605	Gainesville, FL	104		03062	Nashua, NH	2
78732	Austin (West), TX	101		98275	Mukilteo, WA	3
76002	Arlington, TX	92		98226	Bellingham, WA	3
79606	Abilene, TX	89		98273	Mount Vernon, WA	3
75028	Flower Mound, TX	88		54403	Wausau, WI	4
75791	Tyler, TX	87		91354	Santa Clarita, CA	5
95694	Winters, CA	82		92688	Rancho Santa Margarita, CA	5
32073	Orange Park, FL	82		98501	Olympia, WA	6
33594	Valrico, FL	81		15108	Coraopolis–Moon Township, PA	7
HOTTER				**COOLER**		
77479	Sugar Land, TX	81		54313	Green Bay, WI	7
36695	West Mobile, AL	81		54911	Appleton, WI	7
95630	Folsom, CA	77		02760	North Attleboro, MA	8
74012	Broken Arrow, OK	70		98607	Vancouver-Camas, WA	8
29212	Irmo, SC	64		53186	Waukesha, WI	9
67212	Wichita (West), KS	62		53044	Sheboygan, WI	9
87122	Albuquerque (Sandia Heights), NM	61		11730	East Islip, NY	10
72758	Rogers, AR	60		14534	Pittsford, NY	11
84037	Kaysville, UT	58		49426	Hudsonville, MI	11
84321	Logan, UT	58		02067	Sharon, MA	12
97526	Grants Pass, OR	54		53532	DeForest, WI	12
89523	Reno, NV	52		99516	Anchorage, AK	12
89423	Minden, NV	50		58104	Fargo, ND	12
37343	Hixson, TN	49		43537	Maumee, OH	13
66049	Lawrence, KS	45		01824	Chelmsford, MA	15
83616	Eagle, ID	43		55044	Lakeville, MN	15
23233	Richmond-Tuckahoe, VA	41		43026	Hilliard, OH	15
66216	Shawnee, KS	40		97405	Eugene, OR	15
65203	Columbia, MO	39		46060	Noblesville, IN	15
68022	Elkhorn, NE	38		55902	Rochester, MN	15

Source: NOAA/National Climatic Data Center

Commute & Transportation

A family lifestyle, no matter how rich or pleasant, must exist within an infrastructure that supports a family's "comings and goings" for work and for pleasure. Aside from the very wealthy or the fortunate few who work at home on a regular basis, someone in the family must get back and forth between a home and an employer. Even for those not commuting for work, access to conveniences and activities is important.

As suburban growth has led more and more residents farther and farther into the suburbs—in pursuit of economical housing, country settings, and modern housing and schools—commutes have become increasingly long and difficult. Average commute times are up almost 10% since 2003, from 22.6 to almost 25 minutes. The amount of "urban sprawl" has become acute in some areas, and a trip to any modest shopping facility or commercial area is often 5 or 10 miles away, if not farther. And the way most suburbs have spread almost indiscriminately into the hinterlands, large-scale scheduled public transportation is difficult and rare.

The inevitable result is that progressively greater amounts of family time and financial resources are spent on the commute and other driving chores. As part of our assessment of lifestyle, we examine commute times, transport infrastructure, and costs to analyze how they trade off against the benefits of an area.

Area Highlights

- Average Daily Commute Time. Collected by the U.S. Census and updated each year in the American Community Survey, this statistic represents the average *one-way* commute in minutes for the metro area. See Table 4.63. Not surprisingly, the shortest commutes are found in smaller towns, like Sheboygan, Wisconsin; Rochester, Minnesota; and most college towns, while longer commutes are found in populous and spread-out

TABLE 4.62 WARMEST WINTERS		
Days < 32 degrees		
U.S. AVERAGE: 88		
WARMEST		
92354	Loma Linda, CA	0
91354	Santa Clarita, CA	0
92688	Rancho Santa Margarita, CA	0
33326	Weston, FL	0
75791	Tyler, TX	1
32605	Gainesville, FL	2
33594	Valrico, FL	4
32073	Orange Park, FL	12
95630	Folsom, CA	17
36695	West Mobile, AL	19
WARMER		
78232	Hollywood Park, TX	22
78732	Austin (West), TX	23
77479	Sugar Land, TX	24
95694	Winters, CA	25
98275	Mukilteo, WA	32
98226	Bellingham, WA	32
98273	Mount Vernon, WA	32
75028	Flower Mound, TX	39
76002	Arlington, TX	41
98607	Vancouver-Camas, WA	44
23456	Virginia Beach, VA	54
97405	Eugene, OR	54
79606	Abilene, TX	56
30075	Roswell, GA	59
29212	Irmo, SC	60
35758	Madison, AL	65
29650	Greer, SC	68
28105	Matthews, NC	71
37922	Farragut, TN	71
37343	Hixson, TN	75

Source: NOAA/National Climatic Data Center

urban areas. The average commute time of 31 minutes for Atlanta in our Roswell, Georgia, example isn't surprising, given how far it has spread away from the city core. In our interviews, we asked where most people go for work and how long it takes them to get there, and we reported the answers in chapter 5's narratives.

- Percent Commute by Auto. This is the U.S. Census estimate of what percent of the population uses a single-occupant automobile to get to work.

- Per Capita Average Daily Transit Miles. From the Federal Urban Mass Transit Administration, we received the figures that represent the number of seat-miles (that is, the number of seats on available transit vehicles times the route miles they travel, a measure of capacity) of public transportation available per person in an area. Essentially, this measures the size and scheduled frequency of the public transportation

resources—bus, rail, and ferry—available in the area. The larger urban areas dominate in this subcategory, with West Nyack and East Islip, New York, heading the list along with Mukilteo, Washington, in the transit-rich Seattle area. See Table 4.64.

- Annual Auto Insurance Premium. Let's switch gears to the cost of operating an automobile. The National Association of Insurance Commissioners gave us estimated annual auto insurance premiums for an average vehicle for an average driver in each area. The range is surprisingly wide, from $1,600 to $2,200 in New York, New Jersey, Massachusetts, and California down to $600 to $700 in the upper Midwest. See Table 4.65.

- Gas, Cost Per Gallon. Few topics made the 2005 headlines more often than gasoline prices, and we expect them to be a topic of conversation for years to come. In September 2005, when prices hit their 2005 peak, prices ranged from $2.65 per gallon (Anchorage, Alaska, a big oil-producing state) to the mid-$3.30s on the East Coast. See Table 4.66.

Neighborhood Highlights

- Percent of Commutes < 30 minutes: The U.S. Census population surveys collect enough data to chart not only average commute times but also high and low extremes. Reported at the neighborhood level are the population percentages reporting a commute of less than 30 minutes and a commute greater than 1 hour. These percentages talk as much or more about the real commute stress and time commitments in an area as the averages. Not surprisingly, neighborhoods with a predominance of less than 30-minute commutes are in smaller cities and towns. When you see a high percentage of less than 30-minute commutes in a large area—such as in Evendale, Ohio; Hilliard, Ohio; or Vancouver-Camas, Washington—you can assume there's a good road system and/or a healthy concentration of jobs in the immediate area.

- Percent of Commutes > 1 hour: This statistic represents the other end of the scale, exceptionally long and time-consuming commutes most likely to create stress, eat into family time, and stretch daycare arrangements. In this book, no more

TABLE 4.63 SHORTEST AND LONGEST COMMUTE TIMES						
Average One-Way Commute Time						
U.S. AVERAGE: 24.7 MINUTES						
SHORTEST				**LONGEST**		
58104	Fargo, ND	16.2		10994	West Nyack, NY	38.9
55902	Rochester, MN	16.3		11730	East Islip, NY	33
79606	Abilene, TX	16.4		20170	Herndon, VA	32.8
84321	Logan, UT	16.8		20878	Gaithersburg, MD	32.8
53044	Sheboygan, WI	16.9		60047	Lake Zurich, IL	31.5
57702	Rapid City, SD	17.3		60302	Oak Park, IL	31.5
54313	Green Bay, WI	17.5		08824	Kendall Park, NJ	31.3
47906	West Lafayette, IN	17.7		30075	Roswell, GA	31.2
52241	Coralville, IA	17.7		92354	Loma Linda, CA	31.1
65203	Columbia, MO	17.8		07039	Livingston, NJ	30.8
SHORTER				**LONGER**		
54911	Appleton, WI	18.1		21045	Columbia, MD	29.8
54403	Wausau, WI	18.4		91354	Santa Clarita, CA	29.4
67212	Wichita (West), KS	19.1		77479	Sugar Land, TX	29
89523	Reno, NV	19.2		19382	West Chester, PA	28.7
50325	West Des Moines–Clive, IA	19.3		07648	Norwood, NJ	28.6
66049	Lawrence, KS	19.4		75028	Flower Mound, TX	27.9
68022	Elkhorn, NE	19.4		02067	Sharon, MA	27.7
99516	Anchorage, AK	19.5		33326	Weston, FL	27.4
72758	Rogers, AR	19.5		22602	Winchester, VA	27.3
53532	DeForest, WI	19.6		98275	Mukilteo, WA	27.3
97405	Eugene, OR	19.9		92688	Rancho Santa Margarita, CA	27.2
97526	Grants Pass, OR	19.9		01824	Chelmsford, MA	26.9
83616	Eagle, ID	20		76002	Arlington, TX	26.8
43537	Maumee, OH	20.2		32073	Orange Park, FL	26.6
24018	Roanoke, VA	20.5		80104	Castle Rock, CO	26.5
49426	Hudsonville, MI	20.6		80220	Denver (Park Hill), CO	26.5
98226	Bellingham, WA	20.7		28105	Matthews, NC	26.1
14068	Getzville, NY	20.8		95630	Folsom, CA	26.1
14534	Pittsford, NY	21.1		37064	Franklin, TN	25.8
32605	Gainesville, FL	21.1		33594	Valrico, FL	25.6

Source: U.S. Census 2000/American Community Survey 2004

than 20% of any population in any neighborhood fall into this category, but more residents in certain areas will have long commutes, such as in Kendall Park, New Jersey; Santa Clarita, California; and East Islip, New York, among others. More positively, 80 of our 100 Best Places had less than 10% of the population in the 1-hour-plus category.

Health & Safety

Hopefully, you and your loved ones won't have to think about or experience on a day-to-day basis this final major category. Yet health and safety are extremely important factors for all residents of an area—and for families with children in particular.

Like lifestyle factors, many health and safety issues are difficult to measure because they're somewhat intangible. How safe is a physical infrastructure from accidents? Does it have appropriate fences, signs, and other safeguards? How safe is the behavior of residents? Do they drive too fast? Do external forces like climate add to physical hazards in an area? Mountain lions? Disease-bearing insects? Are there major sources of pollution or environmental degradation? It's hard to judge these factors with any precision. Moreover, just because an area "looks" good or has a solid past, it doesn't mean you're completely safe from the next criminal or tornado or drowning accident.

We take a look not only at crime and health *hazards*, but also at the health *resources* available in an area to deal with problems and the cost of those resources. Be aware that these facts and our analysis of them will only provide you with an overview; individuals with special health needs and safety concerns should do more research and talk to residents and healthcare professionals in the area.

TABLE 4.64 PUBLIC TRANSPORTATION		
Daily Mass Transit Miles per Capita		
U.S. AVERAGE: 7.9		
MOST PUBLIC TRANSIT		
10994	West Nyack, NY	62.9
98275	Mukilteo, WA	39.4
11730	East Islip, NY	32.4
02067	Sharon, MA	27.4
60047	Lake Zurich, IL	26.5
60302	Oak Park, IL	26.5
07648	Norwood, NJ	24.9
07039	Livingston, NJ	24.9
08824	Kendall Park, NJ	24.9
20878	Gaithersburg, MD	24.4
MORE PUBLIC TRANSIT		
20170	Castle Rock, CO	24.4
80104	Denver (Park Hill), CO	24.3
80220	Olympia, WA	24.3
98501	Vancouver-Camas, WA	23.5
98607	Coraopolis–Moon Township, PA	21.9
15108	Hollywood Park, TX	21.4
78232	Winchester, VA	20.9
22602	Kaysville, UT	20.7
84037	Santa Clarita, CA	19.5
91354	Austin (West), TX	18.9
78732	West Chester, PA	18.1
19382	Columbia, MD	17.4
21045	Arden-Brandywine, DE	17.2
19810	Roswell, GA	16.9
30075	DeForest, WI	16.7
53532	Flower Mound, TX	16.4
75028	Eugene, OR	16.2
97405	Weston, FL	15.5
33326	Sugar Land, TX	15.5
77479	West Des Moines–Clive, IA	15.1

Source: Federal Highway Administration, 2004

TABLE 4.65 AUTO INSURANCE COST		
Annual Premium per Auto		
U.S. AVERAGE: $1314		
LOWEST COST		
57702	Rapid City, SD	$646
58104	Fargo, ND	$647
52241	Coralville, IA	$656
50325	West Des Moines–Clive, IA	$681
83616	Eagle, ID	$709
54403	Wausau, WI	$750
54313	Green Bay, WI	$753
53044	Sheboygan, WI	$758
66049	Lawrence, KS	$758
54911	Appleton, WI	$775
LOWER COST		
53532	DeForest, WI	$780
47906	West Lafayette, IN	$782
67212	Wichita (West), KS	$787
22901	Charlottesville, VA	$792
24018	Roanoke, VA	$800
84321	Logan, UT	$820
35758	Madison, AL	$823
72758	Rogers, AR	$830
36695	West Mobile, AL	$833
27513	Cary, NC	$834
37922	Farragut, TN	$834
65203	Columbia, MO	$836
28105	Matthews, NC	$844
23233	Richmond-Tuckahoe, VA	$848
29212	Irmo, SC	$856
97405	Eugene, OR	$867
97526	Grants Pass, OR	$870
46060	Noblesville, IN	$871
45241	Evendale, OH	$873
23456	Virginia Beach, VA	$878

Source: National Association of Insurance Commissioners, 2005

Presentation Tables

The area presentation tables divide Health & Safety into four sections: Crime, Health, Healthcare, and Healthcare Cost. There isn't a lot of health or crime data available at the neighborhood level, and much of the healthcare infrastructure makes more sense to examine at the area level anyway.

For an example of neighborhood and area statistics on health and safety, see Table 4.67 and 4.68.

Crime

Whether or not you've been a victim, the incidence of serious crime in an area must be considered. The measurement of crime rates has been a contributing factor to a rather dramatic decrease in violent and nonviolent crime rates over the past 10 years. The rate of decrease has slowed, but for the past 4 years, average crime rates have continued to drop by 7% to 10% after a sharper drop in the late 1990s. The reasons aren't completely clear, but they're probably the result of a combination of factors including an improved economy, improved law enforcement, and more effective housing and urban development programs for economically disadvantaged citizens.

Crime rates are higher in warmer climates and in areas in the southern part of the United States. Areas with very warm climates like Miami, Florida; Memphis, Tennessee; and Baton Rouge, Louisiana, have persistently high violent crime rates, and while the rates drop as you move into smaller cities, they're still relatively high. Other areas in the South—in Texas, Arizona, South Carolina, and Florida, for example—also have high nonviolent, or property, crime rates. The reasons for this aren't completely clear either but probably involve opportunity (more favorable weather), temperament, stress, and the presence of economically disadvantaged groups in these areas.

The Federal Bureau of Investigation (FBI) collects fairly detailed crime statistics at the metro area level for

TABLE 4.66 GASOLINE PRICES		
Cost per Gallon Including Taxes		
U.S. AVERAGE: 3.05		
LOWEST COST		
99516	Anchorage, AK	$2.65
36695	West Mobile, AL	$2.76
98607	Vancouver-Camas, WA	$2.80
55902	Rochester, MN	$2.80
55044	Lakeville, MN	$2.84
84037	Kaysville, UT	$2.87
98501	Olympia, WA	$2.87
84321	Logan, UT	$2.89
40503	Lexington, KY	$2.90
78232	Hollywood Park, TX	$2.90
LOWER COST		
98275	Mukilteo, WA	$2.91
97405	Eugene, OR	$2.91
78732	Austin (West), TX	$2.92
54313	Green Bay, WI	$2.93
83616	Eagle, ID	$2.95
54403	Wausau, WI	$2.95
33326	Weston, FL	$2.96
79606	Abilene, TX	$2.96
72758	Rogers, AR	$2.97
99223	Spokane, WA	$2.97
92688	Rancho Santa Margarita, CA	$2.97
77479	Sugar Land, TX	$2.97
74012	Broken Arrow, OK	$2.97
43537	Maumee, OH	$2.98
76002	Arlington, TX	$2.98
32605	Gainesville, FL	$2.99
75791	Tyler, TX	$2.99
43026	Hilliard, OH	$2.99
49426	Hudsonville, MI	$3.00
46060	Noblesville, IN	$3.00

Source: American Automobile Association, October 2005

violent crime, defined as murder, rape, robbery, and assault, and for nonviolent, or *property* crime, defined as burglary, theft, and auto theft. We pick up those statistics and present them at the area level.

We recognize, and want to reinforce, that area level crime statistics probably won't match your personal experience in a neighborhood. The neighborhoods we chose are safer than the urban area they surround. Columbia, Maryland, for example, is much safer than the Baltimore area as a whole. To evaluate crime risk for specific neighborhoods, we relied on data from an organization known as CAP Index, Inc. (Crime Against Persons/Property), which makes a business of evaluating loss, risk, and crime vulnerability in individual locales across the U.S. and Canada.

Area Highlights

- Violent Crime Rate is a single figure for each metro area representing combined murder, rape, robbery, and assault incidents reported per 100,000 residents. For example, the "513" figure for the Atlanta area means 513 incidents occur per year per 100,000 residents, which is almost right at the national average. Our metro areas ranged from 883 for Columbia, Maryland (not *in* Columbia, but in the Greater Baltimore area), to 54 incidents in Grants Pass, Oregon. See Table 4.69.

- Change in Violent Crime shows the trend in violent crime incidents from 1998 to 2003. The biggest drop we saw was 23% in Albuquerque, New Mexico, followed by 22% in Madison (Huntsville), Alabama; Matthews (Charlotte), North Carolina; and West Lafayette, Indiana. This drop may be less meaningful in small places like West Lafayette because of the small number of crimes in the first place. See Table 4.70.

- Property Crime Rate combines incidents of burglary, theft, and auto theft and averages just less than 3,800 incidents per 100,000 residents across the country. The areas featuring lower rates are highlighted in Table 4.71.

- Change in Property Crime has experienced steady declines in most areas, and all but 18 areas on the 100 Best Places list have experienced a decrease. In fact, some of the biggest decreases were in areas in the South with (at one time) high property crime rates. See Table 4.72.

Neighborhood Highlights

- Violent Crime Risk is calculated for each locale based on material obtained from a professional risk-assessment firm known as CAP Index, Inc. CAP builds elaborate predictive models based on past crime statistics and an assortment of mathematically modeled predictive factors tied to the social and economic composition of an area. CAP uses the FBI classifications for violent crime—murder, rape, assault, and robbery. A

TABLE 4.67 ATLANTA, GA AREA HIGHLIGHTS SEGMENT HEALTH & SAFETY					
CRIME & ENVIRNOMENTAL ISSUES	**AREA**	**U.S. AVG**	**HEALTHCARE & COST**		
Violent Crime Rate	513	517	Physicians per Capita	217	254.3
Change in Violent Crime	-28.80%	-7.50%	Pediatricians per Capita	20.4	16.9
Property Crime Rate	4320	3783	Hospital Beds per Capita	249.2	239.7
Change in Property Crime	-23.40%	-10.10%	No. of Teaching Hospitals	11	1.9
Air Quality Score	32	44	Healthcare Cost Index	104.4	100
Water Quality Score	51	33	Cost per Doctor Visit	$70	$74
Pollen/Allergy Score	63	61	Cost per Dentist Visit	$66	$67
Stress Score	82	49	Cost per Hospital Room	$677	$702
Cancer Mortality Rate	166.2	168.9			

TABLE 4.68 ROSWELL, GA NEIGHBORHOOD HIGHLIGHTS SEGMENT	
HEALTH & SAFETY	
Health Rating (Area)	3
Stress Score (Area)	8
Violent Crime Risk	29
Property Crime Risk	32

CAP score of 100 means that the neighborhood has risk approximately equal to the national average. A score of 50 means that the locale has a crime risk of one-half the national average, while a score of 200 represents twice the average. Scores below 50 are considered very low crime risk, while the label "high risk" applies only to places exceeding 500. A small handful of scores exceeded 200; most are below 100.

- Property Crime Risk is the CAP Index assessment for property crime, including burglary, theft, and auto theft. Scores are interpreted in a manner similar to the Violent Crime Risk.

Health

Aside from crimes, which are outcomes of human behavior, the other major set of hazards to family health and safety arise from disease and environmental factors that can cause poor health. In studying disease rates from the U.S. Department of Health and Human Services Centers for Disease Control and Prevention (CDC), we don't see that much difference among places

TABLE 4.69 VIOLENT CRIME RATE Incidents per 100K Residents U.S. AVERAGE: 517		
LOWEST VIOLENT CRIME		
97526	Grants Pass, OR	54
84321	Logan, UT	63
98273	Mount Vernon, WA	86
54911	Appleton, WI	93
53044	Sheboygan, WI	98
58104	Fargo, ND	100
06470	Newtown, CT	107
22602	Winchester, VA	112
03062	Nashua, NH	127
54403	Wausau, WI	155
LOWER VIOLENT CRIME		
89423	Minden, NV	168
17402	York, PA	195
08824	Kendall Park, NJ	195
55902	Rochester, MN	196
11730	East Islip, NY	197
54313	Green Bay, WI	199
47906	West Lafayette, IN	211
53532	DeForest, WI	222
17601	Lancaster, PA	230
98226	Bellingham, WA	240
72758	Rogers, AR	241
07648	Norwood, NJ	243
18018	Bethlehem, PA	250
50325	West Des Moines–Clive, IA	253
80526	Fort Collins, CO	261
97405	Eugene, OR	263
98501	Olympia, WA	263
22901	Charlottesville, VA	275
92688	Rancho Santa Margarita, CA	277
83616	Eagle, ID	287

Source: FBI Uniform Crime Reports, 2003

TABLE 4.70 CHANGE IN VIOLENT CRIME			
% Crime Decrease 2000–2004 Metro Level Data			
U.S. AVERAGE: -7.5%			
LARGEST DECREASE			
97526	Grants Pass, OR		-53%
68022	Elkhorn, NE		-44%
60047	Lake Zurich, IL		-41%
60302	Oak Park, IL		-41%
10994	West Nyack, NY		-41%
63304	St. Charles, MO		-37%
22901	Charlottesville, VA		-36%
98607	Vancouver-Camas, WA		-36%
95694	Winters, CA		-35%
27513	Cary, NC		-34%
LARGER DECREASE			
07039	Livingston, NJ		-33%
01824	Chelmsford, MA		-33%
53044	Sheboygan, WI		-32%
97405	Eugene, OR		-32%
32605	Gainesville, FL		-31%
99223	Spokane, WA		-31%
17402	York, PA		-29%
58104	Fargo, ND		-29%
30075	Roswell, GA		-29%
53532	DeForest, WI		-29%
52241	Coralville, IA		-28%
29650	Greer, SC		-27%
55902	Rochester, MN		-26%
37343	Hixson, TN		-24%
87122	Albuquerque (Sandia Heights), NM		-23%
35758	Madison, AL		-22%
28105	Matthews, NC		-22%
47906	West Lafayette, IN		-22%
32073	Orange Park, FL		-21%
92688	Rancho Santa Margarita, CA		-21%

Source: FBI Uniform Crime Reports, 2003

TABLE 4.71 PROPERTY CRIME		
Incidents per 100K Residents Metro Level Data		
U.S. AVERAGE: 3783		
LOWEST PROPERTY CRIME		
97526	Grants Pass, OR	1196
06470	Newtown, CT	1592
84321	Logan, UT	1804
98273	Mount Vernon, WA	1832
11730	East Islip, NY	1845
01824	Chelmsford, MA	1872
54911	Appleton, WI	1952
08824	Kendall Park, NJ	2020
03062	Nashua, NH	2028
22602	Winchester, VA	2035
LOWER PROPERTY CRIME		
07648	Norwood, NJ	2057
10994	West Nyack, NY	2154
22901	Charlottesville, VA	2253
17402	York, PA	2289
54403	Wausau, WI	2359
17601	Lancaster, PA	2362
55902	Rochester, MN	2372
15108	Coraopolis–Moon Township, PA	2408
89423	Minden, NV	2412
92688	Rancho Santa Margarita, CA	2464
58104	Fargo, ND	2481
18018	Bethlehem, PA	2538
54313	Green Bay, WI	2566
52241	Coralville, IA	2653
72758	Rogers, AR	2762
07039	Livingston, NJ	2824
24018	Roanoke, VA	2835
19382	West Chester, PA	2837
02760	North Attleboro, MA	2854
53532	DeForest, WI	2932

Source: FBI Uniform Crime Reports, 2003

for incidence of flu, measles, or other diseases, nor most chronic diseases like arthritis or heart disease. But we do see and feel differences in the environmental factors among places.

Measurable differences among places occur for air and water quality and for pollens and other allergy-causing agents. We also subscribe to the notion that high stress lowers resistance to disease and makes people *feel* less healthy than they otherwise might be. Therefore, in the heath category, we break out scores, developed by Sperling's BestPlaces, by air quality, water quality, pollen and allergies, and our "stress score"—a compilation of several factors that create or build stress among residents. Finally, we take a look at cancer mortality rates in the areas, which, while low, do show some differences, which may be part environmental and part behavioral, as in smoking tobacco.

In choosing the 100 best places to raise your family, we gave a degree of consideration to these health factors, especially stress and air quality, but did not weight them as heavily as other factors. We point them out in the data so that those particularly sensitive to certain factors, like pollen and allergies, can be informed enough to make their own choices among the 100 best places.

Area Highlights

Air quality, water quality, and pollen and allergy factors occur mainly at area levels. In other words, you won't find significant differences among neighborhoods within an area, so we don't report these specifics at the neighborhood levels. While some environmental factors, especially the "stress" factors, may be locally driven, we weren't able to get enough factual detail to bring the scoring to a neighborhood level, so we present the stress score at an area level as well.

TABLE 4.72 CHANGE IN PROPERTY CRIME		
% Crime Decrease 2000–2004 Metro Level Data		
U.S. AVERAGE: -10.1%		
LARGEST DECREASE		
32605	Gainesville, FL	-47%
97526	Grants Pass, OR	-41%
87122	Albuquerque (Sandia Heights), NM	-34%
10994	West Nyack, NY	-32%
27513	Cary, NC	-32%
57702	Rapid City, SD	-31%
22901	Charlottesville, VA	-30%
33326	Weston, FL	-28%
54313	Green Bay, WI	-27%
21045	Columbia, MD	-26%
LARGER DECREASE		
80027	Louisville, CO	-25%
06470	Newtown, CT	-25%
54911	Appleton, WI	-25%
37064	Franklin, TN	-24%
60047	Lake Zurich, IL	-24%
60302	Oak Park, IL	-24%
19382	West Chester, PA	-24%
30075	Roswell, GA	-23%
65203	Columbia, MO	-23%
17402	York, PA	-23%
07039	Livingston, NJ	-21%
11730	East Islip, NY	-20%
52241	Coralville, IA	-20%
55044	Lakeville, MN	-20%
32073	Orange Park, FL	-19%
63304	St. Charles, MO	-19%
18018	Bethlehem, PA	-19%
97405	Eugene, OR	-18%
29650	Greer, SC	-18%
08824	Kendall Park, NJ	-18%

Source: FBI Uniform Crime Reports, 2003

TABLE 4.73 AIR QUALITY SCORE		
Metro Area Level Data		
U.S. AVERAGE: 45		
HIGHEST AIR QUALITY		
23456	Virginia Beach, VA	67
22901	Charlottesville, VA	66
24018	Roanoke, VA	66
89423	Minden, NV	60
23233	Richmond-Tuckahoe, VA	59
22602	Winchester, VA	58
40503	Lexington, KY	52
47906	West Lafayette, IN	51
52241	Coralville, IA	49
84321	Logan, UT	48
HIGHER AIR QUALITY		
54911	Appleton, WI	47
50325	West Des Moines–Clive, IA	45
37922	Farragut, TN	45
57702	Rapid City, SD	45
79606	Abilene, TX	44
55902	Rochester, MN	44
65203	Columbia, MO	44
37343	Hixson, TN	44
14534	Pittsford, NY	43
98273	Mount Vernon, WA	43
95694	Winters, CA	43
58104	Fargo, ND	42
53044	Sheboygan, WI	42
37064	Franklin, TN	42
20878	Gaithersburg, MD	41
20170	Herndon, VA	41
54403	Wausau, WI	41
02760	North Attleboro, MA	40
66049	Lawrence, KS	40
98501	Olympia, WA	40

Source: Sperling's BestPlaces

- Air Quality Score is a composite score, with 0 being the worst and 100 being the best, incorporating several measurable chemical pollutants from data obtained from the U.S. Environmental Protection Agency (EPA). Such pollutants include a series of airborne volatile organic and other hydrocarbon compounds, sulfur and nitrogen pollutants, particulates, and ozone. Because it measures a complete set of chemical pollutants, it may not match air quality "scores" you see on TV weather reports, and it may also not match your visual experience. But places with good air circulation or relatively few pollution sources, like Virginia Beach, Virginia, or West Lafayette, Indiana, score well while places like Santa Clarita, California, score poorly. Some places, such as Vancouver-Camas, Washington, or Bellingham, Washington, have excellent air quality *most* of

the year but get mediocre scores because of nearby paper mills and occasional periods of stagnant air, mainly in summer. See Table 4.73.

- Water Quality Score is like the Air Quality Score because it, too, measures chemical pollution, not visual pollution. It measures the chemical quality of watershed runoff or drainage water, not necessarily the quality of drinking water, including naturally occurring minerals, turbidity, sediments, and man-made pollutants. Agricultural and mine waste can influence this score, which is also taken on a 0 to 100 basis with 100 being best.

- Pollen/Allergy Score is a highlight for the estimated 30% of the U.S. population that suffers from the effects of one or more airborne allergies. The 0 to 100 score compiles several types of allergens, including grass and tree pollen and

TABLE 4.74 POLLEN-ALLERGY SCORE Metro Area Level Data		
U.S. AVERAGE: 61.2		
LOWEST ALLERGY		
54313	Green Bay, WI	28
58104	Fargo, ND	30
54911	Appleton, WI	30
53532	DeForest, WI	34
54403	Wausau, WI	36
98607	Vancouver-Camas, WA	36
53044	Sheboygan, WI	37
50325	West Des Moines–Clive, IA	40
91354	Santa Clarita, CA	42
53186	Waukesha, WI	42
LOWER ALLERGY		
99223	Spokane, WA	42
01824	Chelmsford, MA	44
92688	Rancho Santa Margarita, CA	45
83616	Eagle, ID	45
19810	Arden-Brandywine, DE	45
55902	Rochester, MN	46
52241	Coralville, IA	46
98501	Olympia, WA	47
55044	Lakeville, MN	47
17402	York, PA	47
98273	Mount Vernon, WA	48
98226	Bellingham, WA	48
98275	Mukilteo, WA	48
49426	Hudsonville, MI	49
33326	Weston, FL	49
68022	Elkhorn, NE	50
92354	Loma Linda, CA	51
03062	Nashua, NH	52
57702	Rapid City, SD	52
43537	Maumee, OH	53

Source: Sperling's BestPlaces

TABLE 4.75 STRESS SCORE Metro Area Level Data		
U.S. AVERAGE: 49		
LOWEST STRESS		
58104	Fargo, ND	0
55902	Rochester, MN	1
54403	Wausau, WI	3
53044	Sheboygan, WI	3
17601	Lancaster, PA	3
11730	East Islip, NY	4
57702	Rapid City, SD	5
08824	Kendall Park, NJ	5
06470	Newtown, CT	7
66049	Lawrence, KS	7
LOWER STRESS		
79606	Abilene, TX	7
54911	Appleton, WI	9
47906	West Lafayette, IN	10
07648	Norwood, NJ	13
72758	Rogers, AR	16
52241	Coralville, IA	18
65203	Columbia, MO	18
18018	Bethlehem, PA	20
80526	Fort Collins, CO	21
53532	DeForest, WI	23
50325	West Des Moines–Clive, IA	25
54313	Green Bay, WI	27
14068	Getzville, NY	28
68022	Elkhorn, NE	29
92688	Rancho Santa Margarita, CA	31
17402	York, PA	31
03062	Nashua, NH	31
24018	Roanoke, VA	33
55044	Lakeville, MN	35
02067	Sharon, MA	36

Source: Sperling's BestPlaces

mold and mold spores. However, this score, and the stress score, works a little differently than the others in that the *lowest* number is best. Areas in the upper Midwest tend to score best, while places in Texas, Colorado, and California, with large areas of grassland, winds, and relatively little air-clearing rain, tend to score poorly. See Table 4.74.

- Stress Score is a composite of eight factors gathered from other sources and compiled by Sperling's BestPlaces. Factors include divorce rate, commute time, unemployment rate, crime rates, suicide rate, alcohol use rate, days feeling depressed (a CDC compilation), and cloudy days. The score is 0 to 100 with 0 representing the lowest stress levels. Naturally this score creates a *proxy* for stress; it's impossible to measure actual stress in an area, and these stress factors may apply to

some individuals or families more than others. But the resulting scores pinpoint the larger, more crowded cities with longer commutes as stressful, and less "complex" places like Fargo, North Dakota, on the most favored list. See Table 4.75.

- Cancer Mortality Rate, as mentioned above, can be taken as an indicator of both environmental and behavioral health factors, such as smoking, that may be present in an area. The actual measure, compiled by the CDC, is fairly complex, including an age weighting (older people are more likely to get cancer, so the figure is driven proportionally higher when *younger* people show higher disease incidence). With a U.S. average of 169 persons per 100,000 per year, we see figures ranging from a high of 195 in Eastern cities like Columbia, Maryland, and Kendall Park, New Jersey, down to 133 to 135 in Utah and Colorado.

TABLE 4.76 HEALTH RATING Metro Area Level Data		
10 BEING THE BEST		
55902	Rochester, MN	10
24018	Roanoke, VA	10
52241	Coralville, IA	10
29212	Irmo, SC	10
22901	Charlottesville, VA	10
53532	DeForest, WI	10
58104	Fargo, ND	9
54403	Wausau, WI	9
53044	Sheboygan, WI	9
40503	Lexington, KY	8
54911	Appleton, WI	8
37922	Farragut, TN	8
54313	Green Bay, WI	8
72758	Rogers, AR	8
27513	Cary, NC	8
50325	West Des Moines–Clive, IA	8
23233	Richmond-Tuckahoe, VA	8
37343	Hixson, TN	8
80027	Louisville, CO	8

Source: Sperling's BestPlaces

Neighborhood Highlights

We don't present any health data at the neighborhood level, but instead report two composite area scores in the neighborhood table for reference as you consider other neighborhood facts:

- The Health Rating is a Sperling's BestPlaces composite of health hazards and healthcare resources. It is a 1 to 10 rating, with 10 being the highest and 1 being the lowest. Places like Rochester, Minnesota, and Roanoke, Virginia, score well not only for their health characteristics but also for their facilities, such as good hospitals or clinics. See Table 4.76.

- Stress Score is simply a repeat of the Stress Score reported at the area level, except it has been rounded to a single-digit (1 to 10) figure, listed in the neighborhood tables for handy comparison.

Healthcare

From the causes of health problems we move to the solutions—the resources available locally in the form of healthcare professionals and facilities in an area.

Area Highlights

The following statistics are reported at area levels, mainly because that's how they are collected by our sources, but also because they reflect, convenience aside, the true healthcare infrastructure available to residents of a neighborhood.

TABLE 4.77 PHYSICIANS PER CAPITA Metro Area Level Data		
U.S. AVERAGE: 254		
MOST PHYSICIANS		
55902	Rochester, MN	1083
52241	Coralville, IA	594
22901	Charlottesville, VA	479
65203	Columbia, MO	473
32605	Gainesville, FL	469
02067	Sharon, MA	377
11730	East Islip, NY	359
53532	DeForest, WI	337
24018	Roanoke, VA	329
07648	Norwood, NJ	327
MORE PHYSICIANS		
75791	Tyler, TX	318
80027	Louisville, CO	297
21045	Columbia, MD	294
40503	Lexington, KY	292
19382	West Chester, PA	291
27513	Cary, NC	290
57702	Rapid City, SD	288
99516	Anchorage, AK	283
10994	West Nyack, NY	281
20170	Herndon, VA	273
20878	Gaithersburg, MD	273
07039	Livingston, NJ	266
98275	Mukilteo, WA	265
15108	Coraopolis–Moon Township, PA	263
08824	Kendall Park, NJ	261
53186	Waukesha, WI	259
37922	Farragut, TN	256
95694	Winters, CA	252
37064	Franklin, TN	251
06470	Newtown, CT	250

Source: American Medical Association, 2004

- Physicians Per Capita represents the total number of accredited physicians, generalists, and specialists in an area per 100,000 residents. Data comes from the American Medical Association. The Mayo Clinic makes Rochester, Minnesota, number one, but remember, not all of its physicians are practicing healthcare providers for patients; some are dedicated to research. Strong scores occur for college towns and for certain small regional health centers like Tyler, Texas, and Rapid City, South Dakota. See Table 4.77.

- Pediatricians Per Capita is similar to Physicians Per Capita except that it counts only those in the pediatric specialty. The highest numbers tend to be found in larger cities and college towns. See Table 4.78.

- Hospital Beds Per Capita indirectly measures the presence of hospitals and hospital facilities. The

TABLE 4.78 PEDIATRICIANS PER CAPITA Metro Area Level Data		
U.S. AVERAGE: 16.9		
MOST PEDIATRICIANS		
52241	Coralville, IA	108
55902	Rochester, MN	91
22901	Charlottesville, VA	80
32605	Gainesville, FL	79
65203	Columbia, MO	58
02067	Sharon, MA	52
27513	Cary, NC	50
11730	East Islip, NY	49
07648	Norwood, NJ	45
53532	DeForest, WI	45
MORE PEDIATRICIANS		
10994	West Nyack, NY	45
45241	Evendale, OH	43
40503	Lexington, KY	39
21045	Columbia, MD	39
08824	Kendall Park, NJ	38
07039	Livingston, NJ	37
14534	Pittsford, NY	36
20170	Herndon, VA	36
20878	Gaithersburg, MD	36
19382	West Chester, PA	35
02760	North Attleboro, MA	34
68022	Elkhorn, NE	34
19810	Arden-Brandywine, DE	33
46060	Noblesville, IN	33
37064	Franklin, TN	32
43026	Hilliard, OH	31
63304	St. Charles, MO	30
95694	Winters, CA	30
14068	Getzville, NY	30
23233	Richmond-Tuckahoe, VA	30

Source: American Medical Association, 2004

TABLE 4.79 HOSPITAL BEDS PER CAPITA Metro Area Level Data		
U.S. AVERAGE: 240		
MOST BEDS		
55902	Rochester, MN	963
52241	Coralville, IA	861
65203	Columbia, MO	859
24018	Roanoke, VA	747
14068	Getzville, NY	674
22602	Winchester, VA	652
37343	Hixson, TN	600
32605	Gainesville, FL	587
23233	Richmond-Tuckahoe, VA	576
40503	Lexington, KY	568
MORE BEDS		
22901	Charlottesville, VA	543
15108	Coraopolis–Moon Township, PA	535
43537	Maumee, OH	528
68022	Elkhorn, NE	513
79606	Abilene, TX	495
21045	Columbia, MD	494
54403	Wausau, WI	491
75791	Tyler, TX	488
10994	West Nyack, NY	476
07039	Livingston, NJ	476
63304	St. Charles, MO	474
11730	East Islip, NY	473
36695	West Mobile, AL	469
14534	Pittsford, NY	469
29212	Irmo, SC	465
02067	Sharon, MA	450
18018	Bethlehem, PA	441
35758	Madison, AL	439
47906	West Lafayette, IN	438
37064	Franklin, TN	432

Source: U.S. Dept of Health & Human Services, 2004

(VALUE) Cost of Health Insurance

As collectors, packagers, and distributors of facts, we applaud those in industry who go the extra step to collect and publish important comparative facts on their products. Not long before we started our analysis, **eHealthinsurance. com**, a leading health insurance marketing organization and web portal, released a study on the cost of health insurance across the country. As healthcare costs have climbed and more people find themselves self-employed due to today's corporate downsizing, the cost of healthcare is increasingly represented to many of us as a health insurance premium.

The original eHealthinsurance.com study covered the cost of single coverage, but we asked if they could provide data on *family* health insurance. We received the information shown in Table 4.83, and the results are quite interesting. The most expensive places to get hospital and doctor care are not necessarily the most expensive places to buy health insurance. Health insurance premiums, by their nature, also factor in the frequency of use (claims) and competition. Thus, we see an intriguing assortment of premiums based on eHealthinsurance.com's analysis of the lowest premium in each area for our "model" family of four.

We want to thank eHealthinsurance.com and encourage them (along with others) to continue to shine a light on important comparative facts.

TABLE 4.80 TEACHING HOSPITALS		
U.S. AVERAGE: 49		
MOST		
10994	West Nyack, NY	64
60047	Lake Zurich, IL	57
60302	Oak Park, IL	57
19382	West Chester, PA	51
91354	Santa Clarita, CA	48
02067	Sharon, MA	36
11730	East Islip, NY	20
20170	Herndon, VA	20
20878	Gaithersburg, MD	20
77479	Sugar Land, TX	19
MORE		
15108	Coraopolis–Moon Township, PA	18
21045	Columbia, MD	18
63304	St. Charles, MO	18
80104	Castle Rock, CO	18
80220	Denver (Park Hill), CO	18
75028	Flower Mound, TX	17
07039	Livingston, NJ	16
55044	Lakeville, MN	16
66216	Shawnee, KS	15
53186	Waukesha, WI	14
33594	Valrico, FL	11
23456	Virginia Beach, VA	11
30075	Roswell, GA	11
14068	Getzville, NY	10
43026	Hilliard, OH	10
45241	Evendale, OH	10
46060	Noblesville, IN	9
02760	North Attleboro, MA	9
78232	Hollywood Park, TX	9
92354	Loma Linda, CA	9

Source: U.S. Dept of Health & Human Services, 2004

figure, reported by the U.S. Department of Health and Human Services, is stated on a similar basis to the presence of physicians: number of beds per 100,000 residents. The highest figures are found in Rochester, Minnesota, college towns, and other regional health centers. With the advent of outpatient care and ever-shortening hospital stays, this fact is decreasing in importance over time. See Table 4.79.

- Number of Teaching Hospitals reflects the number of hospitals in an area set up to teach doctors or to provide residency. The statistic can be used as a proxy for the breadth and depth of staff, available resources, specialties, and overall quality of hospitals in an area. College towns and large city areas score the highest, but we see strengths in many mid-size Midwestern cities like St. Louis, Missouri, (metro area for St. Charles); Kansas City, Kansas (Shawnee); and Pittsburgh, Pennsylvania (Coraopolis–Moon Township). See Table 4.80.

Healthcare Cost

Our last topic—but certainly not the least important, especially for families footing the bill—is healthcare cost. The steady upward march of basic healthcare pricing—including physician services, hospital care, prescription drugs, and various test procedures and treatments—has far outpaced inflation and has been consistently in the news. What is also coming into the spotlight is the increasing portion of these costs borne by individuals and families through higher insurance premiums, co-pays, coinsurance, and deterioration of retirees' health benefits. While we've seen a slowing in healthcare costs, the shift of burden to the consumer seems nowhere near letting up.

In this book, we present an assortment of healthcare barometers collected and reported at the area level. There are substantial differences among areas, particularly for hospital costs.

Area Highlights

- Healthcare Cost Index captures all healthcare costs, including doctors, hospitals, treatments, and supplies, and shows them as an index similar to the Cost of Living Index, where 100 represents the national average. This fact, like COL, comes from the Bureau of Labor Statistics and is presented at the area level. Strikingly, healthcare costs in more expensive areas like New York, Boston, and California are almost twice that of less expensive areas mainly in the South and in Texas. See Table 4.81.

- Cost per Doctor Visit is an approximation of what a typical short doctor visit costs, excluding prescriptions and other medical services. This fact and the next two were generated by the American Chamber of Commerce Research Association. The highest costs, which run about $100, are found in larger cities like the Boston area and a few smaller places in the West like Albuquerque, New Mexico. Lower costs, again, are found in the South and in Florida.

- Cost per Dentist Visit comes from the same source and reflects an ordinary dentist visit and checkup without additional services like X-rays.

- Cost per Hospital Room shows an exceptionally wide range. There may be some differences in how the data is collected; some reports may include some services that others don't. But the

TABLE 4.81 HIGHEST AND LOWEST HEALTHCARE COST INDEXES
Second Quarter 2005

U.S. AVERAGE: 100

LEAST EXPENSIVE			MOST EXPENSIVE		
37064	Franklin, TN	82	10994	West Nyack, NY	177
22602	Winchester, VA	86	11730	East Islip, NY	164
36695	West Mobile, AL	87	99516	Anchorage, AK	159
78232	Hollywood Park, TX	88	95694	Winters, CA	156
32073	Orange Park, FL	88	95630	Folsom, CA	150
37343	Hixson, TN	88	06470	Newtown, CT	149
37922	Farragut, TN	89	07648	Norwood, NJ	145
32605	Gainesville, FL	90	02760	North Attleboro, MA	135
84037	Kaysville, UT	90	55044	Lakeville, MN	130
23233	Richmond-Tuckahoe, VA	90	98501	Olympia, WA	127

LESS EXPENSIVE			MORE EXPENSIVE		
84321	Logan, UT	90	02067	Sharon, MA	127
35758	Madison, AL	90	92354	Loma Linda, CA	127
17402	York, PA	91	98275	Mukilteo, WA	126
66049	Lawrence, KS	92	80104	Castle Rock, CO	126
72758	Rogers, AR	92	80220	Denver (Park Hill), CO	126
57702	Rapid City, SD	92	01824	Chelmsford, MA	125
52241	Coralville, IA	92	98607	Vancouver-Camas, WA	122
79606	Abilene, TX	93	97405	Eugene, OR	122
75791	Tyler, TX	93	89423	Minden, NV	121
29212	Irmo, SC	93	92688	Rancho Santa Margarita, CA	120
15108	Coraopolis–Moon Township, PA	93	07039	Livingston, NJ	119
17601	Lancaster, PA	93	91354	Santa Clarita, CA	119
23456	Virginia Beach, VA	93	99223	Spokane, WA	119
24018	Roanoke, VA	94	98226	Bellingham, WA	119
65203	Columbia, MO	94	98273	Mount Vernon, WA	118
47906	West Lafayette, IN	94	80027	Louisville, CO	118
45241	Evendale, OH	95	08824	Kendall Park, NJ	117
49426	Hudsonville, MI	96	33326	Weston, FL	117
29650	Greer, SC	96	89523	Reno, NV	117
21045	Columbia, MD	96	60047	Lake Zurich, IL	115

Source: U.S. Bureau of Labor Statistics, 2005

(TIPS) Measuring Healthcare Quality

A new study, released in 2005 through the New England Journal of Medicine, evaluates the *quality* of hospital care in 40 different regions under the government-sponsored Hospital Quality Alliance Program. Treatments and treatment success are analyzed for heart attack, congestive heart failure, and pneumonia. The 2003 Medicare Law that brought prescription drug benefits also provided funds to hospitals that report their data. Ninety-nine percent of U.S. hospitals now report their data, compared to a third who did so before the law was passed. The results can be seen at the DHHS website (www.hospitalcompare.hhs.gov). Unfortunately, this site isn't set up for easy comparisons among areas, and the technical jargon is a bit difficult to understand, but it's clearly a step in the right direction.

The study made headlines as one of the first to dig into healthcare quality, and frankly, to look at what you get for your money. Similar evaluations are in various stages of development for physicians and individual healthcare providers. An organization known as "Bridges to Excellence" (www.bridgestoexcellence.org) has pilot programs in four major U.S. cities to collect physician treatment and outcome data. We expect this to lead to quality metrics and perhaps to a form of an "approval seal" for individual physicians, but it's still in early testing stages and is facing some resistance in the medical community. *Bottom line:* While statistics remain elusive today, we expect that to change in the next few years, allowing future editions of this book to include more in-depth facts and analysis on healthcare quality.

TABLE 4.82 HIGHEST AND LOWEST HOSPITAL COST
Estimated Total Cost per Day
U.S. AVERAGE: $787

LEAST EXPENSIVE			MOST EXPENSIVE		
37064	Franklin, TN	$335	08824	Kendall Park, NJ	$4,440
36695	West Mobile, AL	$357	07648	Norwood, NJ	$3,408
54911	Appleton, WI	$438	07039	Livingston, NJ	$3,360
17402	York, PA	$440	95630	Folsom, CA	$2,249
24018	Roanoke, VA	$480	10994	West Nyack, NY	$1,818
49426	Hudsonville, MI	$510	19382	West Chester, PA	$1,809
27513	Cary, NC	$515	11730	East Islip, NY	$1,639
53186	Waukesha, WI	$516	92688	Rancho Santa Margarita, CA	$1,549
20878	Gaithersburg, MD	$531	92354	Loma Linda, CA	$1,484
20170	Herndon, VA	$531	55044	Lakeville, MN	$1,442

LESS EXPENSIVE			MORE EXPENSIVE		
54403	Wausau, WI	$533	02067	Sharon, MA	$1,437
29212	Irmo, SC	$533	92354	Loma Linda, CA	$1,437
32073	Orange Park, FL	$561	98275	Mukilteo, WA	$1,430
72758	Rogers, AR	$588	80104	Castle Rock, CO	$1,322
53044	Sheboygan, WI	$589	80220	Denver (Park Hill), CO	$1,301
23233	Richmond-Tuckahoe, VA	$598	01824	Chelmsford, MA	$1,248
68022	Elkhorn, NE	$610	98607	Vancouver-Camas, WA	$1,107
53532	De Forest, WI	$612	97405	Eugene, OR	$1,028
28105	Matthews, NC	$614	89423	Minden, NV	$1,023
37922	Farragut, TN	$621	92688	Rancho Santa Margarita, CA	$1,013
78732	Austin (West), TX	$622	07039	Livingston, NJ	$997
98226	Bellingham, WA	$624	91354	Santa Clarita, CA	$997
46060	Noblesville, IN	$625	99223	Spokane, WA	$994
79606	Abilene, TX	$625	98226	Bellingham, WA	$991
84037	Kaysville, UT	$631	98273	Mount Vernon, WA	$990
43026	Hilliard, OH	$632	80027	Louisville, CO	$987
22901	Charlottesville, VA	$634	08824	Kendall Park, NJ	$985
29650	Greer, SC	$636	33326	Weston, FL	$979
63304	St Charles, MO	$646	89523	Reno, NV	$979
66049	Lawrence, KS	$649	60047	Lake Zurich, IL	$963

Source: American Chamber of Commerce Research Association, 2005

differences—over $4,000 per day in New Jersey compared to $500 to 600 per day in Florida, Texas, and other places in the South—are striking. See Table 4.82. Those families paying directly for medical services or paying for their own insurance should pay close attention to these statistics. Even "next-tier" places like California, Washington, and Colorado are almost twice as expensive as national averages.

TABLE 4.83 COST OF HEALTH INSURANCE
$ PER MONTH, PPO, FAMILY OF 4, PARENTS AGE 35-40

	HIGHEST				LOWEST		
	AREA	MONTHLY PREMIUM	HEALTH PLAN		AREA	MONTHLY PREMIUM	HEALTH PLAN
55902	Rochester, MN	$676	Celtic 80/20	45241	Evendale, OH	$362	Golden Rule 0/0 100 Plan
68022	Elkhorn, NE	$661	Celtic PPO 80/20	17402	York, PA	$360	Golden Rule 0/0 100 Plan
33326	Weston, FL	$615	Humana One	20170	Herndon, VA	$358	BCBS-T Sel Sav
83616	Eagle, ID	$591	BC-ID PPO1000	74012	Broken Arrow, OK	$352	BCBS-WI 1K
28105	Matthews, NC	$551	Fortis PPO Xtra	53044	Sheboygan, WI	$346	Golden Rule 0/0 100 Plan
79606	Abilene, TX	$526	HumanaOne w/Copay	15108	Coraopolis–Moon Township, PA	$340	Golden Rule 0/0 100 Plan
30075	Roswell, GA	$521	Aetna PPO 1500	23456	Virginia Beach, VA	$335	Anthem
99516	Anchorage, AK	$505	Golden Rule Saver 80	22602	Winchester, VA	$330	BCBS-T Sel Sav
98226	Bellingham, WA	$482	LifeWise Passport 50	75028	Flower Mound, TX	$330	BCBS-T Sel Sav
98273	Mount Vernon, WA	$482	LifeWise Passport 50	75791	Tyler, TX	$330	BCBS-T Sel Sav
98275	Mukilteo, WA	$482	LifeWise Passport 50	76002	Arlington, TX	$330	BCBS-T Sel Sav
98501	Olympia, WA	$482	LifeWise Passport 50	78232	Hollywood Park, TX	$330	BCBS-T Sel Sav
98607	Vancouver-Camas, WA	$482	LifeWise Passport 50	78732	Austin (West), TX	$327	Humana One
99223	Spokane, WA	$482	LifeWise Passport 50	65203	Columbia, MO	$322	Anthem Plan 1
37343	Hixson, TN	$479	Humana One	40503	Lexington, KY	$321	Golden Rule Saver 80
66049	Lawrence, KS	$476	Humana One Ind	72758	Rogers, AR	$321	Aetna PPO 1500
57702	Rapid City, SD	$473	BCBS-IL ADV 1K	95630	Folsom, CA	$320	BCBS-SC Plan 4
58104	Fargo, ND	$473	BCBS-IL ADV 1K	29212	Irmo, SC	$320	BCBS-SC Plan 4
54911	Appleton, WI	$462	Medica Direct 1K	29650	Greer, SC	$320	Golden Rule 0/0 100 Plan
55044	Lakeville, MN	$462	Medica Direct 1K	24018	Roanoke, VA	$317	BCBS-T Sel Sav
18018	Bethlehem, PA	$457	Golden Rule 0/0 100 Plan	77479	Sugar Land, TX	$316	BCBS-NM BlueChoice Plus
80220	Denver (Park Hill), CO	$454	HumanaOne w/Copay	87122	Albuquerque (Sandia Heights), NM	$314	Golden Rule Saver 80
23233	Richmond-Tuckahoe, VA	$454	Golden Rule 0/0 100 Plan	53186	Waukesha, WI	$312	Golden Rule 0/0 100 Plan
46060	Noblesville, IN	$449	Anthem Plan 1	22901	Charlottesville, VA	$280	Golden Rule Saver 80
37922	Farragut, TN	$437	Humana One	32073	Orange Park, FL	$280	IHC SelMed Base
80526	Fort Collins, CO	$433	HumanaOne w/Copay	84037	Kaysville, UT	$280	IHC SelMed Base
54313	Green Bay, WI	$428	BCBS-WI 1K	84321	Logan, UT	$275	Golden Rule Saver 80
80027	Louisville, CO	$426	Pacificare Signature Options	53532	DeForest, WI	$270	Golden Rule Saver 80
80104	Castle Rock, CO	$426	Pacificare Signature Options	36695	West Mobile, AL	$267	Golden Rule Saver 80
97405	Eugene, OR	$421	Regence BCBS Blue Selection Basic	54403	Wausau, WI	$264	BCBS Carefirst
97526	Grants Pass, OR	$421	Regence BCBS Blue Selection Basic	20878	Gaithersburg, MD	$264	BCBS Carefirst
19382	West Chester, PA	$420	Golden Rule 0/0 100 Plan	21045	Columbia, MD	$237	Golden Rule Saver 80
27513	Cary, NC	$418	AMS Med1 Sec	33594	Valrico, FL	$231	BC Life & Health Basic PPO
37064	Franklin, TN	$418	Humana One	91354	Santa Clarita, CA	$228	Golden Rule Saver 80
43537	Maumee, OH	$408	MedMutual 1000	35758	Madison, AL	$219	Golden Rule Saver 80
06470	Newtown, CT	$406	Golden Rule Copay 45	66216	Shawnee, KS	$216	Golden Rule Saver 80
47906	West Lafayette, IN	$399	Anthem Plan 1	67212	Wichita (West), KS	$212	BC Life & Health Basic PPO
89423	Minden, NV	$397	Anthem BluePreferred 1000-35-80/50	95694	Winters, CA	$210	BC Life & Health Basic PPO
89523	Reno, NV	$397	Anthem BluePreferred 1000-35-80/50	92354	Loma Linda, CA	$204	BC Life & Health Basic PPO
63304	St. Charles, MO	$379	Humana 20/20	92688	Rancho Santa Margarita, CA	$202	Golden Rule Saver 80
32605	Gainesville, FL	$375	Humana One	60302	Oak Park, IL	$200	Golden Rule Saver 80
17601	Lancaster, PA	$374	Golden Rule* 0/0 Plan 100	52241	Coralville, IA	$193	Golden Rule Saver 80
43026	Hilliard, OH	$364	MedMutual 1000	60047	Lake Zurich, IL	$184	Golden Rule Saver 80
49426	Hudsonville, MI	$364	MedMutual 1000	50325	West Des Moines–Clive, IA	$141	Golden Rule Saver 80

NOTES: All plans are based on best rate available for family of four (Gender/Age = M/38; F/36; M/10; F/6).
All plans are based on $1,000 deductible level for a family of four (or next higher deductible when 2-member maximum is noted).

PLANS: *Golden Rule Plan 100 (Network: UnitedHealthcare Choice Plus)
BCBS = Blue Cross Blue Shield
BC = Blue Cross
IHC = Intermountain Health Care
DATA for NY, MA, and DE not available.

Source: eHealthinsurance.com, 2005

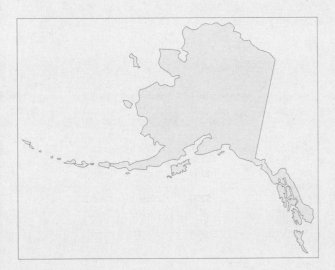

part

III

100 Best Places to Raise Your Family

Abilene, TX

Area Type: Small city

Zip Code: 79606

Metro Area: Abilene, TX

Metro Area Type: Smallest

Location: 180 miles west of Dallas–Fort Worth Metroplex along I-20

Time Zone: Central Standard Time

Pros:

Small-town flavor
Affordable cost of living
Local recreation and arts

Cons:

Isolation
Summer heat
Lack of career opportunities

"The spirit of the Texas Frontier lives and breathes in Abilene, which in the span of a century transformed itself from tent city to cultural center, cow-town to college town, all without losing the flavors of the past." So states the informative and accurate website for Abilene's Convention and Visitor's Bureau (www.abilene.com/visitors).

Today's Abilene is a classic small Western town located under big Western skies at the gateway to the large, dry expanse known as West Texas. Laid out on a perfect east-west–north-south grid with low brick buildings, the classic downtown area is bisected by the Union Pacific Railroad (formerly known as the Texas & Pacific Railroad)—its station lies right at the heart of town. Small cafes and restaurants, particularly to the north, abound. Aside from the medium-size Mall of Abilene to the southwest, downtown remains the commercial and cultural center of the city. Older inner neighborhoods give way to attractive suburbs, mainly to the north, south, and southwest. The Wylie school district area to the southwest has the best schools and newest homes in the area.

Dyess Air Force Base—far and away Abilene's largest economic driver—not only avoided the downsizing ax but may, in fact, expand. It gives a stabilizing influence to the economy, and adds a large number of stay-at-home moms who have formed a strong social community of their own. In addition to Dyess, there is a large Blue Cross/Blue Shield claims processing center, and oil and gas and ranching are important. There are a few small manufacturing businesses and small colleges, but Abilene is not considered a center for corporate career growth.

For a town its size and for the region, Abilene has an unusually complete set of arts and amenities. Some, like Frontier Village and the historic village at Buffalo Gap, and the Stasney's Cook ranch, are tied directly to the area's Western heritage. But surprisingly, there are several quality museums and theater companies, a full-time symphony, a ballet company, and a classical chorus. The area has a friendly small-town feel, and offers some facilities you might expect to find only in bigger places.

Standard of Living   The cost of living is extremely attractive and among the lowest in U.S. metro areas. In the chosen and slightly more upscale Wylie area, the Cost of Living Index is 84. Homes run $80 to $120 per square foot, and while the "sweet spot" is around $200K, many good family homes are available from $150K to $170K. Most homes are on open lots or have a few oak, mesquite, or pecan trees around them. Few have basements. Property taxes in the Wylie area run about 2.2%, nominally high but not bad considering low valuations and the absence of state income tax.

Education   The Wylie School District consistently scores well and is well regarded in the community, although locals point out that the other schools are good too. Wylie HS has fewer than 1,000 students and scores 12 to 25 points above state averages. Three small colleges and two large technical/vocational schools give some higher education and local interest, again a bit beyond what one might expect in a small Plains town.

Lifestyle   The various Western heritage sites, with history exhibits and events, offer family entertainment and cultural opportunities. Downtown, The Grace Museum (www.thegracemuseum.org) is a multipurpose art, children's, and historical museum. The interesting and unique National Center for Children's Illustrated Literature, located near The Grace Museum, contains exhibits of children's book art and offers many creative activities related to children's stories and graphic arts. Dyess Air Force Base has an air and military museum and hosts occasional family events. Two auto racetracks and a skate park are popular with older children.

ABILENE, TX	
NEIGHBORHOOD HIGHLIGHTS	
PEOPLE	
Population	17,952
15-yr Population Growth	4.60%
5-yr Population Growth	-1.10%
% Married w/Children	32.60%
% Single w/Children	8.80%
No. of Households	7,282
Median Age	35.6
Avg. Household Size	2.44
Diversity Measure	30
STANDARD OF LIVING	
Median Household Income	$48,793
% Household Income > $100K	11%
Projected Future Job Growth	7%
Cost of Living Index	84
Buying Power Index	132
Weekly Daycare Cost	$110
Median Home Price	$129,200
"Sweet Spot" Home Price	$200,000
Home Price Ratio	2.6
Median Age of Homes	17
% Homes Owned	59%
Effective Property Tax Rate	2.20%
Estimated Property Tax Bill	$3,520
EDUCATION	
% High School Graduates	94%
% 4-yr Degree	23%
% Graduate or Professional Degree	13%
$ Invested per Pupil	$4,298
Student/Teacher Ratio	16.1
Primary Test Score Percentile	109.9
Secondary Test Score Percentile	107
% Subsidized School Lunch	18.10%
% Attending Public School	80.60%
LIFESTYLE	
Leisure Rating (Area)	3
Arts & Culture Rating (Area)	6
Climate Rating (Area)	9
Physical Setting Rating	2
Downtown Core Rating	6
% Commute < 30 Min.	89%
% Commute > 1 Hour	3%
HEALTH & SAFETY	
Health Rating (Area)	6
Stress Score (Area)	1
Violent Crime Risk	80
Property Crime Risk	89

Commutes are simply a non-issue; nothing is more than 15 minutes away. There is commuter air service nearby, mainly to the Dallas–Fort Worth hub, but many travelers need to drive 3 hours to Dallas–Fort Worth or west to Midland International Airport for more airlines and better service.

Abilene is mostly dry, with only 65 days of precipitation each year, and comprises flat to gently rolling prairie and farmland dotted by deciduous trees, especially near creeks. On the border between dryer Plains continental climates to the northwest and more humid climates to the southeast, the area does experience large weather variations, though prolonged winter extremes are rare.

Health & Safety   The crime risk is moderate. Healthcare facilities are typical for this size of town, and stress levels are very low.

Nearby Neighborhoods   The Wylie area lies on the southwest side of town outside of US 83, and has the best balance of features for families. There are slightly more upscale areas directly south of town, and new growth has started to emerge to the north. All of these areas are within a 6-mile radius of the city center.

ABILENE, TX
AREA HIGHLIGHTS

PEOPLE

SIZE & DIVERSITY	AREA	U.S. AVG	FAMILY DEMOGRAPHICS	AREA	U.S. AVG
Population	125,108		% Married	55.50%	53.80%
15-yr Population Growth	4.60%	4.40%	% Single	44.50%	46.20%
Diversity Measure	43	54	% Divorced	7.30%	10.20%
% Religiously Observant	67%	50%	% Separated	2.30%	2.10%
% Catholic	7%	22%	% Married w/Children	36.30%	27.90%
% Protestant	60%	25%	% Single w/Children	7.90%	9.40%
% Jewish	0%	2%	% Married, No Children	27.70%	31.00%
% Other	0%	1%	% Single, No Children	28.10%	31.70%

STANDARD OF LIVING

INCOME, EMPLOYMENT & TAXES	AREA	U.S. AVG	COST OF LIVING & HOUSING	AREA	U.S. AVG
Median Household Income	$36,024	$44,684	Cost of Living Index	80.4	100
Household Income Growth	3.10%	6.10%	Buying Power Index	100	100
Unemployment Rate	3.10%	5.10%	Median Home Price	$114,500	$208,500
Recent Job Growth	2.20%	1.30%	Home Price Ratio	3.2	4.7
Projected Future Job Growth	5.60%	10.50%	Home Price Appreciation	9.60%	13.60%
State Income Tax Rate	0%	5.00%	% Homes Owned	58.80%	64.10%
State Sales Tax Rate	8.30%	6.00%	Median Rent	$522	$792

EDUCATION

ATTAINMENT & ACHIEVEMENT	AREA	U.S. AVG	RESOURCES & INVESTMENT	AREA	U.S. AVG
% High School Graduate	76.40%	83.90%	No. of Highly Ranked Universities	0	1
% 2-yr Graduate	5.60%	7.10%	$ Invested per Pupil	$5,370	$6,058
% 4-yr Graduate	20.80%	17.20%	Student/Teacher Ratio	13.3	15.9
% Graduate or Professional Degree	6.50%	9.90%	State University In-State Tuition	$5,735	$4,917
% Attending Public School	96.80%	84.30%			
75th Percentile State University SAT Score (Verbal)	540	477			
75th Percentile State University SAT Score (Math)	570	478			
75th Percentile State University ACT Score	23	20			

LIFESTYLE

RECREATION, ARTS & CULTURE	AREA	U.S. AVG	INFRASTRUCTURE & FACILITIES	AREA	U.S. AVG
Professional Sports Rating	2	4	No. of Public Libraries	3	28
Zoos & Aquariums Rating	3	3	Library Volumes Per Capita	1.9	2.8
Amusement Park Rating	1	3	No. of Warehouse Clubs	3	4
Professional Theater Rating	1	3	No. of Starbucks	1	5
Overall Museum Rating	3	6	Golf Course Rating	2	4
Science Museum Rating	1	4	National Park Rating	1	3
Children's Museum Rating	4	3	Sq. Mi. Inland Water	2	4

CLIMATE			COMMUTE & TRANSPORTATION		
Days Mostly Sunny	246	212	Avg. Daily Commute Time	16.4	24.7
Annual Days Precipitation	65	111	% Commute by Auto	75%	77.70%
Annual Days > 90°F	89	38	Per Capita Avg. Daily Transit Miles	5.3	7.9
Annual Days < 32°F	56	88	Annual Auto Insurance Premium	$1,204	$1,314
July Relative Humidity	59	69	Gas, Cost per Gallon	$2.96	$3.05

HEALTH & SAFETY

CRIME & ENVIRNOMENTAL ISSUES	AREA	U.S. AVG	HEALTHCARE & COST	AREA	U.S. AVG
Violent Crime Rate	372	517	Physicians per Capita	224.2	254.3
Change in Violent Crime	-19.80%	-7.50%	Pediatricians per Capita	12	16.9
Property Crime Rate	4213	3783	Hospital Beds per Capita	494.6	239.7
Change in Property Crime	-2.20%	-10.10%	No. of Teaching Hospitals	0	1.9
Air Quality Score	44	44	Healthcare Cost Index	92.5	100
Water Quality Score	100	33	Cost per Doctor Visit	$70	$74
Pollen/Allergy Score	78	61	Cost per Dentist Visit	$55	$67
Stress Score	7	49	Cost per Hospital Room	$625	$702
Cancer Mortality Rate	151.3	168.9			

Albuquerque (Sandia Heights), NM

Area Type: Outer suburb

Zip Code: 87122

Metro Area: Albuquerque, NM

Metro Area Type: Mid-size

Location: 14 miles northeast of downtown Albuquerque

Time Zone: Mountain Standard Time

Pros:
Strong economy
Healthy climate
Unique history and culture

Cons:
Economic cycles
Growth and sprawl
Isolation

Albuquerque—the "Ballooning Capital of the World"—has clear skies, tranquil weather, lots of open space, and a vast colorful landscape of high mountains and desert through which the Rio Grande river valley and snow-capped Sangre de Christo mountains run in a north–south direction. Albuquerque sits on the Rio Grande at the foot of the mountains where the major east–west trade routes intersect.

Albuquerque's history and culture are as interesting as its geography. It's one of the oldest continuously inhabited places in the country. First visited by Europeans in 1598, Albuquerque was established in 1706 as a villa for the Spanish governor. A fascinating mixture of Native American, Hispanic, and Anglo cultures has been evolving since then and has influenced the area's food, architecture, and lifestyle. The modern mix of high-tech research facilities headed up by the gigantic Sandia National Laboratory creates a social and economic environment unlike any other in the United States. These days, in addition to an attractive physical and business climate, Albuquerque is a major transportation hub with at least 30 trucking companies and the BNSF (Burlington Northern Santa Fe) railroad's major operations in the city. These factors have helped to establish Albuquerque as a regional manufacturing center, and today, despite some post-2000 tech industry dislocations, it continues to be a very attractive place for manufacturing, research, and other knowledge-based enterprises.

Both modern and historic buildings fill downtown Albuquerque's streets. Where the historic Route 66 crosses the Rio Grande, the attractive and historic Old Town area offers opportunities to walk around, eat, browse in galleries, and shop. East of the Old Town, the historic and cultural significance of Route 66 is further celebrated in the Nob Hill–Highland district, with more interesting architecture and plenty of entertainment just to the east of the University of New Mexico (UNM) campus. The large Kirtland Air Force Base anchors the southern part of the city. Newer and somewhat sprawling suburbs have emerged on the rising river plain to the west. The specific neighborhood we recommend as a best place to raise your family is known loosely as Sandia Heights, northeast of the city in a scenic area at the foot of the Sangre de Christo mountains with a strong family orientation—the percentage of married-with-children households is 32.4%.

Standard of Living   The ready availability of land in this area and the low cost of construction have created a construction boom, and many of Albuquerque's larger suburbs feature some of the lowest housing costs in the West. The metro area median home price of $172K is well under the national average. In the north and northeast sections of town, where costs are higher, home prices are still a reasonable $140 to $150 per square foot. Good family homes start at about $250K with a "sweet spot" in the mid $300Ks. The Cost of Living Index in the Sandia Heights area is 131, but high incomes bring a strong Buying Power Index of 169. Lower cost profiles are available in other parts of the city. Effective property taxes vary by area and school choice, but most are just above 1%. New Mexico is one of the nation's most solvent governments, which has many benefits, including a recent sales tax repeal on food purchases.

Education   Viewed overall, the populace in general is well educated and Albuquerque schools rate slightly higher than national averages across most testing criteria. Educational achievement is especially strong in Sandia Heights—64% of the population in the area has a 4-year or graduate degree.

Lifestyle   Albuquerque's relative isolation (the nearest metropolis, Phoenix, is 370 miles away), altitude (higher than Denver at 5,314 feet), and a vast natural landscape surrounding the city engender a unique sense of community and a healthy, active lifestyle. Cultural amenities include an array of historical museums, plus science and cultural centers devoted to geology, Native American culture, natural history, Hispanic culture, and astronomy. The Albuquerque Biological Park is an excellent facility containing a zoo, a botanical garden, and the notable Albuquerque Aquarium. There are also several fine art museums and two children's museums. A full symphony orchestra and several active smaller chamber groups highlight a strong performing arts scene. The city provides a full program of seasonal sports and outdoor activities, and of course there's a gigantic annual hot-air balloon festival. Albuquerque is also (literally) full of rocket scientists, a fact that could account for the city's model rocketry program, the meteoritic museum, and the name of the local AAA baseball team: the Isotopes.

Commutes vary, and some traffic congestion occurs from the larger suburbs on the northwest side of town. Sandia Heights is about 20 minutes from downtown. The Sandia lab and other high-tech industries are south of town, and cross-town commutes can take longer.

Albuquerque sits in the shallow valley of the Rio Grande, surrounded by high desert on three sides and the Sangre de Cristo to the east. The climate is high desert continental with four seasons and abundant sunshine. Summers are warm and dry with cool evenings, and winters are variable but typically dry.

Health & Safety   Violent and property crime rates in the Albuquerque area are high but on a downward trend, and crime risk as measured by the "CAP" index in the Sandia Heights area is quite low. Air quality is good and stress factors are very low. Healthcare facilities in Albuquerque are well regarded, and include several trauma centers and special-treatment centers, the UNM teaching hospital, and the UNM Cancer Research and Treatment Center.

Nearby Neighborhoods   Large subdivisions and planned communities spread mainly to the north and west. The enormous Rio Rancho area, across the river to the northwest, is one of the largest and most affordable places to live, but it means longer commutes to most city areas. Other attractive city neighborhoods worth considering are east of downtown and the University of New Mexico.

ALBUQUERQUE (SANDIA HEIGHTS), NM NEIGHBORHOOD HIGHLIGHTS	
PEOPLE	
Population	13,719
15-yr Population Growth	23.60%
5-yr Population Growth	6.70%
% Married w/Children	32.4%
% Single w/Children	6.1%
No. of Households	4,955
Median Age	38.1
Avg. Household Size	2.73
Diversity Measure	34
STANDARD OF LIVING	
Median Household Income	$98,844
% Household Income > $100K	46%
Projected Future Job Growth	15%
Cost of Living Index	131
Buying Power Index	169
Weekly Daycare Cost	$144
Median Home Price	$332,800
"Sweet Spot" Home Price	$350,000
Home Price Ratio	3.4
Median Age of Homes	7.7
% Homes Owned	82%
Effective Property Tax Rate	1%
Estimated Property Tax Bill	$3,500
EDUCATION	
% High School Graduates	98%
% 4-yr Degree	29%
% Graduate or Professional Degree	35%
$ Invested per Pupil	$4,590
Student/Teacher Ratio	20.4
Primary Test Score Percentile	110.5
Secondary Test Score Percentile	130.7
% Subsidized School Lunch	7.50%
% Attending Public School	77.30%
LIFESTYLE	BEST
Leisure Rating (Area)	7
Arts & Culture Rating (Area)	8
Climate Rating (Area)	9
Physical Setting Rating	8
Downtown Core Rating	7
% Commute < 30 Min.	72%
% Commute > 1 Hour	4%
HEALTH & SAFETY	
Health Rating (Area)	3
Stress Score (Area)	9
Violent Crime Risk	36
Property Crime Risk	44

ALBUQUERQUE, NM
AREA HIGHLIGHTS

PEOPLE

SIZE & DIVERSITY	AREA	U.S. AVG	FAMILY DEMOGRAPHICS	AREA	U.S. AVG
Population	764,583		% Married	54.60%	53.80%
15-yr Population Growth	31.10%	4.40%	% Single	45.40%	46.20%
Diversity Measure	60	54	% Divorced	9.40%	10.20%
% Religiously Observant	54%	50%	% Separated	2%	2.10%
% Catholic	36%	22%	% Married w/Children	31.90%	27.90%
% Protestant	17%	25%	% Single w/Children	12.70%	9.40%
% Jewish	1%	2%	% Married, No Children	25.60%	31.00%
% Other	0%	1%	% Single, No Children	29.80%	31.70%

STANDARD OF LIVING

INCOME, EMPLOYMENT & TAXES	AREA	U.S. AVG	COST OF LIVING & HOUSING	AREA	U.S. AVG
Median Household Income	$41,401	$44,684	Cost of Living Index	90.5	100
Household Income Growth	4.40%	6.10%	Buying Power Index	102	100
Unemployment Rate	4.40%	5.10%	Median Home Price	$171,700	$208,500
Recent Job Growth	2.70%	1.30%	Home Price Ratio	4.1	4.7
Projected Future Job Growth	17.90%	10.50%	Home Price Appreciation	8.70%	13.60%
State Income Tax Rate	7.10%	5.00%	% Homes Owned	63.60%	64.10%
State Sales Tax Rate	5.70%	6.00%	Median Rent	$699	$792

EDUCATION

ATTAINMENT & ACHIEVEMENT	AREA	U.S. AVG	RESOURCES & INVESTMENT	AREA	U.S. AVG
% High School Graduate	81.50%	83.90%	No. of Highly Ranked Universities	1	1
% 2-yr Graduate	8.50%	7.10%	$ Invested per Pupil	$4,869	$6,058
% 4-yr Graduate	20.10%	17.20%	Student/Teacher Ratio	16.1	15.9
% Graduate or Professional Degree	13.60%	9.90%	State University In-State Tuition	$3,738	$4,917
% Attending Public School	89.40%	84.30%			
75th Percentile State University SAT Score (Verbal)	470	477			
75th Percentile State University SAT Score (Math)	460	478			
75th Percentile State University ACT Score	19	20			

LIFESTYLE

RECREATION, ARTS & CULTURE	AREA	U.S. AVG	INFRASTRUCTURE & FACILITIES	AREA	U.S. AVG
Professional Sports Rating	3	4	No. of Public Libraries	33	28
Zoos & Aquariums Rating	6	3	Library Volumes Per Capita	2.7	2.8
Amusement Park Rating	5	3	No. of Warehouse Clubs	4	4
Professional Theater Rating	1	3	No. of Starbucks	20	5
Overall Museum Rating	7	6	Golf Course Rating	3	4
Science Museum Rating	9	4	National Park Rating	5	3
Children's Museum Rating	8	3	Sq. Mi. Inland Water	1	4

CLIMATE			COMMUTE & TRANSPORTATION		
Days Mostly Sunny	283	212	Avg. Daily Commute Time	22.9	24.7
Annual Days Precipitation	59	111	% Commute by Auto	72%	77.70%
Annual Days > 90°F	61	38	Per Capita Avg. Daily Transit Miles	8.9	7.9
Annual Days < 32°F	123	88	Annual Auto Insurance Premium	$1,632	$1,314
July Relative Humidity	43	69	Gas, Cost per Gallon	$3.06	$3.05

HEALTH & SAFETY

CRIME & ENVIRNOMENTAL ISSUES	AREA	U.S. AVG	HEALTHCARE & COST	AREA	U.S. AVG
Violent Crime Rate	815	517	Physicians per Capita	312.7	254.3
Change in Violent Crime	-23.40%	-7.50%	Pediatricians per Capita	20.3	16.9
Property Crime Rate	4903	3783	Hospital Beds per Capita	301.2	239.7
Change in Property Crime	-34.10%	-10.10%	No. of Teaching Hospitals	4	1.9
Air Quality Score	23	44	Healthcare Cost Index	107	100
Water Quality Score	49	33	Cost per Doctor Visit	$99	$74
Pollen/Allergy Score	74	61	Cost per Dentist Visit	$97	$67
Stress Score	86	49	Cost per Hospital Room	$724	$702
Cancer Mortality Rate	153.6	168.9			

Anchorage, AK

Area Type: Small City

Zip Code: 99516

Metro Area: Anchorage, AK

Metro Area Type: Smaller

Location: 10 miles south of downtown Anchorage

Time Zone: Alaska Standard Time

Pros:
Attractive setting
Outdoor recreation
Favorable tax climate

Cons:
Cost of housing
Dreary fall and winter seasons
Some summer tourist impact

Myth: Anchorage is near the Arctic, and winters are terrible. Reality: Anchorage faces warm ocean currents, and vast mountain ranges keep out much of the Arctic cold. Yes, winters are cool and wet, but Anchorage temperatures are often milder than those of the Continental heartland.

Myth: You never see the sun in winter. Reality: It's cloudy, but even the shortest winter days are almost 6 hours, and the 19-hour summer days with near-perfect 70°F weather more than make up for lost winter daytime.

Myth: The oil boom drove prices up in Anchorage, and you can't afford to live there. Reality: There are no sales or income taxes, and established Alaska citizens get annual dividend payments typically amounting to $1,000 from a trust fund created to manage and distribute oil profits left over after financing public needs.

Perhaps these myths were spread by the locals and transplants who discovered Anchorage's secrets and wanted to keep the truth to themselves. Today's Anchorage is a vibrant, progressive, and diverse picture-perfect postcard city at the confluence of two sea-level fjordlike canyons at the base of snow-capped 7,000-foot mountains. Reshaped by the 1964 Good Friday earthquake, the downtown area is fairly attractive and modern with a nice waterfront and plenty to do in all seasons. It's also quiet and serene with a strong community feel and a full set of recreational and cultural amenities available in town. It never feels crowded and you seldom have to wait in line for anything, except maybe during a tourist rush in summer. Once outside the city, the pristine water and mountainous wilderness is paradise for outdoor adventurers.

Most city neighborhoods here are attractive and livable for families. The area known locally as "South Anchorage" has a strong family preponderance (48% married with children) and attractive housing set on gentle, winding, wooded streets.

Standard of Living   The cost of living is high (COL Index 134) but not exceptional by West Coast standards. High local wages and incomes adjust for some locally higher prices, giving a comfortable Buying Power Index of 179. Major employers include the military (Elmendorf AFB); basic industries such as fishing, forestry, and oil; hospitals; and schools. Transportation is also important: Sitting on the shortest route to Japan and much of Asia, Anchorage is currently the largest air cargo hub in the United States. Distribution and import-export businesses create many jobs. Housing is in somewhat short supply and expensive, with typical family homes mostly $400K and higher. But the tax climate and oil dividend help household finances, and property taxes are a modest 1.3% to 1.6%. You might expect staple items like milk to be more expensive in such a location, but recent price checks found them comparable to other areas. In fact, estimated weekly grocery costs for a family of 4 were recently estimated at around $100, not far off of national averages.

Education   With a population approaching 250,000, Anchorage offers some elements of a bigger city and some of a smaller town. Education is one of its "small town" qualities: Local schools are commended for their personalized, one-on-one approach to education and strong teacher-student-parent relationships. Although low population sizes may make figures less meaningful, schools in the South Anchorage area test well above state averages. The University of Alaska at Anchorage (14,000 students) and Alaska Pacific University (700 students) both have attractive campuses and bring some college flavor to the city.

ANCHORAGE, AK NEIGHBORHOOD HIGHLIGHTS	
PEOPLE	
Population	22,670
15-yr Population Growth	20.50%
5-yr Population Growth	4.80%
% Married w/Children	47.6%
% Single w/Children	5.9%
No. of Households	7,603
Median Age	34.6
Avg. Household Size	3
Diversity Measure	18
STANDARD OF LIVING	
Median Household Income	$107,470
% Household Income > $100K	48%
Projected Future Job Growth	13%
Cost of Living Index	134
Buying Power Index	179
Weekly Daycare Cost	$200
Median Home Price	$340,000
"Sweet Spot" Home Price	$400,000
Home Price Ratio	3.2
Median Age of Homes	18.1
% Homes Owned	88%
Effective Property Tax Rate	1.40%
Estimated Property Tax Bill	$5,600
EDUCATION	
% High School Graduates	97%
% 4-yr Degree	31%
% Graduate or Professional Degree	20%
$ Invested per Pupil	$6,598
Student/Teacher Ratio	18.3
Primary Test Score Percentile	143.5
Secondary Test Score Percentile	N/A
% Subsidized School Lunch	6.40%
% Attending Public School	86.70%
LIFESTYLE	
Leisure Rating (Area)	7
Arts & Culture Rating (Area)	7
Climate Rating (Area)	1
Physical Setting Rating	10
Downtown Core Rating	5
% Commute < 30 Min.	79%
% Commute > 1 Hour	4%
HEALTH & SAFETY	
Health Rating (Area)	2
Stress Score (Area)	10
Violent Crime Risk	50
Property Crime Risk	57

Lifestyle   Although damp, cool weather is fairly common, Anchorage residents spend a lot of time outdoors in the city and its surroundings. Long, pleasant summer days support all kinds of outdoor activity. Abundant opportunities for downhill and cross-country skiing, as well as snowmobiling, are available practically in town. Cultural amenities exceed expectations. The impressive Alaska Performing Arts Center hosts a complete assortment of performing arts programs. It's just a short trip downtown to the Museum of History and Art and its Children's Gallery and the local science museum "Imaginarium." The 25-acre Alaska Zoo in South Anchorage is open all year. Community activities occur throughout the year, and Anchorage, a melting pot for people from all over the "lower 48" and much of the Pacific Rim, is a friendly, gregarious place.

Commutes within the area are simply a non-issue; traffic is modest and flows well, and the city is easy to get around. But some locals complain of isolation from other "mainland" cities; it's a long flight to anywhere else.

The climate is complex and unique. The strong marine influence brings clouds at all times of the year, but precipitation doesn't occur very often (112 days per year), and it's mainly light and misty. Most of it occurs during the fall and winter, with modest amounts of snow in winter, usually staying on the ground in the deepest winter months. Bitter cold spells do occur but are seldom persistent. Spring and summer are beautiful with many sunny days, which helps compensate for the sometimes dark and gloomy winters.

Health & Safety   The area crime risk is statistically moderate to high, but residents think the neighborhood is quite safe and the local "CAP" crime risk index confirms their instincts. As a center covering a large region, Anchorage has a good assortment of healthcare facilities. The physical environment, beyond winter gloom and resulting stress factors, is healthy.

Nearby Neighborhoods   Most of the Anchorage area is suitable for families. New multiunit housing is bringing more options to the downtown area.

ANCHORAGE, AK
AREA HIGHLIGHTS
PEOPLE

SIZE & DIVERSITY	AREA	U.S. AVG	FAMILY DEMOGRAPHICS	AREA	U.S. AVG
Population	272,687		% Married	54.70%	53.80%
15-yr Population Growth	20.50%	4.40%	% Single	45.30%	46.20%
Diversity Measure	49	54	% Divorced	12.50%	10.20%
% Religiously Observant	37%	50%	% Separated	3.40%	2.10%
% Catholic	9%	22%	% Married w/Children	34.30%	27.90%
% Protestant	27%	25%	% Single w/Children	11.30%	9.40%
% Jewish	1%	2%	% Married, No Children	22%	31.00%
% Other	0%	1%	% Single, No Children	32.40%	31.70%

STANDARD OF LIVING

INCOME, EMPLOYMENT & TAXES	AREA	U.S. AVG	COST OF LIVING & HOUSING	AREA	U.S. AVG
Median Household Income	$61,595	$44,684	Cost of Living Index	114.1	100
Household Income Growth	4.80%	6.10%	Buying Power Index	121	100
Unemployment Rate	4.80%	5.10%	Median Home Price	$219,700	$208,500
Recent Job Growth	4.30%	1.30%	Home Price Ratio	3.6	4.7
Projected Future Job Growth	14.30%	10.50%	Home Price Appreciation	12%	13.60%
State Income Tax Rate	0%	5.00%	% Homes Owned	45.40%	64.10%
State Sales Tax Rate	0%	6.00%	Median Rent	$916	$792

EDUCATION

ATTAINMENT & ACHIEVEMENT	AREA	U.S. AVG	RESOURCES & INVESTMENT	AREA	U.S. AVG
% High School Graduate	92.30%	83.90%	No. of Highly Ranked Universities	0	1
% 2-yr Graduate	12.70%	7.10%	$ Invested per Pupil	$6,669	$6,058
% 4-yr Graduate	28.60%	17.20%	Student/Teacher Ratio	22.5	15.9
% Graduate or Professional Degree	13%	9.90%	State University In-State Tuition	$3,517	$4,917
% Attending Public School	92.20%	84.30%			
75th Percentile State University SAT Score (Verbal)	440	477			
75th Percentile State University SAT Score (Math)	440	478			
75th Percentile State University ACT Score	18	20			

LIFESTYLE

RECREATION, ARTS & CULTURE	AREA	U.S. AVG	INFRASTRUCTURE & FACILITIES	AREA	U.S. AVG
Professional Sports Rating	3	4	No. of Public Libraries	6	28
Zoos & Aquariums Rating	3	3	Library Volumes Per Capita	2.4	2.8
Amusement Park Rating	1	3	No. of Warehouse Clubs	5	4
Professional Theater Rating	10	3	No. of Starbucks	3	5
Overall Museum Rating	5	6	Golf Course Rating	1	4
Science Museum Rating	6	4	National Park Rating	9	3
Children's Museum Rating	7	3	Sq. Mi. Inland Water	4	4

CLIMATE			COMMUTE & TRANSPORTATION		
Days Mostly Sunny	131	212	Avg. Daily Commute Time	19.5	24.7
Annual Days Precipitation	112	111	% Commute by Auto	70%	77.70%
Annual Days > 90°F	12	38	Per Capita Avg. Daily Transit Miles	13.1	7.9
Annual Days < 32°F	192	88	Annual Auto Insurance Premium	$1,377	$1,314
July Relative Humidity	71	69	Gas, Cost per Gallon	$2.65	$3.05

HEALTH & SAFETY

CRIME & ENVIRNOMENTAL ISSUES	AREA	U.S. AVG	HEALTHCARE & COST	AREA	U.S. AVG
Violent Crime Rate	679	517	Physicians per Capita	297.8	254.3
Change in Violent Crime	5.80%	-7.50%	Pediatricians per Capita	24.7	16.9
Property Crime Rate	4548	3783	Hospital Beds per Capita	269.8	239.7
Change in Property Crime	-1.40%	-10.10%	No. of Teaching Hospitals	1	1.9
Air Quality Score	27	44	Healthcare Cost Index	159.1	100
Water Quality Score	49	33	Cost per Doctor Visit	$106	$74
Pollen/Allergy Score	57	61	Cost per Dentist Visit	$104	$67
Stress Score	97	49	Cost per Hospital Room	$985	$702
Cancer Mortality Rate	170.2	168.9			

Appleton, WI

Area Type: Small city

Zip Code: 54911

Metro Area: Appleton-Oshkosh-Neenah, WI

Metro Area Type: Small

Location: East-central Wisconsin at north end of Lake Winnebago

Time Zone: Central Standard Time

Pros:

Small-town flavor
Cost of living and housing
Crime and safety

Cons:

Winter climate
Educational attainment
Property tax rates

The largest city in Wisconsin's "Paper Valley," Appleton offers a safe, active, and prosperous context for raising a family. Appleton is one of a group of small cities in Fox River Valley in east-central Wisconsin, including Neenah and Oshkosh, which surround Lake Winnebago through which the Fox River flows. Appleton is 50 miles southwest of Green Bay, the well-known city and Lake Michigan outlet of the Fox River. The area is full of fun recreation, particularly watersports and activities in the lakes and woods nearby.

Appleton itself has a clean, attractive, and "alive" downtown, surrounded by pleasant residential neighborhoods, an excellent waterfront, and attractive suburbs mainly to the northeast and northwest. Lawrence University—a small liberal arts college listed in the 2005 edition of the Princeton Review's book *The Best 357 Colleges*—brings 1,500 students and a strong college influence to the area, as well as slightly more ethnic and cultural diversity than what's present in neighboring towns. Appleton has more than its share of recreational and arts resources, and, as the birthplace of Harry Houdini, there's a sense of humor mixed in.

Employment is diverse enough but dominated by high-paying industrial jobs at paper mills and a few other manufacturing firms like Pierce Manufacturing (maker of fire engines). The Kimberly-Clark Corporation world headquarters and research laboratories are in nearby Neenah, and some local manufacturers make equipment for the paper industry. Outside firms have discovered the high work ethic and relatively low costs of the area, and future job growth is projected at a robust 17%. Although the paper industry has been a steady employer, there are some concerns about how a downturn would affect employment. Average income levels in the area remain low but buying power is fine. The percentage of married-with-children households is a strong 27.4%.

Standard of Living On a national scale, the Cost of Living Index of 91 is very attractive. Full-featured homes cost $100 to $110 per square foot, with full basements, fireplaces, and other features. Older family homes close to town cost $150K to $200K, and prices reach the low $200Ks in the suburban areas. A four-bedroom, three-bath, 3,500-square-foot Cape Cod on a wooded lot near the city is $235K, and that same amount buys a 2,400-square-foot, two-story colonial a little farther out. Property tax rates are a minor concern at 2.1% to 2.2%.

Education Local schools are all considered above average by the students' parents and most have newer facilities, but test scores tend to run close to, and just slightly above, state averages. For a city with heavy industry, local 4-year degree attainment of 21% is good, and in addition to Lawrence University, the University of Wisconsin Fox Valley campus in Menasha, just to the south, adds to the higher education scene.

Lifestyle Activities and daily life are typical of Wisconsin. There are plenty of parks, and watersports like fishing and boating are big. Skating, snowmobiling, and even iceboating are popular in the winter. Wisconsin's famous Friday fish fries are an important part of community life. The many and varied attractions in the area include a small game zoo in nearby Greenville; Erb Park, a large city park and public pool; Wisconsin Timber Rattlers minor-league baseball; hiking and climbing at High Cliff State Park; an IMAX theater; and strong community athletics programs. The Houdini Historic Center and the Abracadabra Magic Shop provide some magic, and the Fox City Children's Museum is considered to be one of the best in the region. When not engaged in one of these activities, Appletonians lead a neighborly, small-town life. Those getting out of town go to Green Bay or the Wisconsin

Dells 1 hour away, or to the Door Peninsula or northern Wisconsin.

Commutes are generally short and simple. Some make the 10-minute commute to Kimberly-Clark in Neenah; otherwise, commutes and traffic are not significant issues.

The area is mostly flat valley plains with low, rolling, densely wooded hills. The climate is categorically continental with significant winter weather and snow cover, but summers are fairly pleasant with cool evenings.

Health & Safety Crime risk is low and a recent Farmers Insurance study named Appleton one of the 10 most secure areas in the United States. The local healthcare infrastructure is well regarded and anchored by two area hospitals. Air quality and stress scores are both favorable.

Nearby Neighborhoods Most areas of Appleton offer attractive housing and convenient access to the city. The more city-like area just east of town (zip code 54911) is quiet, green, and dignified; it's somewhat upscale but still affordable. North of Highway 41 Business is more suburban. Grand Chute to the northwest and Menasha to the south are also worth a look.

APPLETON, WI NEIGHBORHOOD HIGHLIGHTS	
PEOPLE	
Population	29,690
15-yr Population Growth	20.50%
5-yr Population Growth	5.20%
% Married w/Children	27.4%
% Single w/Children	8.1%
No. of Households	11,691
Median Age	36.8
Avg. Household Size	2.37
Diversity Measure	17
STANDARD OF LIVING	
Median Household Income	$45,629
% Household Income > $100K	8%
Projected Future Job Growth	17%
Cost of Living Index	90.2%
Buying Power Index	113
Weekly Daycare Cost	$143
Median Home Price	$131,400
"Sweet Spot" Home Price	$200,000
Home Price Ratio	2.9
Median Age of Homes	44.1
% Homes Owned	61%
Effective Property Tax Rate	2.20%
Estimated Property Tax Bill	$4,400
EDUCATION	
% High School Graduates	87%
% 4-yr Degree	21%
% Graduate or Professional Degree	8%
$ Invested per Pupil	$6,305
Student/Teacher Ratio	15.6
Primary Test Score Percentile	101.9
Secondary Test Score Percentile	110.3
% Subsidized School Lunch	24.40%
% Attending Public School	74.10%
LIFESTYLE	
Leisure Rating (Area)	5
Arts & Culture Rating (Area)	2
Climate Rating (Area)	2
Physical Setting Rating	5
Downtown Core Rating	6
% Commute < 30 Min.	86%
% Commute > 1 Hour	2%
HEALTH & SAFETY	BEST
Health Rating (Area)	8
Stress Score (Area)	1
Violent Crime Risk	50
Property Crime Risk	78

APPLETON-OSHKOSH-NEENAH, WI
AREA HIGHLIGHTS
PEOPLE

SIZE & DIVERSITY	AREA	U.S. AVG	FAMILY DEMOGRAPHICS	AREA	U.S. AVG
Population	372,110		% Married	62%	53.80%
15-yr Population Growth	18.30%	4.40%	% Single	38%	46.20%
Diversity Measure	12	54	% Divorced	6%	10.20%
% Religiously Observant	70%	50%	% Separated	1.30%	2.10%
% Catholic	40%	22%	% Married w/Children	33.20%	27.90%
% Protestant	30%	25%	% Single w/Children	7.10%	9.40%
% Jewish	0%	2%	% Married, No Children	33%	31.00%
% Other	0%	1%	% Single, No Children	26.70%	31.70%

STANDARD OF LIVING

INCOME, EMPLOYMENT & TAXES	AREA	U.S. AVG	COST OF LIVING & HOUSING	AREA	U.S. AVG
Median Household Income	$50,633	$44,684	Cost of Living Index	86.5	100
Household Income Growth	3.60%	6.10%	Buying Power Index	131	100
Unemployment Rate	3.60%	5.10%	Median Home Price	$129,600	$208,500
Recent Job Growth	2%	1.30%	Home Price Ratio	2.6	4.7
Projected Future Job Growth	14.40%	10.50%	Home Price Appreciation	6.10%	13.60%
State Income Tax Rate	6.90%	5.00%	% Homes Owned	75.50%	64.10%
State Sales Tax Rate	5%	6.00%	Median Rent	$563	$792

EDUCATION

ATTAINMENT & ACHIEVEMENT	AREA	U.S. AVG	RESOURCES & INVESTMENT	AREA	U.S. AVG
% High School Graduate	83.40%	83.90%	No. of Highly Ranked Universities	1	1
% 2-yr Graduate	9.30%	7.10%	$ Invested per Pupil	$6,418	$6,058
% 4-yr Graduate	12.60%	17.20%	Student/Teacher Ratio	15.7	15.9
% Graduate or Professional Degree	4.20%	9.90%	State University In-State Tuition	$5,862	$4,917
% Attending Public School	84.50%	84.30%			
75th Percentile State University SAT Score (Verbal)	N/A	477			
75th Percentile State University SAT Score (Math)	N/A	478			
75th Percentile State University ACT Score	26	20			

LIFESTYLE

RECREATION, ARTS & CULTURE	AREA	U.S. AVG	INFRASTRUCTURE & FACILITIES	AREA	U.S. AVG
Professional Sports Rating	4	4	No. of Public Libraries	18	28
Zoos & Aquariums Rating	1	3	Library Volumes Per Capita	3.6	2.8
Amusement Park Rating	1	3	No. of Warehouse Clubs	1	4
Professional Theater Rating	1	3	No. of Starbucks	4	5
Overall Museum Rating	7	6	Golf Course Rating	4	4
Science Museum Rating	4	4	National Park Rating	1	3
Children's Museum Rating	1	3	Sq. Mi. Inland Water	10	4

CLIMATE			COMMUTE & TRANSPORTATION		
Days Mostly Sunny	192	212	Avg. Daily Commute Time	18.1	24.7
Annual Days Precipitation	120	111	% Commute by Auto	77%	77.70%
Annual Days > 90°F	7	38	Per Capita Avg. Daily Transit Miles	9	7.9
Annual Days < 32°F	163	88	Annual Auto Insurance Premium	$1,008	$1,314
July Relative Humidity	73	69	Gas, Cost per Gallon	$3.04	$3.05

HEALTH & SAFETY

CRIME & ENVIRNOMENTAL ISSUES	AREA	U.S. AVG	HEALTHCARE & COST	AREA	U.S. AVG
Violent Crime Rate	93	517	Physicians per Capita	198.9	254.3
Change in Violent Crime	0%	-7.50%	Pediatricians per Capita	13	16.9
Property Crime Rate	1952	3783	Hospital Beds per Capita	317.7	239.7
Change in Property Crime	-24.90%	-10.10%	No. of Teaching Hospitals	3	1.9
Air Quality Score	47	44	Healthcare Cost Index	102	100
Water Quality Score	31	33	Cost per Doctor Visit	$82	$74
Pollen/Allergy Score	30	61	Cost per Dentist Visit	$66	$67
Stress Score	9	49	Cost per Hospital Room	$438	$702
Cancer Mortality Rate	160	168.9			

Arden-Brandywine, DE

Area Type: Inner suburb

Zip Code: 19810

Metro Area: Wilmington, DE

Metro Area Type: Mid-size

Location: 7 miles northeast of downtown Wilmington along I-95

Time Zone: Eastern Standard Time

Pros:
Historic interest and museums
Central location
Low property taxes

Cons:
Entertainment
Low job growth
Some environmental issues

Most of us are used to defining a city, town, or other governmental unit in terms of specific mapped geographic boundaries. But in northern Delaware, the "Brandywine Hundred" is really an area defined in terms of available guns and gunners. Back in Revolutionary War days, districts were defined as territory large enough to muster 100 men with rifles into a militia.

The name survives today, and now Brandywine Hundred encompasses four zip codes north of Wilmington, Delaware. It exists as a mainly unincorporated and residential area of New Castle County, which, as "the first county in the first state," comprises the top third of Delaware. By East Coast standards, the few layers of government here mean that taxes are among the lowest in the region. Other advantages to this area include attractive housing, good education, and a strategic East Coast location more than suitable for families. In fact, the percentage of married-with-children households is 26.3%.

The Wilmington area may be the East Coast's best-kept secret. Of course, it's well-known as the origin and primary location for DuPont chemical complex. And it has a unique legal and tax environment that makes it a premier place for large American corporations to incorporate and manage their legal affairs. A major banking industry presence is here as well, led by the likes of MBNA, JPMorgan Chase, and pharmaceutical giant Astra-Zeneca. In other words, there's a stable employment base of high-paying jobs here. On the flipside of the coin, low taxes and less crowding compared to other East Coast cities lead to a relatively attractive cost-of-living profile. At the same time, strong business endowments and a traditional commitment to the arts have given the area a notable set of visual and performing arts venues, as well as some excellent museums.

The location—which is central to a few East Coast centers—is another big plus. By car, Philadelphia is 40 minutes away. New York is 2½ hours north, Baltimore is an hour south, and Washington, DC, is just about another hour south. Straight north is historic eastern Pennsylvania, and, depending on where you want to go, you can reach the Atlantic shore and Delaware Bay in a half-hour to 1½ hours.

A small stream winding its way down from Pennsylvania known as the Brandywine River flows into the Delaware River at Wilmington. In its attractive valley, the DuPont family first started making gunpowder, and eventually located a large mansion known as Winterthur upstream from their industrial empire in Wilmington proper. Since then, largely thanks to DuPont and other generous endowments, the area has become studded with museums and parks with many activities and exhibits of unique historic interest. In the 1890s, a sculptor and an architect from Philadelphia got together to found a utopian community in the back-to-basics Arts and Crafts tradition meant to counteract the Victorian excesses of the day. Ultimately, a planned community—with sensible housing on leased lots—low taxes, and a strong community presence was formed. "You're Welcome Hither" is its motto, and the name of the small town is Arden. Two others, called Ardencroft and Arden Town, came along, giving residents some choices, and eventually the Brandywine Hundred filled in with solid residential homes in a mainly wooded setting.

Standard of Living The Cost of Living Index is 117, which seems high at first glance, but not when compared to nicer areas in or around East Coast cities. Such a cost-of-living profile is more likely to support stay-at-home parenthood than that in many other coastal areas. Job growth is a relatively low 10%, but we think the area's attractions and cost profile will add more business to the already stable base. Good family homes typically start in the low $300Ks on a ½ acre. Land in the Arden community is actually leased, which helps residents to get more home for the money. Most homes

ARDEN-BRANDYWINE, DE
NEIGHBORHOOD HIGHLIGHTS

PEOPLE
Population	26,432
15-yr Population Growth	17.50%
5-yr Population Growth	3.80%
% Married w/Children	26.3%
% Single w/Children	6.2%
No. of Households	10,475
Median Age	41.4
Avg. Household Size	2.48
Diversity Measure	23

STANDARD OF LIVING
Median Household Income	$72,168
% Household Income > $100K	28%
Projected Future Job Growth	10%
Cost of Living Index	117
Buying Power Index	137
Weekly Daycare Cost	$203
Median Home Price	$324,400
"Sweet Spot" Home Price	$325,000
Home Price Ratio	4.5
Median Age of Homes	33.6
% Homes Owned	78%
Effective Property Tax Rate	0.80%
Estimated Property Tax Bill	$2,600

EDUCATION
% High School Graduates	93%
% 4-yr Degree	27%
% Graduate or Professional Degree	18%
$ Invested per Pupil	$7,185
Student/Teacher Ratio	16.2
Primary Test Score Percentile	104.8
Secondary Test Score Percentile	107.3
% Subsidized School Lunch	27.40%
% Attending Public School	61.90%

LIFESTYLE
Leisure Rating (Area)	4
Arts & Culture Rating (Area)	4
Climate Rating (Area)	5
Physical Setting Rating	5
Downtown Core Rating	3
% Commute < 30 Min.	69%
% Commute > 1 Hour	5%

HEALTH & SAFETY
Health Rating (Area)	6
Stress Score (Area)	7
Violent Crime Risk	31
Property Crime Risk	31

on the category and grade. The schools are attractively sized, with 1,100 to 1,200 students in the high schools and 200 to 400 students in the elementary schools. The University of Delaware is in Newark, 15 miles west, and it has a branch campus in Wilmington.

Lifestyle The lifestyle in and around Wilmington is generally quiet, diverse, and interesting. Parks in the Brandywine Valley and toward the shore provide a variety of outdoor activities. The Wilmington waterfront is being enhanced with new restaurants and entertainment venues, but entertainment is not currently one of the area's strengths. However, there are a number of museums, including the Hagley Museum and historic site, the Delaware Natural History Museum, and the Brandywine River Museum. The Delaware Toy and Miniature Museum, Brandywine Park and Zoo, and Delaware History Center add interest for children. For adults, the DuPont Winterthur estate (now an art museum) and the Brandywine Gardens are assets. Performing arts are very strong and centered around the Delaware Center for Performing Arts, an attractively renovated 1871 theater. Two hours south, Rehoboth Beach is an excellent old East Coast beach resort town.

Commutes into downtown are easy, often taking less than 10 minutes. Some residents commute 35 to 40 minutes north to Philadelphia and especially to its western suburbs near West Chester; the tax climate (no sales tax, lower property taxes) favors living in Delaware and crossing the border for work. Amtrak service along the coast is excellent, and air service out of Philadelphia is 35 minutes away and now features discount carriers.

The area lies on a flat to rolling wooded coastal plain rising slowly toward the Pennsylvania border. The climate has a strong marine influence: relatively warm winters with less snow compared to the region and some summer cooling, although periods of sticky summer weather do occur each year. Fog is common.

Health & Safety Crime statistics for the Wilmington area are lower than those for other cities in the region. There is a higher incidence of cancer in the region, which may be linked to its chemical industry, but the Arden-Brandywine area is far enough away (and upwind) to avoid the effects. Health services are available on a scale appropriate to the size of the community.

Nearby Neighborhoods Abundant choices of suburbs and small towns, including Talleyville, Devonshire, and Graylyn Crest, exist throughout the relatively large Brandywine Hundred area north to the Pennsylvania border.

were built in or before the 1970s, and they feature mature landscaping and traditional East Coast styles. Property taxes are an exceptionally modest (for the region) 0.80%, and there is no state sales tax.

Education The Brandywine School District is one of the tops in Delaware, with solid test scores and extracurricular programs. Typical high-school test scores run 8% to 32% above state averages, depending

WILMINGTON, DE AREA HIGHLIGHTS

PEOPLE

SIZE & DIVERSITY	AREA	U.S. AVG	FAMILY DEMOGRAPHICS	AREA	U.S. AVG
Population	614,922		% Married	54%	53.80%
15-yr Population Growth	20.10%	4.40%	% Single	46%	46.20%
Diversity Measure	41	54	% Divorced	8.10%	10.20%
% Religiously Observant	43%	50%	% Separated	3.70%	2.10%
% Catholic	23%	22%	% Married w/Children	26.20%	27.90%
% Protestant	18%	25%	% Single w/Children	10.70%	9.40%
% Jewish	2%	2%	% Married, No Children	30.10%	31.00%
% Other	1%	1%	% Single, No Children	33.10%	31.70%

STANDARD OF LIVING

INCOME, EMPLOYMENT & TAXES	AREA	U.S. AVG	COST OF LIVING & HOUSING	AREA	U.S. AVG
Median Household Income	$55,626	$44,684	Cost of Living Index	95.2	100
Household Income Growth	4.10%	6.10%	Buying Power Index	131	100
Unemployment Rate	4.10%	5.10%	Median Home Price	$176,300	$208,500
Recent Job Growth	1.20%	1.30%	Home Price Ratio	3.2	4.7
Projected Future Job Growth	9.80%	10.50%	Home Price Appreciation	14.80%	13.60%
State Income Tax Rate	8.20%	5.00%	% Homes Owned	67.50%	64.10%
State Sales Tax Rate	0%	6.00%	Median Rent	$802	$792

EDUCATION

ATTAINMENT & ACHIEVEMENT	AREA	U.S. AVG	RESOURCES & INVESTMENT	AREA	U.S. AVG
% High School Graduate	80.60%	83.90%	No. of Highly Ranked Universities	1	1
% 2-yr Graduate	8.30%	7.10%	$ Invested per Pupil	$7,214	$6,058
% 4-yr Graduate	18.60%	17.20%	Student/Teacher Ratio	17.6	15.9
% Graduate or Professional Degree	10.10%	9.90%	State University In-State Tuition	$6,954	$4,917
% Attending Public School	74.50%	84.30%			
75th Percentile State University SAT Score (Verbal)	540	477			
75th Percentile State University SAT Score (Math)	560	478			
75th Percentile State University ACT Score	24	20			

LIFESTYLE

RECREATION, ARTS & CULTURE	AREA	U.S. AVG	INFRASTRUCTURE & FACILITIES	AREA	U.S. AVG
Professional Sports Rating	8	4	No. of Public Libraries	23	28
Zoos & Aquariums Rating	4	3	Library Volumes Per Capita	2.3	2.8
Amusement Park Rating	4	3	No. of Warehouse Clubs	3	4
Professional Theater Rating	8	3	No. of Starbucks	5	5
Overall Museum Rating	7	6	Golf Course Rating	7	4
Science Museum Rating	4	4	National Park Rating	2	3
Children's Museum Rating	2	3	Sq. Mi. Inland Water	6	4

CLIMATE			COMMUTE & TRANSPORTATION		
Days Mostly Sunny	201	212	Avg. Daily Commute Time	24.9	24.7
Annual Days Precipitation	123	111	% Commute by Auto	77%	77.70%
Annual Days > 90°F	18	38	Per Capita Avg. Daily Transit Miles	16.9	7.9
Annual Days < 32°F	102	88	Annual Auto Insurance Premium	$1,557	$1,314
July Relative Humidity	70	69	Gas, Cost per Gallon	$3.23	$3.05

HEALTH & SAFETY

CRIME & ENVIRNOMENTAL ISSUES	AREA	U.S. AVG	HEALTHCARE & COST	AREA	U.S. AVG
Violent Crime Rate	606	517	Physicians per Capita	256	254.3
Change in Violent Crime	129.20%	-7.50%	Pediatricians per Capita	26.4	16.9
Property Crime Rate	3323	3783	Hospital Beds per Capita	345.7	239.7
Change in Property Crime	-16.40%	-10.10%	No. of Teaching Hospitals	5	1.9
Air Quality Score	33	44	Healthcare Cost Index	110.9	100
Water Quality Score	21	33	Cost per Doctor Visit	$67	$74
Pollen/Allergy Score	45	61	Cost per Dentist Visit	$83	$67
Stress Score	65	49	Cost per Hospital Room	$785	$702
Cancer Mortality Rate	187.7	168.9			

Arlington, TX

Area Type: Outer suburb

Zip Code: 76002

Metro Area: Fort Worth–Arlington, TX

Metro Area Type: Large

Location: 23 miles southeast of downtown Fort Worth along US 287 and Joe Pool Lake

Time Zone: Central Standard Time

Pros:
Cost of living and housing
Recreation
Central location

Cons:
Growth and sprawl
Traffic
Unattractive landscape

"Baseball, hot dogs, apple pie, and Chevrolet." This well-worn General Motors advertising jingle could well be adopted today by the booming Dallas–Fort Worth mega-suburb of Arlington. The city's red, white, and blue website, www.ci.arlington.tx.us, even builds up its All-American image.

Baseball. Home to the Texas Rangers, the brand-new Ameriquest Field—an architectural gem—brings more than baseball games to the area. There's also the unique Legends of the Game baseball museum and a nice outdoor park—all located along Nolan Ryan Expressway.

Hot dogs and *apple pie.* You can get your fill of these goodies at Ameriquest, as well as at the flagship 205-acre Six Flags Over Texas amusement park and its sister Six Flags Hurricane Harbor water park.

Chevrolet. The 250-acre GM plant founded in 1951 is the largest such in Texas, producing about 250,000 vehicles per year, mostly Chevrolets, and currently employing 3,000 people.

In population and area, the sprawling Dallas–Fort Worth Metroplex is one of the largest cities in the United States. Texans like to do things big, and sitting between the two "anchor" cities adjacent to Fort Worth is the mega-suburb of Arlington. Spanning 140 square miles and 12 zip codes, Arlington is at once a self-sufficient city and a major bedroom community for the rest of the booming metro area. The biggest growth spurt was in the 1970s, and today the area is almost fully developed, with miles of commercial and residential developments to suit all needs. Families looking for big-city amenities can go to Fort Worth or Dallas, but there's also plenty to do closer to home: take in a Rangers game, explore local parks and water facilities, or visit one of several local museums.

The so-called "Metroplex" is an enormous regional commercial and cultural center for the south-central part of the United States with a broad spectrum of employment and a complete set of big-city amenities. The Arlington area spreads across I-30 and I-20, the two main east–west routes between the major cities. Affordable housing is plentiful in typical suburban settings, but the neighborhood (zip code 76002) we've chosen as a best place—at the southeast corner of the Arlington area adjacent to Joe Pool Lake—is newer and more upscale than the rest of the area yet still affordable. It also has a strong contingent of families (44% of households are married with children).

Standard of Living   Affordable living costs and home prices, especially in a place with so many conveniences, make this area very attractive. The Cost of Living Index is a modest 93, and moderately high household incomes bring a Buying Power Index of 170. Employment is steady and growing. General Motors and other operational jobs are here, as well as a vast white-collar employment base mostly to the northwest in Fort Worth and to the northeast in the "in-between" cities toward the Dallas–Fort Worth International Airport. Some family homes are available below $140K with the "sweet spot" somewhere between $160K and $200K for modern brick-fronted homes, most less than 10 years old, in the typical multiple-gable Texas style on attractive but fairly small lots. Per-square-foot costs for most homes are under $70, among the lowest found in any area and the lowest for a large metro area. Property tax rates may be the only bad news at 3.0% to 3.2%, but tax bills aren't excessive due to low valuations and no state income tax. Daycare is also very affordable at under $500 per month, but while cheap, the real headline is that Arlington is suitable for single-earner families.

Education   Arlington schools are somewhat more of a mixed bag than some other places in Texas we examined, but performance is generally solid and test scores range from at to slightly above state averages. The University of Texas at Arlington brings 25,000 students to the area and makes some of its resources available to the public.

Lifestyle The Arlington lifestyle is fast paced and busy, but it's easy to escape along the miles of residential streets blanketing the area. Active recreation is everywhere. The Six Flags and Ameriquest parks draw people from surrounding communities, and would be regular destinations for local families except for high ticket prices. Other attractive local destinations include the Silver Legacy Living Science Center, an interactive science museum, and the 1,300-acre River Legacy park along the Trinity River. Arlington Skatium is a large facility for all types of skating, and watersports are available at the Joe Pool Lake and adjacent parks. Boosted by the university, Arlington has a number of minor performing and visual arts venues, with bigger and better cultural opportunities available in Fort Worth and Dallas.

Growth and sprawl have produced some traffic issues, especially during rush hours, and commuters traveling to Dallas, Fort Worth, and cities in between can expect 30-minute and occasionally longer commutes.

The landscape is flat and generally lacks interest. There are some areas of unattractive commercial sprawl, but new parks have helped improve the physical appearance. The climate is a mix of continental and subtropical influences, with four distinct seasons. Summers are hot, still, and humid; winters are variable.

Health & Safety Fort Worth area crime rates are about average, but the "CAP" crime risk assessment for Arlington is quite low. Healthcare facilities are abundant in the metro area and there are two hospitals in Arlington.

Nearby Neighborhoods The 12 zip codes in the Arlington area each offer a slightly different mix of housing, and a few other neighborhoods are even more affordable than the 76002 area. Some attractive inner suburbs lie inside the I-620 beltway to the southwest of Fort Worth, and areas to the northeast including Keller and moving east toward Grapevine are more upscale. You might also want to read p. 196 for information on Flower Mound, Texas.

ARLINGTON, TX NEIGHBORHOOD HIGHLIGHTS	
PEOPLE	
Population	7,808
15-yr Population Growth	35.70%
5-yr Population Growth	9.80%
% Married w/Children	44.2%
% Single w/Children	8.6%
No. of Households	2,521
Median Age	28.3
Avg. Household Size	3.12
Diversity Measure	63
STANDARD OF LIVING	
Median Household Income	$71,192
% Household Income > $100K	13%
Projected Future Job Growth	20%
Cost of Living Index	93.1
Buying Power Index	170
Weekly Daycare Cost	$128
Median Home Price	$150,600
"Sweet Spot" Home Price	$180,000
Home Price Ratio	2.1
Median Age of Homes	3.8
% Homes Owned	89%
Effective Property Tax Rate	3.10%
Estimated Property Tax Bill	$5,580
EDUCATION	
% High School Graduates	90%
% 4-yr Degree	23%
% Graduate or Professional Degree	5%
$ Invested per Pupil	$4,274
Student/Teacher Ratio	15.6
Primary Test Score Percentile	103.3
Secondary Test Score Percentile	106.1
% Subsidized School Lunch	28.80%
% Attending Public School	88%
LIFESTYLE	
Leisure Rating (Area)	8
Arts & Culture Rating (Area)	6
Climate Rating (Area)	9
Physical Setting Rating	2
Downtown Core Rating	2
% Commute < 30 Min.	44%
% Commute > 1 Hour	10%
HEALTH & SAFETY	
Health Rating (Area)	1
Stress Score (Area)	9
Violent Crime Risk	39
Property Crime Risk	41

FORT WORTH–ARLINGTON, TX
AREA HIGHLIGHTS
PEOPLE

SIZE & DIVERSITY	AREA	U.S. AVG	FAMILY DEMOGRAPHICS	AREA	U.S. AVG
Population	1,878,334		% Married	56.70%	53.80%
15-yr Population Growth	38.30%	4.40%	% Single	43.30%	46.20%
Diversity Measure	50	54	% Divorced	10%	10.20%
% Religiously Observant	52%	50%	% Separated	3.90%	2.10%
% Catholic	10%	22%	% Married w/Children	30.80%	27.90%
% Protestant	40%	25%	% Single w/Children	10.60%	9.40%
% Jewish	0%	2%	% Married, No Children	28.30%	31.00%
% Other	1%	1%	% Single, No Children	30.20%	31.70%

STANDARD OF LIVING

INCOME, EMPLOYMENT & TAXES	AREA	U.S. AVG	COST OF LIVING & HOUSING	AREA	U.S. AVG
Median Household Income	$46,923	$44,684	Cost of Living Index	83.3	100
Household Income Growth	5.20%	6.10%	Buying Power Index	126	100
Unemployment Rate	5.20%	5.10%	Median Home Price	$124,600	$208,500
Recent Job Growth	1.20%	1.30%	Home Price Ratio	2.7	4.7
Projected Future Job Growth	18.10%	10.50%	Home Price Appreciation	11.10%	13.60%
State Income Tax Rate	0%	5.00%	% Homes Owned	60.80%	64.10%
State Sales Tax Rate	7.70%	6.00%	Median Rent	$732	$792

EDUCATION

ATTAINMENT & ACHIEVEMENT	AREA	U.S. AVG	RESOURCES & INVESTMENT	AREA	U.S. AVG
% High School Graduate	79.70%	83.90%	No. of Highly Ranked Universities	1	1
% 2-yr Graduate	8.80%	7.10%	$ Invested per Pupil	$4,983	$6,058
% 4-yr Graduate	23.10%	17.20%	Student/Teacher Ratio	15.9	15.9
% Graduate or Professional Degree	8%	9.90%	State University In-State Tuition	$5,735	$4,917
% Attending Public School	92.90%	84.30%			
75th Percentile State University SAT Score (Verbal)	540	477			
75th Percentile State University SAT Score (Math)	570	478			
75th Percentile State University ACT Score	23	20			

LIFESTYLE

RECREATION, ARTS & CULTURE	AREA	U.S. AVG	INFRASTRUCTURE & FACILITIES	AREA	U.S. AVG
Professional Sports Rating	8	4	No. of Public Libraries	51	28
Zoos & Aquariums Rating	7	3	Library Volumes Per Capita	2.2	2.8
Amusement Park Rating	9	3	No. of Warehouse Clubs	5	4
Professional Theater Rating	9	3	No. of Starbucks	40	5
Overall Museum Rating	7	6	Golf Course Rating	7	4
Science Museum Rating	7	4	National Park Rating	1	3
Children's Museum Rating	10	3	Sq. Mi. Inland Water	4	4

CLIMATE			COMMUTE & TRANSPORTATION		
Days Mostly Sunny	234	212	Avg. Daily Commute Time	26.8	24.7
Annual Days Precipitation	79	111	% Commute by Auto	79%	77.70%
Annual Days > 90°F	92	38	Per Capita Avg. Daily Transit Miles	5.5	7.9
Annual Days < 32°F	41	88	Annual Auto Insurance Premium	$1,326	$1,314
July Relative Humidity	67	69	Gas, Cost per Gallon	$2.98	$3.05

HEALTH & SAFETY

CRIME & ENVIRNOMENTAL ISSUES	AREA	U.S. AVG	HEALTHCARE & COST	AREA	U.S. AVG
Violent Crime Rate	437	517	Physicians per Capita	161.1	254.3
Change in Violent Crime	-15.80%	-7.50%	Pediatricians per Capita	13.9	16.9
Property Crime Rate	4840	3783	Hospital Beds per Capita	226.9	239.7
Change in Property Crime	2.50%	-10.10%	No. of Teaching Hospitals	4	1.9
Air Quality Score	20	44	Healthcare Cost Index	100.1	100
Water Quality Score	91	33	Cost per Doctor Visit	$73	$74
Pollen/Allergy Score	87	61	Cost per Dentist Visit	$59	$67
Stress Score	87	49	Cost per Hospital Room	$658	$702
Cancer Mortality Rate	173	168.9			

Austin (West), TX

Area Type: Outer suburb

Zip Code: 78732

Metro Area: Austin–San Marcos, TX

Metro Area Type: Mid-size

Location: 20 miles northwest of downtown Austin

Time Zone: Central Standard Time

Pros:

Entertainment and culture
Strong economy
Education

Cons:

Growth and sprawl
Summer heat
Long commutes

Say, "Best place to live in Texas," and a good number of Texans will fire back, without hesitation, "Austin." Say, "Best place to live in the Austin area," and most Texans, as well as most Austiners will get a puzzled look on their face. You'll likely get more than one answer.

Austin—known worldwide as "the live music capital of the world"—is an attractive city and college town with much to do, strong employment, and great neighborhoods. Austin has two centers: the attractive small-town–feeling downtown and the 50,000-plus main campus of the top-rated University of Texas. In the downtown area, sitting astride the banks of the Texas edition of the Colorado River, city blocks surround the Capitol with a mix of old and new buildings. Toward the river, between 3rd and 6th streets, are older warehouse and commercial buildings: the so-called Warehouse District, which is full of restaurants and small music venues crossing the spectrum from country to hip-hop, with almost everything in between.

Growth is one of the area's hallmarks, with a list-leading 72% population growth since 1990. One catalyst is Michael Dell, who started his now–world-leading personal computer manufacturing business in a University of Texas dorm room in the mid-1980s. This story of entrepreneurial growth and spirit is noteworthy in its own right, but also says a lot about Austin. Not surprisingly, technology is a big economic driver today. Dell, major semiconductor firms, data service providers, and other technology research and manufacturing operations are clustered around the city, around the university campus, and along I-35 toward Round Rock to the north. Austin is regarded as an excellent place to do business, with an educated workforce, low taxes, and plenty to keep folks busy in their spare time.

Most of Austin's growth has spread north and west into the relatively scenic beginnings of the "hill country." Areas south and east are largely flat and uninteresting. Almost immediately out of town, newer suburbs and subdivisions spring up along Loop 1 (commonly called MoPac) and west toward such long-established communities as Rollingwood and West Lake Hills, and along the Colorado River toward Greenshores and Four Points. These communities have a broad range of housing in attractive settings with good schools and local resources; and all work for families. North of Austin toward Round Rock is Pflugerville, a bedroom community for commuters to both Austin and Round Rock. Any of these areas are great for families, but as a best place, we like the somewhat upscale 78732 area to the west, near the large Lake Travis. It includes a large planned community known as Steiner Ranch and 37% of the area's residents are married with children.

Standard of Living   The Cost of Living Index is 125, high on a Texas scale but reflecting the larger suburban homes available in the area. Despite the high COL, elevated incomes drive the Buying Power Index to a scorching 196. The area may be a bit more prosperous than others on our list of 100 best places, but this shouldn't scare prospective families away because there are many other good neighborhoods, of varying price ranges, in the Austin area. Keep in mind that the high median home price of the zip code we chose is driven up by a few pockets of very expensive homes. Most homes run about $100 per square foot, very reasonable on a national scale and attractive because of their high quality. Many are newer, brick-faced structures on attractive treed lots that are larger than our 2,200-square-foot benchmark. A 3,500-square-foot, four-bedroom home on a ¼ acre with a gourmet kitchen, wood floors, a butler's pantry, and a game room was recently listed for $339K in a community association with a swimming pool and recreation center. Texas property tax rates are high, and range from 2.5% to 3.1% in the Austin area,

AUSTIN (WEST), TX NEIGHBORHOOD HIGHLIGHTS	
PEOPLE	
Population	4,082
15-yr Population Growth	50.90%
5-yr Population Growth	7.10%
% Married w/Children	37%
% Single w/Children	5.8%
No. of Households	1,564
Median Age	31.9
Avg. Household Size	2.61
Diversity Measure	25
STANDARD OF LIVING	**BEST**
Median Household Income	$109,331
% Household Income > $100K	55%
Projected Future Job Growth	21%
Cost of Living Index	125
Buying Power Index	196
Weekly Daycare Cost	$145
Median Home Price	$295,900
"Sweet Spot" Home Price	$240,000
Home Price Ratio	2.7
Median Age of Homes	5.8
% Homes Owned	89%
Effective Property Tax Rate	3%
Estimated Property Tax Bill	$7,200
EDUCATION	
% High School Graduates	96%
% 4-yr Degree	48%
% Graduate or Professional Degree	18%
$ Invested per Pupil	$4,716
Student/Teacher Ratio	16.3
Primary Test Score Percentile	118.6
Secondary Test Score Percentile	100.8
% Subsidized School Lunch	3.10%
% Attending Public School	71%
LIFESTYLE	
Leisure Rating (Area)	5
Arts & Culture Rating (Area)	8
Climate Rating (Area)	9
Physical Setting Rating	5
Downtown Core Rating	6
% Commute < 30 Min.	41%
% Commute > 1 Hour	2%
HEALTH & SAFETY	
Health Rating (Area)	2
Stress Score (Area)	6
Violent Crime Risk	63
Property Crime Risk	56

but low property valuations and lack of state income tax more than make up for the high property tax rates; the total tax burden is quite low.

Education Strong local schools in this area are set against an outstanding backdrop of educational attainment at the university. Cedar Park High School was recognized for advanced placement performance by the Texas state Gold Performance Acknowledgment system and is also noted for its strong arts and extracurricular programs. Test scores run 12 to 25 points above state averages at all levels, and are frequently recognized as "exemplary" by the state education administration.

Lifestyle Downtown is alive with entertainment and nightlife. For daytime visitors, the riverfront offers several attractions, including a pair of large waterfront parks and a good children's museum. On the north edge of downtown, bordering on the university campus, is the Bob Bullock Texas State History Museum, and, with its living, breathing exhibits, it's more of a family attraction than most museums. Outdoor recreation opportunities are abundant, especially on the northwest side of town; watersports on Travis Lake lead the way. The university brings numerous resources to town. Some complain that the area's biggest attractions are geared more toward adults than children, but most find plenty for entire families to do.

As the city spreads west and up the I-35 corridor, some commutes can take 30 minutes or longer.

Austin sits between flat lowlands to the southeast and hills and limestone outcroppings along the numerous rivers, creeks, and washes to the west. The landscape has a dry appearance with scattered trees. The climate is subtropical with hot, humid summers and generally mild winters that include an occasional cold snap. Long periods of heavy rain can occur as Gulf moisture collides with northerly air masses. Aside from these rains, outdoor activities are possible most of the year.

Health & Safety The crime rate is moderate, which is fairly typical for a college town. Healthcare facilities are adequate, and include a modern children's hospital that serves a large region of Texas.

Nearby Neighborhoods Most attractive family neighborhoods are on the north and west sides of Austin. Families looking for more modest home prices or to be closer to a Round Rock job should look at Pflugerville.

AUSTIN–SAN MARCOS, TX
AREA HIGHLIGHTS

PEOPLE

SIZE & DIVERSITY	AREA	U.S. AVG	FAMILY DEMOGRAPHICS	AREA	U.S. AVG
Population	1,412,271		% Married	53.30%	53.80%
15-yr Population Growth	71.90%	4.40%	% Single	46.70%	46.20%
Diversity Measure	54	54	% Divorced	9.40%	10.20%
% Religiously Observant	45%	50%	% Separated	3.20%	2.10%
% Catholic	18%	22%	% Married w/Children	28.10%	27.90%
% Protestant	25%	25%	% Single w/Children	10%	9.40%
% Jewish	1%	2%	% Married, No Children	26.40%	31.00%
% Other	0%	1%	% Single, No Children	35.40%	31.70%

STANDARD OF LIVING

INCOME, EMPLOYMENT & TAXES	AREA	U.S. AVG	COST OF LIVING & HOUSING	AREA	U.S. AVG
Median Household Income	$52,146	$44,684	Cost of Living Index	91.1	100
Household Income Growth	4.20%	6.10%	Buying Power Index	128	100
Unemployment Rate	4.20%	5.10%	Median Home Price	$166,800	$208,500
Recent Job Growth	1.40%	1.30%	Home Price Ratio	3.2	4.7
Projected Future Job Growth	21.80%	10.50%	Home Price Appreciation	2%	13.60%
State Income Tax Rate	0%	5.00%	% Homes Owned	58%	64.10%
State Sales Tax Rate	7.90%	6.00%	Median Rent	$912	$792

EDUCATION

ATTAINMENT & ACHIEVEMENT	AREA	U.S. AVG	RESOURCES & INVESTMENT	AREA	U.S. AVG
% High School Graduate	81%	83.90%	No. of Highly Ranked Universities	1	1
% 2-yr Graduate	7.10%	7.10%	$ Invested per Pupil	$5,243	$6,058
% 4-yr Graduate	27.50%	17.20%	Student/Teacher Ratio	14.8	15.9
% Graduate or Professional Degree	12.50%	9.90%	State University In-State Tuition	$5,735	$4,917
% Attending Public School	94.50%	84.30%			
75th Percentile State University SAT Score (Verbal)	540	477			
75th Percentile State University SAT Score (Math)	570	478			
75th Percentile State University ACT Score	23	20			

LIFESTYLE

RECREATION, ARTS & CULTURE	AREA	U.S. AVG	INFRASTRUCTURE & FACILITIES	AREA	U.S. AVG
Professional Sports Rating	3	4	No. of Public Libraries	44	28
Zoos & Aquariums Rating	1	3	Library Volumes Per Capita	2.4	2.8
Amusement Park Rating	1	3	No. of Warehouse Clubs	4	4
Professional Theater Rating	1	3	No. of Starbucks	37	5
Overall Museum Rating	8	6	Golf Course Rating	4	4
Science Museum Rating	7	4	National Park Rating	1	3
Children's Museum Rating	6	3	Sq. Mi. Inland Water	4	4

CLIMATE			COMMUTE & TRANSPORTATION		
Days Mostly Sunny	231	212	Avg. Daily Commute Time	25.5	24.7
Annual Days Precipitation	82	111	% Commute by Auto	73%	77.70%
Annual Days > 90°F	101	38	Per Capita Avg. Daily Transit Miles	18.1	7.9
Annual Days < 32°F	23	88	Annual Auto Insurance Premium	$1,316	$1,314
July Relative Humidity	67	69	Gas, Cost per Gallon	$2.92	$3.05

HEALTH & SAFETY

CRIME & ENVIRNOMENTAL ISSUES	AREA	U.S. AVG	HEALTHCARE & COST	AREA	U.S. AVG
Violent Crime Rate	354	517	Physicians per Capita	196.1	254.3
Change in Violent Crime	-11.30%	-7.50%	Pediatricians per Capita	17.7	16.9
Property Crime Rate	4382	3783	Hospital Beds per Capita	212.3	239.7
Change in Property Crime	-2.50%	-10.10%	No. of Teaching Hospitals	3	1.9
Air Quality Score	28	44	Healthcare Cost Index	105.9	100
Water Quality Score	82	33	Cost per Doctor Visit	$77	$74
Pollen/Allergy Score	76	61	Cost per Dentist Visit	$69	$67
Stress Score	56	49	Cost per Hospital Room	$622	$702
Cancer Mortality Rate	154	168.9			

Bellingham, WA

Area Type: Small city

Zip Code: 98226

Metro Area: Bellingham, WA

Metro Area Type: Smaller

Location: 90 miles north of Seattle along I-5

Time Zone: Pacific Standard Time

Pros:
Attractive setting
Outdoor recreation
Pleasant summers

Cons:
Economic cycles
High home prices
Dreary winters

You have to love a town that issues a press release every month summarizing the previous month's weather. Of course, there's plenty to talk about in Bellingham besides the weather, but it's fair to say that life here moves at a somewhat more relaxed pace than in Seattle. The attractive setting and slower pace have proven to be a major draw for many different population groups, including retirees and, more recently, families. Located in a scenic Puget Sound setting between Seattle and Vancouver, British Columbia, Bellingham and Whatcom County have grown some 41% since 1990. The influx has caused housing prices to nearly double in 5 years, making them expensive by national standards but still reasonable for the West Coast.

Bellingham is about halfway (60 miles each way) between Vancouver (60 minutes) and Seattle (90 minutes). Locals like to say it's a perfect location for those who prefer to travel to large cities rather than live in them. The setting is gorgeous—looking west across Bellingham Bay into the Puget Sound, the San Juan Islands rise into a picture-postcard setting of mountainous forms rising from the water, with interesting shadows at all times of the day and especially at sunset. Heavy coniferous forests cover the landscape except for some agricultural areas to the north, and the Cascades rise rapidly to the east to the 11,000-foot Mount Baker and the North Cascades National Park. The area is paradise for outdoor recreation, including fishing, clamming, hiking, mountain biking, and skiing.

Downtown Bellingham is a clean, attractive, and walkable center for commercial and shopping activity. The historic Whatcom County Museum, housed in a classic brick Victorian structure that overlooks the bay and shipping port, is a center for various local arts activities, including some at the small children's museum next door. A short drive to the south along Bellingham Bay brings one to the historic gaslight town of Fairhaven, with shops, bookstores, cafes, minor arts

venues, and the modern Alaska Ferry Terminal at water's edge. Farther south along Chuckanut Drive (SR 11) are Fairhaven Park and the excellent shoreline Larrabee State Park. This area is dotted with beautiful bayview home sites in some moderately expensive family neighborhoods.

The best and most affordable family residential areas are east of town up the hill toward Lake Whatcom. Newer suburbs and planned commercial centers reflect an intelligent design and architectural touch. Particularly noteworthy is the Barkley Center development, a supermarket-anchored strip mall cleverly designed to mimic a country downtown street surrounded by other mixed-use commercial buildings. The prevailing Northwest Craftsman home design is tastefully mixed with newer homes of several styles ranging from farmhouse to Southern Plantation to Cape Cod to Chateau, most set on attractive wooded lots, some with views of Lake Whatcom or Bellingham Bay.

Employment has been uncertain at times. Basic forest products industries go through cycles, and there have been sizable layoffs at a local Georgia Pacific pulp and paper mill. The area is an important center for oil refining, commercial shipping, and aluminum production, but these industries have given somewhat inconsistent employment. Nonetheless, the area's strategic location makes it attractive to businesses seeking U.S. and Canadian markets. Recent job growth is a very healthy 5.6% and future job growth is projected at 21%.

Standard of Living The Cost of Living Index is 109, which is high but not so high by West Coast standards. Homebuilding has been on the rise in response to the influx of newcomers, mainly retirees and people from California seeking lower living costs. This activity has updated the available housing stock, which since 2000 had primarily consisted of new condominiums; most single-family homes had been built prior to 1970. But today, you'll find a large number of newer homes, most on small wooded lots, available in the high $300Ks. Property taxes average 1.2%, lower than the national averages, and Washington has no income tax.

Education All districts serving Bellingham test at or near the state averages and above the national averages. The Bellingham School District itself is somewhat better than others in the area, with scores that are almost always 10% to 15% above state averages. Educational attainment is relatively high for an area once tied to basic industries, with 21% possessing 4-year degrees and 11% with graduate degrees. Western Washington University, just south of downtown, brings 12,000 students with strengths in education and environmental studies curricula.

Lifestyle Bellingham has a large harbor, and Bellingham Bay's calm, though cold, waters support many water recreation activities. The city's extensive park system and recreation program acquire and maintain open spaces. There are miles of well-groomed hiking trails here, as well as numerous classes and group activities. The mountains to the east offer extensive trails, hiking, and skiing. The Mount Baker ski area is just a 40-minute drive east. Bellingham, in fact, is surrounded by many 1-hour trips to interesting and scenic places. Short ferry trips take weekenders to the San Juan Islands, excellent for biking and quaint small-town activities. Arts and cultural activities are available in Seattle and Vancouver.

Commutes within Bellingham aren't an issue, except for the few people making an hour or so commute into the northern Seattle suburbs south of Everett. Bellingham is a port for several cruise lines, including the Inside Passage Alaskan Ferry service to seven destinations in Alaska as far north as Skagway. This service is part of the Alaskan Marine Highway System, which has routes following the spectacular Alaskan coastline into the Aleutian Islands.

The climate is coastal marine, with cool, partly cloudy summers sufficiently dry for most outdoor activity. Winter is cloudy and wet with occasional freezing temperatures and snow, but lingering snow is not the norm. However, the area's compromise factor might be its 220-plus cloudy days and 160 days of precipitation (mostly light rain) per year.

Health & Safety Crime rates are near national averages. The coastal location and active weather bring fresh air at most times, although paper mill odors linger

BELLINGHAM, WA NEIGHBORHOOD HIGHLIGHTS	
PEOPLE	
Population	61,135
15-yr Population Growth	41%
5-yr Population Growth	8%
% Married w/Children	26.9%
% Single w/Children	9.7%
No. of Households	23,777
Median Age	36.9
Avg. Household Size	2.6
Diversity Measure	25
STANDARD OF LIVING	
Median Household Income	$45,914
% Household Income > $100K	11%
Projected Future Job Growth	21%
Cost of Living Index	109
Buying Power Index	94
Weekly Daycare Cost	$125
Median Home Price	$320,100
"Sweet Spot" Home Price	$375,000
Home Price Ratio	7
Median Age of Homes	19.9
% Homes Owned	67%
Effective Property Tax Rate	1.20%
Estimated Property Tax Bill	$4,500
EDUCATION	
% High School Graduates	90%
% 4-yr Degree	21%
% Graduate or Professional Degree	11%
$ Invested per Pupil	$5,415
Student/Teacher Ratio	19.2
Primary Test Score Percentile	112.4
Secondary Test Score Percentile	113
% Subsidized School Lunch	36.60%
% Attending Public School	87.70%
LIFESTYLE	
Leisure Rating (Area)	6
Arts & Culture Rating (Area)	2
Climate Rating (Area)	8
Physical Setting Rating	9
Downtown Core Rating	7
% Commute < 30 Min.	78%
% Commute > 1 Hour	4%
HEALTH & SAFETY	
Health Rating (Area)	7
Stress Score (Area)	8
Violent Crime Risk	100
Property Crime Risk	152

in some weather conditions. Healthcare facilities are adequate for this size of city and improving.

Nearby Neighborhoods The best residential neighborhoods are east and southeast. The Fairhaven and Chuckanut Drive area to the south has many restored Victorian homes in a beautiful setting, but it's more expensive and has more retirees than Bellingham.

BELLINGHAM, WA
AREA HIGHLIGHTS
PEOPLE

SIZE & DIVERSITY	AREA	U.S. AVG	FAMILY DEMOGRAPHICS	AREA	U.S. AVG
Population	180,167		% Married	59.70%	53.80%
15-yr Population Growth	41%	4.40%	% Single	40.30%	46.20%
Diversity Measure	25	54	% Divorced	9.40%	10.20%
% Religiously Observant	29%	50%	% Separated	2.40%	2.10%
% Catholic	8%	22%	% Married w/Children	28.20%	27.90%
% Protestant	21%	25%	% Single w/Children	8.40%	9.40%
% Jewish	0%	2%	% Married, No Children	31.50%	31.00%
% Other	0%	1%	% Single, No Children	32%	31.70%

STANDARD OF LIVING

INCOME, EMPLOYMENT & TAXES	AREA	U.S. AVG	COST OF LIVING & HOUSING	AREA	U.S. AVG
Median Household Income	$41,760	$44,684	Cost of Living Index	96.1	100
Household Income Growth	4.70%	6.10%	Buying Power Index	97	100
Unemployment Rate	4.70%	5.10%	Median Home Price	$203,500	$208,500
Recent Job Growth	5.60%	1.30%	Home Price Ratio	4.9	4.7
Projected Future Job Growth	22.20%	10.50%	Home Price Appreciation	19.40%	13.60%
State Income Tax Rate	0%	5.00%	% Homes Owned	59.60%	64.10%
State Sales Tax Rate	6.50%	6.00%	Median Rent	$693	$792

EDUCATION

ATTAINMENT & ACHIEVEMENT	AREA	U.S. AVG	RESOURCES & INVESTMENT	AREA	U.S. AVG
% High School Graduate	84.80%	83.90%	No. of Highly Ranked Universities	0	1
% 2-yr Graduate	9.40%	7.10%	$ Invested per Pupil	$5,593	$6,058
% 4-yr Graduate	21.70%	17.20%	Student/Teacher Ratio	19.7	15.9
% Graduate or Professional Degree	8.90%	9.90%	State University In-State Tuition	$5,286	$4,917
% Attending Public School	90.60%	84.30%			
75th Percentile State University SAT Score (Verbal)	520	477			
75th Percentile State University SAT Score (Math)	550	478			
75th Percentile State University ACT Score	23	20			

LIFESTYLE

RECREATION, ARTS & CULTURE	AREA	U.S. AVG	INFRASTRUCTURE & FACILITIES	AREA	U.S. AVG
Professional Sports Rating	2	4	No. of Public Libraries	11	28
Zoos & Aquariums Rating	1	3	Library Volumes Per Capita	3.3	2.8
Amusement Park Rating	1	3	No. of Warehouse Clubs	3	4
Professional Theater Rating	1	3	No. of Starbucks	10	5
Overall Museum Rating	5	6	Golf Course Rating	1	4
Science Museum Rating	3	4	National Park Rating	10	3
Children's Museum Rating	5	3	Sq. Mi. Inland Water	5	4

CLIMATE			COMMUTE & TRANSPORTATION		
Days Mostly Sunny	136	212	Avg. Daily Commute Time	20.8	24.7
Annual Days Precipitation	160	111	% Commute by Auto	73%	77.70%
Annual Days > 90°F	3	38	Per Capita Avg. Daily Transit Miles	14.4	7.9
Annual Days < 32°F	32	88	Annual Auto Insurance Premium	$1,273	$1,314
July Relative Humidity	74	69	Gas, Cost per Gallon	$3.08	$3.05

HEALTH & SAFETY

CRIME & ENVIRNOMENTAL ISSUES	AREA	U.S. AVG	HEALTHCARE & COST	AREA	U.S. AVG
Violent Crime Rate	240	517	Physicians per Capita	223.7	254.3
Change in Violent Crime	-19.20%	-7.50%	Pediatricians per Capita	15.3	16.9
Property Crime Rate	4936	3783	Hospital Beds per Capita	121.6	239.7
Change in Property Crime	-6.30%	-10.10%	No. of Teaching Hospitals	0	1.9
Air Quality Score	33	44	Healthcare Cost Index	118.5	100
Water Quality Score	60	33	Cost per Doctor Visit	$78	$74
Pollen/Allergy Score	48	61	Cost per Dentist Visit	$81	$67
Stress Score	83	49	Cost per Hospital Room	$624	$702
Cancer Mortality Rate	153.2	168.9			

Bethlehem, PA

Area Type: Small city

Zip Code: 18018

Metro Area: Allentown-Bethlehem-Easton, PA

Metro Area Type: Mid-size

Location: Eastern PA, 70 miles north of Philadelphia, along the Lehigh River

Time Zone: Eastern Standard Time

Pros:
Historic interest
Central location
Diverse population

Cons:
Economic cycles
Older infrastructure
Educational attainment

Few places were hit harder by late-20th-century economic and industrial transitions than Bethlehem, Pennsylvania, and the surrounding area. The 1990s collapse of Bethlehem Steel left this town of 70,000 with a gigantic 1,500-acre abandoned steel mill site resembling something from a Star Wars film. And it left an equally large hole in the economy. Other area employers, like AT&T/Lucent, have hardly fared better. Take all that, together with an aging infrastructure and population, and one might be tempted to write off the area altogether.

Not so fast. Today's Bethlehem has rebounded nicely from this industrial Armageddon, and in fact a unique combination of history, location, and community spirit makes it a very attractive place for families—especially for patient families looking for something different and diverse, for an earlier-era feel mixed with the resources for modern living.

Interestingly, Bethlehem Steel once imported workers into the country from different parts of Europe, which has ultimately left a strong imprint on today's community. Downtown Bethlehem feels like a European city—the German and Moravian influence on the town's historic buildings is striking. The downtown area sits attractively on a bluff above the Lehigh River. Two colleges, Lehigh University and the smaller Moravian College, bring an active, educated college influence to the area along with a number of arts facilities. The area is an interesting mix of old and new, young and elderly, families and nonfamilies (the married-with-children percentage is 18.4), educated and working class. And the kicker is this: Bethlehem is a mere 85 miles due west of New York City. It's also within commuting distance of many New Jersey employers and is gradually growing a new commercial base of its own. Bethlehem is a "where the puck is going" story.

Standard of Living   The area as a whole has a modest Cost of Living Index of 92.5, making it quite affordable considering its proximity to the more expensive areas of New Jersey and New York. Home prices vary around the area, and more family homes are found a few miles north and east of town. Family homes cost from the high $100Ks to mid $200Ks in areas close to the city, and rise to the high $200Ks in the more country-like areas toward Easton. There are a number of attractive older homes close to town. Reasonable property taxes range from 1.0% to 1.2%. Employment is still a bit of a question mark, with future job growth projected at 5%. But a number of smaller industries have moved into the series of industrial parks located near Lehigh University to the south, and it's reasonable to expect a migration of businesses and jobs from other East Coast areas.

Education   Schools have shown inconsistent performances, and local public schools score near to slightly below state averages. But the area is investing in and expanding its schools and most residents have a favorable impression of the local education system. In Bethlehem, 4-year degree attainment is only 15%, reflecting the older, industrial heritage. But that number rises in the eastern suburbs (18%–20%), and the area exudes a stronger educational presence than those figures indicate. Like the economy, education isn't perfect, but it's improving.

Lifestyle   Community activities, church events, festivals, sports, and the arts are popular here. There are 20 different local theaters and theater groups, as well as numerous arts events and traveling acts hosted by the colleges. The annual Christmas celebration is world famous. There is one large central public swimming pool with five neighborhood pools; all are available for

BETHLEHEM, PA
NEIGHBORHOOD HIGHLIGHTS

PEOPLE

Population	32,604
15-yr Population Growth	12%
5-yr Population Growth	4.50%
% Married w/Children	18.4%
% Single w/Children	7.4%
No. of Households	13,754
Median Age	40.2
Avg. Household Size	2.22
Diversity Measure	28

STANDARD OF LIVING

Median Household Income	$41,964
% Household Income > $100K	7%
Projected Future Job Growth	5%
Cost of Living Index	92.5
Buying Power Index	103
Weekly Daycare Cost	$107
Median Home Price	$154,300
"Sweet Spot" Home Price	$220,000
Home Price Ratio	3.7
Median Age of Homes	51
% Homes Owned	56%
Effective Property Tax Rate	1.20%
Estimated Property Tax Bill	$2,640

EDUCATION

% High School Graduates	82%
% 4-yr Degree	15%
% Graduate or Professional Degree	9%
$ Invested per Pupil	$6,435
Student/Teacher Ratio	15.3
Primary Test Score Percentile	89.3
Secondary Test Score Percentile	86.9
% Subsidized School Lunch	36.80%
% Attending Public School	62.80%

LIFESTYLE

Leisure Rating (Area)	8
Arts & Culture Rating (Area)	6
Climate Rating (Area)	3
Physical Setting Rating	3
Downtown Core Rating	6
% Commute < 30 Min.	81%
% Commute > 1 Hour	5%

HEALTH & SAFETY

Health Rating (Area)	6
Stress Score (Area)	2
Violent Crime Risk	149
Property Crime Risk	139

minimal charges. Even bigger and better, Dorney Park & Wildwater Kingdom in the adjacent city of Allentown, Pennsylvania, draws families from other parts of the East Coast. And the Dutch Springs Aquapark offers more family water-related activities and camping. For travelers, New York, Philadelphia, and the Poconos are an hour away, and the Jersey shore is just a bit farther.

Residents working in town, in nearby Allentown, or in Easton have short commutes. It's about a 45-minute drive to the nearest commercial areas in New Jersey. And it is possible to commute to New York; some do it on a well-utilized private bus service.

The Bethlehem area is located in the Lehigh Valley, running between parallel mountain ridges. It's mostly hilly and heavily wooded, especially to the east. Climate is variable in all seasons, but mountains to the north provide some shelter from harsh winter weather.

Health & Safety Reported crime statistics and risk assessments are inconsistent, but locals don't seem concerned. Health facilities are excellent for a community of this size and location. The relatively low stress score of 20 is far lower than that of many big city areas nearby, and reflects, in part, a decline in employment issues and concerns.

Nearby Neighborhoods City neighborhoods run mainly north and east, with some areas across the Lehigh River near the university to the south. The city then gives way to a more rural area with nice homes east of town between Bethlehem and Easton. The Palmer Township area just to the west of Easton is a little more upscale.

ALLENTOWN-BETHLEHEM-EASTON, PA
AREA HIGHLIGHTS

PEOPLE

SIZE & DIVERSITY	AREA	U.S. AVG	FAMILY DEMOGRAPHICS	AREA	U.S. AVG
Population	669,798		% Married	58.80%	53.80%
15-yr Population Growth	12.60%	4.40%	% Single	41.20%	46.20%
Diversity Measure	25	54	% Divorced	6.60%	10.20%
% Religiously Observant	63%	50%	% Separated	2.90%	2.10%
% Catholic	31%	22%	% Married w/Children	27.20%	27.90%
% Protestant	30%	25%	% Single w/Children	7.50%	9.40%
% Jewish	1%	2%	% Married, No Children	34.20%	31.00%
% Other	0%	1%	% Single, No Children	31.10%	31.70%

STANDARD OF LIVING

INCOME, EMPLOYMENT & TAXES	AREA	U.S. AVG	COST OF LIVING & HOUSING	AREA	U.S. AVG
Median Household Income	$47,005	$44,684	Cost of Living Index	98.2	100
Household Income Growth	5.40%	6.10%	Buying Power Index	107	100
Unemployment Rate	5.40%	5.10%	Median Home Price	$249,100	$208,500
Recent Job Growth	2.20%	1.30%	Home Price Ratio	5.3	4.7
Projected Future Job Growth	5.90%	10.50%	Home Price Appreciation	13.10%	13.60%
State Income Tax Rate	3.80%	5.00%	% Homes Owned	73%	64.10%
State Sales Tax Rate	6%	6.00%	Median Rent	$671	$792

EDUCATION

ATTAINMENT & ACHIEVEMENT	AREA	U.S. AVG	RESOURCES & INVESTMENT	AREA	U.S. AVG
% High School Graduate	79.20%	83.90%	No. of Highly Ranked Universities	2	1
% 2-yr Graduate	8%	7.10%	$ Invested per Pupil	$6,369	$6,058
% 4-yr Graduate	13.90%	17.20%	Student/Teacher Ratio	17.8	15.9
% Graduate or Professional Degree	7.20%	9.90%	State University In-State Tuition	$10,856	$4,917
% Attending Public School	85.80%	84.30%			
75th Percentile State University SAT Score (Verbal)	530	477			
75th Percentile State University SAT Score (Math)	560	478			
75th Percentile State University ACT Score		20			

LIFESTYLE

RECREATION, ARTS & CULTURE	AREA	U.S. AVG	INFRASTRUCTURE & FACILITIES	AREA	U.S. AVG
Professional Sports Rating	5	4	No. of Public Libraries	22	28
Zoos & Aquariums Rating	1	3	Library Volumes Per Capita	2.2	2.8
Amusement Park Rating	7	3	No. of Warehouse Clubs	4	4
Professional Theater Rating	6	3	No. of Starbucks	1	5
Overall Museum Rating	9	6	Golf Course Rating	5	4
Science Museum Rating	6	4	National Park Rating	3	3
Children's Museum Rating	2	3	Sq. Mi. Inland Water	2	4

CLIMATE			COMMUTE & TRANSPORTATION		
Days Mostly Sunny	206	212	Avg. Daily Commute Time	23.6	24.7
Annual Days Precipitation	133	111	% Commute by Auto	79%	77.70%
Annual Days > 90°F	16	38	Per Capita Avg. Daily Transit Miles	8	7.9
Annual Days < 32°F	127	88	Annual Auto Insurance Premium	$1,284	$1,314
July Relative Humidity	71	69	Gas, Cost per Gallon	$3.22	$3.05

HEALTH & SAFETY

CRIME & ENVIRNOMENTAL ISSUES	AREA	U.S. AVG	HEALTHCARE & COST	AREA	U.S. AVG
Violent Crime Rate	250	517	Physicians per Capita	280.5	254.3
Change in Violent Crime	-1.50%	-7.50%	Pediatricians per Capita	15.2	16.9
Property Crime Rate	2538	3783	Hospital Beds per Capita	440.5	239.7
Change in Property Crime	-18.60%	-10.10%	No. of Teaching Hospitals	6	1.9
Air Quality Score	39	44	Healthcare Cost Index	103	100
Water Quality Score	46	33	Cost per Doctor Visit	$62	$74
Pollen/Allergy Score	59	61	Cost per Dentist Visit	$75	$67
Stress Score	20	49	Cost per Hospital Room	$887	$702
Cancer Mortality Rate	174.9	168.9			

Broken Arrow, OK

Area Type: Outer suburb	**Pros:**
Zip Code: 74012	Cost of living
Metro Area: Tulsa, OK	Cost of housing
Metro Area Type: Mid-size	Arts and culture
Location: 15 miles southeast of downtown Tulsa	**Cons:**
Time Zone: Central Standard Time	Unattractive setting
	Vigorous climate
	Low educational attainment

"Where the South meets the West" is a phrase often heard about Tulsa, and it makes sense. The Ozark Mountains lie just east, and a strong Bible Belt influence, a laid-back demeanor, and the charm of tree-lined streets and historic neighborhoods all recall the "South." On the other hand, the oil industry, ranches, terrain, and climate all suggest the "West." As a regional and cultural mixing place for the two regions, boosted by strong oil endowments, Tulsa has evolved into a surprising cultural center for the region, and is considered by many a well-kept secret. In some ways, the city is like a small-scale Dallas, Fort Worth, Kansas City, or Denver—with many of the same kinds of amenities, a strong job market, good schools, inexpensive housing in "power" subdivisions, but without the traffic, fast pace, and stress. Tulsa blends the advantages of these larger areas with a small-town lifestyle.

Downtown Tulsa is modern with mid-rise skyscrapers, pockets of historic neighborhoods, and an attractive and evolving waterfront. The city is noted for its urban architecture, including a collection of Art Deco buildings such as the Tulsa Union Depot, which is expected to become the home for the Oklahoma Jazz Hall of Fame, as well as more modern buildings such as those designed by World Trade Center designer Minoru Yamasaki and a new convention center designed by Cesar Pelli. The economy evolved first as a ranching center and cultural center for local Native American populations. Later, in the 1920s, it boomed with the oil industry as Skelly, Phillips, Getty, and Sinclair, among others, all established major operations here. An active Chamber of Commerce brought in water supplies, opened up the waterfront as America's most inland port, and introduced the aviation industry into the area.

Today's Tulsa is diversified, but strong employment opportunities continue to come from the oil and technology industries. The latter include Boeing and major companies involved in fiber optics communications and satellite TV networks, rounded out by large manufacturers Kimberly-Clark and Whirlpool. Tulsa has a business-friendly climate; the costs of doing business are 20% below U.S. averages, and the Chamber has made the most of it. It won the national best-in-class award among metro area chambers in 2004.

Once an area of ranches and farms surrounding a small town, Broken Arrow first evolved into a bedroom community for Tulsa, and is now becoming more economically self-sufficient, though many workers still make the 15-minute commute to the city. Grid streets, with an assortment of shops, surround the small historic downtown area. Residential neighborhoods spread in all directions—many are modern and open with solid houses not unlike those found in Texas, and many are set in attractive golf course communities. Broken Arrow is full of young families; the married-with-children percentage is 41.2%.

Standard of Living Living costs in this part of this country are generally very attractive, and Tulsa and Broken Arrow are no exception. At 87.5, the Cost of Living Index is among the lowest on our list of 100 best places. Relatively high levels of professional employment and moderate incomes give a Buying Power Index of 138. Excellent family homes, some approaching 3,000 square feet, can be found under $200K, and the high incomes make quality housing quite affordable. The Home Price Ratio of 2.3 is tied for second lowest among the 100 best places in this book. Property taxes are a very reasonable 0.75% to 1.0%.

Education Schools in the area are strong, and education was one of the major factors driving us to choose Broken Arrow over its neighbors. Extracurricular activities and sports programs are considered by locals to be especially strong, with elementary and middle-school test scores well above state averages. Higher education opportunities are available nearby at the University of Tulsa, as well as at a handful of smaller colleges not too far away—including three Bible colleges.

Lifestyle Broken Arrow is suburban and traditional. The area is said to be a "youth sports capital" because team sports like soccer and baseball are big among high-school students. Shopping resources are expanding through the area, and locals are excited to have a new Bass Pro Shop outdoor superstore. Local parks and recreation facilities are above average and well utilized. Nothing too surprising here, really, except perhaps the deep and varied arts and museum amenities of Tulsa. They include the Philbrook Museum of Art and its noted Native American art collection, the Tulsa Zoo, and the Tulsa Performing Arts Center, noted especially for its music attractions. A few miles down the Arkansas River in Jenks is the brand-new Oklahoma Aquarium and the River Crossing, an area of waterfront parks, restaurants, and an amphitheater. Out-of-town getaways, mainly to the north and east, abound. You can access the "Green Country" hills of northeast Oklahoma, several large lakes, and eventually the Ozarks and the music theme park of Branson, Missouri.

The area is spreading in all directions, but an effective grid structure and good roads make most commutes a 15-minute affair. Broken Arrow is a bit isolated from other cities though: The Dallas Metroplex is a 4-hour drive; Kansas City is 5 hours away.

The natural area is mostly flat and open, though green most of the year. The climate is continental, and while the area is far enough north to escape intense tropical humidity, air mass collisions bring highly changeable weather in all seasons and strong storms. That said, 228 days of sunshine each year make up for some of these effects.

Health & Safety Crime risk is very low. Broken Arrow has its own St. Francis Hospital. The city is known for progressive environmental quality management programs.

Nearby Neighborhoods Owasso to the north is probably the fastest growing suburb but is connected by only one road and may face some traffic issues. Bixby and Jenks, both south along the river, are attractive and worth a look. Big oil money brought large classic homes to the "uptown" area (actually south of downtown), and good older homes are available here and on the north side.

BROKEN ARROW, OK
NEIGHBORHOOD HIGHLIGHTS

PEOPLE	
Population	47,711
15-yr Population Growth	13.10%
5-yr Population Growth	1%
% Married w/Children	41.2%
% Single w/Children	9.3%
No. of Households	16,845
Median Age	33.1
Avg. Household Size	2.82
Diversity Measure	29

STANDARD OF LIVING	
Median Household Income	$55,799
% Household Income > $100K	12%
Projected Future Job Growth	9%
Cost of Living Index	87.5
Buying Power Index	138
Weekly Daycare Cost	$122
Median Home Price	$124,000
"Sweet Spot" Home Price	$190,000
Home Price Ratio	2.3
Median Age of Homes	19.2
% Homes Owned	72%
Effective Property Tax Rate	1%
Estimated Property Tax Bill	$1,900

EDUCATION	
% High School Graduates	90%
% 4-yr Degree	23%
% Graduate or Professional Degree	8%
$ Invested per Pupil	$4,256
Student/Teacher Ratio	19.8
Primary Test Score Percentile	117.8
Secondary Test Score Percentile	0
% Subsidized School Lunch	30%
% Attending Public School	81.10%

LIFESTYLE	
Leisure Rating (Area)	4
Arts & Culture Rating (Area)	7
Climate Rating (Area)	8
Physical Setting Rating	1
Downtown Core Rating	3
% Commute < 30 Min.	73%
% Commute > 1 Hour	2%

HEALTH & SAFETY	
Health Rating (Area)	3
Stress Score (Area)	7
Violent Crime Risk	37
Property Crime Risk	45

TULSA, OK
AREA HIGHLIGHTS

PEOPLE

SIZE & DIVERSITY	AREA	U.S. AVG	FAMILY DEMOGRAPHICS	AREA	U.S. AVG
Population	825,091		% Married	57.40%	53.80%
15-yr Population Growth	17.10%	4.40%	% Single	42.60%	46.20%
Diversity Measure	43	54	% Divorced	11.40%	10.20%
% Religiously Observant	52%	50%	% Separated	2.60%	2.10%
% Catholic	5%	22%	% Married w/Children	27.90%	27.90%
% Protestant	46%	25%	% Single w/Children	10.20%	9.40%
% Jewish	0%	2%	% Married, No Children	29.80%	31.00%
% Other	0%	1%	% Single, No Children	32.10%	31.70%

STANDARD OF LIVING

INCOME, EMPLOYMENT & TAXES	AREA	U.S. AVG	COST OF LIVING & HOUSING	AREA	U.S. AVG
Median Household Income	$39,941	$44,684	Cost of Living Index	82.5	100
Household Income Growth	4.50%	6.10%	Buying Power Index	108	100
Unemployment Rate	4.50%	5.10%	Median Home Price	$117,400	$208,500
Recent Job Growth	2.50%	1.30%	Home Price Ratio	2.9	4.7
Projected Future Job Growth	10.30%	10.50%	Home Price Appreciation	1.80%	13.60%
State Income Tax Rate	7%	5.00%	% Homes Owned	62.60%	64.10%
State Sales Tax Rate	7.40%	6.00%	Median Rent	$640	$792

EDUCATION

ATTAINMENT & ACHIEVEMENT	AREA	U.S. AVG	RESOURCES & INVESTMENT	AREA	U.S. AVG
% High School Graduate	78.70%	83.90%	No. of Highly Ranked Universities	1	1
% 2-yr Graduate	8.50%	7.10%	$ Invested per Pupil	$4,635	$6,058
% 4-yr Graduate	17.40%	17.20%	Student/Teacher Ratio	17	15.9
% Graduate or Professional Degree	6.80%	9.90%	State University In-State Tuition	$4,515	$4,917
% Attending Public School	90.80%	84.30%			
75th Percentile State University SAT Score (Verbal)	N/A	477			
75th Percentile State University SAT Score (Math)	N/A	478			
75th Percentile State University ACT Score	23	20			

LIFESTYLE

RECREATION, ARTS & CULTURE	AREA	U.S. AVG	INFRASTRUCTURE & FACILITIES	AREA	U.S. AVG
Professional Sports Rating	3	4	No. of Public Libraries	40	28
Zoos & Aquariums Rating	6	3	Library Volumes Per Capita	2.6	2.8
Amusement Park Rating	1	3	No. of Warehouse Clubs	4	4
Professional Theater Rating	5	3	No. of Starbucks	6	5
Overall Museum Rating	6	6	Golf Course Rating	5	4
Science Museum Rating	5	4	National Park Rating	1	3
Children's Museum Rating	7	3	Sq. Mi. Inland Water	7	4

CLIMATE			COMMUTE & TRANSPORTATION		
Days Mostly Sunny	228	212	Avg. Daily Commute Time	21.5	24.7
Annual Days Precipitation	90	111	% Commute by Auto	77%	77.70%
Annual Days > 90°F	70	38	Per Capita Avg. Daily Transit Miles	6.5	7.9
Annual Days < 32°F	85	88	Annual Auto Insurance Premium	$1,456	$1,314
July Relative Humidity	52	69	Gas, Cost per Gallon	$2.97	$3.05

HEALTH & SAFETY

CRIME & ENVIRONMENTAL ISSUES	AREA	U.S. AVG	HEALTHCARE & COST	AREA	U.S. AVG
Violent Crime Rate	634	517	Physicians per Capita	237.7	254.3
Change in Violent Crime	-10.90%	-7.50%	Pediatricians per Capita	15.3	16.9
Property Crime Rate	4496	3783	Hospital Beds per Capita	327.6	239.7
Change in Property Crime	2%	-10.10%	No. of Teaching Hospitals	6	1.9
Air Quality Score	26	44	Healthcare Cost Index	99	100
Water Quality Score	62	33	Cost per Doctor Visit	$100	$74
Pollen/Allergy Score	72	61	Cost per Dentist Visit	$59	$67
Stress Score	74	49	Cost per Hospital Room	$670	$702
Cancer Mortality Rate	172	168.9			

Cary, NC

Area Type: Outer suburb

Zip Code: 27513

Metro Area: Raleigh–Durham–Chapel Hill, NC

Metro Area Type: Large

Location: 12 miles west of downtown Raleigh

Time Zone: Eastern Standard Time

Pros:
Strong economy
Education
Diversity

Cons:
Growth and sprawl
Lack of public transportation
Summer heat and humidity

BEST OF THE BEST

Cary, a large incorporated suburb, sits west of Raleigh and just south of I-40, the "leg" of the triangle between Raleigh and Chapel Hill. With 30.3% of households married with children, Cary is the family "hub." But the area at large has much to offer families; it comprises three interesting cities, three major universities, one world-famous technology park devoted to research and development, and a state capital. In other words, the famous Raleigh–Durham–Chapel Hill "Research Triangle" has just about everything except a world-class ski resort. This is the cultural, intellectual, and economic center of North Carolina and a large area of the South.

Major nearby universities include the University of North Carolina in Chapel Hill, Duke University in Durham, and the North Carolina State University's Raleigh campus. Chapel Hill, farthest west, has the most distinct college-town flavor, with an attractive small "college town USA" core and homes spread through surrounding wooded suburbs. The older-economy Durham still reflects a tobacco industry legacy, but has modernized somewhat with newer buildings downtown and a modest influx of new business. The Duke campus has a strong Ivy League feel. Raleigh, the state capital, is probably the least interesting of the three, although it has the strongest complement of historic sites and museums. Research Triangle Park (www.rtp.org) is an enormous, beautifully landscaped 7,000-acre complex housing premier facilities for 100 major world corporations and research agencies.

Due to this area's many strengths—solid universities, assorted high-paying professional jobs, a relatively low cost of living, a warm climate in the winter, and local cultural interests—many people move here from other areas of the country, particularly from the northeast, as well as from around the world. A vibrant arts scene exists, along with a strong community bond among the people arriving from elsewhere. Locals marvel at the Triad's informal, laid-back friendliness, and note that newcomers have no trouble quickly adapting to it.

Standard of Living Those not working at the Research Triangle Park, in the state government, or at a university will still find plenty of work in and around Cary. Commercial and industrial parks host regional offices and facilities for a variety of leading U.S. firms. The city is home to the SAS Institute, a leading supplier of statistical analysis software and consulting services. The city calls itself the "Technology Town of North Carolina." A relatively low cost of living is one of the area's draws, although comparatively Cary is a bit more upscale and expensive than some of its neighbors; it has a Cost of Living Index of 112. College towns and areas with high-paying technology jobs typically have costly housing—but not Triad and Cary. Good family homes start under $200K. A centrally located new 2,200-square-foot colonial on a ¼ acre is $230K, and $340K gets a 2,900-square-foot Plantation-style home on a ½ acre. Property taxes run about 1%, but daycare—at approximately $650 per month—is slightly more expensive than in other areas in the South.

Education Not surprisingly, the university and research park provide a strong educational backdrop, and fully 39% of Cary's population has a 4-year degree. Another 29% have graduate or professional-level education. Schools are solid, and the local Wake County Public School District was recently voted third best in the nation.

Lifestyle Cultural and recreational opportunities are abundant. Cary has a very active Parks, Recreation & Cultural Resources Department, maintaining over 20 parks, 6 bikeways, and numerous trails in the area. Highlights include the Koka Booth Amphitheater at Regency Park and the 310-acre Bond Park and Bond

CARY, NC
NEIGHBORHOOD HIGHLIGHTS

PEOPLE

Population	42,613
15-yr Population Growth	68.80%
5-yr Population Growth	14.60%
% Married w/Children	30.3%
% Single w/Children	5.6%
No. of Households	16,168
Median Age	31.2
Avg. Household Size	2.61
Diversity Measure	36

STANDARD OF LIVING

Median Household Income	$73,034
% Household Income > $100K	31%
Projected Future Job Growth	21%
Cost of Living Index	112
Buying Power Index	145
Weekly Daycare Cost	$159
Median Home Price	$242,300
"Sweet Spot" Home Price	$230,000
Home Price Ratio	3.3
Median Age of Homes	9.2
% Homes Owned	65%
Effective Property Tax Rate	1%
Estimated Property Tax Bill	$2,300

EDUCATION BEST

% High School Graduates	96%
% 4-yr Degree	39%
% Graduate or Professional Degree	29%
$ Invested per Pupil	$4,847
Student/Teacher Ratio	15.6
Primary Test Score Percentile	109.6
Secondary Test Score Percentile	113
% Subsidized School Lunch	28.60%
% Attending Public School	80%

LIFESTYLE

Leisure Rating (Area)	4
Arts & Culture Rating (Area)	8
Climate Rating (Area)	6
Physical Setting Rating	5
Downtown Core Rating	5
% Commute < 30 Min.	70%
% Commute > 1 Hour	3%

HEALTH & SAFETY BEST

Health Rating (Area)	8
Stress Score (Area)	5
Violent Crime Risk	83
Property Crime Risk	82

Park Community Center. The department manages an unusually full schedule of arts events, concerts, and activities. Beyond Cary, recreation is strong across the state, either west toward the mountains or east toward coastal areas about 3 hours away. Just north of Raleigh, the Falls Lake State Park on a 38,000-acre lake offers water and other outdoor recreation. Cultural opportunities abound at the university and nearby museums in Raleigh. The Exploris science and history museum is one of the best of its kind. The universities supply most of the spectator sports, but there's also a professional NHL team and a AAA minor-league team amusingly named the Durham Bulls.

Area growth and the assortment of places to live have created some traffic issues, and commutes to the Research Triangle can take 20 to 40 minutes. Fortunately, there are alternative back road routes. Cary is close to Raleigh-Durham Airport, a benefit for frequent business travelers.

The area is located at the edge of the flat Piedmont Plateau; hillier and more densely wooded areas start in the Raleigh area toward the west. Some influence from the nearby water and mountains provides a stable climate with a few periods of summer heat; winters are relatively mild with an occasional dusting of snow or ice and temperatures seldom fall below 20°F.

Health & Safety The crime risk is moderately low and the area has been recognized nationally for its law enforcement and safety programs. Healthcare facilities are modern and strengthened by university centers and the "WakeMed" (Western Wake County Medical Center) in Cary.

Nearby Neighborhoods A quieter and more upscale lifestyle can be found in Chapel Hill. Morrisville, just west of Cary, is also a bit more upscale and closer to the research park, but it's also close enough to the airport to have some noise issues. Apex, another suburb just west, is an attractive choice for families as well.

RALEIGH–DURHAM–CHAPEL HILL, NC
AREA HIGHLIGHTS

PEOPLE

SIZE & DIVERSITY	AREA	U.S. AVG	FAMILY DEMOGRAPHICS	AREA	U.S. AVG
Population	1,328,951		% Married	51.60%	53.80%
15-yr Population Growth	57%	4.40%	% Single	48.40%	46.20%
Diversity Measure	49	54	% Divorced	7.40%	10.20%
% Religiously Observant	40%	50%	% Separated	4.60%	2.10%
% Catholic	7%	22%	% Married w/Children	25.40%	27.90%
% Protestant	32%	25%	% Single w/Children	10.20%	9.40%
% Jewish	1%	2%	% Married, No Children	27.90%	31.00%
% Other	1%	1%	% Single, No Children	36.50%	31.70%

STANDARD OF LIVING

INCOME, EMPLOYMENT & TAXES	AREA	U.S. AVG	COST OF LIVING & HOUSING	AREA	U.S. AVG
Median Household Income	$49,562	$44,684	Cost of Living Index	100.1	100
Household Income Growth	3.30%	6.10%	Buying Power Index	111	100
Unemployment Rate	3.30%	5.10%	Median Home Price	$185,200	$208,500
Recent Job Growth	1%	1.30%	Home Price Ratio	3.7	4.7
Projected Future Job Growth	20.70%	10.50%	Home Price Appreciation	4.60%	13.60%
State Income Tax Rate	7%	5.00%	% Homes Owned	63.70%	64.10%
State Sales Tax Rate	4%	6.00%	Median Rent	$779	$792

EDUCATION

ATTAINMENT & ACHIEVEMENT	AREA	U.S. AVG	RESOURCES & INVESTMENT	AREA	U.S. AVG
% High School Graduate	80.40%	83.90%	No. of Highly Ranked Universities	2	1
% 2-yr Graduate	10.40%	7.10%	$ Invested per Pupil	$5,390	$6,058
% 4-yr Graduate	23.40%	17.20%	Student/Teacher Ratio	15.5	15.9
% Graduate or Professional Degree	12.10%	9.90%	State University In-State Tuition	$4,282	$4,917
% Attending Public School	91.10%	84.30%			
75th Percentile State University SAT Score (Verbal)	530	477			
75th Percentile State University SAT Score (Math)	570	478			
75th Percentile State University ACT Score	23	20			

LIFESTYLE

RECREATION, ARTS & CULTURE	AREA	U.S. AVG	INFRASTRUCTURE & FACILITIES	AREA	U.S. AVG
Professional Sports Rating	5	4	No. of Public Libraries	41	28
Zoos & Aquariums Rating	4	3	Library Volumes Per Capita	2.2	2.8
Amusement Park Rating	1	3	No. of Warehouse Clubs	5	4
Professional Theater Rating	6	3	No. of Starbucks	20	5
Overall Museum Rating	8	6	Golf Course Rating	6	4
Science Museum Rating	7	4	National Park Rating	1	3
Children's Museum Rating	6	3	Sq. Mi. Inland Water	2	4

CLIMATE			COMMUTE & TRANSPORTATION		
Days Mostly Sunny	220	212	Avg. Daily Commute Time	24.9	24.7
Annual Days Precipitation	112	111	% Commute by Auto	75%	77.70%
Annual Days > 90°F	25	38	Per Capita Avg. Daily Transit Miles	4.9	7.9
Annual Days < 32°F	82	88	Annual Auto Insurance Premium	$1,084	$1,314
July Relative Humidity	71	69	Gas, Cost per Gallon	$3.14	$3.05

HEALTH & SAFETY

CRIME & ENVIRNOMENTAL ISSUES	AREA	U.S. AVG	HEALTHCARE & COST	AREA	U.S. AVG
Violent Crime Rate	369	517	Physicians per Capita	417.6	254.3
Change in Violent Crime	-34.20%	-7.50%	Pediatricians per Capita	33.4	16.9
Property Crime Rate	3522	3783	Hospital Beds per Capita	352.4	239.7
Change in Property Crime	-31.60%	-10.10%	No. of Teaching Hospitals	6	1.9
Air Quality Score	37	44	Healthcare Cost Index	104.7	100
Water Quality Score	86	33	Cost per Doctor Visit	$86	$74
Pollen/Allergy Score	65	61	Cost per Dentist Visit	$80	$67
Stress Score	45	49	Cost per Hospital Room	$515	$702
Cancer Mortality Rate	161.2	168.9			

Castle Rock, CO

Area Type: Suburban town

Zip Code: 80104

Metro Area: Denver, CO

Metro Area Type: Large

Location: 30 miles south of Denver along I-25

Time Zone: Mountain Standard Time

Pros:
Attractive setting
Outdoor recreation
Small-town feel

Cons:
Long commutes
Cost of living
Growth and sprawl

"It's not easy being a realtor here; not many people are moving out," a real estate agent in Castle Rock says. After all, good schools, abundant outdoor activities, a growing social infrastructure, and easy (if long) commutes to Denver and Colorado Springs provide plenty of reasons to stay.

Castle Rock was established in 1881, 5 years after Colorado was granted statehood, and its historic downtown area offers a link to its past. That downtown mostly consists of smaller shops and city homes, while most of the larger commercial establishments are located north of town. Newer homes, of which there are many, are on all sides of town, except to the west, which is largely undeveloped. The "Rock" in Castle Rock is a formation that sits on a hill a half-mile north of the downtown area, easily visible from anywhere in town.

Castle Rock is nearly midway between Denver and Colorado Springs, on the main north–south corridor that runs through the eastern foothills of the Rockies. The expansion of Denver's tech industry to the south has made Castle Rock a convenient base for tech workers who want access to Denver's attractions but would prefer to live outside the city. Denver, of course, offers all the amenities of a modern metropolis: professional sports, fine restaurants, a well-regarded orchestra, and a large number of museums and other cultural attractions. Colorado Springs to the south is probably best known as the home of the United States Air Force Academy, but nearby are a number of spectacular outdoor locations as one ascends the Front Range, including Pike's Peak and Royal Gorge.

Although Castle Rock has a historic core, most of the area's infrastructure and residents are quite new on the scene. Growth is rampant—nearly 60% of the current population has lived there for 5 years or less, and over 80% of the homes are newly occupied in the last 10 years. It's a "new" old town, filled with educated young families. Almost 50% of the population has achieved a 4-year degree or beyond and 36% of households are categorized as married with children.

Standard of Living The last 5 years have seen rapid development in Castle Rock. Good-sized homes, well-planned subdivisions, and new construction are the norm, but a few older homes come onto the market occasionally. Lot sizes are larger in the older areas. Family homes start around $200K and are typically priced at, or slightly above, $100 per square foot. The "sweet spot" is $250K to $275K and many of the homes in this range are in the 3,000-square-foot range. While home prices are fairly attractive, especially considering the proximity to Denver, the overall cost of living is high, with a COL Index of 133. Growth pressure is strong, which means that there are some concerns over potential sprawl and crowding, and the growth combined with state statutory tax limits has caused some public finance concerns. But the strengthening commercial tax base has, so far, carried much of the additional burden. Douglas County property tax rates are a low 0.8%.

Education Rapid population growth does have an influence on schools, but the Douglas County Board of Education has generally kept up, placing schools high on the priority list. Pupil-teacher ratios are "higher than we would like" according to one parent, but are still under the national average. Overall achievement tests for Castle Rock schools are well above national and state averages. The district offers extensive Advanced Placement (AP) classes and a wide variety of co-curricular and technical programs, including agriculture, industrial technology, and performing arts.

Lifestyle Castle Rock is an excellent place for outdoor enthusiasts. Despite an average annual snowfall of 63 inches, there are nearly 250 sunny days and only 16 inches of rain per year. The town offers extensive recreational facilities, including two outdoor pools and one indoor pool, a recreation center, and a good municipal golf course. This place takes golf seriously. There are no fewer than seven championship courses within a 20-minute drive, and the municipal junior golf program has over 250 participants every summer. Skiing, naturally, is popular here, and Castle Rock is well situated for access to the many resorts along the Front Range. The town sponsors various public arts initiatives, including a museum and live theater. The county fairgrounds (in town) maintain an active calendar of events. In terms of shopping, you'll find big box retailers, and an outlet mall was recently added to the scene. Downtown Denver is an increasingly crowded 40-minute drive north; extensive south-side suburbs and commercial areas near Littleton are closer.

Commutes are long but relatively easy: Most workers in the area make the 25- to 35-minute drive north to the Denver Tech Center area or other commercial centers in Denver's south suburbs.

Although located at 6,200 feet, the town is not subject to the bitter cold or severe blizzards found at similar elevations elsewhere in Colorado. Summers are pleasant, with highs averaging in the mid-80s. Cool evenings and low humidity are typical in the region of mostly open, hilly terrain with seasonal streams and generally thin, high-desert vegetation. Front Range views on the clearest days are spectacular.

Health & Safety   Denver crime statistics are moderate, but crime risk in Castle Rock is far lower. Air quality is typically better in this area than in Denver, as well. The nearest hospital to Castle Rock is 10 minutes north in Lone Tree near the new E-470 beltway.

Nearby Neighborhoods   North of Castle Rock is Castle Pines, a smaller and pricier enclave of larger homes and country-club properties. Littleton choices are extensive and somewhat less expensive, but be prepared to trade the small-town feel for a more typical suburban lifestyle.

CASTLE ROCK, CO
NEIGHBORHOOD HIGHLIGHTS

PEOPLE

Population	41,386
15-yr Population Growth	294%
5-yr Population Growth	35.40%
% Married w/Children	35.6%
% Single w/Children	8.9%
No. of Households	14,519
Median Age	32.9
Avg. Household Size	2.82
Diversity Measure	17

STANDARD OF LIVING

Median Household Income	$78,438
% Household Income > $100K	34%
Projected Future Job Growth	52%
Cost of Living Index	133
Buying Power Index	132
Weekly Daycare Cost	$140
Median Home Price	$240,000
"Sweet Spot" Home Price	$260,000
Home Price Ratio	3.1
Median Age of Homes	9.4
% Homes Owned	79%
Effective Property Tax Rate	0.80%
Estimated Property Tax Bill	$2,002

EDUCATION

% High School Graduates	95%
% 4-yr Degree	32%
% Graduate or Professional Degree	14%
$ Invested per Pupil	$4,905
Student/Teacher Ratio	15.4
Primary Test Score Percentile	112.5
Secondary Test Score Percentile	136.9
% Subsidized School Lunch	4.80%
% Attending Public School	81.90%

LIFESTYLE

	BEST
Leisure Rating (Area)	9
Arts & Culture Rating (Area)	10
Climate Rating (Area)	5
Physical Setting Rating	8
Downtown Core Rating	6
% Commute < 30 Min.	47%
% Commute > 1 Hour	8%

HEALTH & SAFETY

Health Rating (Area)	5
Stress Score (Area)	7
Violent Crime Risk	22
Property Crime Risk	30

DENVER, CO
AREA HIGHLIGHTS
PEOPLE

SIZE & DIVERSITY	AREA	U.S. AVG	FAMILY DEMOGRAPHICS	AREA	U.S. AVG
Population	2,233,818		% Married	53.50%	53.80%
15-yr Population Growth	56.90%	4.40%	% Single	46.50%	46.20%
Diversity Measure	46	54	% Divorced	11.70%	10.20%
% Religiously Observant	39%	50%	% Separated	3.30%	2.10%
% Catholic	18%	22%	% Married w/Children	26.50%	27.90%
% Protestant	18%	25%	% Single w/Children	10.20%	9.40%
% Jewish	2%	2%	% Married, No Children	26.80%	31.00%
% Other	0%	1%	% Single, No Children	36.40%	31.70%

STANDARD OF LIVING

INCOME, EMPLOYMENT & TAXES	AREA	U.S. AVG	COST OF LIVING & HOUSING	AREA	U.S. AVG
Median Household Income	$54,167	$44,684	Cost of Living Index	112.2	100
Household Income Growth	5%	6.10%	Buying Power Index	108	100
Unemployment Rate	5%	5.10%	Median Home Price	$248,400	$208,500
Recent Job Growth	3.40%	1.30%	Home Price Ratio	4.6	4.7
Projected Future Job Growth	14.70%	10.50%	Home Price Appreciation	3.90%	13.60%
State Income Tax Rate	5%	5.00%	% Homes Owned	61.30%	64.10%
State Sales Tax Rate	7%	6.00%	Median Rent	$973	$792

EDUCATION

ATTAINMENT & ACHIEVEMENT	AREA	U.S. AVG	RESOURCES & INVESTMENT	AREA	U.S. AVG
% High School Graduate	87.30%	83.90%	No. of Highly Ranked Universities	2	1
% 2-yr Graduate	9.80%	7.10%	$ Invested per Pupil	$5,796	$6,058
% 4-yr Graduate	29.20%	17.20%	Student/Teacher Ratio	19.3	15.9
% Graduate or Professional Degree	12.80%	9.90%	State University In-State Tuition	$4,341	$4,917
% Attending Public School	90.80%	84.30%			
75th Percentile State University SAT Score (Verbal)	530	477			
75th Percentile State University SAT Score (Math)	550	478			
75th Percentile State University ACT Score	23	20			

LIFESTYLE

RECREATION, ARTS & CULTURE	AREA	U.S. AVG	INFRASTRUCTURE & FACILITIES	AREA	U.S. AVG
Professional Sports Rating	9	4	No. of Public Libraries	63	28
Zoos & Aquariums Rating	7	3	Library Volumes Per Capita	2.6	2.8
Amusement Park Rating	7	3	No. of Warehouse Clubs	5	4
Professional Theater Rating	10	3	No. of Starbucks	83	5
Overall Museum Rating	9	6	Golf Course Rating	7	4
Science Museum Rating	7	4	National Park Rating	3	3
Children's Museum Rating	7	3	Sq. Mi. Inland Water	3	4

CLIMATE			COMMUTE & TRANSPORTATION		
Days Mostly Sunny	246	212	Avg. Daily Commute Time	26.5	24.7
Annual Days Precipitation	88	111	% Commute by Auto	73%	77.70%
Annual Days > 90°F	32	38	Per Capita Avg. Daily Transit Miles	24.3	7.9
Annual Days < 32°F	163	88	Annual Auto Insurance Premium	$1,924	$1,314
July Relative Humidity	53	69	Gas, Cost per Gallon	$3.02	$3.05

HEALTH & SAFETY

CRIME & ENVIRNOMENTAL ISSUES	AREA	U.S. AVG	HEALTHCARE & COST	AREA	U.S. AVG
Violent Crime Rate	391	517	Physicians per Capita	264.3	254.3
Change in Violent Crime	1.80%	-7.50%	Pediatricians per Capita	20.2	16.9
Property Crime Rate	4367	3783	Hospital Beds per Capita	251.4	239.7
Change in Property Crime	3.70%	-10.10%	No. of Teaching Hospitals	18	1.9
Air Quality Score	26	44	Healthcare Cost Index	125.8	100
Water Quality Score	88	33	Cost per Doctor Visit	$96	$74
Pollen/Allergy Score	85	61	Cost per Dentist Visit	$77	$67
Stress Score	70	49	Cost per Hospital Room	$979	$702
Cancer Mortality Rate	152.8	168.9			

Charlottesville, VA

Area Type: Small college town

Zip Code: 22901

Metro Area: Charlottesville, VA

Metro Area Type: Small

Location: West-central Virginia at the base of the Blue Ridge Mountains 75 miles northwest of Richmond

Time Zone: Eastern Standard Time

Pros:
Attractive downtown and setting
Historic context
Education

Cons:
Rising home prices
Rapid growth
Air service

"Don't make us number one again—we just don't need the growth!" Such was the somewhat ironic response of a Chamber of Commerce board member we contacted about Charlottesville's qualities as a family place. Rest assured, we won't rank Charlottesville number one this time, as we did in our 2004 book *Cities Ranked & Rated,* but for many of the same reasons that previously put it on top, Charlottesville is hard to pass up as a best place for families.

More than 200 years ago, Thomas Jefferson saw the attractive Blue Ridge foothill area as the "Eden of the United States" and an ideal place for his mountaintop Monticello home. A few years later, he founded the University of Virginia in view of Monticello adjacent to downtown Charlottesville, then mainly a transportation gateway to the Blue Ridge and Shenandoah Valley to the west. Today, "C-ville" remains a citadel to American education, history, and architecture; it's an exceptional college town with a rich blend of east and south.

The beautiful campus is centered on Jefferson's original "Academical village." Its 24,000 students, colorful leaves, and prominent football and soccer teams create some truly picturesque and fun autumn weekends. Separated by a railroad embankment and bridge, Charlottesville has two downtowns: (1) University Avenue at the northern boundary of the campus and (2) the traditional downtown area with plenty of entertainment, shopping, and events. This traditional downtown area has regained its destination status with recent reinvestments in the pedestrian mall, a theater restoration, an amphitheater, a skating center, and the Virginia Discovery Museum.

Attractive and historic older neighborhoods surround the city, many housing university professors, fraternity members, and students. North of town, along the four-lane US 29, is an attractively executed retail and hospitality strip with access roads and setbacks, giving way to planned residential communities like Forest Lake. These neighborhoods, carved out of old estates, feature lakes and lots of wooded open space separating winding streets and avenues, looking little like typical American big-city suburbs. The best family housing is in these areas, and there are other similar developments west of the city. In other directions, particularly south, Charlottesville has retained a distinctly rural character, and in almost all parts of town, good planning and community synthesis on growth issues are evident. However, growth pressure brought by the area's attractiveness, intellectual climate, and proximity to Washington, DC, is an issue, forcing increased home prices and traffic, and it's not likely to abate soon.

Standard of Living As evidenced by the current unemployment rate of 2%, Charlottesville offers one of the most stable employment environments in the country, with jobs coming from the university, local healthcare facilities, pharmaceutical and biotech research groups, defense contractors, and a General Electric robotics joint venture, among others. The Cost of Living Index at 111 is reasonable, but it reflects an increasing influx of new residents and a degree of growth pressure. Likewise, home prices remain tolerable but are growing fast; most family homes start in the mid $300K to low $400K range, and more expensive homes are appearing as more wealth moves into the area. Most homes are beautifully set and have a distinctly Southern appearance. The Home Price Ratio of 5.6 reads higher than reality because of diminished student incomes. Property taxes range a reasonable 0.75% in Albemarle County to 1.1% within the city limits.

CHARLOTTESVILLE, VA NEIGHBORHOOD HIGHLIGHTS	
PEOPLE	
Population	34,275
15-yr Population Growth	30.20%
5-yr Population Growth	12%
% Married w/Children	20.9%
% Single w/Children	9.2%
No. of Households	15,287
Median Age	38
Avg. Household Size	2.27
Diversity Measure	33
STANDARD OF LIVING	
Median Household Income	$54,104
% Household Income > $100K	18%
Projected Future Job Growth	12%
Cost of Living Index	111
Buying Power Index	109
Weekly Daycare Cost	$140
Median Home Price	$304,300
"Sweet Spot" Home Price	$375,000
Home Price Ratio	5.6
Median Age of Homes	23.4
% Homes Owned	55%
Effective Property Tax Rate	1.10%
Estimated Property Tax Bill	$7,875
EDUCATION	BEST
% High School Graduates	91%
% 4-yr Degree	26%
% Graduate or Professional Degree	28%
$ Invested per Pupil	$6,640
Student/Teacher Ratio	12.4
Primary Test Score Percentile	99.1
Secondary Test Score Percentile	101.3
% Subsidized School Lunch	26.60%
% Attending Public School	80.40%
LIFESTYLE	
Leisure Rating (Area)	3
Arts & Culture Rating (Area)	6
Climate Rating (Area)	7
Physical Setting Rating	7
Downtown Core Rating	10
% Commute < 30 Min.	85%
% Commute > 1 Hour	2%
HEALTH & SAFETY	
Health Rating (Area)	10
Stress Score (Area)	4
Violent Crime Risk	88
Property Crime Risk	87

Education Few places exhibit the intellectual stimulation of Charlottesville, and the combined 4-year and graduate degree attainment exceeds 50%. The schools bond well with the university, offering strong academic programs as well as a holistic approach to education emphasizing extracurricular activities and personal development in areas other than grade-point averages. As an example, the schools are known for award-winning music programs.

Lifestyle The university attracts cultural amenities including art exhibits, theater performances, and concerts. The area is a museum of architecture and early American history. Downtown and the university areas offer vibrant, diverse, and affordable entertainment. Numerous parks and open spaces surround the city with summer programs, splash pools, and playgrounds. Outdoor recreation is mainly west in the Blue Ridge, with the Shenandoah National Park, George Washington National Forest, and the Blue Ridge Parkway. Orchards and horse farms spread in all directions, and horseback riding is a popular pastime. The newer Barracks Road Shopping Center, northwest of downtown, meets many shopping needs with 80-plus stores. The 2-hour trip to the Washington, DC, area takes 2½ to 3 hours due to congestion and growth, but it's still within reach. Other options include the King's Dominion amusement park 80 miles east near Richmond, and the Virginia Beach area 3 hours east.

Local commutes aren't an issue, and few residents regularly commute to other cities. Some work independently but are tied to clients or hiring organizations in the DC area and may make the trip occasionally. As with many other Virginia cities, proximity to DC hurts local air service.

Wooded mountains and rolling land characterize most of the area, becoming more mountainous to the west and flatter and more agricultural to the east. The mountains and ocean to the east modify the continental, four-season climate and block the harshest effects. The region enjoys relatively pleasant weather year-round.

Health & Safety The crime risk is moderate and typical for a college town. Between the university hospital and the not-for-profit Martha Jefferson hospital complex, healthcare is well covered and affordable.

Nearby Neighborhoods The best family areas are mainly in the north, but areas close to downtown are very attractive as well, although more expensive. New developments to the west along Barracks Road are also good choices, and areas south and east have a more rural feel with pockets of more expensive homes, many with acreage.

CHARLOTTESVILLE, VA
AREA HIGHLIGHTS

PEOPLE

SIZE & DIVERSITY	AREA	U.S. AVG	FAMILY DEMOGRAPHICS	AREA	U.S. AVG
Population	165,999		% Married	54%	53.80%
15-yr Population Growth	33.60%	4.40%	% Single	46%	46.20%
Diversity Measure	34	54	% Divorced	6.80%	10.20%
% Religiously Observant	36%	50%	% Separated	3.40%	2.10%
% Catholic	6%	22%	% Married w/Children	28.40%	27.90%
% Protestant	29%	25%	% Single w/Children	9.40%	9.40%
% Jewish	1%	2%	% Married, No Children	29.10%	31.00%
% Other	0%	1%	% Single, No Children	33.10%	31.70%

STANDARD OF LIVING

INCOME, EMPLOYMENT & TAXES	AREA	U.S. AVG	COST OF LIVING & HOUSING	AREA	U.S. AVG
Median Household Income	$49,916	$44,684	Cost of Living Index	110.5	100
Household Income Growth	2%	6.10%	Buying Power Index	101	100
Unemployment Rate	2%	5.10%	Median Home Price	$301,500	$208,500
Recent Job Growth	1.20%	1.30%	Home Price Ratio	6	4.7
Projected Future Job Growth	13.50%	10.50%	Home Price Appreciation	17.20%	13.60%
State Income Tax Rate	5.80%	5.00%	% Homes Owned	65.90%	64.10%
State Sales Tax Rate	3.50%	6.00%	Median Rent	$744	$792

EDUCATION

ATTAINMENT & ACHIEVEMENT	AREA	U.S. AVG	RESOURCES & INVESTMENT	AREA	U.S. AVG
% High School Graduate	74.30%	83.90%	No. of Highly Ranked Universities	1	1
% 2-yr Graduate	6.50%	7.10%	$ Invested per Pupil	$6,316	$6,058
% 4-yr Graduate	19.60%	17.20%	Student/Teacher Ratio	12.7	15.9
% Graduate or Professional Degree	14.20%	9.90%	State University In-State Tuition	$5,838	$4,917
% Attending Public School	83.60%	84.30%			
75th Percentile State University SAT Score (Verbal)	540	477			
75th Percentile State University SAT Score (Math)	560	478			
75th Percentile State University ACT Score	N/A	20			

LIFESTYLE

RECREATION, ARTS & CULTURE	AREA	U.S. AVG	INFRASTRUCTURE & FACILITIES	AREA	U.S. AVG
Professional Sports Rating	2	4	No. of Public Libraries	9	28
Zoos & Aquariums Rating	1	3	Library Volumes Per Capita	3	2.8
Amusement Park Rating	1	3	No. of Warehouse Clubs	3	4
Professional Theater Rating	1	3	No. of Starbucks	5	5
Overall Museum Rating	6	6	Golf Course Rating	1	4
Science Museum Rating	2	4	National Park Rating	4	3
Children's Museum Rating	6	3	Sq. Mi. Inland Water	2	4

CLIMATE			COMMUTE & TRANSPORTATION		
Days Mostly Sunny	218	212	Avg. Daily Commute Time	22.8	24.7
Annual Days Precipitation	125	111	% Commute by Auto	67%	77.70%
Annual Days > 90°F	19	38	Per Capita Avg. Daily Transit Miles	5.7	7.9
Annual Days < 32°F	94	88	Annual Auto Insurance Premium	$1,030	$1,314
July Relative Humidity	69	69	Gas, Cost per Gallon	$3.25	$3.05

HEALTH & SAFETY

CRIME & ENVIRNOMENTAL ISSUES	AREA	U.S. AVG	HEALTHCARE & COST	AREA	U.S. AVG
Violent Crime Rate	275	517	Physicians per Capita	821.1	254.3
Change in Violent Crime	-36.20%	-7.50%	Pediatricians per Capita	48	16.9
Property Crime Rate	2253	3783	Hospital Beds per Capita	543.5	239.7
Change in Property Crime	-30.30%	-10.10%	No. of Teaching Hospitals	1	1.9
Air Quality Score	66	44	Healthcare Cost Index	98.5	100
Water Quality Score	74	33	Cost per Doctor Visit	$86	$74
Pollen/Allergy Score	63	61	Cost per Dentist Visit	$70	$67
Stress Score	38	49	Cost per Hospital Room	$634	$702
Cancer Mortality Rate	159.1	168.9			

Chelmsford, MA

Area Type: Suburban town

Zip Code: 01824

Metro Area: Lowell, MA

Metro Area Type: Smaller

Location: 33 miles northwest of downtown Boston

Time Zone: Eastern Standard Time

Pros:
Strong economy and incomes
Attractive homes
Local sports and recreation

Cons:
Low future job growth
Narrow tax base
Area cost of living

Central to some of the best employment and lifestyle resources in the Boston area at a moderate cost, Chelmsford is one of the top selections among a large assortment of good family suburbs in this area. A quiet, built-out residential suburb surrounding a small-town core, Chelmsford has a spacious feel. It's green in summer, gorgeous in spring and fall, and, well, winter is winter. The downtown has a town square with banks, restaurants, and small shops. About 65% of the population is married, and 30% has children. There is a sprinkling of singles and older couples in the area.

Five miles north is the larger, historic, and revitalized textile mill town of Lowell, providing some quality recreation and, more recently, some jobs as the area recovers and grows out of its long textile slump. Boston is a long but still reasonable commute southeast from Chelmsford and many residents head north into New Hampshire for recreation and short getaways. Recent road improvements have made Boston and its stronger areas of employment on the north side more accessible.

Boston's numerous amenities and resources are further described in the discussion of Sharon, Massachusetts (p. 349). Boston may have a long rush-hour commute, but its resources are all within reach at other times and are quite accessible for an evening outing. Although corporate shifts and the recent technology slowdown slowed job growth in the Boston area as a whole, you're close to some job growth in and around Chelmsford. Some of the best area job prospects lie along the famed "Route 128" (I-95) beltway and its commercial and technology centers, near Burlington 13 miles southeast. Nearby cultural and historic resources include the Lowell National Historical Park, historic sites in Lexington and Concord, and the well-regarded Children's Discovery Museum and Science Discovery Museum in Acton. Chelmsford is relatively close to the northeastern shore; beach towns such as Gloucester, Rockport, and Salem are close enough for recreational trips.

Standard of Living Chelmsford is a middle-of-the-road suburb, less expensive than many nearby neighborhoods and most neighborhoods closer to the city. Typical family homes run in the mid $400K range, about $200 to $250 per square foot. Most homes are colonial or ranch style, and are comparatively new for the Boston area (median age of 36 years). Most are on ½-acre to 1-acre lots, but minimum lot sizes for new construction are 1 acre, consistent with the spacious feel of the area. The Cost of Living Index is 148, moderate for the Boston metro area. Median household income is just over $82,000, making family-style homes affordable for most.

Most Chelmsford workers are employed in the various large and small technology and financial services firms dotting the immediate area and the Route 128/I-95 loop. Fewer than 20% of residents make the 40-minute commute into Boston. But the area's lack of local industry and commerce makes it vulnerable to high property taxes. Rates of $11 per $1,000 (1.1%) are still relatively low on a local and national scale, but property values and assessments have been rising.

Education Over 27% of local residents possess a 4-year degree and another 18% have completed graduate or professional education. Local schools are viewed as "solid" and the Chelmsford School District, with eight schools and 5,700 students, consistently scores 10% to 20% above average on MCAS (Massachusetts Comprehensive Assessment) tests.

Lifestyle Chelmsford is quiet and quintessentially suburban with abundant youth sports and activities year-round. Minor-league baseball is played in Lowell, and the nearby Tsongas Arena hosts a minor-league hockey team. The greater area has an exceptional variety of things to do, and day or weekend trips to Boston and other points of interest in the suburbs, along the coast, on Cape Cod, or in other parts of New England are common. Winter sports buffs welcome abundant snows and head north to New Hampshire ski areas, many within 2 hours. Shoppers drive north year-round to avoid sales tax at the Pheasant Lane Mall, 15 miles outside of Nashua, New Hampshire.

Commutes have improved some on the north side of the Boston area. For most commuters headed south, the crowded US 3 is the first leg of the trip and the only leg for those headed to the Route 128 loop. A recent widening has brought some relief. For those headed farther south into Boston, the route of choice is I-93, and the famed "Big Dig" project has put much of this freeway underground and has added capacity. Taken together, these improvements have helped the downtown commute but it is still long, and many prefer to commute by rail. Downtown Boston is about 40 minutes by train and Route 128 commercial centers near Burlington and Woburn are about 25 minutes south by car. More Chelmsford commuters travel by auto (88%) than in most other Boston suburbs—because they are commuting to other suburbs, not downtown.

Chelmsford is in an area of gently rolling and mostly deciduous woods. The climate is complex, given to summer and winter extremes. Chelmsford is far enough inland to receive some of the region's harsher weather, and winter snow is persistent.

Health & Safety   Lowell metro area crime rates are very low, but the moderate Chelmsford crime risk more closely tracks that of Boston. Healthcare facilities are abundant, though expensive, nearby and in the Boston area. While the pace of local life is relaxing, the Boston area can be stressful for those not used to an East Coast big city.

Nearby Neighborhoods   Tewksbury to the east and Westford just to the west are comparable communities. For another $100K to $150K for a home, prospective residents may want to consider Acton or Concord to the south. For more historic interest and more of a "city" feel, Lowell is an attractive choice.

CHELMSFORD, MA
NEIGHBORHOOD HIGHLIGHTS

PEOPLE

Population	25,415
15-yr Population Growth	4.70%
5-yr Population Growth	-0.10%
% Married w/Children	29.6%
% Single w/Children	6.1%
No. of Households	9,429
Median Age	38.6
Avg. Household Size	2.66
Diversity Measure	14

STANDARD OF LIVING

Median Household Income	$82,209
% Household Income > $100K	32%
Projected Future Job Growth	6%
Cost of Living Index	148
Buying Power Index	125
Weekly Daycare Cost	$240
Median Home Price	$399,200
"Sweet Spot" Home Price	$450,000
Home Price Ratio	4.9
Median Age of Homes	37.5
% Homes Owned	83%
Effective Property Tax Rate	1.1%
Estimated Property Tax Bill	$5,400

EDUCATION

% High School Graduates	93%
% 4-yr Degree	27%
% Graduate or Professional Degree	18%
$ Invested per Pupil	$6,545
Student/Teacher Ratio	15.5
Primary Test Score Percentile	90.2
Secondary Test Score Percentile	72
% Subsidized School Lunch	3.90%
% Attending Public School	83.70%

LIFESTYLE

Leisure Rating (Area)	8
Arts & Culture Rating (Area)	6
Climate Rating (Area)	1
Physical Setting Rating	5
Downtown Core Rating	6
% Commute < 30 Min.	60%
% Commute > 1 Hour	7%

HEALTH & SAFETY

Health Rating (Area)	5
Stress Score (Area)	5
Violent Crime Risk	115
Property Crime Risk	76

LOWELL, MA
AREA HIGHLIGHTS

PEOPLE

SIZE & DIVERSITY	AREA	U.S. AVG	FAMILY DEMOGRAPHICS	AREA	U.S. AVG
Population	302,059		% Married	54.50%	53.80%
15-yr Population Growth	7.70%	4.40%	% Single	45.50%	46.20%
Diversity Measure	25	54	% Divorced	6.80%	10.20%
% Religiously Observant	73%	50%	% Separated	2.90%	2.10%
% Catholic	54%	22%	% Married w/Children	31.50%	27.90%
% Protestant	11%	25%	% Single w/Children	9.20%	9.40%
% Jewish	8%	2%	% Married, No Children	28.10%	31.00%
% Other	1%	1%	% Single, No Children	31.20%	31.70%

STANDARD OF LIVING

INCOME, EMPLOYMENT & TAXES	AREA	U.S. AVG	COST OF LIVING & HOUSING	AREA	U.S. AVG
Median Household Income	$65,906	$44,684	Cost of Living Index	113.4	100
Household Income Growth	3.30%	6.10%	Buying Power Index	130	100
Unemployment Rate	3.30%	5.10%	Median Home Price	$239,100	$208,500
Recent Job Growth	0.90%	1.30%	Home Price Ratio	3.6	4.7
Projected Future Job Growth	5.10%	10.50%	Home Price Appreciation	10.50%	13.60%
State Income Tax Rate	6%	5.00%	% Homes Owned	69.90%	64.10%
State Sales Tax Rate	5%	6.00%	Median Rent	$1,161	$792

EDUCATION

ATTAINMENT & ACHIEVEMENT	AREA	U.S. AVG	RESOURCES & INVESTMENT	AREA	U.S. AVG
% High School Graduate	85.60%	83.90%	No. of Highly Ranked Universities	0	1
% 2-yr Graduate	10.50%	7.10%	$ Invested per Pupil	$7,033	$6,058
% 4-yr Graduate	24.20%	17.20%	Student/Teacher Ratio	15.4	15.9
% Graduate or Professional Degree	12.80%	9.90%	State University In-State Tuition	$9,186	$4,917
% Attending Public School	86.40%	84.30%			
75th Percentile State University SAT Score (Verbal)	510	477			
75th Percentile State University SAT Score (Math)	520	478			
75th Percentile State University ACT Score	21	20			

LIFESTYLE

RECREATION, ARTS & CULTURE	AREA	U.S. AVG	INFRASTRUCTURE & FACILITIES	AREA	U.S. AVG
Professional Sports Rating	8	4	No. of Public Libraries	12	28
Zoos & Aquariums Rating	3	3	Library Volumes Per Capita	2.8	2.8
Amusement Park Rating	5	3	No. of Warehouse Clubs	5	4
Professional Theater Rating	8	3	No. of Starbucks	2	5
Overall Museum Rating	6	6	Golf Course Rating	5	4
Science Museum Rating	3	4	National Park Rating	2	3
Children's Museum Rating	3	3	Sq. Mi. Inland Water	4	4

CLIMATE			COMMUTE & TRANSPORTATION		
Days Mostly Sunny	197	212	Avg. Daily Commute Time	26.9	24.7
Annual Days Precipitation	137	111	% Commute by Auto	82%	77.70%
Annual Days > 90°F	15	38	Per Capita Avg. Daily Transit Miles	5	7.9
Annual Days < 32°F	120	88	Annual Auto Insurance Premium	$1,700	$1,314
July Relative Humidity	68	69	Gas, Cost per Gallon	$3.15	$3.05

HEALTH & SAFETY

CRIME & ENVIRNOMENTAL ISSUES	AREA	U.S. AVG	HEALTHCARE & COST	AREA	U.S. AVG
Violent Crime Rate	327	517	Physicians per Capita	387.9	254.3
Change in Violent Crime	-32.60%	-7.50%	Pediatricians per Capita	34	16.9
Property Crime Rate	1872	3783	Hospital Beds per Capita	401.2	239.7
Change in Property Crime	-16.60%	-10.10%	No. of Teaching Hospitals	0	1.9
Air Quality Score	12	44	Healthcare Cost Index	125.4	100
Water Quality Score	44	33	Cost per Doctor Visit	$98	$74
Pollen/Allergy Score	44	61	Cost per Dentist Visit	$87	$67
Stress Score	46	49	Cost per Hospital Room	$997	$702
Cancer Mortality Rate	184.6	168.9			

Columbia, MD

Area Type: Outer suburb/exurb

Zip Code: 21045

Metro Area: Baltimore, MD

Metro Area Type: Large

Location: 20 miles southwest of downtown Baltimore just west of I-95

Time Zone: Eastern Standard Time

Pros:

Effective community planning
Central location
Strong sense of community

Cons:

Long commutes
Rising costs
Growth pressure

BEST OF THE BEST

In 1964, Jim Rouse—the developer of Boston's Faneuil Hall and Harbor Place who is considered by many to be the founder of urban renewal—had a vision. He foresaw a city specifically planned to take advantage of its excellent location between two vibrant U.S. cities: Washington, DC, and Baltimore. The new city would avoid the problems of uncontrolled growth and be "a good place to live and work" with local jobs, amenities, recreation, and a strong sense of community aided by livable infrastructure.

Area farms were acquired into a blind trust much like the Disney Orlando properties were more famously a few years later. Forty years and 100,000 residents later, the community has matured into a well-kept East Coast secret of 14,000 acres with almost 5,300 acres of parkland and open space. The area has a town center (and a large mall) and is divided into nine self-contained villages with shopping and local necessities, parks, recreational facilities, and interconnecting roads and bike paths. Each village has a mix of single-family homes and townhouses. People meet socially at central mailbox kiosks and village centers, and many who grow up in the area return to further family and community ties. According to locals, the area's design and implementation really works.

Ideally, residents would work right in Columbia, but most employment is outside the area. Two-earner families commonly find one earner working in Baltimore and the other in the DC area (45 min. and 1 hr., respectively). More tend to work in the DC area despite the relative convenience of Baltimore. Recent commercial development around the nearby (10 miles) Baltimore-Washington International Airport has provided jobs, not to mention good air service for traveling professionals and Southwest Airlines for discount-fare seekers.

The area has a married-with-children percentage of 34.2%.

Standard of Living Despite the uniqueness and strengths of the community, the cost of living is relatively moderate for its location within this major East Coast area. The Cost of Living Index is 115, and good family homes are available in the upper $300Ks to mid $400Ks. Condos and townhouses sufficient for families (some with four bedrooms and basements) are blended in and typically run in the high $200Ks and low $300Ks. Most homes are typical split-levels and colonials (most, if not all, of which are 1960s and 1970s vintages) on ¼- to ½-acre wooded lots. Newer homes are available, but most are over $500K and typically on smaller lots, between ⅕ and ¼ acre. Incomes are strong and the Buying Power Index is a high 149, although this figure is probably achieved, in large part, through two-earner household incomes. Property taxes are about 0.75%, but the community association provides many services and recreational amenities that cost approximately 0.60% more, making the total taxes higher than in some other areas but not unreasonable for the region.

Education Schools are highly regarded, and consistently test 13% to 20% above state averages in the Maryland School Assessment. Not surprising in a planned community, school sizes are reasonable, with the larger high schools having 1,100 to 1,500 students. The educational context is strong, with 33% of residents having a 4-year degree; another 26% have graduate degrees. There is also a local community college.

Lifestyle The Columbia Association, as an incorporated nonprofit community association, operates a large set of recreational facilities for local residents, financed by association fees and modest additional membership

COLUMBIA, MD NEIGHBORHOOD HIGHLIGHTS	
PEOPLE	
Population	40,321
15-yr Population Growth	42.40%
5-yr Population Growth	7.60%
% Married w/Children	34.2%
% Single w/Children	11.0%
No. of Households	15,565
Median Age	33.9
Avg. Household Size	2.6
Diversity Measure	56
STANDARD OF LIVING	
Median Household Income	$76,424
% Household Income > $100K	27%
Projected Future Job Growth	25%
Cost of Living Index	115
Buying Power Index	149
Weekly Daycare Cost	$219
Median Home Price	$350,800
"Sweet Spot" Home Price	$400,000
Home Price Ratio	4.6
Median Age of Homes	22.3
% Homes Owned	67%
Effective Property Tax Rate	1.40%
Estimated Property Tax Bill	$5,400
EDUCATION	
% High School Graduates	94%
% 4-yr Degree	33%
% Graduate or Professional Degree	26%
$ Invested per Pupil	$7,188
Student/Teacher Ratio	12.9
Primary Test Score Percentile	138
Secondary Test Score Percentile	144.5
% Subsidized School Lunch	22.50%
% Attending Public School	81.90%
LIFESTYLE	**BEST**
Leisure Rating (Area)	9
Arts & Culture Rating (Area)	9
Climate Rating (Area)	4
Physical Setting Rating	4
Downtown Core Rating	7
% Commute < 30 Min.	54%
% Commute > 1 Hour	12%
HEALTH & SAFETY	
Health Rating (Area)	4
Stress Score (Area)	7
Violent Crime Risk	38
Property Crime Risk	34

and 4 indoor swimming pools. "Tot lots"—meaning playgrounds, 163 of them—dot the area. You'll also find a horse center, a zoo, a large park with fields for team sports, an ice rink, two golf courses, several museums, a few outdoor arts venues hosting outdoor concerts in the summer, and the Jim Rouse Theater for the Performing Arts with various theater and music events. Beyond recreation, a 230-store mall and several movie theaters are in the area. Top-notch attractions are available in the Baltimore area. The attractively redeveloped waterfront features the National Aquarium, one of the country's best. Spectator and participation sports are king, and the classic Camden Yards baseball facility is a noted icon of American sport.

Although the area was designed around a local live-and-work concept, most current residents commute and commute times can be long. Car-pool lanes help, and the MARC (Maryland Area Regional Commuter) line runs commuter trains to DC and Baltimore from nearby Jessup, 5 miles away. Some use a bus service to the Washington Metro at Silver Spring. Traffic, once hardly an issue due to good planning, has emerged as an occasional local complaint.

The area is gently rolling with mixed farmland, developed areas, and dense woods. The climate is coastal continental with four distinct seasons a bit moderated by water to the east. That water and mountains to the north moderate winter snows but large storms approaching from the south can bring occasionally heavy snow.

Health & Safety Crime rates in the Baltimore metro area run high, but crime risk as assessed in the "CAP" score is very low. The Howard County General Hospital, affiliated with Johns Hopkins in Baltimore, anchors a good set of healthcare facilities directly in Columbia.

Nearby Neighborhoods You can choose a village within the planned Columbia community according to taste and budget. The older "Owen Brown" community is among the more affordable, while River Hill is newer, more expensive, and attracting many younger families. Outside of the planned Columbia area, Ellicot City to the north offers an equivalent lifestyle and cost.

fees. Area parks offer plenty of water, bike trails, and walking paths. There are three lakes and over 80 miles of pathways. The Association runs 24 community centers with recreational facilities, including 23 outdoor

BALTIMORE, MD
AREA HIGHLIGHTS

PEOPLE

SIZE & DIVERSITY	AREA	U.S. AVG	FAMILY DEMOGRAPHICS	AREA	U.S. AVG
Population	2,639,213		% Married	53.30%	53.80%
15-yr Population Growth	13.80%	4.40%	% Single	46.70%	46.20%
Diversity Measure	48	54	% Divorced	7%	10.20%
% Religiously Observant	44%	50%	% Separated	5.20%	2.10%
% Catholic	21%	22%	% Married w/Children	28.30%	27.90%
% Protestant	18%	25%	% Single w/Children	10.30%	9.40%
% Jewish	4%	2%	% Married, No Children	30.30%	31.00%
% Other	1%	1%	% Single, No Children	31.10%	31.70%

STANDARD OF LIVING

INCOME, EMPLOYMENT & TAXES	AREA	U.S. AVG	COST OF LIVING & HOUSING	AREA	U.S. AVG
Median Household Income	$56,986	$44,684	Cost of Living Index	107.3	100
Household Income Growth	4.60%	6.10%	Buying Power Index	119	100
Unemployment Rate	4.60%	5.10%	Median Home Price	$264,700	$208,500
Recent Job Growth	2.30%	1.30%	Home Price Ratio	4.6	4.7
Projected Future Job Growth	13%	10.50%	Home Price Appreciation	21%	13.60%
State Income Tax Rate	7.50%	5.00%	% Homes Owned	67.90%	64.10%
State Sales Tax Rate	5.10%	6.00%	Median Rent	$847	$792

EDUCATION

ATTAINMENT & ACHIEVEMENT	AREA	U.S. AVG	RESOURCES & INVESTMENT	AREA	U.S. AVG
% High School Graduate	81.20%	83.90%	No. of Highly Ranked Universities	7	1
% 2-yr Graduate	7.40%	7.10%	$ Invested per Pupil	$6,846	$6,058
% 4-yr Graduate	21.10%	17.20%	Student/Teacher Ratio	16.8	15.9
% Graduate or Professional Degree	12.80%	9.90%	State University In-State Tuition	$7,410	$4,917
% Attending Public School	82.10%	84.30%			
75th Percentile State University SAT Score (Verbal)	560	477			
75th Percentile State University SAT Score (Math)	590	478			
75th Percentile State University ACT Score	N/A	20			

LIFESTYLE

RECREATION, ARTS & CULTURE	AREA	U.S. AVG	INFRASTRUCTURE & FACILITIES	AREA	U.S. AVG
Professional Sports Rating	9	4	No. of Public Libraries	82	28
Zoos & Aquariums Rating	10	3	Library Volumes Per Capita	3.6	2.8
Amusement Park Rating	5	3	No. of Warehouse Clubs	9	4
Professional Theater Rating	10	3	No. of Starbucks	29	5
Overall Museum Rating	10	6	Golf Course Rating	8	4
Science Museum Rating	9	4	National Park Rating	3	3
Children's Museum Rating	9	3	Sq. Mi. Inland Water	9	4

CLIMATE			COMMUTE & TRANSPORTATION		
Days Mostly Sunny	205	212	Avg. Daily Commute Time	29.8	24.7
Annual Days Precipitation	112	111	% Commute by Auto	73%	77.70%
Annual Days > 90°F	31	38	Per Capita Avg. Daily Transit Miles	17.2	7.9
Annual Days < 32°F	100	88	Annual Auto Insurance Premium	$1,430	$1,314
July Relative Humidity	67	69	Gas, Cost per Gallon	$3.30	$3.05

HEALTH & SAFETY

CRIME & ENVIRNOMENTAL ISSUES	AREA	U.S. AVG	HEALTHCARE & COST	AREA	U.S. AVG
Violent Crime Rate	883	517	Physicians per Capita	379.4	254.3
Change in Violent Crime	-17.10%	-7.50%	Pediatricians per Capita	30.2	16.9
Property Crime Rate	3818	3783	Hospital Beds per Capita	493.5	239.7
Change in Property Crime	-26.10%	-10.10%	No. of Teaching Hospitals	18	1.9
Air Quality Score	37	44	Healthcare Cost Index	95.9	100
Water Quality Score	50	33	Cost per Doctor Visit	$79	$74
Pollen/Allergy Score	65	61	Cost per Dentist Visit	$73	$67
Stress Score	71	49	Cost per Hospital Room	$750	$702
Cancer Mortality Rate	194.7	168.9			

Columbia, MO

Area Type: Small college town

Zip Code: 65203

Metro Area: Columbia, MO

Metro Area Type: Smaller

Location: Central Missouri, 125 miles west of St. Louis along I-70

Time Zone: Central Standard Time

Pros:

College-town amenities
Parks and recreation
Healthcare

Cons:

Lack of entertainment (especially in summer)
Isolation
Recent job growth

Coastal dwellers sometimes refer to the central part of the United States as "the fly-over part" of the country. Missouri, in the heart of this fly-over territory, has St. Louis in the east, Kansas City in the west, and lots of small towns along the Missouri River and I-70 in between. The largest of these by far is Columbia, or "College Town USA," which houses Columbia College, Stephens College, and the University of Missouri. The 90,000 residents in this well-educated small Midwestern town are friendly and welcoming—so welcoming, in fact, that newcomers are common; 30% of Columbia's nonstudent population has lived in the area for 5 years or less.

Columbia is set in the gently rolling plains at the edge of the Missouri Valley. Imagine a quiet little town with 40,000 college students, and you've got Columbia. Eight of the top 11 employers are in the public sector, but numerous private firms and healthcare facilities employ some two-thirds of the work force. Private employers include light manufacturing, biotech research, telecommunications, and insurance—among whom State Farm and Shelter are the largest. While recent employment dipped a bit, the private sector expects strong growth in the next 5 years, and the city is building infrastructure to support the expected increase in population.

Columbia is clean and well managed with strong Midwestern roots and just a hint of the South, offering a moderate, low-stress pace of life in an academic, middle-America location. The chosen zip code (65203) lies mainly west of the town and campus, and contains a mix of older homes in a city-neighborhood environment and newer suburbs to the west. The married-with-children percentage is 25%, which is fairly high for a college town.

Standard of Living Columbia's basic cost indexes are lower than national averages, which is unusual for a college town. The COL Index for the southwest neighborhood is just over 96. Because it's a college town, median household income statistics are likely understated, but the bottom line is that the standard of living is healthy for working families. Homes are attractive and fairly priced, with the "sweet spot" for a new family home running about $200K. Good but somewhat smaller homes are available starting at $150K, while $250K might land you a 3,000-square-foot home with extras. Many of the older homes closer to town are better values. Property taxes are low at around 1%.

Education The presence of two large universities ("Mizzou" and Columbia College) in a relatively small town cannot be overestimated; over 50% of Columbia residents have 4-year or advanced degrees. Columbia's school system performs significantly better than the state average on standardized tests. Student-teacher ratios are under 15 at most schools and SAT scores are significantly higher than national averages. Columbia schools also produce a very high percentage of National Merit Scholars.

Lifestyle Columbia offers a fair variety of entertainment opportunities, although most are tied to the universities. When summer arrives, things slow down a lot. Biking is very popular, and not just around campus. The city has a 30-mile network of bike paths and trails used by students, commuters, exercisers, and leisure riders. The city is also located on the Katy Trail, a reconditioned rail trail crossing the state from St. Louis to Kansas City. Beyond these features, Columbia has an excellent park and recreation system with notable facilities, including a nationally recognized skate park and roller hockey arena. There are six outdoor swimming pools and lakes and two indoor aquatic centers. The "ARC" or Activity and Recreation Center Water Zone is an elegant 13,000-square-foot indoor water park with slides, play structures, and a hydrotherapy pool opened just 4 years ago. Columbia is well situated for hunting, fishing, and watersports at the area's many nearby lakes. To get from downtown to "the country" takes no more than 15 minutes by car. Downtown Columbia is safe and has some interesting shopping, but high-end retail is sparse. Those needing a big-city fix from time to time (or a major airport) can travel to St. Louis, 90 minutes away.

The only downfall here may be that the weather's not for everyone—Columbia's summer heat and humidity last from early June to late September, with frequent rain. In fact, you can count on about 3 inches of rain every month of the year. Columbia also gets about 2 feet of snow per year, but most accumulations are less than half an inch. Spring and fall temperatures are very pleasant.

Health & Safety   Property crime rates are close to national averages, not uncommon for a college town, and most of these crimes are probably of a lesser severity than in other places. Air quality, health, and stress scores are all favorable. The area is known for its excellent healthcare facilities: Columbia has nearly 750 physicians in a town of 90,000, three times as many per capita compared to the nation on average, and twice the number of hospital beds. Healthcare costs are below national averages.

Nearby Neighborhoods   The areas south and west of town have newer and more attractive homes, while the homes in the 65202 zip code on the east side are less expensive and more modest in appearance.

COLUMBIA, MO NEIGHBORHOOD HIGHLIGHTS	
PEOPLE	
Population	47,459
15-yr Population Growth	25.80%
5-yr Population Growth	4.40%
% Married w/Children	24.9%
% Single w/Children	10.2%
No. of Households	19,763
Median Age	34.1
Avg. Household Size	2.41
Diversity Measure	30
STANDARD OF LIVING	
Median Household Income	$46,667
% Household Income > $100K	15%
Projected Future Job Growth	20%
Cost of Living Index	96.2
Buying Power Index	108
Weekly Daycare Cost	$155
Median Home Price	$177,600
"Sweet Spot" Home Price	$200,000
Home Price Ratio	3.8
Median Age of Homes	23.4
% Homes Owned	58%
Effective Property Tax Rate	1%
Estimated Property Tax Bill	$2,000
EDUCATION	
% High School Graduates	93%
% 4-yr Degree	29%
% Graduate or Professional Degree	27%
$ Invested per Pupil	$5,146
Student/Teacher Ratio	13.9
Primary Test Score Percentile	123.9
Secondary Test Score Percentile	210.5
% Subsidized School Lunch	25.20%
% Attending Public School	86.10%
LIFESTYLE	
Leisure Rating (Area)	3
Arts & Culture Rating (Area)	7
Climate Rating (Area)	4
Physical Setting Rating	4
Downtown Core Rating	6
% Commute < 30 Min.	84%
% Commute > 1 Hour	3%
HEALTH & SAFETY	BEST
Health Rating (Area)	7
Stress Score (Area)	2
Violent Crime Risk	72
Property Crime Risk	74

COLUMBIA, MO
AREA HIGHLIGHTS

PEOPLE

SIZE & DIVERSITY	AREA	U.S. AVG	FAMILY DEMOGRAPHICS	AREA	U.S. AVG
Population	141,367		% Married	49.80%	53.80%
15-yr Population Growth	25.80%	4.40%	% Single	50.20%	46.20%
Diversity Measure	27	54	% Divorced	8.50%	10.20%
% Religiously Observant	41%	50%	% Separated	2%	2.10%
% Catholic	7%	22%	% Married w/Children	24.60%	27.90%
% Protestant	33%	25%	% Single w/Children	10%	9.40%
% Jewish	0%	2%	% Married, No Children	25.80%	31.00%
% Other	1%	1%	% Single, No Children	39.50%	31.70%

STANDARD OF LIVING

INCOME, EMPLOYMENT & TAXES	AREA	U.S. AVG	COST OF LIVING & HOUSING	AREA	U.S. AVG
Median Household Income	$40,813	$44,684	Cost of Living Index	91.3	100
Household Income Growth	2.40%	6.10%	Buying Power Index	100	100
Unemployment Rate	2.40%	5.10%	Median Home Price	$153,700	$208,500
Recent Job Growth	-0.50%	1.30%	Home Price Ratio	3.8	4.7
Projected Future Job Growth	15.50%	10.50%	Home Price Appreciation	7.40%	13.60%
State Income Tax Rate	6%	5.00%	% Homes Owned	60.60%	64.10%
State Sales Tax Rate	4.20%	6.00%	Median Rent	$557	$792

EDUCATION

ATTAINMENT & ACHIEVEMENT	AREA	U.S. AVG	RESOURCES & INVESTMENT	AREA	U.S. AVG
% High School Graduate	85.10%	83.90%	No. of Highly Ranked Universities	1	1
% 2-yr Graduate	6.90%	7.10%	$ Invested per Pupil	$5,234	$6,058
% 4-yr Graduate	22.70%	17.20%	Student/Teacher Ratio	14.5	15.9
% Graduate or Professional Degree	15.20%	9.90%	State University In-State Tuition	$6,622	$4,917
% Attending Public School	92.20%	84.30%			
75th Percentile State University SAT Score (Verbal)	540	477			
75th Percentile State University SAT Score (Math)	540	478			
75th Percentile State University ACT Score	23	20			

LIFESTYLE

RECREATION, ARTS & CULTURE	AREA	U.S. AVG	INFRASTRUCTURE & FACILITIES	AREA	U.S. AVG
Professional Sports Rating	2	4	No. of Public Libraries	4	28
Zoos & Aquariums Rating	1	3	Library Volumes Per Capita	2.7	2.8
Amusement Park Rating	1	3	No. of Warehouse Clubs	3	4
Professional Theater Rating	1	3	No. of Starbucks	0	5
Overall Museum Rating	4	6	Golf Course Rating	2	4
Science Museum Rating	4	4	National Park Rating	1	3
Children's Museum Rating	1	3	Sq. Mi. Inland Water	2	4

CLIMATE			COMMUTE & TRANSPORTATION		
Days Mostly Sunny	191	212	Avg. Daily Commute Time	17.8	24.7
Annual Days Precipitation	109	111	% Commute by Auto	67%	77.70%
Annual Days > 90°F	39	38	Per Capita Avg. Daily Transit Miles	5	7.9
Annual Days < 32°F	108	88	Annual Auto Insurance Premium	$1,087	$1,314
July Relative Humidity	69	69	Gas, Cost per Gallon	$3.06	$3.05

HEALTH & SAFETY

CRIME & ENVIRNOMENTAL ISSUES	AREA	U.S. AVG	HEALTHCARE & COST	AREA	U.S. AVG
Violent Crime Rate	351	517	Physicians per Capita	746.2	254.3
Change in Violent Crime	-1.60%	-7.50%	Pediatricians per Capita	33.3	16.9
Property Crime Rate	3272	3783	Hospital Beds per Capita	858.6	239.7
Change in Property Crime	-23.20%	-10.10%	No. of Teaching Hospitals	2	1.9
Air Quality Score	44	44	Healthcare Cost Index	94.1	100
Water Quality Score	60	33	Cost per Doctor Visit	$74	$74
Pollen/Allergy Score	55	61	Cost per Dentist Visit	$56	$67
Stress Score	18	49	Cost per Hospital Room	$750	$702
Cancer Mortality Rate	154.4	168.9			

Coralville, IA

Area Type: College-town suburb

Zip Code: 52241

Metro Area: Iowa City, IA

Metro Area Type: Small

Location: 4 miles west of downtown Iowa City along US 6

Time Zone: Central Standard Time

Pros:

Small-town feel
College-town amenities
Education

Cons:

Recent employment declines
Isolation
Harsh winters

Most U.S. maps don't draw a boundary line around the "Midwest"—a familiar term, but one that's not easily defined. *Activity:* Get out a map and draw a circle around *your* definition of this territory. Next, point your pencil to the center of this space. If your pencil isn't pointing to Iowa City, Iowa, it's probably pointing to somewhere very close. Suffice it to say, the rich agricultural, industrial, and sociological area commonly called the Midwest includes the fertile lowlands between the Great Lakes and the Great Plains, encompassing Iowa, Illinois, and parts of Minnesota, Wisconsin, Nebraska, Kansas, Missouri, Indiana, and Ohio, among others.

The so-called "Heart of the Saints" region occupies the center of a 600-mile north–south "Avenue of the Saints" (now US 218) corridor between St. Louis, Missouri, and St. Paul, Minnesota. The region includes such eastern Iowa towns as Cedar Rapids, Cedar Falls–Waterloo, the Amana Colonies, and the Iowa City–Coralville area. At Iowa City, the Avenue crosses I-80, the state's—and the Midwest's—major east–west artery. But as the center of this great region, is the Iowa City skyline dominated by towering grain elevators, rail sidings, and food processing plants? You might expect that, and indeed, there are a few such facilities serving local agricultural interests, but that's where the image ends. Instead, the top-rated University of Iowa brings 30,000 students and a progressive small-town lifestyle to this interesting and cosmopolitan town of 60,000 full-time residents, and the "skyline" consists of limestone and brick academic buildings with a golden dome in the center, small commercial downtown streets, and the long, low buildings of modern new-economy industry.

Iowa City's attractive downtown campus is located along the Iowa River surrounded by tree-lined grid streets. The waterfront is attractive, lively, historic, and walkable, with plenty of entertainment and interesting small retail establishments that are pretty much what you'd expect to find in a college town. Football weekends are electric—and hectic—but otherwise, the pace of life might be described as just right: It's not too slow and not too fast. Attractive older neighborhoods to the east give way to some smaller newer suburbs and industrial parks hosting a small assortment of biotech research and other light industry facilities. The older neighborhoods in the University Heights area, just to the west of the river, are quickly giving way to the newer and more commercial areas at the north and west along US 6, the original artery.

About 4 miles west of downtown lies the small town of Coralville, originally a mill town along the Iowa River. Today, with 17,000 residents (up from 1,000 in 1950), it is one of Iowa's fastest growing towns. The demographic mix is diverse, with 19% of households married with children, a strong presence of single students, and a number of retirees in the mix (in 2005, Coralville was selected by *Money Magazine* as a "Best Place to Retire"). Anchored by the beautifully renovated Town Center and the new Coral Ridge Mall, the suburban neighborhoods—spreading west and north across I-80—offer convenience and access to a great college town at a reasonable price.

Standard of Living   College towns typically are more expensive than others in the region, and Iowa City–Coralville is no exception. But the "premium" is relatively modest. The Cost of Living Index of 97, while high for the region, is attractive on a national scale. Good homes can be found under $200K with a "sweet spot" for family homes in the mid to high $200Ks. Property taxes work out to about 1.6% and are a bit

CORALVILLE, IA NEIGHBORHOOD HIGHLIGHTS	
PEOPLE	
Population	15,942
15-yr Population Growth	20.80%
5-yr Population Growth	4.60%
% Married w/Children	18.5%
% Single w/Children	8.0%
No. of Households	6,878
Median Age	32
Avg. Household Size	2.21
Diversity Measure	26
STANDARD OF LIVING	
Median Household Income	$39,766
% Household Income > $100K	11%
Projected Future Job Growth	10%
Cost of Living Index	96.9
Buying Power Index	88
Weekly Daycare Cost	$150
Median Home Price	$171,600
"Sweet Spot" Home Price	$275,000
Home Price Ratio	4.3
Median Age of Homes	20.3
% Homes Owned	46%
Effective Property Tax Rate	1.60%
Estimated Property Tax Bill	$4,400
EDUCATION	
% High School Graduates	96%
% 4-yr Degree	30%
% Graduate or Professional Degree	22%
$ Invested per Pupil	$5,646
Student/Teacher Ratio	16
Primary Test Score Percentile	109.1
Secondary Test Score Percentile	0
% Subsidized School Lunch	21.20%
% Attending Public School	88.50%
LIFESTYLE	
Leisure Rating (Area)	1
Arts & Culture Rating (Area)	6
Climate Rating (Area)	3
Physical Setting Rating	3
Downtown Core Rating	5
% Commute < 30 Min.	83%
% Commute > 1 Hour	3%
HEALTH & SAFETY	BEST
Health Rating (Area)	10
Stress Score (Area)	2
Violent Crime Risk	109
Property Crime Risk	103

Education Education is, not surprisingly, strong at all levels. In Coralville, more than 50% of residents possess at least a 4-year degree. The Iowa City West High School is a bit crowded, but it offers robust and balanced academics and extracurricular programs, many synchronized with the local university. New schools currently being built to the north, in North Liberty, should alleviate some of the crowding.

Lifestyle "Midwestern, but with a college-town flair" is a fair description of this area. Although much of Coralville has a typical suburban feel, areas along the river and in the old "Strip," a historic downtown district, offer good entertainment, restaurants, and other activities. The 120-store Coral Ridge Mall isn't just a shopping destination—it also houses the Iowa Children's Museum, along with a skating rink and numerous other things to do. Beyond the mall, a full set of city park and recreation activities are also available, with an excellent new aquatic center and an indoor gym set up for kids where "parents can actually relax." Bike trails along the Iowa River and lakes to the north of Coralville provide some opportunities for outdoor recreation. The university provides all forms of entertainment and many museums—locals mention not only their quality but also the affordable cost (usually free) of these amenities.

Commutes into downtown and to the industrial areas to the east are easy and seldom take more than 15 minutes. Aside from Des Moines, an assortment of larger cities lie 250 to 300 miles in all directions but can be hard to get to in winter, and air service is limited.

For the region, the area is relatively scenic, with a mix of flat and rolling farms and woodlands surrounding river valleys. The climate is continental with warm, humid summers and cold, rigorous, variable, and often snowy winters.

Health & Safety Crime risk is moderate and typical for college towns but not a factor for most Coralville residents. With three local hospitals, including the university's hospital, healthcare services are excellent.

Nearby Neighborhoods If you're looking for more of a "city" lifestyle, closer to the campus and college activities, the inner neighborhoods east are excellent and the attractive older homes are quite affordable. Affordable suburban environments, still close enough to the city's attractions, can be found to the north and east toward I-80.

lower than those in Iowa City itself. Daycare is about $600 per month. College towns can also present some employment issues particularly for those not in education or healthcare fields, and recent employment statistics have been weak; but a small diverse industrial base should lead to improved employment opportunities.

IOWA CITY, IA
AREA HIGHLIGHTS

PEOPLE

SIZE & DIVERSITY	AREA	U.S. AVG	FAMILY DEMOGRAPHICS	AREA	U.S. AVG
Population	116,097		% Married	54.20%	53.80%
15-yr Population Growth	20.80%	4.40%	% Single	45.80%	46.20%
Diversity Measure	20	54	% Divorced	6.90%	10.20%
% Religiously Observant	37%	50%	% Separated	1.20%	2.10%
% Catholic	16%	22%	% Married w/Children	28.70%	27.90%
% Protestant	20%	25%	% Single w/Children	6.40%	9.40%
% Jewish	1%	2%	% Married, No Children	28.20%	31.00%
% Other	0%	1%	% Single, No Children	36.70%	31.70%

STANDARD OF LIVING

INCOME, EMPLOYMENT & TAXES	AREA	U.S. AVG	COST OF LIVING & HOUSING	AREA	U.S. AVG
Median Household Income	$40,344	$44,684	Cost of Living Index	88.6	100
Household Income Growth	3.90%	6.10%	Buying Power Index	102	100
Unemployment Rate	3.90%	5.10%	Median Home Price	$131,800	$208,500
Recent Job Growth	-2.40%	1.30%	Home Price Ratio	3.3	4.7
Projected Future Job Growth	9.20%	10.50%	Home Price Appreciation	6.20%	13.60%
State Income Tax Rate	7.90%	5.00%	% Homes Owned	65.90%	64.10%
State Sales Tax Rate	5%	6.00%	Median Rent	$648	$792

EDUCATION

ATTAINMENT & ACHIEVEMENT	AREA	U.S. AVG	RESOURCES & INVESTMENT	AREA	U.S. AVG
% High School Graduate	90.80%	83.90%	No. of Highly Ranked Universities	1	1
% 2-yr Graduate	11.80%	7.10%	$ Invested per Pupil	$5,599	$6,058
% 4-yr Graduate	28.20%	17.20%	Student/Teacher Ratio	17.2	15.9
% Graduate or Professional Degree	16.90%	9.90%	State University In-State Tuition	$5,396	$4,917
% Attending Public School	91.30%	84.30%			
75th Percentile State University SAT Score (Verbal)	530	477			
75th Percentile State University SAT Score (Math)	540	478			
75th Percentile State University ACT Score	22	20			

LIFESTYLE

RECREATION, ARTS & CULTURE	AREA	U.S. AVG	INFRASTRUCTURE & FACILITIES	AREA	U.S. AVG
Professional Sports Rating	2	4	No. of Public Libraries	5	28
Zoos & Aquariums Rating	1	3	Library Volumes Per Capita	3.6	2.8
Amusement Park Rating	1	3	No. of Warehouse Clubs	1	4
Professional Theater Rating	1	3	No. of Starbucks	2	5
Overall Museum Rating	5	6	Golf Course Rating	2	4
Science Museum Rating	3	4	National Park Rating	1	3
Children's Museum Rating	1	3	Sq. Mi. Inland Water	2	4

CLIMATE			COMMUTE & TRANSPORTATION		
Days Mostly Sunny	194	212	Avg. Daily Commute Time	17.7	24.7
Annual Days Precipitation	107	111	% Commute by Auto	67%	77.70%
Annual Days > 90°F	16	38	Per Capita Avg. Daily Transit Miles	13.8	7.9
Annual Days < 32°F	157	88	Annual Auto Insurance Premium	$853	$1,314
July Relative Humidity	73	69	Gas, Cost per Gallon	$3.07	$3.05

HEALTH & SAFETY

CRIME & ENVIRNOMENTAL ISSUES	AREA	U.S. AVG	HEALTHCARE & COST	AREA	U.S. AVG
Violent Crime Rate	394	517	Physicians per Capita	1084.4	254.3
Change in Violent Crime	-28%	-7.50%	Pediatricians per Capita	58.9	16.9
Property Crime Rate	2653	3783	Hospital Beds per Capita	860.7	239.7
Change in Property Crime	-19.70%	-10.10%	No. of Teaching Hospitals	2	1.9
Air Quality Score	49	44	Healthcare Cost Index	92	100
Water Quality Score	73	33	Cost per Doctor Visit	$73	$74
Pollen/Allergy Score	46	61	Cost per Dentist Visit	$55	$67
Stress Score	18	49	Cost per Hospital Room	$712	$702
Cancer Mortality Rate	156.7	168.9			

Coraopolis—Moon Township, PA

Area Type: Suburban town/Outer suburb

Zip Code: 15108

Metro Area: Pittsburgh, PA

Metro Area Type: Large

Location: 18 miles west of downtown Pittsburgh

Time Zone: Eastern Standard Time

Pros:
Attractive setting
Strong, revitalizing urban area
Good schools

Cons:
Spells of clouds and rain
Economic cycles
Possible airport noise

Few cities have gone through as big a transition as Pittsburgh has during the last 30 years. Years ago, the area's steel and related industries had created a sooty, dirty atmosphere with smoke trapped in the area's river valleys. There was a gritty look and feel almost everywhere. Today, the big blast furnaces are mostly gone (one remains) and the economy has rapidly transitioned into a new-age economy with banks, financial institutions, pharmaceutical companies, and science and technology research firms leading the way. Pittsburgh balances its elements of old and new, and offers opportunities in commerce and industry as well as cultural, educational, and recreational amenities.

Coraopolis is an old industrial town located just a few miles down the Ohio River from the "Point"—the convergence of the Allegheny and Monongahela Rivers, which define today's downtown Pittsburgh. The current revitalized town has become attractive to professional singles and couples, but its older infrastructure and still-developing school system make the city itself a little less than perfect for families. However, just south on the plateau above the river valley, Moon Township and several adjacent townships have a commercial base and a suburban mix that's well suited for family life.

Pittsburgh's strength lies in endowments left from the past, a strong civic pride, and healthy businesses that have grown and continue to choose to call the area home. The Carnegie and Mellon endowments have supported numerous excellent facilities, including the highly-rated university of their names. "The Carnegie" complex hosts the Carnegie Science Center, Carnegie Museum of Art, Carnegie Museum of Natural History, Carnegie Music Hall, and Carnegie Library. The science and performing arts centers stand out, as do performing organizations such as the Pittsburgh Symphony. The University of Pittsburgh and several good smaller colleges round out a strong higher education scene. The downtown area is attractive and has once again become an entertainment and cultural destination. Corporate offices for PNC Bank, Mellon Financial, food giant Heinz Corporation, industrialists PPG Industries and Alcoa, and pharmaceutical maker Mylan Laboratories anchor the downtown area and the area-wide job base. A variety of neighborhoods fan out in all directions up the rivers and in the hills surrounding the city.

Standard of Living   Homes in the Moon Township area are plentiful and attractively priced. Good family homes on ½ acres with basements start at about $225K and the "sweet spot" is in the $250K to $275K range. Property tax rates are high at about 2.5%, but they support high quality services and amenities. The cost of living index is at par at 100, attractive for a good family area. Economic diversity provides a stable job environment and, recently, there's been strong job and income growth. Pharmaceutical giant GlaxoSmithKline and Bayer Chemical employ a large number of people in the immediate area. While future job growth projections are still low at 1%, we feel these figures understate the potential of the immediate area, particularly on top of the plateau in Moon Township.

Education   Schools are among the first things you hear about when talking to local residents. The Moon Area School District features six top-rated schools with a total of 3,600 students. Test scores consistently run 15% to 30% higher than state averages. The Robert Morris University provides a local higher education presence in addition to the many good schools in the Pittsburgh area.

Lifestyle   Parks are available for family activities and nearby shopping malls serve purchasing needs. Beyond the downtown museums, the noted Pittsburgh Zoo and

PPG Aquarium and Pittsburgh Children's Museum provide more family activities. The hilly countryside and rivers have numerous spots for hiking and boating activities. Sports are big in the area, stimulated by strong professional teams such as the Steelers, Pirates, and Penguins franchises.

Most jobs are within 10 to 12 miles of the Moon Township area. Downtown commutes are easy and usually take no more than 25 to 30 minutes. Park-and-ride facilities feed a good and well-utilized bus system. The Pittsburgh International Airport lies just to the west creating some noise at times. Most local residents are used to it.

The landscape is rolling to hilly, especially near the rivers and south of the Moon Township area. The climate is humid continental with warm summers and variable winters. The area does get periods of clouds and moderate precipitation from Lake Erie to the north, but major storms are infrequent.

Health & Safety Crime in the Pittsburgh area has dropped significantly as the city has cleaned up, and crime risk in the Coraopolis area itself is very low. Healthcare facilities are adequate, and large teaching medical centers are available near universities downtown.

Nearby Neighborhoods The Pittsburgh area offers a number of choices. Adjacent townships on the west side (Robinson and Kennedy, for example) are similar, and most growth is happening toward the west side. Sewickley Heights, just across the Ohio River, is more upscale, and a number of good older neighborhoods can be found north of the rivers and downtown near Allison Park and McCandless.

CORAOPOLIS–MOON TOWNSHIP, PA NEIGHBORHOOD HIGHLIGHTS	
PEOPLE	
Population	36,762
15-yr Population Growth	-6.40%
5-yr Population Growth	-2.40%
% Married w/Children	23.2%
% Single w/Children	7.5%
No. of Households	14,580
Median Age	38.9
Avg. Household Size	2.38
Diversity Measure	14
STANDARD OF LIVING	
Median Household Income	$54,708
% Household Income > $100K	15%
Projected Future Job Growth	1%
Cost of Living Index	100
Buying Power Index	122
Weekly Daycare Cost	$172
Median Home Price	$160,900
"Sweet Spot" Home Price	$260,000
Home Price Ratio	2.9
Median Age of Homes	33.9
% Homes Owned	69%
Effective Property Tax Rate	2.50%
Estimated Property Tax Bill	$6,500
EDUCATION	
% High School Graduates	89%
% 4-yr Degree	21%
% Graduate or Professional Degree	10%
$ Invested per Pupil	$7,992
Student/Teacher Ratio	15.2
Primary Test Score Percentile	110.5
Secondary Test Score Percentile	124
% Subsidized School Lunch	6.60%
% Attending Public School	72.70%
LIFESTYLE	
Leisure Rating (Area)	9
Arts & Culture Rating (Area)	10
Climate Rating (Area)	3
Physical Setting Rating	4
Downtown Core Rating	6
% Commute < 30 Min.	71%
% Commute > 1 Hour	5%
HEALTH & SAFETY	
Health Rating (Area)	5
Stress Score (Area)	6
Violent Crime Risk	32
Property Crime Risk	50

PITTSBURGH, PA
AREA HIGHLIGHTS

PEOPLE

SIZE & DIVERSITY	AREA	U.S. AVG	FAMILY DEMOGRAPHICS	AREA	U.S. AVG
Population	2,330,180		% Married	55.30%	53.80%
15-yr Population Growth	-2.30%	4.40%	% Single	44.70%	46.20%
Diversity Measure	20	54	% Divorced	6.60%	10.20%
% Religiously Observant	66%	50%	% Separated	3.10%	2.10%
% Catholic	42%	22%	% Married w/Children	24.70%	27.90%
% Protestant	23%	25%	% Single w/Children	8.30%	9.40%
% Jewish	2%	2%	% Married, No Children	31.90%	31.00%
% Other	0%	1%	% Single, No Children	34.80%	31.70%

STANDARD OF LIVING

INCOME, EMPLOYMENT & TAXES	AREA	U.S. AVG	COST OF LIVING & HOUSING	AREA	U.S. AVG
Median Household Income	$40,992	$44,684	Cost of Living Index	87.9	100
Household Income Growth	5.20%	6.10%	Buying Power Index	104	100
Unemployment Rate	5.20%	5.10%	Median Home Price	$118,500	$208,500
Recent Job Growth	2.80%	1.30%	Home Price Ratio	2.9	4.7
Projected Future Job Growth	5.20%	10.50%	Home Price Appreciation	5.50%	13.60%
State Income Tax Rate	4.60%	5.00%	% Homes Owned	69.60%	64.10%
State Sales Tax Rate	6%	6.00%	Median Rent	$639	$792

EDUCATION

ATTAINMENT & ACHIEVEMENT	AREA	U.S. AVG	RESOURCES & INVESTMENT	AREA	U.S. AVG
% High School Graduate	79.40%	83.90%	No. of Highly Ranked Universities	5	1
% 2-yr Graduate	7.30%	7.10%	$ Invested per Pupil	$6,954	$6,058
% 4-yr Graduate	12.70%	17.20%	Student/Teacher Ratio	17.3	15.9
% Graduate or Professional Degree	6.20%	9.90%	State University In-State Tuition	$10,856	$4,917
% Attending Public School	86.20%	84.30%			
75th Percentile State University SAT Score (Verbal)	530	477			
75th Percentile State University SAT Score (Math)	560	478			
75th Percentile State University ACT Score	N/A	20			

LIFESTYLE

RECREATION, ARTS & CULTURE	AREA	U.S. AVG	INFRASTRUCTURE & FACILITIES	AREA	U.S. AVG
Professional Sports Rating	7	4	No. of Public Libraries	128	28
Zoos & Aquariums Rating	8	3	Library Volumes Per Capita	2.7	2.8
Amusement Park Rating	6	3	No. of Warehouse Clubs	4	4
Professional Theater Rating	10	3	No. of Starbucks	36	5
Overall Museum Rating	9	6	Golf Course Rating	9	4
Science Museum Rating	9	4	National Park Rating	2	3
Children's Museum Rating	5	3	Sq. Mi. Inland Water	4	4

CLIMATE			COMMUTE & TRANSPORTATION		
Days Mostly Sunny	161	212	Avg. Daily Commute Time	25.3	24.7
Annual Days Precipitation	152	111	% Commute by Auto	75%	77.70%
Annual Days > 90°F	7	38	Per Capita Avg. Daily Transit Miles	21.4	7.9
Annual Days < 32°F	124	88	Annual Auto Insurance Premium	$1,451	$1,314
July Relative Humidity	68	69	Gas, Cost per Gallon	$3.10	$3.05

HEALTH & SAFETY

CRIME & ENVIRNOMENTAL ISSUES	AREA	U.S. AVG	HEALTHCARE & COST	AREA	U.S. AVG
Violent Crime Rate	360	517	Physicians per Capita	343.1	254.3
Change in Violent Crime	15.60%	-7.50%	Pediatricians per Capita	19.6	16.9
Property Crime Rate	2408	3783	Hospital Beds per Capita	534.7	239.7
Change in Property Crime	0.30%	-10.10%	No. of Teaching Hospitals	18	1.9
Air Quality Score	29	44	Healthcare Cost Index	93	100
Water Quality Score	50	33	Cost per Doctor Visit	$65	$74
Pollen/Allergy Score	73	61	Cost per Dentist Visit	$61	$67
Stress Score	61	49	Cost per Hospital Room	$781	$702
Cancer Mortality Rate	185.2	168.9			

DeForest, WI

Area Type: College-town suburb

Zip Code: 53532

Metro Area: Madison, WI

Metro Area Type: Small

Location: 13 miles north of Madison, WI

Time Zone: Central Standard Time

Pros:
Attractive homes
Nearby college-town amenities
Strong employment

Cons:
Winter climate
Property tax rates
Home prices

DeForest, a small country town of 12,000 to thenorth of Madison, Wisconsin, is known as the "North Star" of Dane County. Madison—well-known as the state capital and home to the University of Wisconsin—often attracts attention as a good place to live, but DeForest offers more affordable housing plus full access to the features and amenities of the Madison area.

The attractive downtown area sits uniquely among, around, and between Lake Monona and Lake Mendota. In 2004, *Prevention* magazine voted it the second-best walking city of its size, and with good reason. The city has many special architectural highlights, including several Frank Lloyd Wright buildings, the largest and best known being a local convention hall on the lakeshore called the Monona Terrace Center. But Wright's influence hardly stops at the city limits; his home and studio west in Spring Green is a world-class attraction. In the college-town area nearby, there's plenty of cultural enrichment in an intellectually stimulating environment. In spite of minor knocks against the area, such as its winter climate, the area is considered a great place to live.

Locals don't like to think of DeForest as a "bedroom community," but many of them commute to the Madison area. Having said that, small businesses in DeForest employ some residents, and there are more small businesses in the nearby towns of Sun Prairie and Marshall. In Waterloo, 30 miles east, the Trek Corporation bicycle factory provides jobs as well. The married-with-children percentage of households is 38.5%.

Standard of Living   Residents are employed in a variety of ways here. People work for small firms that produce appliance parts and injection molded plastics, as well as for wholesaling and distribution facilities. Insurer American Family Insurance has a 500,000-square-foot corporate headquarters, and naturally the university and state governments provide steady employment. Particularly with Madison in the mix, the job base is diverse and unemployment is a very low 2.2%. Homes are attractively priced compared to Madison (about 10% less) but are still high for the Midwest. Good family homes start in the $250K range and rise quickly into the $300Ks and even $400Ks. Property taxes of 2.5% aren't cheap, but they're lower than in Madison.

Education   Local test scores run 5 to 20 points above state averages depending on grade and subject. The university provides plenty of local programs and educational resources, and a library was recently added in DeForest.

Lifestyle   The Madison area is politically and culturally diverse, busy, exciting, and full of entertainment. University sports are comparable to professional sports in other cities. Numerous family-oriented activities and venues are available, including the Henry Vilas Zoo and the Madison Children's Museum. Other museums and performing arts are available on the UW campus. Outdoor recreation is plentiful during the winter and summer; in addition to the two Madison lakes, there are plenty of parks and bike trails around the city. The well-known Wisconsin Dells area is 40 miles to the northwest, and Chicago is about 3 hours to the southeast.

It takes about 10 minutes to get to Madison from DeForest, and area commutes in general are not an issue.

The setting comprises rolling farmland and hills with scattered deciduous woods. You'll experience four definite seasons here, with variable and frequently cold winter weather and warm, humid summers with thunderstorms, but very pleasant spring and fall seasons.

DE FOREST, WI	
NEIGHBORHOOD HIGHLIGHTS	
PEOPLE	
Population	12,196
15-yr Population Growth	23.60%
5-yr Population Growth	6.30%
% Married w/Children	38.5%
% Single w/Children	8.2%
No. of Households	4,340
Median Age	33.5
Avg. Household Size	2.82
Diversity Measure	8
STANDARD OF LIVING	
Median Household Income	$64,523
% Household Income > $100K	15%
Projected Future Job Growth	13%
Cost of Living Index	104
Buying Power Index	139
Weekly Daycare Cost	$120
Median Home Price	$221,600
"Sweet Spot" Home Price	$325,000
Home Price Ratio	3.4
Median Age of Homes	19.1
% Homes Owned	78%
Effective Property Tax Rate	2.50%
Estimated Property Tax Bill	$8,125
EDUCATION	
% High School Graduates	92%
% 4-yr Degree	19%
% Graduate or Professional Degree	6%
$ Invested per Pupil	$6,911
Student/Teacher Ratio	13.7
Primary Test Score Percentile	107.1
Secondary Test Score Percentile	102.7
% Subsidized School Lunch	11.20%
% Attending Public School	89.90%
LIFESTYLE	
Leisure Rating (Area)	4
Arts & Culture Rating (Area)	9
Climate Rating (Area)	2
Physical Setting Rating	4
Downtown Core Rating	9
% Commute < 30 Min.	64%
% Commute > 1 Hour	7%
HEALTH & SAFETY	BEST
Health Rating (Area)	10
Stress Score (Area)	2
Violent Crime Risk	31
Property Crime Risk	71

Health & Safety   Crime is low in DeForest, and the area enjoys excellent medical facilities and university hospital facilities. The stress score is low.

Nearby Neighborhoods   The area around Madison is dotted with small towns. Sun Prairie is growing faster and is newer than DeForest though not as attractive. Closer to downtown Madison, the Maple Bluff area is older and more upscale with fewer families. Good new neighborhoods are also growing to the west of downtown Madison.

MADISON, WI
AREA HIGHLIGHTS

PEOPLE

SIZE & DIVERSITY	AREA	U.S. AVG	FAMILY DEMOGRAPHICS	AREA	U.S. AVG
Population	453,582		% Married	53.80%	53.80%
15-yr Population Growth	23.60%	4.40%	% Single	46.20%	46.20%
Diversity Measure	23	54	% Divorced	7.60%	10.20%
% Religiously Observant	52%	50%	% Separated	2%	2.10%
% Catholic	28%	22%	% Married w/Children	27.60%	27.90%
% Protestant	23%	25%	% Single w/Children	7.90%	9.40%
% Jewish	1%	2%	% Married, No Children	28%	31.00%
% Other	0%	1%	% Single, No Children	36.50%	31.70%

STANDARD OF LIVING

INCOME, EMPLOYMENT & TAXES	AREA	U.S. AVG	COST OF LIVING & HOUSING	AREA	U.S. AVG
Median Household Income	$52,663	$44,684	Cost of Living Index	94.9	100
Household Income Growth	2.20%	6.10%	Buying Power Index	124	100
Unemployment Rate	2.20%	5.10%	Median Home Price	$220,100	$208,500
Recent Job Growth	2.60%	1.30%	Home Price Ratio	4.2	4.7
Projected Future Job Growth	11.50%	10.50%	Home Price Appreciation	10.50%	13.60%
State Income Tax Rate	6.90%	5.00%	% Homes Owned	62.60%	64.10%
State Sales Tax Rate	5.50%	6.00%	Median Rent	$746	$792

EDUCATION

ATTAINMENT & ACHIEVEMENT	AREA	U.S. AVG	RESOURCES & INVESTMENT	AREA	U.S. AVG
% High School Graduate	90.50%	83.90%	No. of Highly Ranked Universities	0	1
% 2-yr Graduate	12.80%	7.10%	$ Invested per Pupil	$7,553	$6,058
% 4-yr Graduate	26.40%	17.20%	Student/Teacher Ratio	13.9	15.9
% Graduate or Professional Degree	12.90%	9.90%	State University In-State Tuition	$5,862	$4,917
% Attending Public School	90.90%	84.30%			
75th Percentile State University SAT Score (Verbal)	N/A	477			
75th Percentile State University SAT Score (Math)	N/A	478			
75th Percentile State University ACT Score	26	20			

LIFESTYLE

RECREATION, ARTS & CULTURE	AREA	U.S. AVG	INFRASTRUCTURE & FACILITIES	AREA	U.S. AVG
Professional Sports Rating	2	4	No. of Public Libraries	26	28
Zoos & Aquariums Rating	6	3	Library Volumes Per Capita	3.8	2.8
Amusement Park Rating	1	3	No. of Warehouse Clubs	3	4
Professional Theater Rating	1	3	No. of Starbucks	9	5
Overall Museum Rating	7	6	Golf Course Rating	3	4
Science Museum Rating	2	4	National Park Rating	1	3
Children's Museum Rating	5	3	Sq. Mi. Inland Water	4	4

CLIMATE			COMMUTE & TRANSPORTATION		
Days Mostly Sunny	190	212	Avg. Daily Commute Time	19.9	24.7
Annual Days Precipitation	117	111	% Commute by Auto	70%	77.70%
Annual Days > 90°F	12	38	Per Capita Avg. Daily Transit Miles	16.4	7.9
Annual Days < 32°F	164	88	Annual Auto Insurance Premium	$1,014	$1,314
July Relative Humidity	73	69	Gas, Cost per Gallon	$3.07	$3.05

HEALTH & SAFETY

CRIME & ENVIRNOMENTAL ISSUES	AREA	U.S. AVG	HEALTHCARE & COST	AREA	U.S. AVG
Violent Crime Rate	222	517	Physicians per Capita	477.1	254.3
Change in Violent Crime	-28.60%	-7.50%	Pediatricians per Capita	30	16.9
Property Crime Rate	2932	3783	Hospital Beds per Capita	358.6	239.7
Change in Property Crime	-14.50%	-10.10%	No. of Teaching Hospitals	3	1.9
Air Quality Score	25	44	Healthcare Cost Index	105.4	100
Water Quality Score	48	33	Cost per Doctor Visit	$75	$74
Pollen/Allergy Score	34	61	Cost per Dentist Visit	$72	$67
Stress Score	23	49	Cost per Hospital Room	$612	$702
Cancer Mortality Rate	155.1	168.9			

Denver (Park Hill), CO

Area Type: City neighborhood

Zip Code: 80220

Metro Area: Denver, CO

Metro Area Type: Large

Location: 4 miles east of downtown Denver along Colfax Ave. (US 40)

Time Zone: Mountain Standard Time

Pros:

Community feel and historic interest
Parks and recreation
Convenience to downtown Denver

Cons:

Aging infrastructure
Air quality
High home prices

Cities can be treasure-troves for families, with intellectually stimulating activities, beautifully historic buildings, and a diverse population. The downside is that they also have crime, as well as social, educational, and infrastructure problems. Further, and maybe because of these issues, many city neighborhoods have few families compared to national averages. But the Park Hill neighborhood, east of downtown Denver, Colorado, is a great choice, with a blend of solid infrastructure, good amenities, safety, and a strong presence of families.

The list of attractions starts with Denver itself—a large, thriving, and vibrant regional center situated at the gateway to the Rocky Mountains, which rise impressively to the city's west. The commercial part of downtown, on the east bank of the South Platte River, is clean and modern with skyscrapers and a strong "downtown America" feel. More interesting is the so-called "LoDo" (lower downtown) area to the northwest of downtown, a nicely revitalized section of historic buildings converted to lofts and various creative enterprises centered on the Union Station rail passenger facility and the new but retro-looking Coors Field stadium. Denver itself has major-league sports, arts, museums, shopping, and cultural activities that draw visitors from a vast area of the western United States. City and county governments are combined into a unified government, giving above-average regional planning and, among other things, the largest park system of any U.S. city.

Moving east from downtown along US 40, known locally as Colfax Avenue, you'll first encounter wealthy areas with high-rises and numerous professional singles and couples. The intersection of Colfax and the major north–south Colorado Avenue is anchored by the large "City Park," a full-featured urban retreat including golf, lakes, museums, and an excellent playground usable most of the year. Crossing Colorado Boulevard to the east, Park Hill begins with wide tree-lined grid streets and a mix of attractive homes—many classic Craftsman bungalows—built mainly in the 1900 to 1920 period. North–south streets are named alphabetically: Albion, Birch, Cherry, Dahlia, and so on. The east–west 17th Avenue Parkway bisects the area with beautiful mature trees on a median wide enough for football or soccer, and there are two other such boulevards running through the neighborhood. Just to the northeast, the old Stapleton airport site, once a source of noise, is now being redeveloped into a planned residential and commercial community known as Forest City Stapleton. Park Hill itself is socioeconomically diverse and has a married-with-children percentage of 16%, which is relatively high for this type of neighborhood.

Standard of Living Not surprising for a quality neighborhood in an excellent city, Park Hill looks somewhat upscale and expensive at first glance. That said, it is actually economically diverse and affordable to many families who can make minor trade-offs. Most homes are smaller than our 2,200-square-foot family standard, and $150 to $225 per square foot is a comparatively steep price guideline. Homeowners may also have to deal with maintenance issues of older homes and neighborhoods, but most homes have a lot of charm, nice yards, and basements. The Cost of Living Index is 137. In part because of the presence of a number of retirees, working incomes are stronger than statistics show, and Buying Power looks weaker than it really is for most families. There are a number of stay-at-home parents. Property tax assessments and rates are complex, but they work out to a favorable effective rate of just over 0.5% of market value.

Education   Almost half of the population possesses at least a 4-year degree. Residents may choose a school for their children to attend among a handful of Denver Public School choices with Park Hill Elementary and East High among the popular choices. Test scores are a mixed bag among the different schools in the area, but local parents are positive on academics and the overall experience. Colorado also has an excellent network of colleges and universities.

Lifestyle   Park Hill offers solid community bonds and convenience to city facilities, sort of like stepping back into the early 20th century. Short bus rides, bike trips, and walks go to a variety of destinations, and these trips are safe and easy. The Cherry Creek Mall is a short 10-minute bus ride south, and the Denver Zoo and Museum of Nature and Science are in City Park, mentioned earlier. Downtown Denver itself is a 20-minute bus ride. Kids can buy a pass to ride buses all summer for $10. The abundance of outdoor recreation opportunities in the Front Range of the Rockies is well-known and among the best anywhere.

The 20-minute downtown commute is often done by bus and preserves a lot of family time often devoted to family and neighborhood activities. A family can get along with minimal use of a car.

Park Hill itself is relatively flat (despite the name) and slopes gently westward toward the South Platte Basin. The Rocky Mountains rise dramatically about 15 miles west. The climate is continental and dry with mountain shelter from the harshest winter weather and mostly pleasant summers with a few hot spells.

Health & Safety   Crime risk is moderate to high, typical for a city neighborhood, but parents feel quite safe on the streets and in city buses. As might be expected in a regional center, area healthcare facilities are diverse and excellent. The basin location adjacent to mountains can trap air and create some air-quality problems such as smog and haze.

Nearby Neighborhoods   The Denver area is full of choices (see Castle Rock and Louisville-Lafayette, CO, on p. 148 and 274). East of Park Hill is the more moderately priced and suburban Aurora, and there are good older neighborhoods just to the south nearing the Cherry Creek area.

DENVER (PARK HILL), CO NEIGHBORHOOD HIGHLIGHTS	
PEOPLE	
Population	36,460
15-yr Population Growth	19.10%
5-yr Population Growth	0.40%
% Married w/Children	16.0%
% Single w/Children	9.9%
No. of Households	15,684
Median Age	35.5
Avg. Household Size	2.16
Diversity Measure	61
STANDARD OF LIVING	
Median Household Income	$49,291
% Household Income > $100K	19%
Projected Future Job Growth	5%
Cost of Living Index	137
Buying Power Index	74
Weekly Daycare Cost	$181
Median Home Price	$275,000
"Sweet Spot" Home Price	$350,000
Home Price Ratio	5.6
Median Age of Homes	53.8
% Homes Owned	58%
Effective Property Tax Rate	0.50%
Estimated Property Tax Bill	$1,750
EDUCATION	
% High School Graduates	87%
% 4-yr Degree	27%
% Graduate or Professional Degree	22%
$ Invested per Pupil	$5,665
Student/Teacher Ratio	15.7
Primary Test Score Percentile	65.6
Secondary Test Score Percentile	52.3
% Subsidized School Lunch	55.30%
% Attending Public School	73.70%
LIFESTYLE	
Leisure Rating (Area)	9
Arts & Culture Rating (Area)	10
Climate Rating (Area)	5
Physical Setting Rating	5
Downtown Core Rating	9
% Commute < 30 Min.	66%
% Commute > 1 Hour	4%
HEALTH & SAFETY	
Health Rating (Area)	5
Stress Score (Area)	7
Violent Crime Risk	178
Property Crime Risk	100

DENVER, CO
AREA HIGHLIGHTS

PEOPLE

SIZE & DIVERSITY	AREA	U.S. AVG	FAMILY DEMOGRAPHICS	AREA	U.S. AVG
Population	2,233,818		% Married	53.50%	53.80%
15-yr Population Growth	56.90%	4.40%	% Single	46.50%	46.20%
Diversity Measure	46	54	% Divorced	11.70%	10.20%
% Religiously Observant	39%	50%	% Separated	3.30%	2.10%
% Catholic	18%	22%	% Married w/Children	26.50%	27.90%
% Protestant	18%	25%	% Single w/Children	10.20%	9.40%
% Jewish	2%	2%	% Married, No Children	26.80%	31.00%
% Other	0%	1%	% Single, No Children	36.40%	31.70%

STANDARD OF LIVING

INCOME, EMPLOYMENT & TAXES	AREA	U.S. AVG	COST OF LIVING & HOUSING	AREA	U.S. AVG
Median Household Income	$54,167	$44,684	Cost of Living Index	112.2	100
Household Income Growth	5%	6.10%	Buying Power Index	108	100
Unemployment Rate	5%	5.10%	Median Home Price	$248,400	$208,500
Recent Job Growth	3.40%	1.30%	Home Price Ratio	4.6	4.7
Projected Future Job Growth	14.70%	10.50%	Home Price Appreciation	3.90%	13.60%
State Income Tax Rate	5%	5.00%	% Homes Owned	61.30%	64.10%
State Sales Tax Rate	7%	6.00%	Median Rent	$973	$792

EDUCATION

ATTAINMENT & ACHIEVEMENT	AREA	U.S. AVG	RESOURCES & INVESTMENT	AREA	U.S. AVG
% High School Graduate	87.30%	83.90%	No. of Highly Ranked Universities	2	1
% 2-yr Graduate	9.80%	7.10%	$ Invested per Pupil	$5,796	$6,058
% 4-yr Graduate	29.20%	17.20%	Student/Teacher Ratio	19.3	15.9
% Graduate or Professional Degree	12.80%	9.90%	State University In-State Tuition	$4,341	$4,917
% Attending Public School	90.80%	84.30%			
75th Percentile State University SAT Score (Verbal)	530	477			
75th Percentile State University SAT Score (Math)	550	478			
75th Percentile State University ACT Score	23	20			

LIFESTYLE

RECREATION, ARTS & CULTURE	AREA	U.S. AVG	INFRASTRUCTURE & FACILITIES	AREA	U.S. AVG
Professional Sports Rating	9	4	No. of Public Libraries	63	28
Zoos & Aquariums Rating	7	3	Library Volumes Per Capita	2.6	2.8
Amusement Park Rating	7	3	No. of Warehouse Clubs	5	4
Professional Theater Rating	10	3	No. of Starbucks	83	5
Overall Museum Rating	9	6	Golf Course Rating	7	4
Science Museum Rating	7	4	National Park Rating	3	3
Children's Museum Rating	7	3	Sq. Mi. Inland Water	3	4

CLIMATE			COMMUTE & TRANSPORTATION		
Days Mostly Sunny	246	212	Avg. Daily Commute Time	26.5	24.7
Annual Days Precipitation	88	111	% Commute by Auto	73%	77.70%
Annual Days > 90°F	32	38	Per Capita Avg. Daily Transit Miles	24.3	7.9
Annual Days < 32°F	163	88	Annual Auto Insurance Premium	$1,924	$1,314
July Relative Humidity	53	69	Gas, Cost per Gallon	$3.02	$3.05

HEALTH & SAFETY

CRIME & ENVIRNOMENTAL ISSUES	AREA	U.S. AVG	HEALTHCARE & COST	AREA	U.S. AVG
Violent Crime Rate	391	517	Physicians per Capita	264.3	254.3
Change in Violent Crime	1.80%	-7.50%	Pediatricians per Capita	20.2	16.9
Property Crime Rate	4367	3783	Hospital Beds per Capita	251.4	239.7
Change in Property Crime	3.70%	-10.10%	No. of Teaching Hospitals	18	1.9
Air Quality Score	26	44	Healthcare Cost Index	125.8	100
Water Quality Score	88	33	Cost per Doctor Visit	$96	$74
Pollen/Allergy Score	85	61	Cost per Dentist Visit	$77	$67
Stress Score	70	49	Cost per Hospital Room	$979	$702
Cancer Mortality Rate	152.8	168.9			

Eagle, ID

Area Type: Outer suburb

Zip Code: 83616

Metro Area: Boise, ID

Metro Area Type: Small

Location: 11 miles northwest of downtown Boise

Time Zone: Mountain Standard Time

Pros:
Outdoor recreation
Attractive setting
Attractive downtown

Cons:
Growth and sprawl
Air quality
Low diversity

This once-agricultural area on the north edge of the Snake River Plain, beautifully set against the Boise Mountains to the north, is rapidly changing. Of course, Eagle still claims big Western skies, dry and sunny days, mountain views, distance from major highways, and old farmhouses. But the world has discovered Eagle (along with many of the communities surrounding Boise). You'll find a number of migrating Californians here, looking for a less expensive and cleaner way of life. The farm fields (most anyway) have turned into subdivisions, though into more attractive and less dense ones compared to those in other such communities. A cute, refreshed downtown area functions well as a local hangout, and residents walk or bike to it along the area's well-planned sidewalks and trails. Yes, the area has grown 66% in 14 years and growth pressure is extreme, but for the most part, local planning has handled it well. Concerns still remain about traffic, water supply, and some unsavory activities in local schools, but today's Eagle "works," especially for those who have relocated from more crowded areas. There are a lot of reasons for a family to fall in love with Eagle. And many have—32% of households are married with children.

Nearby Boise has for years been a clean, attractive capital city and agricultural center with some university influence from Boise State University. It has a typically western downtown with wide, tree-lined grid streets. Older brick buildings mix with modern steel and glass structures. The city photographs well against its mountain backdrop. Restored older areas of town, including the North End and the Farmer's Market area west of downtown, are interesting and offer a lot to do on the weekends. But the minor entertainment and arts amenities available locally aren't the full story: Boise lies at the doorstep of some of the best outdoor recreation opportunities in the country, mainly in the Boise National Forest and mountain areas to the north. Highlights include the Sawtooth National Recreation Area, the Sun Valley area near Ketchum, and the mountain/lake town of McCall.

Standard of Living   The job climate is still strong, although some concerns have recently surfaced. State government, the university, and food processors (including the enormous J.R. Simplot of French fry fame) provide a solid base, and high-tech companies provide the kicker—Hewlett-Packard (despite downsizing) and semiconductor giant Micron Technology are the biggies, among others. Future job growth is still projected at 22%. Home prices are rising, but they're still relatively reasonable on a western U.S. scale; good family homes run $120 to $150 per square foot with a "sweet spot" in the low to mid $300Ks. Most homes are quite new and well outfitted. The cost of living for the Boise area is attractive (COL Index 86.5) and close to the cost of living in Eagle (COL Index 110). Effective property tax rates are about 1.8%.

Education   Area schools are very good, although some problems associated with urban environments reputably have crept in. Locals and local officials are aware of these issues, and the community is trying to improve the situation. Test scores typically run 10% to 20% above state averages with strong college prep and extracurricular activities. Crowding has been an issue, but current facilities are modernizing and expanding.

Lifestyle   Outdoor activities, both in town and in the excellent nearby wilderness, dominate life here. The Snake River Plain is an excellent place to bicycle, and the Snake River itself provides water recreation opportunities, as does the Payette River to the north. For after-work and weekend skiing, locals head up to Bogus Basin just 45 minutes away. Day and weekend getaways to outlying areas like McCall, Sun Valley, Sawtooth

EAGLE, ID	
NEIGHBORHOOD HIGHLIGHTS	
PEOPLE	
Population	16,844
15-yr Population Growth	61.60%
5-yr Population Growth	10.50%
% Married w/Children	32.4%
% Single w/Children	10.1%
No. of Households	5,717
Median Age	34.1
Avg. Household Size	2.93
Diversity Measure	9
STANDARD OF LIVING	
Median Household Income	$67,160
% Household Income > $100K	24%
Projected Future Job Growth	22%
Cost of Living Index	110
Buying Power Index	139
Weekly Daycare Cost	$95
Median Home Price	$264,100
"Sweet Spot" Home Price	$350,000
Home Price Ratio	3.9
Median Age of Homes	9.1
% Homes Owned	84%
Effective Property Tax Rate	1.80%
Estimated Property Tax Bill	$6,300
EDUCATION	
% High School Graduates	94%
% 4-yr Degree	27%
% Graduate or Professional Degree	12%
$ Invested per Pupil	$3,834
Student/Teacher Ratio	19.4
Primary Test Score Percentile	118.9
Secondary Test Score Percentile	98.1
% Subsidized School Lunch	10.70%
% Attending Public School	86.20%
LIFESTYLE	
Leisure Rating (Area)	6
Arts & Culture Rating (Area)	7
Climate Rating (Area)	6
Physical Setting Rating	8
Downtown Core Rating	6
% Commute < 30 Min.	66%
% Commute > 1 Hour	2%
HEALTH & SAFETY	
Health Rating (Area)	5
Stress Score (Area)	5
Violent Crime Risk	82
Property Crime Risk	112

Wilderness, and Snake River rafting areas are plentiful. Area museums and cultural attractions are modest, but the Discovery Center Idaho is a good choice for children and science enthusiasts.

Until recently, nobody complained about Boise commutes—in fact, they were a relief especially to people who moved here from California. But traffic along major arteries has become denser, and some of the major employers, like Micron, are east of town. Downtown commutes can take 30 to 40 minutes.

The Snake River Plain is flat to gently rolling with benches and bluffs defined by the Boise and Snake rivers. The climate is dry with four seasons. The 2,800-foot altitude gives generally pleasant summer days and cool evenings, but the valley location can bring 100°F heat occasionally. Winters are mild with a few cold spells but temperatures seldom drop below zero.

Health & Safety   Crime risk is moderate, and healthcare facilities are average for this type of area. At times, the valley landform and temperature inversions can create air-quality problems.

Nearby Neighborhoods   Particularly as growth spreads west in the valley, many good neighborhoods are available for families. Meridian just to the south is less expensive but has a more crowded feel and a weaker educational environment. Many families are moving to Nampa or Caldwell to the west, both of which have a rural small-town feel and attractive newer homes. These communities may be "where the puck is going."

BOISE, ID
AREA HIGHLIGHTS

PEOPLE

SIZE & DIVERSITY	AREA	U.S. AVG	FAMILY DEMOGRAPHICS	AREA	U.S. AVG
Population	490,561		% Married	58.90%	53.80%
15-yr Population Growth	66.10%	4.40%	% Single	41.10%	46.20%
Diversity Measure	23	54	% Divorced	10.20%	10.20%
% Religiously Observant	44%	50%	% Separated	2.30%	2.10%
% Catholic	12%	22%	% Married w/Children	30.50%	27.90%
% Protestant	31%	25%	% Single w/Children	10%	9.40%
% Jewish	0%	2%	% Married, No Children	29.50%	31.00%
% Other	0%	1%	% Single, No Children	30%	31.70%

STANDARD OF LIVING

INCOME, EMPLOYMENT & TAXES	AREA	U.S. AVG	COST OF LIVING & HOUSING	AREA	U.S. AVG
Median Household Income	$45,313	$44,684	Cost of Living Index	86.5	100
Household Income Growth	4.50%	6.10%	Buying Power Index	117	100
Unemployment Rate	4.50%	5.10%	Median Home Price	$161,800	$208,500
Recent Job Growth	3.40%	1.30%	Home Price Ratio	3.6	4.7
Projected Future Job Growth	26.90%	10.50%	Home Price Appreciation	7.30%	13.60%
State Income Tax Rate	8.20%	5.00%	% Homes Owned	67.70%	64.10%
State Sales Tax Rate	5%	6.00%	Median Rent	$654	$792

EDUCATION

ATTAINMENT & ACHIEVEMENT	AREA	U.S. AVG	RESOURCES & INVESTMENT	AREA	U.S. AVG
% High School Graduate	81.50%	83.90%	No. of Highly Ranked Universities	1	1
% 2-yr Graduate	11.20%	7.10%	$ Invested per Pupil	$4,582	$6,058
% 4-yr Graduate	21.40%	17.20%	Student/Teacher Ratio	19.1	15.9
% Graduate or Professional Degree	7.60%	9.90%	State University In-State Tuition	$3,520	$4,917
% Attending Public School	94%	84.30%			
75th Percentile State University SAT Score (Verbal)	450	477			
75th Percentile State University SAT Score (Math)	425	478			
75th Percentile State University ACT Score	18	20			

LIFESTYLE

RECREATION, ARTS & CULTURE	AREA	U.S. AVG	INFRASTRUCTURE & FACILITIES	AREA	U.S. AVG
Professional Sports Rating	3	4	No. of Public Libraries	15	28
Zoos & Aquariums Rating	1	3	Library Volumes Per Capita	2.2	2.8
Amusement Park Rating	1	3	No. of Warehouse Clubs	3	4
Professional Theater Rating	1	3	No. of Starbucks	13	5
Overall Museum Rating	5	6	Golf Course Rating	2	4
Science Museum Rating	5	4	National Park Rating	2	3
Children's Museum Rating	1	3	Sq. Mi. Inland Water	2	4

CLIMATE			COMMUTE & TRANSPORTATION		
Days Mostly Sunny	214	212	Avg. Daily Commute Time	20.2	24.7
Annual Days Precipitation	91	111	% Commute by Auto	77%	77.70%
Annual Days > 90°F	43	38	Per Capita Avg. Daily Transit Miles	3.4	7.9
Annual Days < 32°F	124	88	Annual Auto Insurance Premium	$922	$1,314
July Relative Humidity	57	69	Gas, Cost per Gallon	$2.95	$3.05

HEALTH & SAFETY

CRIME & ENVIRNOMENTAL ISSUES	AREA	U.S. AVG	HEALTHCARE & COST	AREA	U.S. AVG
Violent Crime Rate	287	517	Physicians per Capita	213.3	254.3
Change in Violent Crime	-6.60%	-7.50%	Pediatricians per Capita	12.1	16.9
Property Crime Rate	3458	3783	Hospital Beds per Capita	236.2	239.7
Change in Property Crime	-14.80%	-10.10%	No. of Teaching Hospitals	3	1.9
Air Quality Score	28	44	Healthcare Cost Index	111.7	100
Water Quality Score	24	33	Cost per Doctor Visit	$76	$74
Pollen/Allergy Score	45	61	Cost per Dentist Visit	$68	$67
Stress Score	53	49	Cost per Hospital Room	$714	$702
Cancer Mortality Rate	148.9	168.9			

East Islip, NY

Area Type: Suburban town/outer suburb	**Pros:**
Zip Code: 11730	Attractive shorefront location
Metro Area: Nassau-Suffolk, NY (Long Island)	Good schools
Metro Area Type: Large	Air service
Location: 50 miles east of Manhattan	**Cons:**
Time Zone: Eastern Standard Time	Long commute
	High taxes
	Limited homes for sale

"It's like being in the Hamptons, only closer in." Maybe this local resident is exaggerating a bit, but not by much. East Islip is about halfway out on the 120-mile Long Island, and its shorefront location offers many of the same recreation opportunities and the kind of pleasant lifestyle found in its fancier neighbors to the east. Though a long way at 50 miles, the commute to New York is relatively easy and the area offers an attractive blend of conveniences, shoreline amenities, and moderate costs—all of which makes it a good place for families. Accordingly, married-with-children households account for 34.5% of all households.

East Islip is one of a long series of typical shorefront towns lying along the south of Long Island. A small downtown commercial district lies to the south of the Long Island Railroad commute route. Numerous parks, beaches, boating, and shore facilities are found near the water, and nicer, more expensive homes appear in this vicinity. Moving away from the water, homes turn into the typical suburban variety found all over the island. The 1950s were the "heyday" for building here. Today, the area is mostly built up and growth has slowed to 4% since 2000 (less than 1% per year), but there is still some new building in the area. Traveling east or west to nearby neighborhoods, it isn't always clear when you've left one and entered another.

Long Island is a dizzying east–west array of suburbs and small cities extending from the New York eastern boroughs of Brooklyn and Queens to the far reaches of the Hamptons and Montauk to the east. Numerous east–west transportation routes provide access to the world-class amenities in New York, and the nearby Long Island MacArthur Airport, served by Southwest Airlines, gives local residents convenient low-cost air service not found in many parts of New York.

Standard of Living As with most of the New York area, living in East Islip isn't cheap. At just over 150, the Cost of Living Index is high on a national scale but moderate for the region. Relatively high incomes keep the Buying Power Index at 117, but we've seen higher figures—more buying power and probably more two-earner families—in nearby areas. Home prices have escalated rapidly in recent years; but good homes can be found in the $450K to $500K range, and some adequate starters can be found starting at $350K. Split levels, ranches, and colonial-style homes are common. Jobs are a mix, with about half of residents commuting into the New York City area and others working in nearby Long Island businesses and professional offices. Defense contractors are the largest private employers. Employment in the region is steady if not rapidly growing. Property taxes run 1.5% to 2%, depending on specific locale, producing $6,000 to $12,000 annual tax bills, a consideration for new residents.

Education Local residents consider schools to be good across the board. The East Islip Unified School District is small (seven schools; 5,300 students) and test scores are in the mid to high 90s on New York State Regents Exams. Elementary and middle schools typically test 15 to 25 points higher than state averages.

Lifestyle Water and water-related local parks provide a focal point for local family recreation. Boating, boating clubs, and city beaches (which require proof of local residency) are very popular. Hecksher State Park, located within city limits at the shore, has fish hatcheries, hiking, boating, and an amphitheater for concerts (including the New York Philharmonic), children's theater, and other events. The adjacent Conetquot River State Park nature preserve is another attraction. Barrier islands lie offshore from this part of Long Island, and the Robert Moses State Park at the outer end of the largest island offers miles of state beaches just 10 miles away. Just offshore, accessible by boat or air, is Fire Island. The New York Islanders bring NHL hockey and the Long Island Ducks offer minor-league baseball; in nearby New York City, major-league sports, as well as arts and entertainment activities, are all within reach.

The Montauk Branch of the Long Island Railroad, now part of New York's Metropolitan Transit Authority, is the main commute route. City commutes take just over an hour into Manhattan's Penn Station.

Long Island itself is a large glacial moraine, and the area is largely flat with gradual rises toward the center. Most areas near East Islip and to the west are built up. The climate is humid continental with strong moderating water influences and cool summertime breezes. Extreme cold is relatively rare with almost no below-zero temperature readings.

Health & Safety   Crime risk is moderate and not out of line for the region. The Southside Hospital in nearby Bayside is one of the largest on Long Island. On a national scale, healthcare costs are high, but they're reasonable for the New York area.

Nearby Neighborhoods   There are literally hundreds of neighborhood choices on Long Island. Close by, West Islip and Great River are similar to East Islip. Old Bethpage, inland, is slightly more upscale. About 20 miles closer to New York, Merrick, and Massapequa are worth a look.

EAST ISLIP, NY NEIGHBORHOOD HIGHLIGHTS	
PEOPLE	
Population	16,638
15-yr Population Growth	11.60%
5-yr Population Growth	4%
% Married w/Children	34.5%
% Single w/Children	7.3%
No. of Households	5,454
Median Age	36
Avg. Household Size	3.04
Diversity Measure	13
STANDARD OF LIVING	
Median Household Income	$79,409
% Household Income > $100K	29%
Projected Future Job Growth	7%
Cost of Living Index	151
Buying Power Index	117
Weekly Daycare Cost	$215
Median Home Price	$476,000
"Sweet Spot" Home Price	$500,000
Home Price Ratio	6
Median Age of Homes	39.4
% Homes Owned	86%
Effective Property Tax Rate	2%
Estimated Property Tax Bill	$10,000
EDUCATION	
% High School Graduates	91%
% 4-yr Degree	16%
% Graduate or Professional Degree	13%
$ Invested per Pupil	$10,935
Student/Teacher Ratio	18.2
Primary Test Score Percentile	107.7
Secondary Test Score Percentile	108.9
% Subsidized School Lunch	5.70%
% Attending Public School	79.60%
LIFESTYLE	
Leisure Rating (Area)	10
Arts & Culture Rating (Area)	9
Climate Rating (Area)	8
Physical Setting Rating	6
Downtown Core Rating	6
% Commute < 30 Min.	56%
% Commute > 1 Hour	17%
HEALTH & SAFETY	
Health Rating (Area)	4
Stress Score (Area)	0
Violent Crime Risk	102
Property Crime Risk	57

NASSAU-SUFFOLK, NY
AREA HIGHLIGHTS

PEOPLE

SIZE & DIVERSITY	AREA	U.S. AVG	FAMILY DEMOGRAPHICS	AREA	U.S. AVG
Population	2,815,129		% Married	56.80%	53.80%
15-yr Population Growth	8%	4.40%	% Single	43.20%	46.20%
Diversity Measure	39	54	% Divorced	5.40%	10.20%
% Religiously Observant	72%	50%	% Separated	2.80%	2.10%
% Catholic	52%	22%	% Married w/Children	29.80%	27.90%
% Protestant	8%	25%	% Single w/Children	7.40%	9.40%
% Jewish	11%	2%	% Married, No Children	34.40%	31.00%
% Other	1%	1%	% Single, No Children	27.90%	31.70%

STANDARD OF LIVING

INCOME, EMPLOYMENT & TAXES	AREA	U.S. AVG	COST OF LIVING & HOUSING	AREA	U.S. AVG
Median Household Income	$74,969	$44,684	Cost of Living Index	149.9	100
Household Income Growth	3.60%	6.10%	Buying Power Index	112	100
Unemployment Rate	3.60%	5.10%	Median Home Price	$467,700	$208,500
Recent Job Growth	0.70%	1.30%	Home Price Ratio	6.2	4.7
Projected Future Job Growth	7.30%	10.50%	Home Price Appreciation	15.90%	13.60%
State Income Tax Rate	7.10%	5.00%	% Homes Owned	72.60%	64.10%
State Sales Tax Rate	4%	6.00%	Median Rent	$1,225	$792

EDUCATION

ATTAINMENT & ACHIEVEMENT	AREA	U.S. AVG	RESOURCES & INVESTMENT	AREA	U.S. AVG
% High School Graduate	87.40%	83.90%	No. of Highly Ranked Universities	2	1
% 2-yr Graduate	9.70%	7.10%	$ Invested per Pupil	$11,562	$6,058
% 4-yr Graduate	22.10%	17.20%	Student/Teacher Ratio	14.5	15.9
% Graduate or Professional Degree	15.60%	9.90%	State University In-State Tuition	$5,966	$4,917
% Attending Public School	87.50%	84.30%			
75th Percentile State University SAT Score (Verbal)	520	477			
75th Percentile State University SAT Score (Math)	550	478			
75th Percentile State University ACT Score	24	20			

LIFESTYLE

RECREATION, ARTS & CULTURE	AREA	U.S. AVG	INFRASTRUCTURE & FACILITIES	AREA	U.S. AVG
Professional Sports Rating	10	4	No. of Public Libraries	126	28
Zoos & Aquariums Rating	7	3	Library Volumes Per Capita	6.3	2.8
Amusement Park Rating	6	3	No. of Warehouse Clubs	9	4
Professional Theater Rating	9	3	No. of Starbucks	64	5
Overall Museum Rating	10	6	Golf Course Rating	10	4
Science Museum Rating	10	4	National Park Rating	4	3
Children's Museum Rating	7	3	Sq. Mi. Inland Water	9	4

CLIMATE			COMMUTE & TRANSPORTATION		
Days Mostly Sunny	219	212	Avg. Daily Commute Time	33	24.7
Annual Days Precipitation	125	111	% Commute by Auto	73%	77.70%
Annual Days > 90°F	10	38	Per Capita Avg. Daily Transit Miles	32.4	7.9
Annual Days < 32°F	85	88	Annual Auto Insurance Premium	$2,025	$1,314
July Relative Humidity	68	69	Gas, Cost per Gallon	$3.32	$3.05

HEALTH & SAFETY

CRIME & ENVIRNOMENTAL ISSUES	AREA	U.S. AVG	HEALTHCARE & COST	AREA	U.S. AVG
Violent Crime Rate	197	517	Physicians per Capita	428	254.3
Change in Violent Crime	17.70%	-7.50%	Pediatricians per Capita	40	16.9
Property Crime Rate	1845	3783	Hospital Beds per Capita	473.2	239.7
Change in Property Crime	-20.40%	-10.10%	No. of Teaching Hospitals	20	1.9
Air Quality Score	14	44	Healthcare Cost Index	164.4	100
Water Quality Score	60	33	Cost per Doctor Visit	$79	$74
Pollen/Allergy Score	62	61	Cost per Dentist Visit	$76	$67
Stress Score	4	49	Cost per Hospital Room	$1,639	$702
Cancer Mortality Rate	190.4	168.9			

Elkhorn, NE

Area Type: Suburban town

Zip Code: 68022

Metro Area: Omaha, NE-IA

Metro Area Type: Mid-size

Location: 17 miles west of downtown Omaha

Time Zone: Central Standard Time

Pros:
Cost of living
Improving downtown
Education

Cons:
Harsh winters
Recreation
Isolation

A classic mid-size, mid-American, mid–almost everything city, Omaha sits on the west bank of the Missouri River as that river defines the border between Nebraska and Iowa. Omaha got its start as a river trading post and came into prominence as the chosen departure point for the Union Pacific Railroad on its transcontinental journey west. Now, Omaha is clean and prosperous with a refreshed downtown area and new waterfront development in place but continually in progress. The area, according to a local resident, is a "good place to earn a living without the stress," and it's starting to be discovered as a good alternative location for business with a laid-back lifestyle and a Western flair.

Downtown Omaha is typical mid-America, with unremarkable old and new office buildings centered on the broad, classically named Dodge Street, otherwise known as US 6. New condominium projects and a proposed larger harbor and marina project have spiffed up the once industrial and railroad-centered waterfront. The new Qwest Center, at once a convention center and sports and performing arts arena, has turned Omaha into a favored convention venue and a place that hosts concerts, indoor rodeos, and ice hockey—to name only a few of many events. Just west and south is the Old Market area, a reused district of old warehouses with shops and an assortment of small entertainment venues. West of downtown, Dodge Street rises onto a ridge area known as Dundee with stately older homes and a view of the city; it is here that billionaire Warren Buffett and other unassuming Omaha millionaires make their homes. Some say that Omaha has more millionaires per capita than any other U.S. city. We're not sure about this, but the healthy economy and modest living costs make it seem possible.

Farther west along Dodge Street, the downtown and nice inner neighborhoods give way to standard mid-20th-century commercial and residential districts, with a large commercial complex at the junction with the I-680 beltway. Another 5 miles west, Dodge Street gradually enters the Platte River Valley and the setting becomes more rural; just north of Dodge Street lies the small village of Elkhorn, once a railroad stop and now a prosperous suburb. Downtown Elkhorn is small and historic but not a major attraction. However, the attractive homes, quiet semi-rural life, convenience to town, and good schools make it a good community for families—39% of households are married with children.

Standard of Living Employment is steady with low unemployment and moderate job growth, thanks to large industries like ConAgra, Union Pacific, Mutual of Omaha, and Berkshire Hathaway in Omaha. The Cost of Living Index is close to the U.S. average, but housing is notably attractive and affordable. Typical per-square-foot costs for family homes run $85 to $90 for existing homes to $100 and up for new construction. The "sweet spot" is $175K to $200K, and $260K can buy a 3,200-square-foot 14-year old colonial on an acre with trees. Property tax rates run a relatively high 2.5%, but are assessed against modest valuations.

Education Area schools are considered excellent, among the tops in the state. Elkhorn High has only 900 students and tests about 10% above state averages. Other schools in the system also fared well. Creighton University and the University of Nebraska-Omaha are nearby, and the Lincoln-based University of Nebraska, 50 miles away, casts a long collegiate shadow—especially on football weekends.

Lifestyle Expect an assortment of small parks and state recreation areas, although not quite as many park and water-based activities as in other Midwest cities. There are a number of local pools and minor amusement facilities and one fairly large one, Funplex, in

ELKHORN, NE
NEIGHBORHOOD HIGHLIGHTS

PEOPLE

Population	9,613
15-yr Population Growth	15.80%
5-yr Population Growth	4%
% Married w/Children	38.8%
% Single w/Children	9.6%
No. of Households	3,130
Median Age	34.1
Avg. Household Size	3.02
Diversity Measure	5

STANDARD OF LIVING

	BEST
Median Household Income	$75,816
% Household Income > $100K	25%
Projected Future Job Growth	13%
Cost of Living Index	99.2
Buying Power Index	171
Weekly Daycare Cost	$130
Median Home Price	$187,900
"Sweet Spot" Home Price	$190,000
Home Price Ratio	2.5
Median Age of Homes	22.1
% Homes Owned	89%
Effective Property Tax Rate	2.50%
Estimated Property Tax Bill	$4,750

EDUCATION

% High School Graduates	95%
% 4-yr Degree	23%
% Graduate or Professional Degree	10%
$ Invested per Pupil	$4,674
Student/Teacher Ratio	15
Primary Test Score Percentile	116.4
Secondary Test Score Percentile	115.2
% Subsidized School Lunch	11.40%
% Attending Public School	90.20%

LIFESTYLE

Leisure Rating (Area)	5
Arts & Culture Rating (Area)	8
Climate Rating (Area)	2
Physical Setting Rating	4
Downtown Core Rating	5
% Commute < 30 Min.	69%
% Commute > 1 Hour	2%

HEALTH & SAFETY

Health Rating (Area)	7
Stress Score (Area)	3
Violent Crime Risk	17
Property Crime Risk	32

nearby Papillion. Omaha has a number of small but high-quality arts amenities, including the Omaha Symphony, the Omaha Opera, and the Joslyn Art Museum, and a well-regarded zoo, the Henry Dourly Zoo. Outdoor concerts in the Old Market area and larger events in the Qwest Center create a fairly active music scene. The nearest large city is Kansas City, 2½ hours south.

Commutes are typically easy. From Elkhorn, it's 30 minutes to downtown, and the area's grid layout provides alternative routes. Elkhorn has good access to the commercial areas on the west side of town.

Elkhorn sits in the Platte Valley west of the low ridge dividing it from the Missouri River. The valley is generally flat and agricultural with areas of dense woods. The climate is vigorous with rapid changes, especially in winter. Temperature ranges and seasons are typical of a continental climate.

Health & Safety Crime risk is very low, with the lowest "CAP" violent crime risk among the best places in this book. Healthcare facilities are considered excellent with notably high hospital beds per capita. Stress scores are low, reflecting the relatively steady pace of life in the area.

Nearby Neighborhoods There are many choices around the western and southwestern periphery of Omaha. Waterloo, 2 miles west from Elkhorn, has a nice downtown area and smaller suburbs, with a new lakefront planned community in the works. A small area of more upscale suburban homes lies just east in the Boys Town area west of I-680, and the Dundee area offers good value ($300K–$400K homes) for those wanting more of a city experience.

OMAHA, NE
AREA HIGHLIGHTS

PEOPLE

SIZE & DIVERSITY	AREA	U.S. AVG	FAMILY DEMOGRAPHICS	AREA	U.S. AVG
Population	752,597		% Married	60.30%	53.80%
15-yr Population Growth	18.10%	4.40%	% Single	39.70%	46.20%
Diversity Measure	30	54	% Divorced	7.60%	10.20%
% Religiously Observant	51%	50%	% Separated	1.70%	2.10%
% Catholic	24%	22%	% Married w/Children	31.80%	27.90%
% Protestant	26%	25%	% Single w/Children	8.70%	9.40%
% Jewish	1%	2%	% Married, No Children	31.10%	31.00%
% Other	0%	1%	% Single, No Children	28.40%	31.70%

STANDARD OF LIVING

INCOME, EMPLOYMENT & TAXES	AREA	U.S. AVG	COST OF LIVING & HOUSING	AREA	U.S. AVG
Median Household Income	$47,673	$44,684	Cost of Living Index	88.5	100
Household Income Growth	3.90%	6.10%	Buying Power Index	121	100
Unemployment Rate	3.90%	5.10%	Median Home Price	$137,300	$208,500
Recent Job Growth	1.30%	1.30%	Home Price Ratio	2.9	4.7
Projected Future Job Growth	14.50%	10.50%	Home Price Appreciation	5%	13.60%
State Income Tax Rate	6.70%	5.00%	% Homes Owned	67.50%	64.10%
State Sales Tax Rate	6%	6.00%	Median Rent	$650	$792

EDUCATION

ATTAINMENT & ACHIEVEMENT	AREA	U.S. AVG	RESOURCES & INVESTMENT	AREA	U.S. AVG
% High School Graduate	86.70%	83.90%	No. of Highly Ranked Universities	1	1
% 2-yr Graduate	10.50%	7.10%	$ Invested per Pupil	$5,382	$6,058
% 4-yr Graduate	19%	17.20%	Student/Teacher Ratio	15.7	15.9
% Graduate or Professional Degree	7.20%	9.90%	State University In-State Tuition	$5,268	$4,917
% Attending Public School	84.30%	84.30%			
75th Percentile State University SAT Score (Verbal)	510	477			
75th Percentile State University SAT Score (Math)	530	478			
75th Percentile State University ACT Score	22	20			

LIFESTYLE

RECREATION, ARTS & CULTURE	AREA	U.S. AVG	INFRASTRUCTURE & FACILITIES	AREA	U.S. AVG
Professional Sports Rating	3	4	No. of Public Libraries	33	28
Zoos & Aquariums Rating	8	3	Library Volumes Per Capita	2.8	2.8
Amusement Park Rating	1	3	No. of Warehouse Clubs	4	4
Professional Theater Rating	8	3	No. of Starbucks	10	5
Overall Museum Rating	7	6	Golf Course Rating	5	4
Science Museum Rating	5	4	National Park Rating	2	3
Children's Museum Rating	7	3	Sq. Mi. Inland Water	4	4

CLIMATE			COMMUTE & TRANSPORTATION		
Days Mostly Sunny	220	212	Avg. Daily Commute Time	19.4	24.7
Annual Days Precipitation	99	111	% Commute by Auto	76%	77.70%
Annual Days > 90°F	38	38	Per Capita Avg. Daily Transit Miles	6.1	7.9
Annual Days < 32°F	138	88	Annual Auto Insurance Premium	$1,309	$1,314
July Relative Humidity	68	69	Gas, Cost per Gallon	$3.26	$3.05

HEALTH & SAFETY

CRIME & ENVIRNOMENTAL ISSUES	AREA	U.S. AVG	HEALTHCARE & COST	AREA	U.S. AVG
Violent Crime Rate	447	517	Physicians per Capita	333.8	254.3
Change in Violent Crime	-44.10%	-7.50%	Pediatricians per Capita	24	16.9
Property Crime Rate	4809	3783	Hospital Beds per Capita	512.5	239.7
Change in Property Crime	1.80%	-10.10%	No. of Teaching Hospitals	7	1.9
Air Quality Score	39	44	Healthcare Cost Index	98.1	100
Water Quality Score	58	33	Cost per Doctor Visit	$80	$74
Pollen/Allergy Score	50	61	Cost per Dentist Visit	$59	$67
Stress Score	29	49	Cost per Hospital Room	$610	$702
Cancer Mortality Rate	176	168.9			

Eugene, OR

Area Type: Small college town

Zip Code: 97405

Metro Area: Eugene-Springfield, OR

Metro Area Type: Smaller

Location: At the south end of Willamette Valley, 110 miles south of Portland

Time Zone: Pacific Standard Time

Pros:
Attractive setting and downtown
Arts and culture
Outdoor recreation

Cons:
Wet winters
Current unemployment
Some crime issues

The name "Fighting Ducks," bestowed on its University of Oregon sports teams, says a lot about Eugene, its nature-rich setting its good-natured residents and its moist climate. A clean university town at the southern end of the flat, expansive agricultural Willamette Valley and surrounded on three sides by heavily forested mountains, Eugene is sort of an "ecotopean" ideal of what a city should look like.

In addition to being a transportation and forest products center, Eugene also serves a large agricultural area. The top-rated University of Oregon brings 20,000 students along with arts and entertainment. More recently, smaller high-tech firms have entered the mix. Older economy industries are slowly declining, but the university as well as technology and some newer small manufacturers have kept the economy on track if not rapidly growing. More recently, Eugene has seen an influx of empty nesters and early retirees migrating from more expensive West Coast areas.

The downtown area is clean, modern, and functional, with tree-lined streets and healthy businesses arranged in a grid pattern. A small historic district surrounds the rail station and has become a retail and entertainment attraction as the "5th Street Market." The Willamette River takes a rest from the rapid Cascade descent east of town, and flows just north of the historic area. Waterfront parks and bike trails are everywhere, and the city is known as being bike-friendly. The large and creatively designed waterfront Skinner Butte Park is a central attraction just north of downtown. The 2,500-seat Hult Center for the Performing Arts is a first-class host to multiple performances, including the symphony, ballet, and opera. The attractive university campus is just east, and good residential areas lie mainly to the south and southwest with a small pocket across the river to the north. While there is a connector, the freeway passes largely unnoticed to the east of town. There

is a modern mall, but sprawl in its typical monotonous and land-gobbling forms is well contained and largely absent. Industrial areas lie mainly to the northwest and to the east in Springfield, and again have little impact on the Eugene townscape itself.

Eugene has a bit of an eclectic, leftover-hippie flavor, which lends quite a different vibe than you'll find in the surrounding area; it's sort of a "blue" island in the "red" sea of rural Oregon. Although ethnic diversity is fairly low by West Coast standards, cultural diversity is quite high and there's always plenty to do, from the traditional to the avant-garde. Whether it's football and fishing or chai tea and New Age medicine that turns you on, you'll find it in Eugene.

Standard of Living Considering that Eugene is a West Coast college town, the Cost of Living Index of 107 is reasonable. Home prices have risen with an overall trend in the region, but good family homes can be found in the high $200K to low $300K range. Development restrictions and geography yield a more varied set of home designs and vintages than is found in most areas. Reported income levels are low, but that data is influenced by the student presence and a still-large contingent of mill and other blue-collar workers. Admittedly, the corporate professional job environment isn't spectacular; many residents work for the university or in one of the area's small businesses. Effective property tax rates run 1.3% to 1.8%.

Education The university forms a strong educational base and, not surprisingly, local public schools are closely tied to it. Local primary- and secondary-school test scores are typically 10% to 20% above average, and the combined neighborhood 4-year and graduate educational attainment is 47%.

Lifestyle Days spent in town or in the wild countryside are equally pleasant. The downtown area and campus are alive most evenings and weekends with plenty of activities. Local parks, pools, and playground facilities are well above average. There is a "Science Factory" children's museum and planetarium. The city of Eugene has an active Department of Library, Recreation & Cultural Services that provides facility "hardware" as well as activity "software" in the form of events and community programs. The city area gives way quickly to natural habitat in the form of the nearby Spencer Butte Park, the wild MacKenzie River watershed to the east, and the rugged Oregon Coast 60 mountainous miles west at Florence.

Most areas can be accessed in 15 minutes, which means that commutes aren't a concern. Portland is about 3 hours north, and major trunk carriers serve the local Eugene airport. The Amtrak Cascades rail service connects Eugene with other Valley cities, Portland, and Seattle with modern equipment and a comfortable, scenic ride.

Valley areas to the north are flat and open, mostly farm- and grazing lands. Thick coniferous forests lie to the east, south, and west. The climate is marine but coastal ranges block strong storms. The Cascades to the east block most harsh continental air masses, resulting in dry, warm summers with cool evenings and only the occasional hot spell, and cool, persistently wet winters. Most of the 158 annual "days mostly sunny" occur in or near summertime, indicating the weather gloom of other seasons. The good news is infrequent snow, and outdoor activities are feasible most of the year.

Health & Safety Crime risk, particularly property crime, is slightly higher than ideal, but it's fairly characteristic of college towns. Air quality is good except for brief stagnant summer periods. Local healthcare facilities are adequate though not outstanding for a college town, and they tend to be more expensive than average.

Nearby Neighborhoods Most neighborhoods around the city offer quality family housing with little difference in price. The 97405 zip code area includes most residential options south of the city.

EUGENE, OR NEIGHBORHOOD HIGHLIGHTS	
PEOPLE	
Population	44,928
15-yr Population Growth	17.20%
5-yr Population Growth	2.70%
% Married w/Children	23.5%
% Single w/Children	9.6%
No. of Households	18,511
Median Age	39.1
Avg. Household Size	2.39
Diversity Measure	17
STANDARD OF LIVING	
Median Household Income	$46,158
% Household Income > $100K	16%
Projected Future Job Growth	11%
Cost of Living Index	107
Buying Power Index	96
Weekly Daycare Cost	$125
Median Home Price	$255,600
"Sweet Spot" Home Price	$300,000
Home Price Ratio	5.5
Median Age of Homes	30.2
% Homes Owned	66%
Effective Property Tax Rate	1.80%
Estimated Property Tax Bill	$5,400
EDUCATION	
% High School Graduates	94%
% 4-yr Degree	26%
% Graduate or Professional Degree	21%
$ Invested per Pupil	$6,026
Student/Teacher Ratio	21.8
Primary Test Score Percentile	123.2
Secondary Test Score Percentile	107.6
% Subsidized School Lunch	29.80%
% Attending Public School	88.10%
LIFESTYLE	
Leisure Rating (Area)	8
Arts & Culture Rating (Area)	6
Climate Rating (Area)	6
Physical Setting Rating	7
Downtown Core Rating	9
% Commute < 30 Min.	82%
% Commute > 1 Hour	3%
HEALTH & SAFETY	
Health Rating (Area)	5
Stress Score (Area)	10
Violent Crime Risk	100
Property Crime Risk	117

EUGENE-SPRINGFIELD, OR
AREA HIGHLIGHTS

PEOPLE

SIZE & DIVERSITY	AREA	U.S. AVG	FAMILY DEMOGRAPHICS	AREA	U.S. AVG
Population	331,594		% Married	58.60%	53.80%
15-yr Population Growth	17.20%	4.40%	% Single	41.40%	46.20%
Diversity Measure	21	54	% Divorced	10.70%	10.20%
% Religiously Observant	25%	50%	% Separated	2.80%	2.10%
% Catholic	5%	22%	% Married w/Children	26.10%	27.90%
% Protestant	18%	25%	% Single w/Children	10.40%	9.40%
% Jewish	1%	2%	% Married, No Children	32.80%	31.00%
% Other	0%	1%	% Single, No Children	30.70%	31.70%

STANDARD OF LIVING

INCOME, EMPLOYMENT & TAXES	AREA	U.S. AVG	COST OF LIVING & HOUSING	AREA	U.S. AVG
Median Household Income	$38,082	$44,684	Cost of Living Index	95.4	100
Household Income Growth	6.50%	6.10%	Buying Power Index	89	100
Unemployment Rate	6.50%	5.10%	Median Home Price	$192,400	$208,500
Recent Job Growth	1.80%	1.30%	Home Price Ratio	5.1	4.7
Projected Future Job Growth	10.90%	10.50%	Home Price Appreciation	15%	13.60%
State Income Tax Rate	9%	5.00%	% Homes Owned	65.70%	64.10%
State Sales Tax Rate	0%	6.00%	Median Rent	$687	$792

EDUCATION

ATTAINMENT & ACHIEVEMENT	AREA	U.S. AVG	RESOURCES & INVESTMENT	AREA	U.S. AVG
% High School Graduate	81.50%	83.90%	No. of Highly Ranked Universities	0	1
% 2-yr Graduate	9.70%	7.10%	$ Invested per Pupil	$5,941	$6,058
% 4-yr Graduate	17.70%	17.20%	Student/Teacher Ratio	20.7	15.9
% Graduate or Professional Degree	8.50%	9.90%	State University In-State Tuition	$5,490	$4,917
% Attending Public School	92.80%	84.30%			
75th Percentile State University SAT Score (Verbal)	490	477			
75th Percentile State University SAT Score (Math)	500	478			
75th Percentile State University ACT Score	N/A	20			

LIFESTYLE

RECREATION, ARTS & CULTURE	AREA	U.S. AVG	INFRASTRUCTURE & FACILITIES	AREA	U.S. AVG
Professional Sports Rating	2	4	No. of Public Libraries	8	28
Zoos & Aquariums Rating	1	3	Library Volumes Per Capita	2.6	2.8
Amusement Park Rating	1	3	No. of Warehouse Clubs	3	4
Professional Theater Rating	1	3	No. of Starbucks	8	5
Overall Museum Rating	6	6	Golf Course Rating	2	4
Science Museum Rating	6	4	National Park Rating	8	3
Children's Museum Rating	1	3	Sq. Mi. Inland Water	4	4

CLIMATE			COMMUTE & TRANSPORTATION		
Days Mostly Sunny	158	212	Avg. Daily Commute Time	19.9	24.7
Annual Days Precipitation	137	111	% Commute by Auto	74%	77.70%
Annual Days > 90°F	15	38	Per Capita Avg. Daily Transit Miles	15.5	7.9
Annual Days < 32°F	54	88	Annual Auto Insurance Premium	$1,127	$1,314
July Relative Humidity	72	69	Gas, Cost per Gallon	$2.91	$3.05

HEALTH & SAFETY

CRIME & ENVIRNOMENTAL ISSUES	AREA	U.S. AVG	HEALTHCARE & COST	AREA	U.S. AVG
Violent Crime Rate	263	517	Physicians per Capita	218.1	254.3
Change in Violent Crime	-31.60%	-7.50%	Pediatricians per Capita	15.1	16.9
Property Crime Rate	5022	3783	Hospital Beds per Capita	206.5	239.7
Change in Property Crime	-18.50%	-10.10%	No. of Teaching Hospitals	0	1.9
Air Quality Score	15	44	Healthcare Cost Index	122.2	100
Water Quality Score	60	33	Cost per Doctor Visit	$82	$74
Pollen/Allergy Score	64	61	Cost per Dentist Visit	$72	$67
Stress Score	98	49	Cost per Hospital Room	$723	$702
Cancer Mortality Rate	160.2	168.9			

Evendale, OH

Area Type: Inner suburb

Zip Code: 45241

Metro Area: Cincinnati-Hamilton-Middletown, OH-KY-IN

Metro Area Type: Large

Location: 15 miles north of downtown Cincinnati along I-75

Time Zone: Eastern Standard Time

Pros:
Local recreation and sports
Attractive, affordable housing
Arts and culture

Cons:
Hot, humid summers
Low job growth
Nearby growth and sprawl

Cincinnati delivers something different than most other cities in the midwest. It sits—literally and figuratively—at a crossroads of north and south; east and west; Old World and New World. This transportation and cultural gateway between the industrial North and rural South—sometimes called the "northernmost Southern city"—dates back to Underground Railroad days.

Influenced by a large influx of German and Italian immigrants in the late 19th century, the city is a patchwork of interesting architecture and historic neighborhoods interspersed by plain, unremarkable subdivisions and industrial areas. Exceptional and nationally noted arts resources are available, including classical music, theater, and museum facilities. And for a city its size, professional sports activities are well-known and widely enjoyed by area residents. Cincinnati's downtown area has declined in recent years, but it's still a destination to visit with activities along the riverfront, especially on the Kentucky side of the Ohio River. Mount Adams, a San Francisco–like area of bars, lounges, and restaurants that often overlook the river, provides nightlife. You'll also find cultural amenities in the large hilltop Eden Park overlooking the Ohio.

The area has a strong industrial base, but not in steel, autos, or auto parts. Instead, it houses the likes of Procter & Gamble and an assortment of smaller household products manufacturers, machine tool firms, and other mid-size businesses ranging from investment managers to publishers. It is said to have more Fortune 500 headquarters *per capita* than any other U.S. city. More recently, a mix of U.S. plants for Asian manufacturers has augmented these traditional industries. The employment base is solid and less subject to cycles than in other Midwest areas, but it isn't growing rapidly.

The inner suburb of Evendale is located directly north of downtown at the eastern edge of the Mill Creek Valley commercial/industrial center. Evendale is one of a series of attractive suburbs spreading mainly east and north, including Blue Ash, Montgomery, and several formerly rural areas north of the I-275 beltway. We like Evendale best because it provides a good mix of attractive and affordable housing, local recreation, and general conveniences, while being less expensive than some of the "power" suburbs to the north and east.

Evendale grew up mainly in the 1960s and 1970s, although attractive new homes arrived on the scene as the remaining dairy farms sold out. The population is a bit older and tends to include more empty nesters than some other nearby neighborhoods, but Evendale has excellent family resources and housing. Its married-with-children percentage of households is 31.4%.

At Evendale's western boundary, General Electric Aircraft Engines Group has a huge plant that provides jobs and adds to the local tax base. There isn't a distinct downtown area, but the exemplary Evendale Recreation Center and adjacent municipal buildings serve as a city center. While accelerating urban sprawl, mainly to the north and northeast, has hurt the downtown Cincinnati economy and has led to rapidly lengthening commutes, Evendale's central location has spared it much of the negative impact of this growth.

Standard of Living Cincinnati residents generally enjoy strong incomes and a low cost of living. While industry and employment in the immediate area are relatively flat, the metro area is growing rapidly, especially to the north and northeast, providing a number of new jobs within an easy (and usually reverse) commute. Quality affordable housing is one of the area's main attractions. A solid four-bedroom, two-story home with a basement on a wooded ½ acre of land can be found for under $300K. The local Cost of Living Index is 107, only modestly higher than that of the area as a whole, with a strong Buying Power Index of 140. While gradually increasing over the past few years, the cost of living is still quite reasonable considering the amenities available in the metro area. Thanks

EVENDALE, OH
NEIGHBORHOOD HIGHLIGHTS

PEOPLE

Population	23,776
15-yr Population Growth	-6%
5-yr Population Growth	-3.60%
% Married w/Children	31.4%
% Single w/Children	7.6%
No. of Households	9,557
Median Age	39.7
Avg. Household Size	2.44
Diversity Measure	18

STANDARD OF LIVING

Median Household Income	$66,560
% Household Income > $100K	27%
Projected Future Job Growth	4%
Cost of Living Index	107
Buying Power Index	140
Weekly Daycare Cost	$174
Median Home Price	$220,500
"Sweet Spot" Home Price	$280,000
Home Price Ratio	3.3
Median Age of Homes	21.6
% Homes Owned	75%
Effective Property Tax Rate	1.30%
Estimated Property Tax Bill	$3,640

EDUCATION

% High School Graduates	91%
% 4-yr Degree	27%
% Graduate or Professional Degree	17%
$ Invested per Pupil	$7,236
Student/Teacher Ratio	12.3
Primary Test Score Percentile	114.2
Secondary Test Score Percentile	113.3
% Subsidized School Lunch	28.20%
% Attending Public School	69.40%

LIFESTYLE

Leisure Rating (Area)	8
Arts & Culture Rating (Area)	10
Climate Rating (Area)	3
Physical Setting Rating	4
Downtown Core Rating	3
% Commute < 30 Min.	75%
% Commute > 1 Hour	2%

HEALTH & SAFETY

Health Rating (Area)	1
Stress Score (Area)	9
Violent Crime Risk	106
Property Crime Risk	54

mainly to GE's presence and recent tax law changes at the state level, local property tax rates are just over 1.3%—the lowest among several nearby communities.

Education   Evendale is part of the Princeton City School system, which is widely diverse and recognized in the area for strong academic and other programs. Test scores are above the state averages, although families looking for the strongest schools in the area might look to the more expensive Blue Ash just to the east. Evendale's population is well educated; 27% have 4-year degrees and another 17% have graduate or professional degrees.

Lifestyle   Convenience is one of Evendale's advantages. You can get to almost anywhere, including downtown, in 15 to 20 minutes. While the city's traffic problems have moved to the north and east along the I-71 and I-275 corridors, Evendale is tucked neatly inside of both. Many residents work in the Blue Ash Industrial Park just 5 minutes east.

The Cincinnati area is vibrant and full of recreational and arts activities. Northern Kentucky is developing a strong recreation base as well, with the likes of Covington Landing and the brand-new Newport Aquarium. It has also redeveloped its historic downtown streets into a fine entertainment district. Very large remodeled malls on the north side have developed into destinations, but unfortunately at the expense of the city center. The Hamilton County Park system is arguably one of the country's finest, and Evendale sits within 3 miles of two of its flagship parks.

The local recreation center, financed in part by a strong tax base, offers resources including a gym and top-notch aquatic center at a very modest cost to local residents. Kings Island, a first-class amusement park, is about a half-hour north. Residents not finding enough to do in the Cincinnati area will find plenty of short getaways in Kentucky and southern Indiana.

The area comprises gently rolling deciduous woods, flattening into more open farmland to the north. The climate is highly variable with periods of muggy summer heat and winter rains with short cold snaps. Although some locals dislike the weather, outdoor activities are possible much of the year. Residents just learn to carry umbrellas and coats.

Health & Safety   Although there have been a few crime issues downtown, crime risk in Evendale is moderate to low. Healthcare facilities include a major hospital in nearby Montgomery and a strong hospital complex near the university.

Nearby Neighborhoods   Families seeking a slightly more upscale lifestyle might look at communities to the north and east. Blue Ash and Montgomery offer many of the same amenities as Evendale and have more attractive downtown cores, but homes are more expensive. Mason to the north is one of the "hot" areas and has a nice downtown, but here, too, homes have gotten quite expensive. Improved highway access and new infrastructure have made Northern Kentucky areas like Highland Heights and Taylor Mill attractive as well.

CINCINNATI-HAMILTON-MIDDLETOWN, OH-KY-IN
AREA HIGHLIGHTS

PEOPLE

SIZE & DIVERSITY	AREA	U.S. AVG	FAMILY DEMOGRAPHICS	AREA	U.S. AVG
Population	1,680,102		% Married	54.70%	53.80%
15-yr Population Growth	15.60%	4.40%	% Single	45.30%	46.20%
Diversity Measure	28	54	% Divorced	9.30%	10.20%
% Religiously Observant	46%	50%	% Separated	2.70%	2.10%
% Catholic	22%	22%	% Married w/Children	28.30%	27.90%
% Protestant	22%	25%	% Single w/Children	11.40%	9.40%
% Jewish	1%	2%	% Married, No Children	27.30%	31.00%
% Other	0%	1%	% Single, No Children	32.20%	31.70%

STANDARD OF LIVING

INCOME, EMPLOYMENT & TAXES	AREA	U.S. AVG	COST OF LIVING & HOUSING	AREA	U.S. AVG
Median Household Income	$47,700	$44,684	Cost of Living Index	87.8	100
Household Income Growth	5%	6.10%	Buying Power Index	122	100
Unemployment Rate	5%	5.10%	Median Home Price	$148,500	$208,500
Recent Job Growth	0%	1.30%	Home Price Ratio	3.1	4.7
Projected Future Job Growth	11.60%	10.50%	Home Price Appreciation	5.40%	13.60%
State Income Tax Rate	7%	5.00%	% Homes Owned	65.30%	64.10%
State Sales Tax Rate	5.50%	6.00%	Median Rent	$698	$792

EDUCATION

ATTAINMENT & ACHIEVEMENT	AREA	U.S. AVG	RESOURCES & INVESTMENT	AREA	U.S. AVG
% High School Graduate	75.60%	83.90%	No. of Highly Ranked Universities	1	1
% 2-yr Graduate	6.90%	7.10%	$ Invested per Pupil	$5,950	$6,058
% 4-yr Graduate	15.10%	17.20%	Student/Teacher Ratio	17.6	15.9
% Graduate or Professional Degree	8.10%	9.90%	State University In-State Tuition	$7,542	$4,917
% Attending Public School	79.60%	84.30%			
75th Percentile State University SAT Score (Verbal)	520	477			
75th Percentile State University SAT Score (Math)	550	478			
75th Percentile State University ACT Score	23	20			

LIFESTYLE

RECREATION, ARTS & CULTURE	AREA	U.S. AVG	INFRASTRUCTURE & FACILITIES	AREA	U.S. AVG
Professional Sports Rating	6	4	No. of Public Libraries	83	28
Zoos & Aquariums Rating	7	3	Library Volumes Per Capita	4.6	2.8
Amusement Park Rating	9	3	No. of Warehouse Clubs	7	4
Professional Theater Rating	8	3	No. of Starbucks	23	5
Overall Museum Rating	9	6	Golf Course Rating	8	4
Science Museum Rating	7	4	National Park Rating	1	3
Children's Museum Rating	10	3	Sq. Mi. Inland Water	3	4

CLIMATE			COMMUTE & TRANSPORTATION		
Days Mostly Sunny	177	212	Avg. Daily Commute Time	24.6	24.7
Annual Days Precipitation	131	111	% Commute by Auto	76%	77.70%
Annual Days > 90°F	28	38	Per Capita Avg. Daily Transit Miles	12	7.9
Annual Days < 32°F	98	88	Annual Auto Insurance Premium	$1,135	$1,314
July Relative Humidity	70	69	Gas, Cost per Gallon	$3.00	$3.05

HEALTH & SAFETY

CRIME & ENVIRNOMENTAL ISSUES	AREA	U.S. AVG	HEALTHCARE & COST	AREA	U.S. AVG
Violent Crime Rate	383	517	Physicians per Capita	294.8	254.3
Change in Violent Crime	8.90%	-7.50%	Pediatricians per Capita	28.7	16.9
Property Crime Rate	4135	3783	Hospital Beds per Capita	286.1	239.7
Change in Property Crime	2.60%	-10.10%	No. of Teaching Hospitals	10	1.9
Air Quality Score	38	44	Healthcare Cost Index	95.3	100
Water Quality Score	32	33	Cost per Doctor Visit	$65	$74
Pollen/Allergy Score	60	61	Cost per Dentist Visit	$66	$67
Stress Score	86	49	Cost per Hospital Room	$682	$702
Cancer Mortality Rate	191	168.9			

Fargo, ND

Area Type: Small city

Zip Code: 58104

Metro Area: Fargo-Moorhead, ND-MN

Metro Area Type: Small

Location: Along I-94 at the North Dakota–Minnesota border

Time Zone: Central Standard Time

Pros:
Economic stability
Educated population
Health and healthcare

Cons:
Winter climate
Isolation
Low diversity

Admittedly, it's cold in Fargo in the winter. Approximately 54 days per year (1 in 7) the temperature falls below zero. Daytime temperatures rise above freezing only 6 days each winter. But Fargo, in spite of its weather, is a great place to raise a family. And ironically, it has something to do with warmth. If you can't find friends in Fargo, it's your attitude, not theirs. Maybe it's the collective winter huddle against the biting north wind. Maybe it's the distance from the big-city rat race, but Fargo is one of the most genuinely friendly places in the country. According to local resident Don Kilander, a former state senator, Fargo is "large enough to hide, but small enough to stay involved."

And where else can you attend a minor-league baseball game for six bucks per adult ticket, sit 10 feet from the field, and watch abundant family entertainment between innings as the Fargo-Moorhead Redhawks whip the Sioux Falls Canaries 20 to 2? It costs less than going to the movies in most places. It isn't that Fargo is a town of baseball fanatics—indeed, hockey gets as much or more participation. Baseball is just one great example of the many family-accessible things to do here.

The so-called "Metrocog" area includes Fargo and West Fargo, North Dakota, along with Moorhead and Dilworth, Minnesota, to the east of the Red River. That river, one of the few U.S. rivers flowing south to north, forms a shallow valley in which downtown Fargo is located. Because the drainage area is large, spring thaws and storms can send it infamously over its banks, but the area's cities are well protected.

Behind riverfront levees, downtown Fargo is clean and has a traditional Midwestern feel. Modern buildings mix with well-kept older brick structures. New residential and shopping districts are sprucing up the Fargo waterfront. And across the river in Moorhead, there are parks and the Heritage Hjemkomst Interpretive Center, a major Scandinavian history attraction. The attractive and modern land-grant North Dakota State University campus lies at the north end of downtown, bringing 12,000 students, strong sports programs, and college life to the area. Well-planned suburbs spread in all directions, especially west and south, but all areas of town are livable.

Standard of Living The area's strong economy is anchored by both traditional and innovative farm and farm-equipment businesses. Growth vectors include (1) a favorable business climate with low taxes and an educated workforce and (2) a central location for North American air cargo. Fargo has become an international air cargo hub, and has set up free-trade-zone business parks for small businesses serving international markets. Combined with stable university and healthcare industries, the economic picture yields a 2% unemployment rate and a 19% projected future job-growth rate. The cost of living is reasonable, and good family homes start around $175K but become more plentiful in the $200K to $250K range. Effective property tax rates are about 2%.

Education Schools are good and balanced across the Fargo area. Special efforts have been made to keep elementary schools small and within walking distance. The scoring data we have show performance about at state averages. Educational attainment in the area is high: 33% of people in the selected neighborhood have 4-year degrees and another 12% have graduate or professional degrees.

Lifestyle The relatively short summers are alive with activity, with parks, nearby lakes (mainly in Minnesota), outdoor concerts, festivals, and restaurants. The early-arriving winter brings with it such activities as skating and cross-country skiing. The parks and miles of trails are groomed, and public schools and other facilities are kept open as warming huts. It is said that no Fargo resident hibernates during the bitter windswept winter—in order to stay warm, they just "keep track of where the telephone poles are so they can hide behind them." High schools open their pools to indoor swimming. Indoor venues like the Children's Museum at Yunker Farm and the Fargo Theater kick into full speed. At all times of the year, you can take a day trip to the noted Red River Zoo, acclaimed for its collection of native northern-latitude animals in 32 acres of mostly outdoor habitat. Skiing is available about an hour southeast in Minnesota.

Commutes aren't an issue; Fargo is a 15-minute city. With its large airport, air service is better than average for the size of town. Minneapolis–St. Paul is about 4 hours away.

The shallow Red River Valley is surrounded by mostly level, treeless plains. Summers are pleasant with a few hot days and mostly cool evenings. Winters are cold and can be extreme with strong winds, but are typically sunny and dry. Large snow accumulations are unusual.

Health & Safety   The area scores well in health and safety categories. Metro-area crime risk is very low. Air quality is good, stress levels are very low, and healthcare facilities are well above average.

Nearby Neighborhoods   Residential neighborhoods lie in town on tree-lined, grid-style streets. Most suburban growth goes toward the west and south into the open prairies. We especially like the southwestern bedroom communities of Prairie Rose and Frontier (zip code 58104) because of their more favorable facts but the whole area is livable.

FARGO, ND NEIGHBORHOOD HIGHLIGHTS	
PEOPLE	
Population	16,284
15-yr Population Growth	25%
5-yr Population Growth	4.40%
% Married w/Children	42.8%
% Single w/Children	5.4%
No. of Households	5,923
Median Age	31.9
Avg. Household Size	2.72
Diversity Measure	8
STANDARD OF LIVING	
Median Household Income	$69,310
% Household Income > $100K	23%
Projected Future Job Growth	19%
Cost of Living Index	102
Buying Power Index	152
Weekly Daycare Cost	$130
Median Home Price	$215,900
"Sweet Spot" Home Price	$225,000
Home Price Ratio	3.1
Median Age of Homes	7.8
% Homes Owned	62%
Effective Property Tax Rate	2%
Estimated Property Tax Bill	$4,500
EDUCATION	
% High School Graduates	96%
% 4-yr Degree	33%
% Graduate or Professional Degree	12%
$ Invested per Pupil	$5,024
Student/Teacher Ratio	22.7
Primary Test Score Percentile	99
Secondary Test Score Percentile	100.1
% Subsidized School Lunch	8.70%
% Attending Public School	85.90%
LIFESTYLE	
Leisure Rating (Area)	2
Arts & Culture Rating (Area)	6
Climate Rating (Area)	4
Physical Setting Rating	1
Downtown Core Rating	4
% Commute < 30 Min.	88%
% Commute > 1 Hour	3%
HEALTH & SAFETY	BEST
Health Rating (Area)	9
Stress Score (Area)	0
Violent Crime Risk	37
Property Crime Risk	51

FARGO-MOORHEAD, ND-MN
AREA HIGHLIGHTS

PEOPLE

SIZE & DIVERSITY	AREA	U.S. AVG	FAMILY DEMOGRAPHICS	AREA	U.S. AVG
Population	181,520		% Married	61%	53.80%
15-yr Population Growth	19.20%	4.40%	% Single	39%	46.20%
Diversity Measure	12	54	% Divorced	4.60%	10.20%
% Religiously Observant	59%	50%	% Separated	0.90%	2.10%
% Catholic	16%	22%	% Married w/Children	30.90%	27.90%
% Protestant	43%	25%	% Single w/Children	5.50%	9.40%
% Jewish	0%	2%	% Married, No Children	33%	31.00%
% Other	0%	1%	% Single, No Children	28%	31.70%

STANDARD OF LIVING

INCOME, EMPLOYMENT & TAXES	AREA	U.S. AVG	COST OF LIVING & HOUSING	AREA	U.S. AVG
Median Household Income	$43,342	$44,684	Cost of Living Index	84.5	100
Household Income Growth	2%	6.10%	Buying Power Index	115	100
Unemployment Rate	2%	5.10%	Median Home Price	$132,600	$208,500
Recent Job Growth	3.30%	1.30%	Home Price Ratio	3.1	4.7
Projected Future Job Growth	14.30%	10.50%	Home Price Appreciation	9.10%	13.60%
State Income Tax Rate	3.90%	5.00%	% Homes Owned	71.90%	64.10%
State Sales Tax Rate	5%	6.00%	Median Rent	$524	$792

EDUCATION

ATTAINMENT & ACHIEVEMENT	AREA	U.S. AVG	RESOURCES & INVESTMENT	AREA	U.S. AVG
% High School Graduate	83.40%	83.90%	No. of Highly Ranked Universities	1	1
% 2-yr Graduate	14.60%	7.10%	$ Invested per Pupil	$5,194	$6,058
% 4-yr Graduate	20.10%	17.20%	Student/Teacher Ratio	16.5	15.9
% Graduate or Professional Degree	5.40%	9.90%	State University In-State Tuition	$4,828	$4,917
% Attending Public School	93.60%	84.30%			
75th Percentile State University SAT Score (Verbal)	N/A	477			
75th Percentile State University SAT Score (Math)	N/A	478			
75th Percentile State University ACT Score	20	20			

LIFESTYLE

RECREATION, ARTS & CULTURE	AREA	U.S. AVG	INFRASTRUCTURE & FACILITIES	AREA	U.S. AVG
Professional Sports Rating	2	4	No. of Public Libraries	17	28
Zoos & Aquariums Rating	1	3	Library Volumes Per Capita	2.5	2.8
Amusement Park Rating	1	3	No. of Warehouse Clubs	3	4
Professional Theater Rating	1	3	No. of Starbucks	3	5
Overall Museum Rating	5	6	Golf Course Rating	2	4
Science Museum Rating	1	4	National Park Rating	1	3
Children's Museum Rating	3	3	Sq. Mi. Inland Water	2	4

CLIMATE			COMMUTE & TRANSPORTATION		
Days Mostly Sunny	199	212	Avg. Daily Commute Time	16.2	24.7
Annual Days Precipitation	102	111	% Commute by Auto	63%	77.70%
Annual Days > 90°F	12	38	Per Capita Avg. Daily Transit Miles	5	7.9
Annual Days < 32°F	181	88	Annual Auto Insurance Premium	$841	$1,314
July Relative Humidity	71	69	Gas, Cost per Gallon	$3.04	$3.05

HEALTH & SAFETY

CRIME & ENVIRNOMENTAL ISSUES	AREA	U.S. AVG	HEALTHCARE & COST	AREA	U.S. AVG
Violent Crime Rate	100	517	Physicians per Capita	275.9	254.3
Change in Violent Crime	-29%	-7.50%	Pediatricians per Capita	14.5	16.9
Property Crime Rate	2481	3783	Hospital Beds per Capita	318.9	239.7
Change in Property Crime	-16.10%	-10.10%	No. of Teaching Hospitals	2	1.9
Air Quality Score	42	44	Healthcare Cost Index	98.2	100
Water Quality Score	47	33	Cost per Doctor Visit	$79	$74
Pollen/Allergy Score	30	61	Cost per Dentist Visit	$62	$67
Stress Score	0	49	Cost per Hospital Room	$693	$702
Cancer Mortality Rate	158.1	168.9			

Farragut, TN

Area Type: Outer suburb

Zip Code: 37922 or 37934

Metro Area: Knoxville, TN

Metro Area Type: Mid-size

Location: 10 miles west of downtown Knoxville

Time Zone: Eastern Standard Time

Pros:
Attractive setting
College influence
Nearby recreation

Cons:
Hot, humid summers
Growth pressure
Low diversity

Situated at the crossroads of I-75, I-40, and the Tennessee River in the eastern tip of the state, Knoxville calls to mind Civil War sites, atomic energy, Appalachia, the 1982 World's Fair, and the University of Tennessee. Farragut is a modern suburb to the west of Knoxville, located along the north shore of the large and winding Fort Loudoun Lake. One of the newer neighborhoods in the Knoxville area, it became an incorporated town in 1980, and recently (in 2005) earned its own zip code of 37934.

Knoxville is a not-too-big, not-too-small city of 175,000 shaped by a variety of cultural, recreational, and intellectual influences. The 20,000-student University of Tennessee is tucked into a river bend just south of the downtown core, and adds a strong college influence (especially on football weekends). Forty miles southeast is the entrance to the Great Smoky Mountains National Park and tourist gateways of Pigeon Forge and Gatlinburg. Knoxville has long served as the major northwest gateway to the park, the most visited national park east of the Mississippi. Last, but not least, the U.S. government runs the Tennessee Valley Authority and Oak Ridge National Laboratory at Oak Ridge, just 30 miles west of downtown and 15 miles northwest of Farragut.

In the Tennessee River Valley—in a transition area between the Appalachian foothills to the east and farm country to the west—the Knoxville area is hilly, wooded, and physically attractive. The downtown area, for years unremarkable, has gone through renewal spearheaded by the World's Fair, bringing new riverfront parks and pathways. A number of small but high-quality museums are in the area. The economy is stable and prosperous. Economic drivers include the university and university hospitals, the TVA, and a few major corporate employers, including Alcoa, Kimberly Clark, and (more recently) Home and Garden TV (HGTV). The

favorable tax and business climate continues to attract employers. Consequently, incomes and income growth are strong. As a whole, and despite the college influence, Knoxville is a family city, with over 32% married-with-children households in the metro area. The Farragut area comprises even more: 37% of its households are categorized as married with children.

The Farragut area itself is loosely organized with a town hall and a few local commercial establishments but no real downtown. It sits in the river valley with a mix of wooded hills and open farmland all around and mostly attractive subdivisions and community associations. The area is mainly tied to Knoxville but some residents work in Oak Ridge to the northwest.

Standard of Living As a whole, low taxes and relative uncrowding make Tennessee an affordable place to live—the Knoxville area is no exception. The Cost of Living Index for the Knoxville metro area is a very low 82, and in the more "upscale" Farragut, the COL Index creeps just above the U.S. average to 103. The real story is buying power: High incomes drive the Buying Power Index up to 179. Family home prices run $200K to $250K for an attractive colonial or Georgian with a mountain view; starter homes can be found below $200K. Costs per square foot run $75 to $100. There's no state income tax in Tennessee, and while sales taxes over 8% make up some of the difference, property taxes around 0.75% are quite reasonable. Daycare costs around $125 per week for a preschooler.

Education The university and energy labs exert an influence on education and bring in learned workers, although the Knoxville area as a whole shows only average educational attainment. Four-year degree attainment in Farragut is a healthy 33%, and another 21% of the people have graduate and professional degrees. Local schools are considered the most desirable

FARRAGUT, TN NEIGHBORHOOD HIGHLIGHTS	
PEOPLE	
Population	47,738
15-yr Population Growth	19.20%
5-yr Population Growth	4.70%
% Married w/Children	36.6%
% Single w/Children	7.4%
No. of Households	17,120
Median Age	36.3
Avg. Household Size	2.75
Diversity Measure	12
STANDARD OF LIVING	
Median Household Income	$84,426
% Household Income > $100K	33%
Projected Future Job Growth	13%
Cost of Living Index	103
Buying Power Index	179
Weekly Daycare Cost	$125
Median Home Price	$224,900
"Sweet Spot" Home Price	$225,000
Home Price Ratio	2.7
Median Age of Homes	14.9
% Homes Owned	82%
Effective Property Tax Rate	0.75%
Estimated Property Tax Bill	$ 1,800
EDUCATION	
% High School Graduates	96%
% 4-yr Degree	33%
% Graduate or Professional Degree	21%
$ Invested per Pupil	$4,793
Student/Teacher Ratio	N/A
Primary Test Score Percentile	131
Secondary Test Score Percentile	N/A
% Subsidized School Lunch	N/A
% Attending Public School	76.40%
LIFESTYLE	
Leisure Rating (Area)	6
Arts & Culture Rating (Area)	7
Climate Rating (Area)	4
Physical Setting Rating	5
Downtown Core Rating	5
% Commute < 30 Min.	68%
% Commute > 1 Hour	4%
HEALTH & SAFETY	
Health Rating (Area)	8
Stress Score (Area)	6
Violent Crime Risk	34
Property Crime Risk	55

in the Knoxville area. Primary test scores are well above average; we were unable to obtain scores for area high schools.

Lifestyle The natural surroundings and university provide plenty to do. Farragut has beautiful parks for athletic, children's, and more passive activities; Campbell Station park and its new library are popular local destinations. Water recreation comes in all forms at Fort Loudoun Lake and the Tennessee River. Knoxville is golf country, and a wide variety of other activities and entertainment options are available near the Smoky Mountains park.

Knoxville is a fairly easy 20-minute commute from Farragut, and many locals take back roads to avoid I-40 congestion and truck traffic.

Nearby mountains have a distinct effect on the area's climate. Hot, sticky air gets trapped in the valleys in summer, but cool mountain breezes help. Winters are fairly mild for the latitude, and while snow does occur, it seldom lasts more than a week. Longer periods of rain occur but the mountains shelter the area from severe storms, which are far more frequent in Nashville and to the west.

Health & Safety Crime risk in the area-at-large is moderate, but much lower in the western suburbs. Healthcare facilities are modern and bolstered by the university hospitals; healthcare costs are a very reasonable 89% of national averages.

Nearby Neighborhoods The best suburban neighborhoods lie to the west. Although the Farragut area offers a good variety of housing, golf-course communities offer more upscale alternatives. Families interested in a more urban lifestyle might want to look at older historic homes and bungalows in the city in Sequoia Hills or in Island Home across the river from downtown Knoxville.

KNOXVILLE, TN
AREA HIGHLIGHTS
PEOPLE

SIZE & DIVERSITY	AREA	U.S. AVG	FAMILY DEMOGRAPHICS	AREA	U.S. AVG
Population	724,440		% Married	57.10%	53.80%
15-yr Population Growth	24.80%	4.40%	% Single	42.90%	46.20%
Diversity Measure	17	54	% Divorced	10.20%	10.20%
% Religiously Observant	61%	50%	% Separated	2.40%	2.10%
% Catholic	3%	22%	% Married w/Children	25.70%	27.90%
% Protestant	57%	25%	% Single w/Children	9%	9.40%
% Jewish	0%	2%	% Married, No Children	31.50%	31.00%
% Other	1%	1%	% Single, No Children	33.70%	31.70%

STANDARD OF LIVING

INCOME, EMPLOYMENT & TAXES	AREA	U.S. AVG	COST OF LIVING & HOUSING	AREA	U.S. AVG
Median Household Income	$40,316	$44,684	Cost of Living Index	82.1	100
Household Income Growth	3.50%	6.10%	Buying Power Index	110	100
Unemployment Rate	3.50%	5.10%	Median Home Price	$143,400	$208,500
Recent Job Growth	2.30%	1.30%	Home Price Ratio	3.6	4.7
Projected Future Job Growth	17.50%	10.50%	Home Price Appreciation	6.90%	13.60%
State Income Tax Rate	0%	5.00%	% Homes Owned	64.70%	64.10%
State Sales Tax Rate	8.30%	6.00%	Median Rent	$553	$792

EDUCATION

ATTAINMENT & ACHIEVEMENT	AREA	U.S. AVG	RESOURCES & INVESTMENT	AREA	U.S. AVG
% High School Graduate	71.70%	83.90%	No. of Highly Ranked Universities	1	1
% 2-yr Graduate	6.40%	7.10%	$ Invested per Pupil	$5,334	$6,058
% 4-yr Graduate	15.20%	17.20%	Student/Teacher Ratio	14.6	15.9
% Graduate or Professional Degree	7.30%	9.90%	State University In-State Tuition	$4,748	$4,917
% Attending Public School	91.90%	84.30%			
75th Percentile State University SAT Score (Verbal)	500	477			
75th Percentile State University SAT Score (Math)	500	478			
75th Percentile State University ACT Score	21	20			

LIFESTYLE

RECREATION, ARTS & CULTURE	AREA	U.S. AVG	INFRASTRUCTURE & FACILITIES	AREA	U.S. AVG
Professional Sports Rating	2	4	No. of Public Libraries	35	28
Zoos & Aquariums Rating	5	3	Library Volumes Per Capita	2.1	2.8
Amusement Park Rating	8	3	No. of Warehouse Clubs	4	4
Professional Theater Rating	1	3	No. of Starbucks	7	5
Overall Museum Rating	8	6	Golf Course Rating	5	4
Science Museum Rating	7	4	National Park Rating	8	3
Children's Museum Rating	8	3	Sq. Mi. Inland Water	8	4

CLIMATE			COMMUTE & TRANSPORTATION		
Days Mostly Sunny	202	212	Avg. Daily Commute Time	23.2	24.7
Annual Days Precipitation	128	111	% Commute by Auto	79%	77.70%
Annual Days > 90°F	19	38	Per Capita Avg. Daily Transit Miles	3.9	7.9
Annual Days < 32°F	71	88	Annual Auto Insurance Premium	$1,084	$1,314
July Relative Humidity	71	69	Gas, Cost per Gallon	$3.17	$3.05

HEALTH & SAFETY

CRIME & ENVIRNOMENTAL ISSUES	AREA	U.S. AVG	HEALTHCARE & COST	AREA	U.S. AVG
Violent Crime Rate	514	517	Physicians per Capita	282.8	254.3
Change in Violent Crime	-18.20%	-7.50%	Pediatricians per Capita	22.7	16.9
Property Crime Rate	3974	3783	Hospital Beds per Capita	409.2	239.7
Change in Property Crime	-6%	-10.10%	No. of Teaching Hospitals	1	1.9
Air Quality Score	45	44	Healthcare Cost Index	89	100
Water Quality Score	62	33	Cost per Doctor Visit	$71	$74
Pollen/Allergy Score	61	61	Cost per Dentist Visit	$55	$67
Stress Score	59	49	Cost per Hospital Room	$621	$702
Cancer Mortality Rate	164.4	168.9			

Flower Mound, TX

Area Type: Outer suburb

Zip Code: 75028

Metro Area: Dallas, TX

Metro Area Type: Largest

Location: 30 miles northwest of downtown Dallas between Lake Grapevine and I-35E

Time Zone: Central Standard Time

Pros:
Convenient location
Education
Attractive, affordable housing

Cons:
Growth and sprawl
Some long commutes
Summer heat

BEST OF THE BEST

"Please move your seat backs forward and put your tray tables in the locked and upright position." When you hear this on final approach to the Dallas–Fort Worth International Airport, look out the window. You'll see a sprawling array of new neighborhoods and business properties, many with spectacular new homes, all marked by lollipop-shaped water towers visible for miles both from the air (on a clear day, anyway) and from the largely flat landscape. If the approach is southbound and you're sitting on the right side of the plane, you might see a large oblong lake, with wooded areas and attractively laid-out streets and homes next to it. The water tower in the distance to the southwest reads GRAPEVINE and is set among groups of large brand-new homes. That beautiful suburb under your right wing, with a modernistic water tower of its own, is Flower Mound, Texas.

The regional center known as Dallas–Fort Worth (or just the "Metroplex") needs little introduction. It serves as a commercial center for the south-central part of the United States, and as a regional and national headquarters for many major U.S. corporations. The list of corporate names is too long to list in these pages, and many more companies without major facilities here have a regional branch office in the area. Downtown Dallas's steel-and-glass skyscrapers thrust upward from the middle of a vast prairie, and multiple freeways serve it from all directions like blood vessels to a beating heart. Downtown is busy, modern, and cosmopolitan. Fort Worth, to the west, is more like a typical and somewhat slower paced western or Midwestern city, with its own downtown and a more laid-back look with parks, trees, and older buildings.

Flower Mound sits at the apex of a roughly equilateral triangle, 30 miles to a side, with Fort Worth at the left corner and Dallas at the right. This strategic location between these two cities is important, but the prox-imity to prosperous and sprawling commercial centers—such as Irving, Las Colinas, and Grand Prairie—is even more important to most Metroplex area workers. The DFW airport, only 12 miles south of Flower Mound, is especially convenient for frequent business travelers. Flower Mound itself incorporated as a town in the 1960s, grew into a large 2,300-acre "new town" development in the 1970s, and fought battles throughout to avoid being annexed. After growing 55% over the past 14 years, Flower Mound now exists as a modern, attractive small town and suburb nestled among low mesquite trees. It is most definitely a family place, with excellent schools and a married-with-children percentage of households exceeding 53%, the highest of all 100 best places we discuss in this book.

Standard of Living People from other parts of the United States, particularly coastal locations, will get excited when they see what's available in Flower Mound for the price. The Cost of Living Index is 108, a bit high for the region but low by national standards for a top big-city location. High incomes bring a sizzling Buying Power Index of 193. Home prices are very attractive on a national scale, again for a big-city location, with per-square-foot costs in the $75 to $90 range and a Home Price Ratio of 2.2. The "sweet spot" is $225K, with many homes available for less. Most homes are newer with mature trees, and large homes and lots are available. Property taxes run about 2.8%, which are high but not excessive due to low valuations and the absence of state income tax. Daycare—about $140 per week—is reasonable for a large metro area.

Education Flower Mound schools are part of the Lewisville Independent School District, and are among the best schools in the state. Flower Mound High School received the state's Gold Performance Acknowledgment in seven different categories, the highest number we saw among the Texas neighborhoods we examined. Test scores regularly run 15% to 20% above state averages, and some 34% of students take advanced college-prep courses. Flower Mound Elementary received Commended Performance recognition in all four academic categories from the state of Texas.

Lifestyle Trees, lakes, and parks make Flower Mound one of the most physically beautiful areas in the Metroplex. In fact, the 544 acres of modern and well-equipped parks are linked by a 30-mile trail system. It's possible to get to most parts of the community without using roads. Athletic recreation programs, as well as arts and cultural activities, are excellent and oriented toward youth. Recreational sports programs are extensive for adults as well. The downtown area provides some basic services, and Lewisville, just east, has a larger, older, and more significant downtown area currently undergoing restoration. Outside of the Flower Mound–Lewisville area, outdoor recreation is abundant at Grapevine Lake and Lewisville Lake. Major-league sports, entertainment, arts, and cultural events are found throughout the two main Metroplex cities.

Flower Mound is convenient to most of the Metroplex, but the area is spread out and commutes are long. Driving to downtown Dallas can take 20 to 40 minutes depending on traffic, and Irving is 20 minutes away.

Flower Mound itself is a small hill some 50 feet above the rest of the area bedecked with an abundance of wildflowers; the recognition of this geographic feature should give an idea of the relatively bland landscape in the surrounding area. The climate is a mix of continental and humid subtropical elements, which yields four seasons with warm humid summers that give way to hot spells, variable winters, and wide temperature ranges all year with periods of strong storms.

Health & Safety Crime rates are low, particularly in relation to the metro area, and the Metroplex offers a wide variety of needed health services. Long commutes and fast pace bring a relatively high stress score, and the area's grasslands and winds make it uncomfortable for allergy sufferers.

Nearby Neighborhoods The high-profile Grapevine just south is more upscale. Flashier "power" suburbs with excellent housing and large planned developments, as well as top schools, are also found east in Plano,

FLOWER MOUND, TX NEIGHBORHOOD HIGHLIGHTS	
PEOPLE	
Population	44,246
15-yr Population Growth	94%
5-yr Population Growth	22.50%
% Married w/Children	53.2%
% Single w/Children	7.4%
No. of Households	14,459
Median Age	29.5
Avg. Household Size	3.12
Diversity Measure	24
STANDARD OF LIVING	BEST
Median Household Income	$97,081
% Household Income > $100K	42%
Projected Future Job Growth	26%
Cost of Living Index	108
Buying Power Index	193
Weekly Daycare Cost	$141
Median Home Price	$211,700
"Sweet Spot" Home Price	$225,000
Home Price Ratio	2.2
Median Age of Homes	8.2
% Homes Owned	90%
Effective Property Tax Rate	2.80%
Estimated Property Tax Bill	$6,300
EDUCATION	
% High School Graduates	98%
% 4-yr Degree	39%
% Graduate or Professional Degree	12%
$ Invested per Pupil	$4,720
Student/Teacher Ratio	15.1
Primary Test Score Percentile	109.6
Secondary Test Score Percentile	103.7
% Subsidized School Lunch	4.40%
% Attending Public School	83.80%
LIFESTYLE	
Leisure Rating (Area)	9
Arts & Culture Rating (Area)	9
Climate Rating (Area)	9
Physical Setting Rating	3
Downtown Core Rating	4
% Commute < 30 Min.	42%
% Commute > 1 Hour	7%
HEALTH & SAFETY	
Health Rating (Area)	1
Stress Score (Area)	9
Violent Crime Risk	48
Property Crime Risk	70

Richardson, Allen, and the up-and-coming Mesquite. Abundant neighborhood choices are available throughout the Metroplex, but we prefer Flower Mound for its relative understatement, physical appearance, and location.

DALLAS, TX
AREA HIGHLIGHTS

PEOPLE

SIZE & DIVERSITY	AREA	U.S. AVG	FAMILY DEMOGRAPHICS	AREA	U.S. AVG
Population	3,886,553		% Married	56.10%	53.80%
15-yr Population Growth	55.50%	4.40%	% Single	43.90%	46.20%
Diversity Measure	58	54	% Divorced	9.70%	10.20%
% Religiously Observant	52%	50%	% Separated	4%	2.10%
% Catholic	18%	22%	% Married w/Children	30.20%	27.90%
% Protestant	32%	25%	% Single w/Children	10.90%	9.40%
% Jewish	1%	2%	% Married, No Children	27.30%	31.00%
% Other	1%	1%	% Single, No Children	31.60%	31.70%

STANDARD OF LIVING

INCOME, EMPLOYMENT & TAXES	AREA	U.S. AVG	COST OF LIVING & HOUSING	AREA	U.S. AVG
Median Household Income	$50,996	$44,684	Cost of Living Index	91.2	100
Household Income Growth	5.60%	6.10%	Buying Power Index	125	100
Unemployment Rate	5.60%	5.10%	Median Home Price	$149,100	$208,500
Recent Job Growth	1.30%	1.30%	Home Price Ratio	2.9	4.7
Projected Future Job Growth	20%	10.50%	Home Price Appreciation	3%	13.60%
State Income Tax Rate	0%	5.00%	% Homes Owned	59.70%	64.10%
State Sales Tax Rate	8.20%	6.00%	Median Rent	$862	$792

EDUCATION

ATTAINMENT & ACHIEVEMENT	AREA	U.S. AVG	RESOURCES & INVESTMENT	AREA	U.S. AVG
% High School Graduate	79.30%	83.90%	No. of Highly Ranked Universities	3	1
% 2-yr Graduate	7.70%	7.10%	$ Invested per Pupil	$5,162	$6,058
% 4-yr Graduate	24.90%	17.20%	Student/Teacher Ratio	15.2	15.9
% Graduate or Professional Degree	10.20%	9.90%	State University In-State Tuition	$5,735	$4,917
% Attending Public School	92.50%	84.30%			
75th Percentile State University SAT Score (Verbal)	540	477			
75th Percentile State University SAT Score (Math)	570	478			
75th Percentile State University ACT Score	23	20			

LIFESTYLE

RECREATION, ARTS & CULTURE	AREA	U.S. AVG	INFRASTRUCTURE & FACILITIES	AREA	U.S. AVG
Professional Sports Rating	9	4	No. of Public Libraries	101	28
Zoos & Aquariums Rating	6	3	Library Volumes Per Capita	2.2	2.8
Amusement Park Rating	5	3	No. of Warehouse Clubs	8	4
Professional Theater Rating	10	3	No. of Starbucks	107	5
Overall Museum Rating	9	6	Golf Course Rating	8	4
Science Museum Rating	8	4	National Park Rating	1	3
Children's Museum Rating	8	3	Sq. Mi. Inland Water	7	4

CLIMATE			COMMUTE & TRANSPORTATION		
Days Mostly Sunny	233	212	Avg. Daily Commute Time	27.9	24.7
Annual Days Precipitation	79	111	% Commute by Auto	76%	77.70%
Annual Days > 90°F	88	38	Per Capita Avg. Daily Transit Miles	16.2	7.9
Annual Days < 32°F	39	88	Annual Auto Insurance Premium	$1,949	$1,314
July Relative Humidity	67	69	Gas, Cost per Gallon	$3.00	$3.05

HEALTH & SAFETY

CRIME & ENVIRNOMENTAL ISSUES	AREA	U.S. AVG	HEALTHCARE & COST	AREA	U.S. AVG
Violent Crime Rate	653	517	Physicians per Capita	215.5	254.3
Change in Violent Crime	-10.30%	-7.50%	Pediatricians per Capita	15.8	16.9
Property Crime Rate	5208	3783	Hospital Beds per Capita	263.7	239.7
Change in Property Crime	0%	-10.10%	No. of Teaching Hospitals	17	1.9
Air Quality Score	19	44	Healthcare Cost Index	107.6	100
Water Quality Score	82	33	Cost per Doctor Visit	$72	$74
Pollen/Allergy Score	87	61	Cost per Dentist Visit	$72	$67
Stress Score	94	49	Cost per Hospital Room	$789	$702
Cancer Mortality Rate	166.4	168.9			

Folsom, CA

Area Type: Suburb

Zip Code: 95630

Metro Area: Sacramento, CA

Metro Area Type: Mid-size

Location: 18 miles east of downtown Sacramento along US 50 corridor

Time Zone: Pacific Standard Time

Pros:
- Historic interest
- Nearby outdoor recreation
- Attractive climate

Cons:
- Cost of living and housing
- Growth and traffic issues
- Crowded schools

Folsom started out as a small Gold Rush mining town like many other places in 1850s California. Then it became the terminus of Sacramento Valley Railroad—the first commercial railroad west of the Mississippi—covering the 22 miles from downtown Sacramento to the first Pony Express terminus at the base of the Sierra Nevada. The line was built in hopes of becoming the first leg of the Transcontinental, but that line ultimately went north of Folsom to achieve the easier Donner Summit. Continuing life as a quiet American River mining center, Folsom claimed only 12,000 residents as late as 1980, most living in older homes surrounding the vintage riverfront historic district.

But that was then, and this is now. Currently, Folsom lies within commute distance of the booming Sacramento area and is, relatively speaking, a California bargain compared to coastal cities. Today's population has exploded to 58,000 and the once-open, oak-studded ranch grasslands are covered with a patchwork of subdivisions and shopping areas—most attractive but some not—spreading into the bare foothills rising just east of town. Home prices have likewise grown some 50% in the past 5 years and good family homes typically cost about half a million dollars. To accommodate this development, the city completely overran its infrastructure, particularly near the old downtown and American River. The horrid traffic crossing the narrow World War I–era "Rainbow Bridge" has thankfully been addressed by a new bridge.

Folsom is more than just a bedroom community for the mostly government and service jobs located in and around Sacramento. A large local Intel plant employs 6,500 people, and an assortment of other high-tech firms like Intuit, Apple, and Verizon have facilities in the area. Dozens of others, including health insurers, a large aerospace manufacturer, and an assortment of small businesses, line the so-called "Highway 50 Corridor" into Sacramento. But there is significant competition for these jobs as coastal Californians move in without employment to find lower home prices. Further fueling growth is an influx of immigrants, particularly from Asia, as Sacramento becomes the "first stop" bypassing the Los Angeles and Bay Areas altogether. About 30% of Folsom households are categorized as married with children.

Sacramento—the capital of California—has come a long way from its roots as an agricultural and rail center. The downtown area is clean with attractive, mainly modern buildings and a well-preserved historic district along the Sacramento River. Active tree planting and care have brought a shady, green look to the city and its inner residential districts. As Sacramento has spread to the north, east, and south, it has acquired the resources and amenities of a bigger city, including strong arts programs, professional sports, air service, and healthcare. Despite some growing pains, the area's location between coastal areas and mountains, with a pleasant climate most of the year, is a big plus.

Standard of Living   Folsom's Cost of Living Index is 151, which is 50% above national averages. But the good news is that strong incomes keep the Buying Power Index comfortably above par at 124, and home prices, while typically in the low $500Ks (or $250 per square foot), are starting to slow their relentless march upward. The Home Price Ratio at 6.0 has moved well above the benchmark conventional loan qualification level of 4.86, but is still better than much of the rest of the state. Property tax rates, held down by Proposition 13, are still about 1.2%, and those buying today will pay this rate on the purchase price. Daycare costs about $184 per week, or more than $750 per month.

Education   Area schools are considered excellent. In fact, all schools were rated 10 out of 10 on the combined California Test Score Rating for academics, which

FOLSOM, CA NEIGHBORHOOD HIGHLIGHTS	
PEOPLE	
Population	57,182
15-yr Population Growth	29.90%
5-yr Population Growth	10.50%
% Married w/Children	29.8%
% Single w/Children	8.7%
No. of Households	19,201
Median Age	35.5
Avg. Household Size	2.62
Diversity Measure	46
STANDARD OF LIVING	
Median Household Income	$82,962
% Household Income > $100K	30%
Projected Future Job Growth	13%
Cost of Living Index	151
Buying Power Index	124
Weekly Daycare Cost	$184
Median Home Price	$500,000
"Sweet Spot" Home Price	$525,000
Home Price Ratio	6
Median Age of Homes	9.9
% Homes Owned	73%
Effective Property Tax Rate	1.20%
Estimated Property Tax Bill	$6,300
EDUCATION	
% High School Graduates	89%
% 4-yr Degree	25%
% Graduate or Professional Degree	12%
$ Invested per Pupil	$4,695
Student/Teacher Ratio	21.4
Primary Test Score Percentile	173
Secondary Test Score Percentile	145.1
% Subsidized School Lunch	8.60%
% Attending Public School	83.50%
LIFESTYLE	
Leisure Rating (Area)	9
Arts & Culture Rating (Area)	7
Climate Rating (Area)	9
Physical Setting Rating	3
Downtown Core Rating	5
% Commute < 30 Min.	54%
% Commute > 1 Hour	7%
HEALTH & SAFETY	
Health Rating (Area)	0
Stress Score (Area)	8
Violent Crime Risk	34
Property Crime Risk	33

means that scores are in the top 10% among all California schools when compared with students in the same group. That said, the schools have had some trouble keeping up with the area's growth.

Lifestyle   Folsom and its surroundings offer many outdoor recreation opportunities. The 18,000-acre Folsom Lake reservoir is one of the largest in the state and a watersports paradise, particularly during the hot summers. The American River Bike Trail winds 34 miles to downtown Sacramento through secluded riverbank parklands. The higher Sierra Nevada wilderness areas are an hour's drive east, with excellent hiking, camping, and winter skiing opportunities, and Lake Tahoe is another 20 minutes over Echo Summit along US 50. The old-west downtown Folsom, with numerous antique and craft shops, restaurants, and sidewalk fairs is a pleasant destination, and the small but well-designed Folsom Zoo and the Folsom Aquatic Center are both popular local attractions. History buffs and shoppers will enjoy Old Sacramento and the numerous mining towns all within a day's drive. Sacramento has better than average performing arts and sports activities for a city its size. When you're looking for more to do, what should be a 2-hour drive (though it's often longer) takes you to a treasure-trove in the San Francisco Bay Area.

Commutes within the Folsom area and the outer Highway 50 Corridor are relatively easy, but downtown commuters face increasing traffic and slowdowns. A light rail line, just opened in 2005, should reduce traffic pressure somewhat.

Folsom lies at the eastern edge of California's Central Valley where the foothills start to emerge. The climate is California Mediterranean—winters are cool and wet with only occasional below-freezing temperatures and little snow, while summers are hot, dry, and dusty with frequent 100-plus days.

Health & Safety   Crime risk is very low, especially for the region. The Folsom State Prison, which Johnny Cash made famous, is out of sight and largely out of mind for most Folsom residents. A new Mercy Hospital in Folsom provides healthcare services, but the Sacramento area is one of the nation's most expensive healthcare markets. California is well-known for its air-quality problems, and air quality can be an issue in this part of the Central Valley, particularly in the late summer season.

Nearby Neighborhoods   The sprawling suburbs in West Placer and West El Dorado Counties offer numerous places to live. El Dorado Hills, to the east of Folsom, is more upscale and spread out. Roseville, Rocklin, and Lincoln to the north are booming, but have locked themselves into perpetual traffic problems due to poor planning, and neither has the downtown charm of Folsom.

SACRAMENTO, CA
AREA HIGHLIGHTS
PEOPLE

SIZE & DIVERSITY	AREA	U.S. AVG	FAMILY DEMOGRAPHICS	AREA	U.S. AVG
Population	1,832,338		% Married	56.20%	53.80%
15-yr Population Growth	38.60%	4.40%	% Single	43.80%	46.20%
Diversity Measure	53	54	% Divorced	11.10%	10.20%
% Religiously Observant	36%	50%	% Separated	3.50%	2.10%
% Catholic	18%	22%	% Married w/Children	26.80%	27.90%
% Protestant	17%	25%	% Single w/Children	11%	9.40%
% Jewish	1%	2%	% Married, No Children	31%	31.00%
% Other	0%	1%	% Single, No Children	31.20%	31.70%

STANDARD OF LIVING

INCOME, EMPLOYMENT & TAXES	AREA	U.S. AVG	COST OF LIVING & HOUSING	AREA	U.S. AVG
Median Household Income	$53,610	$44,684	Cost of Living Index	136.1	100
Household Income Growth	4.70%	6.10%	Buying Power Index	88	100
Unemployment Rate	4.70%	5.10%	Median Home Price	$377,400	$208,500
Recent Job Growth	1.20%	1.30%	Home Price Ratio	7	4.7
Projected Future Job Growth	22.40%	10.50%	Home Price Appreciation	25.80%	13.60%
State Income Tax Rate	6%	5.00%	% Homes Owned	58.40%	64.10%
State Sales Tax Rate	7.70%	6.00%	Median Rent	$971	$792

EDUCATION

ATTAINMENT & ACHIEVEMENT	AREA	U.S. AVG	RESOURCES & INVESTMENT	AREA	U.S. AVG
% High School Graduate	85.20%	83.90%	No. of Highly Ranked Universities	0	1
% 2-yr Graduate	14.50%	7.10%	$ Invested per Pupil	$5,233	$6,058
% 4-yr Graduate	24.30%	17.20%	Student/Teacher Ratio	21.6	15.9
% Graduate or Professional Degree	9%	9.90%	State University In-State Tuition	$6,586	$4,917
% Attending Public School	91.40%	84.30%			
75th Percentile State University SAT Score (Verbal)	560	477			
75th Percentile State University SAT Score (Math)	600	478			
75th Percentile State University ACT Score	23	20			

LIFESTYLE

RECREATION, ARTS & CULTURE	AREA	U.S. AVG	INFRASTRUCTURE & FACILITIES	AREA	U.S. AVG
Professional Sports Rating	6	4	No. of Public Libraries	42	28
Zoos & Aquariums Rating	5	3	Library Volumes Per Capita	1.6	2.8
Amusement Park Rating	9	3	No. of Warehouse Clubs	8	4
Professional Theater Rating	9	3	No. of Starbucks	93	5
Overall Museum Rating	8	6	Golf Course Rating	6	4
Science Museum Rating	7	4	National Park Rating	10	3
Children's Museum Rating	2	3	Sq. Mi. Inland Water	9	4

CLIMATE			COMMUTE & TRANSPORTATION		
Days Mostly Sunny	265	212	Avg. Daily Commute Time	26.1	24.7
Annual Days Precipitation	57	111	% Commute by Auto	76%	77.70%
Annual Days > 90°F	77	38	Per Capita Avg. Daily Transit Miles	9.5	7.9
Annual Days < 32°F	17	88	Annual Auto Insurance Premium	$1,719	$1,314
July Relative Humidity	66	69	Gas, Cost per Gallon	$3.03	$3.05

HEALTH & SAFETY

CRIME & ENVIRNOMENTAL ISSUES	AREA	U.S. AVG	HEALTHCARE & COST	AREA	U.S. AVG
Violent Crime Rate	505	517	Physicians per Capita	220.6	254.3
Change in Violent Crime	-14.30%	-7.50%	Pediatricians per Capita	17.5	16.9
Property Crime Rate	4226	3783	Hospital Beds per Capita	210.7	239.7
Change in Property Crime	-10.10%	-10.10%	No. of Teaching Hospitals	7	1.9
Air Quality Score	23	44	Healthcare Cost Index	150.3	100
Water Quality Score	46	33	Cost per Doctor Visit	$74	$74
Pollen/Allergy Score	74	61	Cost per Dentist Visit	$87	$67
Stress Score	78	49	Cost per Hospital Room	$2,249	$702
Cancer Mortality Rate	179.4	168.9			

Fort Collins, CO

Best OF THE BEST

Area Type: Small city

Zip Code: 80526

Metro Area: Fort Collins–Loveland, CO

Metro Area Type: Smaller

Location: West of US 287 southwest of downtown Fort Collins, approximately 60 miles north of Denver

Time Zone: Mountain Standard Time

Pros:

Small-town flavor
Attractive setting
Education

Cons:

Some short-term employment issues
Harsh winters
Growth pressure

Fort Collins has been called an "American Dream Town" by *Outside* magazine, a "Preserve America Community" by the federal Advisory Council on Historic Preservation, and a "Bicycle-Friendly Community" by the League of American Bicyclists. In other words, the town's gotten its fair share of compliments, and deservedly so.

Dramatic, usually snowcapped, peaks of the main Rocky front dominate the town's western horizon, and the popular Rocky Mountain National Park is a mere 40 miles to the southwest. The well-preserved and well-used historic district originated from Colorado's golden Victorian era, and the 28,000-student Colorado State University adds an element of culture and youth, not to mention dozens of small shops, eateries, and activities.

Set in an area known as the Northern Front Range along the Cache de Poudre River, Fort Collins is one of a small group of right-sized towns (see *Nearby Neighborhoods*, on the next page) in the mainly agricultural western edge of the Great Plains near the foot of the Rockies. Large areas of sugar beets, winter wheat, and livestock ranching fill the immediate area and this "Kansas part of Colorado" spreads east for miles. These agricultural interests remain the main economic drivers in nearby Longmont and Greeley. Meanwhile, major firms like Hewlett-Packard and Eastman Kodak came to see the area as a good place to do business and soon the cities, particularly Fort Collins and Loveland, developed as a place for high-tech industry with a large industrial park in an area known as Windsor at the center of the triangle formed by Fort Collins, Loveland, and Greeley. Fort Collins and the university support the high-tech industry base with a technology incubator for small start-up companies.

The area's attractiveness, combined with business opportunities, an agriculture core, and the university, brews a balanced and effective not-too-liberal, not-too-conservative culture. While growth pressures are strong, Fort Collins has retained the charm and character of another time with excellent walking (and biking) on downtown sidewalks, historic buildings, and a neighborly feel. Tourist impact can be strong in the mountain areas west, but it rarely spreads to Fort Collins, which seldom feels crowded. The neighborhood we've chosen as a best place to raise your family lies to the southwest of downtown and comprises 32% of married-with-children households (strong for a college town).

Standard of Living Although the cost of living is a bit high on a national scale (COL Index is 114), Fort Collins is quite affordable considering what it offers and especially compared to the Boulder area just south. Income statistics are probably understated by the presence of students. While there have been some consolidations in the tech industry (notably a plant closing by contract manufacturer Celestica and job jeopardy at both Kodak and HP), the long-term economic picture is buoyed by numerous smaller firms and supports high-paying jobs. Future job growth is projected at a robust 25%. Quality family housing is affordable; good family homes start in the $190Ks with the "sweet spot" near $225K. A variety of ages, sizes, and settings are available. Property taxes are set at a very favorable effective rate just under 1%.

Education The Poudre School District has a good track record for academic achievement and performance improvement, with test scores typically running 9% to 20% above state norms, and a rapidly increasing base of schools rated "excellent" by the state of Colorado. The university provides added educational and extracurricular opportunities. The combined 4-year and graduate degree attainment rate in the Fort Collins area is 50%.

Lifestyle College-town entertainment combined with exceptional outdoor resources means that a variety of recreational options are available here. Fort Collins has an excellent park system covering 600 acres with 20 miles of bike trails. A notable assortment of leisure facilities includes the City Park and Pool with a water play area, Mulberry Pool (indoor), the Edora recreation center (which houses a pool, skate park, and ice rink), three golf courses, and a racquet center. The university attracts a variety of small arts events, and the Lincoln Center theater in town hosts a variety of performances suitable for all ages. There usually isn't much reason to leave "The Fort" except to head west to the Rockies and the historic-turned-tourist town of Estes Park, but Denver is only an hour away with its big-city services and attractions.

Commutes within the Fort Collins area are easy, and it's only 15 to 20 minutes to Loveland or to the Windsor commercial areas.

The landscape in the immediate area is flat to gently rolling prairie. It's green but there are few trees except where abundantly planted in town. The continental climate is somewhat sheltered by the mountains, and it's sunny and very pleasant during three seasons. Winters can be highly variable as warm mountain chinook winds alternate with cold northerly blasts, and the high altitude increases variability year-round.

Health & Safety Crime rates are about average for a college town and don't concern local residents. Adequate healthcare facilities are anchored by three local hospitals and stress factors are low.

Nearby Neighborhoods In addition to Fort Collins, neighborhoods just east of the major north–south artery US 287 are attractive. In many ways, Loveland is as nice as Fort Collins, but it doesn't have the university and its schools don't measure up as well. Greeley is a fine choice as well; it's more agricultural, a bit less expensive, and has the University of Northern Colorado.

FORT COLLINS, CO NEIGHBORHOOD HIGHLIGHTS	
PEOPLE	
Population	45,349
15-yr Population Growth	44.40%
5-yr Population Growth	6.90%
% Married w/Children	32.0%
% Single w/Children	9.4%
No. of Households	17,476
Median Age	32.3
Avg. Household Size	2.61
Diversity Measure	25
STANDARD OF LIVING	
Median Household Income	$52,738
% Household Income > $100K	15%
Projected Future Job Growth	25%
Cost of Living Index	114
Buying Power Index	102
Weekly Daycare Cost	$155
Median Home Price	$245,500
"Sweet Spot" Home Price	$225,000
Home Price Ratio	4.7
Median Age of Homes	14.7
% Homes Owned	63%
Effective Property Tax Rate	1%
Estimated Property Tax Bill	$2,250
EDUCATION	
% High School Graduates	96%
% 4-yr Degree	30%
% Graduate or Professional Degree	20%
$ Invested per Pupil	$4,722
Student/Teacher Ratio	17
Primary Test Score Percentile	121.3
Secondary Test Score Percentile	134.7
% Subsidized School Lunch	15.60%
% Attending Public School	90.50%
LIFESTYLE	BEST
Leisure Rating (Area)	9
Arts & Culture Rating (Area)	6
Climate Rating (Area)	5
Physical Setting Rating	9
Downtown Core Rating	10
% Commute < 30 Min.	80%
% Commute > 1 Hour	5%
HEALTH & SAFETY	
Health Rating (Area)	7
Stress Score (Area)	2
Violent Crime Risk	81
Property Crime Risk	102

FORT COLLINS–LOVELAND, CO
AREA HIGHLIGHTS

PEOPLE

SIZE & DIVERSITY	AREA	U.S. AVG	FAMILY DEMOGRAPHICS	AREA	U.S. AVG
Population	268,872		% Married	57.30%	53.80%
15-yr Population Growth	44.40%	4.40%	% Single	42.70%	46.20%
Diversity Measure	23	54	% Divorced	8.70%	10.20%
% Religiously Observant	39%	50%	% Separated	1.90%	2.10%
% Catholic	13%	22%	% Married w/Children	25.20%	27.90%
% Protestant	25%	25%	% Single w/Children	7.60%	9.40%
% Jewish	0%	2%	% Married, No Children	34%	31.00%
% Other	1%	1%	% Single, No Children	33.20%	31.70%

STANDARD OF LIVING

INCOME, EMPLOYMENT & TAXES	AREA	U.S. AVG	COST OF LIVING & HOUSING	AREA	U.S. AVG
Median Household Income	$49,178	$44,684	Cost of Living Index	103	100
Household Income Growth	4.70%	6.10%	Buying Power Index	107	100
Unemployment Rate	4.70%	5.10%	Median Home Price	$197,500	$208,500
Recent Job Growth	0.80%	1.30%	Home Price Ratio	4	4.7
Projected Future Job Growth	22.60%	10.50%	Home Price Appreciation	4.70%	13.60%
State Income Tax Rate	5%	5.00%	% Homes Owned	54.20%	64.10%
State Sales Tax Rate	3%	6.00%	Median Rent	$750	$792

EDUCATION

ATTAINMENT & ACHIEVEMENT	AREA	U.S. AVG	RESOURCES & INVESTMENT	AREA	U.S. AVG
% High School Graduate	89.40%	83.90%	No. of Highly Ranked Universities	1	1
% 2-yr Graduate	10.90%	7.10%	$ Invested per Pupil	$5,460	$6,058
% 4-yr Graduate	26%	17.20%	Student/Teacher Ratio	18.8	15.9
% Graduate or Professional Degree	15.50%	9.90%	State University In-State Tuition	$4,341	$4,917
% Attending Public School	92.50%	84.30%			
75th Percentile State University SAT Score (Verbal)	530	477			
75th Percentile State University SAT Score (Math)	550	478			
75th Percentile State University ACT Score	23	20			

LIFESTYLE

RECREATION, ARTS & CULTURE	AREA	U.S. AVG	INFRASTRUCTURE & FACILITIES	AREA	U.S. AVG
Professional Sports Rating	4	4	No. of Public Libraries	7	28
Zoos & Aquariums Rating	1	3	Library Volumes Per Capita	3	2.8
Amusement Park Rating	1	3	No. of Warehouse Clubs	4	4
Professional Theater Rating	1	3	No. of Starbucks	9	5
Overall Museum Rating	6	6	Golf Course Rating	2	4
Science Museum Rating	7	4	National Park Rating	10	3
Children's Museum Rating	1	3	Sq. Mi. Inland Water	4	4

CLIMATE			COMMUTE & TRANSPORTATION		
Days Mostly Sunny	246	212	Avg. Daily Commute Time	21.4	24.7
Annual Days Precipitation	88	111	% Commute by Auto	72%	77.70%
Annual Days > 90°F	32	38	Per Capita Avg. Daily Transit Miles	4.9	7.9
Annual Days < 32°F	163	88	Annual Auto Insurance Premium	$1,346	$1,314
July Relative Humidity	53	69	Gas, Cost per Gallon	$3.04	$3.05

HEALTH & SAFETY

CRIME & ENVIRNOMENTAL ISSUES	AREA	U.S. AVG	HEALTHCARE & COST	AREA	U.S. AVG
Violent Crime Rate	261	517	Physicians per Capita	202.5	254.3
Change in Violent Crime	-12.30%	-7.50%	Pediatricians per Capita	12	16.9
Property Crime Rate	3441	3783	Hospital Beds per Capita	188.6	239.7
Change in Property Crime	-4.80%	-10.10%	No. of Teaching Hospitals	1	1.9
Air Quality Score	34	44	Healthcare Cost Index	107.8	100
Water Quality Score	100	33	Cost per Doctor Visit	$75	$74
Pollen/Allergy Score	78	61	Cost per Dentist Visit	$62	$67
Stress Score	21	49	Cost per Hospital Room	$994	$702
Cancer Mortality Rate	133.3	168.9			

Franklin, TN

Area Type: Satellite city

Zip Code: 37064

Metro Area: Nashville, TN

Metro Area Type: Large

Location: 20 miles south of downtown Nashville

Time Zone: Central Standard Time

Pros:
 Attractive downtown
 Historic interest
 Low taxes

Cons:
 Growth pressure
 Urban sprawl
 Relatively high home prices

"Fifteen miles and 100 years down the road from Nashville" is Franklin—an attractive, historic, and dignified oasis just south of Tennessee's second-largest city. A major battle toward the end of the Civil War locked in the historical importance of this small town of 45,000 residents. Thanks to civic pride and a strong preservation movement, the area retains an antebellum look, but modern-day Franklin is a progressive, fun place to live.

Attractive suburbs have sprung up around the city and some local employment, primarily in the insurance industry, has arrived. But many residents of the suburbs commute to Nashville, Spring Hill (home of automaker Saturn) to the south, or Smyrna (home of a large Nissan Motor plant) to the northeast. Nissan, in fact, just announced plans to relocate their North American headquarters from southern California to the Franklin area. Thirty percent of all households are married with children.

Nashville has always been a vibrant and dynamic metropolitan area, and its growth has recently accelerated. A strong downtown revitalization, new major-league sports teams (for example, the NFL Tennessee Titans, NHL Nashville Predators, and Arena Football Nashville Kats), and a new Nashville Zoo have highlighted its increasing scale. The Grand Old Opry, the Country Music Hall of Fame, and numerous recording studios make this the world center for country music, but country music isn't only the entertainment and culture to be found. This so-called "Music City USA" is also known as the "Athens of the South" for its historic Greek Revival architecture and as the "Protestant Vatican" for its Bible printing and location at the center of the Bible Belt. Aside from the nearby auto plants, service industries dominate the economy, including such major national healthcare corporations as Caremark Rx and HCA calling the area home.

Standard of Living   Although far from the least expensive area in the region, Franklin offers reasonable costs and a strong local economy. Employment is robust and future job growth is projected at 30%, among the highest percentage on our list. The area's peaceful location, historic interest, and solid economy have driven home prices upward, but good family residences can be found in the low $300K range. Base property taxes are under 1%. Actual property taxes vary by school district, but they're usually less than 2%. Property assessments have been rising, but the tax climate, led by the absence of an earnings-based state income tax, is otherwise favorable.

Education   Schools are one of area's attractions. There is some overcrowding, but test scores run well above national averages and new school facilities are trying to keep up with population growth. The Tennessee Comprehensive Assessment Program Achievement Tests score students against national achievement averages, and the Grassland Middle School runs 30% to 35% above these averages. Higher education in the Nashville area is led by Vanderbilt and Tennessee State universities.

Lifestyle   The area's well-preserved battlefield and old plantation sites offer cultural interest and a lot to do. Harlansville Farm, a 200-acre horse farm close to town, is being converted into a park. Downtown is lively with an active arts scene and numerous fairs, as well as bluegrass, jazz, and blues music festivals. It's the sort of downtown that lends itself to weekends touring small shops with antiques, ice cream, and local restaurants. For more active recreation, residents head to the Opryland amusement park, check out Nashville sports, or visit Percy Priest Lake to the northeast.

Growth has put some pressure on roads and traffic can be difficult at times. The commute to the Nashville

FRANKLIN, TN	
NEIGHBORHOOD HIGHLIGHTS	
PEOPLE	
Population	43,433
15-yr Population Growth	81.40%
5-yr Population Growth	16%
% Married w/Children	32.3%
% Single w/Children	11.0%
No. of Households	15,546
Median Age	34.9
Avg. Household Size	2.71
Diversity Measure	28
STANDARD OF LIVING	
Median Household Income	$65,177
% Household Income > $100K	22%
Projected Future Job Growth	30%
Cost of Living Index	108
Buying Power Index	135
Weekly Daycare Cost	$154
Median Home Price	$243,600
"Sweet Spot" Home Price	$325,000
Home Price Ratio	3.7
Median Age of Homes	18.4
% Homes Owned	76%
Effective Property Tax Rate	1.80%
Estimated Property Tax Bill	$5,850
EDUCATION	
% High School Graduates	86%
% 4-yr Degree	27%
% Graduate or Professional Degree	11%
$ Invested per Pupil	$5,339
Student/Teacher Ratio	N/A
Primary Test Score Percentile	128.7
Secondary Test Score Percentile	N/A
% Subsidized School Lunch	N/A
% Attending Public School	80.40%
LIFESTYLE	
Leisure Rating (Area)	7
Arts & Culture Rating (Area)	7
Climate Rating (Area)	2
Physical Setting Rating	4
Downtown Core Rating	6
% Commute < 30 Min.	59%
% Commute > 1 Hour	3%
HEALTH & SAFETY	
Health Rating (Area)	7
Stress Score (Area)	8
Violent Crime Risk	66
Property Crime Risk	94

area is still easy at 20 minutes, and an estimated 40% of workers make the trip for work. Others commute 12 miles south to Spring Hill.

Franklin sits in an area of rolling, mixed woods and farmland. The area lies far enough south to avoid winter extremes, and summers are warm and humid. The location on the storm track, with relatively few mountains nearby, can lead to some periods of strong storms and long winter rains.

Health & Safety   Crime in the Nashville area is slightly higher than national averages, and some of it spills over to the Franklin area; but local crime risk remains low to moderate. The Williamson Medical Center is a 140-bed area hospital and Vanderbilt's teaching hospital is in Nashville.

Nearby Neighborhoods   Residential neighborhoods surround Franklin, and those to the north are a bit more upscale and expensive. An alternative to Franklin is the less expensive Spring Hill to the south.

NASHVILLE, TN
AREA HIGHLIGHTS

PEOPLE

SIZE & DIVERSITY	AREA	U.S. AVG	FAMILY DEMOGRAPHICS	AREA	U.S. AVG
Population	1,311,630		% Married	54.80%	53.80%
15-yr Population Growth	38.20%	4.40%	% Single	45.20%	46.20%
Diversity Measure	36	54	% Divorced	9.60%	10.20%
% Religiously Observant	48%	50%	% Separated	3%	2.10%
% Catholic	5%	22%	% Married w/Children	28.50%	27.90%
% Protestant	42%	25%	% Single w/Children	10.20%	9.40%
% Jewish	0%	2%	% Married, No Children	29.10%	31.00%
% Other	1%	1%	% Single, No Children	31%	31.70%

STANDARD OF LIVING

INCOME, EMPLOYMENT & TAXES	AREA	U.S. AVG	COST OF LIVING & HOUSING	AREA	U.S. AVG
Median Household Income	$50,251	$44,684	Cost of Living Index	87.9	100
Household Income Growth	3.90%	6.10%	Buying Power Index	128	100
Unemployment Rate	3.90%	5.10%	Median Home Price	$159,700	$208,500
Recent Job Growth	2.30%	1.30%	Home Price Ratio	3.2	4.7
Projected Future Job Growth	18%	10.50%	Home Price Appreciation	6.20%	13.60%
State Income Tax Rate	0%	5.00%	% Homes Owned	65.90%	64.10%
State Sales Tax Rate	8.20%	6.00%	Median Rent	$697	$792

EDUCATION

ATTAINMENT & ACHIEVEMENT	AREA	U.S. AVG	RESOURCES & INVESTMENT	AREA	U.S. AVG
% High School Graduate	74.80%	83.90%	No. of Highly Ranked Universities	0	1
% 2-yr Graduate	6%	7.10%	$ Invested per Pupil	$5,306	$6,058
% 4-yr Graduate	17.90%	17.20%	Student/Teacher Ratio	15.1	15.9
% Graduate or Professional Degree	8%	9.90%	State University In-State Tuition	$4,748	$4,917
% Attending Public School	87%	84.30%			
75th Percentile State University SAT Score (Verbal)	500	477			
75th Percentile State University SAT Score (Math)	500	478			
75th Percentile State University ACT Score	21	20			

LIFESTYLE

RECREATION, ARTS & CULTURE	AREA	U.S. AVG	INFRASTRUCTURE & FACILITIES	AREA	U.S. AVG
Professional Sports Rating	7	4	No. of Public Libraries	44	28
Zoos & Aquariums Rating	5	3	Library Volumes Per Capita	1.8	2.8
Amusement Park Rating	1	3	No. of Warehouse Clubs	6	4
Professional Theater Rating	1	3	No. of Starbucks	22	5
Overall Museum Rating	9	6	Golf Course Rating	5	4
Science Museum Rating	5	4	National Park Rating	2	3
Children's Museum Rating	1	3	Sq. Mi. Inland Water	4	4

CLIMATE			COMMUTE & TRANSPORTATION		
Days Mostly Sunny	210	212	Avg. Daily Commute Time	25.8	24.7
Annual Days Precipitation	119	111	% Commute by Auto	74%	77.70%
Annual Days > 90°F	37	38	Per Capita Avg. Daily Transit Miles	5.4	7.9
Annual Days < 32°F	75	88	Annual Auto Insurance Premium	$1,410	$1,314
July Relative Humidity	71	69	Gas, Cost per Gallon	$3.11	$3.05

HEALTH & SAFETY

CRIME & ENVIRNOMENTAL ISSUES	AREA	U.S. AVG	HEALTHCARE & COST	AREA	U.S. AVG
Violent Crime Rate	845	517	Physicians per Capita	316.5	254.3
Change in Violent Crime	-14.40%	-7.50%	Pediatricians per Capita	23.1	16.9
Property Crime Rate	4480	3783	Hospital Beds per Capita	432.5	239.7
Change in Property Crime	-23.80%	-10.10%	No. of Teaching Hospitals	5	1.9
Air Quality Score	42	44	Healthcare Cost Index	82.5	100
Water Quality Score	77	33	Cost per Doctor Visit	$69	$74
Pollen/Allergy Score	68	61	Cost per Dentist Visit	$52	$67
Stress Score	82	49	Cost per Hospital Room	$335	$702
Cancer Mortality Rate	162.8	168.9			

Gainesville, FL

Area Type: Small college town

Zip Code: 32605

Metro Area: Gainesville, FL

Metro Area Type: Smaller

Location: North-central Florida, 75 miles southwest of Jacksonville

Time Zone: Eastern Standard Time

Pros:
College-town flavor and amenities
Outdoor recreation
Mild winters

Cons:
Hot, humid summers
Crime rates
Air service

Forget the obvious Floridian images of palm trees, beaches, high-rise condos, golf courses, boat docks, shopping malls, crowded freeways, hotels, motels, souvenir shops, and year-round tourists. Imagine, instead, a small Southern town set in an area of Southern pine forests, with a friendly Southern feel. Envision this small town built around a major university, with medical research labs where academics and professionals from all over the world work. Now you have Gainesville in mind.

It started out as a citrus-growing area, but freezes (yes, they do occur in this northerly and inland location) cut back that trade; and in the first decade of the 20th century, the University of Florida was founded here. This top-rated university brings 36,000 students to town each year. The school and its medical center, a VA hospital, along with a few other government offices, account for some 70% of the jobs in the area. In other words, Gainesville provides a stable employment base. New companies and out-of-towners, including many foreigners, are discovering Gainesville as an attractive spot to live and as a good place to do business. In fact, several new research and high-tech facilities have recently arrived.

Gainesville is a retirement place, but not in the most typical sense. Many early retirees and individuals seeking a second career find what they're looking for in Gainesville's diverse population and business climate. The popular saying goes: "Yes, people retire to Gainesville—and their parents retire to St. Pete."

The area is small enough to be explained and evaluated as a whole, but most family-style housing and living is on the west side spread among several attractive suburbs that are all considered part of Gainesville. The characteristics of zip codes 32605 and 32606 are similar in features, appearance, and housing; 32605 is larger and closer to town and has a married-with-children per-

centage of 27%, which is typical for a good family area in a college town.

Standard of Living   For a college town, living costs are reasonable. The Cost of Living Index is 90.5, and adequate family homes can be found in the low to mid $200Ks, typically $100 to $120 per square foot, for homes on ½-acre wooded lots and larger. Newer construction is more expensive. Interestingly, housing prices are bid up to a degree by parents in other parts of Florida buying homes for their college-student children (and a few roommates)—these parents consider the area a good investment. Property taxes are high at 3%, but the level of city services is also high and there's a $25,000 homestead exemption. Even better, there's no state income tax.

Education   Education at all levels is a main attraction of Gainesville. Local primary and secondary schools work together with the university on curriculum design; resulting coursework is strongly oriented toward college prep work. The schools in this area produce more Merit Scholars per capita than any others in the state of Florida. Test scores typically run 15 to 20 points above state averages, although the high school gets only a "B" from the Florida Department of Education due to slow improvements in scores. The main high school has 2,500 students, which is a large school for a small town, but student-teacher ratios are reasonable at about 17.

Lifestyle   The area features a culturally diverse and outdoor-oriented lifestyle. The university attracts a number of permanent and traveling arts exhibits, as well as various performing groups. Nature and natural history are a common theme. The Florida Museum of Natural History has the largest collection in the southeast. State parks, nature preserves, and nature centers surround the city, with the Cedar Keys area an hour away on the Gulf being the most notable. Nearby lakes offer abundant fishing and swimming and the area has several popular preserves. Sports, particularly football, are big. Jacksonville and St. Augustine (with good beaches and historic sites) are about an hour away; Orlando is 1½ hours away.

Although the area is growing in a spread-out fashion toward the west, there are no real issues with commute, and all areas of the city are easily accessible (except, perhaps, during Gator football weekends).

The natural landscape is mostly flat with forests of live oak and Southern pines. Summer heat can be persistent, as the area is located far from the oceans, but the winter climate is pleasant; and outdoor activities are possible year-round. However, unlike most of Florida, short cold snaps with some below-freezing nights occur each winter.

Health & Safety   Crime risk has been relatively high for a small town, but there are strong signs of improvement in the latest FBI statistics for the Gainesville area. Due to the university, the large VA hospital, and a number of medical research facilities and firms, healthcare is far above average. A major burn unit, a sports injury research facility, and numerous pediatricians are in the area.

Nearby Neighborhoods   There isn't much difference among residential neighborhoods in the area. The university is just west of town, and most family-oriented neighborhoods spread west from there.

GAINESVILLE, FL NEIGHBORHOOD HIGHLIGHTS	
PEOPLE	
Population	23,159
15-yr Population Growth	22.80%
5-yr Population Growth	2.40%
% Married w/Children	27.2%
% Single w/Children	9.5%
No. of Households	9,678
Median Age	38.8
Avg. Household Size	2.39
Diversity Measure	30
STANDARD OF LIVING	
Median Household Income	$55,417
% Household Income > $100K	17%
Projected Future Job Growth	12%
Cost of Living Index	90.5
Buying Power Index	138
Weekly Daycare Cost	$124
Median Home Price	$183,400
"Sweet Spot" Home Price	$240,000
Home Price Ratio	3.3
Median Age of Homes	24.8
% Homes Owned	71%
Effective Property Tax Rate	3.0%
Estimated Property Tax Bill	$7,200
EDUCATION	BEST
% High School Graduates	94%
% 4-yr Degree	24%
% Graduate or Professional Degree	29%
$ Invested per Pupil	$4,932
Student/Teacher Ratio	16.6
Primary Test Score Percentile	100
Secondary Test Score Percentile	90.9
% Subsidized School Lunch	47.80%
% Attending Public School	87.70%
LIFESTYLE	
Leisure Rating (Area)	3
Arts & Culture Rating (Area)	8
Climate Rating (Area)	8
Physical Setting Rating	5
Downtown Core Rating	9
% Commute < 30 Min.	82%
% Commute > 1 Hour	4%
HEALTH & SAFETY	
Health Rating (Area)	7
Stress Score (Area)	6
Violent Crime Risk	205
Property Crime Risk	189

GAINESVILLE, FL
AREA HIGHLIGHTS

PEOPLE

SIZE & DIVERSITY	AREA	U.S. AVG		FAMILY DEMOGRAPHICS	AREA	U.S. AVG
Population	223,090			% Married	45.50%	53.80%
15-yr Population Growth	22.80%	4.40%		% Single	54.50%	46.20%
Diversity Measure	46	54		% Divorced	9.40%	10.20%
% Religiously Observant	34%	50%		% Separated	3.10%	2.10%
% Catholic	7%	22%		% Married w/Children	22%	27.90%
% Protestant	25%	25%		% Single w/Children	11.80%	9.40%
% Jewish	1%	2%		% Married, No Children	24.40%	31.00%
% Other	0%	1%		% Single, No Children	41.90%	31.70%

STANDARD OF LIVING

INCOME, EMPLOYMENT & TAXES	AREA	U.S. AVG		COST OF LIVING & HOUSING	AREA	U.S. AVG
Median Household Income	$33,574	$44,684		Cost of Living Index	84.8	100
Household Income Growth	2%	6.10%		Buying Power Index	89	100
Unemployment Rate	2%	5.10%		Median Home Price	$188,800	$208,500
Recent Job Growth	4%	1.30%		Home Price Ratio	5.6	4.7
Projected Future Job Growth	12.80%	10.50%		Home Price Appreciation	17.60%	13.60%
State Income Tax Rate	0%	5.00%		% Homes Owned	56.80%	64.10%
State Sales Tax Rate	6%	6.00%		Median Rent	$614	$792

EDUCATION

ATTAINMENT & ACHIEVEMENT	AREA	U.S. AVG		RESOURCES & INVESTMENT	AREA	U.S. AVG
% High School Graduate	84%	83.90%		No. of Highly Ranked Universities	0	1
% 2-yr Graduate	11.40%	7.10%		$ Invested per Pupil	$5,183	$6,058
% 4-yr Graduate	22.40%	17.20%		Student/Teacher Ratio	17.7	15.9
% Graduate or Professional Degree	20.10%	9.90%		State University In-State Tuition	$2,955	$4,917
% Attending Public School	90.10%	84.30%				
75th Percentile State University SAT Score (Verbal)	570	477				
75th Percentile State University SAT Score (Math)	590	478				
75th Percentile State University ACT Score	N/A	20				

LIFESTYLE

RECREATION, ARTS & CULTURE	AREA	U.S. AVG		INFRASTRUCTURE & FACILITIES	AREA	U.S. AVG
Professional Sports Rating	2	4		No. of Public Libraries	11	28
Zoos & Aquariums Rating	2	3		Library Volumes Per Capita	3.7	2.8
Amusement Park Rating	1	3		No. of Warehouse Clubs	3	4
Professional Theater Rating	6	3		No. of Starbucks	6	5
Overall Museum Rating	5	6		Golf Course Rating	1	4
Science Museum Rating	4	4		National Park Rating	1	3
Children's Museum Rating	6	3		Sq. Mi. Inland Water	5	4

CLIMATE				COMMUTE & TRANSPORTATION		
Days Mostly Sunny	242	212		Avg. Daily Commute Time	21.1	24.7
Annual Days Precipitation	116	111		% Commute by Auto	70%	77.70%
Annual Days > 90°F	104	38		Per Capita Avg. Daily Transit Miles	9	7.9
Annual Days < 32°F	2	88		Annual Auto Insurance Premium	$1,325	$1,314
July Relative Humidity	74	69		Gas, Cost per Gallon	$2.99	$3.05

HEALTH & SAFETY

CRIME & ENVIRNOMENTAL ISSUES	AREA	U.S. AVG		HEALTHCARE & COST	AREA	U.S. AVG
Violent Crime Rate	857	517		Physicians per Capita	713.8	254.3
Change in Violent Crime	-31.20%	-7.50%		Pediatricians per Capita	48.3	16.9
Property Crime Rate	4396	3783		Hospital Beds per Capita	586.5	239.7
Change in Property Crime	-46.50%	-10.10%		No. of Teaching Hospitals	2	1.9
Air Quality Score	37	44		Healthcare Cost Index	89.5	100
Water Quality Score	45	33		Cost per Doctor Visit	$71	$74
Pollen/Allergy Score	68	61		Cost per Dentist Visit	$75	$67
Stress Score	61	49		Cost per Hospital Room	$788	$702
Cancer Mortality Rate	175.6	168.9				

Gaithersburg, MD

Area Type: Outer suburb/exurb

Zip Code: 20878

Metro Area: Washington, DC-MD-VA-WV

Metro Area Type: Largest

Location: 22 miles northwest of Washington, DC, along I-270

Time Zone: Eastern Standard Time

Pros:

Strong economy and employment
Attractive downtown and setting
Convenience to DC area

Cons:

Cost of living and housing
Growth and sprawl
Commute times

For good reason, the Washington, DC, area has become one of the most attractive places in the country to live. The area bubbles with historic and cultural interest, economic strength, education, entertainment, and diversity—all set within a uniquely attractive downtown setting and surrounding region. The big question is where to live among the area's many good choices.

Across the Potomac, the bustling, sprawling, typically suburban areas of northern Virginia offer a variety of good places to raise your family—including another best place in this book: Herndon, VA (see p. 226). If you're willing to pay more for a quieter, less crowded, more country-like setting in an area of intact historic towns, open spaces, and woods, you might consider the more sedate suburbs in Maryland, including Rockville and Gaithersburg, as well as Silver Spring farther east. These areas are not entirely without growth, sprawl, and traffic issues, but their lower population densities and more developed public transportation into DC reduce the impact.

Our pick, Gaithersburg, is an area of attractive suburbs radiating in all directions from a small town center about 10 miles north of the I-495 beltway and 20 miles from downtown Washington, DC. Just 5 miles closer to DC, Rockville is a major economic center with world-class research facilities, government contractors, and major facilities for such companies as MedImmune, Genentech, and the NASDAQ stock exchange. Although many residents commute to downtown DC, the growth of Rockville and nearby communities has fostered Gaithersburg's transition to more of a self-sufficient exurb convenient to, but not dependent on, DC itself.

Homes in Gaithersburg are attractive but also quite expensive with many choices available in subdivisions and planned developments. Montgomery Village, within the Gaithersburg area, is a unique planned community with many family-sized townhouses. Areas west of I-270, which include our chosen 20878 zip code, are more suburban and spread out with typical single-family homes and a 37.4% married-with-children percentage. Less expensive and more diverse in terms of homes and lifestyles are areas east of I-270; Montgomery Village is part of this mix. Beyond Gaithersburg, the area quickly becomes rural; one would hardly know they were within 30 miles of the bustling U.S. capital.

Standard of Living Typical of the DC area, a strong economy and stable employment combined with the area's attractions have driven up living costs and particularly housing costs. Detached family homes start in the mid $400Ks to the east of I-270 and are more likely in the $500K to $600K range or higher to the west. Planned developments and townhomes support a quality family lifestyle for less than $400K, and many of these townhomes have adequate space, basements, and attractive common areas. Property taxes, collected at both county and state levels, are about 1.2% of assessed value but can be more in some areas. High incomes make the area affordable for many, and two-earner families are common.

Education The educational context is extremely strong, with more than 34% possessing a 4-year degree and fully 30% with graduate-level degrees. Montgomery County schools are considered tops, and most are "magnet" schools available by choice for discerning parents. "A private school education for free" is the sort of comment we heard from parents about Quince Orchard High School. For higher education, the well-respected University of Maryland is nearby in College Park.

GAITHERSBURG, MD NEIGHBORHOOD HIGHLIGHTS	
PEOPLE	
Population	58,062
15-yr Population Growth	20.90%
5-yr Population Growth	5.50%
% Married w/Children	37.4%
% Single w/Children	9.6%
No. of Households	20,564
Median Age	33
Avg. Household Size	2.87
Diversity Measure	61
STANDARD OF LIVING	
Median Household Income	$97,790
% Household Income > $100K	40%
Projected Future Job Growth	11%
Cost of Living Index	159.6
Buying Power Index	137
Weekly Daycare Cost	$241
Median Home Price	$535,600
"Sweet Spot" Home Price	$550,000
Home Price Ratio	5.5
Median Age of Homes	16.3
% Homes Owned	70%
Effective Property Tax Rate	1.20%
Estimated Property Tax Bill	$6,600
EDUCATION	BEST
% High School Graduates	94%
% 4-yr Degree	34%
% Graduate or Professional Degree	30%
$ Invested per Pupil	$8,201
Student/Teacher Ratio	16.9
Primary Test Score Percentile	121.1
Secondary Test Score Percentile	123.3
% Subsidized School Lunch	13.10%
% Attending Public School	78.20%
LIFESTYLE	BEST
Leisure Rating (Area)	10
Arts & Culture Rating (Area)	10
Climate Rating (Area)	4
Physical Setting Rating	6
Downtown Core Rating	8
% Commute < 30 Min.	47%
% Commute > 1 Hour	14%
HEALTH & SAFETY	
Health Rating (Area)	3
Stress Score (Area)	4
Violent Crime Risk	58
Property Crime Risk	48

Lifestyle Parks and athletic fields are readily available. Sports, especially youth team sports, are very popular in the area, and numerous small arts venues, restaurants, and gathering places are available in downtown Gaithersburg, Rockville to the south, and Germantown to the north. Washington is a nice day trip, but most residents find what they need locally. Areas toward the mountains, to the north and west, offer skiing and house numerous historic sites. Chesapeake Bay beaches are an hour away.

DC-area commutes are always an issue, but public transit resources on the Maryland side are well developed, with the Washington Metro system in Rockville and the "MARC" heavy-rail passenger service serving Gaithersburg. Ample car-pool lanes also help. It's possible but challenging to commute to commercial centers in northern Virginia, and a few do it. One complaint we heard was about transience in this area—the tendency for people to move in and out of the area due to changing work assignments.

The area is hilly with mixed farmland, developed areas, and dense woods. The climate is coastal continental with a subtropical influence, which can bring hot and sticky summers. The area is far enough south to escape the harshest winters, but the storm-track location and nearby water can lead to occasional strong winter storms with heavy snow.

Health & Safety The crime risk as reported in the "CAP" index is quite low. The six hospitals in Montgomery County provide a good backup to above-average healthcare services in Gaithersburg.

Nearby Neighborhoods Considerable choices lie within the Gaithersburg area itself, mostly between the more single-family–oriented areas west of I-270 and the more varied neighborhoods and planned developments to the east. The Rockville area to the south is more crowded and built up but also an option.

WASHINGTON, DC-MD-VA-WV
AREA HIGHLIGHTS

PEOPLE

SIZE & DIVERSITY	AREA	U.S. AVG	FAMILY DEMOGRAPHICS	AREA	U.S. AVG
Population	5,276,939		% Married	52.70%	53.80%
15-yr Population Growth	32.30%	4.40%	% Single	47.30%	46.20%
Diversity Measure	59	54	% Divorced	7.30%	10.20%
% Religiously Observant	45%	50%	% Separated	4.50%	2.10%
% Catholic	18%	22%	% Married w/Children	29%	27.90%
% Protestant	21%	25%	% Single w/Children	9.70%	9.40%
% Jewish	3%	2%	% Married, No Children	28.30%	31.00%
% Other	3%	1%	% Single, No Children	32.70%	31.70%

STANDARD OF LIVING

INCOME, EMPLOYMENT & TAXES	AREA	U.S. AVG	COST OF LIVING & HOUSING	AREA	U.S. AVG
Median Household Income	$69,558	$44,684	Cost of Living Index	116	100
Household Income Growth	3.10%	6.10%	Buying Power Index	134	100
Unemployment Rate	3.10%	5.10%	Median Home Price	$429,200	$208,500
Recent Job Growth	2.60%	1.30%	Home Price Ratio	6.2	4.7
Projected Future Job Growth	13.60%	10.50%	Home Price Appreciation	22.40%	13.60%
State Income Tax Rate	9.40%	5.00%	% Homes Owned	65.10%	64.10%
State Sales Tax Rate	11.50%	6.00%	Median Rent	$1,162	$792

EDUCATION

ATTAINMENT & ACHIEVEMENT	AREA	U.S. AVG	RESOURCES & INVESTMENT	AREA	U.S. AVG
% High School Graduate	84.40%	83.90%	No. of Highly Ranked Universities	6	1
% 2-yr Graduate	7.30%	7.10%	$ Invested per Pupil	$7,203	$6,058
% 4-yr Graduate	25.90%	17.20%	Student/Teacher Ratio	15.7	15.9
% Graduate or Professional Degree	16.90%	9.90%	State University In-State Tuition	$7,410	$4,917
% Attending Public School	85.60%	84.30%			
75th Percentile State University SAT Score (Verbal)	560	477			
75th Percentile State University SAT Score (Math)	590	478			
75th Percentile State University ACT Score	N/A	20			

LIFESTYLE

RECREATION, ARTS & CULTURE	AREA	U.S. AVG	INFRASTRUCTURE & FACILITIES	AREA	U.S. AVG
Professional Sports Rating	9	4	No. of Public Libraries	153	28
Zoos & Aquariums Rating	10	3	Library Volumes Per Capita	3	2.8
Amusement Park Rating	2	3	No. of Warehouse Clubs	10	4
Professional Theater Rating	10	3	No. of Starbucks	194	5
Overall Museum Rating	10	6	Golf Course Rating	10	4
Science Museum Rating	10	4	National Park Rating	4	3
Children's Museum Rating	10	3	Sq. Mi. Inland Water	8	4

CLIMATE			COMMUTE & TRANSPORTATION		
Days Mostly Sunny	207	212	Avg. Daily Commute Time	32.8	24.7
Annual Days Precipitation	111	111	% Commute by Auto	66%	77.70%
Annual Days > 90°F	37	38	Per Capita Avg. Daily Transit Miles	24.4	7.9
Annual Days < 32°F	75	88	Annual Auto Insurance Premium	$1,482	$1,314
July Relative Humidity	64	69	Gas, Cost per Gallon	$3.31	$3.05

HEALTH & SAFETY

CRIME & ENVIRNOMENTAL ISSUES	AREA	U.S. AVG	HEALTHCARE & COST	AREA	U.S. AVG
Violent Crime Rate	548	517	Physicians per Capita	332	254.3
Change in Violent Crime	4.10%	-7.50%	Pediatricians per Capita	28.9	16.9
Property Crime Rate	3572	3783	Hospital Beds per Capita	242.5	239.7
Change in Property Crime	-10.50%	-10.10%	No. of Teaching Hospitals	20	1.9
Air Quality Score	41	44	Healthcare Cost Index	111.5	100
Water Quality Score	51	33	Cost per Doctor Visit	$92	$74
Pollen/Allergy Score	69	61	Cost per Dentist Visit	$70	$67
Stress Score	43	49	Cost per Hospital Room	$531	$702
Cancer Mortality Rate	176.8	168.9			

Getzville, NY

Area Type: Outer suburb

Zip Code: 14068

Metro Area: Buffalo–Niagara Falls, NY

Metro Area Type: Mid-size

Location: 17 miles northeast of downtown Buffalo

Time Zone: Eastern Standard Time

Pros:

Schools
Strong community
Summer climate

Cons:

High tax rates
Winter climate
Downtown core

Known as the "City of Good Neighbors," Buffalo offers classic and affordable old city neighborhoods, good schools, and close proximity to major centers of interest in Canada. After many years of economic decline, today's Buffalo area is on a slow rebound and offers good value for durable and opportunistic families.

City neighborhoods give way quickly to Getzville, a pocket of recently developed farmland, and then to East Amherst. These "country-ish" and relatively new suburban neighborhoods are still within 15 to 17 miles of the city center. More than 34% of households are married with children and the area has excellent schools and community services. While expensive for the Buffalo area, Getzville is quite affordable on a national scale.

Economically, Buffalo is best described as a city in transition. Rust-belt industries, corporate relocations, and consolidations took a heavy toll on the economy. For years, the downtown area declined, and many gritty neighborhoods still remain, particularly to the south. But a dedicated group of residents, some with strong philanthropic intentions, stayed put to capitalize on the area's location and strong community roots. And now, downtown redevelopment, especially along the waterfront, has brought citizens (especially young people) back to the city. Major-league sports teams (Buffalo Bills and Buffalo Sabres), plus the minor-league baseball Buffalo Bisons, have further helped bring the community together. Along a new "biomedic corridor" to the north, several new biotech companies have set up labs and facilities. From Getzville, you can get across the Canadian border in 45 minutes. Recreational opportunities abound in Canada, nearby Niagara Falls, and the New York countryside to the east.

Standard of Living   It would stand to reason that a top neighborhood in a mid-size city in an expensive state would have a high Cost of Living Index, yet the COL Index for Getzville is only 108. Home prices are key: High-quality family homes cost about $100 per square foot and the "sweet spot" is $225K to $260K. Lots typically range in size from a ½ acre to a full acre. Average commute times from Getzville are only about 20 minutes and a new connector freeway has further improved access to most of the Buffalo area.

New York taxes are generally high, and local property taxes in the Getzville-Amherst area, when taken as a rate, are quite high at $26 per $1,000. But lower property valuations keep tax bills down, and many services not normally included are covered, like water, sewer, and waste disposal. In addition, the area has a number of publicly funded community centers. Local residents don't currently complain, but rates and assessments bear close watch in the future.

While the economy in general is a lot better off than it was a few years ago, jobs and employment are a concern in the Buffalo area, and that is likely to continue. Several large older employers, like Delphi Corporation (auto parts), still hang on (if just barely), but public and privately funded economic development efforts are starting to pay off. Smaller, newer businesses—biotech, for example—are starting to arrive, attracting a new wave of professional workers. We concede that the job market makes the Buffalo area more suited for the independently employed or the financially intrepid, but low costs and good values make it still worth a look.

Education   Locals rave about the schools, with good reason. The Williamsville City School District consistently scores well. The Heim Elementary and Middle Schools and Williamsburg North High are among the top-rated schools in the state. In this district, 99% of students passed the New York State Regents Exam in

English, and most test scores in the district run 15% to 20% above state averages.

Lifestyle Community activities, with a strong amount of sports thrown into the mix, dominate the scene in this area. The Amherst neighborhood has four community centers, all free to Getzville residents, with a full set of recreational activities, including swimming and hockey. Numerous churches offer free after-school activities for children as well. Short trips take families to Canada, Niagara Falls, and nearby state parks. Cosmopolitan Toronto is only 2 hours away from Buffalo. Performing arts are strong in the Buffalo area, particularly theater and classical music. Summer outdoor concerts and events on the waterfront are commonplace. Winter brings an abundance of winter sports and activities throughout the region.

Commutes are easy, with freeway and surface street alternatives. The geography is interesting, with Lake Erie to the west and Lake Ontario to the north. While the lakes create heavy winter snowfalls at times, they aren't as severe as in New York lakefront cities to the east. Summers can be warm and sticky, but breezes from Lake Erie make late afternoons and evenings pleasant.

Health & Safety The Getzville area has very low crime risk, and the Buffalo area as a whole has low crime rates—especially considering the city's economic transition. Air quality and health resources are strong for the region, and stress factors measure relatively low.

Nearby Neighborhoods Families might also look at Clarence, a more suburban and spread-out area to the east with larger lots of property and lower taxes. The adjacent Amherst area offers a variety of housing and strong community facilities.

GETZVILLE, NY
NEIGHBORHOOD HIGHLIGHTS

PEOPLE

Population	9,952
15-yr Population Growth	-3.30%
5-yr Population Growth	-1.50%
% Married w/Children	34.2%
% Single w/Children	8.6%
No. of Households	2,290
Median Age	34.1
Avg. Household Size	2.77
Diversity Measure	23

STANDARD OF LIVING

Median Household Income	$74,539
% Household Income > $100K	28%
Projected Future Job Growth	2%
Cost of Living Index	108
Buying Power Index	153
Weekly Daycare Cost	$139
Median Home Price	$201,600
"Sweet Spot" Home Price	$240,000
Home Price Ratio	2.7
Median Age of Homes	16.5
% Homes Owned	76%
Effective Property Tax Rate	2.60%
Estimated Property Tax Bill	$6,240

EDUCATION

% High School Graduates	89%
% 4-yr Degree	22%
% Graduate or Professional Degree	21%
$ Invested per Pupil	$8,845
Student/Teacher Ratio	14.3
Primary Test Score Percentile	128.4
Secondary Test Score Percentile	110.4
% Subsidized School Lunch	11.10%
% Attending Public School	46.60%

LIFESTYLE

Leisure Rating (Area)	8
Arts & Culture Rating (Area)	10
Climate Rating (Area)	1
Physical Setting Rating	3
Downtown Core Rating	2
% Commute < 30 Min.	78%
% Commute > 1 Hour	2%

HEALTH & SAFETY

Health Rating (Area)	5
Stress Score (Area)	3
Violent Crime Risk	42
Property Crime Risk	48

BUFFALO–NIAGARA FALLS, NY
AREA HIGHLIGHTS

PEOPLE

SIZE & DIVERSITY	AREA	U.S. AVG	FAMILY DEMOGRAPHICS	AREA	U.S. AVG
Population	1,154,378		% Married	51.80%	53.80%
15-yr Population Growth	-2.90%	4.40%	% Single	48.20%	46.20%
Diversity Measure	30	54	% Divorced	7.10%	10.20%
% Religiously Observant	71%	50%	% Separated	3.30%	2.10%
% Catholic	53%	22%	% Married w/Children	24.20%	27.90%
% Protestant	16%	25%	% Single w/Children	10%	9.40%
% Jewish	2%	2%	% Married, No Children	29.10%	31.00%
% Other	0%	1%	% Single, No Children	35.40%	31.70%

STANDARD OF LIVING

INCOME, EMPLOYMENT & TAXES	AREA	U.S. AVG	COST OF LIVING & HOUSING	AREA	U.S. AVG
Median Household Income	$41,251	$44,684	Cost of Living Index	87.3	100
Household Income Growth	5.70%	6.10%	Buying Power Index	106	100
Unemployment Rate	5.70%	5.10%	Median Home Price	$97,500	$208,500
Recent Job Growth	-0.50%	1.30%	Home Price Ratio	2.4	4.7
Projected Future Job Growth	2%	10.50%	Home Price Appreciation	6.60%	13.60%
State Income Tax Rate	7.10%	5.00%	% Homes Owned	64.50%	64.10%
State Sales Tax Rate	8%	6.00%	Median Rent	$648	$792

EDUCATION

ATTAINMENT & ACHIEVEMENT	AREA	U.S. AVG	RESOURCES & INVESTMENT	AREA	U.S. AVG
% High School Graduate	81.10%	83.90%	No. of Highly Ranked Universities	1	1
% 2-yr Graduate	12%	7.10%	$ Invested per Pupil	$8,605	$6,058
% 4-yr Graduate	15.50%	17.20%	Student/Teacher Ratio	14.5	15.9
% Graduate or Professional Degree	9.10%	9.90%	State University In-State Tuition	$5,966	$4,917
% Attending Public School	84.90%	84.30%			
75th Percentile State University SAT Score (Verbal)	520	477			
75th Percentile State University SAT Score (Math)	550	478			
75th Percentile State University ACT Score	24	20			

LIFESTYLE

RECREATION, ARTS & CULTURE	AREA	U.S. AVG	INFRASTRUCTURE & FACILITIES	AREA	U.S. AVG
Professional Sports Rating	6	4	No. of Public Libraries	64	28
Zoos & Aquariums Rating	5	3	Library Volumes Per Capita	2.7	2.8
Amusement Park Rating	1	3	No. of Warehouse Clubs	5	4
Professional Theater Rating	10	3	No. of Starbucks	14	5
Overall Museum Rating	8	6	Golf Course Rating	6	4
Science Museum Rating	5	4	National Park Rating	1	3
Children's Museum Rating	2	3	Sq. Mi. Inland Water	2	4

CLIMATE			COMMUTE & TRANSPORTATION		
Days Mostly Sunny	159	212	Avg. Daily Commute Time	21.1	24.7
Annual Days Precipitation	168	111	% Commute by Auto	76%	77.70%
Annual Days > 90°F	2	38	Per Capita Avg. Daily Transit Miles	8.9	7.9
Annual Days < 32°F	137	88	Annual Auto Insurance Premium	$1,800	$1,314
July Relative Humidity	73	69	Gas, Cost per Gallon	$3.37	$3.05

HEALTH & SAFETY

CRIME & ENVIRNOMENTAL ISSUES	AREA	U.S. AVG	HEALTHCARE & COST	AREA	U.S. AVG
Violent Crime Rate	448	517	Physicians per Capita	297	254.3
Change in Violent Crime	-4.40%	-7.50%	Pediatricians per Capita	22.4	16.9
Property Crime Rate	2958	3783	Hospital Beds per Capita	674.2	239.7
Change in Property Crime	-15.10%	-10.10%	No. of Teaching Hospitals	10	1.9
Air Quality Score	15	44	Healthcare Cost Index	105.1	100
Water Quality Score	65	33	Cost per Doctor Visit	$61	$74
Pollen/Allergy Score	57	61	Cost per Dentist Visit	$90	$67
Stress Score	28	49	Cost per Hospital Room	$826	$702
Cancer Mortality Rate	190.8	168.9			

Grants Pass, OR

Area Type: Small town

Zip Code: 97526

Metro Area: Grants Pass, OR

Metro Area Type: Smallest

Location: 60 miles north of the California border along I-5

Time Zone: Pacific Standard Time

Pros:
Attractive setting
Outdoor recreation
Crime and safety

Cons:
Growth pressure
Educational attainment
Current unemployment

"It's the Climate!" proclaims a large overhead sign spanning the main drag into downtown Grants Pass. Indeed, the climate is one of the attractions of this well-located small town in the so-called "sun belt of southern Oregon."

In addition, Grants Pass has a classic downtown area now recognized as a National Historic District, with small shops and restaurants. At 900 feet elevation, it's surrounded on all sides by wooded mountains rising 1,000 to 1,500 feet above the city. The Rogue River, bordered by the large Riverside Park, runs through the middle of town. Although distant from major urban areas, Grants Pass is only about 30 miles from the larger and more commercial area of Medford. Also, Ashland—a cultural center and college town—is just another 15 miles south. Grants Pass avoids the sprawl and air-quality issues of Medford and the high costs of Ashland, while sharing many of their benefits.

Grants Pass has been around since 1863, when road builders moving through the rugged scenery north of the Rogue River toward Portland heard of Ulysses S. Grant's victory at Vicksburg. Through most of the 19th and 20th centuries, the town was a mill center and loading point for forest products industries for miles around. As a transportation junction, Grants Pass is where the main coastal California highway joins the north–south interior artery I-5 and its historic US 99 counterpart.

For years, travelers and retirees, mainly from California, headed north to southern Oregon for waterborne vacations on the Rogue River. The Rogue is one of the largest preserved wild and scenic rivers in the country, descending slowly through the Grants Pass area, then more rapidly through the spectacular Hellgate Canyon toward the Pacific. Rafting and river sports, including fishing, support many commercial enterprises, including custom raft manufacturer Sotar. Nearby mountains and national forests broaden the range of possibilities in what has become a recognized outdoor paradise.

Gradually, Californians who recognized the cost-of-living differential and the small-town quality of life started moving to Grants Pass. Local growth policies, the geography, and a relatively flat economy has put boundaries around the influx, but the area is gradually transforming from a basic materials economy into more of a knowledge economy, with small manufacturers, software firms, and healthcare providers steadily employing more people. Many residents run small businesses or work remotely. The State of Oregon and local city planners have created enterprise zones to lure more diverse businesses into the area. More families are moving in, but the demographics are mixed, with many older residents arriving as well, and the average age remains highest among areas we looked at.

Standard of Living After the physical setting and small-town feel, a low cost of living is the third leg of the stool bringing many in from other places, mainly California and the West Coast. The Cost of Living Index is 97, one of few metro-area–sized places on the West Coast below 100 (yes, Grants Pass just barely grew into a metro area in the last U.S. Census Population Survey). Home prices have risen, but an assortment of family homes is available in the high $200Ks to low $300Ks. Future job growth is projected at a modest 13% as economic transformations in progress take hold. Effective property tax rates run 1.3% to 1.4%, and there's no sales tax in Oregon.

Education Local educational attainment, still reflecting years of the working-class mill-based economy, is relatively low; 10% of the population has 4-year

GRANTS PASS, OR NEIGHBORHOOD HIGHLIGHTS	
PEOPLE	
Population	33,803
15-yr Population Growth	27.60%
5-yr Population Growth	5.50%
% Married w/Children	21.1%
% Single w/Children	11.3%
No. of Households	13,916
Median Age	41.3
Avg. Household Size	2.38
Diversity Measure	15
STANDARD OF LIVING	
Median Household Income	$32,952
% Household Income > $100K	6%
Projected Future Job Growth	13%
Cost of Living Index	97.2
Buying Power Index	77
Weekly Daycare Cost	$85
Median Home Price	$190,000
"Sweet Spot" Home Price	$300,000
Home Price Ratio	5.8
Median Age of Homes	25.1
% Homes Owned	61%
Effective Property Tax Rate	1.40%
Estimated Property Tax Bill	$4,200
EDUCATION	
% High School Graduates	84%
% 4-yr Degree	10%
% Graduate or Professional Degree	5%
$ Invested per Pupil	$5,459
Student/Teacher Ratio	21.9
Primary Test Score Percentile	107.5
Secondary Test Score Percentile	94.9
% Subsidized School Lunch	47.60%
% Attending Public School	86.90%
LIFESTYLE	
Leisure Rating (Area)	5
Arts & Culture Rating (Area)	2
Climate Rating (Area)	5
Physical Setting Rating	7
Downtown Core Rating	7
% Commute < 30 Min.	78%
% Commute > 1 Hour	3%
HEALTH & SAFETY	
Health Rating (Area)	3
Stress Score (Area)	9
Violent Crime Risk	17
Property Crime Risk	61

degrees. We expect these numbers to rise rapidly as migration increases. Local schools are growing, but they do a good job overall. Grants Pass High School tests at about state averages, but Highland Elementary School on the north side tests well above the averages. Rogue River Community College is in Grants Pass while Southern Oregon State University is located in Ashland.

Lifestyle Outdoor activities rule, and range from boating, rafting, and fishing to hiking, camping, and mountain biking. Save for some gloomy, wet weather in the winter, the climate supports these activities all year. Local events and races occur on the water and on mountain bike trails, but these areas get busy (although never really crowded) on weekends—and most evenings after work. There are some small local arts amenities, but those wanting more can go to the Shakespeare festivals in Ashland or to the historic gold mining town of Jacksonville 30 miles southeast. Good skiing is found at Mount Ashland at the California border. Excursions to Crater Lake National Park in the Cascades, Oregon Caves National Monument 30 miles southwest, and the Oregon Coast 2 hours away add to the many options, as do the local Wildlife Images wildlife rehabilitation center and the Howling Acres Wolf Sanctuary.

Commutes aren't an issue, considering that most of the town can be accessed within 10 minutes. The trip to Medford takes 30 minutes. Medford has a full-service airport but flights are expensive.

Grants Pass is surrounded by mountains on all sides and is in a border zone between marine Pacific Northwest and the more Mediterranean climate types found to the south. Summers are typical of California—calm, dry, and sunny with an occasional 100°F-plus period—while winters are more "northwest" with frequent rain, some freezing temperatures, and occasional snow. Snow persists in the nearby mountains.

Health & Safety Crime risk is among the lowest of areas we looked at, which rounds out the area's small-town feel. Air quality can suffer during the long summers. The local Three Rivers Hospital is a good-sized complex for the size of town, but healthcare has been oriented toward an older population, and the area rates near the bottom in pediatricians per capita. We expect that to change.

Nearby Neighborhoods The best family areas are on the northwest side of town toward I-5. Those looking for a bigger town environment find many of the same advantages in Medford with a similar cost profile.

GRANTS PASS, OR
AREA HIGHLIGHTS

PEOPLE

SIZE & DIVERSITY	AREA	U.S. AVG	FAMILY DEMOGRAPHICS	AREA	U.S. AVG
Population	79,920		% Married	59.80%	53.80%
15-yr Population Growth	27.60%	4.40%	% Single	40.20%	46.20%
Diversity Measure	19	54	% Divorced	11.60%	10.20%
% Religiously Observant	20%	50%	% Separated	4%	2.10%
% Catholic	3%	22%	% Married w/Children	23.20%	27.90%
% Protestant	12%	25%	% Single w/Children	11.90%	9.40%
% Jewish	0%	2%	% Married, No Children	35.10%	31.00%
% Other	4%	1%	% Single, No Children	29.80%	31.70%

STANDARD OF LIVING

INCOME, EMPLOYMENT & TAXES	AREA	U.S. AVG	COST OF LIVING & HOUSING	AREA	U.S. AVG
Median Household Income	$32,281	$44,684	Cost of Living Index	91.1	100
Household Income Growth	7.50%	6.10%	Buying Power Index	79	100
Unemployment Rate	7.50%	5.10%	Median Home Price	$138,300	$208,500
Recent Job Growth	2.90%	1.30%	Home Price Ratio	4.3	4.7
Projected Future Job Growth	13.10%	10.50%	Home Price Appreciation	12.90%	13.60%
State Income Tax Rate	9%	5.00%	% Homes Owned	67.50%	64.10%
State Sales Tax Rate	0%	6.00%	Median Rent	$597	$792

EDUCATION

ATTAINMENT & ACHIEVEMENT	AREA	U.S. AVG	RESOURCES & INVESTMENT	AREA	U.S. AVG
% High School Graduate	78.60%	83.90%	No. of Highly Ranked Universities	0	1
% 2-yr Graduate	8.90%	7.10%	$ Invested per Pupil	$5,948	$6,058
% 4-yr Graduate	13.80%	17.20%	Student/Teacher Ratio	19.2	15.9
% Graduate or Professional Degree	4.40%	9.90%	State University In-State Tuition	$5,490	$4,917
% Attending Public School	92.70%	84.30%			
75th Percentile State University SAT Score (Verbal)	490	477			
75th Percentile State University SAT Score (Math)	500	478			
75th Percentile State University ACT Score	N/A	20			

LIFESTYLE

RECREATION, ARTS & CULTURE	AREA	U.S. AVG	INFRASTRUCTURE & FACILITIES	AREA	U.S. AVG
Professional Sports Rating	1	4	No. of Public Libraries	4	28
Zoos & Aquariums Rating	1	3	Library Volumes Per Capita	2.3	2.8
Amusement Park Rating	1	3	No. of Warehouse Clubs	1	4
Professional Theater Rating	1	3	No. of Starbucks	0	5
Overall Museum Rating	2	6	Golf Course Rating	2	4
Science Museum Rating	1	4	National Park Rating	7	3
Children's Museum Rating	1	3	Sq. Mi. Inland Water	7	4

CLIMATE			COMMUTE & TRANSPORTATION		
Days Mostly Sunny	196	212	Avg. Daily Commute Time	20	24.7
Annual Days Precipitation	125	111	% Commute by Auto	73%	77.70%
Annual Days > 90°F	54	38	Per Capita Avg. Daily Transit Miles	0	7.9
Annual Days < 32°F	90	88	Annual Auto Insurance Premium	$1,131	$1,314
July Relative Humidity	67	69	Gas, Cost per Gallon	$3.06	$3.05

HEALTH & SAFETY

CRIME & ENVIRNOMENTAL ISSUES	AREA	U.S. AVG	HEALTHCARE & COST	AREA	U.S. AVG
Violent Crime Rate	54	517	Physicians per Capita	149.3	254.3
Change in Violent Crime	-52.90%	-7.50%	Pediatricians per Capita	7.6	16.9
Property Crime Rate	1196	3783	Hospital Beds per Capita	251.8	239.7
Change in Property Crime	-41.50%	-10.10%	No. of Teaching Hospitals	0	1.9
Air Quality Score	35	44	Healthcare Cost Index	113.1	100
Water Quality Score	65	33	Cost per Doctor Visit	$75	$74
Pollen/Allergy Score	58	61	Cost per Dentist Visit	$70	$67
Stress Score	85	49	Cost per Hospital Room	$708	$702
Cancer Mortality Rate	175.2	168.9			

Green Bay, WI

Area Type: Small city

Zip Code: 54313

Metro Area: Green Bay, WI

Metro Area Type: Smaller

Location: Northeastern Wisconsin at the head of Green Bay

Time Zone: Central Standard Time

Pros:
Small-town flavor
Recreation
Sports tradition

Cons:
Winter climate
Isolation
Some employment issues

The "Pack is back" and so is Green Bay. Actually, as a good family city, Green Bay never left. Green Bay serves as a port, industrial, and commercial center for most of northeastern Wisconsin. It's large enough to have desirable services and amenities while small enough to have a pleasant small-town feel. The city's economy has a strong industrial tradition with paper, forest products, shipping, and manufacturing. Insurance, healthcare, education, and newer small businesses have grown. An excellent labor force, low costs, good transportation, and business climate led to its 2004 designation by *Inc. Magazine* as the number-one medium-size place to start a business.

While the economy is important, the story hardly ends there. Today's Green Bay is prosperous, hardworking, and clean, with strong traditions brought forth in both its physical and social structures. There is plenty to do: Green Bay is in the middle of a large area of attractive farmland, water, and woodland, making it a premier center of outdoor activity of all varieties, summer and winter. Arts and recreational resources are strong if not quite at the big-city caliber. Numerous suburbs surround the city, and the Howard-Suamico (zip code 54313) area is in a suburban country/farmland area rising to the west side of town, and has a very high percentage of married-with-children households at 42.4%.

One local resource, of course, easily makes the "big city" grade. The NFL Green Bay Packers are a national institution and local obsession without parallel in all of major-league sports. Fall weekends are packed with excitement, and Lambeau Field is an incomparable shrine, crawling with souvenir shoppers and restaurant-goers even on a hot June weekday. The "Pack" galvanizes and inspires the community and, for that matter, most of Wisconsin.

Standard of Living Although a little more expensive than some other Wisconsin towns, Green Bay is affordable. A new, or almost new, family home in Howard can be purchased in the $200K to $225K range, and the "sweet spot" is around $220K. Less expensive but attractive homes can be found in city areas spreading mainly south toward Ashwaubenon and the Lambeau Field area. Lots are large, usually over a ½ acre and sometimes larger. Property tax rates are relatively low on a Wisconsin scale at about 1.8%. The Cost of Living Index in Howard is a modest 102, and the Buying Power Index is a strong 140. Current unemployment is a modest 3.8%, and while recent current and projected job-growth rates are quite attractive at 4.2% and 16% respectively, one should note that Oneida Tribe Casino has been a major employment force in recent years, bringing some question to true employment viability.

Education Most area schools are well thought of in the community. The Howard-Suamico School District, with seven schools and 4,600 students, is one of the best, often scoring 10 to 15 points above state testing averages. The University of Wisconsin Green Bay anchors the local higher education scene.

Lifestyle The Green Bay area is full of recreational activities. The Green Bay Symphony has been playing for 90 years, and other musical and theater entertainment is easy to find. In addition to performing arts centers in downtown Green Bay, a convention center and the university are by the bay shore. Also nearby is the Bay Beach Amusement Park, offering fun for whole families and special teen nights, and the Bay Beach Wildlife Sanctuary. Near the city on the east side are the Joannes Family Aquatic Center and Joannes Sk8 Park, thought to be the largest concrete skate facility in the state. The Northeastern Wisconsin Zoo, on the northwest side near Howard, is part of a 1,600-acre nature complex. The National Railroad Museum is popular, as is the Children's Museum of Green Bay. Clean, attractive downtown buildings and parkland line the Fox River through downtown. (For someone new to the area, it can be surprising to watch a giant Great Lakes freighter make its way through this setting.) Short drives to the Door Peninsula (a New England–like area to the northeast), the farm country to the west, or the wilderness areas north provide more opportunities for family recreation.

The city sits in a shallow river basin where it empties into Green Bay (the body of water). The land rises gently to the east and west; farmland is mainly to the west. Winters are an issue for those not used to a winter climate. That said, the surrounding topography and Lake Michigan and the physical Green Bay's influence modify the climate somewhat, by reducing amounts of snow and extreme cold compared to nearby areas to the west. Summers are generally cool and pleasant.

Health & Safety   Crime risk is low in the Howard area and reasonably low in the city itself. Three major hospitals are in the area, and recently they've been expanding. Healthcare costs run near national averages, and the area is number one on our best places list as a refuge from pollen and allergy problems.

Nearby Neighborhoods   Good neighborhoods can be found on all sides of the city; but the south and west areas are the best. Ashwaubenon is a mixed residential and commercial area with parks and a shopping mall. Allouez, on the east side of the river close to downtown, is an attractive, historic, and somewhat more upscale city neighborhood.

GREEN BAY, WI NEIGHBORHOOD HIGHLIGHTS	
PEOPLE	
Population	33,100
15-yr Population Growth	21.90%
5-yr Population Growth	4.60%
% Married w/Children	42.4%
% Single w/Children	8.8%
No. of Households	11,465
Median Age	33.9
Avg. Household Size	2.87
Diversity Measure	8
STANDARD OF LIVING	
Median Household Income	$65,848
% Household Income > $100K	17%
Projected Future Job Growth	16%
Cost of Living Index	102
Buying Power Index	140
Weekly Daycare Cost	$130
Median Home Price	$204,500
"Sweet Spot" Home Price	$220,000
Home Price Ratio	3.1
Median Age of Homes	17.7
% Homes Owned	85%
Effective Property Tax Rate	1.80%
Estimated Property Tax Bill	$3,960
EDUCATION	
% High School Graduates	93%
% 4-yr Degree	22%
% Graduate or Professional Degree	7%
$ Invested per Pupil	$5,972
Student/Teacher Ratio	16.5
Primary Test Score Percentile	97
Secondary Test Score Percentile	104.3
% Subsidized School Lunch	11.80%
% Attending Public School	80.60%
LIFESTYLE	
Leisure Rating (Area)	5
Arts & Culture Rating (Area)	5
Climate Rating (Area)	2
Physical Setting Rating	5
Downtown Core Rating	6
% Commute < 30 Min.	87%
% Commute > 1 Hour	3%
HEALTH & SAFETY	
Health Rating (Area)	8
Stress Score (Area)	3
Violent Crime Risk	43
Property Crime Risk	78

GREEN BAY, WI
AREA HIGHLIGHTS
PEOPLE

SIZE & DIVERSITY	AREA	U.S. AVG	FAMILY DEMOGRAPHICS	AREA	U.S. AVG
Population	237,166		% Married	58.80%	53.80%
15-yr Population Growth	21.90%	4.40%	% Single	41.30%	46.20%
Diversity Measure	19	54	% Divorced	6.50%	10.20%
% Religiously Observant	73%	50%	% Separated	1.50%	2.10%
% Catholic	52%	22%	% Married w/Children	32.90%	27.90%
% Protestant	21%	25%	% Single w/Children	7.90%	9.40%
% Jewish	0%	2%	% Married, No Children	29.70%	31.00%
% Other	0%	1%	% Single, No Children	29.50%	31.70%

STANDARD OF LIVING

INCOME, EMPLOYMENT & TAXES	AREA	U.S. AVG	COST OF LIVING & HOUSING	AREA	U.S. AVG
Median Household Income	$49,635	$44,684	Cost of Living Index	85.1	100
Household Income Growth	3.80%	6.10%	Buying Power Index	131	100
Unemployment Rate	3.80%	5.10%	Median Home Price	$159,200	$208,500
Recent Job Growth	4.20%	1.30%	Home Price Ratio	3.2	4.7
Projected Future Job Growth	13.20%	10.50%	Home Price Appreciation	6.50%	13.60%
State Income Tax Rate	6.90%	5.00%	% Homes Owned	72.20%	64.10%
State Sales Tax Rate	5%	6.00%	Median Rent	$587	$792

EDUCATION

ATTAINMENT & ACHIEVEMENT	AREA	U.S. AVG	RESOURCES & INVESTMENT	AREA	U.S. AVG
% High School Graduate	84.50%	83.90%	No. of Highly Ranked Universities	0	1
% 2-yr Graduate	10.60%	7.10%	$ Invested per Pupil	$6,626	$6,058
% 4-yr Graduate	14.90%	17.20%	Student/Teacher Ratio	15.5	15.9
% Graduate or Professional Degree	4.60%	9.90%	State University In-State Tuition	$5,862	$4,917
% Attending Public School	84.70%	84.30%			
75th Percentile State University SAT Score (Verbal)	N/A	477			
75th Percentile State University SAT Score (Math)	N/A	478			
75th Percentile State University ACT Score	26	20			

LIFESTYLE

RECREATION, ARTS & CULTURE	AREA	U.S. AVG	INFRASTRUCTURE & FACILITIES	AREA	U.S. AVG
Professional Sports Rating	6	4	No. of Public Libraries	9	28
Zoos & Aquariums Rating	1	3	Library Volumes Per Capita	1.9	2.8
Amusement Park Rating	1	3	No. of Warehouse Clubs	3	4
Professional Theater Rating	1	3	No. of Starbucks	1	5
Overall Museum Rating	5	6	Golf Course Rating	2	4
Science Museum Rating	1	4	National Park Rating	1	3
Children's Museum Rating	3	3	Sq. Mi. Inland Water	2	4

CLIMATE			COMMUTE & TRANSPORTATION		
Days Mostly Sunny	192	212	Avg. Daily Commute Time	17.5	24.7
Annual Days Precipitation	120	111	% Commute by Auto	79%	77.70%
Annual Days > 90°F	7	38	Per Capita Avg. Daily Transit Miles	9.8	7.9
Annual Days < 32°F	163	88	Annual Auto Insurance Premium	$979	$1,314
July Relative Humidity	73	69	Gas, Cost per Gallon	$2.93	$3.05

HEALTH & SAFETY

CRIME & ENVIRNOMENTAL ISSUES	AREA	U.S. AVG	HEALTHCARE & COST	AREA	U.S. AVG
Violent Crime Rate	199	517	Physicians per Capita	227.5	254.3
Change in Violent Crime	37.20%	-7.50%	Pediatricians per Capita	19.2	16.9
Property Crime Rate	2566	3783	Hospital Beds per Capita	419.3	239.7
Change in Property Crime	-27.30%	-10.10%	No. of Teaching Hospitals	2	1.9
Air Quality Score	33	44	Healthcare Cost Index	100.6	100
Water Quality Score	24	33	Cost per Doctor Visit	$86	$74
Pollen/Allergy Score	28	61	Cost per Dentist Visit	$87	$67
Stress Score	27	49	Cost per Hospital Room	$729	$702
Cancer Mortality Rate	162.3	168.9			

Greer, SC

Area Type: Small town

Zip Code: 29650

Metro Area: Greenville-Spartanburg-Anderson, SC

Metro Area Type: Small

Location: Midway between Greenville and Spartanburg, SC, 40 miles southwest of Charlotte

Time Zone: Eastern Standard Time

Pros:

Small-town flavor
Attractive housing
Recreation

Cons:

Hot, humid summers
Growth pressure
Violent crime

"Most people are very surprised when they come to Greer," a local resident said. Indeed, this town that few have heard of, literally between a triad of cities—Greenville, Spartanburg, and Anderson—and figuratively between Old South and New South, is rapidly developing into a premier family spot in South Carolina's rapidly growing northwest region. More than 36% of the households in this area are married with children.

Greer has about 20,000 residents and holds onto its traditional Southern past. But after the arrival 10 years ago of North America's only BMW assembly plant, Greer also offers numerous amenities, attractive housing, educated workers, and a pleasant physical environment.

Northwest South Carolina, and the Greenville-Spartanburg area in particular, have undergone a rapid economic transition from older textile and agriculture industries to newer manufacturing businesses. The BMW plant and a Michelin plant in Spartanburg are the jewels in the economic crown. Spartanburg has emerged as the economic center of industry and retail commerce, while Greenville is the county seat and cultural center. Greenville features a beautifully restored and award-winning downtown main street, attractive parks especially along the riverfront, and a notable performing arts center featuring the theater, symphony, and other arts-related activities. Anderson, to the south, has meanwhile remained virtually unchanged with a rural, old-industrial Southern small-city feel.

As Greer has experienced fairly rapid growth, the challenge has been to keep up with it. The progressive local city government and such volunteer organizations as the Greer Cultural Arts Council have helped preserve the area's character. But there is still concern among some local residents about the arrival of too much sprawl, cookie-cutter retail stores, and fast-food restaurants into new shopping areas.

Standard of Living   Living costs are reasonable. The Cost of Living Index is at the national average, but housing costs are the major attraction. Per-square-foot costs start at about $75 and rise to $100 for newer homes. Good family homes start in the $150K range, which is one of the lowest price points in this book. Economic transitions have kept area unemployment rates somewhat high at 5.8%, but economic diversity in the region is growing and future job growth is projected at a moderately strong 15%. Property taxes are complex, but they work out to about 1% of a property's value. Day-care costs, at $80 per week, were among the lowest we found during our research.

Education   The local Greer population is well educated; 28% possesses 4-year degrees and another 14% has graduate and professional degrees. Local schools have about 200 to 250 students per grade level. Greer High School tests at state averages on South Carolina's Basic Skills Assessment Program. The middle and elementary schools test more strongly with over 90% of students meeting state standards, about 10% higher than state averages. Clemson University is about 40 miles west in a beautiful college-town setting.

Lifestyle   Greer is expanding around a small downtown area and commercial strip. Most homes are in new subdivisions to the north of town, and many have views of the Appalachians. Local recreation centers on the strong park system—its many sports fields and a large volunteer-built "Kids Planet" section in one of the larger local parks. Simpsonville Park, 10 miles south, is another popular spot, with camps and a skate park. A Frankie's Fun Park amusement center is also nearby in Greenville. Mountains, lakes, and state parks provide

GREER, SC	
NEIGHBORHOOD HIGHLIGHTS	
PEOPLE	
Population	25,161
15-yr Population Growth	25.30%
5-yr Population Growth	5.70%
% Married w/Children	36.5%
% Single w/Children	7.9%
No. of Households	9,587
Median Age	35.5
Avg. Household Size	2.59
Diversity Measure	28
STANDARD OF LIVING	
Median Household Income	$60,592
% Household Income > $100K	24%
Projected Future Job Growth	15%
Cost of Living Index	99.8
Buying Power Index	132
Weekly Daycare Cost	$80
Median Home Price	$184,900
"Sweet Spot" Home Price	$190,000
Home Price Ratio	3.1
Median Age of Homes	14.6
% Homes Owned	67%
Effective Property Tax Rate	1%
Estimated Property Tax Bill	$1,900
EDUCATION	
% High School Graduates	89%
% 4-yr Degree	28%
% Graduate or Professional Degree	14%
$ Invested per Pupil	$4,724
Student/Teacher Ratio	10.2
Primary Test Score Percentile	101.4
Secondary Test Score Percentile	111.7
% Subsidized School Lunch	18%
% Attending Public School	78%
LIFESTYLE	
Leisure Rating (Area)	6
Arts & Culture Rating (Area)	8
Climate Rating (Area)	5
Physical Setting Rating	4
Downtown Core Rating	4
% Commute < 30 Min.	77%
% Commute > 1 Hour	4%
HEALTH & SAFETY	
Health Rating (Area)	7
Stress Score (Area)	7
Violent Crime Risk	75
Property Crime Risk	93

ample outdoor activity and spectacular fall color. Most go to Greenville for performing arts at the Peace Center, and local shopping opportunities are abundant and growing. Bigger city amenities are available in Charlotte, North Carolina, 90 miles northeast and Columbia, South Carolina, 100 miles southeast.

Commutes are easy; it takes 15 minutes to get about anywhere in the tri-cities area. There is local air service at the nearby Greenville-Spartanburg airport, but many drive to Charlotte.

The area is mainly flat and naturally wooded, with hills rising into the Appalachians just outside of town to the northwest. The winter climate is well protected by the mountains, and outdoor activities are feasible much of the year. The area is far enough from the ocean to get periods of strong summer heat and humidity.

Health & Safety Crime risk is moderate and there is evidence that it is improving. Healthcare facilities are adequate and have recently been strengthened by a new hospital in Greer.

Nearby Neighborhoods Greer is the "hot spot" in the tri-cities area, but attractive neighborhoods and subdivisions spread mainly west into Greenville.

GREENVILLE-SPARTANBURG-ANDERSON, SC
AREA HIGHLIGHTS

PEOPLE

SIZE & DIVERSITY	AREA	U.S. AVG	FAMILY DEMOGRAPHICS	AREA	U.S. AVG
Population	1,005,211		% Married	54.70%	53.80%
15-yr Population Growth	21.10%	4.40%	% Single	45.30%	46.20%
Diversity Measure	36	54	% Divorced	7.80%	10.20%
% Religiously Observant	57%	50%	% Separated	4.10%	2.10%
% Catholic	3%	22%	% Married w/Children	26.90%	27.90%
% Protestant	54%	25%	% Single w/Children	10.60%	9.40%
% Jewish	0%	2%	% Married, No Children	30.30%	31.00%
% Other	0%	1%	% Single, No Children	30.70%	31.70%

STANDARD OF LIVING

INCOME, EMPLOYMENT & TAXES	AREA	U.S. AVG	COST OF LIVING & HOUSING	AREA	U.S. AVG
Median Household Income	$38,857	$44,684	Cost of Living Index	84.8	100
Household Income Growth	5.80%	6.10%	Buying Power Index	103	100
Unemployment Rate	5.80%	5.10%	Median Home Price	$121,500	$208,500
Recent Job Growth	3.70%	1.30%	Home Price Ratio	3.1	4.7
Projected Future Job Growth	13.80%	10.50%	Home Price Appreciation	3.90%	13.60%
State Income Tax Rate	7%	5.00%	% Homes Owned	69%	64.10%
State Sales Tax Rate	5%	6.00%	Median Rent	$562	$792

EDUCATION

ATTAINMENT & ACHIEVEMENT	AREA	U.S. AVG	RESOURCES & INVESTMENT	AREA	U.S. AVG
% High School Graduate	70.40%	83.90%	No. of Highly Ranked Universities	3	1
% 2-yr Graduate	8.50%	7.10%	$ Invested per Pupil	$5,108	$6,058
% 4-yr Graduate	14.70%	17.20%	Student/Teacher Ratio	16.4	15.9
% Graduate or Professional Degree	6.70%	9.90%	State University In-State Tuition	$6,416	$4,917
% Attending Public School	91%	84.30%			
75th Percentile State University SAT Score (Verbal)	510	477			
75th Percentile State University SAT Score (Math)	520	478			
75th Percentile State University ACT Score	22	20			

LIFESTYLE

RECREATION, ARTS & CULTURE	AREA	U.S. AVG	INFRASTRUCTURE & FACILITIES	AREA	U.S. AVG
Professional Sports Rating	3	4	No. of Public Libraries	37	28
Zoos & Aquariums Rating	3	3	Library Volumes Per Capita	2.4	2.8
Amusement Park Rating	1	3	No. of Warehouse Clubs	5	4
Professional Theater Rating	1	3	No. of Starbucks	3	5
Overall Museum Rating	8	6	Golf Course Rating	5	4
Science Museum Rating	7	4	National Park Rating	1	3
Children's Museum Rating	1	3	Sq. Mi. Inland Water	2	4

CLIMATE			COMMUTE & TRANSPORTATION		
Days Mostly Sunny	221	212	Avg. Daily Commute Time	22.5	24.7
Annual Days Precipitation	119	111	% Commute by Auto	78%	77.70%
Annual Days > 90°F	29	38	Per Capita Avg. Daily Transit Miles	1.9	7.9
Annual Days < 32°F	68	88	Annual Auto Insurance Premium	$1,162	$1,314
July Relative Humidity	70	69	Gas, Cost per Gallon	$3.11	$3.05

HEALTH & SAFETY

CRIME & ENVIRNOMENTAL ISSUES	AREA	U.S. AVG	HEALTHCARE & COST	AREA	U.S. AVG
Violent Crime Rate	606	517	Physicians per Capita	218.6	254.3
Change in Violent Crime	-27.10%	-7.50%	Pediatricians per Capita	15.6	16.9
Property Crime Rate	3682	3783	Hospital Beds per Capita	312.3	239.7
Change in Property Crime	-18.30%	-10.10%	No. of Teaching Hospitals	3	1.9
Air Quality Score	34	44	Healthcare Cost Index	95.5	100
Water Quality Score	49	33	Cost per Doctor Visit	$79	$74
Pollen/Allergy Score	56	61	Cost per Dentist Visit	$60	$67
Stress Score	66	49	Cost per Hospital Room	$636	$702
Cancer Mortality Rate	161.7	168.9			

Herndon, VA

Area Type: Outer suburb/exurb

Zip Code: 20170

Metro Area: Washington, DC-MD-VA-WV

Metro Area Type: Largest

Location: Along Dulles Toll Road (SR 267), 25 miles west of Washington, DC

Time Zone: Eastern Standard Time

Pros:

Strong economy and employment
Cultural diversity
Education

Cons:

Cost of living and housing
Growth and sprawl
Commute times

Manassas, Tyson's Corner, Chantilly, Arlington, Reston, Herndon. Fairfax County, Loudoun County, Prince William County. Many of these are historic names; all are household names if you know anyone living in the DC area. The sprawling suburbs of Northern Virginia offer a vast, economically rich cornucopia of places to live within a (usually) short distance to Washington, DC, one of the most vibrant and culturally rich cities in the world.

A lengthy series of suburbs and commercial districts spread west from DC along the Dulles Toll Road. This road, originally conceived in the 1970s as an airport-only access road to the once-remote Dulles International Airport, is now a major commute artery. Concrete-and-glass corporate buildings are near the highway, housing such stalwarts as AOL, IBM, Accenture, Nextel, Fannie Mae, Siebel, Oracle, MCI, Unisys, and Northrup Grumman. Companies large and small come for the business-friendly climate, access to the federal government, and educated workforce. The area has become a premier technology and research and development base. Consequently, the area boasts a 1.7% unemployment rate and offers one of the highest income potentials in the United States.

The area's growth and prosperity have brought some of the expected negatives: high home prices, traffic, and long commutes. Although well planned for the most part, the long series of communities spreading west from Arlington through Reston, Herndon, Ashburn, and even out to Leesburg are quintessentially suburban. Reston, in fact, is one of America's premier planned communities, with self-contained centers for shopping and recreation. These communities have become good examples of "exurbs"; many residents of the Herndon area and other areas west have few economic ties with Washington, DC.

But strong cultural ties to the DC area clearly remain. Washington, DC, and its immediate surroundings are as culturally diverse and intellectually stimulating as any big city in the country, and moreover, just plain fun. The Capitol Mall and Smithsonian museum complex (with its amazing 35 million visitors per year) anchor the downtown area. Numerous performing arts and entertainment venues are in the city and spread out to the west. There's no shortage of historical, cultural, educational, and leisure resources for families with children.

Looking at the big picture, the area's negatives are easy to take in stride, considering its economic opportunity, central location, and proximity to the DC area. With so many choices, selecting a specific area is difficult, but we like Herndon for its combination of central location, relatively reasonable housing costs, low-key demeanor, and high number of married-with-children households (38.3%).

Standard of Living The strong job market and the area's attractions have elevated real estate prices, although strong incomes keep the area affordable for prosperous families. Practically speaking, home prices start in the $400Ks and move into the low to mid $500Ks. That amount buys a small two-story colonial on a wooded ¼-acre lot. Prices have appreciated 20% annually and there's some vulnerability to a real estate slowdown, both in values and in the large number of construction and real estate jobs. The Cost of Living Index is 135, but median household incomes exceed $90K and the Buying Power Index is a strong 151. The area has a high percentage of two-earner families, and daycare runs a steep $216 per week. Property taxes are about 1%, plus additional taxes on intangible assets.

Education An educated population, with almost 50% of residents achieving either 4-year or graduate-level degrees, and the intellectual base of the DC area provide strong educational encouragement. It isn't hard to find good schools in northern Virginia, and the education system lures many people to Fairfax County and to Herndon in particular. Herndon's schools are large and a bit crowded, but they consistently score above state averages.

Lifestyle Herndon's small downtown area has undergone revitalization with a new municipal center, town green, and numerous restaurants. There are also typical suburban shopping, eating, and entertainment options. Local parks and bike trails are abundant and well designed. Short drives take a family to area water parks in Reston and Chantilly, county and state parks including the Great Falls State Park along the Potomac, and numerous Civil War historic sites and parks to the south and west toward the Blue Ridge and Shenandoah Valley. Wolf Trap in nearby Vienna and the Nissan Pavilion amphitheater offer top performing acts and concerts. Herndon has its own Friday Night Live event and an assortment of other festivals and live music events.

Traffic and commutes in the area, particularly into DC, can be challenging. Some Herndon residents make the commute to DC, but most work somewhere else in northern Virginia. It takes 45 minutes to an hour by car to reach DC, or you can connect with the well-utilized Metro system 10 miles east in Vienna. The Metro system will likely be extended to the Herndon area in the future, but no specific dates are set.

The mainly flat landscape is mostly developed but sprinkled with deciduous woodlands. The climate is coastal continental with a subtropical influence, which can lead to hot, sticky summers. The area is far enough south to escape the harshest winters, but its storm-track location and nearby water can lead to occasional winter storms with heavy snow.

Health & Safety Crime risk is moderate. Healthcare facilities are strong with numerous teaching hospitals in the area.

Nearby Neighborhoods Reston, which is adjacent to the east, is another good choice, but it's slightly more expensive than Herndon and has fewer families. Many people are moving farther west into Loudoun County to the more upscale Ashburn or farther out to Leesburg. Some also look farther south and west into the less-expensive Prince William County to Manassas or Haymarket, but commutes from these places tend to be more difficult.

HERNDON, VA NEIGHBORHOOD HIGHLIGHTS	
PEOPLE	
Population	39,515
15-yr Population Growth	22.60%
5-yr Population Growth	3.40%
% Married w/Children	38.3%
% Single w/Children	9.1%
No. of Households	12,402
Median Age	31
Avg. Household Size	3.21
Diversity Measure	66
STANDARD OF LIVING	
Median Household Income	$91,379
% Household Income > $100K	39%
Projected Future Job Growth	16%
Cost of Living Index	135
Buying Power Index	151
Weekly Daycare Cost	$216
Median Home Price	$489,700
"Sweet Spot" Home Price	$525,000
Home Price Ratio	5.4
Median Age of Homes	16.4
% Homes Owned	69%
Effective Property Tax Rate	1%
Estimated Property Tax Bill	$5,250
EDUCATION	
% High School Graduates	85%
% 4-yr Degree	30%
% Graduate or Professional Degree	18%
$ Invested per Pupil	$7,116
Student/Teacher Ratio	13
Primary Test Score Percentile	108
Secondary Test Score Percentile	107.3
% Subsidized School Lunch	23.50%
% Attending Public School	80.60%
LIFESTYLE	
Leisure Rating (Area)	10
Arts & Culture Rating (Area)	10
Climate Rating (Area)	4
Physical Setting Rating	3
Downtown Core Rating	6
% Commute < 30 Min.	57%
% Commute > 1 Hour	9%
HEALTH & SAFETY	
Health Rating (Area)	3
Stress Score (Area)	4
Violent Crime Risk	83
Property Crime Risk	77

WASHINGTON, DC-MD-VA-WV
AREA HIGHLIGHTS
PEOPLE

SIZE & DIVERSITY	AREA	U.S. AVG	FAMILY DEMOGRAPHICS	AREA	U.S. AVG
Population	5,276,939		% Married	52.70%	53.80%
15-yr Population Growth	32.30%	4.40%	% Single	47.30%	46.20%
Diversity Measure	59	54	% Divorced	7.30%	10.20%
% Religiously Observant	45%	50%	% Separated	4.50%	2.10%
% Catholic	18%	22%	% Married w/Children	29%	27.90%
% Protestant	21%	25%	% Single w/Children	9.70%	9.40%
% Jewish	3%	2%	% Married, No Children	28.30%	31.00%
% Other	3%	1%	% Single, No Children	32.70%	31.70%

STANDARD OF LIVING

INCOME, EMPLOYMENT & TAXES	AREA	U.S. AVG	COST OF LIVING & HOUSING	AREA	U.S. AVG
Median Household Income	$69,558	$44,684	Cost of Living Index	116	100
Household Income Growth	3.10%	6.10%	Buying Power Index	134	100
Unemployment Rate	3.10%	5.10%	Median Home Price	$429,200	$208,500
Recent Job Growth	2.60%	1.30%	Home Price Ratio	6.2	4.7
Projected Future Job Growth	13.60%	10.50%	Home Price Appreciation	22.40%	13.60%
State Income Tax Rate	9.40%	5.00%	% Homes Owned	65.10%	64.10%
State Sales Tax Rate	11.50%	6.00%	Median Rent	$1,162	$792

EDUCATION

ATTAINMENT & ACHIEVEMENT	AREA	U.S. AVG	RESOURCES & INVESTMENT	AREA	U.S. AVG
% High School Graduate	84.40%	83.90%	No. of Highly Ranked Universities	6	1
% 2-yr Graduate	7.30%	7.10%	$ Invested per Pupil	$7,203	$6,058
% 4-yr Graduate	25.90%	17.20%	Student/Teacher Ratio	15.7	15.9
% Graduate or Professional Degree	16.90%	9.90%	State University In-State Tuition	$5,838	$4,917
% Attending Public School	85.60%	84.30%			
75th Percentile State University SAT Score (Verbal)	540	477			
75th Percentile State University SAT Score (Math)	560	478			
75th Percentile State University ACT Score	N/A	20			

LIFESTYLE

RECREATION, ARTS & CULTURE	AREA	U.S. AVG	INFRASTRUCTURE & FACILITIES	AREA	U.S. AVG
Professional Sports Rating	9	4	No. of Public Libraries	153	28
Zoos & Aquariums Rating	10	3	Library Volumes Per Capita	3	2.8
Amusement Park Rating	2	3	No. of Warehouse Clubs	10	4
Professional Theater Rating	10	3	No. of Starbucks	194	5
Overall Museum Rating	10	6	Golf Course Rating	10	4
Science Museum Rating	10	4	National Park Rating	4	3
Children's Museum Rating	10	3	Sq. Mi. Inland Water	8	4

CLIMATE			COMMUTE & TRANSPORTATION		
Days Mostly Sunny	207	212	Avg. Daily Commute Time	32.8	24.7
Annual Days Precipitation	111	111	% Commute by Auto	66%	77.70%
Annual Days > 90°F	37	38	Per Capita Avg. Daily Transit Miles	24.4	7.9
Annual Days < 32°F	75	88	Annual Auto Insurance Premium	$1,482	$1,314
July Relative Humidity	64	69	Gas, Cost per Gallon	$3.31	$3.05

HEALTH & SAFETY

CRIME & ENVIRNOMENTAL ISSUES	AREA	U.S. AVG	HEALTHCARE & COST	AREA	U.S. AVG
Violent Crime Rate	548	517	Physicians per Capita	332	254.3
Change in Violent Crime	4.10%	-7.50%	Pediatricians per Capita	28.9	16.9
Property Crime Rate	3572	3783	Hospital Beds per Capita	242.5	239.7
Change in Property Crime	-10.50%	-10.10%	No. of Teaching Hospitals	20	1.9
Air Quality Score	41	44	Healthcare Cost Index	111.5	100
Water Quality Score	51	33	Cost per Doctor Visit	$92	$74
Pollen/Allergy Score	69	61	Cost per Dentist Visit	$70	$67
Stress Score	43	49	Cost per Hospital Room	$531	$702
Cancer Mortality Rate	176.8	168.9			

Hilliard, OH

Area Type: Outer suburb

Zip Code: 43026

Metro Area: Columbus, OH

Metro Area Type: Mid-size

Location: 13 miles NW of downtown Columbus outside the I-270 beltway

Time Zone: Eastern Standard Time

Pros:

Convenience
Attractive neighborhoods
Arts and culture

Cons:

Growth and sprawl
Relatively unattractive downtown core (Columbus)
Employment concerns

Columbus, Ohio, a mid-size Midwestern capital city, might be best known for Jack Nicklaus and the Ohio State football program. In fact, it's so typically USA—with a diverse demographic and socioeconomic mix—that it has become a hot spot for market researchers and test marketers. Beyond Ohio State, both its huge campus and its sports complex, there are few standout attractions (even the state capitol is understated). But the city is a great place to raise a family, with a solid mix of economic opportunities, attractive neighborhoods, recreation outlets, and cultural features.

With access to the major markets of the eastern two-thirds of the country, and an educated, diverse workforce, Columbus is a popular place to locate business facilities. Indeed, the influx of small high-tech firms is notable; the Chamber of Commerce claims more information technology workers here than in the high-tech Boston-Cambridge area. There are also corporate headquarters for Wendy's, Cardinal Health, Compuserve, the Limited, and high-tech retailer Micro Center, among others. The state government and university add employment stability. These factors haven't shown up in local employment statistics or projections, but we think the area is on the upswing. The downtown area, while still not a major attraction, has started to come back through redevelopment and renewal.

With few geographic barriers, the city is laid out in a traditional grid. Nicer neighborhoods have grown up mainly to the north and west along the Scioto River and along the I-270 beltway, starting with Worthington and Westerville to the north, Dublin to the northwest, and swinging around west to Hilliard. Today's Hilliard blends its old village core with excellent subdivisions and housing, convenient to all parts of the area and mimicking the more posh but more expensive and less

diverse Dublin to the north. The amount of married-with-children households is 32.5%.

Standard of Living The Cost of Living Index is a moderate 103, and with the area's high incomes, the Buying Power Index is a strong 144. Good family homes, mainly two-story colonials, start around $200K, with basements and attractive if fairly small yards. Property taxes are a moderate 1.25% to 1.5% of the sale price.

Education Many families who are willing to pay a little more for a home move into this area from other parts of Columbus for the area's school system. Ohio state proficiency test scores are 5 to 20 points above state averages at all levels, and 32% of the population possesses 4-year degrees. There's also a strong higher educational shadow cast by Ohio State.

Lifestyle The historic "Old Hilliard" area is gradually becoming more of an attraction, as an assortment of convenient shopping and "big box" retail establishments have grown up along I-270. The 135-acre Municipal Park provides a full range of services, with a community center and gym available for $15 per year and full-size community swimming pools for $115 per year per family. There are ball diamonds and athletic fields throughout the area. Venturing toward Columbus brings families to a good zoo and aquarium, a science museum (COSI, or the Center of Science and Industry), and Wyandot Lake Adventure Park, a major water and amusement park just to the north. Amusement park buffs can drive 2 hours to Cedar Point in Sandusky or King's Island near Cincinnati. Outdoor and nature lovers will like the Hocking Hills area to the southeast. Columbus has a full set of performing arts, and spectator sports are big, although only the NHL Blue Jackets

HILLIARD, OH NEIGHBORHOOD HIGHLIGHTS	
PEOPLE	
Population	48,311
15-yr Population Growth	13.30%
5-yr Population Growth	1.90%
% Married w/Children	32.5%
% Single w/Children	9.7%
No. of Households	18,195
Median Age	31.3
Avg. Household Size	2.65
Diversity Measure	17
STANDARD OF LIVING	
Median Household Income	$66,433
% Household Income > $100K	19%
Projected Future Job Growth	9%
Cost of Living Index	103
Buying Power Index	144
Weekly Daycare Cost	$174
Median Home Price	$205,700
"Sweet Spot" Home Price	$225,000
Home Price Ratio	3.1
Median Age of Homes	8.6
% Homes Owned	70%
Effective Property Tax Rate	1.50%
Estimated Property Tax Bill	$3,375
EDUCATION	
% High School Graduates	93%
% 4-yr Degree	32%
% Graduate or Professional Degree	13%
$ Invested per Pupil	$5,130
Student/Teacher Ratio	16.5
Primary Test Score Percentile	112.8
Secondary Test Score Percentile	118.3
% Subsidized School Lunch	9.70%
% Attending Public School	83.10%
LIFESTYLE	
Leisure Rating (Area)	5
Arts & Culture Rating (Area)	9
Climate Rating (Area)	4
Physical Setting Rating	3
Downtown Core Rating	3
% Commute < 30 Min.	69%
% Commute > 1 Hour	4%
HEALTH & SAFETY	
Health Rating (Area)	3
Stress Score (Area)	7
Violent Crime Risk	30
Property Crime Risk	37

are at the major-league level (some would also accredit such status to Ohio State football). Golf is also popular.

Commutes are easy. Downtown is a 15- to 20-minute drive away, and many residents work along the I-270 corridor. This well-designed and recently expanded freeway provides satisfactory 15- to 30-minute commutes, at least for now.

The immediate landscape varies from flat to gently rolling with some areas of woods mainly near the Scioto River. The climate is changeable with four distinct seasons and few geographic barriers to modify it; expect warm, humid summers and a winter mix with pleasant spring and fall seasons.

Health & Safety Columbus metro area crime statistics show moderate to high rates but local crime risk as measured by the "CAP" index is very low. Healthcare facilities are adequate and strengthened by the facilities at Ohio State.

Nearby Neighborhoods Other places in close proximity to Hilliard are attractive and generally more upscale. Dublin is excellent, but homes run from $100K to $200K and higher. Upper Arlington just to the east toward the city is older and more elegant. Both of these neighborhoods are worth a look for those who can afford them. Westerville, to the north, is a bit more expensive than Hilliard but closer to much of the high-tech employment.

COLUMBUS, OH
AREA HIGHLIGHTS

PEOPLE

SIZE & DIVERSITY	AREA	U.S. AVG	FAMILY DEMOGRAPHICS	AREA	U.S. AVG
Population	1,615,172		% Married	55.40%	53.80%
15-yr Population Growth	24%	4.40%	% Single	44.60%	46.20%
Diversity Measure	33	54	% Divorced	9.50%	10.20%
% Religiously Observant	36%	50%	% Separated	2.60%	2.10%
% Catholic	13%	22%	% Married w/Children	28.40%	27.90%
% Protestant	22%	25%	% Single w/Children	10.50%	9.40%
% Jewish	1%	2%	% Married, No Children	29.30%	31.00%
% Other	0%	1%	% Single, No Children	31.80%	31.70%

STANDARD OF LIVING

INCOME, EMPLOYMENT & TAXES	AREA	U.S. AVG	COST OF LIVING & HOUSING	AREA	U.S. AVG
Median Household Income	$49,029	$44,684	Cost of Living Index	91.9	100
Household Income Growth	5%	6.10%	Buying Power Index	119	100
Unemployment Rate	5%	5.10%	Median Home Price	$155,900	$208,500
Recent Job Growth	-0.90%	1.30%	Home Price Ratio	3.2	4.7
Projected Future Job Growth	12.80%	10.50%	Home Price Appreciation	5%	13.60%
State Income Tax Rate	6.80%	5.00%	% Homes Owned	64.20%	64.10%
State Sales Tax Rate	5.70%	6.00%	Median Rent	$675	$792

EDUCATION

ATTAINMENT & ACHIEVEMENT	AREA	U.S. AVG	RESOURCES & INVESTMENT	AREA	U.S. AVG
% High School Graduate	82.30%	83.90%	No. of Highly Ranked Universities	4	1
% 2-yr Graduate	7.20%	7.10%	$ Invested per Pupil	$6,272	$6,058
% 4-yr Graduate	18.90%	17.20%	Student/Teacher Ratio	17.6	15.9
% Graduate or Professional Degree	9.20%	9.90%	State University In-State Tuition	$7,542	$4,917
% Attending Public School	88.70%	84.30%			
75th Percentile State University SAT Score (Verbal)	520	477			
75th Percentile State University SAT Score (Math)	550	478			
75th Percentile State University ACT Score	23	20			

LIFESTYLE

RECREATION, ARTS & CULTURE	AREA	U.S. AVG	INFRASTRUCTURE & FACILITIES	AREA	U.S. AVG
Professional Sports Rating	5	4	No. of Public Libraries	57	28
Zoos & Aquariums Rating	7	3	Library Volumes Per Capita	4.2	2.8
Amusement Park Rating	4	3	No. of Warehouse Clubs	5	4
Professional Theater Rating	1	3	No. of Starbucks	30	5
Overall Museum Rating	9	6	Golf Course Rating	8	4
Science Museum Rating	9	4	National Park Rating	1	3
Children's Museum Rating	8	3	Sq. Mi. Inland Water	3	4

CLIMATE			COMMUTE & TRANSPORTATION		
Days Mostly Sunny	181	212	Avg. Daily Commute Time	23.2	24.7
Annual Days Precipitation	136	111	% Commute by Auto	79%	77.70%
Annual Days > 90°F	15	38	Per Capita Avg. Daily Transit Miles	9	7.9
Annual Days < 32°F	122	88	Annual Auto Insurance Premium	$1,377	$1,314
July Relative Humidity	70	69	Gas, Cost per Gallon	$2.99	$3.05

HEALTH & SAFETY

CRIME & ENVIRNOMENTAL ISSUES	AREA	U.S. AVG	HEALTHCARE & COST	AREA	U.S. AVG
Violent Crime Rate	465	517	Physicians per Capita	290.7	254.3
Change in Violent Crime	-6.10%	-7.50%	Pediatricians per Capita	20.4	16.9
Property Crime Rate	5210	3783	Hospital Beds per Capita	318.4	239.7
Change in Property Crime	-10.50%	-10.10%	No. of Teaching Hospitals	10	1.9
Air Quality Score	35	44	Healthcare Cost Index	96.5	100
Water Quality Score	44	33	Cost per Doctor Visit	$67	$74
Pollen/Allergy Score	57	61	Cost per Dentist Visit	$62	$67
Stress Score	65	49	Cost per Hospital Room	$632	$702
Cancer Mortality Rate	180.7	168.9			

Hixson, TN

Area Type: Inner suburb

Zip Code: 37343

Metro Area: Chattanooga, TN

Metro Area Type: Smaller

Location: 10 miles north of downtown Chattanooga

Time Zone: Eastern Standard Time

Pros:
Revitalized downtown
Attractive setting and historic interest
Home prices

Cons:
Economic strength
Crime issues
Educational attainment

Distinctly Southern, full of history, and set in the center of the so-called Grand Canyon of the Tennessee River, Chattanooga has always been an interesting place to visit—albeit one with, at times, a questionable economy, a decayed downtown, and a distinctly "old south" character. On the major north–south I-75, Chattanooga has 150,000 residents and lies 100 miles north of the Atlanta area, with no income tax and little of its hustle and bustle.

Visionary local leaders, blending local private contributions with lodging tax and federal funds, recently completed one of the largest downtown revitalizations in the country, bringing international acclaim for bold, well-planned, and rapid renewal. The new city center has brought an improved ambience, and a slow influx of new employment, and on the whole has made the area a better family place.

The ambitious $120-million downtown and waterfront project brought new form and function to the area, and brought residents back into the center city. Headline attractions now include the impressive Tennessee Aquarium, which features the world's largest freshwater tank and is considered one of the best in the country. Other new museums on the waterfront include the noted Hunter Museum of American Art and the Creative Discovery Museum, an above-average children's and science museum with an IMAX theater. An operating railroad museum and riverboat provide more activity.

Hixson is one of several small middle-class suburbs north of the city on the northwest bank of the river nestled against the mountains. A lot of the growth is heading south and east of the city toward East Brainerd, with a new mall and extensive commercial construction. Hixson is quieter, with very attractive housing on heavily wooded, large lots; it has one of the best school systems in the area; and 32.6% of households are married with children.

Standard of Living The low cost of living here is a major attraction. The "sweet spot" for family homes is $175K to $200K. Most are colonial style, on heavily wooded lots of a ½ acre or more. Most resale homes start at about $75 per square foot, with newer construction priced at $100 per square foot. The Cost of Living Index is 90. After overcoming some issues with employment, today's unemployment figures are reasonably healthy. The area has insurers Blue Cross/Blue Shield of Tennessee and Cigna and a major DuPont facility. The downtown project and available federal redevelopment tax credits, combined with some of the area's other location advantages, promise a stronger economic future, especially for areas close to the city. Effective property tax rates are about 1% and daycare is a reasonable $132 per week.

Education The local schools are modestly sized and have a good local reputation, being "one of the main reasons to move to Hixson." Aside from Hixson High School, which has 1,000 students, other schools in the Hamilton County School District in the Hixson area test from slightly above national averages to 25 points above. The University of Tennessee Chattanooga, Tennessee Wesleyan, and a number of smaller community colleges add a higher-education presence.

Lifestyle Hixson is quiet and offers local services, but not a lot to do. Fortunately, downtown Chattanooga is only 10 miles south. The surrounding area is full of history and natural interest. Civil War history is big and the Chickamauga and Chattanooga National Military Park is one of the biggest and oldest Civil War sites in the country. Lookout Mountain, a 2,100-foot mountaintop that overlooks the city, and the large Cherokee

National Forest are highlights of the abundant outdoor recreation here. The broad Tennessee River and Chickamauga Lake provide ample water recreation. In addition to downtown assets already noted, there are a small assortment of local theaters, a symphony, and local live musical performances. When bigger city amenities and services are required, Atlanta is 2 hours away.

Traffic and commutes don't present problems in the Chattanooga area. Most work downtown or in commercial areas east of the city; all are easily accessed by freeways and an adequate supply of passages across the Tennessee River.

Hixson and the city sit in a deep river valley, with wooded mountains and bluffs rising 500 to 2,000 feet on all sides. The climate is moderate. Mountains shelter the area from harsh winters, but the valleys can trap hot, humid air at times in the summer. At 685 feet in elevation and considering the surrounding mountains, the climate here is considered better than in many nearby areas in the south.

Health & Safety   Unfortunately, metro area crime statistics still reflect an older, more economically deprived past, but trends are in the right direction and neighborhood crime risk as reported by the "CAP" score is low. A major new hospital has arrived, and healthcare costs run 10% below national averages.

Nearby Neighborhoods   Signal Mountain, on an upland to the west of Hixson, is smaller and more upscale. New development is bringing subdivisions to the southeast near East Brainerd with less expensive homes but more traffic and typical growth and sprawl.

HIXSON, TN NEIGHBORHOOD HIGHLIGHTS	
PEOPLE	
Population	37,608
15-yr Population Growth	8.70%
5-yr Population Growth	0.80%
% Married w/Children	32.6%
% Single w/Children	9.6%
No. of Households	14,301
Median Age	37.3
Avg. Household Size	2.62
Diversity Measure	15
STANDARD OF LIVING	
Median Household Income	$49,902
% Household Income > $100K	13%
Projected Future Job Growth	7%
Cost of Living Index	90.1
Buying Power Index	124
Weekly Daycare Cost	$132
Median Home Price	$145,400
"Sweet Spot" Home Price	$190,000
Home Price Ratio	2.9
Median Age of Homes	24.6
% Homes Owned	72%
Effective Property Tax Rate	1%
Estimated Property Tax Bill	$1,900
EDUCATION	
% High School Graduates	87%
% 4-yr Degree	19%
% Graduate or Professional Degree	9%
$ Invested per Pupil	$4,802
Student/Teacher Ratio	N/A
Primary Test Score Percentile	123.2
Secondary Test Score Percentile	N/A
% Subsidized School Lunch	N/A
% Attending Public School	79.40%
LIFESTYLE	
Leisure Rating (Area)	4
Arts & Culture Rating (Area)	4
Climate Rating (Area)	2
Physical Setting Rating	5
Downtown Core Rating	6
% Commute < 30 Min.	71%
% Commute > 1 Hour	3%
HEALTH & SAFETY	
Health Rating (Area)	8
Stress Score (Area)	6
Violent Crime Risk	33
Property Crime Risk	64

CHATTANOOGA, TN
AREA HIGHLIGHTS

PEOPLE

SIZE & DIVERSITY	AREA	U.S. AVG	FAMILY DEMOGRAPHICS	AREA	U.S. AVG
Population	477,248		% Married	53.30%	53.80%
15-yr Population Growth	13.30%	4.40%	% Single	46.70%	46.20%
Diversity Measure	30	54	% Divorced	10.80%	10.20%
% Religiously Observant	53%	50%	% Separated	3.20%	2.10%
% Catholic	2%	22%	% Married w/Children	25.10%	27.90%
% Protestant	49%	25%	% Single w/Children	12%	9.40%
% Jewish	0%	2%	% Married, No Children	29.10%	31.00%
% Other	0%	1%	% Single, No Children	33.70%	31.70%

STANDARD OF LIVING

INCOME, EMPLOYMENT & TAXES	AREA	U.S. AVG	COST OF LIVING & HOUSING	AREA	U.S. AVG
Median Household Income	$37,688	$44,684	Cost of Living Index	83.2	100
Household Income Growth	3.60%	6.10%	Buying Power Index	101	100
Unemployment Rate	3.60%	5.10%	Median Home Price	$130,500	$208,500
Recent Job Growth	1.50%	1.30%	Home Price Ratio	3.5	4.7
Projected Future Job Growth	11%	10.50%	Home Price Appreciation	5.90%	13.60%
State Income Tax Rate	0.10%	5.00%	% Homes Owned	63.50%	64.10%
State Sales Tax Rate	7.70%	6.00%	Median Rent	$569	$792

EDUCATION

ATTAINMENT & ACHIEVEMENT	AREA	U.S. AVG	RESOURCES & INVESTMENT	AREA	U.S. AVG
% High School Graduate	68.20%	83.90%	No. of Highly Ranked Universities	1	1
% 2-yr Graduate	6.60%	7.10%	$ Invested per Pupil	$5,075	$6,058
% 4-yr Graduate	15.50%	17.20%	Student/Teacher Ratio	14.1	15.9
% Graduate or Professional Degree	6.40%	9.90%	State University In-State Tuition	$4,748	$4,917
% Attending Public School	84.10%	84.30%			
75th Percentile State University SAT Score (Verbal)	500	477			
75th Percentile State University SAT Score (Math)	500	478			
75th Percentile State University ACT Score	21	20			

LIFESTYLE

RECREATION, ARTS & CULTURE	AREA	U.S. AVG	INFRASTRUCTURE & FACILITIES	AREA	U.S. AVG
Professional Sports Rating	2	4	No. of Public Libraries	14	28
Zoos & Aquariums Rating	8	3	Library Volumes Per Capita	3.4	2.8
Amusement Park Rating	5	3	No. of Warehouse Clubs	3	4
Professional Theater Rating	1	3	No. of Starbucks	2	5
Overall Museum Rating	7	6	Golf Course Rating	3	4
Science Museum Rating	1	4	National Park Rating	2	3
Children's Museum Rating	6	3	Sq. Mi. Inland Water	4	4

CLIMATE			COMMUTE & TRANSPORTATION		
Days Mostly Sunny	213	212	Avg. Daily Commute Time	23.7	24.7
Annual Days Precipitation	121	111	% Commute by Auto	76%	77.70%
Annual Days > 90°F	49	38	Per Capita Avg. Daily Transit Miles	5	7.9
Annual Days < 32°F	75	88	Annual Auto Insurance Premium	$1,360	$1,314
July Relative Humidity	72	69	Gas, Cost per Gallon	$3.06	$3.05

HEALTH & SAFETY

CRIME & ENVIRNOMENTAL ISSUES	AREA	U.S. AVG	HEALTHCARE & COST	AREA	U.S. AVG
Violent Crime Rate	599	517	Physicians per Capita	255.7	254.3
Change in Violent Crime	-24.20%	-7.50%	Pediatricians per Capita	20.6	16.9
Property Crime Rate	4616	3783	Hospital Beds per Capita	600	239.7
Change in Property Crime	3.10%	-10.10%	No. of Teaching Hospitals	3	1.9
Air Quality Score	44	44	Healthcare Cost Index	88.4	100
Water Quality Score	61	33	Cost per Doctor Visit	$85	$74
Pollen/Allergy Score	64	61	Cost per Dentist Visit	$49	$67
Stress Score	62	49	Cost per Hospital Room	$746	$702
Cancer Mortality Rate	171.7	168.9			

Hollywood Park, TX

Area Type: Outer suburb

Zip Code: 78232

Metro Area: San Antonio, TX

Metro Area Type: Mid-size

Location: 14 miles north of San Antonio along US 281

Time Zone: Central Standard Time

Pros:
Cost of living
Education
Nearby city amenities

Cons:
Growth and sprawl
Steady summer heat
Health and safety issues

We probably shouldn't let this out, but several residents in Hollywood Park told us that they don't lock their doors. Admittedly, the crime rate is high and on the rise in parts of San Antonio, but in the attractive northern suburbs it's hardly an issue. What *is* an issue for most new residents is good, inexpensive housing, good schools, a pleasant winter climate, and the ability to enjoy major-league sports and other amenities offered by the San Antonio metro area.

Hollywood Park, 14 miles north of downtown, is an older, well-established neighborhood adjacent to the upscale, old-money Hill Country Village. The residents of both areas enjoy unique homes on large lots filled with mature oaks, providing as much shade as possible in San Antonio. Most of the homes are 40 to 50 years old, well built, and unique in design. The problem is that Hollywood Park isn't large, and homes that come onto the market don't stay on the market for long. The 78232 zip code actually covers several neighborhoods, including some east of US 281 that can't be defined as Hollywood Park. In fact, many of them are attractive and less expensive alternatives to Hollywood Park.

San Antonio—the ninth largest city in the United States—offers a unique mix of cultural amenities that reflect its rich history as a missionary frontier, a trading center, a battleground, and a melting pot. The economy is broad based, with such diverse larger employers as automobile manufacturers, insurance brokers, energy companies, and banks. The city has some challenges ahead of it, not the least of which is to find enough water to support projected population increases (summer water controls here are not unusual), but this issue is less of a concern for the older, established areas such as Hollywood Park and the rest of the 78232 zip code. Most of the growth is spreading to the north and east up US 281 and toward New Braunfels. The 27% of married-with-children households in this area reflects a mix of older and younger families.

Standard of Living   San Antonio's cost-of-living profile is far below the national average, with a notably low metro area Cost of Living Index of 78. Even in the more upscale Hollywood Park, the COL Index is still a reasonable 92. Likewise, home prices in the San Antonio metro area are extremely reasonable, with a "sweet spot" family home—a 20-year-old, four-bedroom, three-bathroom, 2,200-square-foot abode on a ¼-acre lot—costing about $140K on average. The comparable home in Hollywood Park rises to about $210K but probably has a larger lot. This is just over the national median home price, which, in an up-and-coming Sun Belt area like San Antonio, says a lot about how reasonable housing is in the area. Property taxes in Texas are higher than average, at around 2.5%, and sales taxes are also higher than average, but there's no state income tax.

Education   Hollywood Park is served by the Northeast Independent School District, which has very good test scores and a relatively high graduation rate (30% higher than in the area at large). Advanced Placement enrollment is nearly twice the state average and a very high percentage of students take college entrance exams (99% at Reagan High School take the SAT, for example). About 50% of the residents have at least a 4-year degree, and in the area are five 2-year colleges and six 4-year colleges/universities.

Lifestyle   San Antonio offers a great number and variety of entertainment and cultural amenities. There are traditional art, science, and cultural museums, plus a large botanical garden and The Alamo. The local university arts programs also offer a variety of exhibitions and performances at family-friendly prices. Open during the day as a shopping destination, the River Walk

HOLLYWOOD PARK, TX NEIGHBORHOOD HIGHLIGHTS	
PEOPLE	
Population	36,297
15-yr Population Growth	26%
5-yr Population Growth	7.30%
% Married w/Children	26.6%
% Single w/Children	9.5%
No. of Households	14,886
Median Age	37.7
Avg. Household Size	2.41
Diversity Measure	44
STANDARD OF LIVING	
Median Household Income	$66,593
% Household Income > $100K	26%
Projected Future Job Growth	19%
Cost of Living Index	92.3
Buying Power Index	164
Weekly Daycare Cost	$104
Median Home Price	$173,500
"Sweet Spot" Home Price	$210,000
Home Price Ratio	2.6
Median Age of Homes	16.6
% Homes Owned	65%
Effective Property Tax Rate	2.50%
Estimated Property Tax Bill	$5,250
EDUCATION	
% High School Graduates	96%
% 4-yr Degree	30%
% Graduate or Professional Degree	19%
$ Invested per Pupil	$5,286
Student/Teacher Ratio	15.6
Primary Test Score Percentile	108.8
Secondary Test Score Percentile	103
% Subsidized School Lunch	20.70%
% Attending Public School	75.90%
LIFESTYLE	
Leisure Rating (Area)	7
Arts & Culture Rating (Area)	4
Climate Rating (Area)	10
Physical Setting Rating	3
Downtown Core Rating	3
% Commute < 30 Min.	67%
% Commute > 1 Hour	3%
HEALTH & SAFETY	
Health Rating (Area)	0
Stress Score (Area)	8
Violent Crime Risk	63
Property Crime Risk	46

area in downtown is also lively as temperatures drop in the evening. Sea World and Six Flags Fiesta Texas provide traditional family entertainment year-round. Sports are big, and the San Antonio Spurs NBA team commands considerable local attention. Hollywood Park doesn't provide a general recreation program, but the YMCA and other local social organizations offer comparable activities.

Many residents work along one of the two beltways (Hollywood Park is just inside the outer beltway) and commutes can be long in certain traffic conditions, although the reported average commute time of 24 minutes isn't bad. Some residents in the area complain of difficult freeway access from Hollywood Park.

San Antonio sits along the edge of the "hill country" with dry, sparsely treed hills spreading north, while much of the city and areas to the southeast are flat. The climate is mainly continental with a strong subtropical summer influence. Summer in San Antonio starts early; average daily highs are 80°F by the end of March, hover around 98°F through July and August, and don't return below 80°F again until November. Average daily lows in December and January are above freezing, and snow is rare.

Health & Safety Both property and violent crime rates are significantly higher than the national averages in San Antonio, but are moderate to low in the northern suburbs; these areas are considered quite safe. San Antonio does have high stress and especially allergy scores, something to be mindful of if in a susceptible group. The metro area has good healthcare facilities with nine teaching hospitals area-wide and notably low healthcare costs.

Nearby Neighborhoods Areas just to the east of Hollywood Park in unincorporated parts of Bexar County offer lower prices and a wider assortment of homes. The choices aren't as unique as in Hollywood Park and property lots are smaller; but the school district is the same. New, affluent suburbs and planned developments are growing into the hills to the north of SR 1604, which could be particularly good choices if your employer is on the north side of town.

SAN ANTONIO, TX
AREA HIGHLIGHTS

PEOPLE

SIZE & DIVERSITY	AREA	U.S. AVG	FAMILY DEMOGRAPHICS	AREA	U.S. AVG
Population	1,722,117		% Married	55.30%	53.80%
15-yr Population Growth	31.10%	4.40%	% Single	44.70%	46.20%
Diversity Measure	60	54	% Divorced	9.30%	10.20%
% Religiously Observant	63%	50%	% Separated	3.80%	2.10%
% Catholic	39%	22%	% Married w/Children	32.30%	27.90%
% Protestant	23%	25%	% Single w/Children	12.20%	9.40%
% Jewish	1%	2%	% Married, No Children	27.10%	31.00%
% Other	0%	1%	% Single, No Children	28.40%	31.70%

STANDARD OF LIVING

INCOME, EMPLOYMENT & TAXES	AREA	U.S. AVG	COST OF LIVING & HOUSING	AREA	U.S. AVG
Median Household Income	$41,050	$44,684	Cost of Living Index	77.9	100
Household Income Growth	4.70%	6.10%	Buying Power Index	118	100
Unemployment Rate	4.70%	5.10%	Median Home Price	$134,000	$208,500
Recent Job Growth	2.20%	1.30%	Home Price Ratio	3.3	4.7
Projected Future Job Growth	17.50%	10.50%	Home Price Appreciation	5.30%	13.60%
State Income Tax Rate	0%	5.00%	% Homes Owned	60.60%	64.10%
State Sales Tax Rate	6.30%	6.00%	Median Rent	$716	$792

EDUCATION

ATTAINMENT & ACHIEVEMENT	AREA	U.S. AVG	RESOURCES & INVESTMENT	AREA	U.S. AVG
% High School Graduate	75.10%	83.90%	No. of Highly Ranked Universities	0	1
% 2-yr Graduate	8.40%	7.10%	$ Invested per Pupil	$5,639	$6,058
% 4-yr Graduate	18.40%	17.20%	Student/Teacher Ratio	15.2	15.9
% Graduate or Professional Degree	9.70%	9.90%	State University In-State Tuition	$5,735	$4,917
% Attending Public School	91.60%	84.30%			
75th Percentile State University SAT Score (Verbal)	540	477			
75th Percentile State University SAT Score (Math)	570	478			
75th Percentile State University ACT Score	23	20			

LIFESTYLE

RECREATION, ARTS & CULTURE	AREA	U.S. AVG	INFRASTRUCTURE & FACILITIES	AREA	U.S. AVG
Professional Sports Rating	6	4	No. of Public Libraries	32	28
Zoos & Aquariums Rating	7	3	Library Volumes Per Capita	1.4	2.8
Amusement Park Rating	9	3	No. of Warehouse Clubs	5	4
Professional Theater Rating	1	3	No. of Starbucks	23	5
Overall Museum Rating	9	6	Golf Course Rating	5	4
Science Museum Rating	8	4	National Park Rating	2	3
Children's Museum Rating	6	3	Sq. Mi. Inland Water	2	4

CLIMATE			COMMUTE & TRANSPORTATION		
Days Mostly Sunny	227	212	Avg. Daily Commute Time	24.5	24.7
Annual Days Precipitation	81	111	% Commute by Auto	73%	77.70%
Annual Days > 90°F	111	38	Per Capita Avg. Daily Transit Miles	20.9	7.9
Annual Days < 32°F	22	88	Annual Auto Insurance Premium	$1,339	$1,314
July Relative Humidity	67	69	Gas, Cost per Gallon	$2.90	$3.05

HEALTH & SAFETY

CRIME & ENVIRNOMENTAL ISSUES	AREA	U.S. AVG	HEALTHCARE & COST	AREA	U.S. AVG
Violent Crime Rate	485	517	Physicians per Capita	298.8	254.3
Change in Violent Crime	12.70%	-7.50%	Pediatricians per Capita	22.1	16.9
Property Crime Rate	5716	3783	Hospital Beds per Capita	349.3	239.7
Change in Property Crime	0.50%	-10.10%	No. of Teaching Hospitals	9	1.9
Air Quality Score	16	44	Healthcare Cost Index	87.5	100
Water Quality Score	74	33	Cost per Doctor Visit	$70	$74
Pollen/Allergy Score	94	61	Cost per Dentist Visit	$63	$67
Stress Score	79	49	Cost per Hospital Room	$692	$702
Cancer Mortality Rate	164.1	168.9			

Hudsonville, MI

Area Type: Suburban town

Zip Code: 49426

Metro Area: Grand Rapids–Muskegon–Holland, MI

Metro Area Type: Mid-size

Location: 14 miles southwest of downtown Grand Rapids

Time Zone: Central Standard Time

Pros:
Small-town flavor
Recreation, arts, and culture
Cost of living

Cons:
Cold, cloudy winters
Some urban sprawl and growth issues
Isolation

Known locally as "Michigan's Salad Bowl," Hudsonville is an old farming community 14 miles from Grand Rapids—perhaps Michigan's most livable large city (and second-largest city overall). Hudsonville has a town square surrounded by low-density suburbs with a distinct country feel. Locals value this "oasis" of country peace and quiet that's so close to a vibrant city, and many families call the area home. More than 43% of households are married with children.

Like most Michigan cities, Grand Rapids has a past centered on manufacturing. Autos and auto parts were big industries and still support some of the local economy. Nearby hardwood forests brought a flourishing furniture industry, particularly in the first half of the 20th century, which has since evolved toward office furniture. Meanwhile, the city continues to serve a clean, prosperous, Dutch-influenced farming area, which happens to be centered in the nearby town of Holland. Two Dutch entrepreneur families, the Van Andel and De Vos families, started direct-sales giant Amway, and the Meijer family started a major grocery chain. These families have left (and are still leaving) an enormous cultural imprint on the community through endowments and community leadership. An excellent downtown revitalization created a clean and active city center and a 1,500-acre waterfront Millennium Park along the Grand River.

The family endowments have supported outstanding local assets. Along the waterfront is the new Public Museum of Grand Rapids (often called the Van Andel Museum Center), an exceptional museum of area history with top visiting exhibits; DeVos Place, a large convention center; and the Van Andel Arena, which hosts sports and arts events. The De Vos Performance Hall, here too, hosts the symphony, ballet, and opera. The Meijer Gardens, on the east side, host a number of activities for children in addition to outdoor concerts and a 5-acre arboretum under glass.

Away from downtown, the city is clean and typically Midwestern in appearance. Streets are on a grid with wide commercial strips to the south and southwest. It's almost always easy to get around the city. Employment is diverse, with such furniture manufacturers as Steelcase and Herman Miller, Alticor (now the corporate name for Amway), some medical research firms, and a variety of small to medium-size businesses. Job-growth projections are relatively strong at 18% for the region. The area's population, always with a strong European influence, has become more diverse with the arrival of more Asian, African-American, and Hispanic families.

Standard of Living   Considering what's available for the money, this area's cost-of-living profile (COL Index of 83) is excellent on a national scale. Hudsonville is slightly higher at 104. Homes cost $110 to $120 per square foot and full-featured family homes with large yards and basements are available in the low to mid $200Ks. Property tax is very reasonable at about 0.8%, and daycare costs $160 per week.

Education   Schools are good, but face some overcrowding problems as the city grows to the south and west. Test results are good, especially in the middle and elementary schools. At the Forest Grove Elementary School, 4th-grade math test scores were 96% proficient on the Michigan Educational Assessment Program, fully 31 points above the state average.

Lifestyle   Hudsonville has a number of small recreational assets, including its downtown, parks, aquatic center, and libraries (which are actually open on Sunday). Grand Rapids has no shortage of things to do. Arena football, minor-league baseball, hockey, and basketball are area spectator sports. You'll also find a children's museum, a zoo, a planetarium, and an IMAX theater. Shopping is nearby at the Riverview Crossing Mall. The Michigan Shore and its beach areas are 50 miles west, and boating, fishing, hiking, and other options for winter recreation are available in abundance nearby and to the north and northwest. Chicago is 4 hours by car or by ferry (from Muskegon).

Commutes are generally short and simple. There are some minor traffic and growth concerns on the southwest side as commercial and residential activity grows in that direction.

The landscape is a combination of flat and rolling farmland with areas of dense woods with some hilly areas to each side of the Grand River. The climate is continental and variable. Lake Michigan moderates temperatures, bringing less severe cold and better summer weather than in other parts of the state. However, there are about 200 cloudy days per year, and winters can be cool and dreary with snow present at most times.

Health & Safety   Crime risk is moderate in the metro area, but it drops significantly away from the city. Area hospitals are modern and well regarded, and a new heart center recently opened. Healthcare costs are below U.S. averages.

Nearby Neighborhoods   Jenison, to the north and east, is more built up and a little less expensive than Hudsonville, but it has a similar feel. Ada, on the east side, is more upscale and popular with executive families.

HUDSONVILLE, MI
NEIGHBORHOOD HIGHLIGHTS

PEOPLE

Population	29,118
15-yr Population Growth	34.40%
5-yr Population Growth	5.90%
% Married w/Children	43.2%
% Single w/Children	5.4%
No. of Households	9,283
Median Age	32.6
Avg. Household Size	3.12
Diversity Measure	6

STANDARD OF LIVING

Median Household Income	$63,026
% Household Income > $100K	15%
Projected Future Job Growth	18%
Cost of Living Index	104
Buying Power Index	130
Weekly Daycare Cost	$160
Median Home Price	$197,300
"Sweet Spot" Home Price	$235,000
Home Price Ratio	3.1
Median Age of Homes	17.2
% Homes Owned	89%
Effective Property Tax Rate	0.80%
Estimated Property Tax Bill	$ 1,250

EDUCATION

% High School Graduates	90%
% 4-yr Degree	20%
% Graduate or Professional Degree	8%
$ Invested per Pupil	$4,613
Student/Teacher Ratio	18.4
Primary Test Score Percentile	120.8
Secondary Test Score Percentile	107.4
% Subsidized School Lunch	12.80%
% Attending Public School	66.90%

LIFESTYLE

Leisure Rating (Area)	6
Arts & Culture Rating (Area)	7
Climate Rating (Area)	1
Physical Setting Rating	3
Downtown Core Rating	5
% Commute < 30 Min.	74%
% Commute > 1 Hour	2%

HEALTH & SAFETY

Health Rating (Area)	4
Stress Score (Area)	5
Violent Crime Risk	37
Property Crime Risk	76

GRAND RAPIDS–MUSKEGON–HOLLLAND, MI
AREA HIGHLIGHTS

PEOPLE

SIZE & DIVERSITY	AREA	U.S. AVG	FAMILY DEMOGRAPHICS	AREA	U.S. AVG
Population	1,133,127		% Married	58.90%	53.80%
15-yr Population Growth	21.30%	4.40%	% Single	41.10%	46.20%
Diversity Measure	30	54	% Divorced	8.30%	10.20%
% Religiously Observant	49%	50%	% Separated	2.10%	2.10%
% Catholic	16%	22%	% Married w/Children	32.20%	27.90%
% Protestant	32%	25%	% Single w/Children	10.10%	9.40%
% Jewish	0%	2%	% Married, No Children	30%	31.00%
% Other	1%	1%	% Single, No Children	27.70%	31.70%

STANDARD OF LIVING

INCOME, EMPLOYMENT & TAXES	AREA	U.S. AVG	COST OF LIVING & HOUSING	AREA	U.S. AVG
Median Household Income	$46,084	$44,684	Cost of Living Index	89.2	100
Household Income Growth	6.20%	6.10%	Buying Power Index	116	100
Unemployment Rate	6.20%	5.10%	Median Home Price	$139,000	$208,500
Recent Job Growth	2.10%	1.30%	Home Price Ratio	3	4.7
Projected Future Job Growth	15.40%	10.50%	Home Price Appreciation	4.90%	13.60%
State Income Tax Rate	5.40%	5.00%	% Homes Owned	73.40%	64.10%
State Sales Tax Rate	6%	6.00%	Median Rent	$658	$792

EDUCATION

ATTAINMENT & ACHIEVEMENT	AREA	U.S. AVG	RESOURCES & INVESTMENT	AREA	U.S. AVG
% High School Graduate	81%	83.90%	No. of Highly Ranked Universities	1	1
% 2-yr Graduate	10.70%	7.10%	$ Invested per Pupil	$6,324	$6,058
% 4-yr Graduate	15.30%	17.20%	Student/Teacher Ratio	18.5	15.9
% Graduate or Professional Degree	6.40%	9.90%	State University In-State Tuition	$6,999	$4,917
% Attending Public School	85.40%	84.30%			
75th Percentile State University SAT Score (Verbal)	490	477			
75th Percentile State University SAT Score (Math)	515	478			
75th Percentile State University ACT Score	22	20			

LIFESTYLE

RECREATION, ARTS & CULTURE	AREA	U.S. AVG	INFRASTRUCTURE & FACILITIES	AREA	U.S. AVG
Professional Sports Rating	3	4	No. of Public Libraries	62	28
Zoos & Aquariums Rating	5	3	Library Volumes Per Capita	3.5	2.8
Amusement Park Rating	7	3	No. of Warehouse Clubs	5	4
Professional Theater Rating	1	3	No. of Starbucks	8	5
Overall Museum Rating	8	6	Golf Course Rating	7	4
Science Museum Rating	7	4	National Park Rating	1	3
Children's Museum Rating	7	3	Sq. Mi. Inland Water	3	4

CLIMATE			COMMUTE & TRANSPORTATION		
Days Mostly Sunny	163	212	Avg. Daily Commute Time	20.7	24.7
Annual Days Precipitation	144	111	% Commute by Auto	82%	77.70%
Annual Days > 90°F	11	38	Per Capita Avg. Daily Transit Miles	4.8	7.9
Annual Days < 32°F	149	88	Annual Auto Insurance Premium	$1,339	$1,314
July Relative Humidity	73	69	Gas, Cost per Gallon	$3.00	$3.05

HEALTH & SAFETY

CRIME & ENVIRNOMENTAL ISSUES	AREA	U.S. AVG	HEALTHCARE & COST	AREA	U.S. AVG
Violent Crime Rate	453	517	Physicians per Capita	207.6	254.3
Change in Violent Crime	-3%	-7.50%	Pediatricians per Capita	14.9	16.9
Property Crime Rate	3154	3783	Hospital Beds per Capita	283.8	239.7
Change in Property Crime	-13.80%	-10.10%	No. of Teaching Hospitals	6	1.9
Air Quality Score	31	44	Healthcare Cost Index	95.5	100
Water Quality Score	36	33	Cost per Doctor Visit	$69	$74
Pollen/Allergy Score	49	61	Cost per Dentist Visit	$67	$67
Stress Score	53	49	Cost per Hospital Room	$510	$702
Cancer Mortality Rate	164.8	168.9			

Irmo, SC

Area Type: Outer suburb

Zip Code: 29212

Metro Area: Columbia, SC

Metro Area Type: Mid-size

Location: Along I-20 10 miles northwest of downtown Columbia, SC

Time Zone: Eastern Standard Time

Pros:
Appealing setting
Attractive, affordable housing
Nearby recreation

Cons:
Hot, humid summers
Growth pressure
Air service

Close to Lake Murray and the distinctly Southern city of Columbia, Irmo—once a sleepy small town named after a couple of railroad builders—is now a high-end suburb. Lake Murray, a 50,000-acre man-made lake and reservoir built in 1930, sits just to the west of Irmo and is a minor regional vacation destination for boating, fishing, camping, and other outdoor activities. This lake and nearby timberland provide an attractive setting. Downtown Irmo offers an assortment of small restaurants, and attractive new subdivisions have been built to the west near the lake. New retail facilities, some upscale, are along Harbison Boulevard. Thirty-eight percent of all households are married with children.

Columbia, the capital of South Carolina and home to the University of South Carolina, is, in the words of a local resident, "staying Columbia but changing." An attractive alternative to bustling Atlanta and Charlotte, it is growing rapidly but still looks and feels like a Southern town—modestly sized with approximately a half-million residents. Set on a small plateau above the banks of the Congaree River, downtown Columbia is clean, modern, and walkable. The university and its attractive campus are just south of the heart of the city and give a distinct college-town feel, especially on "Gamecock" football weekends.

The stable local economy is driven mainly by the state government, the university, and Fort Jackson, a military installation, but also has an assortment of private industry and manufacturing, including Bose Audio and a Siemens plant. Colonial Life is another large employer. Recent job growth of 6.3% is quite strong, and the future projection of 22% growth is very healthy.

Standard of Living   Particularly for a capital city and college town, Columbia offers a low cost of living with an area-wide Cost of Living Index of 86. The Irmo area's COL is 97, quite reasonable on a national scale. High-quality homes and picturesque settings are available for $75 to $100 per square foot. Good family homes can be had for $175K to $200K, and $250K buys a fairly new, 2,800-square-foot home on a large ½-acre–plus wooded lot. Older 1960s to 1970s homes are mainly ranch and colonial styles, while newer homes are relatively ornate brick "Texas style" contemporaries. Property taxes are just below 1%, and daycare costs about $110 per week. Typical household income levels are strong, and the Buying Power Index is a healthy 147.

Education   The University of South Carolina and the capital city amenities provide a strong educational context; and 31% of Irmo residents have a 4-year degree and another 17% have graduate or professional degrees. Test scores for local schools are 10% above state averages for most subjects at most grade levels, and Irmo High scores over 90% in all categories on the state exit exam.

Lifestyle   Irmo is at once a self-contained community, a vacation spot, and a suburb of Columbia. There is plenty to do locally, particularly if shopping and outdoor lake-related recreation are high on your list. The annual fall "Okra Strut" food festival is a classic and shows off a little of the town's tongue-in-cheek Southern-style humor. In Columbia, the university provides sports, performing arts, nightlife, museums, bookstores, and cafes to suit most interests. The redeveloping "Riverbanks" area hosts a nationally noted zoo, aquarium, and botanical garden. Minor historic sites, museums, and older historic homes are abundant. Columbia residents like their central location at the freeway crossroads of southeast–northwest I-26, east–west I-20, and north–south I-77. These freeways bring an assortment of "getaway" choices: South Carolina beaches are 2

IRMO, SC	
NEIGHBORHOOD HIGHLIGHTS	
PEOPLE	
Population	29,848
15-yr Population Growth	37.90%
5-yr Population Growth	7%
% Married w/Children	37.7%
% Single w/Children	10.7%
No. of Households	11,286
Median Age	35.2
Avg. Household Size	2.61
Diversity Measure	33
STANDARD OF LIVING	
Median Household Income	$63,488
% Household Income > $100K	20%
Projected Future Job Growth	22%
Cost of Living Index	96.7
Buying Power Index	147
Weekly Daycare Cost	$110
Median Home Price	$174,800
"Sweet Spot" Home Price	$190,000
Home Price Ratio	2.8
Median Age of Homes	16.3
% Homes Owned	72%
Effective Property Tax Rate	1%
Estimated Property Tax Bill	$1,900
EDUCATION	
% High School Graduates	95%
% 4-yr Degree	31%
% Graduate or Professional Degree	17%
$ Invested per Pupil	$5,497
Student/Teacher Ratio	13.3
Primary Test Score Percentile	107.5
Secondary Test Score Percentile	91.4
% Subsidized School Lunch	33.60%
% Attending Public School	85.60%
LIFESTYLE	
Leisure Rating (Area)	1
Arts & Culture Rating (Area)	7
Climate Rating (Area)	2
Physical Setting Rating	5
Downtown Core Rating	5
% Commute < 30 Min.	66%
% Commute > 1 Hour	4%
HEALTH & SAFETY	
Health Rating (Area)	10
Stress Score (Area)	5
Violent Crime Risk	35
Property Crime Risk	42

hours away, Charlotte is just over an hour, the Appalachians are a couple of hours north, and Atlanta is 3 hours west.

Downtown Columbia is an easy 15- to 20-minute commute from Irmo, and most employers are in or near the downtown area. The strength of Atlanta and Charlotte as air hubs has pulled away local air service, making it weak for a capital city; most flights depart out of one of the larger cities.

The area is located along the valley confluence of the Congaree and Saluda (which feeds Lake Murray) rivers. While terrain is gently rolling and wooded to the northwest, it's flat and mainly agricultural to the southeast. Mountains to the northwest block strong winter storms, making for mostly pleasant winters, but summers can be hot and sticky.

Health & Safety   Metro-area crime risk is moderate and consistent with the region, but the local "CAP" crime risk indexes are very low. Healthcare facilities are adequate, particularly because of the nearby university and the 318-bed Lexington Medical Center near Irmo on Columbia's northwest side. Healthcare costs are reasonable at 93% of national averages.

Nearby Neighborhoods   Irmo is the strongest family neighborhood in this area, but Dutch Fork is another good choice about 25 minutes from town. Columbia has some excellent inner neighborhoods of old historic homes, including Shandon on the east side. Homes are either restored or restorable, and the neighborhoods are attractive; but there are fewer families in these areas and schools are a mixed picture.

COLUMBIA, SC
AREA HIGHLIGHTS
PEOPLE

SIZE & DIVERSITY	AREA	U.S. AVG	FAMILY DEMOGRAPHICS	AREA	U.S. AVG
Population	565,666		% Married	51%	53.80%
15-yr Population Growth	25.40%	4.40%	% Single	49%	46.20%
Diversity Measure	50	54	% Divorced	7.60%	10.20%
% Religiously Observant	45%	50%	% Separated	4.70%	2.10%
% Catholic	4%	22%	% Married w/Children	29%	27.90%
% Protestant	40%	25%	% Single w/Children	12.50%	9.40%
% Jewish	1%	2%	% Married, No Children	26.60%	31.00%
% Other	0%	1%	% Single, No Children	31.90%	31.70%

STANDARD OF LIVING

INCOME, EMPLOYMENT & TAXES	AREA	U.S. AVG	COST OF LIVING & HOUSING	AREA	U.S. AVG
Median Household Income	$43,177	$44,684	Cost of Living Index	86.4	100
Household Income Growth	4.20%	6.10%	Buying Power Index	112	100
Unemployment Rate	4.20%	5.10%	Median Home Price	$133,700	$208,500
Recent Job Growth	6.30%	1.30%	Home Price Ratio	3.1	4.7
Projected Future Job Growth	14.70%	10.50%	Home Price Appreciation	5.40%	13.60%
State Income Tax Rate	6.90%	5.00%	% Homes Owned	66.40%	64.10%
State Sales Tax Rate	4.90%	6.00%	Median Rent	$625	$792

EDUCATION

ATTAINMENT & ACHIEVEMENT	AREA	U.S. AVG	RESOURCES & INVESTMENT	AREA	U.S. AVG
% High School Graduate	80.30%	83.90%	No. of Highly Ranked Universities	0	1
% 2-yr Graduate	10.50%	7.10%	$ Invested per Pupil	$5,817	$6,058
% 4-yr Graduate	21.50%	17.20%	Student/Teacher Ratio	16.2	15.9
% Graduate or Professional Degree	11%	9.90%	State University In-State Tuition	$6,416	$4,917
% Attending Public School	92.10%	84.30%			
75th Percentile State University SAT Score (Verbal)	510	477			
75th Percentile State University SAT Score (Math)	520	478			
75th Percentile State University ACT Score	22	20			

LIFESTYLE

RECREATION, ARTS & CULTURE	AREA	U.S. AVG	INFRASTRUCTURE & FACILITIES	AREA	U.S. AVG
Professional Sports Rating	3	4	No. of Public Libraries	19	28
Zoos & Aquariums Rating	7	3	Library Volumes Per Capita	3.1	2.8
Amusement Park Rating	1	3	No. of Warehouse Clubs	4	4
Professional Theater Rating	1	3	No. of Starbucks	4	5
Overall Museum Rating	7	6	Golf Course Rating	3	4
Science Museum Rating	6	4	National Park Rating	3	3
Children's Museum Rating	5	3	Sq. Mi. Inland Water	5	4

CLIMATE			COMMUTE & TRANSPORTATION		
Days Mostly Sunny	223	212	Avg. Daily Commute Time	23.5	24.7
Annual Days Precipitation	111	111	% Commute by Auto	75%	77.70%
Annual Days > 90°F	64	38	Per Capita Avg. Daily Transit Miles	4.6	7.9
Annual Days < 32°F	60	88	Annual Auto Insurance Premium	$1,113	$1,314
July Relative Humidity	73	69	Gas, Cost per Gallon	$3.20	$3.05

HEALTH & SAFETY

CRIME & ENVIRNOMENTAL ISSUES	AREA	U.S. AVG	HEALTHCARE & COST	AREA	U.S. AVG
Violent Crime Rate	859	517	Physicians per Capita	291.3	254.3
Change in Violent Crime	0.60%	-7.50%	Pediatricians per Capita	20.7	16.9
Property Crime Rate	4784	3783	Hospital Beds per Capita	464.5	239.7
Change in Property Crime	-11.50%	-10.10%	No. of Teaching Hospitals	2	1.9
Air Quality Score	26	44	Healthcare Cost Index	92.9	100
Water Quality Score	56	33	Cost per Doctor Visit	$71	$74
Pollen/Allergy Score	65	61	Cost per Dentist Visit	$83	$67
Stress Score	50	49	Cost per Hospital Room	$533	$702
Cancer Mortality Rate	166.7	168.9			

Kaysville, UT

Area Type: Outer suburb/suburban town

Zip Code: 84037

Metro Area: Salt Lake City–Ogden, UT

Metro Area Type: Mid-size

Location: Along I-15, 19 miles south of Ogden and 23 miles north of Salt Lake City

Time Zone: Mountain Standard Time

Pros:
Attractive setting and downtown areas
Nearby recreation
Climate

Cons:
Growth and sprawl
Traffic
Entertainment

"It's 15 minutes to the mountains, 15 minutes to the lake, and a half-hour to Salt Lake or to Ogden," say local residents of Kaysville's ideal location.

Once a fort, then an agricultural center of the Mormon pioneers, Kaysville has evolved into an attractive small town and bedroom community tucked into the narrow strip of fertile farmland between the Great Salt Lake and the Wasatch to the east. Drive north from Salt Lake City, and the snowcapped (most of the year, anyway) Wasatch Mountains on your right provide a dramatic backdrop for the clean and attractive suburban communities dotting what was once a mainly agricultural landscape.

The climate, setting, educated population, and strategic position along transportation routes to many points in the West make the Salt Lake City area one of the fastest growing in the United States. Basic industries like mining, metal products, and agriculture prospered for many years, and now new-economy industries are flourishing as well, being often seen as an attractive alternative to the West Coast. A strong religious tradition and work ethic, low costs, and excellent mountain recreation nearby draw many people to the area. Projected future job growth, not surprisingly, is a robust 25%.

Downtown Kaysville is very clean and typically Western with low buildings, wide streets, and a look of quiet prosperity found throughout the Utah region. Along the main street and on the gridlike streets just adjacent are well-maintained historic homes, which then give way to areas of newer suburban houses. The Mormon influence is strong and the family orientation is undeniable (52% of households are married with children). As in many ideal family places, top-notch big-city amenities and services are close by, in this case in Ogden and Salt Lake City.

Standard of Living Hill Air Force Base, just north, is currently the largest employer in the immediate vicinity, employing 15,000 military and nonmilitary personnel. There's also a 175-acre business park in town. Alternately, many residents go north or south to work in Ogden or Salt Lake City. Area employers include such names as Thiokol, Iomega, Levolor, and the IRS, among many smaller manufacturers in the technology, aerospace, and airport equipment fields. Homes are reasonably priced with good-quality building on generous lots; many good family homes start in the $180K to $200K range with the "sweet spot" near $250K. Those looking for larger, 3,000-square-foot–plus homes can find them under $300K. Property taxes run about 1.3%.

Education Schools are modern in structure and traditional in values. The local Davis High School scores the best in the Davis County area, generally 10% to 20% above national averages on Stanford Achievement tests. Some 97% passed the 10th-grade Utah Basic Skills reading test on the first attempt, and 87% passed the math test. Good higher education alternatives lie within 50 miles, including the University of Utah (Salt Lake), Utah State (Logan, to the north), and Brigham Young (Provo).

Lifestyle It's quiet in Kaysville, but local parks and a pair of small amusement and water parks 5 miles north and south provide some recreation. The real recreational opportunities lie east in the mountains and canyons of the Wasatch. World-class skiing is available at an assortment of resorts, and hiking, backpacking, mountain biking, river rafting, and family camping are popular. The Great Salt Lake affords some boating and watersports but it isn't like a typical inland freshwater lake. Salt Lake City is an easy drive, and national parks in southern Utah are spectacular short or long getaways. Salt Lake air service is good and the international airport is easy to get to from Kaysville.

Commutes to local businesses or to Hill AFB are simple, but trips up and down I-15 to the larger cities can be busy at rush hour, especially if one is trying to get south of Salt Lake. Currently, there is little public transportation.

The green and fertile west slope plain quickly gives way to desert conditions at the Great Salt Lake and westward, and to lush alpine mountain settings to the east. The climate is a dry continental, with 232 days of sunshine annually. Summer days are pleasant but occasionally hot with cool evenings brought on by the mountains and the 4,200-foot altitude. Winters are cold, but not severe, with an occasional heavy snow; outdoor activities are seldom impaired for long periods.

Health & Safety The crime risk is low and healthcare facilities are above average. Pollution sources and the mountain barrier can cause air-quality problems at times in the summer and thick haze in winter.

Nearby Neighborhoods Kaysville is one of many suburban areas to be considered in the Salt Lake basin. Attractive neighborhoods lie nearby in all directions and particularly towards Ogden to the north. To the south of Salt Lake City, Sandy and Provo are attractive alternatives, although they're becoming a bit crowded.

KAYSVILLE, UT
NEIGHBORHOOD HIGHLIGHTS

PEOPLE

Population	27,792
15-yr Population Growth	39%
5-yr Population Growth	9.30%
% Married w/Children	52.4%
% Single w/Children	8.1%
No. of Households	7,417
Median Age	29.4
Avg. Household Size	3.76
Diversity Measure	9

STANDARD OF LIVING

Median Household Income	$62,509
% Household Income > $100K	17%
Projected Future Job Growth	25%
Cost of Living Index	107
Buying Power Index	131
Weekly Daycare Cost	$85
Median Home Price	$209,100
"Sweet Spot" Home Price	$250,000
Home Price Ratio	3.3
Median Age of Homes	17.7
% Homes Owned	85%
Effective Property Tax Rate	1.30%
Estimated Property Tax Bill	$3,250

EDUCATION

% High School Graduates	95%
% 4-yr Degree	27%
% Graduate or Professional Degree	11%
$ Invested per Pupil	$3,624
Student/Teacher Ratio	19.4
Primary Test Score Percentile	107.1
Secondary Test Score Percentile	102.4
% Subsidized School Lunch	26.50%
% Attending Public School	94.80%

LIFESTYLE

Leisure Rating (Area)	9
Arts & Culture Rating (Area)	9
Climate Rating (Area)	4
Physical Setting Rating	7
Downtown Core Rating	7
% Commute < 30 Min.	59%
% Commute > 1 Hour	5%

HEALTH & SAFETY

Health Rating (Area)	2
Stress Score (Area)	6
Violent Crime Risk	36
Property Crime Risk	61

SALT LAKE CITY–OGDEN, UT
AREA HIGHLIGHTS

PEOPLE

SIZE & DIVERSITY	AREA	U.S. AVG	FAMILY DEMOGRAPHICS	AREA	U.S. AVG
Population	1,405,136		% Married	56.30%	53.80%
15-yr Population Growth	31.20%	4.40%	% Single	43.70%	46.20%
Diversity Measure	30	54	% Divorced	9.40%	10.20%
% Religiously Observant	70%	50%	% Separated	2.20%	2.10%
% Catholic	5%	22%	% Married w/Children	38%	27.90%
% Protestant	64%	25%	% Single w/Children	10%	9.40%
% Jewish	0%	2%	% Married, No Children	25.20%	31.00%
% Other	0%	1%	% Single, No Children	26.80%	31.70%

STANDARD OF LIVING

INCOME, EMPLOYMENT & TAXES	AREA	U.S. AVG	COST OF LIVING & HOUSING	AREA	U.S. AVG
Median Household Income	$49,037	$44,684	Cost of Living Index	90.4	100
Household Income Growth	4.30%	6.10%	Buying Power Index	121	100
Unemployment Rate	4.30%	5.10%	Median Home Price	$169,900	$208,500
Recent Job Growth	2.30%	1.30%	Home Price Ratio	3.5	4.7
Projected Future Job Growth	18.40%	10.50%	Home Price Appreciation	5.50%	13.60%
State Income Tax Rate	7%	5.00%	% Homes Owned	64.80%	64.10%
State Sales Tax Rate	6%	6.00%	Median Rent	$747	$792

EDUCATION

ATTAINMENT & ACHIEVEMENT	AREA	U.S. AVG	RESOURCES & INVESTMENT	AREA	U.S. AVG
% High School Graduate	87.60%	83.90%	No. of Highly Ranked Universities	0	1
% 2-yr Graduate	12%	7.10%	$ Invested per Pupil	$3,863	$6,058
% 4-yr Graduate	26.20%	17.20%	Student/Teacher Ratio	22.9	15.9
% Graduate or Professional Degree	11.10%	9.90%	State University In-State Tuition	$4,000	$4,917
% Attending Public School	94.40%	84.30%			
75th Percentile State University SAT Score (Verbal)	N/A	477			
75th Percentile State University SAT Score (Math)	N/A	478			
75th Percentile State University ACT Score	21	20			

LIFESTYLE

RECREATION, ARTS & CULTURE	AREA	U.S. AVG	INFRASTRUCTURE & FACILITIES	AREA	U.S. AVG
Professional Sports Rating	6	4	No. of Public Libraries	34	28
Zoos & Aquariums Rating	7	3	Library Volumes Per Capita	2.6	2.8
Amusement Park Rating	3	3	No. of Warehouse Clubs	7	4
Professional Theater Rating	9	3	No. of Starbucks	15	5
Overall Museum Rating	8	6	Golf Course Rating	5	4
Science Museum Rating	7	4	National Park Rating	8	3
Children's Museum Rating	7	3	Sq. Mi. Inland Water	10	4

CLIMATE			COMMUTE & TRANSPORTATION		
Days Mostly Sunny	232	212	Avg. Daily Commute Time	22.4	24.7
Annual Days Precipitation	88	111	% Commute by Auto	74%	77.70%
Annual Days > 90°F	58	38	Per Capita Avg. Daily Transit Miles	19.5	7.9
Annual Days < 32°F	134	88	Annual Auto Insurance Premium	$1,209	$1,314
July Relative Humidity	54	69	Gas, Cost per Gallon	$2.87	$3.05

HEALTH & SAFETY

CRIME & ENVIRNOMENTAL ISSUES	AREA	U.S. AVG	HEALTHCARE & COST	AREA	U.S. AVG
Violent Crime Rate	363	517	Physicians per Capita	240.2	254.3
Change in Violent Crime	-4.40%	-7.50%	Pediatricians per Capita	21.6	16.9
Property Crime Rate	5577	3783	Hospital Beds per Capita	260.5	239.7
Change in Property Crime	-3.70%	-10.10%	No. of Teaching Hospitals	8	1.9
Air Quality Score	23	44	Healthcare Cost Index	89.5	100
Water Quality Score	65	33	Cost per Doctor Visit	$72	$74
Pollen/Allergy Score	60	61	Cost per Dentist Visit	$77	$67
Stress Score	64	49	Cost per Hospital Room	$631	$702
Cancer Mortality Rate	132.5	168.9			

Kendall Park, NJ

Area Type: Outer suburb

Zip Code: 08824

Metro Area: Middlesex–Somerset Hunterdon, NJ

Metro Area Type: Largest

Location: 50 miles southwest of Manhattan

Time Zone: Eastern Standard Time

Pros:
Country setting
Good schools
Central location

Cons:
Long commutes
Lack of downtown district
Little local recreation

Smack in the middle of Middlesex County, which calls itself the "Heart of New Jersey," Kendall Park is a quiet and modest suburban oasis convenient to much of the New York–New Jersey area. In rural fringe along the busy US 1 corridor, Kendall Park is just 9 miles southwest of satellite city New Brunswick and 9 miles northeast of the Princeton area.

An extension of South Brunswick, Kendall Park is a relatively new suburb in the region. Many homes here were built in the 1960s and 1970s, but newer housing is still being constructed today. The number of married-with-children households is high at 36.3%, schools are excellent, incomes are strong, and crime is low; it's a good fit for families, if you don't mind somewhat long commutes to work.

Middlesex County is one of the more prosperous counties in the state, serving as home to the headquarters and/or large facilities of such big companies as Bristol-Myers Squibb Co., Johnson & Johnson, Inc., Dow Jones Company, Inc., American Reinsurance Co., and Merrill Lynch, Inc. Beyond these big players, Middlesex County is home to some 87 industrial parks of all sizes. The area is also home to Princeton University and Rutgers, the largest state university, in New Brunswick. These universities bring a strong intellectual base, and several research facilities are part of the mix of manufacturing and distribution facilities in the area. New York City, with its wide array of activities and services, is about 45 miles to the northeast.

Standard of Living   Smaller, newer, and a little farther out into the country than some other New Jersey suburbs, Kendall Park has a Cost of Living Index of 137, which is relatively low in this part of the country. Homes are still expensive on the national scale, ranging from the mid $450Ks to the low $500Ks. Some homes are available at about $350K. Half-acre wooded lots are common, and styles range from traditional colonials and ranches to more contemporary styles. Property taxes run about 1.8%—high but not much higher than other comparable areas and lower than many. The employment base is steady and diverse, with unemployment rates running a low 3.3% and median household incomes over $100,000. The Buying Power Index is a strong 167.

Education   The South Brunswick School District is well regarded in the area, with modest school sizes and good test scores running 5% to 20% above state averages. The student-teacher ratio of 13.8 is impressive. Locals say that "schools are what sell the homes." The nearby universities influence the area's arts scene and overall diversity.

Lifestyle   Not having much of a town center, Kendall Park residents find most of their entertainment and services in nearby New Brunswick and Princeton. A few minor sports and recreation facilities are in the area, including a skating rink, sports arena, soccer stadium, and small, redeveloped mall. Here too are a YMCA and several libraries, plus a number of historic and recreational parks sprinkled throughout the county. Several Revolutionary War sites and the Delaware and Raritan Canal State Park, with some 70 miles of canalfront parkway, are other interesting attractions. For getaways, the New Jersey Shore is 45 miles to the east (Asbury Park) and Atlantic City is 90 miles to the south.

About 50% of working residents commute into New York City, which takes about an hour. Express buses run into the city, with convenient park-and-ride facilities, and NJ Transit trains run from New Brunswick.

The eastern half of Middlesex County is mainly flat and built up. In the area of Kendall Park and to the west, the landscape becomes rural with woods and

KENDALL PARK, NJ NEIGHBORHOOD HIGHLIGHTS	
PEOPLE	
Population	12,418
15-yr Population Growth	16.90%
5-yr Population Growth	4.70%
% Married w/Children	36.3%
% Single w/Children	6.3%
No. of Households	3,944
Median Age	34.5
Avg. Household Size	3.17
Diversity Measure	43
STANDARD OF LIVING	
Median Household Income	$102,293
% Household Income > $100K	42%
Projected Future Job Growth	6%
Cost of Living Index	137
Buying Power Index	167
Weekly Daycare Cost	$215
Median Home Price	$408,300
"Sweet Spot" Home Price	$500,000
Home Price Ratio	4
Median Age of Homes	24.9
% Homes Owned	88%
Effective Property Tax Rate	1.80%
Estimated Property Tax Bill	$9,000
EDUCATION	
% High School Graduates	94%
% 4-yr Degree	28%
% Graduate or Professional Degree	17%
$ Invested per Pupil	$8,415
Student/Teacher Ratio	13.8
Primary Test Score Percentile	116.4
Secondary Test Score Percentile	106.2
% Subsidized School Lunch	5%
% Attending Public School	81.10%
LIFESTYLE	
Leisure Rating (Area)	9
Arts & Culture Rating (Area)	10
Climate Rating (Area)	6
Physical Setting Rating	4
Downtown Core Rating	4
% Commute < 30 Min.	49%
% Commute > 1 Hour	20%
HEALTH & SAFETY	
Health Rating (Area)	2
Stress Score (Area)	1
Violent Crime Risk	25
Property Crime Risk	32

farmland. The climate is continental with distinct seasons, and some marine influence moderates the temperatures.

Health & Safety Crime risk is low and trending lower. Two university teaching hospitals are available in New Brunswick, and general health resources are good and less expensive than in other parts of the New York–New Jersey area.

Nearby Neighborhoods Families looking in this area should also consider neighborhoods in East and South Brunswick. Though more upscale and farther from New York City, the Princeton area is also an excellent choice for families.

MIDDLESEX–SOMERSET HUNTERDON, NJ
AREA HIGHLIGHTS

PEOPLE

SIZE & DIVERSITY	AREA	U.S. AVG	FAMILY DEMOGRAPHICS	AREA	U.S. AVG
Population	1,231,591		% Married	57.30%	53.80%
15-yr Population Growth	21.10%	4.40%	% Single	42.70%	46.20%
Diversity Measure	49	54	% Divorced	6.40%	10.20%
% Religiously Observant	58%	50%	% Separated	2.40%	2.10%
% Catholic	43%	22%	% Married w/Children	28.60%	27.90%
% Protestant	10%	25%	% Single w/Children	6.50%	9.40%
% Jewish	5%	2%	% Married, No Children	33.70%	31.00%
% Other	1%	1%	% Single, No Children	31.30%	31.70%

STANDARD OF LIVING

INCOME, EMPLOYMENT & TAXES	AREA	U.S. AVG	COST OF LIVING & HOUSING	AREA	U.S. AVG
Median Household Income	$76,726	$44,684	Cost of Living Index	118.7	100
Household Income Growth	3.30%	6.10%	Buying Power Index	145	100
Unemployment Rate	3.30%	5.10%	Median Home Price	$394,100	$208,500
Recent Job Growth	2.60%	1.30%	Home Price Ratio	5.1	4.7
Projected Future Job Growth	14.30%	10.50%	Home Price Appreciation	16%	13.60%
State Income Tax Rate	2.50%	5.00%	% Homes Owned	72%	64.10%
State Sales Tax Rate	6%	6.00%	Median Rent	$1,210	$792

EDUCATION

ATTAINMENT & ACHIEVEMENT	AREA	U.S. AVG	RESOURCES & INVESTMENT	AREA	U.S. AVG
% High School Graduate	86.60%	83.90%	No. of Highly Ranked Universities	2	1
% 2-yr Graduate	7.60%	7.10%	$ Invested per Pupil	$9,491	$6,058
% 4-yr Graduate	26.70%	17.20%	Student/Teacher Ratio	14.4	15.9
% Graduate or Professional Degree	14%	9.90%	State University In-State Tuition	$8,564	$4,917
% Attending Public School	83.50%	84.30%			
75th Percentile State University SAT Score (Verbal)	530	477			
75th Percentile State University SAT Score (Math)	550	478			
75th Percentile State University ACT Score	N/A	20			

LIFESTYLE

RECREATION, ARTS & CULTURE	AREA	U.S. AVG	INFRASTRUCTURE & FACILITIES	AREA	U.S. AVG
Professional Sports Rating	10	4	No. of Public Libraries	56	28
Zoos & Aquariums Rating	4	3	Library Volumes Per Capita	3.9	2.8
Amusement Park Rating	5	3	No. of Warehouse Clubs	6	4
Professional Theater Rating	9	3	No. of Starbucks	12	5
Overall Museum Rating	8	6	Golf Course Rating	9	4
Science Museum Rating	7	4	National Park Rating	3	3
Children's Museum Rating	3	3	Sq. Mi. Inland Water	6	4

CLIMATE			COMMUTE & TRANSPORTATION		
Days Mostly Sunny	216	212	Avg. Daily Commute Time	31.3	24.7
Annual Days Precipitation	128	111	% Commute by Auto	79%	77.70%
Annual Days > 90°F	17	38	Per Capita Avg. Daily Transit Miles	24.9	7.9
Annual Days < 32°F	88	88	Annual Auto Insurance Premium	$1,894	$1,314
July Relative Humidity	67	69	Gas, Cost per Gallon	$3.17	$3.05

HEALTH & SAFETY

CRIME & ENVIRNOMENTAL ISSUES	AREA	U.S. AVG	HEALTHCARE & COST	AREA	U.S. AVG
Violent Crime Rate	195	517	Physicians per Capita	332.7	254.3
Change in Violent Crime	-9.20%	-7.50%	Pediatricians per Capita	31.8	16.9
Property Crime Rate	2020	3783	Hospital Beds per Capita	298.9	239.7
Change in Property Crime	-18.10%	-10.10%	No. of Teaching Hospitals	7	1.9
Air Quality Score	33	44	Healthcare Cost Index	117	100
Water Quality Score	25	33	Cost per Doctor Visit	$66	$74
Pollen/Allergy Score	62	61	Cost per Dentist Visit	$83	$67
Stress Score	5	49	Cost per Hospital Room	$4,440	$702
Cancer Mortality Rate	194.3	168.9			

Lakeville, MN

BEST OF THE BEST

Area Type: Outer suburb

Zip Code: 55044

Metro Area: Minneapolis–St. Paul, MN

Metro Area Type: Large

Location: 27 miles south of downtown Minneapolis along I-35

Time Zone: Central Standard Time

Pros:

Strong economy
Attractive housing
Education

Cons:

Growth and sprawl
Harsh winters
Low diversity

When visiting or doing business in the Twin Cities area, it doesn't take long to pick up on the clean, prosperous, intellectually stimulating way of life present throughout the area. The Twin Cities serve as the regional economic and cultural center for a large region of the upper Midwest as far west as the Rocky Mountains. The cities feel alive, and there's something for everyone within and outside the urban areas.

Adjacent to and divided by the Mississippi River, Minneapolis and St. Paul are both destination-quality cities with entertainment and performing arts. Supposedly, only New York has more performing arts—including theater performances, classical music, and dance companies—per capita. The city wins awards for being the "Most Literate City" and it's full of bookstores, newspapers, libraries, and educational context. The population is well educated: 23% of residents in the metro area have 4-year degrees, which is one of the highest such percentages outside of college towns. The economy is strong and diverse, anchored by 3M, Cargill, General Mills, and Pillsbury. Retailers Target and Best Buy, and a growing number of insurance and financial services firms, also call the area home. The population is very family oriented: 31% of households *across the metro area* are married with children, the highest percentage for a U.S. metro area of this size.

Away from downtown, attractive suburbs spread out in all directions. The inner suburbs of Edina and Richfield, south of Minneapolis, are classic, with tree-lined streets and older but refreshed and lively streetscapes and parks. The area's many lakes serve as centers for excellent city parks. To the north of St. Paul, Maplewood is another good suburb. While these suburbs may not be as affordable nor as family oriented as

some others nearby, they are truly some of America's most attractive neighborhoods for city living.

Farther from downtown, outside the I-494–694 beltway, well-planned outer suburbs have emerged in almost all directions. The list is long and demographics vary somewhat, but almost all are model family neighborhoods with attractive housing, large yards, extensive public spaces, attractive commercial developments, and an expanding array of jobs. We especially like Lakeville, on the south side, because of its good schools, small downtown area, attractive homes, strong family presence (47% of households are married with children), and comfortable suburban feel.

Standard of Living   While there is a growing industrial park in Lakeville, an estimated 75% of residents travel north on I-35 toward downtown or to one of many commercial areas located along the beltway. Future job growth is projected at a robust 29%. There are no predominant employers. Driven somewhat by its attractions and relatively high taxes, the area Cost of Living Index is 102, and for Lakeville, it's 132. The Buying Power Index is 146. The "sweet spot" for a family home here is in the low $300Ks, and this buys a newer 2,600-square-foot colonial or farmhouse-style home with a basement on an open ⅓- to ½-acre tract. Property taxes are around 1%, but Minnesota income and sales taxes are relatively high.

Education   Schools are top-notch, according to locals, with strong focus on academic and extracurricular programs. With a lot of single-earner families in the area, parent involvement and school volunteerism are high. What test scoring data is available shows strong performance, 5% to 20% higher than state averages. The student-teacher ratio of 15.9 is excellent. With 16

4-year colleges and universities in the metro area, there's no shortage of higher-education facilities.

Lifestyle The local community is active and sports oriented. Kids and adults play baseball, soccer, and other family sports at large parks. Major- and minor-league and collegiate sports are widely followed, and you can't go very long without talking about the Twins, Timberwolves, Vikings, or Gophers. Outdoor sports are also popular, led by watersports at the area's many lakes (Lake Marion is one of the bigger local lake-centered parks with beaches, boating, and lifeguard-patrolled swimming). Winter sports include snowmobiling, skating, and cross-country skiing, and the Buck Hill ski area is just 10 minutes away toward the city in Burnsville. Shoppers are 20 minutes from the largest mall in the United States, the Mall of America, and from upscale malls in the Edina area. Family and children's amenities are readily available, and the Minnesota Zoo, 5 miles away in Apple Valley, is especially convenient.

Traffic and commutes are an issue for those working north in the Twin Cities, but are manageable at 30 to 45 minutes to most major work areas. Many commuters travel at off-peak times to avoid the rush.

Lakeville is in a hilly, partially wooded area south of the city. Most developed areas were once open, clear farmland. The climate is northern continental with a wide temperature range; summers are warm and normally pleasant, but winter weather generally stays below freezing with persistent snow and stronger cold snaps. Cold but sunny days are common.

Health & Safety Crime is low in Lakeville and moderately low in the metro area. Healthcare facilities are excellent, if expensive. The prevailing wind direction and lack of trapping geographic features provide good air quality for a big city.

Nearby Neighborhoods In addition to Lakeville, Maple Grove, Apple Valley, and Bloomington are attractive and comparable Minneapolis neighborhoods. Edina, Eden Prairie, and Wayzata to the west are more upscale and very attractive. On the St. Paul side, Maplewood and Woodbury are good options.

LAKEVILLE, MN
NEIGHBORHOOD HIGHLIGHTS

PEOPLE

Population	37,366
15-yr Population Growth	37.70%
5-yr Population Growth	6.50%
% Married w/Children	46.6%
% Single w/Children	8.7%
No. of Households	11,748
Median Age	29.7
Avg. Household Size	3.17
Diversity Measure	8

STANDARD OF LIVING

Median Household Income	$86,314
% Household Income > $100K	31%
Projected Future Job Growth	29%
Cost of Living Index	132
Buying Power Index	146
Weekly Daycare Cost	$202
Median Home Price	$310,100
"Sweet Spot" Home Price	$325,000
Home Price Ratio	3.6
Median Age of Homes	11.5
% Homes Owned	91%
Effective Property Tax Rate	1%
Estimated Property Tax Bill	$3,250

EDUCATION

% High School Graduates	96%
% 4-yr Degree	29%
% Graduate or Professional Degree	9%
$ Invested per Pupil	$5,218
Student/Teacher Ratio	14.9
Primary Test Score Percentile	111.3
Secondary Test Score Percentile	105
% Subsidized School Lunch	10.10%
% Attending Public School	87.80%

LIFESTYLE

Leisure Rating (Area)	9
Arts & Culture Rating (Area)	10
Climate Rating (Area)	1
Physical Setting Rating	4
Downtown Core Rating	8
% Commute < 30 Min.	60%
% Commute > 1 Hour	4%

HEALTH & SAFETY

Health Rating (Area)	4
Stress Score (Area)	4
Violent Crime Risk	24
Property Crime Risk	35

MINNEAPOLIS–ST. PAUL, MN
AREA HIGHLIGHTS

PEOPLE

SIZE & DIVERSITY	AREA	U.S. AVG	FAMILY DEMOGRAPHICS	AREA	U.S. AVG
Population	3,116,206		% Married	56.40%	53.80%
15-yr Population Growth	27.10%	4.40%	% Single	43.60%	46.20%
Diversity Measure	27	54	% Divorced	8%	10.20%
% Religiously Observant	56%	50%	% Separated	1.90%	2.10%
% Catholic	26%	22%	% Married w/Children	30.60%	27.90%
% Protestant	29%	25%	% Single w/Children	8.50%	9.40%
% Jewish	1%	2%	% Married, No Children	28.20%	31.00%
% Other	0%	1%	% Single, No Children	32.70%	31.70%

STANDARD OF LIVING

INCOME, EMPLOYMENT & TAXES	AREA	U.S. AVG	COST OF LIVING & HOUSING	AREA	U.S. AVG
Median Household Income	$60,762	$44,684	Cost of Living Index	102.3	100
Household Income Growth	3.70%	6.10%	Buying Power Index	133	100
Unemployment Rate	3.70%	5.10%	Median Home Price	$237,700	$208,500
Recent Job Growth	2.70%	1.30%	Home Price Ratio	3.9	4.7
Projected Future Job Growth	14.30%	10.50%	Home Price Appreciation	9.30%	13.60%
State Income Tax Rate	7.90%	5.00%	% Homes Owned	71.10%	64.10%
State Sales Tax Rate	7%	6.00%	Median Rent	$928	$792

EDUCATION

ATTAINMENT & ACHIEVEMENT	AREA	U.S. AVG	RESOURCES & INVESTMENT	AREA	U.S. AVG
% High School Graduate	87.70%	83.90%	No. of Highly Ranked Universities	3	1
% 2-yr Graduate	11.40%	7.10%	$ Invested per Pupil	$6,266	$6,058
% 4-yr Graduate	23.20%	17.20%	Student/Teacher Ratio	17.6	15.9
% Graduate or Professional Degree	8.20%	9.90%	State University In-State Tuition	$8,230	$4,917
% Attending Public School	87.30%	84.30%			
75th Percentile State University SAT Score (Verbal)	540	477			
75th Percentile State University SAT Score (Math)	560	478			
75th Percentile State University ACT Score	23	20			

LIFESTYLE

RECREATION, ARTS & CULTURE	AREA	U.S. AVG	INFRASTRUCTURE & FACILITIES	AREA	U.S. AVG
Professional Sports Rating	7	4	No. of Public Libraries	132	28
Zoos & Aquariums Rating	9	3	Library Volumes Per Capita	3.5	2.8
Amusement Park Rating	10	3	No. of Warehouse Clubs	7	4
Professional Theater Rating	10	3	No. of Starbucks	58	5
Overall Museum Rating	10	6	Golf Course Rating	9	4
Science Museum Rating	9	4	National Park Rating	3	3
Children's Museum Rating	8	3	Sq. Mi. Inland Water	10	4

CLIMATE			COMMUTE & TRANSPORTATION		
Days Mostly Sunny	200	212	Avg. Daily Commute Time	23.7	24.7
Annual Days Precipitation	113	111	% Commute by Auto	73%	77.70%
Annual Days > 90°F	15	38	Per Capita Avg. Daily Transit Miles	10.9	7.9
Annual Days < 32°F	158	88	Annual Auto Insurance Premium	$1,487	$1,314
July Relative Humidity	69	69	Gas, Cost per Gallon	$2.84	$3.05

HEALTH & SAFETY

CRIME & ENVIRNOMENTAL ISSUES	AREA	U.S. AVG	HEALTHCARE & COST	AREA	U.S. AVG
Violent Crime Rate	327	517	Physicians per Capita	241.5	254.3
Change in Violent Crime	-18.20%	-7.50%	Pediatricians per Capita	18.8	16.9
Property Crime Rate	3453	3783	Hospital Beds per Capita	271.8	239.7
Change in Property Crime	-19.70%	-10.10%	No. of Teaching Hospitals	16	1.9
Air Quality Score	35	44	Healthcare Cost Index	129.5	100
Water Quality Score	27	33	Cost per Doctor Visit	$87	$74
Pollen/Allergy Score	47	61	Cost per Dentist Visit	$97	$67
Stress Score	35	49	Cost per Hospital Room	$1,442	$702
Cancer Mortality Rate	163.2	168.9			

Lake Zurich, IL

Area Type: Outer suburb/exurb

Zip Code: 60047

Metro Area: Chicago, IL

Metro Area Type: Largest

Location: 40 miles northwest of downtown Chicago along US 12

Time Zone: Central Standard Time

Pros:

Parks and recreation
Strong economy
Education

Cons:

Cost of living
Growth pressure
Some long commutes

When you think of Chicago's booming, bustling suburbs, the household names of Naperville, Schaumburg, Palatine, Aurora, and Carol Stream quickly come to mind. Most likely you've done business with a company in the area, and you probably also know someone who lives there. The booming, bustling Chicago Outer Belt suburban region offers excellent economic opportunity within easy striking distance of one of the great urban areas in the world. The so-called Chicagoland area is hard to beat as a family place.

So where, among the many suburban choices, should an aspiring family look to live? The above suburbs, plus dozens of others, can all work for families. They have attractive suburban homes, usually on developed, flat farmland, with a small downtown or commercial area often surrounding a station on one of the area's many well-developed commuter rail arteries. There are plenty of jobs, plenty of places to shop, and plenty to do. The network of freeways and surface streets takes residents most anywhere in reasonable time, except during rush hour or the summer construction season. Downtown Chicago is 40 minutes away, and offers some of the best arts, culture, and entertainment in the country.

Because of its unique heritage, appearance, community resources, and overall "family" feel, we picked the somewhat upscale Lake Zurich on the northwest side. Speaking loudest to us was the married-with-children percentage of 45%, one of the highest among qualifying places. Sitting on a 250-acre glacial lake by the same name, Lake Zurich originally developed in the 19th century as a farming town, then later as a resort community for Chicago getaways. Suburban growth has caught up, but a legacy remains: The lake and its shore are used as a community center, and an outstanding park and recreation system provides 27 parks that are used year-round by local residents. Team sports, nature activities,

and fitness programs are king. The 41-acre lakefront Paulus Park includes a large "Kids Kingdom" playground supported by local donations and volunteer labor. Public parks are augmented by the new Foglia YMCA. The area has a mix of housing, some of 1900-vintage close in to the village, some in attractive planned developments surrounding the village and lake. The downtown area is undergoing a renewal, bringing in attractive new condo complexes and streetfronts with residential units above.

Standard of Living   Lake Zurich is conveniently situated relative to Chicago and its stronger growth areas on the northwest side. Schaumburg, Palatine, and Rolling Meadows, 8 to 12 miles southeast, feature major business establishments and corporate headquarters, and Lake Zurich itself has a 420-acre industrial park with a diverse mix of businesses. Employment growth projections are moderately strong at almost 18%, and median household incomes are a very high $107K. Living costs are high but not excessive for the Chicago area, with a COL Index of 156. Home prices start in the mid $300Ks, with a "sweet spot" in the $400K to $450K range, which is high but not unreasonable considering the area and the available amenities. Local industry keeps a lid on effective property tax rates at about 1.7%.

Education   The local Lake Zurich Community Unit School District provides a complete academic and extracurricular educational environment. Scores on Illinois Standards Achievement Tests exceed state averages by 10% to 30%, and more than three in four high-school graduates go on to college. Fully 50% of the Lake Zurich–area's residents have a 4-year or graduate degree.

Lifestyle   Local parks and community centers offer abundant family opportunities, and the downtown

LAKE ZURICH, IL	
NEIGHBORHOOD HIGHLIGHTS	
PEOPLE	
Population	41,046
15-yr Population Growth	34.20%
5-yr Population Growth	7.50%
% Married w/Children	44.9%
% Single w/Children	4.9%
No. of Households	12,810
Median Age	33.1
Avg. Household Size	3.2
Diversity Measure	19
STANDARD OF LIVING	
Median Household Income	$106,023
% Household Income > $100K	51%
Projected Future Job Growth	18%
Cost of Living Index	156
Buying Power Index	146
Weekly Daycare Cost	$190
Median Home Price	$411,000
"Sweet Spot" Home Price	$425,000
Home Price Ratio	3.9
Median Age of Homes	18.1
% Homes Owned	91%
Effective Property Tax Rate	1.70%
Estimated Property Tax Bill	$7,225
EDUCATION	
% High School Graduates	95%
% 4-yr Degree	33%
% Graduate or Professional Degree	17%
$ Invested per Pupil	$5,249
Student/Teacher Ratio	15.4
Primary Test Score Percentile	133
Secondary Test Score Percentile	111.5
% Subsidized School Lunch	3.80%
% Attending Public School	79.40%
LIFESTYLE	
Leisure Rating (Area)	10
Arts & Culture Rating (Area)	10
Climate Rating (Area)	3
Physical Setting Rating	3
Downtown Core Rating	8
% Commute < 30 Min.	43%
% Commute > 1 Hour	12%
HEALTH & SAFETY	
Health Rating (Area)	1
Stress Score (Area)	8
Violent Crime Risk	29
Property Crime Risk	31

renewal promises to bring in more activities. For shopping, the Deer Park Town Center and the Shops of Kildeer are nearby. In addition to Lake Zurich itself, water recreation is available at a series of state parks and lakes to the north and into Wisconsin, where downhill skiing is also available. As for arts, culture, and entertainment, few places beat the Chicago assortment. Along the Michigan shore one finds the Navy Pier amusement area, Grant Park, the Art Institute of Chicago, the "Magnificent Mile" shopping district on Michigan Avenue, and the Museum of Science and Industry south of town. Performing arts are world-class, and professional sports are a passion for fans despite being only infrequently rewarded with winning teams. There is a treasure-trove of interesting architecture all around the city.

For residents who work in Lake Zurich or nearby outer-belt communities, auto commutes are a reasonable 15 to 30 minutes. Driving to Chicago is longer and more difficult, but the Northwestern rail service runs out of nearby Barrington, just 5 miles away. The train ride into Chicago takes about an hour.

Around Lake Zurich, the physical environment is generally flat, developed farmland with some trees. The climate is continental with a mild lake influence. Expect humid summers, brisk winters, and frequent weather changes.

Health & Safety   For the large metro area, crime is relatively moderate and improving. In Lake Zurich, crime risk as indicated by the "CAP" score is very low. Local healthcare facilities are abundant, and a moderately sized hospital with pediatric facilities is just west of town.

Nearby Neighborhoods   Deer Park, Barrington, and Kildeer are near Lake Zurich and are good neighborhoods but don't have as strong a set of community resources. To the west, Cary offers newer and somewhat less expensive housing, but it's another 8 miles away from the city. Closer in is Elk Grove Village, an attractive planned suburb with a more mixed, older, less family-centric population profile.

CHICAGO, IL
AREA HIGHLIGHTS

PEOPLE

SIZE & DIVERSITY	AREA	U.S. AVG	FAMILY DEMOGRAPHICS	AREA	U.S. AVG
Population	8,541,230		% Married	53.20%	53.80%
15-yr Population Growth	18.60%	4.40%	% Single	46.80%	46.20%
Diversity Measure	57	54	% Divorced	7.90%	10.20%
% Religiously Observant	57%	50%	% Separated	2.80%	2.10%
% Catholic	39%	22%	% Married w/Children	27.90%	27.90%
% Protestant	14%	25%	% Single w/Children	9.90%	9.40%
% Jewish	3%	2%	% Married, No Children	28.20%	31.00%
% Other	1%	1%	% Single, No Children	33.60%	31.70%

STANDARD OF LIVING

INCOME, EMPLOYMENT & TAXES	AREA	U.S. AVG	COST OF LIVING & HOUSING	AREA	U.S. AVG
Median Household Income	$55,785	$44,684	Cost of Living Index	113.8	100
Household Income Growth	5.80%	6.10%	Buying Power Index	110	100
Unemployment Rate	5.80%	5.10%	Median Home Price	$265,000	$208,500
Recent Job Growth	1.50%	1.30%	Home Price Ratio	4.8	4.7
Projected Future Job Growth	9%	10.50%	Home Price Appreciation	10.60%	13.60%
State Income Tax Rate	3%	5.00%	% Homes Owned	65.80%	64.10%
State Sales Tax Rate	8%	6.00%	Median Rent	$903	$792

EDUCATION

ATTAINMENT & ACHIEVEMENT	AREA	U.S. AVG	RESOURCES & INVESTMENT	AREA	U.S. AVG
% High School Graduate	82.90%	83.90%	No. of Highly Ranked Universities	5	1
% 2-yr Graduate	8.40%	7.10%	$ Invested per Pupil	$6,567	$6,058
% 4-yr Graduate	23.20%	17.20%	Student/Teacher Ratio	17.6	15.9
% Graduate or Professional Degree	12%	9.90%	State University In-State Tuition	$7,944	$4,917
% Attending Public School	84.80%	84.30%			
75th Percentile State University SAT Score (Verbal)	N/A	477			
75th Percentile State University SAT Score (Math)	N/A	478			
75th Percentile State University ACT Score	25	20			

LIFESTYLE

RECREATION, ARTS & CULTURE	AREA	U.S. AVG	INFRASTRUCTURE & FACILITIES	AREA	U.S. AVG
Professional Sports Rating	9	4	No. of Public Libraries	291	28
Zoos & Aquariums Rating	10	3	Library Volumes Per Capita	3.8	2.8
Amusement Park Rating	10	3	No. of Warehouse Clubs	10	4
Professional Theater Rating	10	3	No. of Starbucks	225	5
Overall Museum Rating	10	6	Golf Course Rating	10	4
Science Museum Rating	10	4	National Park Rating	2	3
Children's Museum Rating	10	3	Sq. Mi. Inland Water	3	4

CLIMATE			COMMUTE & TRANSPORTATION		
Days Mostly Sunny	197	212	Avg. Daily Commute Time	31.5	24.7
Annual Days Precipitation	123	111	% Commute by Auto	70%	77.70%
Annual Days > 90°F	21	38	Per Capita Avg. Daily Transit Miles	26.5	7.9
Annual Days < 32°F	119	88	Annual Auto Insurance Premium	$1,417	$1,314
July Relative Humidity	67	69	Gas, Cost per Gallon	$3.04	$3.05

HEALTH & SAFETY

CRIME & ENVIRNOMENTAL ISSUES	AREA	U.S. AVG	HEALTHCARE & COST	AREA	U.S. AVG
Violent Crime Rate	631	517	Physicians per Capita	292.1	254.3
Change in Violent Crime	-40.60%	-7.50%	Pediatricians per Capita	20.8	16.9
Property Crime Rate	3452	3783	Hospital Beds per Capita	326.6	239.7
Change in Property Crime	-23.80%	-10.10%	No. of Teaching Hospitals	57	1.9
Air Quality Score	16	44	Healthcare Cost Index	114.8	100
Water Quality Score	38	33	Cost per Doctor Visit	$88	$74
Pollen/Allergy Score	58	61	Cost per Dentist Visit	$67	$67
Stress Score	77	49	Cost per Hospital Room	$1,437	$702
Cancer Mortality Rate	183.4	168.9			

Lancaster, PA

Area Type: Small city

Zip Code: 17601

Metro Area: Lancaster, PA

Metro Area Type: Smaller

Location: Southeastern Pennsylvania on US 30, 80 miles west of Philadelphia

Time Zone: Eastern Standard Time

Pros:

Diverse employment base
Attractive housing and home prices
Convenient to major East Coast cities

Cons:

Low educational attainment
Lack of entertainment
Too traditional for some

With its small-town prosperity and traditions, Lancaster is, in many ways, a blast from the past. As an anchor city to the famed Pennsylvania Dutch Country, Lancaster attracts a lot of tourists—especially because of its old-world activities and ambience. These same activities provide a diverse and unusually manufacturing-oriented economic base for residents. Lancaster offers low living costs and plenty of things for families to do locally, plus convenience to some of the major economic centers of the East—Baltimore, Philadelphia, and Washington, DC.

At one time during the Revolutionary War, Lancaster was the largest inland city in the colonies. Not surprisingly, the downtown area retains some historic charm and is a regular destination for most locals. The most family-oriented suburbs spread north of the city and the recently upgraded US 30 bypass. About 28% of the households in this area are married with children. The nearby countryside is mainly agricultural and dotted with small farms, particularly to the east, where most of the Amish and Pennsylvania Dutch country is located. Many larger city services and amenities are available in Harrisburg, 30 miles northwest, and Baltimore is an easy 75-mile drive south.

There are over 900 manufacturing companies in Lancaster County producing more than 50,000 jobs. The economic base is oriented toward smaller and medium-size businesses, many employing 20 to 100 people in various forms of light manufacturing. A wide range of manufactured products come from the area, including electronics, packaging, flooring, cabinets, printed materials, machine tools and parts, and rubber boots. Although the job base is not growing particularly fast, it remains steady and diverse.

Standard of Living   Family homes on wooded ½-acre lots cost somewhere in the low $200K range, around $100 per square foot. Upgraded homes run $280K to $300K. The Home Price Ratio, our benchmark of home prices against local incomes, is very good at 3.4. Property taxes run about 1.5%. The Cost of Living Index is 99.1, very low for the region. Local businesses are prosperous, and the recent job growth of 2.7% is strong for a manufacturing-oriented economy. Future job growth of 8% is comparable to national averages in the United States. Tourism is another relatively stable source of income.

Education   Reflecting the more traditional and agrarian lifestyle, the population of the metro area as a whole is relatively less educated than many areas examined in this book. About 13% of the metro area population has a 4-year degree, and 74% possesses a high-school diploma. In the chosen zip code area of 17601, 28% of the population has 4-year college degrees, and 89% are high-school graduates. The area around Lancaster has a notably large number of highly ranked primary and secondary schools, and the local Manheim Township School District shows state test scores consistently 10% to 22% above state averages, but other schools are less consistent. Some less traditional families might consider the schools' rules and policies, such as dress codes, outdated.

Lifestyle   Historic sites are abundant, from individual downtown buildings to the Gettysburg National Military Park 50 miles west. Local performing arts, particularly theater, are abundant throughout the area. The downtown Lancaster Central Marketplace is one of the country's oldest farmers' marketplaces and a popular gathering place on the weekends. Relatively new to the scene are the minor-league baseball Lancaster Barnstormers and the $20-million stadium where they play (which also serves as a popular concert venue).

For a town its size, Lancaster has good museums, including the Hands On House Children's Museum and the North Museum of Natural History & Science. Interesting for the grown-ups, but probably less so for the kids, are the Lancaster Cultural History Museum, the Lancaster Newspapers Museum, and the National Watch and Clock Museum in Columbia just west. Train buffs will enjoy the Strasburg Rail Road and the Railroad Museum of Pennsylvania in Strasburg 15 miles southeast. If that isn't sweet enough, Hershey, Pennsylvania, and its chocolate factory are a 40-minute drive north.

Not surprisingly, commutes and commute times are hardly an issue for Lancaster residents. Geographically, the area is mainly flat with areas of gently rolling hills and farmland. The eastern continental climate is humid, but gets some moderating influence from the mountains to the north and water to the southeast.

Health & Safety   Crime risk is generally low. Stress factors are largely absent, and the area in fact has one of the lowest stress scores we examined. Healthcare facilities are average for this type of area.

Nearby Neighborhoods   The northern suburbs of Lancaster are probably the best family places in the area. Other family-friendly towns and cities in the region include Lebanon, Hershey, and York (see p. 412).

LANCASTER, PA NEIGHBORHOOD HIGHLIGHTS	
PEOPLE	
Population	47,301
15-yr Population Growth	15.30%
5-yr Population Growth	3.50%
% Married w/Children	28.1%
% Single w/Children	6.1%
No. of Households	18,586
Median Age	40.9
Avg. Household Size	2.47
Diversity Measure	66
STANDARD OF LIVING	
Median Household Income	$60,084
% Household Income > $100K	18%
Projected Future Job Growth	8%
Cost of Living Index	99.1
Buying Power Index	136
Weekly Daycare Cost	$162
Median Home Price	$204,200
"Sweet Spot" Home Price	$220,000
Home Price Ratio	3.4
Median Age of Homes	27.3
% Homes Owned	73%
Effective Property Tax Rate	1.50%
Estimated Property Tax Bill	$3,300
EDUCATION	
% High School Graduates	89%
% 4-yr Degree	28%
% Graduate or Professional Degree	13%
$ Invested per Pupil	$6,640
Student/Teacher Ratio	16.6
Primary Test Score Percentile	93.5
Secondary Test Score Percentile	77.6
% Subsidized School Lunch	11.40%
% Attending Public School	78.10%
LIFESTYLE	
Leisure Rating (Area)	6
Arts & Culture Rating (Area)	0
Climate Rating (Area)	3
Physical Setting Rating	3
Downtown Core Rating	2
% Commute < 30 Min.	79%
% Commute > 1 Hour	4%
HEALTH & SAFETY	
Health Rating (Area)	3
Stress Score (Area)	0
Violent Crime Risk	85
Property Crime Risk	88

LANCASTER, PA
AREA HIGHLIGHTS

PEOPLE

SIZE & DIVERSITY	AREA	U.S. AVG	FAMILY DEMOGRAPHICS	AREA	U.S. AVG
Population	487,332		% Married	61.30%	53.80%
15-yr Population Growth	15.30%	4.40%	% Single	38.70%	46.20%
Diversity Measure	21	54	% Divorced	5.60%	10.20%
% Religiously Observant	48%	50%	% Separated	2.70%	2.10%
% Catholic	10%	22%	% Married w/Children	32.50%	27.90%
% Protestant	38%	25%	% Single w/Children	7.10%	9.40%
% Jewish	1%	2%	% Married, No Children	33.90%	31.00%
% Other	0%	1%	% Single, No Children	26.40%	31.70%

STANDARD OF LIVING

INCOME, EMPLOYMENT & TAXES	AREA	U.S. AVG	COST OF LIVING & HOUSING	AREA	U.S. AVG
Median Household Income	$50,197	$44,684	Cost of Living Index	92.3	100
Household Income Growth	3.40%	6.10%	Buying Power Index	122	100
Unemployment Rate	3.40%	5.10%	Median Home Price	$162,900	$208,500
Recent Job Growth	2.70%	1.30%	Home Price Ratio	3.2	4.7
Projected Future Job Growth	10.20%	10.50%	Home Price Appreciation	10.30%	13.60%
State Income Tax Rate	2.80%	5.00%	% Homes Owned	72.40%	64.10%
State Sales Tax Rate	6%	6.00%	Median Rent	$643	$792

EDUCATION

ATTAINMENT & ACHIEVEMENT	AREA	U.S. AVG	RESOURCES & INVESTMENT	AREA	U.S. AVG
% High School Graduate	73.80%	83.90%	No. of Highly Ranked Universities	0	1
% 2-yr Graduate	5.20%	7.10%	$ Invested per Pupil	$6,075	$6,058
% 4-yr Graduate	12.50%	17.20%	Student/Teacher Ratio	16.6	15.9
% Graduate or Professional Degree	5.50%	9.90%	State University In-State Tuition	$10,856	$4,917
% Attending Public School	79.90%	84.30%			
75th Percentile State University SAT Score (Verbal)	530	477			
75th Percentile State University SAT Score (Math)	560	478			
75th Percentile State University ACT Score	N/A	20			

LIFESTYLE

RECREATION, ARTS & CULTURE	AREA	U.S. AVG	INFRASTRUCTURE & FACILITIES	AREA	U.S. AVG
Professional Sports Rating	4	4	No. of Public Libraries	17	28
Zoos & Aquariums Rating	1	3	Library Volumes Per Capita	1.6	2.8
Amusement Park Rating	3	3	No. of Warehouse Clubs	4	4
Professional Theater Rating	1	3	No. of Starbucks	1	5
Overall Museum Rating	7	6	Golf Course Rating	3	4
Science Museum Rating	3	4	National Park Rating	1	3
Children's Museum Rating	4	3	Sq. Mi. Inland Water	3	4

CLIMATE			COMMUTE & TRANSPORTATION		
Days Mostly Sunny	193	212	Avg. Daily Commute Time	21.7	24.7
Annual Days Precipitation	125	111	% Commute by Auto	73%	77.70%
Annual Days > 90°F	24	38	Per Capita Avg. Daily Transit Miles	7.1	7.9
Annual Days < 32°F	107	88	Annual Auto Insurance Premium	$1,292	$1,314
July Relative Humidity	67	69	Gas, Cost per Gallon	$3.22	$3.05

HEALTH & SAFETY

CRIME & ENVIRNOMENTAL ISSUES	AREA	U.S. AVG	HEALTHCARE & COST	AREA	U.S. AVG
Violent Crime Rate	230	517	Physicians per Capita	181.7	254.3
Change in Violent Crime	12.20%	-7.50%	Pediatricians per Capita	8.3	16.9
Property Crime Rate	2362	3783	Hospital Beds per Capita	238.1	239.7
Change in Property Crime	-14.40%	-10.10%	No. of Teaching Hospitals	2	1.9
Air Quality Score	20	44	Healthcare Cost Index	93.2	100
Water Quality Score	20	33	Cost per Doctor Visit	$62	$74
Pollen/Allergy Score	53	61	Cost per Dentist Visit	$72	$67
Stress Score	3	49	Cost per Hospital Room	$790	$702
Cancer Mortality Rate	160.7	168.9			

Lawrence, KS

Area Type: Small college town

Zip Code: 66049

Metro Area: Lawrence, KS

Metro Area Type: Smaller

Location: 40 miles west of Kansas City along I-70

Time Zone: Central Standard Time

Pros:
College-town flavor
Cost of living
Diversity

Cons:
Long commutes
Some sprawl and retail displacement
Rising living costs

If you repeatedly hear the word "Jayhawks," you're probably getting close to Lawrence, or "Larryville" as it's sometimes called, in east-central Kansas. The Jayhawks—the nationally recognized and locally worshipped athletic teams of the top-rated University of Kansas—are a dominant force in the community.

Lawrence, a college-town sort of place with low costs and a laid-back lifestyle (except on football weekends), sits in an area of flat, fertile farmland on the southwest shore of the winding Kansas River. The downtown area is adjacent to the river and its flood-control levees. Just to the southwest of the city core on a hill is the university campus, overlooking expanses of nearby farmland almost like a Medieval castle. From there, the city spreads south and west through attractive older neighborhoods and country clubs, reaching still farther west into newer suburbs just north of Clinton Lake. The zip code (66049) we selected for this book lies west of town with the area's highest married-with-children percentage (27%), high for a college town. Some suburbs are also springing up east of town to take advantage of shorter commutes to the Kansas City area. Most residents consider the area to be well planned, but larger mass retailers and chain restaurants have put some pressure on downtown merchants.

In recent years, Lawrence, with its pleasant combination of small-town and college-town style, lower costs, and laid-back lifestyle (except on football weekends), has become attractive to professionals commuting to the western parts of the Kansas City area—the "KCK" area—home to numerous high-tech and other companies. Convenience to the KC airport, also on the west side of town, has brought some frequent business travelers to Lawrence as well. This "bedroom community" transition has been handled well and hasn't caused any problems so far, but some residents would like to see more employment in the immediate area and less commuting.

As one might suspect, the university provides a lot to do, and Lawrence takes on a political and cultural bent in contrast to most of the conservative rural areas around it and even Kansas City. Culturally, it is very diverse, and it's part of the only Kansas county that voted Democratic in the 2004 Presidential election. This diversity and cultural orientation attracts many residents from KC and even the Topeka area to the west and brings a lot in the way of events and entertainment.

Standard of Living   For a college town, Lawrence has a reasonable Cost of Living Index (103), but locals express concern about rising prices as more noncollege residents discover the area. Good single-family homes start in the $170K to $180K range and can be found more easily for $200K to $225K. Effective property tax rates are about 1.3%. Employment is found at the university, but most professional employment opportunities are found in the Kansas City area or with the state government in Topeka 25 miles west.

Education   The University of Kansas exudes a strong educational influence in the area. The Lawrence Free State High School (the name referring to the pre–Civil War controversies over slavery) is relatively new and is right-sized at about 1,300 students, who score 7% to 15% above state averages. Schools work closely with the university to offer college-credit opportunities, and athletic programs—especially football and basketball—are modeled after the university's highly successful teams. The unique Haskell Indian Nations University for native Americans opened in 1984. Educational attainment in the area is very high: 55% of residents have a 4-year or graduate degree.

LAWRENCE, KS
NEIGHBORHOOD HIGHLIGHTS

PEOPLE

Population	21,234
15-yr Population Growth	25.70%
5-yr Population Growth	2.80%
% Married w/Children	27.4%
% Single w/Children	6.9%
No. of Households	8,603
Median Age	33.8
Avg. Household Size	2.48
Diversity Measure	22

STANDARD OF LIVING

Median Household Income	$52,207
% Household Income > $100K	17%
Projected Future Job Growth	12%
Cost of Living Index	103
Buying Power Index	119
Weekly Daycare Cost	$147
Median Home Price	$212,100
"Sweet Spot" Home Price	$210,000
Home Price Ratio	4.1
Median Age of Homes	14.5
% Homes Owned	60%
Effective Property Tax Rate	1.30%
Estimated Property Tax Bill	$2,730

EDUCATION

% High School Graduates	96%
% 4-yr Degree	31%
% Graduate or Professional Degree	24%
$ Invested per Pupil	$5,823
Student/Teacher Ratio	16.2
Primary Test Score Percentile	100
Secondary Test Score Percentile	116.9
% Subsidized School Lunch	18.40%
% Attending Public School	90.30%

LIFESTYLE

Leisure Rating (Area)	0
Arts & Culture Rating (Area)	6
Climate Rating (Area)	3
Physical Setting Rating	2
Downtown Core Rating	5
% Commute < 30 Min.	70%
% Commute > 1 Hour	4%

HEALTH & SAFETY

Health Rating (Area)	4
Stress Score (Area)	1
Violent Crime Risk	88
Property Crime Risk	75

Lifestyle   Major university towns offer a lot for families, and Lawrence is no exception. Excellent parks, campus museums, and entertainment facilities are available. The city runs an excellent and very family-oriented indoor and outdoor Aquatic Center. The University attracts an assortment of traveling arts and cultural events. There is an annual Renaissance Fair. Numerous historic sites and reenactments commemorate events in the area's Civil War and especially pre–Civil War history.

Within Lawrence, commutes aren't a problem. An estimated 40% of the working population drives to "KCK," which takes 30 minutes to an hour, depending on the specific destination and the time of day.

The weather in Lawrence is variable with periods of 100°F-plus temperatures in summer and blustery winter cold. Strong storms, particularly in spring and summer, punctuate the transitions between air masses from the dry northern plains and humid Gulf region.

Health & Safety   The crime risk is moderate but not atypical for college towns. Healthcare facilities, led by the Lawrence Memorial Hospital, are above average, and additional options are available in Kansas City.

Nearby Neighborhoods   The western part of the Lawrence area (zip code 66049) is probably the most family oriented and comfortable while still being quite affordable. There are attractive older residential areas in town as well. Areas to the east will probably experience growth as more area residents commute to Kansas City and a new planned highway is built.

LAWRENCE, KS
AREA HIGHLIGHTS

PEOPLE

SIZE & DIVERSITY	AREA	U.S. AVG		FAMILY DEMOGRAPHICS	AREA	U.S. AVG
Population	102,786			% Married	50.90%	53.80%
15-yr Population Growth	25.70%	4.40%		% Single	49.10%	46.20%
Diversity Measure	28	54		% Divorced	7.20%	10.20%
% Religiously Observant	29%	50%		% Separated	1.30%	2.10%
% Catholic	7%	22%		% Married w/Children	26.60%	27.90%
% Protestant	21%	25%		% Single w/Children	8%	9.40%
% Jewish	0%	2%		% Married, No Children	28%	31.00%
% Other	0%	1%		% Single, No Children	37.40%	31.70%

STANDARD OF LIVING

INCOME, EMPLOYMENT & TAXES	AREA	U.S. AVG		COST OF LIVING & HOUSING	AREA	U.S. AVG
Median Household Income	$40,026	$44,684		Cost of Living Index	90.9	100
Household Income Growth	4.30%	6.10%		Buying Power Index	99	100
Unemployment Rate	4.30%	5.10%		Median Home Price	$149,500	$208,500
Recent Job Growth	4.90%	1.30%		Home Price Ratio	3.7	4.7
Projected Future Job Growth	11.90%	10.50%		Home Price Appreciation	6.50%	13.60%
State Income Tax Rate	6.40%	5.00%		% Homes Owned	62.40%	64.10%
State Sales Tax Rate	6%	6.00%		Median Rent	$626	$792

EDUCATION

ATTAINMENT & ACHIEVEMENT	AREA	U.S. AVG		RESOURCES & INVESTMENT	AREA	U.S. AVG
% High School Graduate	89.30%	83.90%		No. of Highly Ranked Universities	0	1
% 2-yr Graduate	5.70%	7.10%		$ Invested per Pupil	$5,900	$6,058
% 4-yr Graduate	26.30%	17.20%		Student/Teacher Ratio	14.4	15.9
% Graduate or Professional Degree	18.10%	9.90%		State University In-State Tuition	$4,737	$4,917
% Attending Public School	95.40%	84.30%				
75th Percentile State University SAT Score (Verbal)	N/A	477				
75th Percentile State University SAT Score (Math)	N/A	478				
75th Percentile State University ACT Score	21	20				

LIFESTYLE

RECREATION, ARTS & CULTURE	AREA	U.S. AVG		INFRASTRUCTURE & FACILITIES	AREA	U.S. AVG
Professional Sports Rating	2	4		No. of Public Libraries	3	28
Zoos & Aquariums Rating	1	3		Library Volumes Per Capita	3.2	2.8
Amusement Park Rating	1	3		No. of Warehouse Clubs	1	4
Professional Theater Rating	1	3		No. of Starbucks	1	5
Overall Museum Rating	5	6		Golf Course Rating	1	4
Science Museum Rating	4	4		National Park Rating	1	3
Children's Museum Rating	1	3		Sq. Mi. Inland Water	3	4

CLIMATE				COMMUTE & TRANSPORTATION		
Days Mostly Sunny	205	212		Avg. Daily Commute Time	19.4	24.7
Annual Days Precipitation	96	111		% Commute by Auto	74%	77.70%
Annual Days > 90°F	45	38		Per Capita Avg. Daily Transit Miles	0	7.9
Annual Days < 32°F	123	88		Annual Auto Insurance Premium	$985	$1,314
July Relative Humidity	68	69		Gas, Cost per Gallon	$3.10	$3.05

HEALTH & SAFETY

CRIME & ENVIRNOMENTAL ISSUES	AREA	U.S. AVG		HEALTHCARE & COST	AREA	U.S. AVG
Violent Crime Rate	412	517		Physicians per Capita	180.6	254.3
Change in Violent Crime	25.70%	-7.50%		Pediatricians per Capita	6.8	16.9
Property Crime Rate	4925	3783		Hospital Beds per Capita	176.5	239.7
Change in Property Crime	5.70%	-10.10%		No. of Teaching Hospitals	0	1.9
Air Quality Score	40	44		Healthcare Cost Index	91.5	100
Water Quality Score	45	33		Cost per Doctor Visit	$69	$74
Pollen/Allergy Score	74	61		Cost per Dentist Visit	$59	$67
Stress Score	7	49		Cost per Hospital Room	$649	$702
Cancer Mortality Rate	141.5	168.9				

Lexington, KY

Area Type: Inner suburb

Zip Code: 40503

Metro Area: Lexington, KY

Metro Area Type: Smaller

Location: Central Kentucky, 80 miles south of Cincinnati and 75 miles east of Louisville

Time Zone: Eastern Standard Time

Pros:

Historic, attractive downtown
College-town influence
Beautiful countryside

Cons:

Growth and sprawl
Traffic
Some crime issues

When we asked residents about Lexington, they described their hometown with phrases like these: "size of a larger city, sense of a small town," and "city merged with the country." Surrounded by horse farms at the center of the "bluegrass" part of the Bluegrass State, Lexington is a unique mixture of country town and a grown-up city, old and new, North and South.

The countryside is beautiful. Large horse farms surround the city on all sides, but particularly to the north and east. Rolling hills, miles of well-maintained board fences, and stately homes are typical. The Kentucky Horse Park, a 1,000-acre shrine to horses and the region's horse heritage, is just north of town. Unfortunately, some horse farms to the south are starting to sell out to developers, and sprawling areas of unattractive, small lots have sprung up in these areas. But so far it doesn't detract from the quality of the area nor take much away from the excellent surroundings.

The distinctly Southern downtown area is full of Georgian brick structures with black shutters, white trim, and wrought-iron fencing and lighting. A few modern buildings, including a new performing arts center, sit in the vibrant and walkable city center. Here one also finds a new convention center, the Lexington Children's Museum, and plenty of entertainment. In fact, Lexington was rated number eight on *Prevention* magazine's list of the country's "Most Walkable Cities."

The University of Kentucky, with 20,000 students, is located south of downtown. Transylvania University, a liberal arts college with 1,100 students, lies just northeast of downtown in one of the most historic areas. Both give a strong college-town influence to the area. The University of Kentucky also adds strong healthcare facilities to the area, and, of course, is center stage for the city and state's fanatical devotion to basketball.

Economically, Lexington is tied to the university, agriculture, and horses. But in the past few years, the area has also been recognized for its good workforce, educated population, low cost of doing business, and after-work attractions for residents. Just north of town is Lexmark, Inc., the printer manufacturer, and a little farther north in Georgetown is Toyota's largest U.S. plant. Today, the area attracts a number of smaller businesses as well. The job situation is stable and current unemployment is low.

The selected neighborhood (zip code 40503) is the university area on the south side inside the beltway near downtown. The outer portion of this area has excellent housing for the money, and the area is convenient to most of the city. The married-with-children percentage of households is 25.4% and would likely be much higher without the university influence.

Standard of Living   Current employment is solid, job-growth figures are strong, and the Cost of Living Index is a modest 93. Incomes are moderate, and the reported figures are probably understated due to the college influence. Home prices are reasonable; good family homes cost between $200K and $250K with some older starters available in the $180Ks. The area is built up and considered desirable; some newcomers may find the selection of available homes to be limited at times. Aside from students, residents tend to stay for a long time. Property taxes run about 1.4%.

Education   The university influence and a well-educated population create a context for good schools. The Fayette County School District Schools cover the area, and Lafayette High School in the south area runs 12% to 17% above state averages and receives praise from the community. New schools are being built in most areas of town, successfully keeping up with growth.

Lifestyle The university, along with an assortment of in-town recreation and arts amenities, provides plenty to do. Museums and children's activities are abundant, including an aviation museum, the Explorium of Lexington children's museum, and a children's art museum and theater. Outdoor movies are shown at Jacobsen Park, a large city park east of town with an amphitheater, paddle boating, rock climbing, and state-of-the-art playground equipment.

Short drives from the city bring families to a wide assortment of destinations, many not well-known on a national scale but above average nonetheless. These include Daniel Boone's Boonesborough, Fort Harrod in Harrodsburg, the Natural Bridge State Park, the Red River Gorge, the Kentucky River Valley, and cave country and Lake Cumberland to the south. Additionally, Kentucky has one of the best state park systems in the country. Excellent amusement parks can be found in Louisville and north of Cincinnati. In fact, Cincinnati—with even more activities, including major-league sports—is just 75 miles north of Lexington. Air service into the area was once poor, but a recent airport expansion has begun to bring in more and better choices.

Commutes aren't much of an issue, although those living on the south side and traveling to larger corporate sites on the north (Lexmark and Toyota, for example) may face a bit of traffic and a 30-minute commute. A bigger concern is the growth to the southeast, which is some distance to most areas of employment.

Health & Safety Crime and crime risk are moderate on a national scale but a bit high for the region. The university and other healthcare facilities are excellent, serving most of the eastern half of Kentucky, with some specialties serving a wider area. Lexington is far enough away from major industrial areas, both north and south, to have excellent air quality.

Nearby Neighborhoods Houses on the west side are more plentiful, smaller, and less expensive than the university area, as are homes in the growing areas to the southeast. But both areas lack the wooded lots and sense of place that are common in the inner neighborhoods closer to the city. Georgetown, 10 miles north and home to Toyota, is a good alternative with a small-town environment.

LEXINGTON, KY NEIGHBORHOOD HIGHLIGHTS	
PEOPLE	
Population	27,922
15-yr Population Growth	18.20%
5-yr Population Growth	2.20%
% Married w/Children	25.4%
% Single w/Children	7.1%
No. of Households	11,947
Median Age	38
Avg. Household Size	2.29
Diversity Measure	18
STANDARD OF LIVING	
Median Household Income	$44,401
% Household Income > $100K	12%
Projected Future Job Growth	10%
Cost of Living Index	93
Buying Power Index	111
Weekly Daycare Cost	$140
Median Home Price	$156,000
"Sweet Spot" Home Price	$225,000
Home Price Ratio	3.5
Median Age of Homes	36.9
% Homes Owned	67%
Effective Property Tax Rate	1.40%
Estimated Property Tax Bill	$3,150
EDUCATION	
% High School Graduates	93%
% 4-yr Degree	22%
% Graduate or Professional Degree	19%
$ Invested per Pupil	$5,856
Student/Teacher Ratio	16
Primary Test Score Percentile	99.5
Secondary Test Score Percentile	120.7
% Subsidized School Lunch	25.60%
% Attending Public School	83.40%
LIFESTYLE	
Leisure Rating (Area)	2
Arts & Culture Rating (Area)	8
Climate Rating (Area)	4
Physical Setting Rating	4
Downtown Core Rating	5
% Commute < 30 Min.	82%
% Commute > 1 Hour	3%
HEALTH & SAFETY	
Health Rating (Area)	8
Stress Score (Area)	5
Violent Crime Risk	109
Property Crime Risk	86

LEXINGTON, KY
AREA HIGHLIGHTS
PEOPLE

SIZE & DIVERSITY	AREA	U.S. AVG	FAMILY DEMOGRAPHICS	AREA	U.S. AVG
Population	500,869		% Married	50.40%	53.80%
15-yr Population Growth	24.60%	4.40%	% Single	49.60%	46.20%
Diversity Measure	26	54	% Divorced	9.40%	10.20%
% Religiously Observant	48%	50%	% Separated	2.70%	2.10%
% Catholic	7%	22%	% Married w/Children	27%	27.90%
% Protestant	40%	25%	% Single w/Children	9.70%	9.40%
% Jewish	0%	2%	% Married, No Children	28.60%	31.00%
% Other	0%	1%	% Single, No Children	34.70%	31.70%

STANDARD OF LIVING

INCOME, EMPLOYMENT & TAXES	AREA	U.S. AVG	COST OF LIVING & HOUSING	AREA	U.S. AVG
Median Household Income	$39,520	$44,684	Cost of Living Index	87	100
Household Income Growth	3.20%	6.10%	Buying Power Index	102	100
Unemployment Rate	3.20%	5.10%	Median Home Price	$144,800	$208,500
Recent Job Growth	4.30%	1.30%	Home Price Ratio	3.7	4.7
Projected Future Job Growth	13%	10.50%	Home Price Appreciation	4.90%	13.60%
State Income Tax Rate	7.90%	5.00%	% Homes Owned	56.90%	64.10%
State Sales Tax Rate	6%	6.00%	Median Rent	$571	$792

EDUCATION

ATTAINMENT & ACHIEVEMENT	AREA	U.S. AVG	RESOURCES & INVESTMENT	AREA	U.S. AVG
% High School Graduate	78.20%	83.90%	No. of Highly Ranked Universities	5	1
% 2-yr Graduate	6.70%	7.10%	$ Invested per Pupil	$5,478	$6,058
% 4-yr Graduate	23.30%	17.20%	Student/Teacher Ratio	19.1	15.9
% Graduate or Professional Degree	14.50%	9.90%	State University In-State Tuition	$5,240	$4,917
% Attending Public School	87.10%	84.30%			
75th Percentile State University SAT Score (Verbal)	510	477			
75th Percentile State University SAT Score (Math)	510	478			
75th Percentile State University ACT Score	22	20			

LIFESTYLE

RECREATION, ARTS & CULTURE	AREA	U.S. AVG	INFRASTRUCTURE & FACILITIES	AREA	U.S. AVG
Professional Sports Rating	3	4	No. of Public Libraries	12	28
Zoos & Aquariums Rating	1	3	Library Volumes Per Capita	2.1	2.8
Amusement Park Rating	1	3	No. of Warehouse Clubs	3	4
Professional Theater Rating	1	3	No. of Starbucks	4	5
Overall Museum Rating	8	6	Golf Course Rating	4	4
Science Museum Rating	5	4	National Park Rating	1	3
Children's Museum Rating	7	3	Sq. Mi. Inland Water	2	4

CLIMATE			COMMUTE & TRANSPORTATION		
Days Mostly Sunny	197	212	Avg. Daily Commute Time	21.2	24.7
Annual Days Precipitation	130	111	% Commute by Auto	72%	77.70%
Annual Days > 90°F	16	38	Per Capita Avg. Daily Transit Miles	3.9	7.9
Annual Days < 32°F	97	88	Annual Auto Insurance Premium	$1,143	$1,314
July Relative Humidity	70	69	Gas, Cost per Gallon	$2.90	$3.05

HEALTH & SAFETY

CRIME & ENVIRNOMENTAL ISSUES	AREA	U.S. AVG	HEALTHCARE & COST	AREA	U.S. AVG
Violent Crime Rate	361	517	Physicians per Capita	379.7	254.3
Change in Violent Crime	-19.20%	-7.50%	Pediatricians per Capita	25	16.9
Property Crime Rate	4064	3783	Hospital Beds per Capita	568.4	239.7
Change in Property Crime	-5%	-10.10%	No. of Teaching Hospitals	4	1.9
Air Quality Score	52	44	Healthcare Cost Index	98.4	100
Water Quality Score	61	33	Cost per Doctor Visit	$69	$74
Pollen/Allergy Score	62	61	Cost per Dentist Visit	$70	$67
Stress Score	51	49	Cost per Hospital Room	$674	$702
Cancer Mortality Rate	169.3	168.9			

Livingston, NJ

Area Type: Inner suburb

Zip Code: 07039

Metro Area: Newark, NJ, Metropolitan Division, New York Metro Area

Metro Area Type: Largest

Location: 23 miles west of Manhattan

Time Zone: Eastern Standard Time

Pros:
Schools
Community centers, parks
Attractive housing

Cons:
High taxes
High home prices
Long commutes and no direct rail service

"Most people don't move, and after their kids go away to college, they come back to Livingston." According to a local resident, this is how things work in Livingston, New Jersey.

The benefits of living near New York City—cultural and intellectual stimulation, a wide range of commercial and employment opportunities, and the vast assortment of things to do—are well-known. The challenge is to figure out *where* in the area to live. To find a place that's safe, not too far from work, and affordable, families look to New Jersey, parts of southern New York along the Hudson River or on Long Island, and parts of Connecticut. We chose Livingston because it offers a combination of benefits: a strong sense of community (31% of households in the area are married with children), an attractive setting and infrastructure, strong schools, and convenience to the city, all at costs reasonable for the area. Situated along I-280 due west of Manhattan and Newark, Livingston is a planned community, and the town center has recently received a facelift. Homes are set attractively on reasonably large, wooded lots and the area has an old, dignified suburban feel.

Naturally, there is far more to say about the New York area than can be said here. Cultural amenities are among the finest in the world, with Broadway theater, the New York Philharmonic, and the Metropolitan Museum of Art—just to name a few. As a financial and commercial center, New York City is unmatched, and the northern New Jersey area adds a lot of manufacturing and research industry to the economic mix. Northern New Jersey is a vast assortment of adjacent suburbs and small towns located along major highway and rail transportation corridors. The suburban complex abruptly turns to farmland about 40 miles west of the city, a testimony to New Jersey's strong land-use planning initiatives.

Standard of Living The "sweet spot" for attractive family homes in Livingston is in the $500K to $600K range, although good older starter homes can be found for $450K to $500K. The Cost of Living Index is 164, not low by any means but not as high as 200-plus readings found in many nearby areas. While these figures are moderate, it clearly requires a good income to support a family, and median household incomes are a healthy $102K. Most Livingston workers are professionals who work in such fields as finance, law, or pharmaceutical industries. Property taxes run about 1.2%, a reasonable percentage but one that can still end up being high due to home values.

Education Schools are cited as one of the best reasons to move to the area. Academic focus is strong, and New Jersey Proficiency Test scores run from 13% to 25% above state averages. The student-teacher ratio of 14.1 suggests small class sizes, and the school sizes are moderate, too. Livingston Senior High School (grades 9–12) has approximately 1,450 students.

Lifestyle Strong community resources—including two town pools, two recreation centers, summer camp programs, a YMCA, and the Livingston Mall—provide plenty to do right in town. A family pool membership costs about $250 per year. Local service organizations and schools bring busloads of kids to Broadway shows and other city venues. With various local grants and an active "In Town Livingston" Business Improvement District group, the central strip is undergoing renovation and is getting new signage and businesses. Readers will enjoy the new Livingston Public Library and the local Borders bookstore.

Any suburban New Jersey resident must be concerned with commutes. An estimated 40% to 50% of workers travel to Manhattan, a 55-minute ride by express bus. Others drive 15 minutes to Harrison, close to Newark,

LIVINGSTON, NJ
NEIGHBORHOOD HIGHLIGHTS

PEOPLE

Population	27,364
15-yr Population Growth	2.40%
5-yr Population Growth	0.40%
% Married w/Children	31.2%
% Single w/Children	6.7%
No. of Households	9,272
Median Age	39.5
Avg. Household Size	2.94
Diversity Measure	32

STANDARD OF LIVING

Median Household Income	$102,228
% Household Income > $100K	50%
Projected Future Job Growth	0%
Cost of Living Index	164
Buying Power Index	144
Weekly Daycare Cost	$257
Median Home Price	$514,400
"Sweet Spot" Home Price	$550,000
Home Price Ratio	5
Median Age of Homes	41.3
% Homes Owned	94%
Effective Property Tax Rate	1.20%
Estimated Property Tax Bill	$6,600

EDUCATION

% High School Graduates	94%
% 4-yr Degree	31%
% Graduate or Professional Degree	27%
$ Invested per Pupil	$11,466
Student/Teacher Ratio	14.1
Primary Test Score Percentile	115.2
Secondary Test Score Percentile	108.7
% Subsidized School Lunch	0.80%
% Attending Public School	74.60%

LIFESTYLE

Leisure Rating (Area)	9
Arts & Culture Rating (Area)	9
Climate Rating (Area)	5
Physical Setting Rating	3
Downtown Core Rating	3
% Commute < 30 Min.	56%
% Commute > 1 Hour	16%

HEALTH & SAFETY

Health Rating (Area)	2
Stress Score (Area)	4
Violent Crime Risk	38
Property Crime Risk	41

and take the New Jersey Transit/PATH (rail) into the city. Some residents drive to nearby suburban locations for jobs within New Jersey.

The area has mostly rolling, wooded hills with a few small lakes and reservoirs to the southwest. Winters are typical for the East Coast, with warm, muggy summers and cool, wet, variable winters. The nearby ocean moderates temperatures somewhat, and temperatures and precipitation depend a lot on wind direction.

Health & Safety Crime risk is low, particularly for an inner suburban area. The St. Barnabas Medical Center, a teaching hospital, adds strength to the local healthcare system.

Nearby Neighborhoods Communities for families are abundant in this area, and each one offers a different flavor and mix of costs and features. Summit to the south is wealthier and more bohemian. Morristown to the west offers more of a small-town feel, but is expensive and farther from New York City and most large areas of employment in northern New Jersey. West Orange is also worth a look.

NEWARK, NJ, METROPOLITAN DIVISION, NEW YORK METRO AREA
AREA HIGHLIGHTS

PEOPLE

SIZE & DIVERSITY	AREA	U.S. AVG	FAMILY DEMOGRAPHICS	AREA	U.S. AVG
Population	2,079,05		% Married	54.30%	53.80%
15-yr Population Growth	8.90%	4.40%	% Single	45.70%	46.20%
Diversity Measure	57	54	% Divorced	6.20%	10.20%
% Religiously Observant	58%	50%	% Separated	3.60%	2.10%
% Catholic	39%	22%	% Married w/Children	28.40%	27.90%
% Protestant	11%	25%	% Single w/Children	9.10%	9.40%
% Jewish	7%	2%	% Married, No Children	31.10%	31.00%
% Other	1%	1%	% Single, No Children	31.50%	31.70%

STANDARD OF LIVING

INCOME, EMPLOYMENT & TAXES	AREA	U.S. AVG	COST OF LIVING & HOUSING	AREA	U.S. AVG
Median Household Income	$60,902	$44,684	Cost of Living Index	129.7	100
Household Income Growth	4.30%	6.10%	Buying Power Index	105	100
Unemployment Rate	4.30%	5.10%	Median Home Price	$414,400	$208,500
Recent Job Growth	1.30%	1.30%	Home Price Ratio	6.8	4.7
Projected Future Job Growth	5.70%	10.50%	Home Price Appreciation	13.10%	13.60%
State Income Tax Rate	2.50%	5.00%	% Homes Owned	67.50%	64.10%
State Sales Tax Rate	6%	6.00%	Median Rent	$1,020	$792

EDUCATION

ATTAINMENT & ACHIEVEMENT	AREA	U.S. AVG	RESOURCES & INVESTMENT	AREA	U.S. AVG
% High School Graduate	84.60%	83.90%	No. of Highly Ranked Universities	3	1
% 2-yr Graduate	7.20%	7.10%	$ Invested per Pupil	$10,159	$6,058
% 4-yr Graduate	25.80%	17.20%	Student/Teacher Ratio	14.5	15.9
% Graduate or Professional Degree	13.10%	9.90%	State University In-State Tuition	$8,564	$4,917
% Attending Public School	83.90%	84.30%			
75th Percentile State University SAT Score (Verbal)	530	477			
75th Percentile State University SAT Score (Math)	550	478			
75th Percentile State University ACT Score	N/A	20			

LIFESTYLE

RECREATION, ARTS & CULTURE	AREA	U.S. AVG	INFRASTRUCTURE & FACILITIES	AREA	U.S. AVG
Professional Sports Rating	10	4	No. of Public Libraries	114	28
Zoos & Aquariums Rating	8	3	Library Volumes Per Capita	3.8	2.8
Amusement Park Rating	7	3	No. of Warehouse Clubs	4	4
Professional Theater Rating	10	3	No. of Starbucks	21	5
Overall Museum Rating	9	6	Golf Course Rating	10	4
Science Museum Rating	9	4	National Park Rating	4	3
Children's Museum Rating	9	3	Sq. Mi. Inland Water	7	4

CLIMATE			COMMUTE & TRANSPORTATION	AREA	U.S. AVG
Days Mostly Sunny	207	212	Avg. Daily Commute Time	30.8	24.7
Annual Days Precipitation	129	111	% Commute by Auto	75%	77.70%
Annual Days > 90°F	20	38	Per Capita Avg. Daily Transit Miles	24.9	7.9
Annual Days < 32°F	87	88	Annual Auto Insurance Premium	$2,123	$1,314
July Relative Humidity	65	69	Gas, Cost per Gallon	$3.16	$3.05

HEALTH & SAFETY

CRIME & ENVIRNOMENTAL ISSUES	AREA	U.S. AVG	HEALTHCARE & COST	AREA	U.S. AVG
Violent Crime Rate	450	517	Physicians per Capita	325	254.3
Change in Violent Crime	-33.10%	-7.50%	Pediatricians per Capita	30.3	16.9
Property Crime Rate	2824	3783	Hospital Beds per Capita	475.8	239.7
Change in Property Crime	-20.90%	-10.10%	No. of Teaching Hospitals	16	1.9
Air Quality Score	33	44	Healthcare Cost Index	119.1	100
Water Quality Score	21	33	Cost per Doctor Visit	$69	$74
Pollen/Allergy Score	63	61	Cost per Dentist Visit	$83	$67
Stress Score	42	49	Cost per Hospital Room	$3,360	$702
Cancer Mortality Rate	187	168.9			

Logan, UT

Area Type: Small college town

Zip Code: 84321

Metro Area: Logan, UT

Metro Area Type: Smallest

Location: 90 miles northeast of Salt Lake City along US 89/91

Time Zone: Mountain Standard Time

Pros:
Attractive setting
Inexpensive homes
College-town feel

Cons:
Isolation
Harsh winters
Entertainment

Because it wasn't on a main route to anywhere, the beautiful Cache Valley wasn't discovered until 1859, more than 10 years after Mormons had settled the wide, fertile, and more familiar valley west of the Wasatch Range. Surrounded by mountains on three sides and facing due north into Idaho, the Cache Valley existed for years as a predominantly Mormon agricultural area, with the town of Logan at its southern end. Logan served as a mill town and the area's economic nucleus for years.

Then the small Brigham Young College was established in 1878. Some 10 years later, the Lund Act provided for the land-grant Agricultural College of Utah, which set forth in 1890 with a faculty of eight. Eventually, that school became Utah State University, and its 20,000 students currently add a strong college flavor to this town of about 50,000 inhabitants.

Today, Logan is a near-ideal blend of small-town and college-town elements, set beautifully against the mountains, with a clean city core, a pleasant climate (in three seasons, anyway), and a better-than-average economic base for a college town. Businesses in the area range from high-tech manufacturing companies and biomedical research and production firms to printing and food processing plants. Convergys, Tyco, Pepperidge Farms, Moore Business Forms, and Herff-Jones Yearbooks are some of the more familiar names, and many are located in the Logan Industrial Quadrangle near the small airport north of town. Recent job growth of 4.8% and future job growth of 25% prove the new economic strength of the area.

The picture-book downtown area recalls the Old West as it runs along the wide north–south Main Street, lined with older commercial establishments, a few theaters, and restaurants. Grid streets lie mostly to the east and up a gentle grade toward the university with nice older homes and clean neighborhoods. There aren't many trees in the dry Cache Valley, but these older streets are heavily shaded. A small canyon separates the campus from River Heights to the southeast of the city. Good family homes and neighborhoods are found not only in River Heights but throughout the area. The married-with-children percentage of households is quite high for a college town at 31%. For more information about this area, visit the area's noteworthy Chamber of Commerce website at www.cachechamber.com.

Standard of Living The Cost of Living Index is 92, modest for a small town in an attractive area. Housing is really the headline here. Good family homes start around $150K with a wide selection in the $170K to $225K range. Property taxes are a modest 1.1%, and while incomes and the Buying Power Index are moderated by the student population, those working in the area's businesses should prosper economically.

Education Utah State provides a strong educational backdrop. That said, there is still a large and traditional agricultural base, so educational attainment levels are lower than in some college towns. Local schools test average to well above average, with the River Heights Elementary and Hillcrest Elementary east of town near the university showing the best scores. The university itself is highly regarded and a bargain at about $4,000 per year in state tuition.

Lifestyle Downtown is quiet and easily accessed by foot or bike, and Logan is one of those places where cars are for many only a part-time necessity. While the college does bring a fair amount of arts and cultural interest, typical family entertainment venues are modest. The real "holy grail" of family entertainment lies in the vast recreational paradise surrounding the city, with mountains, hiking trails, white water, skiing, and boating opportunities on the enormous Bear Lake located 40 miles northeast. Families looking for bigger-city amenities will find them in the Ogden and Salt Lake City areas.

Traditional commutes for work are hardly an issue; it takes 10 minutes to get anywhere in town and there are few traffic signals to impede progress. While Logan is only 45 miles from Ogden and 90 miles from Salt Lake City, the drive across the Wellsville Mountains is windy and can be difficult in winter, and there is little air service out of Logan.

The area immediately around Logan is mainly flat but foothills start almost immediately out of town, especially to the east. The climate is high and dry, with pleasant summer days, cool evenings, and cold and mainly dry winters. As the Cache Valley opens to the north, periods of harsher winter weather with snow and cold snaps occur each winter.

Health & Safety Crime risk is predictably low. Healthcare is good for a small town with a regional hospital, and air quality is excellent.

Nearby Neighborhoods In-town neighborhoods east of Main Street, the River Heights area, and North Logan offer the highest number of alternatives for families. Lifestyles, as well as the major facts and figures, are largely the same among all, but those looking to be closer to a city should consider Ogden and Kaysville (see p. 244).

LOGAN, UT NEIGHBORHOOD HIGHLIGHTS	
PEOPLE	
Population	40,860
15-yr Population Growth	38.90%
5-yr Population Growth	6.60%
% Married w/Children	30.9%
% Single w/Children	6.6%
No. of Households	13,025
Median Age	28.6
Avg. Household Size	2.96
Diversity Measure	29
STANDARD OF LIVING	
Median Household Income	$32,921
% Household Income > $100K	6%
Projected Future Job Growth	25%
Cost of Living Index	92.1
Buying Power Index	80
Weekly Daycare Cost	$105
Median Home Price	$156,000
"Sweet Spot" Home Price	$200,000
Home Price Ratio	4.7
Median Age of Homes	29.6
% Homes Owned	46%
Effective Property Tax Rate	1.10%
Estimated Property Tax Bill	$2,200
EDUCATION	
% High School Graduates	89%
% 4-yr Degree	21%
% Graduate or Professional Degree	12%
$ Invested per Pupil	$3,745
Student/Teacher Ratio	17
Primary Test Score Percentile	139.1
Secondary Test Score Percentile	87.3
% Subsidized School Lunch	42.40%
% Attending Public School	96.20%
LIFESTYLE	
Leisure Rating (Area)	7
Arts & Culture Rating (Area)	2
Climate Rating (Area)	3
Physical Setting Rating	8
Downtown Core Rating	6
% Commute < 30 Min.	87%
% Commute > 1 Hour	3%
HEALTH & SAFETY	
Health Rating (Area)	5
Stress Score (Area)	6
Violent Crime Risk	80
Property Crime Risk	97

LOGAN, UT
AREA HIGHLIGHTS

PEOPLE

SIZE & DIVERSITY	AREA	U.S. AVG	FAMILY DEMOGRAPHICS	AREA	U.S. AVG
Population	97,467		% Married	62.20%	53.80%
15-yr Population Growth	38.90%	4.40%	% Single	37.80%	46.20%
Diversity Measure	24	54	% Divorced	3.70%	10.20%
% Religiously Observant	85%	50%	% Separated	0.90%	2.10%
% Catholic	2%	22%	% Married w/Children	45.30%	27.90%
% Protestant	82%	25%	% Single w/Children	4.80%	9.40%
% Jewish	0%	2%	% Married, No Children	25.30%	31.00%
% Other	1%	1%	% Single, No Children	24.60%	31.70%

STANDARD OF LIVING

INCOME, EMPLOYMENT & TAXES	AREA	U.S. AVG	COST OF LIVING & HOUSING	AREA	U.S. AVG
Median Household Income	$40,843	$44,684	Cost of Living Index	90.7	100
Household Income Growth	3%	6.10%	Buying Power Index	101	100
Unemployment Rate	3%	5.10%	Median Home Price	$148,200	$208,500
Recent Job Growth	4.80%	1.30%	Home Price Ratio	3.6	4.7
Projected Future Job Growth	25.40%	10.50%	Home Price Appreciation	6.30%	13.60%
State Income Tax Rate	7%	5.00%	% Homes Owned	71.80%	64.10%
State Sales Tax Rate	6.20%	6.00%	Median Rent	$577	$792

EDUCATION

ATTAINMENT & ACHIEVEMENT	AREA	U.S. AVG	RESOURCES & INVESTMENT	AREA	U.S. AVG
% High School Graduate	90.50%	83.90%	No. of Highly Ranked Universities	0	1
% 2-yr Graduate	8.40%	7.10%	$ Invested per Pupil	$3,655	$6,058
% 4-yr Graduate	28.10%	17.20%	Student/Teacher Ratio	20.6	15.9
% Graduate or Professional Degree	11.40%	9.90%	State University In-State Tuition	$4,000	$4,917
% Attending Public School	99.70%	84.30%			
75th Percentile State University SAT Score (Verbal)	N/A	477			
75th Percentile State University SAT Score (Math)	N/A	478			
75th Percentile State University ACT Score	21	20			

LIFESTYLE

RECREATION, ARTS & CULTURE	AREA	U.S. AVG	INFRASTRUCTURE & FACILITIES	AREA	U.S. AVG
Professional Sports Rating	4	4	No. of Public Libraries	7	28
Zoos & Aquariums Rating	4	3	Library Volumes Per Capita	3.1	2.8
Amusement Park Rating	1	3	No. of Warehouse Clubs	4	4
Professional Theater Rating	3	3	No. of Starbucks	0	5
Overall Museum Rating	4	6	Golf Course Rating	2	4
Science Museum Rating	5	4	National Park Rating	8	3
Children's Museum Rating	4	3	Sq. Mi. Inland Water	10	4

CLIMATE			COMMUTE & TRANSPORTATION		
Days Mostly Sunny	232	212	Avg. Daily Commute Time	16.8	24.7
Annual Days Precipitation	92	111	% Commute by Auto	65%	77.70%
Annual Days > 90°F	58	38	Per Capita Avg. Daily Transit Miles	3.2	7.9
Annual Days < 32°F	134	88	Annual Auto Insurance Premium	$1,066	$1,314
July Relative Humidity	54	69	Gas, Cost per Gallon	$2.89	$3.05

HEALTH & SAFETY

CRIME & ENVIRNOMENTAL ISSUES	AREA	U.S. AVG	HEALTHCARE & COST	AREA	U.S. AVG
Violent Crime Rate	63	517	Physicians per Capita	146.3	254.3
Change in Violent Crime	60.40%	-7.50%	Pediatricians per Capita	13.6	16.9
Property Crime Rate	1804	3783	Hospital Beds per Capita	186.1	239.7
Change in Property Crime	102.20%	-10.10%	No. of Teaching Hospitals	0	1.9
Air Quality Score	48	44	Healthcare Cost Index	90.1	100
Water Quality Score	47	33	Cost per Doctor Visit	$60	$74
Pollen/Allergy Score	60	61	Cost per Dentist Visit	$56	$67
Stress Score	64	49	Cost per Hospital Room	$678	$702
Cancer Mortality Rate	135.2	168.9			

Loma Linda, CA

Area Type: Exurb

Zip Code: 92354

Metro Area: Riverside–San Bernardino, CA

Metro Area Type: Large

Location: 60 miles east of Los Angeles

Time Zone: Pacific Standard Time

Pros:
Relative affordability
Job growth
Pleasant winters

Cons:
Air quality
Some long commutes
Some crime and crime risk

Larger than nine U.S. states, San Bernardino County is 90% low desert with desert mountains that stretch from the eastern fringes of the Los Angeles area to the Nevada state line. The 10% of land at the southwest corner of the county, where all the people live, is home to Loma Linda and a series of other cities that make up what is now referred to popularly (and by many local governments) as the Inland Empire.

The Inland Empire consists of mainly flat valleys surrounded to the north by the steep San Bernardino Mountains rising to 10,000-foot peaks, and the dry Santa Ana Mountains and several smaller mountain ranges to the south. Freeways crisscross the area, with I-10 (San Bernardino Fwy.) and I-210 (Foothill Fwy.) running east–west and crossing the north–south I-15 (Ontario Fwy.) and "the 91" (SR 91), otherwise known as the Riverside Freeway. Ontario, Rancho Cucamonga, Fontana, San Bernardino, and Riverside—among others—line these freeways with an extensive infrastructure of horizontally built manufacturing, commercial, and retail activity that mixes with housing developments up to the base of the mountains. These areas were once desert and agricultural centers for citrus growing, but no longer. The town of Riverside still has remnants of the old fruit loading sheds along the old Santa Fe railroad, but that's about the only reminder of a peaceful, agrarian history.

Loma Linda, an older small town whose name means "beautiful hill" in Spanish, has an interesting mix of new and old, urban and rural. In the early 1900s, a number of health facilities sprang up. They later morphed into the two Seventh-Day Adventist hospitals and a medical college that have become the town's main local economic engines. Most Loma Linda residents are employed in the large light-industrial areas to the west and to the south in Riverside. The larger Riverside–San Bernardino area has enjoyed one of the country's largest job booms in the past 5 years, with over 110,000 new jobs being added in the area. Many of the employers here need space for warehousing and manufacturing, and in contrast to most of the LA area, land is available in the Inland Empire.

Because of the relatively available land and the long commute distance from LA, home prices remained relatively reasonable for years. But more recently, the area has been one of the strongest new housing markets in the United States. This has led to an increase in the number of residential construction jobs and (not surprisingly) a low vacancy rate and a blip in the housing prices. Over the long term, with newer homes coming onto the market and the departure of the transient construction labor, rents and home prices should stabilize at a level most professionals can afford.

Standard of Living   The city of Loma Linda is dominated by the Loma Linda University Medical Center (a teaching hospital run by the Seventh-Day Adventist Church), a veteran's hospital, and various medical support businesses. But most residents commute somewhere else for work, likely west toward Ontario. Not surprisingly, recent job growth has been strong at 3.6%.

For home prices, standard southern California rules apply, meaning that, statewide, average homes are more expensive relative to incomes than anywhere else in the United States. That said, a "benchmark" family home in this area costs $400K to $450K. This is less than most other urban-exurban areas in California, but with the moderate incomes enjoyed locally, the Home Price Ratio is a very high 8.3. While there is more of a mix of ages and styles in Loma Linda than some surrounding areas, lot sizes are small and extras like basements are rare. Property taxes are regulated by California's Proposition 13 and are just above 1%, but will still produce sizable tax bills.

LOMA LINDA, CA
NEIGHBORHOOD HIGHLIGHTS

PEOPLE

Population	20,457
15-yr Population Growth	35.40%
5-yr Population Growth	12.40%
% Married w/Children	25.9%
% Single w/Children	11.2%
No. of Households	7,750
Median Age	37.2
Avg. Household Size	2.53
Diversity Measure	72

STANDARD OF LIVING

Median Household Income	$43,876
% Household Income > $100K	11%
Projected Future Job Growth	18%
Cost of Living Index	123
Buying Power Index	80
Weekly Daycare Cost	$145
Median Home Price	$363,000
"Sweet Spot" Home Price	$425,000
Home Price Ratio	8.3
Median Age of Homes	24.6
% Homes Owned	39%
Effective Property Tax Rate	1.10%
Estimated Property Tax Bill	$4,675

EDUCATION

% High School Graduates	87%
% 4-yr Degree	22%
% Graduate or Professional Degree	21%
$ Invested per Pupil	$4,452
Student/Teacher Ratio	20.3
Primary Test Score Percentile	78.2
Secondary Test Score Percentile	101
% Subsidized School Lunch	54.60%
% Attending Public School	58.70%

LIFESTYLE

Leisure Rating (Area)	9
Arts & Culture Rating (Area)	7
Climate Rating (Area)	10
Physical Setting Rating	3
Downtown Core Rating	1
% Commute < 30 Min.	75%
% Commute > 1 Hour	8%

HEALTH & SAFETY

Health Rating (Area)	1
Stress Score (Area)	7
Violent Crime Risk	279
Property Crime Risk	233

Education   Educational attainment levels are quite high, with 44% of the population having at least a 4-year degree. The local Redlands Unified school district reports achievement indexes and graduation rates that are higher than national averages, and the area's high school gets a 9-out-of-10 Academic Performance Index rating from the State of California. The Loma Linda University and Medical Center is a local higher-education highlight, and the Los Angeles area has numerous colleges and universities within an hour's drive.

Lifestyle   Despite having no "downtown" area to speak of, the community retains the feeling of its small-town roots, with friendly residents and some quaint shops. Some life in town revolves around the hospitals, and many of the healthcare graduates remain in Loma Linda. With 268 sunny days a year, outdoor activities are abundant but the heat and dry conditions can limit the possibilities somewhat. Two nearby lakes allow boating and fishing and are popular powerboating areas, but shade is sparse. Hiking, at least in the summertime, is almost a survival sport (winter/spring conditions are much better). Winter skiing (yes, in Southern California) in the Mount Baldy ski area just 30 miles northwest is popular, and the golf/boating/resort spot of Palm Springs is just an hour to the southeast.

The city has two newer business parks to accommodate future growth and, like many Inland Empire towns, is actively recruiting new businesses. Unless you're working in Loma Linda or nearby in Redlands or San Bernardino, your commute will probably be west toward Ontario—and, unfortunately, that commute can be crowded and frustrating, taking as much as an hour. The "91" commute to Riverside can also be crowded. Local traffic is a problem at times, as surface street patterns haven't changed in many years even though the population has increased greatly. To head farther west into LA county, driving north to San Bernardino to catch the Metrolink rail service is the best idea.

The desert is clearly in charge of the area's climate. Loma Linda receives fewer than 14 inches of rain—almost all during the winter. Summer daytime highs usually exceed 90°F, and 100°F days are common. Winter snows, while in plain sight in the San Bernardino area, are nonexistent locally.

Health & Safety   Local crime rates and crime risk are higher than national averages, but there has been some recent progress in lowering them. Air quality suffers greatly from Loma Linda's location (downwind of Los Angeles), and high temperatures and stagnant wind conditions can lead to significant problems in the summer. But the climate is benign and healthcare is excellent.

Nearby Neighborhoods   Close by is the area of Redlands, home to the private liberal arts University of Redlands, and offering a housing mix similar to Loma Linda's. San Bernardino is a much larger town with some less expensive, but less attractive, neighborhoods. Schools in San Bernardino are not up to Loma Linda's standard.

RIVERSIDE–SAN BERNARDINO, CA
AREA HIGHLIGHTS
PEOPLE

SIZE & DIVERSITY	AREA	U.S. AVG	FAMILY DEMOGRAPHICS	AREA	U.S. AVG
Population	3,793,081		% Married	56%	53.80%
15-yr Population Growth	47.50%	4.40%	% Single	44%	46.20%
Diversity Measure	63	54	% Divorced	9.80%	10.20%
% Religiously Observant	42%	50%	% Separated	4%	2.10%
% Catholic	27%	22%	% Married w/Children	28.90%	27.90%
% Protestant	14%	25%	% Single w/Children	11.90%	9.40%
% Jewish	1%	2%	% Married, No Children	28.50%	31.00%
% Other	1%	1%	% Single, No Children	30.80%	31.70%

STANDARD OF LIVING

INCOME, EMPLOYMENT & TAXES	AREA	U.S. AVG	COST OF LIVING & HOUSING	AREA	U.S. AVG
Median Household Income	$47,554	$44,684	Cost of Living Index	122.4	100
Household Income Growth	5%	6.10%	Buying Power Index	87	100
Unemployment Rate	5%	5.10%	Median Home Price	$367,600	$208,500
Recent Job Growth	3.60%	1.30%	Home Price Ratio	7.7	4.7
Projected Future Job Growth	22.10%	10.50%	Home Price Appreciation	28.70%	13.60%
State Income Tax Rate	6%	5.00%	% Homes Owned	53.90%	64.10%
State Sales Tax Rate	7.30%	6.00%	Median Rent	$752	$792

EDUCATION

ATTAINMENT & ACHIEVEMENT	AREA	U.S. AVG	RESOURCES & INVESTMENT	AREA	U.S. AVG
% High School Graduate	76.10%	83.90%	No. of Highly Ranked Universities	0	1
% 2-yr Graduate	11.60%	7.10%	$ Invested per Pupil	$5,048	$6,058
% 4-yr Graduate	15.40%	17.20%	Student/Teacher Ratio	22.4	15.9
% Graduate or Professional Degree	7.90%	9.90%	State University In-State Tuition	$6,586	$4,917
% Attending Public School	93.60%	84.30%			
75th Percentile State University SAT Score (Verbal)	560	477			
75th Percentile State University SAT Score (Math)	600	478			
75th Percentile State University ACT Score	23	20			

LIFESTYLE

RECREATION, ARTS & CULTURE	AREA	U.S. AVG	INFRASTRUCTURE & FACILITIES	AREA	U.S. AVG
Professional Sports Rating	9	4	No. of Public Libraries	78	28
Zoos & Aquariums Rating	5	3	Library Volumes Per Capita	1.3	2.8
Amusement Park Rating	7	3	No. of Warehouse Clubs	9	4
Professional Theater Rating	5	3	No. of Starbucks	109	5
Overall Museum Rating	9	6	Golf Course Rating	10	4
Science Museum Rating	10	4	National Park Rating	10	3
Children's Museum Rating	8	3	Sq. Mi. Inland Water	7	4

CLIMATE			COMMUTE & TRANSPORTATION		
Days Mostly Sunny	268	212	Avg. Daily Commute Time	31.1	24.7
Annual Days Precipitation	35	111	% Commute by Auto	72%	77.70%
Annual Days > 90°F	20	38	Per Capita Avg. Daily Transit Miles	6.7	7.9
Annual Days < 32°F	0	88	Annual Auto Insurance Premium	$1,791	$1,314
July Relative Humidity	69	69	Gas, Cost per Gallon	$3.03	$3.05

HEALTH & SAFETY

CRIME & ENVIRNOMENTAL ISSUES	AREA	U.S. AVG	HEALTHCARE & COST	AREA	U.S. AVG
Violent Crime Rate	544	517	Physicians per Capita	142.5	254.3
Change in Violent Crime	-16%	-7.50%	Pediatricians per Capita	10.1	16.9
Property Crime Rate	3691	3783	Hospital Beds per Capita	202.3	239.7
Change in Property Crime	-3.30%	-10.10%	No. of Teaching Hospitals	9	1.9
Air Quality Score	12	44	Healthcare Cost Index	127.2	100
Water Quality Score	49	33	Cost per Doctor Visit	$70	$74
Pollen/Allergy Score	51	61	Cost per Dentist Visit	$82	$67
Stress Score	68	49	Cost per Hospital Room	$1,484	$702
Cancer Mortality Rate	164.2	168.9			

Louisville, CO

BEST OF THE BEST

Area Type: Outer suburb/suburban town

Zip Code: 80027

Metro Area: Denver, CO

Metro Area Type: Large

Location: Along US 36, 10 miles southeast of Boulder and 15 miles northwest of Denver

Time Zone: Mountain Standard Time

Pros:
Attractive setting
Convenient to Boulder and Denver
Education

Cons:
Uncertain job market
Some long commutes
Housing availability

A few years back, the TV sitcom *Dharma and Greg* featured a liberal, New Age wife and a conservative, suit-clad husband. We don't know exactly where they lived in TV land, but they—or a real-life couple like them—would be quite comfortable in Louisville. Approximately halfway between the more traditional northwest suburbs of Denver and the progressive New Age college town of Boulder, Louisville may be just the place for families with middle-of-the-road politics. It's also a good pick for families with jobs in one of the many local firms, or in Boulder or Denver.

Louisville is a town of about 25,000 middle-class, well-educated residents who enjoy living in a smaller town with great schools, a country lifestyle, and easy access to the amenities of the larger Colorado cities. The setting is open and beautiful, on a rising plateau 10 miles from the major upward thrust of the Rockies. Louisville lies along the main route between Denver and Boulder, ideally situated to capture their advantages but to avoid the crowding of Denver and the expenses of Boulder. Boulder does cast a shadow on home prices, but they are still much more reasonable in Louisville than in Boulder itself, and many who work in Boulder live in Louisville or one of the neighboring communities. Those making their way to Denver will have an easy commute if headed downtown or to the northern suburbs and a more difficult one if headed to the Denver Tech Center and other areas south.

The Boulder economy is anchored by the University of Colorado and an assortment of technology and service firms surrounding it. But don't discount Louisville employment opportunities—there are many, led by Storage Technology with their headquarters, research, and manufacturing operations; major facilities for IBM, EDS, Sun Microsystems, Bell Aerospace, and Interlocken; and an assortment of smaller new-economy companies seeking educated workers in a good business climate and attractive setting. While employment seems

secure overall, the technology sector, particularly for StorageTek and Sun, who recently announced a merger, is less certain. Recent downturns and consolidations have led to job losses in the area and at other technology centers nearby in Loveland and Fort Collins.

Louisville and its neighbors have a clean, mostly suburban appearance, with small historic downtowns (the area was a coal-mining center until the 1950s) and spacious suburbs spreading mostly northeast of US 36, along a high bluff looking west toward Boulder. Unlike some of its neighbors closer to Denver, growth moratoriums have effectively avoided overbuilding and ugly sprawl, and much of the area feels as much like a country town as a bedroom suburb. Some commercial and retail establishments have moved in, but the area doesn't feel overbuilt. Thirty-four percent of households are married with children.

Standard of Living The Boulder "shadow" is evident in the Cost of Living Index, high at 145 but not as high as most areas in and around Boulder (some are as high as 181). Family home prices start at about $250K, and the "sweet spot" is at about $350K. Many homes, particularly those built before 1990, are on lots of a ¼ acre or more and have basements. Many have mountain views. The somewhat restrictive Boulder County growth policy has limited new construction and kept things attractive, but has also created some housing shortages. Prices rise substantially in Boulder. Property taxes are reasonable (around 1%) and the growth controls have also benefited by keeping special assessments at a minimum.

Education Louisville has a well-educated population; about 60% of residents have at least a 4-year degree (40% undergraduate, 24% graduate or professional degrees). An emphasis on educational attainment is apparent in the local school district: Boulder Valley school district graduates over 95% of its entrants and its state standardized test scores are significantly higher than state averages in every category. The district's overall achievement index is some 80% higher than the national index used by the State of Colorado as its benchmark. The University of Colorado exerts a strong influence on education and culture.

Lifestyle An affordable suburb of a large, cosmopolitan city with social and cultural attractions usually sounds like an attractive proposition. As a suburb of two such cities, Louisville also benefits from the fact that Denver and Boulder are different. There's a broad range of entertainment, including museums, performing arts, and sports events, as well as excellent dining options.

Louisville has its own active downtown area with small shops, but going to a mall means a short drive toward Denver or Boulder. Louisville intends to maintain 20% of its land as accessible park space. The city has several attractive parks, 1,300 acres of green space, 22 miles of trails, and an excellent recreation center with a pool, a 160-foot water slide, and an indoor track and gym. Much of the outdoor lifestyle here revolves around the mountains and winter sports, mainly skiing. There are 10 excellent ski areas within 100 miles of town. A season ski pass doesn't go wasted, with a solid 6-month season and sometimes even longer.

Denver downtown commutes take about 35 minutes in average traffic, and Boulder is about 15 minutes away. Denver commutes may improve if the planned rail service becomes a reality. Also helpful, the local transit district recently set up a large park-and-ride facility in nearby Westminster. Louisville is on the airport side of town, which makes the area favorable for business travelers, and a new highway loop in that direction just opened.

High altitude, low humidity, and its mountain-base location bring variability to Louisville's four-season continental climate. Summer temperatures are pleasant with large swings between evening and daytime temperatures, sometimes up to 50 degrees, and periods of thunderstorms especially in early summer. Winters are cool with occasional cold blasts. Heavy snow is more likely to fall in late autumn or spring. Downslope mountain chinook winds can bring warm days even in winter, and stagnant high-pressure systems can result in 100°F-plus summer temperatures.

Health & Safety The local crime risk ("CAP") scores are very low. Air quality is generally good and better than in Denver. Water quality is excellent, and healthcare facilities, with the university to the west in Boulder and others to the southeast in Denver, are complete. There's a hospital in Lafayette.

LOUISVILLE, CO NEIGHBORHOOD HIGHLIGHTS	
PEOPLE	
Population	27,248
15-yr Population Growth	23.80%
5-yr Population Growth	-4.20%
% Married w/Children	33.7%
% Single w/Children	8.5%
No. of Households	10,204
Median Age	31.8
Avg. Household Size	2.61
Diversity Measure	24
STANDARD OF LIVING	
Median Household Income	$76,739
% Household Income > $100K	30%
Projected Future Job Growth	13%
Cost of Living Index	145
Buying Power Index	122
Weekly Daycare Cost	$145
Median Home Price	$297,500
"Sweet Spot" Home Price	$350,000
Home Price Ratio	3.9
Median Age of Homes	9.3
% Homes Owned	65%
Effective Property Tax Rate	1%
Estimated Property Tax Bill	$3,500
EDUCATION	**BEST**
% High School Graduates	97%
% 4-yr Degree	40%
% Graduate or Professional Degree	24%
$ Invested per Pupil	$5,124
Student/Teacher Ratio	18.3
Primary Test Score Percentile	125.6
Secondary Test Score Percentile	120.3
% Subsidized School Lunch	4.80%
% Attending Public School	84%
LIFESTYLE	**BEST**
Leisure Rating (Area)	9
Arts & Culture Rating (Area)	6
Climate Rating (Area)	6
Physical Setting Rating	9
Downtown Core Rating	6
% Commute < 30 Min.	70%
% Commute > 1 Hour	5%
HEALTH & SAFETY	
Health Rating (Area)	8
Stress Score (Area)	5
Violent Crime Risk	36
Property Crime Risk	47

Nearby Neighborhoods Lafayette, just northeast, is similar to Louisville in size with older and less expensive homes and a lower-performing (but still good) school district. Boulder offers a typical college-town lifestyle in an excellent setting with great schools, but you pay the price. Denver (Park Hill) and Castle Rock are also good choices for families. See p. 172 and p. 148.

DENVER, CO
AREA HIGHLIGHTS

PEOPLE

SIZE & DIVERSITY	AREA	U.S. AVG	FAMILY DEMOGRAPHICS	AREA	U.S. AVG
Population	278,917		% Married	50.70%	53.80%
15-yr Population Growth	23.80%	4.40%	% Single	49.30%	46.20%
Diversity Measure	28	54	% Divorced	10.70%	10.20%
% Religiously Observant	47%	50%	% Separated	2.10%	2.10%
% Catholic	20%	22%	% Married w/Children	24.30%	27.90%
% Protestant	21%	25%	% Single w/Children	8.80%	9.40%
% Jewish	5%	2%	% Married, No Children	26.30%	31.00%
% Other	1%	1%	% Single, No Children	40.50%	31.70%

STANDARD OF LIVING

INCOME, EMPLOYMENT & TAXES	AREA	U.S. AVG	COST OF LIVING & HOUSING	AREA	U.S. AVG
Median Household Income	$60,405	$44,684	Cost of Living Index	113.8	100
Household Income Growth	4.40%	6.10%	Buying Power Index	119	100
Unemployment Rate	4.40%	5.10%	Median Home Price	$346,200	$208,500
Recent Job Growth	1.90%	1.30%	Home Price Ratio	5.7	4.7
Projected Future Job Growth	15.90%	10.50%	Home Price Appreciation	4.60%	13.60%
State Income Tax Rate	5%	5.00%	% Homes Owned	51.40%	64.10%
State Sales Tax Rate	3.30%	6.00%	Median Rent	$1,022	$792

EDUCATION

ATTAINMENT & ACHIEVEMENT	AREA	U.S. AVG	RESOURCES & INVESTMENT	AREA	U.S. AVG
% High School Graduate	94.20%	83.90%	No. of Highly Ranked Universities	1	1
% 2-yr Graduate	8.30%	7.10%	$ Invested per Pupil	$4,981	$6,058
% 4-yr Graduate	37.30%	17.20%	Student/Teacher Ratio	18.4	15.9
% Graduate or Professional Degree	23.30%	9.90%	State University In-State Tuition	$4,341	$4,917
% Attending Public School	86.90%	84.30%			
75th Percentile State University SAT Score (Verbal)	530	477			
75th Percentile State University SAT Score (Math)	550	478			
75th Percentile State University ACT Score	23	20			

LIFESTYLE

RECREATION, ARTS & CULTURE	AREA	U.S. AVG	INFRASTRUCTURE & FACILITIES	AREA	U.S. AVG
Professional Sports Rating	8	4	No. of Public Libraries	9	28
Zoos & Aquariums Rating	2	3	Library Volumes Per Capita	3.8	2.8
Amusement Park Rating	2	3	No. of Warehouse Clubs	1	4
Professional Theater Rating	3	3	No. of Starbucks	11	5
Overall Museum Rating	6	6	Golf Course Rating	3	4
Science Museum Rating	5	4	National Park Rating	7	3
Children's Museum Rating	4	3	Sq. Mi. Inland Water	3	4

CLIMATE			COMMUTE & TRANSPORTATION		
Days Mostly Sunny	246	212	Avg. Daily Commute Time	22.4	24.7
Annual Days Precipitation	88	111	% Commute by Auto	69%	77.70%
Annual Days > 90°F	32	38	Per Capita Avg. Daily Transit Miles	0	7.9
Annual Days < 32°F	163	88	Annual Auto Insurance Premium	$1,352	$1,314
July Relative Humidity	53	69	Gas, Cost per Gallon	$3.03	$3.05

HEALTH & SAFETY

CRIME & ENVIRNOMENTAL ISSUES	AREA	U.S. AVG	HEALTHCARE & COST	AREA	U.S. AVG
Violent Crime Rate	302	517	Physicians per Capita	291.8	254.3
Change in Violent Crime	6.50%	-7.50%	Pediatricians per Capita	19	16.9
Property Crime Rate	3285	3783	Hospital Beds per Capita	183.3	239.7
Change in Property Crime	-25%	-10.10%	No. of Teaching Hospitals	1	1.9
Air Quality Score	35	44	Healthcare Cost Index	117.9	100
Water Quality Score	100	33	Cost per Doctor Visit	$75	$74
Pollen/Allergy Score	83	61	Cost per Dentist Visit	$73	$67
Stress Score	48	49	Cost per Hospital Room	$987	$702
Cancer Mortality Rate	136.5	168.9			

Madison, AL

Area Type: Suburban town

Zip Code: 35758

Metro Area: Huntsville, AL

Metro Area Type: Smaller

Location: 13 miles west of downtown Huntsville

Time Zone: Central Standard Time

Pros:
Strong economy
Education
Low housing costs and taxes

Cons:
Infrastructure
Hot, humid summers
Isolation

Not familiar with Huntsville (or Madison)? Suppose we told you that NASA employs 2,600 people in the local George C. Marshall Space Flight Center. The center manages design, construction, and information technology for Space Shuttle and International Space Station programs, and its Huntsville Operations Support Center manages portions of Space Shuttle missions. Wernher von Braun once developed rockets there, and the first satellites that went up in space were designed in the city. We think you might be surprised by this emerging place tucked against the southern end of the Appalachian range along the Tennessee River.

From the birthplace of Alabama to the Space Capital of America, it's been a long and interesting road for Huntsville. The city has gone from the birthplace of Alabama to the Space Capital of America. It started in 1950 when a visionary U.S. senator brought German rocket scientists, including Dr. von Braun, to the local U.S. Army Redstone Arsenal. Fifty years later, today's Huntsville is dominated by space and technology research and is known as an excellent place to do business. There are manufacturing, research and development, and distribution operations for some of the world's leading companies. The laundry list is long— Boeing, Sanmina/SCI, ADTRAN, Intergraph, Teledyne, Lockheed Martin, Toyota, LG Electronics, DIRECTV, Northrup Grumman, and Siemens all have major operations in this small metro area of 360,000 residents. In all, some 220 manufacturing companies employ 32,000 highly skilled workers, and not surprisingly, with so many engineers and scientists, educational attainment figures are very high, especially for the region.

Huntsville is full of "new South" elements in an old South setting. The city is quite attractive, with mostly modern buildings set among a wooded, mountainous backdrop. Prosperity is relatively recent and it shows, with new buildings, shopping malls, museums, arts organizations, schools, and parks popping up throughout the city.

Huntsville is located in Madison County, from which the small historic town and suburb of Madison gets its name. Fittingly, Madison describes itself as "where progress joins preservation." A simple 15-minute drive from downtown Huntsville, Madison has a small historic downtown with old and new shopping amenities, historic homes, and a new farmers' market. Spreading mainly to the north are attractive older and new suburbs thick with woods and rural character and excellent home values. Twenty-eight percent of households are married with children and there's a small-town feeling throughout the community.

Standard of Living The cost of living is a major attraction (COL Index 96) and, taken together with solid incomes and income growth of 12.1%, it creates a strong Buying Power Index of 163. Well-constructed brick homes are available in the $180K to $200K range, many in rural settings on old farmland or nestled into tree-surrounded subdivisions. Property taxes work out to a very low 0.5% to 0.6%, although the low tax rates have led, in part, to some local complaints about roads and road quality. Madison residents just approved a 0.11% tax rate increase for schools. Day care costs are a very modest $106 per week.

Education Schools are a top priority, although some funding issues have created intra-district busing to balance loads. The new school levy brings enough money to build new schools, and the situation should improve. Scores are 10% to 20% above state averages. The local population is highly educated with more than half possessing a 4-year or higher degree; 35% with 4-year degrees and 17% with graduate-level education. The University of Alabama at Huntsville and Alabama A&M provide higher-education facilities.

MADISON, AL
NEIGHBORHOOD HIGHLIGHTS

PEOPLE

Population	32,480
15-yr Population Growth	22.70%
5-yr Population Growth	5.90%
% Married w/Children	28.2%
% Single w/Children	8.2%
No. of Households	12,457
Median Age	32.8
Avg. Household Size	2.61
Diversity Measure	36

STANDARD OF LIVING | BEST |

Median Household Income	$67,775
% Household Income > $100K	22%
Projected Future Job Growth	14%
Cost of Living Index	96
Buying Power Index	163
Weekly Daycare Cost	$106
Median Home Price	$171,400
"Sweet Spot" Home Price	$190,000
Home Price Ratio	2.5
Median Age of Homes	9.7
% Homes Owned	66%
Effective Property Tax Rate	0.60%
Estimated Property Tax Bill	$1,140

EDUCATION

% High School Graduates	94%
% 4-yr Degree	35%
% Graduate or Professional Degree	17%
$ Invested per Pupil	N/A
Student/Teacher Ratio	16.2
Primary Test Score Percentile	150.7
Secondary Test Score Percentile	111.2
% Subsidized School Lunch	17.60%
% Attending Public School	79.20%

LIFESTYLE

Leisure Rating (Area)	1
Arts & Culture Rating (Area)	5
Climate Rating (Area)	2
Physical Setting Rating	6
Downtown Core Rating	6
% Commute < 30 Min.	84%
% Commute > 1 Hour	1%

HEALTH & SAFETY

Health Rating (Area)	4
Stress Score (Area)	4
Violent Crime Risk	88
Property Crime Risk	55

Lifestyle In the words of one local resident, "You're never more than 30 minutes from anything you want to do." Madison offers community-style attractions, one of the best being the local Dublin Park and Recreation Center with its large indoor, outdoor, and kiddie pools. Downtown Huntsville has an unusually strong assortment for children and adults. The EarlyWorks children's history museum is a highlight especially for younger kids, and the U.S. Space and Rocket Center, actually one of the largest tourist attractions in Alabama, has hands-on exhibits and simulated astronaut training experiences. Sci-Quest is a local science museum with a unique 3-D "immersive reality" theater. Local arts, performing arts, and music amenities are all noteworthy, and the Huntsville Museum of Art is in a particularly striking building. We should note that some of the facilities are new and haven't been fully incorporated into arts and leisure statistics. Outside of Huntsville, the Tennessee River and two major lakes on its course provide water recreation, and the area also has outstanding golf courses.

Aside from a few infrastructure issues due to growth and low tax revenues, driving and commutes are relatively easy. Few drives take longer than 15 minutes. Air service is fair. Nashville is about 120 miles north and is the best bet for a nearby larger city; drives to Atlanta (200 miles) and other cities are fairly long and without good direct routes.

The surrounding terrain is flat to gently rolling with some open agricultural areas and dense woods, particularly in the mountains that rise to the north. The climate is humid subtropical with a continental influence. Expect hot, humid summers with frequent thundershowers and generally mild winters with only occasional snow.

Health & Safety The crime risk is low for the region. Healthcare facilities are very good. The Huntsville Hospital just opened a local diagnostic and imaging center in 2005, and there is extensive support for the new Madison Crestwood Hospital, which is in the final planning stages. Stress and air-quality factors are low to moderate.

Nearby Neighborhoods Attractive historic districts are close to downtown and may be good bets for some families. A residential area known as South Huntsville, extending south toward the Tennessee River, has good housing and schools, but it isn't as safe as Madison.

HUNTSVILLE, AL
AREA HIGHLIGHTS

PEOPLE

SIZE & DIVERSITY	AREA	U.S. AVG	FAMILY DEMOGRAPHICS	AREA	U.S. AVG
Population	362,459		% Married	59.90%	53.80%
15-yr Population Growth	23.70%	4.40%	% Single	40.10%	46.20%
Diversity Measure	42	54	% Divorced	8.60%	10.20%
% Religiously Observant	55%	50%	% Separated	2.20%	2.10%
% Catholic	5%	22%	% Married w/Children	31.30%	27.90%
% Protestant	49%	25%	% Single w/Children	9%	9.40%
% Jewish	0%	2%	% Married, No Children	31%	31.00%
% Other	0%	1%	% Single, No Children	28.70%	31.70%

STANDARD OF LIVING

INCOME, EMPLOYMENT & TAXES	AREA	U.S. AVG	COST OF LIVING & HOUSING	AREA	U.S. AVG
Median Household Income	$48,552	$44,684	Cost of Living Index	93.1	100
Household Income Growth	4%	6.10%	Buying Power Index	117	100
Unemployment Rate	4%	5.10%	Median Home Price	$166,700	$208,500
Recent Job Growth	0.50%	1.30%	Home Price Ratio	3.4	4.7
Projected Future Job Growth	14.20%	10.50%	Home Price Appreciation	5%	13.60%
State Income Tax Rate	5%	5.00%	% Homes Owned	67%	64.10%
State Sales Tax Rate	9.20%	6.00%	Median Rent	$523	$792

EDUCATION

ATTAINMENT & ACHIEVEMENT	AREA	U.S. AVG	RESOURCES & INVESTMENT	AREA	U.S. AVG
% High School Graduate	78.40%	83.90%	No. of Highly Ranked Universities	1	1
% 2-yr Graduate	8.80%	7.10%	$ Invested per Pupil	$5,171	$6,058
% 4-yr Graduate	23.70%	17.20%	Student/Teacher Ratio	15.9	15.9
% Graduate or Professional Degree	9.30%	9.90%	State University In-State Tuition	$4,630	$4,917
% Attending Public School	88.60%	84.30%			
75th Percentile State University SAT Score (Verbal)	490	477			
75th Percentile State University SAT Score (Math)	500	478			
75th Percentile State University ACT Score	21	20			

LIFESTYLE

RECREATION, ARTS & CULTURE	AREA	U.S. AVG	INFRASTRUCTURE & FACILITIES	AREA	U.S. AVG
Professional Sports Rating	2	4	No. of Public Libraries	16	28
Zoos & Aquariums Rating	1	3	Library Volumes Per Capita	1.6	2.8
Amusement Park Rating	2	3	No. of Warehouse Clubs	3	4
Professional Theater Rating	1	3	No. of Starbucks	3	5
Overall Museum Rating	5	6	Golf Course Rating	2	4
Science Museum Rating	5	4	National Park Rating	2	3
Children's Museum Rating	1	3	Sq. Mi. Inland Water	2	4

CLIMATE			COMMUTE & TRANSPORTATION		
Days Mostly Sunny	207	212	Avg. Daily Commute Time	21.9	24.7
Annual Days Precipitation	121	111	% Commute by Auto	81%	77.70%
Annual Days > 90°F	38	38	Per Capita Avg. Daily Transit Miles	3	7.9
Annual Days < 32°F	65	88	Annual Auto Insurance Premium	$1,070	$1,314
July Relative Humidity	73	69	Gas, Cost per Gallon	$3.14	$3.05

HEALTH & SAFETY

CRIME & ENVIRNOMENTAL ISSUES	AREA	U.S. AVG	HEALTHCARE & COST	AREA	U.S. AVG
Violent Crime Rate	354	517	Physicians per Capita	206.1	254.3
Change in Violent Crime	-22.10%	-7.50%	Pediatricians per Capita	14.8	16.9
Property Crime Rate	3955	3783	Hospital Beds per Capita	439.4	239.7
Change in Property Crime	-1.30%	-10.10%	No. of Teaching Hospitals	1	1.9
Air Quality Score	36	44	Healthcare Cost Index	90.1	100
Water Quality Score	9	33	Cost per Doctor Visit	$59	$74
Pollen/Allergy Score	67	61	Cost per Dentist Visit	$53	$67
Stress Score	36	49	Cost per Hospital Room	$731	$702
Cancer Mortality Rate	162	168.9			

Matthews, NC

Area Type: Inner suburb

Zip Code: 28105

Metro Area: Charlotte-Gastonia–Rock Hill, NC

Metro Area Type: Large

Location: 10 miles southeast of downtown Charlotte along the US 74 corridor

Time Zone: Eastern Standard Time

Pros:
Attractive housing
Cost of living
Strong economy

Cons:
Long commutes
Growth and sprawl
Hot, humid summers

Charlotte—with its easy pace, strong job market, and urban culture—is at the epicenter of the emerging New South. Once home to the traditional businesses of textile, agriculture, and paper, now the city has morphed into a national financial center, attracting such industry giants as Bank of America, Wachovia, and SunTrust. In fact, more banking institutions are headquartered in Charlotte than in any other U.S. city outside of New York City. The downtown area looks the part, with modern steel-and-glass skyscrapers (the top of the Bank of America headquarters is adorned with a glass rendition of Queen Charlotte's crown). Picturesque, tree-lined neighborhoods reminiscent of the Old South spread along the city's broad, straight arteries to the south, merging into a series of attractive, older suburbs. Matthews, once an isolated fringe town, has emerged as a strong community, with a lot of families (35% married with children) and an attractive mix of old and new infrastructure. The trend continues outside the I-485 beltway, where newer suburbs and commercial districts are expanding outward to encompass some older towns like Indian Trail.

Despite the New South modernity downtown and in the suburbs, Charlotte has not forgotten its Southern roots. Traditional values still hold, and while the city is generally open-minded about personal issues, Protestant religious observance is big in the area. Yet, Northerners admire the open friendliness of area residents, and Charlotte has been called "a small city with big-city stuff."

Standard of Living The area is a treasure-trove of appealing, well-kept housing. Golf-course developments are common, and the landscaped lots look like golf-course homes even if they aren't. Prices for good homes range from $80 to $100 per square foot, and excellent choices for families are available from $180K. Homes

from the 1970s and 1980s have bigger, more wooded lots, often of a ½ acre or more; homes built since are on smaller lots of a ¼ to a ½ acre. Combined city and county property tax is about 1.2%. The Cost of Living Index for the Charlotte area is 91 and for Matthews is 105—very reasonable given income levels. Employment is steady and growing, with an 18% continued job-growth projection.

Education Local educational attainment is a strong 30% for 4-year degrees and another 12% for graduate and professional degrees. The local school system is a plus in the eyes of Charlotte residents. Butler High School tests well, at about 10% over state averages. Those willing to pay more might look at Weddington just to the west, with scores far exceeding state averages. Though the big-name colleges are in the two triad city sets (Raleigh–Durham–Chapel Hill and Greensboro–Winston–Salem–High Point) to the north, the University of North Carolina and Queens University have a strong presence and undeniably enhance the local scene.

Lifestyle The town of Matthews has a strong community feel, with its small but attractive parks, outdoor movies, performances, summer camp programs, and many special events. The Matthews Community Center, converted from a large 1907 schoolhouse, hosts many town activities, local events, art performances, club meetings, and even birthday celebrations and other private parties.

The city of Charlotte has grown up to be a major-league entertainment city, with professional sports (NBA, NFL) and a good assortment of restaurants downtown. While downtown Charlotte itself is a bit sterile, a handful of small yet high-quality museums, a science museum and IMAX complex at Discovery Place, and a new Performing Arts Center are a big draw. Charlotte residents also enjoy the many Mecklenberg County parks just beyond the city, the countryside toward the South Carolina border, or the area north to Lake Norman, the state's largest man-made lake. It only takes 2 or 3 hours to reach Asheville and the mountains to the northwest or the Raleigh-Durham area to the northeast.

Growth has been rapid, and traffic is often snarled along the I-77 corridor into town. But most streets are generally well laid out, and timed for commuters to reach downtown in 30 to 45 minutes. Lack of public transit is also an issue; a new light rail service along the I-77 corridor is being considered, though it may be too far west to impact Matthews residents.

The immediate area is flat to gently rolling, with both developed farmland and thick woods. Mountains to the northwest and the south afford mild winters, and outdoor activities are possible year-round. However, long, hot, humid spells are possible in summer.

Health & Safety   The crime risk in the metro area is relatively high, but the local crime risk as measured by the "CAP" score is low. Major hospital facilities are available in the Charlotte area, and healthcare costs match national averages.

Nearby Neighborhoods   Weddington and Ballantyne offer more established upscale alternatives to the west, while Mint Hill to the east is newer and less expensive. Many home buyers seek out the older Greek Revival or plantation-style gems closer to town, which can go for as little as $200K, but schools in those areas can be inconsistent and merit further investigation.

MATTHEWS, NC NEIGHBORHOOD HIGHLIGHTS	
PEOPLE	
Population	35,528
15-yr Population Growth	50.90%
5-yr Population Growth	11%
% Married w/Children	35.2%
% Single w/Children	7.1%
No. of Households	12,970
Median Age	34.5
Avg. Household Size	2.71
Diversity Measure	29
STANDARD OF LIVING	
Median Household Income	$63,789
% Household Income > $100K	23%
Projected Future Job Growth	18%
Cost of Living Index	105
Buying Power Index	136
Weekly Daycare Cost	$152
Median Home Price	$205,200
"Sweet Spot" Home Price	$220,000
Home Price Ratio	3.2
Median Age of Homes	12.3
% Homes Owned	72%
Effective Property Tax Rate	1.20%
Estimated Property Tax Bill	$2,640
EDUCATION	
% High School Graduates	93%
% 4-yr Degree	30%
% Graduate or Professional Degree	12%
$ Invested per Pupil	$4,996
Student/Teacher Ratio	21.3
Primary Test Score Percentile	104.3
Secondary Test Score Percentile	88.7
% Subsidized School Lunch	20.40%
% Attending Public School	76.90%
LIFESTYLE	
Leisure Rating (Area)	7
Arts & Culture Rating (Area)	7
Climate Rating (Area)	4
Physical Setting Rating	4
Downtown Core Rating	6
% Commute < 30 Min.	51%
% Commute > 1 Hour	5%
HEALTH & SAFETY	
Health Rating (Area)	4
Stress Score (Area)	7
Violent Crime Risk	26
Property Crime Risk	41

CHARLOTTE-GASTONIA–ROCK HILL, NC
AREA HIGHLIGHTS

PEOPLE

SIZE & DIVERSITY	AREA	U.S. AVG	FAMILY DEMOGRAPHICS	AREA	U.S. AVG
Population	1,651,894		% Married	54.60%	53.80%
15-yr Population Growth	44.60%	4.40%	% Single	45.40%	46.20%
Diversity Measure	44	54	% Divorced	7.50%	10.20%
% Religiously Observant	50%	50%	% Separated	4.80%	2.10%
% Catholic	6%	22%	% Married w/Children	27.40%	27.90%
% Protestant	43%	25%	% Single w/Children	10.60%	9.40%
% Jewish	1%	2%	% Married, No Children	30.40%	31.00%
% Other	1%	1%	% Single, No Children	31.60%	31.70%

STANDARD OF LIVING

INCOME, EMPLOYMENT & TAXES	AREA	U.S. AVG	COST OF LIVING & HOUSING	AREA	U.S. AVG
Median Household Income	$45,823	$44,684	Cost of Living Index	90.8	100
Household Income Growth	5.30%	6.10%	Buying Power Index	113	100
Unemployment Rate	5.30%	5.10%	Median Home Price	$145,900	$208,500
Recent Job Growth	3.10%	1.30%	Home Price Ratio	3.2	4.7
Projected Future Job Growth	18.10%	10.50%	Home Price Appreciation	4.40%	13.60%
State Income Tax Rate	7%	5.00%	% Homes Owned	68.10%	64.10%
State Sales Tax Rate	6%	6.00%	Median Rent	$719	$792

EDUCATION

ATTAINMENT & ACHIEVEMENT	AREA	U.S. AVG	RESOURCES & INVESTMENT	AREA	U.S. AVG
% High School Graduate	74.60%	83.90%	No. of Highly Ranked Universities	1	1
% 2-yr Graduate	10.20%	7.10%	$ Invested per Pupil	$5,252	$6,058
% 4-yr Graduate	18.90%	17.20%	Student/Teacher Ratio	16.6	15.9
% Graduate or Professional Degree	7.60%	9.90%	State University In-State Tuition	$4,282	$4,917
% Attending Public School	89.40%	84.30%			
75th Percentile State University SAT Score (Verbal)	530	477			
75th Percentile State University SAT Score (Math)	570	478			
75th Percentile State University ACT Score	23	20			

LIFESTYLE

RECREATION, ARTS & CULTURE	AREA	U.S. AVG	INFRASTRUCTURE & FACILITIES	AREA	U.S. AVG
Professional Sports Rating	5	4	No. of Public Libraries	50	28
Zoos & Aquariums Rating	2	3	Library Volumes Per Capita	2.2	2.8
Amusement Park Rating	5	3	No. of Warehouse Clubs	7	4
Professional Theater Rating	1	3	No. of Starbucks	29	5
Overall Museum Rating	8	6	Golf Course Rating	7	4
Science Museum Rating	8	4	National Park Rating	2	3
Children's Museum Rating	4	3	Sq. Mi. Inland Water	3	4

CLIMATE			COMMUTE & TRANSPORTATION		
Days Mostly Sunny	214	212	Avg. Daily Commute Time	26.1	24.7
Annual Days Precipitation	111	111	% Commute by Auto	78%	77.70%
Annual Days > 90°F	31	38	Per Capita Avg. Daily Transit Miles	3.9	7.9
Annual Days < 32°F	71	88	Annual Auto Insurance Premium	$1,097	$1,314
July Relative Humidity	69	69	Gas, Cost per Gallon	$3.17	$3.05

HEALTH & SAFETY

CRIME & ENVIRNOMENTAL ISSUES	AREA	U.S. AVG	HEALTHCARE & COST	AREA	U.S. AVG
Violent Crime Rate	740	517	Physicians per Capita	199.6	254.3
Change in Violent Crime	-21.80%	-7.50%	Pediatricians per Capita	16.5	16.9
Property Crime Rate	5137	3783	Hospital Beds per Capita	260.6	239.7
Change in Property Crime	-9.60%	-10.10%	No. of Teaching Hospitals	5	1.9
Air Quality Score	35	44	Healthcare Cost Index	100.5	100
Water Quality Score	65	33	Cost per Doctor Visit	$90	$74
Pollen/Allergy Score	68	61	Cost per Dentist Visit	$71	$67
Stress Score	73	49	Cost per Hospital Room	$614	$702
Cancer Mortality Rate	163.9	168.9			

Maumee, OH

Area Type: Inner suburb

Zip Code: 43537

Metro Area: Toledo, OH

Metro Area Type: Mid-size

Location: 9 miles southwest of Toledo along the Maumee River

Time Zone: Eastern Standard Time

Pros:
Convenience
Historic interest
Schools

Cons:
Featureless setting
Cold winters
Older industrial areas

We expect to draw a little fire for including the much-maligned Toledo area in a best-places-to-live list. But we feel a book like this one should bring a few not-so-obvious places to light, and Maumee and the Toledo areas have some pleasant surprises.

Admittedly, the port of Toledo has a typical Great Lakes industrial landscape. Ship terminals, auto assembly plants (Jeep, Ford, GM Powertrain), and glass factories (Owens-Corning, Owens-Illinois, Libby-Owens) abound on the lakefront and near the downtown. Though they have endured some difficult times, these Rust Belt manufacturing industries, especially the glass plants, have actually fared quite well. And mighty industrialists leave mighty endowments, and Toledo, like many other Great Lakes cities, has a generous share of cultural assets for its size.

On the west end of Lake Erie, Toledo's frigid winters are hardly conducive to extensive outdoor activities (it's too flat for skiing), but it gets far less snow than many of its Michigan neighbors to the north, east, and west. And, as suggested by Corporal Klinger in the TV show *M*A*S*H*, Toledo is a true melting pot for working-class civilians whose ethnic influence lends an element of interest to the city. Many of these recent immigrants religiously follow the minor-league Mudhens, and the new Mudhen stadium is quite possibly the best in the minors—and one of the best values in family sports outings anywhere.

West of the city center and adjacent industrial areas, along the Anthony Wayne Parkway and the Maumee River, you'll find a great set of older historic towns and prosperous newer suburbs. Maumee, with strong roots in pre–Civil War America, features a downtown that makes the National Register of Historic Places and has numerous historic Greek Revival homes and others of architectural interest. Maumee has recognized its legacy

and is attracting a diverse cross-section of prosperous families who are looking for good homes of all vintages. Commutes are a non-issue here, and newcomers find the lack of traffic and crowds refreshing. In fact, residents proud of the short travel times call Toledo the "15-minute city." It has a married-with-children percentage of almost 30%, indicating younger adults and more children than one might expect for an older neighborhood.

Standard of Living   Many Maumee residents work locally at the Arrowhead Industrial Park or the new Dana Corporation research laboratory, and an estimated 30,000 work in the greater area. Toledo and its western suburbs have been recognized as a good center for traveling professionals, such as account executives who go mainly to Midwestern accounts by car and occasionally by air. The Cost of Living is an attractive 89, and Maumee tracks national averages at 101. Good family homes start at $150K, while newer homes in the Monclova township to the west climb into the low $200Ks. Property tax rates run about 1.8%, not as high as in some nearby communities because of the strong commercial tax base.

Education   New residents are attracted by the strong academics and high parent involvement in Toledo schools, which, interestingly, are better than at the more upscale Perrysburg across the Maumee River. Test scores for the Maumee School district are consistently above average. In terms of higher education, the area offers the University of Toledo and Bowling Green State University.

Lifestyle   Toledo and Maumee are each working hard to preserve and expand their legacies. Toledo has new waterfront "Metroparks" with events, programs, and bike trails that bring in many visitors. The Toledo Zoo, COSI (the science museum), and the Museum of Art are

MAUMEE, OH NEIGHBORHOOD HIGHLIGHTS	
PEOPLE	
Population	24,292
15-yr Population Growth	-2.50%
5-yr Population Growth	-1%
% Married w/Children	29.7%
% Single w/Children	9.3%
No. of Households	9,910
Median Age	37.5
Avg. Household Size	2.42
Diversity Measure	12
STANDARD OF LIVING	
Median Household Income	$53,633
% Household Income > $100K	15%
Projected Future Job Growth	4%
Cost of Living Index	101
Buying Power Index	116
Weekly Daycare Cost	$150
Median Home Price	$170,000
"Sweet Spot" Home Price	$190,000
Home Price Ratio	3.2
Median Age of Homes	28.6
% Homes Owned	66%
Effective Property Tax Rate	1.80%
Estimated Property Tax Bill	$3,325
EDUCATION	
% High School Graduates	93%
% 4-yr Degree	23%
% Graduate or Professional Degree	10%
$ Invested per Pupil	$6,281
Student/Teacher Ratio	16.2
Primary Test Score Percentile	109.5
Secondary Test Score Percentile	108
% Subsidized School Lunch	13.80%
% Attending Public School	75.40%
LIFESTYLE	
Leisure Rating (Area)	5
Arts & Culture Rating (Area)	9
Climate Rating (Area)	4
Physical Setting Rating	2
Downtown Core Rating	4
% Commute < 30 Min.	82%
% Commute > 1 Hour	3%
HEALTH & SAFETY	
Health Rating (Area)	4
Stress Score (Area)	8
Violent Crime Risk	72
Property Crime Risk	71

all well-known and worthwhile. In fact, in 2005, Toledo was rated by Sperling's BestPlaces as the fifth most "unwired" (wireless) city in the United States. Small businesses and citizens are becoming increasingly tech savvy, and you can find Wi-Fi hot spots at International Park downtown and the Fifth Third Field, home of the Mudhens. There is evidence of change.

Maumee's 13 parks are going through a rebuilding and expansion program, with a major new pool facility opened in 2005. Many Lake Erie parks are easily accessible; the world-class Cedar Point Amusement Park is in Sandusky, 1 hour east; and big-city amenities await 1 hour north in Detroit and 4 hours west in Chicago.

The immediate area is mainly flat farmland with some small wooded areas. The climate is Great Lakes continental, and the potential for cold, cloudy, gloomy winters is more of an issue than rain or snow.

Health & Safety   Crime risk is low to moderate in Maumee, and better than in Toledo as a whole, which as a metro area still shows above-average crime activity. Healthcare facilities are good and less expensive than national averages. St. Luke's Hospital is right in Maumee.

Nearby Neighborhoods   Prices across the river in Perrysburg are a little higher, and schools are not as well regarded. However, despite its older downtown, Perrysburg is actually newer, overall, than Maumee. Its malls and shopping areas are easily accessible from Maumee. Sylvania to the north, or even Bowling Green to the south, offer more of a small, college-town lifestyle.

TOLEDO, OH
AREA HIGHLIGHTS
PEOPLE

SIZE & DIVERSITY	AREA	U.S. AVG	FAMILY DEMOGRAPHICS	AREA	U.S. AVG
Population	616,829		% Married	52.90%	53.80%
15-yr Population Growth	0.70%	4.40%	% Single	47.10%	46.20%
Diversity Measure	33	54	% Divorced	8.90%	10.20%
% Religiously Observant	49%	50%	% Separated	2.30%	2.10%
% Catholic	23%	22%	% Married w/Children	27.70%	27.90%
% Protestant	24%	25%	% Single w/Children	10.70%	9.40%
% Jewish	1%	2%	% Married, No Children	28%	31.00%
% Other	1%	1%	% Single, No Children	33.60%	31.70%

STANDARD OF LIVING

INCOME, EMPLOYMENT & TAXES	AREA	U.S. AVG	COST OF LIVING & HOUSING	AREA	U.S. AVG
Median Household Income	$40,828	$44,684	Cost of Living Index	88.8	100
Household Income Growth	6.70%	6.10%	Buying Power Index	103	100
Unemployment Rate	6.70%	5.10%	Median Home Price	$118,600	$208,500
Recent Job Growth	-2.20%	1.30%	Home Price Ratio	2.9	4.7
Projected Future Job Growth	6.10%	10.50%	Home Price Appreciation	4.30%	13.60%
State Income Tax Rate	7.20%	5.00%	% Homes Owned	67.30%	64.10%
State Sales Tax Rate	6%	6.00%	Median Rent	$571	$792

EDUCATION

ATTAINMENT & ACHIEVEMENT	AREA	U.S. AVG	RESOURCES & INVESTMENT	AREA	U.S. AVG
% High School Graduate	81.10%	83.90%	No. of Highly Ranked Universities	0	1
% 2-yr Graduate	8.90%	7.10%	$ Invested per Pupil	$6,275	$6,058
% 4-yr Graduate	14.70%	17.20%	Student/Teacher Ratio	15.7	15.9
% Graduate or Professional Degree	6.20%	9.90%	State University In-State Tuition	$7,542	$4,917
% Attending Public School	82.30%	84.30%			
75th Percentile State University SAT Score (Verbal)	520	477			
75th Percentile State University SAT Score (Math)	550	478			
75th Percentile State University ACT Score	23	20			

LIFESTYLE

RECREATION, ARTS & CULTURE	AREA	U.S. AVG	INFRASTRUCTURE & FACILITIES	AREA	U.S. AVG
Professional Sports Rating	6	4	No. of Public Libraries	39	28
Zoos & Aquariums Rating	7	3	Library Volumes Per Capita	5.5	2.8
Amusement Park Rating	1	3	No. of Warehouse Clubs	1	4
Professional Theater Rating	1	3	No. of Starbucks	2	5
Overall Museum Rating	6	6	Golf Course Rating	5	4
Science Museum Rating	5	4	National Park Rating	2	3
Children's Museum Rating	1	3	Sq. Mi. Inland Water	2	4

CLIMATE			COMMUTE & TRANSPORTATION		
Days Mostly Sunny	181	212	Avg. Daily Commute Time	20.5	24.7
Annual Days Precipitation	136	111	% Commute by Auto	80%	77.70%
Annual Days > 90°F	13	38	Per Capita Avg. Daily Transit Miles	7.4	7.9
Annual Days < 32°F	145	88	Annual Auto Insurance Premium	$1,381	$1,314
July Relative Humidity	72	69	Gas, Cost per Gallon	$2.98	$3.05

HEALTH & SAFETY

CRIME & ENVIRNOMENTAL ISSUES	AREA	U.S. AVG	HEALTHCARE & COST	AREA	U.S. AVG
Violent Crime Rate	540	517	Physicians per Capita	315.5	254.3
Change in Violent Crime	-0.50%	-7.50%	Pediatricians per Capita	22.4	16.9
Property Crime Rate	5103	3783	Hospital Beds per Capita	527.6	239.7
Change in Property Crime	-5.80%	-10.10%	No. of Teaching Hospitals	7	1.9
Air Quality Score	37	44	Healthcare Cost Index	100.3	100
Water Quality Score	22	33	Cost per Doctor Visit	$73	$74
Pollen/Allergy Score	53	61	Cost per Dentist Visit	$51	$67
Stress Score	84	49	Cost per Hospital Room	$679	$702
Cancer Mortality Rate	179.8	168.9			

Minden-Gardnerville, NV

Area Type: Small town

Zip Code: 89423

Metro Area: Minden-Gardnerville, NV (micropolitan area)

Metro Area Type: Smallest

Location: Western Nevada, 15 miles south of Carson City

Time Zone: Pacific Standard Time

Pros:
> Attractive setting
> Climate and outdoor recreation
> Low taxes

Cons:
> Small employment base
> Cost of living
> Tight housing market

"This is the place!" exclaimed Mormon founder and pioneer Joseph Smith in the 1840s as he descended the Wasatch Mountains into the beautiful Salt Lake Valley. The Mormon nation spread west from there into Carson Valley, at the eastern base of the Sierra Nevada. Today, the flat land of the Carson Valley gradually transitions from desert in the east to alfalfa fields, small housing developments, and the twin towns of Minden and Gardnerville toward the south.

Many people, especially Californians, get their first impressions of the Carson Valley as they descend the windy, 3,500-foot, 10-mile Kingsbury Grade (SR 207) from the Lake Tahoe Basin just west. From the bustling tourist centers and lush forests around Stateline and South Lake Tahoe at 6,200 feet, they first rise to a 7,500-foot crest dotted by expensive cabins and chalets, then overlook and descend into the vast valley to the east almost as if in an airplane. The spectacular view makes it hard to watch the road. The flat land is surrounded by mountains on all sides gradually transitioning to desert toward the east, with alfalfa fields, small housing developments, and the twin towns of Minden and Gardnerville toward the south end of the picture. Once reaching the valley floor, the Sierra rises dramatically across the western horizon as a ridge of 9,000- to 11,000-foot snowcapped peaks.

The excellent combination of setting, nearby attractions, and climate has indeed brought a new breed of settlers in—many looking for a pristine small-town atmosphere near California but away from its crowds, taxes, and cost of living. Small subdivisions, some featuring million-dollar homes, have sprung up in a well-managed growth pattern among the valley's grassland and sagebrush. Possibly echoing the quote from that famous Mormon pioneer, the Starbucks Corporation built a coffee roasting plant in the small town of Minden in 2003. (The employee-oriented Starbucks is renowned for their choosiness about location, with quality of life topping their list.) Many workers commute to the tourist-supported Tahoe Basin; some work for local companies like Starbucks and Bentley Agrodynamics; and others work remotely or telecommute. Life in Minden will reward you with a wholesome small-town environment that combines the best of Western and Midwestern towns. Plus, you'll find a near-infinite supply of outdoor activities and recreation in Lake Tahoe and nearby Nevada parks and historic sites, as well as beautiful mountain vistas.

Standard of Living You may need to be creative to find income in Minden, but job growth is projected at a strong 19%. Hospitality jobs are available in Tahoe, but the commute is a tricky half-hour and most jobs don't pay well. Prospective employees may find work in Carson City or Reno, but Reno is a long commute that is particularly difficult in winter. Much of the land around Minden is Bureau of Land Management and National Forest Service land owned by the federal government, and developers have bought most of the rest, making housing scarce and pricey. Family homes start at $350K and rise quickly into the $400Ks and $500Ks. Homes are on large lots that are a bit barren because of the desert climate. Effective property tax rates range from 0.75% to 1.0%, and Nevada has no state income tax and very low business taxes.

Education Locals praise Minden's schools, with their manageable size, dedicated teachers, and strong values. Scores are well above state averages, and gifted-student programs are available.

Lifestyle Outdoor recreation dominates. Nearby rivers and creeks offer excellent fishing; the Lake Tahoe Basin is a world attraction for hiking, skiing, and watersports; and less-crowded eastern shore areas like Zephyr Cove are particularly attractive to Minden residents. The deep Sierra snows are visible from Minden, but the Kingsbury road is kept open and heavy snow in the Valley is uncommon. Minden and Gardnerville are adding amenities, including parks, local concerts and events, and downtown restaurants. Both downtowns are pleasant and walkable. Carson City, Nevada's capital, offers residents little beyond shopping facilities and the noteworthy Nevada State Railroad Museum. The Stateline area offers an assortment of entertainment, often more geared to adults, and Reno, an hour north, offers entertainment and cultural attractions (see p. 328). Historic Genoa and Virginia City, an excellent living museum and theme experience, make good day trips.

Commutes to surrounding areas can be tedious because of terrain. Severe winter weather can close roads briefly, but the area is far more accessible than it used to be.

Carson Valley is a high-altitude desert with significant water flow from mountains to the west and some Pacific influence. Summers range from warm to hot but with cool evenings and occasional thundershowers. Winters are generally moderate but subject to cold snaps when Continental air masses prevail. Annual rainfall is a mere 8½ inches, most occurring in winter.

Health & Safety Crime is very low. Except during some parts of summer when air trapped in the valley stagnates, air quality is generally good. Local healthcare facilities are modest, but those in Carson City and Reno are accessible.

Nearby Neighborhoods Neighborhoods at the base of the Sierra are more expensive, but good family homes are available north of Minden and south of Gardnerville. Carson City to the north and Dayton to the northeast are less expensive but far less attractive.

MINDEN-GARDNERVILLE, NV NEIGHBORHOOD HIGHLIGHTS

PEOPLE

Population	9,072
15-yr Population Growth	64.30%
5-yr Population Growth	10%
% Married w/Children	29.8%
% Single w/Children	7.9%
No. of Households	3,463
Median Age	40.8
Avg. Household Size	2.59
Diversity Measure	14

STANDARD OF LIVING

Median Household Income	$58,195
% Household Income > $100K	14%
Projected Future Job Growth	19%
Cost of Living Index	120
Buying Power Index	108
Weekly Daycare Cost	$65
Median Home Price	$461,600
"Sweet Spot" Home Price	$450,000
Home Price Ratio	7.9
Median Age of Homes	11.5
% Homes Owned	81%
Effective Property Tax Rate	1%
Estimated Property Tax Bill	$4,500

EDUCATION

% High School Graduates	93%
% 4-yr Degree	15%
% Graduate or Professional Degree	7%
$ Invested per Pupil	$5,855
Student/Teacher Ratio	26.2
Primary Test Score Percentile	128.7
Secondary Test Score Percentile	131
% Subsidized School Lunch	19%
% Attending Public School	91.20%

LIFESTYLE

Leisure Rating (Area)	9
Arts & Culture Rating (Area)	2
Climate Rating (Area)	8
Physical Setting Rating	10
Downtown Core Rating	5
% Commute < 30 Min.	68%
% Commute > 1 Hour	8%

HEALTH & SAFETY

Health Rating (Area)	2
Stress Score (Area)	8
Violent Crime Risk	40
Property Crime Risk	58

MINDEN-GARDNERVILLE, NV
AREA HIGHLIGHTS

PEOPLE

SIZE & DIVERSITY	AREA	U.S. AVG	FAMILY DEMOGRAPHICS	AREA	U.S. AVG
Population	45,394		% Married	63.40%	53.80%
15-yr Population Growth	64.30%	4.40%	% Single	36.60%	46.20%
Diversity Measure	27	54	% Divorced	11.80%	10.20%
% Religiously Observant	23%	50%	% Separated	2.40%	2.10%
% Catholic	12%	22%	% Married w/Children	27.40%	27.90%
% Protestant	10%	25%	% Single w/Children	9.20%	9.40%
% Jewish	0%	2%	% Married, No Children	35.50%	31.00%
% Other	1%	1%	% Single, No Children	27.90%	31.70%

STANDARD OF LIVING

INCOME, EMPLOYMENT & TAXES	AREA	U.S. AVG	COST OF LIVING & HOUSING	AREA	U.S. AVG
Median Household Income	$51,942	$44,684	Cost of Living Index	144.1	100
Household Income Growth	3.40%	6.10%	Buying Power Index	81	100
Unemployment Rate	3.40%	5.10%	Median Home Price	$466,300	$208,500
Recent Job Growth	1.80%	1.30%	Home Price Ratio	9	4.7
Projected Future Job Growth	19.30%	10.50%	Home Price Appreciation	31.20%	13.60%
State Income Tax Rate	0%	5.00%	% Homes Owned	61.30%	64.10%
State Sales Tax Rate	6.80%	6.00%	Median Rent	$863	$792

EDUCATION

ATTAINMENT & ACHIEVEMENT	AREA	U.S. AVG	RESOURCES & INVESTMENT	AREA	U.S. AVG
% High School Graduate	89.30%	83.90%	No. of Highly Ranked Universities	0	1
% 2-yr Graduate	11.60%	7.10%	$ Invested per Pupil	$5,727	$6,058
% 4-yr Graduate	23.40%	17.20%	Student/Teacher Ratio	18	15.9
% Graduate or Professional Degree	9.20%	9.90%	State University In-State Tuition	$3,270	$4,917
% Attending Public School	98.20%	84.30%			
75th Percentile State University SAT Score (Verbal)	450	477			
75th Percentile State University SAT Score (Math)	450	478			
75th Percentile State University ACT Score	18	20			

LIFESTYLE

RECREATION, ARTS & CULTURE	AREA	U.S. AVG	INFRASTRUCTURE & FACILITIES	AREA	U.S. AVG
Professional Sports Rating	1	4	No. of Public Libraries	2	28
Zoos & Aquariums Rating	1	3	Library Volumes Per Capita	2.5	2.8
Amusement Park Rating	2	3	No. of Warehouse Clubs	2	4
Professional Theater Rating	1	3	No. of Starbucks	2	5
Overall Museum Rating	4	6	Golf Course Rating	2	4
Science Museum Rating	4	4	National Park Rating	7	3
Children's Museum Rating	2	3	Sq. Mi. Inland Water	10	4

CLIMATE			COMMUTE & TRANSPORTATION		
Days Mostly Sunny	255	212	Avg. Daily Commute Time	23.5	24.7
Annual Days Precipitation	51	111	% Commute by Auto	79%	77.70%
Annual Days > 90°F	50	38	Per Capita Avg. Daily Transit Miles	0	7.9
Annual Days < 32°F	189	88	Annual Auto Insurance Premium	$1,430	$1,314
July Relative Humidity	50	69	Gas, Cost per Gallon	$3.05	$3.05

HEALTH & SAFETY

CRIME & ENVIRNOMENTAL ISSUES	AREA	U.S. AVG	HEALTHCARE & COST	AREA	U.S. AVG
Violent Crime Rate	168	517	Physicians per Capita	145.1	254.3
Change in Violent Crime	35.10%	-7.50%	Pediatricians per Capita	2.3	16.9
Property Crime Rate	2412	3783	Hospital Beds per Capita	0	239.7
Change in Property Crime	7.70%	-10.10%	No. of Teaching Hospitals	0	1.9
Air Quality Score	60	44	Healthcare Cost Index	120.6	100
Water Quality Score	30	33	Cost per Doctor Visit	$70	$74
Pollen/Allergy Score	63	61	Cost per Dentist Visit	$89	$67
Stress Score	80	49	Cost per Hospital Room	$990	$702
Cancer Mortality Rate	175.2	168.9			

Mount Vernon, WA

Area Type: Small town

Zip Code: 98273

Metro Area: Mount Vernon–Anacortes, WA

Metro Area Type: Smallest

Location: 60 miles north of downtown Seattle along I-5

Time Zone: Pacific Standard Time

Pros:
Attractive setting
Outdoor recreation
Central location

Cons:
Educational attainment
Cost of housing
Some employment concerns

In the early 20th century, Dutch farmers arrived in the fertile Skagit River Delta near Mount Vernon, a small farming community. They recognized the familiar flat, moist, fertile soil in a sheltered, cool climate. Their tulips and daffodils planted among the high-value cash crops and dairies added to the beauty and prosperity of this pristine farm belt flanked by the Olympic Mountains and Puget Sound to the west, San Juan Islands to the northwest, and the Cascade Range to the east. With an economy driven also by fishing, timber, shipbuilding, and oil refining, a constellation of small towns sprang up around Mount Vernon: Burlington and Sedro Wooley to the north, Conway and Stanwood to the south, and Anacortes and La Conner to the west, each having some potential for today's prospective families.

Mount Vernon has a classic rural downtown with small storefronts along the main street. Once negatively impacted by new strip mall development north of town toward Burlington, downtown Mount Vernon has since come back with good bookstores, a natural-foods center, a restored movie theater, restaurants, brewpubs, and the brand-new Children's Museum of Skagit County. Residential areas rise into the evergreen-forested Cascade foothills mostly to the east, with a mix of attractive bungalows and newer family homes and neighborhoods. The large expanse of farmland to the west, though pleasant, has limited residential areas. Mount Vernon's central location is also an attraction: Mountain and Puget Sound recreation are a half-hour away; the town of Bellingham a half-hour north offers some city conveniences; and Seattle and Vancouver, B.C., are both an hour away.

The economy is mixed. Stagnant forest, fishing, and agricultural industries have led to high unemployment, and educational attainment remains statistically low. But its prosperous northern suburbs and overall quality of life suggest improvement. A strong 5.7% recent job growth is in the books, and a moderate 18% 10-year employment growth rate is projected. The Mount Vernon area may not be perfect today, but it is up-and-coming; and we expect it to only improve as a family place.

Standard of Living   It's difficult to find any place on the West Coast with a truly attractive cost profile. The Mount Vernon area is still a bit expensive by national standards but is more reasonable than Seattle. The Cost of Living Index is 105. Incomes, reflecting the rural economy, remain relatively low, giving a poor Buying Power Index of 90. Though a bit scarce, good family homes run from $300K to $350K. More family homes are available in Stanwood and Anacortes, but for about $350K to $400K. Effective property tax rates are about 1.4%.

Education   Each town has its own elementary and secondary schools, and, among the towns, Stanwood, Anacortes, and Conway schools rate better than Mount Vernon's. Neighboring La Conner High School, in fact, scored 17% to 25% higher than state averages. Mount Vernon schools are on an improvement track but still have some ground to cover.

Lifestyle   Outdoor activities—fishing, hiking, skiing, camping, and crabbing—dominate the recreation scene, and participant team sports are also popular. The calm Puget Sound offers excellent boating opportunities. The lush North Cascades National Park and Mount Baker are less than an hour to the east. The flat farmlands are excellent for bicycling, and adventure biking is common in the mountains and in the San Juans. State parks on Whidbey Island to the west and along Chuckanut Drive toward Bellingham offer excellent opportunities to commune with nature, and there are a number of bird and wildlife refuges in the area. There aren't many

MOUNT VERNON, WA NEIGHBORHOOD HIGHLIGHTS	
PEOPLE	
Population	27,410
15-yr Population Growth	39.60%
5-yr Population Growth	7.90%
% Married w/Children	25.0%
% Single w/Children	11.1%
No. of Households	9,935
Median Age	34.8
Avg. Household Size	2.72
Diversity Measure	59
STANDARD OF LIVING	
Median Household Income	$41,962
% Household Income > $100K	9%
Projected Future Job Growth	18%
Cost of Living Index	105
Buying Power Index	90
Weekly Daycare Cost	$132
Median Home Price	$235,400
"Sweet Spot" Home Price	$350,000
Home Price Ratio	5.6
Median Age of Homes	25.8
% Homes Owned	59%
Effective Property Tax Rate	1.40%
Estimated Property Tax Bill	$4,900
EDUCATION	
% High School Graduates	79%
% 4-yr Degree	14%
% Graduate or Professional Degree	7%
$ Invested per Pupil	$5,270
Student/Teacher Ratio	37.3
Primary Test Score Percentile	84.4
Secondary Test Score Percentile	97.3
% Subsidized School Lunch	62.30%
% Attending Public School	91.10%
LIFESTYLE	
Leisure Rating (Area)	5
Arts & Culture Rating (Area)	4
Climate Rating (Area)	7
Physical Setting Rating	9
Downtown Core Rating	5
% Commute < 30 Min.	70%
% Commute > 1 Hour	8%
HEALTH & SAFETY	
Health Rating (Area)	5
Stress Score (Area)	9
Violent Crime Risk	94
Property Crime Risk	114

museums or cultural amenities in Mount Vernon, but Seattle and Vancouver are close enough for day trips, and the popular Amtrak Cascades trains are a good way to get there.

Commutes are not an issue in the Skagit Valley. But an increasing number of commuters head south toward Seattle, especially the northern areas of Everett and Lynnwood. The commute into Seattle is a tedious hour-plus, while the northern commercial areas take 30 to 45 minutes.

The Skagit Delta is completely flat save for the river levees protecting the low-lying farmland from floods. The climate is decidedly marine, cool in summer and wet in winter, with few temperature extremes. The Olympic Mountains protect the area against strong storms from the southwest. Severe weather is uncommon, and outdoor activities are possible most of the year (although there are a lot of cloudy days). Spring, when the tulips are in bloom, is especially spectacular and draws tourists from around the world.

Health & Safety Crime risk is low to moderate throughout the area. Stress factors are minimal, and the air quality by experience is excellent if impaired statistically by the presence of oil refineries in Anacortes. There are three small hospitals.

Nearby Neighborhoods Stanwood is adjacent to popular but upscale Camano Island and has the best family homes and good schools, but the setting and town are not very appealing. Many residents commute to the Seattle area from Stanwood. Anacortes is a ship-building town with two enormous oil refineries, and the old town has a distinct working-class seaport flavor, with small pockets of attractive old and new homes as more people discover the area. It receives a modest economic and recreational boost as the gateway to the San Juans. Conway has good schools but is small with few housing choices. La Conner is an old fishing village enjoying its reincarnation as a tourist destination; it's a pleasant place to live, but a bit more suited to retirees.

MOUNT VERNON–ANACORTES, WA
AREA HIGHLIGHTS

PEOPLE

SIZE & DIVERSITY	AREA	U.S. AVG	FAMILY DEMOGRAPHICS	AREA	U.S. AVG
Population	111,064		% Married	59.30%	53.80%
15-yr Population Growth	39.60%	4.40%	% Single	40.70%	46.20%
Diversity Measure	40	54	% Divorced	11.60%	10.20%
% Religiously Observant	43%	50%	% Separated	2.50%	2.10%
% Catholic	18%	22%	% Married w/Children	24%	27.90%
% Protestant	20%	25%	% Single w/Children	10.80%	9.40%
% Jewish	0%	2%	% Married, No Children	34.10%	31.00%
% Other	5%	1%	% Single, No Children	31.20%	31.70%

STANDARD OF LIVING

INCOME, EMPLOYMENT & TAXES	AREA	U.S. AVG	COST OF LIVING & HOUSING	AREA	U.S. AVG
Median Household Income	$44,319	$44,684	Cost of Living Index	96.5	100
Household Income Growth	6.10%	6.10%	Buying Power Index	103	100
Unemployment Rate	6.10%	5.10%	Median Home Price	$170,100	$208,500
Recent Job Growth	5.70%	1.30%	Home Price Ratio	3.8	4.7
Projected Future Job Growth	18.50%	10.50%	Home Price Appreciation	13.70%	13.60%
State Income Tax Rate	0%	5.00%	% Homes Owned	66.80%	64.10%
State Sales Tax Rate	7.80%	6.00%	Median Rent	$767	$792

EDUCATION

ATTAINMENT & ACHIEVEMENT	AREA	U.S. AVG	RESOURCES & INVESTMENT	AREA	U.S. AVG
% High School Graduate	82.70%	83.90%	No. of Highly Ranked Universities	0	1
% 2-yr Graduate	11.70%	7.10%	$ Invested per Pupil	$5,323	$6,058
% 4-yr Graduate	20%	17.20%	Student/Teacher Ratio	19.5	15.9
% Graduate or Professional Degree	7.50%	9.90%	State University In-State Tuition	$5,286	$4,917
% Attending Public School	95.10%	84.30%			
75th Percentile State University SAT Score (Verbal)	520	477			
75th Percentile State University SAT Score (Math)	550	478			
75th Percentile State University ACT Score	23	20			

LIFESTYLE

RECREATION, ARTS & CULTURE	AREA	U.S. AVG	INFRASTRUCTURE & FACILITIES	AREA	U.S. AVG
Professional Sports Rating	5	4	No. of Public Libraries	6	28
Zoos & Aquariums Rating	5	3	Library Volumes Per Capita	2.4	2.8
Amusement Park Rating	5	3	No. of Warehouse Clubs	6	4
Professional Theater Rating	6	3	No. of Starbucks	4	5
Overall Museum Rating	6	6	Golf Course Rating	5	4
Science Museum Rating	7	4	National Park Rating	10	3
Children's Museum Rating	7	3	Sq. Mi. Inland Water	5	4

CLIMATE			COMMUTE & TRANSPORTATION		
Days Mostly Sunny	136	212	Avg. Daily Commute Time	25.1	24.7
Annual Days Precipitation	152	111	% Commute by Auto	77%	77.70%
Annual Days > 90°F	3	38	Per Capita Avg. Daily Transit Miles	2.1	7.9
Annual Days < 32°F	32	88	Annual Auto Insurance Premium	$1,748	$1,314
July Relative Humidity	74	69	Gas, Cost per Gallon	$3.01	$3.05

HEALTH & SAFETY

CRIME & ENVIRNOMENTAL ISSUES	AREA	U.S. AVG	HEALTHCARE & COST	AREA	U.S. AVG
Violent Crime Rate	86	517	Physicians per Capita	233.4	254.3
Change in Violent Crime	108.50%	-7.50%	Pediatricians per Capita	13.7	16.9
Property Crime Rate	1832	3783	Hospital Beds per Capita	259.1	239.7
Change in Property Crime	20.60%	-10.10%	No. of Teaching Hospitals	0	1.9
Air Quality Score	43	44	Healthcare Cost Index	118.4	100
Water Quality Score	52	33	Cost per Doctor Visit	$78	$74
Pollen/Allergy Score	48	61	Cost per Dentist Visit	$85	$67
Stress Score	91	49	Cost per Hospital Room	$683	$702
Cancer Mortality Rate	165.7	168.9			

Mukilteo, WA

Area Type: Suburban town

Zip Code: 98275

Metro Area: Seattle-Bellevue-Everett, WA

Metro Area Type: Largest

Location: 31 miles north of downtown Seattle along Puget Sound

Time Zone: Pacific Standard Time

Pros:
Attractive setting
Strong economy
Education

Cons:
Cost of living
Tight housing market
Economic cycles

Many of the best places for families that we include in this book are newer, rapidly expanding areas growing at or above the pace of the metro area as a whole. Not so with Mukilteo. Even though the town is fairly new (over half the homes here are less than 10 years old), the growth phase has ended and the housing market is pretty tight. Mukilteo's proximity to Seattle, along with a beautiful landscape, have made it very desirable—yet it's still fairly inexpensive for the Seattle area. There is a strong family presence with 36.4% of households categorized as married with children.

Mukilteo, perched on a bluff above Puget Sound, is a small town and ferry port with a distinct Pacific Northwest character. A small but colorful commercial district is surrounded by well-maintained and restored older homes and has great views of the Puget Sound. Mukilteo is the closest mainland access point to Whidbey Island across the Sound and to the Whidbey ferry docks at the northwest tip of town. The Snohomish County Airport and Boeing's Everett facility are just to the east, which means that noise from aircraft is noticeable at times.

Mukilteo's newcomers are a fairly diverse mix of retirees and West Coast transplants looking for a more relaxed lifestyle. As Seattle expands, mainly to the north and east, Mukilteo is dedicated to maintaining its small-town look and feel.

Standard of Living Incomes are high in the Mukilteo area, but so is the cost of living, with a West Coast–like COL Index of 141. Due to the presence of retirees, working families likely enjoy an income higher than the reported median of $70K per household. Employment in the Seattle area is strong if somewhat cyclical, but recent job growth (4.4%) and job-growth projections (25%) are very strong. Major employers in the area include Boeing, Amazon, and Microsoft. Family homes start around $350K and rise quickly into the $400Ks—about $200 per square foot—high, but not out of sight for Seattle. Abundant hydroelectric power keeps utility costs far below the national average, and there is no state income tax. Effective property taxes are lower than the national average at 1.4%, but sales tax is a high 8.2%.

Education The educational context is strong with over 40% of the Mukilteo population possessing at least a college degree. School-district leadership has experienced some turnover in the past 5 years, and test scores have not been the picture of consistency. They are, however, mostly better than the state average at all grade levels, and the recent trend is upward. Recently, overcrowding has been a significant issue, but two new schools were just opened thanks to $48 million in funding that was approved in 2000. Middle- and high-school expansions are planned. A strong vocational program serves other nearby communities; there are five community colleges within 20 miles; and the University of Washington's main campus is 22 miles south.

Lifestyle The Mukilteo area offers great outdoor opportunities for hikers and bikers. The Cascades to the east, Olympics to the west, and San Juan Islands to the north all offer a bounty of recreational and getaway opportunities. Whidbey is a summer and weekend destination; however, ferry lines can be long (there is a $250-million project underway to expand the terminal). Boating on Puget Sound is excellent, particularly in summer, and there are many freshwater lakes inland as well. Mukilteo's walkable downtown boasts good restaurants—seafood, anyone?—and small shops, and Seattle is only 35 minutes away. Boeing is a 5-minute drive, and trips to downtown Everett and Port Garner will set you back 10 minutes. Bus service is above average, and a new local stop on the "Sounder" commuter rail system is planned for 2007.

Despite stereotypes of the Northwest's climate, the Olympic Mountains actually shelter the area from Pacific storms and some potential rainfall. Despite at least some precipitation nearly half of the days in the year, Mukilteo gets only 38½ inches of total rain annually—which is 7 inches less than, say, Cincinnati. You rarely need to carry an umbrella; and as one local says about inclement weather: "It's the sort of rain where you don't know what to do with your windshield wipers." Mukilteo weather is cloudy and/or foggy 2 of every 3 days from October through May. But summers are beautiful, with 75°F July and August temperatures, and the air is clean year-round.

Health & Safety   Crime risk in Mukilteo is very low. Healthcare facilities are adequate; a medical center and a hospital are within 7 miles of town.

Nearby Neighborhoods   Just east of Mukilteo is the larger and more industrial Everett, with its assortment of older, somewhat less expensive homes. Areas of new construction exist near I-5, attractive but not with Mukilteo's character. The rest of the Seattle area has an extensive assortment of large and small neighborhoods; finding a good balance among community, commute, and cost can be tricky. Bellevue and Issaquah along I-405 are good family areas but more expensive. More modest homes can be found farther south in Renton.

MUKILTEO, WA NEIGHBORHOOD HIGHLIGHTS	
PEOPLE	
Population	20,425
15-yr Population Growth	38.40%
5-yr Population Growth	6.30%
% Married w/Children	36.4%
% Single w/Children	7.6%
No. of Households	7,633
Median Age	34.6
Avg. Household Size	2.71
Diversity Measure	32
STANDARD OF LIVING	
Median Household Income	$67,326
% Household Income > $100K	26%
Projected Future Job Growth	25%
Cost of Living Index	141
Buying Power Index	110
Weekly Daycare Cost	$188
Median Home Price	$358,800
"Sweet Spot" Home Price	$400,000
Home Price Ratio	5.3
Median Age of Homes	14.2
% Homes Owned	65%
Effective Property Tax Rate	1.40%
Estimated Property Tax Bill	$5,600
EDUCATION	
% High School Graduates	96%
% 4-yr Degree	30%
% Graduate or Professional Degree	13%
$ Invested per Pupil	$5,484
Student/Teacher Ratio	20.7
Primary Test Score Percentile	110.5
Secondary Test Score Percentile	104.2
% Subsidized School Lunch	13.60%
% Attending Public School	86.80%
LIFESTYLE	BEST
Leisure Rating (Area)	7
Arts & Culture Rating (Area)	2
Climate Rating (Area)	8
Physical Setting Rating	9
Downtown Core Rating	8
% Commute < 30 Min.	57%
% Commute > 1 Hour	12%
HEALTH & SAFETY	
Health Rating (Area)	5
Stress Score (Area)	10
Violent Crime Risk	49
Property Crime Risk	64

SEATTLE-BELLEVUE-EVERETT, WA
AREA HIGHLIGHTS

PEOPLE

SIZE & DIVERSITY	AREA	U.S. AVG	FAMILY DEMOGRAPHICS	AREA	U.S. AVG
Population	2,500,710		% Married	52.80%	53.80%
15-yr Population Growth	23.60%	4.40%	% Single	47.20%	46.20%
Diversity Measure	39	54	% Divorced	11.60%	10.20%
% Religiously Observant	33%	50%	% Separated	2.70%	2.10%
% Catholic	14%	22%	% Married w/Children	23.90%	27.90%
% Protestant	18%	25%	% Single w/Children	9.10%	9.40%
% Jewish	1%	2%	% Married, No Children	28.30%	31.00%
% Other	0%	1%	% Single, No Children	38.70%	31.70%

STANDARD OF LIVING

INCOME, EMPLOYMENT & TAXES	AREA	U.S. AVG	COST OF LIVING & HOUSING	AREA	U.S. AVG
Median Household Income	$54,298	$44,684	Cost of Living Index	117.1	100
Household Income Growth	5%	6.10%	Buying Power Index	104	100
Unemployment Rate	5%	5.10%	Median Home Price	$310,300	$208,500
Recent Job Growth	4.40%	1.30%	Home Price Ratio	5.7	4.7
Projected Future Job Growth	12.80%	10.50%	Home Price Appreciation	12.20%	13.60%
State Income Tax Rate	0%	5.00%	% Homes Owned	60.40%	64.10%
State Sales Tax Rate	8.20%	6.00%	Median Rent	$834	$792

EDUCATION

ATTAINMENT & ACHIEVEMENT	AREA	U.S. AVG	RESOURCES & INVESTMENT	AREA	U.S. AVG
% High School Graduate	88.70%	83.90%	No. of Highly Ranked Universities	2	1
% 2-yr Graduate	11.80%	7.10%	$ Invested per Pupil	$5,838	$6,058
% 4-yr Graduate	29.90%	17.20%	Student/Teacher Ratio	20.4	15.9
% Graduate or Professional Degree	11.30%	9.90%	State University In-State Tuition	$5,286	$4,917
% Attending Public School	88.10%	84.30%			
75th Percentile State University SAT Score (Verbal)	520	477			
75th Percentile State University SAT Score (Math)	550	478			
75th Percentile State University ACT Score	23	20			

LIFESTYLE

RECREATION, ARTS & CULTURE	AREA	U.S. AVG	INFRASTRUCTURE & FACILITIES	AREA	U.S. AVG
Professional Sports Rating	8	4	No. of Public Libraries	89	28
Zoos & Aquariums Rating	8	3	Library Volumes Per Capita	2.9	2.8
Amusement Park Rating	8	3	No. of Warehouse Clubs	8	4
Professional Theater Rating	10	3	No. of Starbucks	211	5
Overall Museum Rating	9	6	Golf Course Rating	7	4
Science Museum Rating	9	4	National Park Rating	10	3
Children's Museum Rating	10	3	Sq. Mi. Inland Water	8	4

CLIMATE			COMMUTE & TRANSPORTATION		
Days Mostly Sunny	136	212	Avg. Daily Commute Time	27.3	24.7
Annual Days Precipitation	160	111	% Commute by Auto	72%	77.70%
Annual Days > 90°F	3	38	Per Capita Avg. Daily Transit Miles	39.4	7.9
Annual Days < 32°F	32	88	Annual Auto Insurance Premium	$2,100	$1,314
July Relative Humidity	74	69	Gas, Cost per Gallon	$2.91	$3.05

HEALTH & SAFETY

CRIME & ENVIRNOMENTAL ISSUES	AREA	U.S. AVG	HEALTHCARE & COST	AREA	U.S. AVG
Violent Crime Rate	410	517	Physicians per Capita	313.1	254.3
Change in Violent Crime	-6.10%	-7.50%	Pediatricians per Capita	20.7	16.9
Property Crime Rate	5049	3783	Hospital Beds per Capita	191.2	239.7
Change in Property Crime	-12.50%	-10.10%	No. of Teaching Hospitals	9	1.9
Air Quality Score	11	44	Healthcare Cost Index	126.3	100
Water Quality Score	56	33	Cost per Doctor Visit	$84	$74
Pollen/Allergy Score	48	61	Cost per Dentist Visit	$93	$67
Stress Score	98	49	Cost per Hospital Room	$702	$702
Cancer Mortality Rate	170.3	168.9			

Nashua, NH

Area Type: Satellite city

Zip Code: 03062

Metro Area: Nashua, NH

Metro Area Type: Smaller

Location: Southern New Hampshire, 5 miles north of Massachusetts border

Time Zone: Eastern Standard Time

Pros:
Moderate home prices
Low taxes and cost of living
Low crime rates

Cons:
Harsh winters
Long commutes
Public finance challenges

"Just like Massachusetts—only without the taxes, and your home will cost $100,000 less." So say the residents who have moved north to Nashua for the small-town atmosphere just 50 miles north of Boston. For many families, it's a good value proposition: In fact, almost 30% of Nashua households are married with children.

Just north of the Massachusetts border along US 3, Nashua has prospered both as a bedroom community and as an economically independent city. New Hampshire is the only state with no sales tax and no wage-based income tax (they do tax dividends and interest), so families get a boost equivalent to 5.3% (Massachusetts income tax) and 5% (Massachusetts sales tax) just for moving across the border. The downside is that systems dependent on public finance (like schools) may be starved for funds.

Built along the Merrimack River, Nashua is an old city with a typical New England downtown. Imagine historic brick structures with white-framed windows, old converted mills and factory buildings, treed streets, steepled churches, open spaces, and town squares. Past economic malaise and intense suburbanization had resulted in neglect; however, in recent years, the downtown has been rediscovered, and many new shops, restaurants, and entertainment venues have returned. Highway 3 swings west around the city core; the area south and west of this "swing" has the strongest family feel, and close economic ties to Massachusetts with many residents commuting to do business south of the border. Nashua residents boast about their central location: "1 hour to Boston, 1 hour to the coast, and 1 hour to the mountains and skiing."

With low taxes, relatively low labor costs for the region, and few barriers to commerce, New Hampshire is a compelling place for business. Plenty of businesses have indeed settled in the area, including Oracle,

Hewlett-Packard, Lockheed-Martin, and Nashua Corporation, all seeking the educated population and low costs. Employment has lagged somewhat with the technology downturn, but it's still favorable. Population growth has challenged both public finance and the general quality of life, but these challenges have been managed adequately. Recent (and planned) improvements point to a better future for the area's transportation infrastructures.

Standard of Living The Cost of Living Index of 119 is high by national standards but quite attractive for New England. It is possible to buy a good family home in the $250K range, and $350K will get you a very nice one. Homes are typically on ½-acre lots, although some new developments are on a ¼ acre. Comparable homes are $400K to $500K in Massachusetts residential areas just 20 miles south. Downsides include potentially long commutes, high property taxes, and rapidly rising home prices. As in Boston, daycare runs about $800 per month.

For public finance, New Hampshire relies on property tax, which is collected and spent at the state level. Not surprisingly, property tax rates are high and rising, about $20 per $1,000 valuation or 2%, varying by town. When a town needs a new school, property taxes are adjusted to compensate. Frequently, the result is that needed new schools don't get funded right away and school growth lags population growth. Some areas are overcrowded, and some areas, like Merrimack to the north, face large tax increases to pay for new infrastructure.

Education About 24% of local residents possess a 4-year degree and another 14% have achieved graduate or professional levels of education. Schools have faced some growth challenges and disruptions as new schools are completed (the Nashua School District just opened

NASHUA, NH NEIGHBORHOOD HIGHLIGHTS	
PEOPLE	
Population	27,670
15-yr Population Growth	18.70%
5-yr Population Growth	4.70%
% Married w/Children	29.7%
% Single w/Children	5.6%
No. of Households	10,488
Median Age	37
Avg. Household Size	2.6
Diversity Measure	21
STANDARD OF LIVING	
Median Household Income	$73,176
% Household Income > $100K	23%
Projected Future Job Growth	9%
Cost of Living Index	119
Buying Power Index	138
Weekly Daycare Cost	$210
Median Home Price	$291,500
"Sweet Spot" Home Price	$340,000
Home Price Ratio	4
Median Age of Homes	21
% Homes Owned	73%
Effective Property Tax Rate	2%
Estimated Property Tax Bill	$6,800
EDUCATION	
% High School Graduates	91%
% 4-yr Degree	24%
% Graduate or Professional Degree	14%
$ Invested per Pupil	$5,556
Student/Teacher Ratio	16.7
Primary Test Score Percentile	102.2
Secondary Test Score Percentile	124.7
% Subsidized School Lunch	12.60%
% Attending Public School	75.10%
LIFESTYLE	
Leisure Rating (Area)	6
Arts & Culture Rating (Area)	2
Climate Rating (Area)	1
Physical Setting Rating	5
Downtown Core Rating	5
% Commute < 30 Min.	61%
% Commute > 1 Hour	10%
HEALTH & SAFETY	BEST
Health Rating (Area)	3
Stress Score (Area)	3
Violent Crime Risk	29
Property Crime Risk	33

a new high school), and test scores are only average to slightly above average.

Lifestyle Nashua residents lead a typical small-town/suburban life. Downtown is busy, as is the nearby Pheasant Lane Mall (often crowded with Massachusetts shoppers avoiding sales tax). There is a minor-league baseball team, and there are a number of small lakes for watersports. Winter sports enthusiasts have plenty to do—including skiing, snowmobiling, ice-skating, and ice hockey—during the long winters. The area is relatively lacking in arts and cultural amenities, but there is plenty to do in Boston.

Commutes can be a key consideration for Nashua residents. Most commuters travel an hour or less to commercial areas in the northern Boston suburbs. A recent lane addition to US 3 has dropped commuting times considerably—for now, at least. Rail service is planned to begin in the next 2 years using an existing railroad right-of-way, and facilities have just been acquired for a Nashua station.

Nashua lies in a flat valley with some areas of woods. The climate is rigorous, with cold, windy, often snowy winters and occasional severe cold spells. Summers are moderately warm and humid with occasional hot, sticky spells.

Health & Safety Area crime risk is very low. Healthcare facilities are under some capacity pressure, but are adequate. Stress levels are notably lower here than in Massachusetts.

Nearby Neighborhoods Some residents look to the Amherst and Hollis areas to the west; homes have bigger lots and can be about $100K to $200K more expensive.

NASHUA, NH
AREA HIGHLIGHTS

PEOPLE

SIZE & DIVERSITY	AREA	U.S. AVG	FAMILY DEMOGRAPHICS	AREA	U.S. AVG
Population	199,840		% Married	61.70%	53.80%
15-yr Population Growth	18.70%	4.40%	% Single	38.30%	46.20%
Diversity Measure	15	54	% Divorced	7.70%	10.20%
% Religiously Observant	58%	50%	% Separated	2.20%	2.10%
% Catholic	46%	22%	% Married w/Children	35.20%	27.90%
% Protestant	11%	25%	% Single w/Children	7.50%	9.40%
% Jewish	2%	2%	% Married, No Children	30.40%	31.00%
% Other	0%	1%	% Single, No Children	26.90%	31.70%

STANDARD OF LIVING

INCOME, EMPLOYMENT & TAXES	AREA	U.S. AVG	COST OF LIVING & HOUSING	AREA	U.S. AVG
Median Household Income	$59,203	$44,684	Cost of Living Index	108.3	100
Household Income Growth	3.50%	6.10%	Buying Power Index	122	100
Unemployment Rate	3.50%	5.10%	Median Home Price	$228,400	$208,500
Recent Job Growth	1%	1.30%	Home Price Ratio	3.9	4.7
Projected Future Job Growth	10%	10.50%	Home Price Appreciation	12.30%	13.60%
State Income Tax Rate	0%	5.00%	% Homes Owned	73.60%	64.10%
State Sales Tax Rate	0%	6.00%	Median Rent	$776	$792

EDUCATION

ATTAINMENT & ACHIEVEMENT	AREA	U.S. AVG	RESOURCES & INVESTMENT	AREA	U.S. AVG
% High School Graduate	87.90%	83.90%	No. of Highly Ranked Universities	0	1
% 2-yr Graduate	12.10%	7.10%	$ Invested per Pupil	$7,291	$6,058
% 4-yr Graduate	28.40%	17.20%	Student/Teacher Ratio	15	15.9
% Graduate or Professional Degree	11.90%	9.90%	State University In-State Tuition	$9,226	$4,917
% Attending Public School	83.50%	84.30%			
75th Percentile State University SAT Score (Verbal)	510	477			
75th Percentile State University SAT Score (Math)	520	478			
75th Percentile State University ACT Score	N/A	20			

LIFESTYLE

RECREATION, ARTS & CULTURE	AREA	U.S. AVG	INFRASTRUCTURE & FACILITIES	AREA	U.S. AVG
Professional Sports Rating	8	4	No. of Public Libraries	15	28
Zoos & Aquariums Rating	3	3	Library Volumes Per Capita	3.5	2.8
Amusement Park Rating	5	3	No. of Warehouse Clubs	4	4
Professional Theater Rating	8	3	No. of Starbucks	3	5
Overall Museum Rating	4	6	Golf Course Rating	5	4
Science Museum Rating	3	4	National Park Rating	2	3
Children's Museum Rating	3	3	Sq. Mi. Inland Water	4	4

CLIMATE			COMMUTE & TRANSPORTATION		
Days Mostly Sunny	197	212	Avg. Daily Commute Time	25.5	24.7
Annual Days Precipitation	147	111	% Commute by Auto	82%	77.70%
Annual Days > 90°F	2	38	Per Capita Avg. Daily Transit Miles	1	7.9
Annual Days < 32°F	147	88	Annual Auto Insurance Premium	$1,178	$1,314
July Relative Humidity	68	69	Gas, Cost per Gallon	$3.06	$3.05

HEALTH & SAFETY

CRIME & ENVIRNOMENTAL ISSUES	AREA	U.S. AVG	HEALTHCARE & COST	AREA	U.S. AVG
Violent Crime Rate	127	517	Physicians per Capita	204	254.3
Change in Violent Crime	38.20%	-7.50%	Pediatricians per Capita	21.5	16.9
Property Crime Rate	2028	3783	Hospital Beds per Capita	250.7	239.7
Change in Property Crime	-11.50%	-10.10%	No. of Teaching Hospitals	1	1.9
Air Quality Score	28	44	Healthcare Cost Index	112	100
Water Quality Score	60	33	Cost per Doctor Visit	$82	$74
Pollen/Allergy Score	52	61	Cost per Dentist Visit	$78	$67
Stress Score	31	49	Cost per Hospital Room	$1,013	$702
Cancer Mortality Rate	190.1	168.9			

Newtown, CT

Area Type: Small town

Zip Code: 06470

Metro Area: Danbury, CT

Metro Area Type: Smaller

Location: 12 miles east of Danbury, along SR 6

Time Zone: Eastern Standard Time

Pros:
Small-town flavor and setting
Education
Nearby cities

Cons:
Long commutes
High home prices
High cost of living

If you ever have the chance, visit this picture-postcard place in New England, especially during the fall. The large Congregational church and its towering steeple sit atop the highest point in town, and the nearby Main Street corridor is lined with older homes that have deep frontages, some converted into businesses, and others, like the well-patronized Newtown General Store and Newtown Inn, serving travelers and local diners seemingly since the Colonial days. With few traffic lights, sparse traffic streams by at modest speeds along the many two-lane roads winding through dense woods, old farms, and rolling hills. The Housatonic River cuts a shallow valley east of town, and many more church steeples dot the view from the hilltop bluffs overlooking the river.

Newtown is a favored spot for businesses and professionals looking for close access to city markets and resources. Some medium-sized local businesses are right in town, like publisher Taunton Press and the Curtis Packaging Corporation. Travel 13 miles west (as many do for work), and you arrive at Danbury, a solid mid-size town with an assortment of industry, government, and retail jobs (and by the way, one of the lowest crime rates in the country). It doesn't take long to pass through Danbury; another 40 miles of pastoral country highway later, and you're in White Plains, New York, a major corporate center for the likes of IBM. Continue south another 30 miles and you wind up in Manhattan—all told, about 80 miles and 1½ hours from Newtown. It's too far for a daily commute, but an okay drive once in a while. Major corporate centers on the Long Island sound, as well as in Stamford, are about an hour south.

One of the largest towns in Fairfield County, Newtown is well planned and zoned to preserve its rural character. The ½-acre–plus minimums and large setbacks are a strong antidote to the suburban sprawl seen near so many of today's urban areas. It's a bit off the beaten track, but families are finding it; and the married-with-children percentage is a strong 34.7%.

Standard of Living   Based on the description offered so far, the area might sound completely unaffordable—East Coast, rural setting, close to big cities. True, it is expensive, but it's a good value considering what it has to offer. The Cost of Living Index is 165, but it is within the wider New York area after all. Living costs are offset by high incomes, giving a still-respectable Buying Power Index of 138. The availability of high-paying jobs nearby allows for many one-earner families, and it's a viable area for the self-employed who want to stay close to major markets. Family homes start in the mid $350Ks and range from $450K to $500K and higher for larger executive homes. Recently a 1,750-square-foot farmhouse on a ½ acre with a basement, fireplace, and hardwood floors sold for $422K, while $455K secured a two-story 1930s colonial with a basement on 0.72 acres. Effective property taxes are high at 1.9% with high valuations that bring large tax bills, but reasonable state income and sales taxes partially offset these rates.

Education   Schools are top-notch, with strong college-prep and extracurricular programs. Newtown High School won national Blue Ribbon school recognition, and the elementary and middle schools score on average in the high 90% range, as well as significantly above state averages on most proficiency tests. Teachers are so well paid that residents of nearby towns complain of the Newtown School District "stealing" them. Local educational attainment is at a high 31% for 4-year degrees and 20% for graduate degrees, fortifying the strong educational context.

Lifestyle The rural small-town lifestyle is augmented by numerous outdoor activities in town and in nearby state parks. Lakes Lillioniah and Zoar, the Housatonic River, and the Long Island Sound to the south provide water recreation, as do the local aquatic centers and pools, and excellent skiing lies 2 hours north. The Town Hall theater features near-first-run movies for $2, and the nearby Stew Leonard's is a fun and somewhat quirky grocery and seasonal shopping experience. Danbury, with a major mall, is the place to shop for typical retail items and has some cultural amenities, while the New York area opens up an even bigger world of shopping and activities.

Those who don't work in Newtown or Danbury face potentially challenging commutes: Most cities along the Long Island Sound are an hour away on mainly two-lane roads.

The climate is New England continental, but Newtown is close enough to the water to receive some moderating effects. Summers are hot and humid with occasional thundershowers and cooling breezes. In winter, cold northerly air colliding with moist air from the south produces snow, often while New York is getting rain.

Health & Safety The crime risk in the Danbury area is one of the lowest nationwide, and Newtown is better still. Healthcare facilities in the immediate area aren't extensive, but excellent facilities are found a short drive to the east or south. Newtown is a relaxing place to live, and stress scores—except during commute times—are very low.

Nearby Neighborhoods Other nearby towns like Brookfield are worth a look, and the more-typically suburban communities around Danbury are also possibilities.

NEWTOWN, CT NEIGHBORHOOD HIGHLIGHTS	
PEOPLE	
Population	14,974
15-yr Population Growth	9.10%
5-yr Population Growth	2.30%
% Married w/Children	34.7%
% Single w/Children	4.9%
No. of Households	5,020
Median Age	36.4
Avg. Household Size	2.83
Diversity Measure	17
STANDARD OF LIVING	
Median Household Income	$102,105
% Household Income > $100K	44%
Projected Future Job Growth	4%
Cost of Living Index	165
Buying Power Index	138
Weekly Daycare Cost	$200
Median Home Price	$499,200
"Sweet Spot" Home Price	$475,000
Home Price Ratio	4.9
Median Age of Homes	31.3
% Homes Owned	90%
Effective Property Tax Rate	1.90%
Estimated Property Tax Bill	$9,025
EDUCATION	
% High School Graduates	93%
% 4-yr Degree	31%
% Graduate or Professional Degree	20%
$ Invested per Pupil	$7,539
Student/Teacher Ratio	10.9
Primary Test Score Percentile	119.3
Secondary Test Score Percentile	118.5
% Subsidized School Lunch	17.70%
% Attending Public School	79%
LIFESTYLE	BEST
Leisure Rating (Area)	8
Arts & Culture Rating (Area)	6
Climate Rating (Area)	6
Physical Setting Rating	6
Downtown Core Rating	7
% Commute < 30 Min.	52%
% Commute > 1 Hour	13%
HEALTH & SAFETY	
Health Rating (Area)	3
Stress Score (Area)	1
Violent Crime Risk	20
Property Crime Risk	23

DANBURY, CT
AREA HIGHLIGHTS

PEOPLE

SIZE & DIVERSITY	AREA	U.S. AVG	FAMILY DEMOGRAPHICS	AREA	U.S. AVG
Population	223,646		% Married	60%	53.80%
15-yr Population Growth	9.10%	4.40%	% Single	40%	46.20%
Diversity Measure	38	54	% Divorced	7.50%	10.20%
% Religiously Observant	67%	50%	% Separated	1.60%	2.10%
% Catholic	47%	22%	% Married w/Children	30.70%	27.90%
% Protestant	15%	25%	% Single w/Children	6%	9.40%
% Jewish	4%	2%	% Married, No Children	33.30%	31.00%
% Other	1%	1%	% Single, No Children	30%	31.70%

STANDARD OF LIVING

INCOME, EMPLOYMENT & TAXES	AREA	U.S. AVG	COST OF LIVING & HOUSING	AREA	U.S. AVG
Median Household Income	$71,368	$44,684	Cost of Living Index	113.8	100
Household Income Growth	3.60%	6.10%	Buying Power Index	140	100
Unemployment Rate	3.60%	5.10%	Median Home Price	$203,400	$208,500
Recent Job Growth	1.10%	1.30%	Home Price Ratio	2.9	4.7
Projected Future Job Growth	5.20%	10.50%	Home Price Appreciation	14.20%	13.60%
State Income Tax Rate	4.50%	5.00%	% Homes Owned	73.10%	64.10%
State Sales Tax Rate	6%	6.00%	Median Rent	$916	$792

EDUCATION

ATTAINMENT & ACHIEVEMENT	AREA	U.S. AVG	RESOURCES & INVESTMENT	AREA	U.S. AVG
% High School Graduate	91.10%	83.90%	No. of Highly Ranked Universities	0	1
% 2-yr Graduate	8.50%	7.10%	$ Invested per Pupil	$8,149	$6,058
% 4-yr Graduate	31.20%	17.20%	Student/Teacher Ratio	13.9	15.9
% Graduate or Professional Degree	18.90%	9.90%	State University In-State Tuition	$7,490	$4,917
% Attending Public School	86.40%	84.30%			
75th Percentile State University SAT Score (Verbal)	530	477			
75th Percentile State University SAT Score (Math)	550	478			
75th Percentile State University ACT Score	N/A	20			

LIFESTYLE

RECREATION, ARTS & CULTURE	AREA	U.S. AVG	INFRASTRUCTURE & FACILITIES	AREA	U.S. AVG
Professional Sports Rating	10	4	No. of Public Libraries	13	28
Zoos & Aquariums Rating	4	3	Library Volumes Per Capita	4	2.8
Amusement Park Rating	5	3	No. of Warehouse Clubs	4	4
Professional Theater Rating	8	3	No. of Starbucks	5	5
Overall Museum Rating	5	6	Golf Course Rating	8	4
Science Museum Rating	7	4	National Park Rating	3	3
Children's Museum Rating	3	3	Sq. Mi. Inland Water	6	4

CLIMATE			COMMUTE & TRANSPORTATION		
Days Mostly Sunny	188	212	Avg. Daily Commute Time	25.1	24.7
Annual Days Precipitation	128	111	% Commute by Auto	81%	77.70%
Annual Days > 90°F	20	38	Per Capita Avg. Daily Transit Miles	5.7	7.9
Annual Days < 32°F	137	88	Annual Auto Insurance Premium	$1,580	$1,314
July Relative Humidity	68	69	Gas, Cost per Gallon	$3.10	$3.05

HEALTH & SAFETY

CRIME & ENVIRNOMENTAL ISSUES	AREA	U.S. AVG	HEALTHCARE & COST	AREA	U.S. AVG
Violent Crime Rate	107	517	Physicians per Capita	298.6	254.3
Change in Violent Crime	-14.80%	-7.50%	Pediatricians per Capita	25.9	16.9
Property Crime Rate	1592	3783	Hospital Beds per Capita	180.2	239.7
Change in Property Crime	-24.90%	-10.10%	No. of Teaching Hospitals	1	1.9
Air Quality Score	30	44	Healthcare Cost Index	148.9	100
Water Quality Score	39	33	Cost per Doctor Visit	$78	$74
Pollen/Allergy Score	55	61	Cost per Dentist Visit	$90	$67
Stress Score	7	49	Cost per Hospital Room	$1,248	$702
Cancer Mortality Rate	177.1	168.9			

Noblesville, IN

Area Type: Suburban town

Zip Code: 46060

Metro Area: Indianapolis, IN

Metro Area Type: Mid-size

Location: 25 miles north of downtown Indianapolis on SR 37

Time Zone: Eastern Standard Time

BEST OF THE BEST

Pros:
Small-town flavor
Job-growth prospects
Attractive homes

Cons:
Growth and sprawl nearby
Recent job declines
Winter climate

With its classic Midwest downtown, courthouse square, wrought-iron decor, period lamps, French Second Empire clock tower, cobblestone streets, and period ice-cream parlor, Noblesville, Indiana, could come from a Norman Rockwell painting. Indeed, so close to Indianapolis, the best-of-both-worlds Noblesville offers a lot for families—and with over 33% of the population married with children, many have apparently accepted the offer.

Noblesville's classic lines blend well with the rising star of Indianapolis. "Indy" is the most vibrant and big-time of the large Midwest capitals, a set including Columbus, Lansing, Springfield, and Des Moines. Years of well-planned downtown renewal driven by the combined city-county "Unigov" structure, along with an attractive business climate and strong professional sports (NBA Pacers, NFL Colts, Indianapolis 500), have brought this once plain, quiet, and somewhat rundown area well forward from its old regional nickname of "India-noplace."

Today's Indy has a strong, diverse job base with some recent sluggishness as old-economy industries like autos and auto parts retrench. The area has made a transition from manufacturing to a knowledge-based economy. Pharmaceutical giant Eli Lilly is the largest private employer. A broad high-tech industry base specializes in industrial automation and software. Two major book publishing houses weigh in to complete the picture. Job growth is projected at a very robust 29%. Indy has evolved into a cultural center, with well-acclaimed museums, static arts, performing arts, symphony, and a first-class children's museum. The downtown is clean, lively, and walkable with excellent sports venues and higher educational facilities.

Indy's major growth is to the north and northwest, and Noblesville is at the end of the northward push. Other more well-known suburbs include Carmel and Fishers. But it's Noblesville that retains a true small-town feeling, and "people are more friendly and genuine here than in Texas," according to one Texas transplant. About 50% of residents commute to Indy. There is substantial local industry with small to medium-sized manufacturers of rubber, plastics, and other industrial goods, mostly located in a 3,600-acre industrial park. Firestone Industrial Products is a big area employer. The downtown is classic and well-preserved with good planning. Retail sprawl is kept to the SR 37 corridor east of town, but locals are still concerned about growth pressure. Altogether, though, strong incomes, low costs, and local amenities make Noblesville an ideal place for families.

Standard of Living   Standard of living indicators are strong: Median household incomes of $62K and a low cost of living (COL Index 98) produce a Buying Power Index of 143. Home prices—and values—are excellent, and the Home Price Ratio is a favorable 2.8. The "sweet spot" for family homes (many with basements) is $180K to $220K, around $75 per square foot, many with basements. A building boom in the late '70s/early '80s saw the growth of larger homes on ½-acre wooded lots to the northwest; another boom in 1999–2000 brought smaller lots with fewer trees and more modern homes to the northeast and south. A 5-year-old, 2,800-square-foot two-story contemporary on ⅓ of an acre in a newer subdivision goes for $176K. There are also many attractive older homes near the town center. Property tax rates work out to just below 2%, a high rate, but low valuations make for low tax bills.

Education   Four-year degree attainment is 27% with another 11% claiming post-graduate degrees. Within an hour's drive are four strong colleges and universities: Indiana University, Purdue University, IUPUI (Indiana and Purdue's joint campus in Indy), and Butler

NOBLESVILLE, IN NEIGHBORHOOD HIGHLIGHTS	
PEOPLE	
Population	55,079
15-yr Population Growth	112.70%
5-yr Population Growth	26.80%
% Married w/Children	33.4%
% Single w/Children	8.8%
No. of Households	19,869
Median Age	33.8
Avg. Household Size	2.69
Diversity Measure	7
STANDARD OF LIVING	
Median Household Income	$62,555
% Household Income > $100K	20%
Projected Future Job Growth	29%
Cost of Living Index	97.7
Buying Power Index	143
Weekly Daycare Cost	$170
Median Home Price	$176,800
"Sweet Spot" Home Price	$200,000
Home Price Ratio	2.8
Median Age of Homes	18
% Homes Owned	74%
Effective Property Tax Rate	2%
Estimated Property Tax Bill	$4,000
EDUCATION	
% High School Graduates	90%
% 4-yr Degree	27%
% Graduate or Professional Degree	11%
$ Invested per Pupil	$5,237
Student/Teacher Ratio	18.4
Primary Test Score Percentile	126.1
Secondary Test Score Percentile	122.9
% Subsidized School Lunch	21.10%
% Attending Public School	85.80%
LIFESTYLE	
Leisure Rating (Area)	8
Arts & Culture Rating (Area)	9
Climate Rating (Area)	5
Physical Setting Rating	2
Downtown Core Rating	8
% Commute < 30 Min.	53%
% Commute > 1 Hour	5%
HEALTH & SAFETY	
Health Rating (Area)	1
Stress Score (Area)	8
Violent Crime Risk	29
Property Crime Risk	57

University. Primary and secondary test scores run 20% above state averages. Schools carry a full curriculum of arts, music, and physical education. The "Focus" program is available for gifted children starting in 3rd grade.

Lifestyle Diversions abound both in town and in Indianapolis. Noblesville Parks & Recreation markets itself as "Your Vacation in Town" for good reason. Its flagship Forest Park on 150 acres has golf, miniature golf, and a resort-like water park with three pools and waterslides. The Indiana Transportation Museum originates train excursions from the park. The city hosts activities year-round and summer day camps for $30 to $45 per week. The Verizon Wireless Music Center is an outdoor pavilion bringing in Jimmy Buffett and other similar acts. The all-volunteer Noblesville Cultural Arts Commission sponsors local plays, music, and a Shakespeare Festival. Connor Prairie is a large living-history museum just south in Fishers. It's hard to live in Indiana without getting involved with basketball, mainly at the large indoor-outdoor basketball center. Families play together at the many nearby lakes, small parks, and Brown County State Park, 70 miles south. When Indy isn't enough, Chicago is 3 hours away.

Commutes from Noblesville aren't a big issue: Downtown Indy is only 30 minutes away. Locals are a bit edgy about their future, and downtown Noblesville *is* occasionally crowded—bad if you're trying to park, but actually a good sign of a prosperous city overall.

The immediate area is mainly flat farmland with some woods. The climate is continental with four distinct seasons and a Great Lakes influence. Extreme heat is rare, and some summer and winter storms can be intense.

Health & Safety Crime is not an issue. There is a hospital in town and another in Carmel, and downtown Indianapolis is well supplied with medical facilities, including the Indiana University Medical School.

Nearby Neighborhoods Friendly inter-neighborhood competition between Carmel, Fishers, and Noblesville breeds the notion that the more upscale Carmel is for "yuppies," while Fishers is for "DINKs" (double income no kids), and Noblesville is for families. Those considering the area should probably check out all three, as well as spots along I-65 northwest of Indy.

INDIANAPOLIS, IN
AREA HIGHLIGHTS

PEOPLE

SIZE & DIVERSITY	AREA	U.S. AVG	FAMILY DEMOGRAPHICS	AREA	U.S. AVG
Population	1,700,201		% Married	58.40%	53.80%
15-yr Population Growth	30.80%	4.40%	% Single	41.60%	46.20%
Diversity Measure	32	54	% Divorced	10%	10.20%
% Religiously Observant	41%	50%	% Separated	2%	2.10%
% Catholic	12%	22%	% Married w/Children	30%	27.90%
% Protestant	28%	25%	% Single w/Children	10%	9.40%
% Jewish	1%	2%	% Married, No Children	30.60%	31.00%
% Other	0%	1%	% Single, No Children	29.30%	31.70%

STANDARD OF LIVING

INCOME, EMPLOYMENT & TAXES	AREA	U.S. AVG	COST OF LIVING & HOUSING	AREA	U.S. AVG
Median Household Income	$48,830	$44,684	Cost of Living Index	83.4	100
Household Income Growth	4.80%	6.10%	Buying Power Index	131	100
Unemployment Rate	4.80%	5.10%	Median Home Price	$124,600	$208,500
Recent Job Growth	-1.70%	1.30%	Home Price Ratio	2.6	4.7
Projected Future Job Growth	14.20%	10.50%	Home Price Appreciation	3.40%	13.60%
State Income Tax Rate	4.10%	5.00%	% Homes Owned	69.90%	64.10%
State Sales Tax Rate	5%	6.00%	Median Rent	$655	$792

EDUCATION

ATTAINMENT & ACHIEVEMENT	AREA	U.S. AVG	RESOURCES & INVESTMENT	AREA	U.S. AVG
% High School Graduate	82.10%	83.90%	No. of Highly Ranked Universities	1	1
% 2-yr Graduate	7.50%	7.10%	$ Invested per Pupil	$6,249	$6,058
% 4-yr Graduate	15.80%	17.20%	Student/Teacher Ratio	18	15.9
% Graduate or Professional Degree	8.70%	9.90%	State University In-State Tuition	$6,777	$4,917
% Attending Public School	87.40%	84.30%			
75th Percentile State University SAT Score (Verbal)	490	477			
75th Percentile State University SAT Score (Math)	500	478			
75th Percentile State University ACT Score	22	20			

LIFESTYLE

RECREATION, ARTS & CULTURE	AREA	U.S. AVG	INFRASTRUCTURE & FACILITIES	AREA	U.S. AVG
Professional Sports Rating	7	4	No. of Public Libraries	69	28
Zoos & Aquariums Rating	7	3	Library Volumes Per Capita	3.5	2.8
Amusement Park Rating	1	3	No. of Warehouse Clubs	6	4
Professional Theater Rating	8	3	No. of Starbucks	48	5
Overall Museum Rating	9	6	Golf Course Rating	7	4
Science Museum Rating	8	4	National Park Rating	1	3
Children's Museum Rating	10	3	Sq. Mi. Inland Water	2	4

CLIMATE			COMMUTE & TRANSPORTATION		
Days Mostly Sunny	191	212	Avg. Daily Commute Time	23.9	24.7
Annual Days Precipitation	122	111	% Commute by Auto	80%	77.70%
Annual Days > 90°F	15	38	Per Capita Avg. Daily Transit Miles	6.3	7.9
Annual Days < 32°F	122	88	Annual Auto Insurance Premium	$1,132	$1,314
July Relative Humidity	73	69	Gas, Cost per Gallon	$3.00	$3.05

HEALTH & SAFETY

CRIME & ENVIRNOMENTAL ISSUES	AREA	U.S. AVG	HEALTHCARE & COST	AREA	U.S. AVG
Violent Crime Rate	548	517	Physicians per Capita	319	254.3
Change in Violent Crime	-20.90%	-7.50%	Pediatricians per Capita	22.3	16.9
Property Crime Rate	3938	3783	Hospital Beds per Capita	374.5	239.7
Change in Property Crime	-1.40%	-10.10%	No. of Teaching Hospitals	9	1.9
Air Quality Score	37	44	Healthcare Cost Index	98.7	100
Water Quality Score	15	33	Cost per Doctor Visit	$76	$74
Pollen/Allergy Score	73	61	Cost per Dentist Visit	$62	$67
Stress Score	75	49	Cost per Hospital Room	$625	$702
Cancer Mortality Rate	178.2	168.9			

North Attleboro, MA

Area Type: Outer suburb/suburban town

Zip Code: 02760

Metro Area: Providence, RI

Metro Area Type: Large

Location: 15 miles northeast of downtown Providence

Time Zone: Eastern Standard Time

Pros:
Central location
Attractive homes
Local sports and recreation

Cons:
Low job growth
Housing costs
Long commutes

Football, baseball, and basketball dominate most conversations in North Attleboro. Baseball diamonds are filled every day and evening during the summer. Fall weekends are all about the NFL's New England Patriots in nearby Foxboro and local "Big Red" high-school football games against rival Attleboro and others. This sports-minded mecca is a perfect family place, and, to that end, approximately 28% of households are married with children.

North Attleboro, with its mix of residential housing built up around a small town, is nested strategically between the major economic and cultural centers of Boston and Providence. The town is just 40 miles southwest of downtown Boston, still accessible by rail. Jobs in the south and west sides of Boston are also within reach.

Boston may be a bit far for an evening expedition, but its amenities are available and convenient for family weekend outings. (For more information on Boston's numerous amenities and resources, see the discussion of Sharon, Massachusetts, on p. 349.) The south side of Boston has experienced more economic challenges than the area as a whole, but it is also going through more revitalization, particularly near the South Shore and areas near Brockton. Providence has endured many years of economic malaise, but holds some promise as more businesses acknowledge its strategic location between New York and Boston.

Some North Attleboro residents look south to Providence and the rest of Rhode Island for employment and amenities. While high on a national scale, Massachusetts taxes and cost of living are generally lower than in Rhode Island. Though overshadowed by Boston, Providence has a revitalized downtown and a number of first-class amenities all its own, including numerous activities on the Narragansett Bay and in Newport, Rhode Island, to the south.

Standard of Living North Attleboro offers a good balance between cost and lifestyle. The area is less expensive than many other family neighborhoods closer to the city. Family homes run in the low $400K range and in the low $200s per square foot, quite affordable for the larger metro area. Homes are mostly New England colonials with an assortment of older homes, ranch style, and contemporaries. There are many $700K to $1M homes in the area, and several New England Patriots players even live nearby. Lot sizes tend to be a 1/3 to a 1/2 acre. Undeveloped spaces with abundant trees and several lakes make the area feel uncrowded. The local Cost of Living Index is 134, modest for the region. Median household incomes are also lower than in many other Boston suburbs, likely reflecting the presence of younger, single-earner families and some working-class families.

Future job growth, reflecting increased business south of Boston, is 6%, a bit higher than the 5% projected for the Boston area as a whole; but recent job trends are less than stellar. Most workers commute to the north. North Attleboro does not have a strong property tax base, but, at $9.29 per $1,000 (0.9%), the rates are quite reasonable. As in most of the Boston area, parents can expect to pay about $200 per week ($800 to $900 per month) for daycare.

Education North Attleboro is very proud of its schools. The North Attleboro School District features seven right-sized elementary schools, a middle school, and a high school. North Attleboro High has 1,140 students. MCAS test scores range 5% to 20% higher than state averages. Sports programs are big, and parents are noticeably involved in volunteering and fundraising activities. Over 22% of local residents possess a 4-year degree, and 88% are high-school graduates.

Lifestyle Typical family activities, including sports outings and weekends at the shore, are common for North Attleboro residents. The historic downtown is vibrant and popular. The relatively new Emerald Square Mall provides convenient shopping about 3 miles south at I-295. Recreational fields can be found in the many parks. The World War I Veterans Memorial Park just outside of town offers hiking and rock climbing. Small lakes provide jet-skiing, small boat launches, and ice-skating.

Most North Attleboro residents commute to the abundant industrial centers around Marlboro, Foxboro, and Franklin to the north or to the southern portions of the I-95/Route 128 commercial centers. There is a newer industrial park in North Attleboro. The commute to downtown Boston is long but you can take a train from the Attleboro station. Only 78% of metro-area commuters travel by auto.

North Attleboro is mainly flat and wooded. The climate is varied and somewhat moderated by water to the south and east. Measurable precipitation occurs about 1 day in 3, and occasional noreasters approach from the south.

Health & Safety Crime risk is notably low. Nearby healthcare facilities are abundant, though expensive.

Nearby Neighborhoods Other neighborhoods in the area include Franklin, Massachusetts, and the many smaller neighborhoods north of Providence. Cumberland Hill, Rhode Island, just to the west, is slightly cheaper but farther from jobs and job growth.

NORTH ATTLEBORO, MA NEIGHBORHOOD HIGHLIGHTS	
PEOPLE	
Population	25,503
15-yr Population Growth	8.30%
5-yr Population Growth	2.50%
% Married w/Children	28.4%
% Single w/Children	9.4%
No. of Households	9,913
Median Age	35.1
Avg. Household Size	2.57
Diversity Measure	9
STANDARD OF LIVING	
Median Household Income	$67,084
% Household Income > $100K	18%
Projected Future Job Growth	6%
Cost of Living Index	134
Buying Power Index	116
Weekly Daycare Cost	$198
Median Home Price	$413,700
"Sweet Spot" Home Price	$400,000
Home Price Ratio	6.2
Median Age of Homes	30.5
% Homes Owned	65%
Effective Property Tax Rate	0.90%
Estimated Property Tax Bill	$3,720
EDUCATION	
% High School Graduates	88%
% 4-yr Degree	22%
% Graduate or Professional Degree	10%
$ Invested per Pupil	$4,853
Student/Teacher Ratio	14.2
Primary Test Score Percentile	111.6
Secondary Test Score Percentile	97.1
% Subsidized School Lunch	8%
% Attending Public School	79.80%
LIFESTYLE	
Leisure Rating (Area)	9
Arts & Culture Rating (Area)	8
Climate Rating (Area)	3
Physical Setting Rating	3
Downtown Core Rating	5
% Commute < 30 Min.	60%
% Commute > 1 Hour	12%
HEALTH & SAFETY	
Health Rating (Area)	2
Stress Score (Area)	4
Violent Crime Risk	38
Property Crime Risk	54

PROVIDENCE, RI
AREA HIGHLIGHTS

PEOPLE

SIZE & DIVERSITY	AREA	U.S. AVG	FAMILY DEMOGRAPHICS	AREA	U.S. AVG
Population	1,223,610		% Married	53%	53.80%
15-yr Population Growth	8%	4.40%	% Single	47%	46.20%
Diversity Measure	27	54	% Divorced	7.30%	10.20%
% Religiously Observant	63%	50%	% Separated	2.30%	2.10%
% Catholic	52%	22%	% Married w/Children	27%	27.90%
% Protestant	9%	25%	% Single w/Children	8.70%	9.40%
% Jewish	2%	2%	% Married, No Children	30.20%	31.00%
% Other	0%	1%	% Single, No Children	34.20%	31.70%

STANDARD OF LIVING

INCOME, EMPLOYMENT & TAXES	AREA	U.S. AVG	COST OF LIVING & HOUSING	AREA	U.S. AVG
Median Household Income	$50,205	$44,684	Cost of Living Index	105.4	100
Household Income Growth	4.30%	6.10%	Buying Power Index	107	100
Unemployment Rate	4.30%	5.10%	Median Home Price	$291,600	$208,500
Recent Job Growth	-0.30%	1.30%	Home Price Ratio	5.8	4.7
Projected Future Job Growth	3%	10.50%	Home Price Appreciation	15.60%	13.60%
State Income Tax Rate	7.40%	5.00%	% Homes Owned	63.10%	64.10%
State Sales Tax Rate	6.90%	6.00%	Median Rent	$788	$792

EDUCATION

ATTAINMENT & ACHIEVEMENT	AREA	U.S. AVG	RESOURCES & INVESTMENT	AREA	U.S. AVG
% High School Graduate	78.40%	83.90%	No. of Highly Ranked Universities	1	1
% 2-yr Graduate	9%	7.10%	$ Invested per Pupil	$7,469	$6,058
% 4-yr Graduate	20.50%	17.20%	Student/Teacher Ratio	12.6	15.9
% Graduate or Professional Degree	11.10%	9.90%	State University In-State Tuition	$9,186	$4,917
% Attending Public School	83.60%	84.30%			
75th Percentile State University SAT Score (Verbal)	510	477			
75th Percentile State University SAT Score (Math)	520	478			
75th Percentile State University ACT Score	21	20			

LIFESTYLE

RECREATION, ARTS & CULTURE	AREA	U.S. AVG	INFRASTRUCTURE & FACILITIES	AREA	U.S. AVG
Professional Sports Rating	5	4	No. of Public Libraries	80	28
Zoos & Aquariums Rating	6	3	Library Volumes Per Capita	3.3	2.8
Amusement Park Rating	3	3	No. of Warehouse Clubs	4	4
Professional Theater Rating	10	3	No. of Starbucks	12	5
Overall Museum Rating	10	6	Golf Course Rating	5	4
Science Museum Rating	7	4	National Park Rating	1	3
Children's Museum Rating	5	3	Sq. Mi. Inland Water	7	4

CLIMATE			COMMUTE & TRANSPORTATION		
Days Mostly Sunny	205	212	Avg. Daily Commute Time	22.6	24.7
Annual Days Precipitation	134	111	% Commute by Auto	78%	77.70%
Annual Days > 90°F	8	38	Per Capita Avg. Daily Transit Miles	12.2	7.9
Annual Days < 32°F	123	88	Annual Auto Insurance Premium	$1,577	$1,314
July Relative Humidity	68	69	Gas, Cost per Gallon	$3.22	$3.05

HEALTH & SAFETY

CRIME & ENVIRNOMENTAL ISSUES	AREA	U.S. AVG	HEALTHCARE & COST	AREA	U.S. AVG
Violent Crime Rate	362	517	Physicians per Capita	262.9	254.3
Change in Violent Crime	15.90%	-7.50%	Pediatricians per Capita	21.1	16.9
Property Crime Rate	2854	3783	Hospital Beds per Capita	352.9	239.7
Change in Property Crime	-12.20%	-10.10%	No. of Teaching Hospitals	9	1.9
Air Quality Score	40	44	Healthcare Cost Index	135	100
Water Quality Score	50	33	Cost per Doctor Visit	$100	$74
Pollen/Allergy Score	61	61	Cost per Dentist Visit	$76	$67
Stress Score	38	49	Cost per Hospital Room	$1,023	$702
Cancer Mortality Rate	188	168.9			

Norwood, NJ

Area Type: Suburban town

Zip Code: 07648

Metro Area: Bergen/Passaic Metropolitan Division, New York Metro Area

Metro Area Type: Largest

Location: 23 miles northwest of midtown Manhattan

Time Zone: Eastern Standard Time

Pros:
Attractive housing
Schools
Convenient to New York City

Cons:
High home prices
Low future job growth
Long commutes

"It feels like the country, but you're only 15 miles from Manhattan." Such is the motto of north Bergen County residents living to the west of the Palisades Parkway. The area is striking—woods, lakes, open spaces, stately homes on large lots—all about 15 minutes from the George Washington (GW) bridge to New York City.

Norwood is in the center of a cluster of small northern Bergen County towns, including Harrington Park, Demarest, Closter, Old Tappan, and, a little farther south, Bergenfield, Teaneck, and Paramus. Norwood is about 2 miles south of New York's Rockland County and about 2 miles west of the Hudson River and the Palisades Parkway. A family-oriented place, over 33% of households are married with children. A downtown strip along Livingston Street has a good balance of commercial and consumer businesses. Except for occasionally heavy traffic on the main drag, the town is fairly quiet. But it all comes at a price: Norwood is the most expensive place included in *Best Places to Raise Your Family* with a Cost of Living Index of 191.

Most family needs, including employment, can be met a few miles south in Paramus if not closer. The Palisades Parkway and GW bridge make Manhattan uniquely accessible from north Bergen County, especially at non–rush hour times. It really is possible—with minimal stress and time—to go into the city for dinner or a show. Weekend jaunts up the Hudson or across the river on the Tappan Zee Bridge are usually easy and relatively traffic free.

Standard of Living Good places in major metro areas are expensive, and this is one of the best places in one of the most sought-after metro areas. Home prices and taxes figure heavily into the high cost of living. Good family homes cost $600K to $650K, although adequate smaller, pre-1920 homes can be had for $550K. Homes are generally built well on sizable lots. Property taxes are 1.6%, but a small assortment of local businesses the likes of which aren't found in many of the surrounding communities contribute to the tax base and keep rates a bit lower. In an area of million-dollar homes (and even higher in Upper Saddle River and other places to the west), Norwood provides good value despite the large price tag.

Education Schools are one of the area's strengths. The local Norwood Boro School has 569 students in grades K–8 and posts excellent test scores, as much as 29% above state averages. The school emphasizes arts, foreign languages, and other specialty studies above and beyond state curriculum requirements. The following appears in the Norwood School curriculum statement: "Music and art have increased in their importance. Think of it, ancient civilizations are best remembered by their great works of visual art, architecture, music, drama, literature, poetry, etc. Today, we dignify the arts with a comprehensive approach that includes production, history, aesthetic criticism, technical, and stylistic elements." Need we say more?

Lifestyle Norwood and nearby boroughs are fairly quiet, but there's plenty of action to the south. Borough centers have a number of restaurants and cafes that serve as local hangouts. Amenities are available at the Paramus Mall, and the New Jersey Children's Museum, also in Paramus, is a fine facility targeted to kids 8 and under. For older children who are curious about industrial history and technology, the Paterson Industrial Museum, located in an old locomotive factory, is a good bet.

The commute to Manhattan is a consideration. It takes about 15 minutes to make it to the GW, but traffic down the Henry Hudson/West Side Parkway can be slow; 30 to 40 minutes should be allowed by car (park-

NORWOOD, NJ	
NEIGHBORHOOD HIGHLIGHTS	
PEOPLE	
Population	5,885
15-yr Population Growth	9.40%
5-yr Population Growth	2.10%
% Married w/Children	33.2%
% Single w/Children	5.6%
No. of Households	1,885
Median Age	39.2
Avg. Household Size	2.99
Diversity Measure	36
STANDARD OF LIVING	
Median Household Income	$100,881
% Household Income > $100K	47%
Projected Future Job Growth	5%
Cost of Living Index	191
Buying Power Index	116
Weekly Daycare Cost	$265
Median Home Price	$631,000
"Sweet Spot" Home Price	$625,000
Home Price Ratio	6.3
Median Age of Homes	33.3
% Homes Owned	82%
Effective Property Tax Rate	1.60%
Estimated Property Tax Bill	$10,000
EDUCATION	
% High School Graduates	91%
% 4-yr Degree	29%
% Graduate or Professional Degree	14%
$ Invested per Pupil	$8,456
Student/Teacher Ratio	13.8
Primary Test Score Percentile	111.1
Secondary Test Score Percentile	115
% Subsidized School Lunch	1%
% Attending Public School	75.40%
LIFESTYLE	
Leisure Rating (Area)	10
Arts & Culture Rating (Area)	7
Climate Rating (Area)	5
Physical Setting Rating	5
Downtown Core Rating	6
% Commute < 30 Min.	43%
% Commute > 1 Hour	15%
HEALTH & SAFETY	
Health Rating (Area)	3
Stress Score (Area)	1
Violent Crime Risk	39
Property Crime Risk	49

ing costs should be considered, too.) Many commuters drive a few miles to Westwood or Oradell Park to connect with the New Jersey Transit rail system, a 40-minute commute, which still isn't bad for the region. About 50% of workers are estimated to travel to Manhattan, 5% work at home, and most of the rest head farther south in New Jersey.

The area is mostly flat and wooded with small lakes and streams and some open space. Weather is typical for the East Coast, with warm, muggy summers and cool, wet, variable winters. The nearby ocean does moderate temperatures.

Health & Safety Crime risk is low and healthcare resources are adequate but predictably expensive. The somewhat rural lifestyle results in low stress scores for the region.

Nearby Neighborhoods The small boroughs nearby offer much of the same experience as Norwood, though prices and taxes may be somewhat higher. Paramus to the south is busier and more crowded, but homes may be $50K to $100K cheaper.

BERGEN-PASSAIC METROPOLITAN DIVISION, NEW YORK METRO AREA
AREA HIGHLIGHTS

PEOPLE

SIZE & DIVERSITY	AREA	U.S. AVG	FAMILY DEMOGRAPHICS	AREA	U.S. AVG
Population	1,403,425		% Married	55%	53.80%
15-yr Population Growth	8.30%	4.40%	% Single	45%	46.20%
Diversity Measure	52	54	% Divorced	5.90%	10.20%
% Religiously Observant	66%	50%	% Separated	3%	2.10%
% Catholic	46%	22%	% Married w/Children	26.70%	27.90%
% Protestant	10%	25%	% Single w/Children	7.40%	9.40%
% Jewish	7%	2%	% Married, No Children	33.10%	31.00%
% Other	2%	1%	% Single, No Children	32.80%	31.70%

STANDARD OF LIVING

INCOME, EMPLOYMENT & TAXES	AREA	U.S. AVG	COST OF LIVING & HOUSING	AREA	U.S. AVG
Median Household Income	$63,392	$44,684	Cost of Living Index	144.3	100
Household Income Growth	4%	6.10%	Buying Power Index	98	100
Unemployment Rate	4%	5.10%	Median Home Price	$407,400	$208,500
Recent Job Growth	1.90%	1.30%	Home Price Ratio	6.4	4.7
Projected Future Job Growth	4.90%	10.50%	Home Price Appreciation	15.60%	13.60%
State Income Tax Rate	2.50%	5.00%	% Homes Owned	67%	64.10%
State Sales Tax Rate	6%	6.00%	Median Rent	$1,132	$792

EDUCATION

ATTAINMENT & ACHIEVEMENT	AREA	U.S. AVG	RESOURCES & INVESTMENT	AREA	U.S. AVG
% High School Graduate	82.90%	83.90%	No. of Highly Ranked Universities	1	1
% 2-yr Graduate	6.70%	7.10%	$ Invested per Pupil	$10,178	$6,058
% 4-yr Graduate	24.90%	17.20%	Student/Teacher Ratio	14.5	15.9
% Graduate or Professional Degree	12.60%	9.90%	State University In-State Tuition	$8,564	$4,917
% Attending Public School	79.50%	84.30%			
75th Percentile State University SAT Score (Verbal)	530	477			
75th Percentile State University SAT Score (Math)	550	478			
75th Percentile State University ACT Score	N/A	20			

LIFESTYLE

RECREATION, ARTS & CULTURE	AREA	U.S. AVG	INFRASTRUCTURE & FACILITIES	AREA	U.S. AVG
Professional Sports Rating	10	4	No. of Public Libraries	84	28
Zoos & Aquariums Rating	7	3	Library Volumes Per Capita	4.2	2.8
Amusement Park Rating	5	3	No. of Warehouse Clubs	6	4
Professional Theater Rating	8	3	No. of Starbucks	22	5
Overall Museum Rating	8	6	Golf Course Rating	9	4
Science Museum Rating	7	4	National Park Rating	3	3
Children's Museum Rating	9	3	Sq. Mi. Inland Water	6	4

CLIMATE			COMMUTE & TRANSPORTATION		
Days Mostly Sunny	207	212	Avg. Daily Commute Time	28.6	24.7
Annual Days Precipitation	129	111	% Commute by Auto	73%	77.70%
Annual Days > 90°F	20	38	Per Capita Avg. Daily Transit Miles	24.9	7.9
Annual Days < 32°F	87	88	Annual Auto Insurance Premium	$1,907	$1,314
July Relative Humidity	65	69	Gas, Cost per Gallon	$3.15	$3.05

HEALTH & SAFETY

CRIME & ENVIRNOMENTAL ISSUES	AREA	U.S. AVG	HEALTHCARE & COST	AREA	U.S. AVG
Violent Crime Rate	243	517	Physicians per Capita	371.8	254.3
Change in Violent Crime	-6.50%	-7.50%	Pediatricians per Capita	38.5	16.9
Property Crime Rate	2057	3783	Hospital Beds per Capita	381.2	239.7
Change in Property Crime	-16.70%	-10.10%	No. of Teaching Hospitals	4	1.9
Air Quality Score	24	44	Healthcare Cost Index	144.6	100
Water Quality Score	34	33	Cost per Doctor Visit	$66	$74
Pollen/Allergy Score	62	61	Cost per Dentist Visit	$80	$67
Stress Score	13	49	Cost per Hospital Room	$3,408	$702
Cancer Mortality Rate	188.5	168.9			

Oak Park, IL

Area Type: City neighborhood

Zip Code: 60302

Metro Area: Chicago, IL

Metro Area Type: Largest

Location: 11 miles due west of downtown Chicago

Time Zone: Central Standard Time

Pros:
Attractive downtown
Historic and architectural interest
Diversity

Cons:
Cost of living
High property taxes
Some crime issues

Frank Lloyd Wright had it right when he eschewed the fast-paced, rapidly growing Chicago cityscape in the mid-1880s in favor of the utopian and then mostly rural Oak Park. He started a family a few years later in the studio and home he built on the corner of Forest and Chicago Avenues in the expanding community.

When Wright arrived, Oak Park's downtown was already established and centered around the railroad and new commuter rail system now known as the "El." Oak Park is near the west end of the Green Line, which shuttles commuters to the "Loop" (downtown Chicago). The downtown itself is classic, with attractive storefronts, eateries, a major library, and the world-famous Unity Temple on Lake Street, giving way to more modern retail establishments in River Forest just west. The town surrounds the 4-acre Scoville Park, site of numerous festivals and weekend events through the summer. A perfect grid of dignified tree-lined streets moves north from downtown; notable Wright master-pieces are interspersed with the many older Victorian "painted lady" beauties. Past Chicago Avenue, the more moderately priced suburban homes and parks are well suited for family life.

The population is diverse, with older residents, young families, touring Wright aficionados, and many ethnic and religious groups working cohesively to better the community through its schools, service clubs, and organizations. The town boasts more than 300 neighborhood block parties each year. Predictably high living costs aside, it is a near-perfect place for those families seeking a city lifestyle.

Standard of Living The attractive historic homes, strong community and schools, and proximity to Chicago all account for the COL Index of 125. The number of landmark historic homes drives the median home price upward, but a close look reveals good older family homes in the mid $400K to lower $500K range, especially moving a few blocks north of the historic center. Homes are as interesting and diverse as the population, and one might discover great potential in a promising fixer-upper. The local commercial and industrial tax base is low, and community-proud residents have voted in park levies and other enhancements. As a result, effective local tax rates are a high 3%, and with relatively high property valuations, total tax bills are among the largest we found. Many jobs are based in downtown Chicago and in some of the inner suburbs to the north and south; but the employment base is mature, and projected job growth is low. Median household incomes are also low, likely reflecting a number of retirees and economically disadvantaged persons in the area. That said, high-paying professional jobs are easy to find for those who qualify.

Education A strong educational context is indeed present in the area that was the birthplace of Ernest Hemingway and was home to many of Chicago's early-20th-century elite. About 32% of Oak Park residents have a 4-year degree and fully another 31% have graduate-level degrees—one of the highest combined attainment figures anywhere outside of college towns. Despite a large percentage of economically disadvantaged students, Oak Park–River Forest High School scores above state averages.

Lifestyle Leisure means playing sports in one of the more than 20 local parks, or hanging out in a bakery or cafe downtown, at the library, or at the Ridgeland Common pool, park, and ice rink just east of downtown. Most of Chicago's main attractions are accessible by El or other forms of public transport, and Oak Park is one of those places where a family car can sit in the garage for days at a time.

Most commuters take the El downtown; it's about a 15-minute ride, with ample bus connections at both ends. Because Oak Park is inside both beltways, most suburban commutes are against major traffic flows, and the well-designed grid streets offer plenty of alternate routes.

Oak Park is generally flat and heavily wooded with mature trees planted along roadways and in yards. The climate is continental, with four distinct highly variable seasons, humid summers, cold winters with occasionally heavy snow and bitter cold snaps, and a moderating lake influence at times.

Health & Safety   Crime risk in Oak Park is higher than in other areas we have selected, and there are some rougher inner-city neighborhoods not far away; still, locals do not seem troubled by it. Healthcare facilities in Oak Park and the Chicago area are excellent.

Nearby Neighborhoods   Oak Park has a truly unique history and profile; few of its neighbors have Oak Park's charm and value. Riverside to the south, designed by Frederick Law Olmstead of New York Central Park fame, is another architectural and historic gem. Attractive older communities exist to the north of Chicago toward Evanston, but affordable single-family units are hard to find. Farther out, the lifestyle changes considerably to a more typical modern suburban setup. Families should look at Elk Grove Village and places north and west—see Lake Zurich, Illinois (p. 253).

OAK PARK, IL NEIGHBORHOOD HIGHLIGHTS	
PEOPLE	
Population	32,157
15-yr Population Growth	4.40%
5-yr Population Growth	-0.90%
% Married w/Children	19.3%
% Single w/Children	10.4%
No. of Households	14,719
Median Age	37.2
Avg. Household Size	2.17
Diversity Measure	47
STANDARD OF LIVING	
Median Household Income	$60,774
% Household Income > $100K	27%
Projected Future Job Growth	0%
Cost of Living Index	125.3
Buying Power Index	109
Weekly Daycare Cost	$155
Median Home Price	$322,000
"Sweet Spot" Home Price	$500,000
Home Price Ratio	5.3
Median Age of Homes	57
% Homes Owned	51%
Effective Property Tax Rate	3%
Estimated Property Tax Bill	$15,000
EDUCATION	
% High School Graduates	95%
% 4-yr Degree	32%
% Graduate or Professional Degree	31%
$ Invested per Pupil	$7,037
Student/Teacher Ratio	14.9
Primary Test Score Percentile	76.8
Secondary Test Score Percentile	63.8
% Subsidized School Lunch	15.20%
% Attending Public School	70.70%
LIFESTYLE	BEST
Leisure Rating (Area)	10
Arts & Culture Rating (Area)	10
Climate Rating (Area)	3
Physical Setting Rating	3
Downtown Core Rating	8
% Commute < 30 Min.	39%
% Commute > 1 Hour	8%
HEALTH & SAFETY	
Health Rating (Area)	1
Stress Score (Area)	8
Violent Crime Risk	531
Property Crime Risk	143

CHICAGO, IL
AREA HIGHLIGHTS

PEOPLE

SIZE & DIVERSITY	AREA	U.S. AVG	FAMILY DEMOGRAPHICS	AREA	U.S. AVG
Population	8,541,230		% Married	53.20%	53.80%
15-yr Population Growth	18.60%	4.40%	% Single	46.80%	46.20%
Diversity Measure	57	54	% Divorced	7.90%	10.20%
% Religiously Observant	57%	50%	% Separated	2.80%	2.10%
% Catholic	39%	22%	% Married w/Children	27.90%	27.90%
% Protestant	14%	25%	% Single w/Children	9.90%	9.40%
% Jewish	3%	2%	% Married, No Children	28.20%	31.00%
% Other	1%	1%	% Single, No Children	33.60%	31.70%

STANDARD OF LIVING

INCOME, EMPLOYMENT & TAXES	AREA	U.S. AVG	COST OF LIVING & HOUSING	AREA	U.S. AVG
Median Household Income	$55,785	$44,684	Cost of Living Index	113.8	100
Household Income Growth	5.80%	6.10%	Buying Power Index	110	100
Unemployment Rate	5.80%	5.10%	Median Home Price	$265,000	$208,500
Recent Job Growth	1.50%	1.30%	Home Price Ratio	4.8	4.7
Projected Future Job Growth	9%	10.50%	Home Price Appreciation	10.60%	13.60%
State Income Tax Rate	3%	5.00%	% Homes Owned	65.80%	64.10%
State Sales Tax Rate	8%	6.00%	Median Rent	$903	$792

EDUCATION

ATTAINMENT & ACHIEVEMENT	AREA	U.S. AVG	RESOURCES & INVESTMENT	AREA	U.S. AVG
% High School Graduate	82.90%	83.90%	No. of Highly Ranked Universities	5	1
% 2-yr Graduate	8.40%	7.10%	$ Invested per Pupil	$6,567	$6,058
% 4-yr Graduate	23.20%	17.20%	Student/Teacher Ratio	17.6	15.9
% Graduate or Professional Degree	12%	9.90%	State University In-State Tuition	$7,944	$4,917
% Attending Public School	84.80%	84.30%			
75th Percentile State University SAT Score (Verbal)	N/A	477			
75th Percentile State University SAT Score (Math)	N/A	478			
75th Percentile State University ACT Score	25	20			

LIFESTYLE

RECREATION, ARTS & CULTURE	AREA	U.S. AVG	INFRASTRUCTURE & FACILITIES	AREA	U.S. AVG
Professional Sports Rating	9	4	No. of Public Libraries	291	28
Zoos & Aquariums Rating	10	3	Library Volumes Per Capita	3.8	2.8
Amusement Park Rating	10	3	No. of Warehouse Clubs	10	4
Professional Theater Rating	10	3	No. of Starbucks	225	5
Overall Museum Rating	10	6	Golf Course Rating	10	4
Science Museum Rating	10	4	National Park Rating	2	3
Children's Museum Rating	10	3	Sq. Mi. Inland Water	3	4

CLIMATE			COMMUTE & TRANSPORTATION		
Days Mostly Sunny	197	212	Avg. Daily Commute Time	31.5	24.7
Annual Days Precipitation	123	111	% Commute by Auto	70%	77.70%
Annual Days > 90°F	21	38	Per Capita Avg. Daily Transit Miles	26.5	7.9
Annual Days < 32°F	119	88	Annual Auto Insurance Premium	$1,417	$1,314
July Relative Humidity	67	69	Gas, Cost per Gallon	$3.04	$3.05

HEALTH & SAFETY

CRIME & ENVIRNOMENTAL ISSUES	AREA	U.S. AVG	HEALTHCARE & COST	AREA	U.S. AVG
Violent Crime Rate	631	517	Physicians per Capita	292.1	254.3
Change in Violent Crime	-40.60%	-7.50%	Pediatricians per Capita	20.8	16.9
Property Crime Rate	3452	3783	Hospital Beds per Capita	326.6	239.7
Change in Property Crime	-23.80%	-10.10%	No. of Teaching Hospitals	57	1.9
Air Quality Score	16	44	Healthcare Cost Index	114.8	100
Water Quality Score	38	33	Cost per Doctor Visit	$88	$74
Pollen/Allergy Score	58	61	Cost per Dentist Visit	$67	$67
Stress Score	77	49	Cost per Hospital Room	$1,437	$702
Cancer Mortality Rate	183.4	168.9			

Olympia, WA

Area Type: Small capital city

Zip Code: 98501

Metro Area: Olympia, WA

Metro Area Type: Smaller

Location: 60 miles southwest of Seattle along I-5

Time Zone: Pacific Standard Time

Pros:
Attractive setting
Mild climate
Education

Cons:
Clouds and rain
Some long commutes
Low job diversity

"It's the water," touted the once-popular beer of the same name as this vibrant, lush, green capital city. Although the brewery is no longer in operation, the phrase still applies to the gorgeous waterways and inlets of southern Puget Sound. And it isn't *just* the water. The landscape, carpeted by dense green fir forests, is accented by the beautiful and mostly snowcapped Olympic Mountains to the north and the stunning 14,000-foot Mount Rainier to the east.

At the southern end of Puget Sound, Olympia is a town that, like many other Pacific Northwest seaports, has strong ties to the foresting and fishing industries. While those industries have flourished and ebbed, Olympia's steadier role has been that of state capital and, to a lesser degree, college town—thanks to the 4,300-student Evergreen State College. The downtown sits on a small peninsula that juts out into the Sound. One resident described it as "the next San Francisco," but declined to offer a timeline for the actual transition.

At 43,000 residents, Olympia has a decidedly small-town feel. Government is the town's main business, and state and local governments employ some 65% of the area's residents. Forestry, fishing, construction, and manufacturing make up less than 10%. Some employment is found at the military installations of Fort Lewis and McChord AFB toward Tacoma. These days, the Port of Olympia is less trafficked as a shipping center; most shipping activity is in Tacoma or Seattle, leaving a port area in transition (could San Francisco's waterfront with its Fisherman's Wharf and Pier 39 makeovers be the model for the port's future?). There is an active arts community, and local college students drum up some nightlife. But the pervasive atmosphere is forest-floor quiet, and those looking for more entertainment options will find them in Seattle. Before venturing into nearby national parks and forests, check the local Parks, Arts and Recreation department to see what's happening in the 700 acres of parks and waterfront in town.

Olympia offers a quiet natural beauty and amenities in a nice small-town package, close to the major urban hubs of Seattle and Tacoma but without their traffic, crowding, and high prices. The military bases act as a barrier to Tacoma's sprawl, allowing Olympia to remain essentially a standalone city. With careful land use that includes a grid-street pattern and individual larger lots in lieu of massive housing developments, Olympia prospers as an old-style Pacific Northwest town: clean and built on the water, it has lots of trees, strong neighborhood associations, and a good number of residents who are here for the long haul.

Standard of Living As government agencies make up most of the job base, those seeking private employment may have to trek up the road to Tacoma or into Seattle's southern outskirts. This commute can be rough, particularly near Tacoma. However, recent job growth and job projections are strong at 4.6% and 21% respectively, and Olympia is "ripe" for economic growth. Home prices in Olympia, though reasonable by West Coast and Puget Sound standards, have risen as much as 30% last year alone. Good family homes start at about $250K with a "sweet spot" around $350K, or about $150 to $160 per square foot. As large suburban developments aren't the rule here, style varies by home and small custom homes are common. Recently, many smaller Puget Sound towns have become hot markets for summer-home seekers and Californians (some retirees, some not) cashing out and looking for a better quality of life. Effective property tax rates are 1.5%; and, while sales tax is higher than national averages, Washington has no state income tax.

Education The educational context is strong, with 36% of residents having at least a 4-year degree. The Olympia School District performed significantly better than the state averages on both state and national standardized tests across all grade levels and in all subjects.

OLYMPIA, WA NEIGHBORHOOD HIGHLIGHTS	
PEOPLE	
Population	36,133
15-yr Population Growth	39.30%
5-yr Population Growth	8.40%
% Married w/Children	23.8%
% Single w/Children	11.3%
No. of Households	15,139
Median Age	36.5
Avg. Household Size	2.39
Diversity Measure	22
STANDARD OF LIVING	
Median Household Income	$49,173
% Household Income > $100K	13%
Projected Future Job Growth	21%
Cost of Living Index	108
Buying Power Index	101
Weekly Daycare Cost	$140
Median Home Price	$203,500
"Sweet Spot" Home Price	$350,000
Home Price Ratio	4.1
Median Age of Homes	26.3
% Homes Owned	60%
Effective Property Tax Rate	1.50%
Estimated Property Tax Bill	$5,250
EDUCATION	
% High School Graduates	93%
% 4-yr Degree	23%
% Graduate or Professional Degree	13%
$ Invested per Pupil	$5,671
Student/Teacher Ratio	27.5
Primary Test Score Percentile	113.5
Secondary Test Score Percentile	110.3
% Subsidized School Lunch	23.40%
% Attending Public School	88.40%
LIFESTYLE	
Leisure Rating (Area)	8
Arts & Culture Rating (Area)	3
Climate Rating (Area)	5
Physical Setting Rating	8
Downtown Core Rating	8
% Commute < 30 Min.	77%
% Commute > 1 Hour	5%
HEALTH & SAFETY	
Health Rating (Area)	6
Stress Score (Area)	9
Violent Crime Risk	97
Property Crime Risk	125

Teachers here have an average of 16 years' experience and 70% have a Master's degree or higher. Liberal arts–oriented Evergreen State specializes in such subjects as environmental studies, public administration, and teaching.

Lifestyle   The outdoors reign supreme. More than 50 city, state, and national parks lie within an hour's drive of town. The rugged and remote Olympic National Park offers excellent hiking, lodges, and rainforest preserves on the west slopes and along US 101. Attractive Pacific coastal areas lie about an hour west, and the various inlets along the Sound offer a range of small towns and water recreation for fun day trips. Mount Rainier National Park and the vast Wenatchee National Forest lie east, with abundant whitewater activities, hiking, and skiing. Cultural amenities include the acclaimed Hands On Children's Museum, the State Capitol museum and campus, a regional symphony orchestra and performing arts center with an active and well-supported series, a professional theatre group, and a biannual arts festival.

Commutes aren't an issue for those working in the Olympia area. Those traveling to Tacoma can count on a 45-minute drive, and Seattle is 90 minutes away. Sea-Tac airport is halfway between Seattle and Tacoma, about a 70-minute drive.

The terrain is low wooded hills penetrated by inlets, bays, and streams. The strong marine climate yields beautiful summers with temperatures rarely above 80 and relatively mild winters with average lows in the 30s. Occasional cold fronts blast temperatures into the teens or 20s. Olympia has a typical coastal Northwest precipitation pattern: 210 days with rain, but only 51 inches of actual annual rainfall, in fine mists that don't faze outdoor enthusiasts.

Health & Safety   Crime rates are about on par with national averages. Air quality is also good. Providence St. Peter Hospital, several medical centers, and a specialty children's hospital are all 5 minutes from downtown.

Nearby Neighborhoods   Our chosen zip code in Olympia extends from downtown several miles south through Tumwater, a faster growing and more commercial area along I-5 offering some newer homes in a more suburban style. Lacey, to the east, has less expensive and generally less appealing housing. Schools in the Tumwater and Lacey areas test consistently lower than those in Olympia.

OLYMPIA, WA
AREA HIGHLIGHTS

PEOPLE

SIZE & DIVERSITY	AREA	U.S. AVG	FAMILY DEMOGRAPHICS	AREA	U.S. AVG
Population	224,673		% Married	53.20%	53.80%
15-yr Population Growth	39.30%	4.40%	% Single	46.80%	46.20%
Diversity Measure	29	54	% Divorced	10.70%	10.20%
% Religiously Observant	27%	50%	% Separated	2.60%	2.10%
% Catholic	9%	22%	% Married w/Children	30.90%	27.90%
% Protestant	18%	25%	% Single w/Children	11%	9.40%
% Jewish	0%	2%	% Married, No Children	29.50%	31.00%
% Other	0%	1%	% Single, No Children	28.60%	31.70%

STANDARD OF LIVING

INCOME, EMPLOYMENT & TAXES	AREA	U.S. AVG	COST OF LIVING & HOUSING	AREA	U.S. AVG
Median Household Income	$48,608	$44,684	Cost of Living Index	98.6	100
Household Income Growth	4.70%	6.10%	Buying Power Index	110	100
Unemployment Rate	4.70%	5.10%	Median Home Price	$193,100	$208,500
Recent Job Growth	4.60%	1.30%	Home Price Ratio	4	4.7
Projected Future Job Growth	16.20%	10.50%	Home Price Appreciation	14.20%	13.60%
State Income Tax Rate	0%	5.00%	% Homes Owned	66.10%	64.10%
State Sales Tax Rate	6.50%	6.00%	Median Rent	$747	$792

EDUCATION

ATTAINMENT & ACHIEVEMENT	AREA	U.S. AVG	RESOURCES & INVESTMENT	AREA	U.S. AVG
% High School Graduate	87.60%	83.90%	No. of Highly Ranked Universities	0	1
% 2-yr Graduate	13.90%	7.10%	$ Invested per Pupil	$6,035	$6,058
% 4-yr Graduate	22.40%	17.20%	Student/Teacher Ratio	19.5	15.9
% Graduate or Professional Degree	11.80%	9.90%	State University In-State Tuition	$5,286	$4,917
% Attending Public School	94.90%	84.30%			
75th Percentile State University SAT Score (Verbal)	520	477			
75th Percentile State University SAT Score (Math)	550	478			
75th Percentile State University ACT Score	23	20			

LIFESTYLE

RECREATION, ARTS & CULTURE	AREA	U.S. AVG	INFRASTRUCTURE & FACILITIES	AREA	U.S. AVG
Professional Sports Rating	7	4	No. of Public Libraries	27	28
Zoos & Aquariums Rating	3	3	Library Volumes Per Capita	2.7	2.8
Amusement Park Rating	3	3	No. of Warehouse Clubs	3	4
Professional Theater Rating	3	3	No. of Starbucks	8	5
Overall Museum Rating	7	6	Golf Course Rating	3	4
Science Museum Rating	3	4	National Park Rating	7	3
Children's Museum Rating	5	3	Sq. Mi. Inland Water	6	4

CLIMATE			COMMUTE & TRANSPORTATION		
Days Mostly Sunny	137	212	Avg. Daily Commute Time	24.4	24.7
Annual Days Precipitation	163	111	% Commute by Auto	74%	77.70%
Annual Days > 90°F	6	38	Per Capita Avg. Daily Transit Miles	23.5	7.9
Annual Days < 32°F	89	88	Annual Auto Insurance Premium	$1,280	$1,314
July Relative Humidity	71	69	Gas, Cost per Gallon	$2.87	$3.05

HEALTH & SAFETY

CRIME & ENVIRNOMENTAL ISSUES	AREA	U.S. AVG	HEALTHCARE & COST	AREA	U.S. AVG
Violent Crime Rate	263	517	Physicians per Capita	231.6	254.3
Change in Violent Crime	8.80%	-7.50%	Pediatricians per Capita	12.6	16.9
Property Crime Rate	3385	3783	Hospital Beds per Capita	200.3	239.7
Change in Property Crime	-14.10%	-10.10%	No. of Teaching Hospitals	1	1.9
Air Quality Score	40	44	Healthcare Cost Index	127.3	100
Water Quality Score	50	33	Cost per Doctor Visit	$74	$74
Pollen/Allergy Score	47	61	Cost per Dentist Visit	$95	$67
Stress Score	90	49	Cost per Hospital Room	$1,107	$702
Cancer Mortality Rate	167.7	168.9			

Orange Park, FL

Area Type: Outer suburb

Zip Code: 32073

Metro Area: Jacksonville, FL

Metro Area Type: Mid-size

Location: 20 miles south of downtown Jacksonville

Time Zone: Eastern Standard Time

Pros:
Outdoor recreation
Schools
Economic growth

Cons:
Sprawl, growth, construction
Area crime
Hot, humid summers

As North Florida's major commercial and cultural center, Jacksonville has the most "northern" look and feel of Florida's large cities. Jacksonville is 25 miles south of the Georgia border and about 15 miles inland from the Atlantic along the St. John's River, a wide, slow, meandering river flowing north from near the center of the state. The modern city offers a complete blend of recreation and commercial activity with glass skyscrapers at the center and miles of beach and parkland mainly to the east and south.

Major corporations with offices in the city include CSX Transportation, Publix Markets, Blue Cross/Blue Shield of Florida, Xerox, BellSouth, AT&T, and a number of financial firms and defense contractors. The Navy has a strong presence, and the city is home to a branch of the Mayo Clinic. Employment is strong with current job growth of 3.6% and job growth projected at a robust 26%.

The city is *of, by, for,* and *on* the water, and water-based recreation abounds. The city has an attractive riverfront and a number of activities, restaurants, museums, and exhibits close by. The city joined the major leagues with the arrival of the Jacksonville Jaguars, and has always been a golf area, hosting the Tournament Players Championship. Historic St. Augustine, a popular weekend getaway, also features the World Golf Hall of Fame. The city does also have some top-notch museums and indoor amenities.

Orange Park is a relatively plain, quiet, family-oriented suburban neighborhood south of downtown along the St. John's River. Area growth is rapid and has caused some growing pains (mostly in the form of traffic jams) as construction tries to keep up with demand. Orange Park is new enough that there isn't really a downtown area, but some town centers can be found in planned developments on Fleming Island to the south. Thirty-three percent of Orange Park households are married with children.

Standard of Living For a major coastal metropolitan area in a desirable state, Jacksonville has a relatively low cost of living with an index of 97.7. Home prices are still reasonable, though escalating fast, with a good deal of availability. Prices run $100 to $130 per square foot, and family homes typically start at $220K; but for $250K to $320K you can have the pick of the litter. Many older starters are available for less, and waterfront locations command a lot more. Many homes are on wooded lots. Property taxes are $18 per $1,000, or 1.8%, not unreasonable for Florida. The low cost of living drives a healthy Buying Power Index of 135 with a median household income of $59K, suggesting that one-earner families can do well. If not, daycare costs are moderate at $156 per week for a preschooler.

Education Schools rate well in Orange Park. Clay County as a whole is known for having some of the best schools in the state. Ridgeview High gets a "B" from the Florida Department of Education, with test scores 10% to 15% above the state average. Orange Park Elementary gets an "A," testing fully 20 to 30 points above state averages and fully 40% above in 6th-grade math. Jacksonville University and the University of North Florida add a bit of a college presence.

Lifestyle Outdoor recreation and beach activities reign. Families frequently make the 30-minute trip to "Jax Beach" (Jacksonville Beach) on the Atlantic. Orange Park and Fleming Island parks provide local recreation, while longer trips take families to St. Augustine (40 miles) or to Orlando (about 2 hours).

Commutes can be a bit challenging, as the roads are often close to maximum capacity. Bridge traffic is frequently bottlenecked. Downtown commutes take 35 to 40 minutes, and there are few public transportation alternatives.

The terrain is level with some open land and wooded areas. The climate is subtropical with a coastal and continental influence, and is good for outdoor activity most of the year. Coastal breezes occasionally cool the warm and humid summers. Winters are typically mild but the area is far enough north to get a few short cold snaps. Interestingly, hurricanes are a bigger risk north and south of the area; a major one hasn't hit Jacksonville since 1964.

Health & Safety Crime is a bit high, and the area has some history of racial tension. Area healthcare is considered very strong, especially with the Mayo Clinic in town, and costs are a favorable 88% of national averages.

Nearby Neighborhoods Small suburban neighborhoods dot the area, particularly to the south and east. Some developments with small homes are more geared to retirees than families. Housing on Fleming Island is worth examining, but the area is a bit more expensive and located farther—and across one more bridge—from downtown Jacksonville.

ORANGE PARK, FL NEIGHBORHOOD HIGHLIGHTS	
PEOPLE	
Population	58,093
15-yr Population Growth	55.10%
5-yr Population Growth	16.70%
% Married w/Children	33.4%
% Single w/Children	10.1%
No. of Households	20,929
Median Age	35.9
Avg. Household Size	2.72
Diversity Measure	35
STANDARD OF LIVING	
Median Household Income	$59,002
% Household Income > $100K	17%
Projected Future Job Growth	26%
Cost of Living Index	97.7
Buying Power Index	135
Weekly Daycare Cost	$156
Median Home Price	$234,200
"Sweet Spot" Home Price	$280,000
Home Price Ratio	4
Median Age of Homes	18.4
% Homes Owned	68%
Effective Property Tax Rate	1.80%
Estimated Property Tax Bill	$5,040
EDUCATION	
% High School Graduates	92%
% 4-yr Degree	19%
% Graduate or Professional Degree	11%
$ Invested per Pupil	$4,458
Student/Teacher Ratio	17.2
Primary Test Score Percentile	108.6
Secondary Test Score Percentile	104.9
% Subsidized School Lunch	25.40%
% Attending Public School	84.30%
LIFESTYLE	
Leisure Rating (Area)	3
Arts & Culture Rating (Area)	2
Climate Rating (Area)	5
Physical Setting Rating	4
Downtown Core Rating	5
% Commute < 30 Min.	51%
% Commute > 1 Hour	6%
HEALTH & SAFETY	
Health Rating (Area)	1
Stress Score (Area)	9
Violent Crime Risk	49
Property Crime Risk	63

JACKSONVILLE, FL
AREA HIGHLIGHTS

PEOPLE

SIZE & DIVERSITY	AREA	U.S. AVG	FAMILY DEMOGRAPHICS	AREA	U.S. AVG
Population	1,201,362		% Married	53.80%	53.80%
15-yr Population Growth	35.30%	4.40%	% Single	46.20%	46.20%
Diversity Measure	45	54	% Divorced	11%	10.20%
% Religiously Observant	43%	50%	% Separated	3.90%	2.10%
% Catholic	9%	22%	% Married w/Children	28.50%	27.90%
% Protestant	33%	25%	% Single w/Children	12.40%	9.40%
% Jewish	1%	2%	% Married, No Children	26.60%	31.00%
% Other	0%	1%	% Single, No Children	32.60%	31.70%

STANDARD OF LIVING

INCOME, EMPLOYMENT & TAXES	AREA	U.S. AVG	COST OF LIVING & HOUSING	AREA	U.S. AVG
Median Household Income	$46,394	$44,684	Cost of Living Index	90.6	100
Household Income Growth	4.30%	6.10%	Buying Power Index	115	100
Unemployment Rate	4.30%	5.10%	Median Home Price	$200,800	$208,500
Recent Job Growth	3.60%	1.30%	Home Price Ratio	4.3	4.7
Projected Future Job Growth	17.70%	10.50%	Home Price Appreciation	14.60%	13.60%
State Income Tax Rate	0%	5.00%	% Homes Owned	61.40%	64.10%
State Sales Tax Rate	6%	6.00%	Median Rent	$732	$792

EDUCATION

ATTAINMENT & ACHIEVEMENT	AREA	U.S. AVG	RESOURCES & INVESTMENT	AREA	U.S. AVG
% High School Graduate	78.80%	83.90%	No. of Highly Ranked Universities	2	1
% 2-yr Graduate	9.60%	7.10%	$ Invested per Pupil	$4,985	$6,058
% 4-yr Graduate	17.30%	17.20%	Student/Teacher Ratio	19.2	15.9
% Graduate or Professional Degree	7%	9.90%	State University In-State Tuition	$2,955	$4,917
% Attending Public School	86.30%	84.30%			
75th Percentile State University SAT Score (Verbal)	570	477			
75th Percentile State University SAT Score (Math)	590	478			
75th Percentile State University ACT Score	N/A	20			

LIFESTYLE

RECREATION, ARTS & CULTURE	AREA	U.S. AVG	INFRASTRUCTURE & FACILITIES	AREA	U.S. AVG
Professional Sports Rating	6	4	No. of Public Libraries	27	28
Zoos & Aquariums Rating	8	3	Library Volumes Per Capita	2.7	2.8
Amusement Park Rating	1	3	No. of Warehouse Clubs	6	4
Professional Theater Rating	1	3	No. of Starbucks	26	5
Overall Museum Rating	8	6	Golf Course Rating	6	4
Science Museum Rating	5	4	National Park Rating	2	3
Children's Museum Rating	1	3	Sq. Mi. Inland Water	10	4

CLIMATE			COMMUTE & TRANSPORTATION		
Days Mostly Sunny	226	212	Avg. Daily Commute Time	26.6	24.7
Annual Days Precipitation	116	111	% Commute by Auto	74%	77.70%
Annual Days > 90°F	82	38	Per Capita Avg. Daily Transit Miles	8.6	7.9
Annual Days < 32°F	12	88	Annual Auto Insurance Premium	$1,382	$1,314
July Relative Humidity	75	69	Gas, Cost per Gallon	$3.00	$3.05

HEALTH & SAFETY

CRIME & ENVIRNOMENTAL ISSUES	AREA	U.S. AVG	HEALTHCARE & COST	AREA	U.S. AVG
Violent Crime Rate	755	517	Physicians per Capita	261	254.3
Change in Violent Crime	-21.20%	-7.50%	Pediatricians per Capita	20	16.9
Property Crime Rate	4564	3783	Hospital Beds per Capita	273.9	239.7
Change in Property Crime	-19.30%	-10.10%	No. of Teaching Hospitals	6	1.9
Air Quality Score	25	44	Healthcare Cost Index	87.7	100
Water Quality Score	27	33	Cost per Doctor Visit	$56	$74
Pollen/Allergy Score	65	61	Cost per Dentist Visit	$59	$67
Stress Score	91	49	Cost per Hospital Room	$561	$702
Cancer Mortality Rate	188.9	168.9			

Pittsford, NY

Area Type: Inner suburb/suburban town

Zip Code: 14534

Metro Area: Rochester, NY

Metro Area Type: Mid-size

Location: 9 miles southeast of downtown Rochester

Time Zone: Eastern Standard Time

Pros:
Attractive local town center
Arts, cultural, and children's resources
Attractive homes and home prices

Cons:
Snow
Clouds and rain
High property tax rates

It's easy to overlook a place like Rochester when searching for the best place for your family. Snow, snow, and more snow. Fading Great Lakes Rust Belt economy. Eastman Kodak withering and laying off workers as business goes digital.

Although there is a lot of snow, and there have been business transitions, an inside look at Rochester uncovers something better than what shows on the surface. Kodak, the area's largest employer, has furloughed workers but is entering the digital imaging market at full speed and hiring new workers in that skill area. New tech and biotech firms are also hiring. Rochester has some of the best cultural and children's assets found in any city its size, and for that matter, in many larger cities. Why? Because of Rochester's leadership in science and technology research. Kodak, the Rochester Institute of Technology, the University of Rochester, Xerox, and numerous others have left a scientific imprint and endowments that continue to attract new businesses, cultural resources, and educated residents.

Pittsford is a historic town located along the Erie Canal just to the southeast of Rochester. Most of Rochester's growth has moved southeast beyond Pittsford. Today's downtown Pittsford features a vibrant commercial district with parks, canal-front trails, canal boat rides, and winter ice-skating. A complement of older and newer homes surrounds the downtown, with large, wooded lots, and a country-town feel atypical of a location only 9 miles from a major city. Most of the area's big shopping and modern sprawl have leapfrogged Pittsford to the southeast, so residents have convenient access to these facilities without feeling the impact of growth. With a median age of 40.1 years (U.S. average 35.5), the Pittsford population is older than most places we examined, but the 36.2% married-with-children percentage suggests a strong family presence.

Downtown Rochester sits about 5 miles south of Lake Ontario and near the head of Irondequoit Bay. The downtown is typical for a city of its vintage and is going through some renewal as the area recovers from its economic dip. Endowments and civic commitments have supported first-class museums and acquisition of open space for new parks. An enhanced downtown waterfront hosts many activities, especially during summer months. Museums are one of the area's strongest calling cards; for example, the Strong Museum's "National Museum of Play," with its renowned National Toy Hall of Fame, rates as one of *Child Magazine*'s top 10 children's museums in the country. The Rochester Museum and Science Center and the New York Museum of Transportation also make the list.

Standard of Living   Pittsford is one of those places that, while a bit expensive for the area, is quite inexpensive on a national scale, and it is possible to enjoy a surprisingly high standard of living on a moderate income. The Cost of Living Index of 113 isn't bad for a top neighborhood. Homes run about $100 per square foot and a nice family home can be purchased in the low $200Ks. A four-bedroom, 2,600-square-foot, two-story colonial with a basement on a wooded ½ acre recently listed for $245K. Strong household incomes give a Buying Power Index of 181 and a Home Price Ratio of 2.5, among the best of areas surveyed. Property taxes are high at $28 to $32 per $1,000; but valuations are low, and revenues support snow removal and other needed services.

Education   One might expect good schools, and the Pittsford City School District doesn't disappoint. New York State Regents exam scores are in the high 90s and test scores typically exceed state averages by 20 to 30 points. School ratios and sizes are comfortably small,

PITTSFORD, NY NEIGHBORHOOD HIGHLIGHTS	
PEOPLE	
Population	30,053
15-yr Population Growth	3%
5-yr Population Growth	0%
% Married w/Children	36.2%
% Single w/Children	5.8%
No. of Households	10,913
Median Age	39.8
Avg. Household Size	2.71
Diversity Measure	18
STANDARD OF LIVING	BEST
Median Household Income	$89,247
% Household Income > $100K	43%
Projected Future Job Growth	4%
Cost of Living Index	113
Buying Power Index	181
Weekly Daycare Cost	$174
Median Home Price	$221,000
"Sweet Spot" Home Price	$220,000
Home Price Ratio	2.5
Median Age of Homes	29.3
% Homes Owned	90%
Effective Property Tax Rate	3.20%
Estimated Property Tax Bill	$7,040
EDUCATION	
% High School Graduates	96%
% 4-yr Degree	33%
% Graduate or Professional Degree	31%
$ Invested per Pupil	$9,397
Student/Teacher Ratio	16.7
Primary Test Score Percentile	126.2
Secondary Test Score Percentile	122.3
% Subsidized School Lunch	1.50%
% Attending Public School	77.30%
LIFESTYLE	
Leisure Rating (Area)	8
Arts & Culture Rating (Area)	8
Climate Rating (Area)	1
Physical Setting Rating	3
Downtown Core Rating	7
% Commute < 30 Min.	79%
% Commute > 1 Hour	3%
HEALTH & SAFETY	
Health Rating (Area)	4
Stress Score (Area)	4
Violent Crime Risk	22
Property Crime Risk	34

with only 900 students in Pittsford Sutherland High. College-prep and sports programs are well-regarded by local residents. The local universities are well above average.

Lifestyle Pittsford families have plenty of activities to choose from year-round. Summers are particularly active, with numerous festivals, boating, Lake Ontario shore activities, and playtime at local parks. Winter sports activities are plentiful too, and good skiing is available at Bristol Mountain 35 minutes south. Every year the "Cold Rush" festival brings some energy to the area's long winters. Beyond Rochester, day trips will lead you to parks, nearby agricultural areas, and wineries. As we noted earlier, museums and performing arts are above average and well patronized.

Pittsford is convenient to all locations in Rochester, and commutes seldom take more than 15 minutes. Many travel downtown, others to industrial parks and commercial areas to the south along the city's above-average freeway system.

The landscape is mainly flat near the lake and hilly to the south with farmland and dense deciduous forest. The climate is humid continental with warm but not unbearable summers and wet, snowy winters. The 182 days of measurable precipitation—1 in 2 days each year—are too much for some. Periods of heavy snow do occur, but residents are accustomed to it and local snow removal and road maintenance are efficient.

Health & Safety Crime risk in Pittsford and Rochester is generally low; Pittsford has one of the lowest "CAP" crime risk scores we observed. The lakeside location brings good air quality. Healthcare resources score well with teaching hospitals at the University of Rochester and the Strong Memorial Hospital.

Nearby Neighborhoods Pittsford is fairly unique in the area for its combination of small-town flavor, good housing, and prime location. Families seeking older and slightly more upscale surroundings might look west to Brighton. Also west, Spencerport has attractive and less expensive housing, and, on the east side, many choose to live closer to the lake in Webster.

ROCHESTER, NY
AREA HIGHLIGHTS

PEOPLE

SIZE & DIVERSITY	AREA	U.S. AVG	FAMILY DEMOGRAPHICS	AREA	U.S. AVG
Population	1,101,188		% Married	54.30%	53.80%
15-yr Population Growth	3.70%	4.40%	% Single	45.70%	46.20%
Diversity Measure	31	54	% Divorced	7.10%	10.20%
% Religiously Observant	51%	50%	% Separated	4.10%	2.10%
% Catholic	32%	22%	% Married w/Children	27.80%	27.90%
% Protestant	16%	25%	% Single w/Children	10%	9.40%
% Jewish	2%	2%	% Married, No Children	29.40%	31.00%
% Other	0%	1%	% Single, No Children	32.70%	31.70%

STANDARD OF LIVING

INCOME, EMPLOYMENT & TAXES	AREA	U.S. AVG	COST OF LIVING & HOUSING	AREA	U.S. AVG
Median Household Income	$45,985	$44,684	Cost of Living Index	88.4	100
Household Income Growth	5%	6.10%	Buying Power Index	116	100
Unemployment Rate	5%	5.10%	Median Home Price	$110,700	$208,500
Recent Job Growth	-1%	1.30%	Home Price Ratio	2.4	4.7
Projected Future Job Growth	5.10%	10.50%	Home Price Appreciation	4.30%	13.60%
State Income Tax Rate	7.10%	5.00%	% Homes Owned	67.70%	64.10%
State Sales Tax Rate	6.80%	6.00%	Median Rent	$687	$792

EDUCATION

ATTAINMENT & ACHIEVEMENT	AREA	U.S. AVG	RESOURCES & INVESTMENT	AREA	U.S. AVG
% High School Graduate	82.40%	83.90%	No. of Highly Ranked Universities	2	1
% 2-yr Graduate	12.50%	7.10%	$ Invested per Pupil	$8,436	$6,058
% 4-yr Graduate	16.90%	17.20%	Student/Teacher Ratio	13.7	15.9
% Graduate or Professional Degree	9.70%	9.90%	State University In-State Tuition	$5,966	$4,917
% Attending Public School	90.10%	84.30%			
75th Percentile State University SAT Score (Verbal)	520	477			
75th Percentile State University SAT Score (Math)	550	478			
75th Percentile State University ACT Score	24	20			

LIFESTYLE

RECREATION, ARTS & CULTURE	AREA	U.S. AVG	INFRASTRUCTURE & FACILITIES	AREA	U.S. AVG
Professional Sports Rating	3	4	No. of Public Libraries	78	28
Zoos & Aquariums Rating	5	3	Library Volumes Per Capita	4	2.8
Amusement Park Rating	6	3	No. of Warehouse Clubs	8	4
Professional Theater Rating	6	3	No. of Starbucks	13	5
Overall Museum Rating	9	6	Golf Course Rating	7	4
Science Museum Rating	7	4	National Park Rating	1	3
Children's Museum Rating	7	3	Sq. Mi. Inland Water	4	4

CLIMATE			COMMUTE & TRANSPORTATION		
Days Mostly Sunny	170	212	Avg. Daily Commute Time	21.1	24.7
Annual Days Precipitation	182	111	% Commute by Auto	76%	77.70%
Annual Days > 90°F	11	38	Per Capita Avg. Daily Transit Miles	6.7	7.9
Annual Days < 32°F	135	88	Annual Auto Insurance Premium	$1,765	$1,314
July Relative Humidity	73	69	Gas, Cost per Gallon	$3.21	$3.05

HEALTH & SAFETY

CRIME & ENVIRNOMENTAL ISSUES	AREA	U.S. AVG	HEALTHCARE & COST	AREA	U.S. AVG
Violent Crime Rate	293	517	Physicians per Capita	308.8	254.3
Change in Violent Crime	3.80%	-7.50%	Pediatricians per Capita	25.9	16.9
Property Crime Rate	3377	3783	Hospital Beds per Capita	469.1	239.7
Change in Property Crime	-6.70%	-10.10%	No. of Teaching Hospitals	7	1.9
Air Quality Score	43	44	Healthcare Cost Index	102.4	100
Water Quality Score	54	33	Cost per Doctor Visit	$67	$74
Pollen/Allergy Score	67	61	Cost per Dentist Visit	$83	$67
Stress Score	43	49	Cost per Hospital Room	$1,322	$702
Cancer Mortality Rate	171.5	168.9			

Rancho Santa Margarita, CA

Area Type: Exurb

Zip Code: 92688

Metro Area: Orange County, CA

Metro Area Type: Large

Location: 22 miles south of Santa Ana, 50 miles southeast of downtown Los Angeles

Time Zone: Pacific Standard Time

Pros:

Excellent schools
Good climate
Strong sense of community

Cons:

High home prices
Growth, sprawl, crowding
Air quality

Many of the places included in this book, in addition to providing the fundamentals for a healthy family life, come complete with a long and sometimes colorful history that gives their residents a real sense of place. Other, newer areas have just begun to create their own history, and they often reflect the demands of a more modern lifestyle.

Rancho Santa Margarita, officially incorporated at the start of the millennium, is one of the latter. A thoroughly planned community, it sits in a valley just to the east of Mission Viejo tucked in against the Santa Ana mountains. And while the area does have a ranching past, that was then, this is now, and few quiet old ranchos are found in Rancho Santa Margarita today. Conceived as an "urban village," Rancho Santa Margarita's general plan governs all development in this small (pop. 50,000), largely residential community. The town and most of the surrounding subdivisions exhibit the hallmarks of a modern planned community: integrated architectural design, professional landscaping and maintenance, and efficient layout. What it may lack in quirky charm, it makes up for with a beautiful setting, abundant green space, strong community involvement, and one of the most livable climates in the country.

All of this, of course, comes at a price. Southern Orange County has some of the most expensive homes in the region, and Rancho Santa Margarita is near the top of the scale. That said, Orange County pricing overall has risen consistently for 10 years, and Rancho Santa Margarita isn't exorbitant on a relative scale. Those considering a move from outside the region, however, should allow time for sticker-shock recovery after the initial house-hunting trip.

Standard of Living Rancho Santa Margarita's household income of nearly twice the national average reflects the high percentage of professional and executive workers. The Cost of Living Index, at 156, and most components of that index are close to their national averages. The glaring exception is housing, which costs nearly three times the national average. The benchmark family home in Rancho Santa Margarita will set you back around $650K. In addition, some areas have special tax assessments that raise the overall property tax rate to as high as 2%, high for Proposition 13–regulated California and which, on a $650K or higher base, hurts.

On the plus side, homes are well-built, and the neighborhood is immaculate with good zoning controls and great schools. Over 70% of the homes on the market date from 1990 or later and very few homes were built prior to 1980. The employment base in Orange County is very diverse, with high-tech defense contractors, some manufacturing, and regional offices of major corporations. There were some economic "down" cycles as defense and certain high-tech players consolidated, but this is largely past. Irvine, some 15 miles to the west, is a modern and attractive corporate employment center.

Education Rancho Santa Margarita is in the Saddleback Valley Unified school district, which includes the communities of Mission Viejo, Laguna Hills, and Lake Forest. The district has consistently been among the best performers in the state, with current SAT test scores significantly higher than the state and national averages. The district includes 10 National Blue Ribbon Schools, and over 90% of graduates go on to higher education. Schools are large and student-teacher ratios are somewhat higher than average, owing mostly to the recent growth in the area.

Lifestyle The ocean to the west and mountains to the east offer great outdoor recreation. In fact, given a little luck with traffic, one can spend a winter morning skiing at Big Bear and the afternoon surfing at Newport

Beach. Though not many people actually do this, the fascination with the *possibility* looms large.

Anecdotes aside, there really is very little that you cannot do with Rancho Santa Margarita as your base. Hiking, biking, boating, fishing, golfing, surfing, skiing, mountain climbing, open-water sailing, whale-watching . . . the list of opportunities within an hour of town goes on and on; and the weather is near-perfect year-round. Obviously, the attractions of Los Angeles are an easy drive (except during commute times), and San Diego is about the same distance south. The city itself has many parks and activities, and, if you still have some money left after paying the mortgage, Las Vegas (which is also trying its hand at family recreation) is a 4-hour drive to the northeast.

Commutes to Irvine, the area's major employment base, are a relatively easy (by Southern California standards) 15 minutes. John Wayne Airport is just 10 minutes away, making Rancho Santa Margarita a good base for folks whose jobs require domestic travel.

Southern California is well-known for its agreeable climate, and Rancho Santa Margarita is no exception. Average July highs are a moderate 82°F with only 5 summer days over 90°F, and January lows average 44°F with just occasional rain. There are 258 sunny days per year, and there would be more save for low stratus clouds off the ocean (known locally as "fog"), which keep summer mornings and evenings cool.

Health & Safety   Crime rates are below the national average and low for California as well. As with many southern California communities with mountains to the east, trapped and poorly circulated air brings serious air-quality problems. Stress and allergy scores, however, are relatively low.

Nearby Neighborhoods   Mission Viejo to the west is an established area of somewhat older and less expensive homes and a good alternative to Rancho Santa Margarita. Other more modest suburbs can be found to the north and noncoastal west. Coastal areas, and Yorba Linda at the mountain gate toward Riverside, are more upscale.

RANCHO SANTA MARGARITA, CA NEIGHBORHOOD HIGHLIGHTS	
PEOPLE	
Population	44,596
15-yr Population Growth	23.90%
5-yr Population Growth	5%
% Married w/Children	32.6%
% Single w/Children	7.2%
No. of Households	16,135
Median Age	29.2
Avg. Household Size	2.77
Diversity Measure	48
STANDARD OF LIVING	
Median Household Income	$81,230
% Household Income > $100K	30%
Projected Future Job Growth	13%
Cost of Living Index	156
Buying Power Index	117
Weekly Daycare Cost	$200
Median Home Price	$523,800
"Sweet Spot" Home Price	$650,000
Home Price Ratio	6.4
Median Age of Homes	6.8
% Homes Owned	73%
Effective Property Tax Rate	2%
Estimated Property Tax Bill	$13,000
EDUCATION	
% High School Graduates	95%
% 4-yr Degree	32%
% Graduate or Professional Degree	12%
$ Invested per Pupil	$4,660
Student/Teacher Ratio	24.2
Primary Test Score Percentile	175.4
Secondary Test Score Percentile	94.5
% Subsidized School Lunch	5.40%
% Attending Public School	83%
LIFESTYLE	BEST
Leisure Rating (Area)	10
Arts & Culture Rating (Area)	5
Climate Rating (Area)	10
Physical Setting Rating	4
Downtown Core Rating	2
% Commute < 30 Min.	47%
% Commute > 1 Hour	10%
HEALTH & SAFETY	
Health Rating (Area)	4
Stress Score (Area)	3
Violent Crime Risk	23
Property Crime Risk	30

ORANGE COUNTY, CA
AREA HIGHLIGHTS
PEOPLE

SIZE & DIVERSITY	AREA	U.S. AVG		FAMILY DEMOGRAPHICS	AREA	U.S. AVG
Population	2,987,591			% Married	51.70%	53.80%
15-yr Population Growth	23.90%	4.40%		% Single	48.30%	46.20%
Diversity Measure	61	54		% Divorced	10%	10.20%
% Religiously Observant	45%	50%		% Separated	3.10%	2.10%
% Catholic	27%	22%		% Married w/Children	27%	27.90%
% Protestant	14%	25%		% Single w/Children	9.10%	9.40%
% Jewish	2%	2%		% Married, No Children	28.30%	31.00%
% Other	1%	1%		% Single, No Children	35.60%	31.70%

STANDARD OF LIVING

INCOME, EMPLOYMENT & TAXES	AREA	U.S. AVG		COST OF LIVING & HOUSING	AREA	U.S. AVG
Median Household Income	$64,416	$44,684		Cost of Living Index	167.5	100
Household Income Growth	2.90%	6.10%		Buying Power Index	86	100
Unemployment Rate	2.90%	5.10%		Median Home Price	$696,100	$208,500
Recent Job Growth	1.80%	1.30%		Home Price Ratio	10.8	4.7
Projected Future Job Growth	13.30%	10.50%		Home Price Appreciation	6.20%	13.60%
State Income Tax Rate	6%	5.00%		% Homes Owned	58%	64.10%
State Sales Tax Rate	7.20%	6.00%		Median Rent	$1,317	$792

EDUCATION

ATTAINMENT & ACHIEVEMENT	AREA	U.S. AVG		RESOURCES & INVESTMENT	AREA	U.S. AVG
% High School Graduate	86.60%	83.90%		No. of Highly Ranked Universities	1	1
% 2-yr Graduate	13.70%	7.10%		$ Invested per Pupil	$5,119	$6,058
% 4-yr Graduate	31.10%	17.20%		Student/Teacher Ratio	22.9	15.9
% Graduate or Professional Degree	14.10%	9.90%		State University In-State Tuition	$6,586	$4,917
% Attending Public School	87.80%	84.30%				
75th Percentile State University SAT Score (Verbal)	560	477				
75th Percentile State University SAT Score (Math)	600	478				
75th Percentile State University ACT Score	23	20				

LIFESTYLE

RECREATION, ARTS & CULTURE	AREA	U.S. AVG		INFRASTRUCTURE & FACILITIES	AREA	U.S. AVG
Professional Sports Rating	10	4		No. of Public Libraries	53	28
Zoos & Aquariums Rating	5	3		Library Volumes Per Capita	1.9	2.8
Amusement Park Rating	10	3		No. of Warehouse Clubs	8	4
Professional Theater Rating	5	3		No. of Starbucks	127	5
Overall Museum Rating	8	6		Golf Course Rating	8	4
Science Museum Rating	7	4		National Park Rating	10	3
Children's Museum Rating	5	3		Sq. Mi. Inland Water	4	4

CLIMATE				COMMUTE & TRANSPORTATION		
Days Mostly Sunny	258	212		Avg. Daily Commute Time	27.2	24.7
Annual Days Precipitation	40	111		% Commute by Auto	78%	77.70%
Annual Days > 90°F	5	38		Per Capita Avg. Daily Transit Miles	8.2	7.9
Annual Days < 32°F	0	88		Annual Auto Insurance Premium	$1,421	$1,314
July Relative Humidity	71	69		Gas, Cost per Gallon	$2.97	$3.05

HEALTH & SAFETY

CRIME & ENVIRNOMENTAL ISSUES	AREA	U.S. AVG		HEALTHCARE & COST	AREA	U.S. AVG
Violent Crime Rate	277	517		Physicians per Capita	263.2	254.3
Change in Violent Crime	-21.10%	-7.50%		Pediatricians per Capita	21	16.9
Property Crime Rate	2464	3783		Hospital Beds per Capita	268.5	239.7
Change in Property Crime	-8.70%	-10.10%		No. of Teaching Hospitals	7	1.9
Air Quality Score	2	44		Healthcare Cost Index	119.5	100
Water Quality Score	65	33		Cost per Doctor Visit	$91	$74
Pollen/Allergy Score	45	61		Cost per Dentist Visit	$77	$67
Stress Score	31	49		Cost per Hospital Room	$1,549	$702
Cancer Mortality Rate	166.3	168.9				

Rapid City, SD

Area Type: Small city

Zip Code: 57702

Metro Area: Rapid City, SD

Metro Area Type: Smallest

Location: Western South Dakota at the edge of the Black Hills

Time Zone: Mountain Standard Time

Pros:
Outdoor recreation
Attractive downtown
Cost of living, low taxes

Cons:
Isolation
Tourist impact
Possible military base closure

Like an island in the center of a vast sea, Rapid City is an isolated but attractive, self-confident, and fundamentally Western town at the eastern base of South Dakota's Black Hills. It isn't for everyone, but its slow pace and low cost of living do appeal to adventurous and outdoorsy families. And it's certainly family-oriented: Fully 29.3% of households in the area are married with children.

Rapid City's heritage dates back to the late-1800s gold-mining boom in the nearby Black Hills; towns like Keystone and Deadwood made their mark in early frontier history and still exist as historic tourist attractions. During the wealth-producing years and Victorian-era heyday, these towns attracted Easterners who built solid, and, for the time, sophisticated cities with elegant hotels, performing arts, and libraries. The ore held out longer than in most boom towns; in fact, the Homestake Gold Mine, the oldest, largest, and deepest gold mine in the Western Hemisphere, just closed in 2001. As a result, these towns never became ghost towns as did so many in the Rockies and Nevada; instead, mining slowly gave way to tourism as many travelers discovered the pristine beauty and fascinating history of the Hills.

The results of this increased tourism are both good and bad. The smaller towns and the Rapid City core remained intact, and Deadwood in particular is well-preserved and full of historic interest. Rapid City is still quite functional today with an excellent Main Street of older buildings, a genuine historic feel, and a strong arts tradition. However, much of the tourist development is tacky "tourist sprawl" with low-end souvenir shops in towns like nearby Keystone. That said, the Black Hills beyond the impressive Mount Rushmore memorial are as good as any national park anywhere and are an outstanding source of weekend and after-supper jaunts.

Standard of Living   The narrow job base in Rapid City is a concern. Ellsworth Air Force Base, northeast of town, is the largest employer, but it was barely spared in the last round of base closures and there is continuing talk of it. The Rapid City Regional Hospital is the second-largest employer, employing almost 2,800; and the tourist industry employs most of the rest. There is no strong industrial or commercial base. Professionals moving to the area may have to rely on self-employment or telecommuting. South Dakota has an excellent business climate with low business taxes and no personal or corporate income tax. Living costs are very low, and good family homes are available for $175K to $200K. Real property tax rates run about 2% but on low valuations. Utility costs are also among the lowest in the nation.

Education   Area schools are modestly sized and generally test well. Grade 11 students at Stevens High School tested in the 85th percentile nationally for math and 69th for reading. West Middle School students tested 13% to 18% above state averages. Higher education is not a particularly strong suit, but there is the South Dakota School of Mines and Technology as well as Black Hills State in nearby Spearfish.

Lifestyle   Outdoor recreation is the centerpiece of family entertainment and life in Rapid City. Black Hills mountain sports are the rule: camping, hiking, climbing, trout fishing, kayaking, and, in winter, skiing, snowmobiling, ice fishing, and skating. Tourists do crowd the Black Hills in summer, but there are still out-of-the-way spots. During the rest of the year, the Black Hills area is like a private park for Rapid City residents. In town, the Main Street area is fun, with antique shops, ice-cream parlors, and restaurants. The Dahl Performing Arts Center, owned by the city, hosts 60 musical and

RAPID CITY, SD
NEIGHBORHOOD HIGHLIGHTS

PEOPLE

Population	30,791
15-yr Population Growth	13.90%
5-yr Population Growth	4.60%
% Married w/Children	29.3%
% Single w/Children	8.3%
No. of Households	12,393
Median Age	38.5
Avg. Household Size	2.45
Diversity Measure	11

STANDARD OF LIVING

Median Household Income	$51,689
% Household Income > $100K	12%
Projected Future Job Growth	14%
Cost of Living Index	97.8
Buying Power Index	122
Weekly Daycare Cost	$80
Median Home Price	$181,400
"Sweet Spot" Home Price	$190,000
Home Price Ratio	3.5
Median Age of Homes	25.4
% Homes Owned	70%
Effective Property Tax Rate	2%
Estimated Property Tax Bill	$3,800

EDUCATION

% High School Graduates	93%
% 4-yr Degree	25%
% Graduate or Professional Degree	12%
$ Invested per Pupil	$4,363
Student/Teacher Ratio	17.9
Primary Test Score Percentile	94.9
Secondary Test Score Percentile	139
% Subsidized School Lunch	34.10%
% Attending Public School	87.10%

LIFESTYLE

Leisure Rating (Area)	5
Arts & Culture Rating (Area)	0
Climate Rating (Area)	1
Physical Setting Rating	6
Downtown Core Rating	7
% Commute < 30 Min.	84%
% Commute > 1 Hour	3%

HEALTH & SAFETY

Health Rating (Area)	7
Stress Score (Area)	1
Violent Crime Risk	64
Property Crime Risk	102

performance arts events each year. There are plenty of small community parks and centers, and a large active YMCA has over 10,000 members.

Commute problems are nonexistent; locals complain when it takes 15 minutes to get somewhere. The bigger issue is distance to other places: Denver is the closest city of any size at 400 miles away. Air service is good but not particularly cheap.

Rapid City sits in an area where different climate influences converge from the north, west, and south, yielding mostly pleasant but highly dynamic weather patterns. Strong chinook winds off the Black Hills and Rocky Mountains farther west produce short periods of extreme dry heat, and southerly moisture flows can make it humid. Winter snows and bitter cold snaps can be intense, but snow rarely stays for more than a week.

Health & Safety   Crime risk is low and not much of a concern. The regional hospital offers excellent and affordable healthcare.

Nearby Neighborhoods   Most areas of town are attractive and affordable. The air base and modest commercial development spreads to the northeast. Older neighborhoods to the south of town are appealing; some of the newer and slightly more upscale areas are to the southwest toward the mountains (zip code 57702); and the north side of town is also worth a look.

RAPID CITY, SD
AREA HIGHLIGHTS
PEOPLE

SIZE & DIVERSITY	AREA	U.S. AVG	FAMILY DEMOGRAPHICS	AREA	U.S. AVG
Population	92,631		% Married	65.30%	53.80%
15-yr Population Growth	13.90%	4.40%	% Single	34.70%	46.20%
Diversity Measure	26	54	% Divorced	7.80%	10.20%
% Religiously Observant	63%	50%	% Separated	1.60%	2.10%
% Catholic	28%	22%	% Married w/Children	31.10%	27.90%
% Protestant	35%	25%	% Single w/Children	7.40%	9.40%
% Jewish	0%	2%	% Married, No Children	33.60%	31.00%
% Other	0%	1%	% Single, No Children	27.90%	31.70%

STANDARD OF LIVING

INCOME, EMPLOYMENT & TAXES	AREA	U.S. AVG	COST OF LIVING & HOUSING	AREA	U.S. AVG
Median Household Income	$42,112	$44,684	Cost of Living Index	89.6	100
Household Income Growth	3.30%	6.10%	Buying Power Index	105	100
Unemployment Rate	3.30%	5.10%	Median Home Price	$140,800	$208,500
Recent Job Growth	1.70%	1.30%	Home Price Ratio	3.3	4.7
Projected Future Job Growth	11.50%	10.50%	Home Price Appreciation	8.90%	13.60%
State Income Tax Rate	0%	5.00%	% Homes Owned	57%	64.10%
State Sales Tax Rate	6%	6.00%	Median Rent	$609	$792

EDUCATION

ATTAINMENT & ACHIEVEMENT	AREA	U.S. AVG	RESOURCES & INVESTMENT	AREA	U.S. AVG
% High School Graduate	83.40%	83.90%	No. of Highly Ranked Universities	0	1
% 2-yr Graduate	8.10%	7.10%	$ Invested per Pupil	$4,715	$6,058
% 4-yr Graduate	16.80%	17.20%	Student/Teacher Ratio	16.2	15.9
% Graduate or Professional Degree	5.10%	9.90%	State University In-State Tuition	$4,802	$4,917
% Attending Public School	91.60%	84.30%			
75th Percentile State University SAT Score (Verbal)	N/A	477			
75th Percentile State University SAT Score (Math)	N/A	478			
75th Percentile State University ACT Score	20	20			

LIFESTYLE

RECREATION, ARTS & CULTURE	AREA	U.S. AVG	INFRASTRUCTURE & FACILITIES	AREA	U.S. AVG
Professional Sports Rating	2	4	No. of Public Libraries	4	28
Zoos & Aquariums Rating	5	3	Library Volumes Per Capita	1.7	2.8
Amusement Park Rating	1	3	No. of Warehouse Clubs	3	4
Professional Theater Rating	1	3	No. of Starbucks	1	5
Overall Museum Rating	6	6	Golf Course Rating	2	4
Science Museum Rating	7	4	National Park Rating	10	3
Children's Museum Rating	1	3	Sq. Mi. Inland Water	2	4

CLIMATE			COMMUTE & TRANSPORTATION		
Days Mostly Sunny	205	212	Avg. Daily Commute Time	17.3	24.7
Annual Days Precipitation	96	111	% Commute by Auto	70%	77.70%
Annual Days > 90°F	32	38	Per Capita Avg. Daily Transit Miles	3.9	7.9
Annual Days < 32°F	169	88	Annual Auto Insurance Premium	$840	$1,314
July Relative Humidity	71	69	Gas, Cost per Gallon	$3.05	$3.05

HEALTH & SAFETY

CRIME & ENVIRNOMENTAL ISSUES	AREA	U.S. AVG	HEALTHCARE & COST	AREA	U.S. AVG
Violent Crime Rate	345	517	Physicians per Capita	316.7	254.3
Change in Violent Crime	-1.90%	-7.50%	Pediatricians per Capita	13.1	16.9
Property Crime Rate	3806	3783	Hospital Beds per Capita	405.6	239.7
Change in Property Crime	-30.70%	-10.10%	No. of Teaching Hospitals	1	1.9
Air Quality Score	45	44	Healthcare Cost Index	91.8	100
Water Quality Score	42	33	Cost per Doctor Visit	$62	$74
Pollen/Allergy Score	52	61	Cost per Dentist Visit	$65	$67
Stress Score	5	49	Cost per Hospital Room	$697	$702
Cancer Mortality Rate	158.9	168.9			

Reno, NV

Area Type: Outer suburb

Zip Code: 89523

Metro Area: Reno, NV

Metro Area Type: Mid-size

Location: 7 miles west of downtown Reno along I-80

Time Zone: Pacific Standard Time

Pros:
    Attractive setting
    Outdoor recreation
    Pleasant climate

Cons:
    Growth and sprawl
    Rising home prices
    Tourist impact

Reno has long been a popular destination for Westerners with a little money in their pockets. Now thousands of California transplants—and major employers along with them—seeking lower taxes, better living costs, less crowding, and the great outdoors are taking a gamble on the "Biggest Little City in the World." This claim made by the large overhead sign on Virginia Street is slowly being realized, and the happy result is a more livable and self-sufficient city, far less dependent on the gaming and vacation industries than its flashier neighbor to the south. In the past few years, Amazon, Wal-Mart, and others have made major commitments to the area, and the once-cyclical gaming industry accounts for less than half of the Washoe County economy. High-tech and manufacturing industries have moved in to capitalize on the attractive location, low cost of doing business, and educated population base. Reno's growth as a regional distribution center is due largely to its location at the western edge of Nevada's high desert where I-80 meets the Sierra Nevada mountains—next stop: all points California.

The majority of the casinos are downtown, where the Truckee River, I-80, and the Union Pacific Railroad pass. Downtown is clean, and renewal efforts include relocating the railroad below street grade and building an excellent waterfront park and recreation area along the fast-flowing Truckee. Some crowded and relatively unattractive commercial zones are found close to downtown and particularly to the south and east along the major arteries, but older, established residential neighborhoods to the southwest are pleasant. Reno is also a college town, with the 10,000-student University of Nevada-Reno campus just north of downtown.

Reno is set against the dramatic eastern escarpment of the Sierra Nevada mountains, and views to the west are of snow-capped mountains and Douglas fir forest. Elevation changes within the city itself are dramatic, providing sweeping views of the Reno basin from many

neighborhoods. The best neighborhoods lie to the west and south; the chosen zip code of 89523 lies north of I-80 and west of both McCarran Boulevard and the town. A hilly and mainly desert area turned modern suburbia, the area has good schools, plenty of services, a married-with-children percentage of 36%, and nice views of the mountains and city that might remind some of the Colorado Front Range suburbs near Denver.

Standard of Living   Reno has traditionally been one of the more affordable cities out West, but recent California newcomers and subsequent growth have pushed housing prices upward dramatically, with year-to-year increases as much as 40%. There is a shortage of entry-level homes, and prices of $200 per square foot and higher are commonplace. The "sweet spot" for family homes has pushed well over $400K, but that's still attractive relative to other parts of the West and especially California. Some may not care for the California-style homes on small lots in large subdivisions. Property taxes run about 1.3% with a statutory cap near that level. The overall Cost of Living Index for Reno is a reasonable 117, reflecting low tax rates, as well as low transportation and healthcare costs, but housing costs are expected to continue to rise as new jobs and California transplants create demand for housing.

The gaming industry is still among major employers, with nearly 50% of the workforce employed in gaming-associated hotels, casinos, restaurants, and nightclubs. Current unemployment is 3% and recent job growth is 4.3%. Amazon, Wal-Mart, and other corporate migrants add to future job prospects, with a conservative 12% expected job growth rate projection.

Education   Schools in the Reno area all rate well. In the neighborhood identified with the 89523 zip code, schools test consistently 20% or more above state averages, and school facilities are modern and attractive. The University of Nevada-Reno contributes a college element with its campus just east of the chosen zip code area.

Lifestyle Reno offers a broad range of year-round outdoor activities. In the summer and fall, camping, fishing, hunting, golf, rafting, and kayaking are all easily accessible within minutes of town. Rock climbing and mountain biking are also very popular. In winter and spring, some of the best downhill and cross-country skiing in the country is less than an hour's drive away. Lake Tahoe is just 45 minutes away and is a spectacular destination for all forms of outdoor recreation and other entertainment. By law, casino gaming is restricted to adults, but the Circus Circus casino in Reno also caters to children with many popular and family-oriented shows and features. Although the area isn't generally considered a cultural hot spot, there is a growing complement of arts resources, especially performing arts, some in conjunction with the university. The historic and well-preserved Comstock Lode mining town of Virginia City remains a popular local weekend destination.

Most Reno commutes are less than 20 minutes, but increasing volumes of traffic are becoming an issue. Notably, the city has good air service, and major carriers serve Chicago, Salt Lake City, Phoenix, and most California cities, with some discount carrier service.

Reno sits in a shallow basin just east of the main Sierra ridge, with dry, rain-shadow mountains spreading in other directions. The Sierra rain shadow and the 4,400-foot elevation, combined with an inland location, lead to a dry, sunny, and pleasant climate most of the year, with 255 sunny days, a few sharp cold snaps, and some snow.

Health & Safety Violent and property crime rates and estimated risks are both somewhat higher than national averages. While air quality is usually quite good, the topography lends itself to some periods of air stagnation and unattractive haze, mainly in summer and winter. Healthcare resources are adequate with six hospitals in the area.

Nearby Neighborhoods The better residential neighborhoods are west and southwest of town. More upscale areas are found south toward Lake Tahoe along US 395 at the junction with the Mount Rose Highway (SR 431). Sparks, just east of Reno on I-80, is more industrial but may see eventual growth. Areas in the Lake Tahoe Basin are far more expensive.

RENO, NV NEIGHBORHOOD HIGHLIGHTS	
PEOPLE	
Population	19,408
15-yr Population Growth	49.50%
5-yr Population Growth	12.20%
% Married w/Children	36.3%
% Single w/Children	7.5%
No. of Households	7,389
Median Age	33.8
Avg. Household Size	2.61
Diversity Measure	30
STANDARD OF LIVING	
Median Household Income	$61,263
% Household Income > $100K	17%
Projected Future Job Growth	12%
Cost of Living Index	117
Buying Power Index	118
Weekly Daycare Cost	$132
Median Home Price	$465,500
"Sweet Spot" Home Price	$450,000
Home Price Ratio	7.6
Median Age of Homes	7.1
% Homes Owned	59%
Effective Property Tax Rate	1.30%
Estimated Property Tax Bill	$5,850
EDUCATION	
% High School Graduates	95%
% 4-yr Degree	26%
% Graduate or Professional Degree	13%
$ Invested per Pupil	$4,896
Student/Teacher Ratio	19.2
Primary Test Score Percentile	123.2
Secondary Test Score Percentile	123.4
% Subsidized School Lunch	13.90%
% Attending Public School	90.10%
LIFESTYLE	**BEST**
Leisure Rating (Area)	7
Arts & Culture Rating (Area)	5
Climate Rating (Area)	8
Physical Setting Rating	7
Downtown Core Rating	6
% Commute < 30 Min.	88%
% Commute > 1 Hour	2%
HEALTH & SAFETY	
Health Rating (Area)	3
Stress Score (Area)	7
Violent Crime Risk	168
Property Crime Risk	158

RENO, NV
AREA HIGHLIGHTS

PEOPLE

SIZE & DIVERSITY	AREA	U.S. AVG	FAMILY DEMOGRAPHICS	AREA	U.S. AVG
Population	380,754		% Married	53%	53.80%
15-yr Population Growth	49.50%	4.40%	% Single	47%	46.20%
Diversity Measure	43	54	% Divorced	14.70%	10.20%
% Religiously Observant	28%	50%	% Separated	3%	2.10%
% Catholic	16%	22%	% Married w/Children	23.90%	27.90%
% Protestant	11%	25%	% Single w/Children	11.20%	9.40%
% Jewish	1%	2%	% Married, No Children	27.20%	31.00%
% Other	0%	1%	% Single, No Children	37.70%	31.70%

STANDARD OF LIVING

INCOME, EMPLOYMENT & TAXES	AREA	U.S. AVG	COST OF LIVING & HOUSING	AREA	U.S. AVG
Median Household Income	$47,402	$44,684	Cost of Living Index	106.8	100
Household Income Growth	3%	6.10%	Buying Power Index	99	100
Unemployment Rate	3%	5.10%	Median Home Price	$357,400	$208,500
Recent Job Growth	4.30%	1.30%	Home Price Ratio	7.5	4.7
Projected Future Job Growth	12.30%	10.50%	Home Price Appreciation	31.80%	13.60%
State Income Tax Rate	0%	5.00%	% Homes Owned	56.30%	64.10%
State Sales Tax Rate	6.80%	6.00%	Median Rent	$852	$792

EDUCATION

ATTAINMENT & ACHIEVEMENT	AREA	U.S. AVG	RESOURCES & INVESTMENT	AREA	U.S. AVG
% High School Graduate	82%	83.90%	No. of Highly Ranked Universities	0	1
% 2-yr Graduate	10.60%	7.10%	$ Invested per Pupil	$5,235	$6,058
% 4-yr Graduate	21.20%	17.20%	Student/Teacher Ratio	19.5	15.9
% Graduate or Professional Degree	8.40%	9.90%	State University In-State Tuition	$3,270	$4,917
% Attending Public School	93.10%	84.30%			
75th Percentile State University SAT Score (Verbal)	450	477			
75th Percentile State University SAT Score (Math)	450	478			
75th Percentile State University ACT Score	18	20			

LIFESTYLE

RECREATION, ARTS & CULTURE	AREA	U.S. AVG	INFRASTRUCTURE & FACILITIES	AREA	U.S. AVG
Professional Sports Rating	2	4	No. of Public Libraries	13	28
Zoos & Aquariums Rating	1	3	Library Volumes Per Capita	2.3	2.8
Amusement Park Rating	5	3	No. of Warehouse Clubs	3	4
Professional Theater Rating	1	3	No. of Starbucks	16	5
Overall Museum Rating	5	6	Golf Course Rating	2	4
Science Museum Rating	5	4	National Park Rating	8	3
Children's Museum Rating	4	3	Sq. Mi. Inland Water	10	4

CLIMATE			COMMUTE & TRANSPORTATION		
Days Mostly Sunny	255	212	Avg. Daily Commute Time	19.2	24.7
Annual Days Precipitation	49	111	% Commute by Auto	70%	77.70%
Annual Days > 90°F	52	38	Per Capita Avg. Daily Transit Miles	14.6	7.9
Annual Days < 32°F	189	88	Annual Auto Insurance Premium	$1,482	$1,314
July Relative Humidity	50	69	Gas, Cost per Gallon	$3.06	$3.05

HEALTH & SAFETY

CRIME & ENVIRNOMENTAL ISSUES	AREA	U.S. AVG	HEALTHCARE & COST	AREA	U.S. AVG
Violent Crime Rate	517	517	Physicians per Capita	271.8	254.3
Change in Violent Crime	15.60%	-7.50%	Pediatricians per Capita	12.9	16.9
Property Crime Rate	4518	3783	Hospital Beds per Capita	305.8	239.7
Change in Property Crime	1.70%	-10.10%	No. of Teaching Hospitals	1	1.9
Air Quality Score	33	44	Healthcare Cost Index	116.6	100
Water Quality Score	40	33	Cost per Doctor Visit	$69	$74
Pollen/Allergy Score	63	61	Cost per Dentist Visit	$89	$67
Stress Score	72	49	Cost per Hospital Room	$963	$702
Cancer Mortality Rate	180.7	168.9			

Richmond-Tuckahoe, VA

Area Type: Small capital city

Zip Code: 23233

Metro Area: Richmond, VA

Metro Area Type: Mid-size

Location: 15 miles west of downtown Richmond

Time Zone: Eastern Standard Time

Pros:
Central location
Cost of living
Schools

Cons:
Downtown area
Growth and sprawl
Lack of entertainment

Centered between Virginia's main attractions and Washington, DC, Richmond is a quiet capital city and commercial center with distinct historical and Southern roots. The broad, shallow James River flowing past the downtown makes for an attractive waterfront and adds to a relatively peaceful experience of modest pace—compared to the bustling 'burbs of northern Virginia just 100 miles north.

Fire destroyed most of Richmond at the end of the Civil War, but—excluding its somewhat uninteresting downtown core—Richmond is a very appealing place. It's dotted with important sites like the State Capital, the Governor's Mansion, and the Museum of the Confederacy, and areas in need of some work are slated for redevelopment. Shockhoe Slip, an old waterfront warehouse area, has been attractively restored, but much of the downtown is adorned with a bland mix of mid-20th-century concrete and glass structures. The area's economy, for many years tied to the capital and state government, has emerged as a strong commercial center, home to such companies as Circuit City, Capital One, and CarMax, Inc., and a number of smaller high-tech and manufacturing firms choosing to avoid the drawbacks of the DC area while remaining close by. Many of these firms are located in office complexes outside of town, while downtown remains mainly a government and legal center for the state.

To the west of town, older and very attractive residential neighborhoods are laid out in a grid along the river and Patterson Avenue. Farther west, these stately neighborhoods give way to more contemporary but gracious subdivisions as the suburban street bends due west, now more of a broad, attractive boulevard. Tuckahoe is the first of several neighborhoods along Patterson as it heads—seemingly without end—into the western reaches of Henrico County. Small retail clusters and shopping centers form neighborhood centers for com-munities lying mostly north of the road. These communities, with solid housing and strong schools, form a good set of choices for families. The married-with-children percentage is 32.6%.

Standard of Living Compared to Cost of Living Indexes typically in the 130 to 150 range in northern Virginia, the Richmond metro area COL Index of 90 explains the attraction. The Cost of Living rises to almost 110 in the western suburbs, but stable and growing incomes yield a strong Buying Power Index of 155. Homes run typically $120 to $140 per square foot, and, while lot sizes are fairly small at a ¼ to a ½ acre, the homes are mostly southern colonials set among dense, mature trees. Good family homes run in the upper $200Ks to low $300Ks, with some new construction approaching $500K. While not the least expensive in Virginia, these homes represent a good value. Income growth in Richmond is strong, and property taxes are low, typically 1.4% or less.

Education Schools in western Henrico County are considered excellent and score well on Virginia Standards of Learning (SOL) tests. Most schools score well into the 90% proficient range and 10 to 20 points above state averages. Godwin High School scored 96% and 99% respectively on 2003 reading and math tests. Higher education is centered around the University of Richmond (a private liberal arts school) and Virginia Commonwealth University, both giving a minor college-town influence to the city.

Lifestyle The lifestyle is quiet and laid-back at most times. Residents take advantage of the city's first-class museums, including the Virginia Museum of Fine Arts, the State Capitol, Maymont Estate, and the Science Museum of Virginia, all of which draw more than a quarter-million visitors per year. There are several historical sites, a noted children's museum, and a nature

RICHMOND-TUCKAHOE, VA
NEIGHBORHOOD HIGHLIGHTS

PEOPLE

Population	52,967
15-yr Population Growth	26.90%
5-yr Population Growth	5.40%
% Married w/Children	31.4%
% Single w/Children	7.3%
No. of Households	20,631
Median Age	36.8
Avg. Household Size	2.48
Diversity Measure	20

STANDARD OF LIVING

Median Household Income	$76,854
% Household Income > $100K	29%
Projected Future Job Growth	12%
Cost of Living Index	110
Buying Power Index	155
Weekly Daycare Cost	$140
Median Home Price	$289,500
"Sweet Spot" Home Price	$300,000
Home Price Ratio	3.8
Median Age of Homes	14.6
% Homes Owned	69%
Effective Property Tax Rate	1.40%
Estimated Property Tax Bill	$4,200

EDUCATION

% High School Graduates	96%
% 4-yr Degree	36%
% Graduate or Professional Degree	21%
$ Invested per Pupil	$5,306
Student/Teacher Ratio	16.2
Primary Test Score Percentile	123.2
Secondary Test Score Percentile	112.1
% Subsidized School Lunch	6.10%
% Attending Public School	77.80%

LIFESTYLE

Leisure Rating (Area)	5
Arts & Culture Rating (Area)	9
Climate Rating (Area)	4
Physical Setting Rating	5
Downtown Core Rating	5
% Commute < 30 Min.	69%
% Commute > 1 Hour	4%

HEALTH & SAFETY

Health Rating (Area)	8
Stress Score (Area)	5
Violent Crime Risk	31
Property Crime Risk	31

center and aquarium in the area. Paramount King's Dominion is a large amusement park 30 miles north in Doswell, and from there, activities spread in all directions—an hour to Charlottesville to the west; 2 hours to Virginia Beach, Williamsburg, or the DC area to the east and north; a little farther to North Carolina's Outer Banks.

Although quite spread out, roads are well-engineered, and traffic and commute flows are generally not a problem. The large corporate office parks are a 10- to 15-minute commute to the I-295 beltway north in the Glen Allen area, and downtown Richmond is 30 to 40 minutes.

The area, just where the coastal plain meets the Piedmont Hills, is gently rolling and heavily forested on both sides of the river. The climate is modified continental with some ocean influence. The area does have four seasons, but winters are reasonable with infrequent bitter cold, snow, or prolonged accumulation, while summers can be hot and muggy.

Health & Safety Measured by the "CAP" index, crime risk is very low. Healthcare is better than average, with teaching hospitals and healthcare facilities tied to Virginia Commonwealth University. Area healthcare costs are reasonable at 90% of the U.S. average.

Nearby Neighborhoods The suburban area is large and without great variation; it becomes a matter of picking a community and a subdivision. South of the river across the "Nickel Bridge" is Westover Hills, a very attractive, hilly, wooded, and somewhat more expensive area.

RICHMOND, VA
AREA HIGHLIGHTS
PEOPLE

SIZE & DIVERSITY	AREA	U.S. AVG	FAMILY DEMOGRAPHICS	AREA	U.S. AVG
Population	1,047,366		% Married	52.60%	53.80%
15-yr Population Growth	24.30%	4.40%	% Single	47.40%	46.20%
Diversity Measure	49	54	% Divorced	7.50%	10.20%
% Religiously Observant	44%	50%	% Separated	5.10%	2.10%
% Catholic	6%	22%	% Married w/Children	26.10%	27.90%
% Protestant	36%	25%	% Single w/Children	10.50%	9.40%
% Jewish	2%	2%	% Married, No Children	29.90%	31.00%
% Other	0%	1%	% Single, No Children	30.80%	31.70%

STANDARD OF LIVING

INCOME, EMPLOYMENT & TAXES	AREA	U.S. AVG	COST OF LIVING & HOUSING	AREA	U.S. AVG
Median Household Income	$54,197	$44,684	Cost of Living Index	90.3	100
Household Income Growth	3.80%	6.10%	Buying Power Index	134	100
Unemployment Rate	3.80%	5.10%	Median Home Price	$198,400	$208,500
Recent Job Growth	2.30%	1.30%	Home Price Ratio	3.7	4.7
Projected Future Job Growth	12.60%	10.50%	Home Price Appreciation	13.50%	13.60%
State Income Tax Rate	5.80%	5.00%	% Homes Owned	66.80%	64.10%
State Sales Tax Rate	4.40%	6.00%	Median Rent	$810	$792

EDUCATION

ATTAINMENT & ACHIEVEMENT	AREA	U.S. AVG	RESOURCES & INVESTMENT	AREA	U.S. AVG
% High School Graduate	75%	83.90%	No. of Highly Ranked Universities	0	1
% 2-yr Graduate	6.80%	7.10%	$ Invested per Pupil	$5,653	$6,058
% 4-yr Graduate	17.90%	17.20%	Student/Teacher Ratio	14.7	15.9
% Graduate or Professional Degree	9.50%	9.90%	State University In-State Tuition	$5,838	$4,917
% Attending Public School	92%	84.30%			
75th Percentile State University SAT Score (Verbal)	540	477			
75th Percentile State University SAT Score (Math)	560	478			
75th Percentile State University ACT Score	N/A	20			

LIFESTYLE

RECREATION, ARTS & CULTURE	AREA	U.S. AVG	INFRASTRUCTURE & FACILITIES	AREA	U.S. AVG
Professional Sports Rating	3	4	No. of Public Libraries	51	28
Zoos & Aquariums Rating	1	3	Library Volumes Per Capita	3.1	2.8
Amusement Park Rating	8	3	No. of Warehouse Clubs	7	4
Professional Theater Rating	8	3	No. of Starbucks	17	5
Overall Museum Rating	9	6	Golf Course Rating	5	4
Science Museum Rating	7	4	National Park Rating	2	3
Children's Museum Rating	7	3	Sq. Mi. Inland Water	6	4

CLIMATE			COMMUTE & TRANSPORTATION		
Days Mostly Sunny	210	212	Avg. Daily Commute Time	24.3	24.7
Annual Days Precipitation	113	111	% Commute by Auto	72%	77.70%
Annual Days > 90°F	41	38	Per Capita Avg. Daily Transit Miles	7.5	7.9
Annual Days < 32°F	85	88	Annual Auto Insurance Premium	$1,102	$1,314
July Relative Humidity	72	69	Gas, Cost per Gallon	$3.12	$3.05

HEALTH & SAFETY

CRIME & ENVIRNOMENTAL ISSUES	AREA	U.S. AVG	HEALTHCARE & COST	AREA	U.S. AVG
Violent Crime Rate	411	517	Physicians per Capita	314.4	254.3
Change in Violent Crime	-18.70%	-7.50%	Pediatricians per Capita	22.5	16.9
Property Crime Rate	3922	3783	Hospital Beds per Capita	576.4	239.7
Change in Property Crime	-15%	-10.10%	No. of Teaching Hospitals	4	1.9
Air Quality Score	59	44	Healthcare Cost Index	89.6	100
Water Quality Score	80	33	Cost per Doctor Visit	$77	$74
Pollen/Allergy Score	66	61	Cost per Dentist Visit	$68	$67
Stress Score	50	49	Cost per Hospital Room	$598	$702
Cancer Mortality Rate	177.8	168.9			

Roanoke, VA

Area Type: Small city

Zip Code: 24018

Metro Area: Roanoke, VA

Metro Area Type: Smaller

Location: 4 miles southwest of downtown Roanoke, in southwestern Virginia along the Blue Ridge mountains

Time Zone: Eastern Standard Time

Pros:
Attractive downtown and setting
Historic interest
Healthcare

Cons:
Some growth pressure
Air service
Low educational attainment

In 1953, the last steam locomotive to be built for a U.S. mainline railroad rolled off the shop floor of the gargantuan Norfolk & Western Railway shops adjacent to downtown Roanoke. The railway, headquartered in the city, was the area's main employer, and the endless coal trains from the western mines to the ports at Norfolk were the lifeblood of this—at the time—relatively uninteresting place.

A lot has changed since 1953. This nicely sized city of 100,000 residents situated in the Roanoke Valley, a shallow but attractive valley in the heart of the Blue Ridge Mountains, has done a lot right in recent years and is an attractive place for families. Traditionally a Southern city located at the eastern gateway to a major section of Appalachia, recent migration from many areas of the country has given a more cosmopolitan flavor and more cultural diversity. That said, it remains Virginia at its finest: full of tradition, prosperous, dignified, and touched with Southern charm.

The downtown area is classic America, a mix of modestly sized newer commercial buildings and older 19th- and early-20th-century brick warehouses and storefronts. It is clean, fully inhabited, and a great walking city. The historic areas around Market Square downtown come alive daily (except Sunday) with a farmer's market that has operated since 1882. Numerous quality shops and the restored Center in the Square performing arts venue attract residents, particularly on the weekends. The Center in the Square, a restored 1910-era warehouse, is noteworthy for the quality of not only the restoration but also the performing acts and museums using it.

The economic base is diverse, with an attractive climate for small and medium-sized manufacturers. Major employers include the railroad industry, Johnson & Johnson, and GE just to the west in Salem, but the

assortment of smaller employers is the real economic story. The Carilion Health Foundation, a major employer, operates an assortment of area healthcare providers, including a major hospital, healthcare training facilities, and a cancer center. The current unemployment rate is 2.7%, but job growth is projected at 3%, a figure we suspect will be easy to beat.

Standard of Living The low cost of living is one of the attractions, and the COL Index of 95 compares well with other parts of Virginia and the east. A recent surge of new home building to the northwest has kept prices moderate and supply plentiful. Good family homes can be had here starting in the high $100Ks, and $100 per square foot is the norm for most of the area. Daycare is a very reasonable $112 per week. Property tax rates are 1.2%, also reasonable, particularly with modest valuations. Above-average income levels and low cost of living give a Buying Power Index of 146.

Education Schools are good and attractively sized at 200 to 250 students per grade level on both the north and the southwest sides. The local student-teacher ratio is a strong 12. Test scores (6%–15% above state averages) and overall 4-year degree attainment run stronger in the 24018 zip code on the southwest side. New schools have just been built on both the north and the south sides, and school infrastructure is generally keeping up with growth. Big names in higher education are absent; but the local private liberal arts Hollins University is a top-rated school of 800 students, and Virginia Tech lies just down the road in Blacksburg.

Lifestyle Roanoke is casual, easy, and fun. Adding to the city highlights mentioned above are the Virginia Museum of Transportation and a strong city park and recreation system. There is an ice rink, and even a professional minor-league hockey team, giving a subtle hint of the area's newfound popularity with transplants, particularly from the Northeast. The city is culturally very open and stimulating with an actively supported arts and music community. Roanoke is a tad less conservative than most other Virginia cities with strong yet diverse religious beliefs, but still maintains close ties to tradition. The city limits quickly give way to top recreational amenities, including Smith Lake and hiking and nature outposts in the Blue Ridge mountains. For big-city amenities, most travel to the DC area 4 hours to the northeast.

Commutes are a non-issue: It seldom takes more than 15 to 20 minutes to get anywhere in Roanoke. Local residents do complain about air service, which is commuter-only and expensive, and many drive to Greensboro, North Carolina, to get better service and prices.

The Roanoke Valley is relatively flat; the surrounding terrain is hilly to mountainous and wooded. The mountains and slightly higher elevation (1,176 feet) give more pleasant summers and protected winters than many other Virginia and East Coast areas.

Health & Safety   Crime risk is low and air quality is well above average. Healthcare facilities are some of the best anywhere for a city of this size, anchored by the Carilion healthcare complex.

Nearby Neighborhoods   Most of the Roanoke area is quite livable; residential areas flank the city to the southwest and northwest, with most of the growth in the north area. Although we gave a slight edge to the southwest side toward Cave Spring due to the availability of better education and presence of families with children (25%), the northwest area is worth a look too.

ROANOKE, VA NEIGHBORHOOD HIGHLIGHTS	
PEOPLE	
Population	29,645
15-yr Population Growth	10.60%
5-yr Population Growth	2.20%
% Married w/Children	24.7%
% Single w/Children	6.2%
No. of Households	12,488
Median Age	40.5
Avg. Household Size	2.37
Diversity Measure	10
STANDARD OF LIVING	
Median Household Income	$61,719
% Household Income > $100K	19%
Projected Future Job Growth	3%
Cost of Living Index	94.6
Buying Power Index	146
Weekly Daycare Cost	$112
Median Home Price	$219,000
"Sweet Spot" Home Price	$200,000
Home Price Ratio	3.5
Median Age of Homes	26.9
% Homes Owned	75%
Effective Property Tax Rate	1.2%
Estimated Property Tax Bill	$2,400
EDUCATION	
% High School Graduates	94%
% 4-yr Degree	28%
% Graduate or Professional Degree	15%
$ Invested per Pupil	$5,790
Student/Teacher Ratio	12.2
Primary Test Score Percentile	115.3
Secondary Test Score Percentile	109.4
% Subsidized School Lunch	9.80%
% Attending Public School	82%
LIFESTYLE	
Leisure Rating (Area)	3
Arts & Culture Rating (Area)	8
Climate Rating (Area)	8
Physical Setting Rating	7
Downtown Core Rating	10
% Commute < 30 Min.	82%
% Commute > 1 Hour	3%
HEALTH & SAFETY	BEST
Health Rating (Area)	10
Stress Score (Area)	3
Violent Crime Risk	52
Property Crime Risk	57

RICHMOND, VA
AREA HIGHLIGHTS

PEOPLE

SIZE & DIVERSITY	AREA	U.S. AVG	FAMILY DEMOGRAPHICS	AREA	U.S. AVG
Population	236,155		% Married	51.90%	53.80%
15-yr Population Growth	6.10%	4.40%	% Single	48.10%	46.20%
Diversity Measure	29	54	% Divorced	8.90%	10.20%
% Religiously Observant	55%	50%	% Separated	3.90%	2.10%
% Catholic	4%	22%	% Married w/Children	24.20%	27.90%
% Protestant	50%	25%	% Single w/Children	9.10%	9.40%
% Jewish	0%	2%	% Married, No Children	30%	31.00%
% Other	0%	1%	% Single, No Children	36.70%	31.70%

STANDARD OF LIVING

INCOME, EMPLOYMENT & TAXES	AREA	U.S. AVG	COST OF LIVING & HOUSING	AREA	U.S. AVG
Median Household Income	$44,698	$44,684	Cost of Living Index	95	100
Household Income Growth	2.70%	6.10%	Buying Power Index	105	100
Unemployment Rate	2.70%	5.10%	Median Home Price	$209,600	$208,500
Recent Job Growth	1.90%	1.30%	Home Price Ratio	4.7	4.7
Projected Future Job Growth	6.10%	10.50%	Home Price Appreciation	8.70%	13.60%
State Income Tax Rate	5.80%	5.00%	% Homes Owned	66.80%	64.10%
State Sales Tax Rate	3.50%	6.00%	Median Rent	$586	$792

EDUCATION

ATTAINMENT & ACHIEVEMENT	AREA	U.S. AVG	RESOURCES & INVESTMENT	AREA	U.S. AVG
% High School Graduate	73.10%	83.90%	No. of Highly Ranked Universities	0	1
% 2-yr Graduate	8.70%	7.10%	$ Invested per Pupil	$6,060	$6,058
% 4-yr Graduate	15%	17.20%	Student/Teacher Ratio	13.9	15.9
% Graduate or Professional Degree	7.40%	9.90%	State University In-State Tuition	$5,838	$4,917
% Attending Public School	95.10%	84.30%			
75th Percentile State University SAT Score (Verbal)	540	477			
75th Percentile State University SAT Score (Math)	560	478			
75th Percentile State University ACT Score	N/A	20			

LIFESTYLE

RECREATION, ARTS & CULTURE	AREA	U.S. AVG	INFRASTRUCTURE & FACILITIES	AREA	U.S. AVG
Professional Sports Rating	3	4	No. of Public Libraries	17	28
Zoos & Aquariums Rating	1	3	Library Volumes Per Capita	4	2.8
Amusement Park Rating	1	3	No. of Warehouse Clubs	1	4
Professional Theater Rating	1	3	No. of Starbucks	1	5
Overall Museum Rating	5	6	Golf Course Rating	2	4
Science Museum Rating	5	4	National Park Rating	5	3
Children's Museum Rating	1	3	Sq. Mi. Inland Water	2	4

CLIMATE			COMMUTE & TRANSPORTATION		
Days Mostly Sunny	217	212	Avg. Daily Commute Time	20.6	24.7
Annual Days Precipitation	121	111	% Commute by Auto	76%	77.70%
Annual Days > 90°F	20	38	Per Capita Avg. Daily Transit Miles	6.7	7.9
Annual Days < 32°F	92	88	Annual Auto Insurance Premium	$1,040	$1,314
July Relative Humidity	65	69	Gas, Cost per Gallon	$3.12	$3.05

HEALTH & SAFETY

CRIME & ENVIRNOMENTAL ISSUES	AREA	U.S. AVG	HEALTHCARE & COST	AREA	U.S. AVG
Violent Crime Rate	340	517	Physicians per Capita	394.4	254.3
Change in Violent Crime	-0.10%	-7.50%	Pediatricians per Capita	18.6	16.9
Property Crime Rate	2835	3783	Hospital Beds per Capita	746.7	239.7
Change in Property Crime	-12.30%	-10.10%	No. of Teaching Hospitals	2	1.9
Air Quality Score	66	44	Healthcare Cost Index	93.6	100
Water Quality Score	85	33	Cost per Doctor Visit	$76	$74
Pollen/Allergy Score	53	61	Cost per Dentist Visit	$53	$67
Stress Score	33	49	Cost per Hospital Room	$480	$702
Cancer Mortality Rate	157	168.9			

Rochester, MN

Area Type: Small city

Zip Code: 55902

Metro Area: Rochester, MN

Metro Area Type: Smaller

Location: Southeast Minnesota, 85 miles southeast of Minneapolis–St. Paul

Time Zone: Central Standard Time

Pros:
Attractive housing
Healthcare
Convenience

Cons:
Winter climate
Entertainment
Some corporate downsizing

Mayo Clinic. Healthcare. Rochester, Minnesota. Over the years, these phrases have become synonymous to Minnesotans. The "healthy" small metropolis of Rochester, population 133,000, includes one of the greatest healthcare complexes in the world—the Mayo Clinic and its aligned research facilities. Employing some 2,500 physicians and research scientists, the Mayo Clinic mixes a unique intellectual element and a varied skill set into this solid Midwestern small city. That mix is strengthened by the presence of high-tech industries, notably IBM.

In a shallow valley that spans the Zumbro River, downtown Rochester is clean, fairly modern, and attractive. The city and its healthy economy supports a great park system, with over 3,500 acres of parks, 60 miles of trails, 23 miles of bike trails, two dog parks, several indoor and outdoor pools, and more than 50 playgrounds scattered through and around the city. The Mayo Civic Center hosts conventions, concerts, and performing arts—some 1,300 events each year in total.

No other healthcare complex has the impact on a city that the Mayo Clinic has on Rochester. The Mayo complex, just west of the downtown core, covers some 18 city blocks. Taken together with the affiliated St. Mary's Hospital, the Clinic employs some 42,000 workers in total (a gigantic influence in an area of 130,000). Some 400,000 people from all over the world come to the clinic for treatment or as visitors each year, supporting a large hospitality industry in Rochester. IBM at one point employed 5,000 workers but has since downsized. Many displaced workers have relocated to other tech and contract manufacturing firms in the area. Agribusiness, food processing, and the local school system round out the area's employment picture.

Standard of Living Living costs in the Rochester metro area are comparable to national averages, and the

Cost of Living Index for the more upscale southwest side is 116. Although the overall COL is high, homes in the area run a very affordable $75 to $100 per square foot, and good starter homes for families are abundant at $200K. The prime choices are in the $250K to $300K range, which buys a generously sized (3,000-square-foot–plus) newer home in the attractive southwest side. Families with moderate incomes fare well, and higher-paid doctors and scientists can live quite comfortably in a classy older home on "Pill Hill," the area's high-end enclave.

Education Minnesota has strong education in general, and the special achievement-oriented context created in Rochester brings excellent educational facilities. The 4-year degree attainment in the southwest neighborhood is 27%, but the graduate-level attainment in the area is *another* 26%, making the combined attainment rate of 53% one of the highest outside a true college town. A large number of "high-end" professional workers are accompanied by highly educated nonworking spouses, fostering a very high volunteer rate in schools and organizations. Test scores for neighborhood schools run 10% to 15% above state averages. There is a Rochester campus of the University of Minnesota.

Lifestyle Parks and recreation figure large in the local lifestyle. Team and individual sports are led by soccer and basketball in the summer and fall, with hockey, skating, and sledding in the winter. Parks, pools, and playgrounds host independent events as well as a number of camps and group activities. Outdoor concerts, some with big-name headliners, are held in the city throughout the summer, and performing arts events, including a symphony and ballet, occur in the Mayo Civic Center. Among the many parks, standouts include Chester Woods with a 190-acre reservoir, Silver Lake Park, and the nature-oriented Quarry Hill Park.

ROCHESTER, MN	
NEIGHBORHOOD HIGHLIGHTS	
PEOPLE	
Population	20,083
15-yr Population Growth	25.20%
5-yr Population Growth	7.20%
% Married w/Children	27.7%
% Single w/Children	4.3%
No. of Households	7,969
Median Age	36
Avg. Household Size	2.45
Diversity Measure	17
STANDARD OF LIVING	
Median Household Income	$65,095
% Household Income > $100K	28%
Projected Future Job Growth	12%
Cost of Living Index	116
Buying Power Index	130
Weekly Daycare Cost	$148
Median Home Price	$239,500
"Sweet Spot" Home Price	$275,000
Home Price Ratio	3.7
Median Age of Homes	26.7
% Homes Owned	70%
Effective Property Tax Rate	1.30%
Estimated Property Tax Bill	$3,575
EDUCATION	
% High School Graduates	94%
% 4-yr Degree	27%
% Graduate or Professional Degree	26%
$ Invested per Pupil	$6,102
Student/Teacher Ratio	14
Primary Test Score Percentile	105.9
Secondary Test Score Percentile	93.2
% Subsidized School Lunch	13.50%
% Attending Public School	74.80%
LIFESTYLE	
Leisure Rating (Area)	7
Arts & Culture Rating (Area)	10
Climate Rating (Area)	1
Physical Setting Rating	4
Downtown Core Rating	4
% Commute < 30 Min.	89%
% Commute > 1 Hour	2%
HEALTH & SAFETY	BEST
Health Rating (Area)	10
Stress Score (Area)	0
Violent Crime Risk	92
Property Crime Risk	287

Excellent outdoor facilities are found in state parks and forests just to the east and south, including Whitewater State Park and the 2-million-acre Richard Dorer Memorial Hardwood Forest. Minneapolis–St. Paul, a short 1½ hours away, is never out of mind for Rochester residents.

Commutes are absolutely no issue; in fact, the ample streets and central location of the Mayo Clinic allow an average commute time of about 16 minutes, the seventh best among over 300 U.S. metropolitan areas. In Rochester, you are never more than 15 minutes from anywhere.

The surrounding terrain is wooded with rolling hills. The climate is continental with four distinct seasons, generally pleasant summers, and rigorous winters with persistent snow cover. Being located toward the northern reaches of the Gulf moisture zone results in periods of rain and stronger storms in all seasons.

Health & Safety   Crime risk is low to moderate, stress factors and air quality are favorable, and, in terms of healthcare facilities, well, we'll say no more.

Nearby Neighborhoods   Growth has sprouted from the city in every direction. The chosen neighborhood, zip code 55902, on the southwest side of town, is most popular among Mayo professionals and employees. It's probably the most desirable area in the city, but areas southeast and northeast are also growing. All nearby neighborhoods are attractive and supported by comparable infrastructure.

ROCHESTER, MN
AREA HIGHLIGHTS

PEOPLE

SIZE & DIVERSITY	AREA	U.S. AVG	FAMILY DEMOGRAPHICS	AREA	U.S. AVG
Population	133,283		% Married	62.10%	53.80%
15-yr Population Growth	25.20%	4.40%	% Single	37.90%	46.20%
Diversity Measure	20	54	% Divorced	6.80%	10.20%
% Religiously Observant	62%	50%	% Separated	1.20%	2.10%
% Catholic	22%	22%	% Married w/Children	33.40%	27.90%
% Protestant	39%	25%	% Single w/Children	7.40%	9.40%
% Jewish	0%	2%	% Married, No Children	30.30%	31.00%
% Other	0%	1%	% Single, No Children	28.90%	31.70%

STANDARD OF LIVING

INCOME, EMPLOYMENT & TAXES	AREA	U.S. AVG	COST OF LIVING & HOUSING	AREA	U.S. AVG
Median Household Income	$57,338	$44,684	Cost of Living Index	97.3	100
Household Income Growth	3%	6.10%	Buying Power Index	132	100
Unemployment Rate	3%	5.10%	Median Home Price	$151,500	$208,500
Recent Job Growth	3.60%	1.30%	Home Price Ratio	2.6	4.7
Projected Future Job Growth	11.70%	10.50%	Home Price Appreciation	6.20%	13.60%
State Income Tax Rate	8%	5.00%	% Homes Owned	74.90%	64.10%
State Sales Tax Rate	7%	6.00%	Median Rent	$745	$792

EDUCATION

ATTAINMENT & ACHIEVEMENT	AREA	U.S. AVG	RESOURCES & INVESTMENT	AREA	U.S. AVG
% High School Graduate	89%	83.90%	No. of Highly Ranked Universities	0	1
% 2-yr Graduate	15.40%	7.10%	$ Invested per Pupil	$5,629	$6,058
% 4-yr Graduate	21.30%	17.20%	Student/Teacher Ratio	16.9	15.9
% Graduate or Professional Degree	10.70%	9.90%	State University In-State Tuition	$8,230	$4,917
% Attending Public School	87.20%	84.30%			
75th Percentile State University SAT Score (Verbal)	540	477			
75th Percentile State University SAT Score (Math)	560	478			
75th Percentile State University ACT Score	23	20			

LIFESTYLE

RECREATION, ARTS & CULTURE	AREA	U.S. AVG	INFRASTRUCTURE & FACILITIES	AREA	U.S. AVG
Professional Sports Rating	2	4	No. of Public Libraries	2	28
Zoos & Aquariums Rating	1	3	Library Volumes Per Capita	0.7	2.8
Amusement Park Rating	1	3	No. of Warehouse Clubs	3	4
Professional Theater Rating	1	3	No. of Starbucks	0	5
Overall Museum Rating	3	6	Golf Course Rating	9	4
Science Museum Rating	1	4	National Park Rating	3	3
Children's Museum Rating	1	3	Sq. Mi. Inland Water	2	4

CLIMATE			COMMUTE & TRANSPORTATION		
Days Mostly Sunny	200	212	Avg. Daily Commute Time	16.3	24.7
Annual Days Precipitation	113	111	% Commute by Auto	74%	77.70%
Annual Days > 90°F	15	38	Per Capita Avg. Daily Transit Miles	7.5	7.9
Annual Days < 32°F	158	88	Annual Auto Insurance Premium	$1,236	$1,314
July Relative Humidity	69	69	Gas, Cost per Gallon	$2.80	$3.05

HEALTH & SAFETY

CRIME & ENVIRNOMENTAL ISSUES	AREA	U.S. AVG	HEALTHCARE & COST	AREA	U.S. AVG
Violent Crime Rate	196	517	Physicians per Capita	1781	254.3
Change in Violent Crime	-26.40%	-7.50%	Pediatricians per Capita	56.3	16.9
Property Crime Rate	2372	3783	Hospital Beds per Capita	963	239.7
Change in Property Crime	-8.70%	-10.10%	No. of Teaching Hospitals	2	1.9
Air Quality Score	44	44	Healthcare Cost Index	113.4	100
Water Quality Score	20	33	Cost per Doctor Visit	$98	$74
Pollen/Allergy Score	46	61	Cost per Dentist Visit	$66	$67
Stress Score	1	49	Cost per Hospital Room	$991	$702
Cancer Mortality Rate	151.5	168.9			

Rogers, AR

Area Type: Small town

Zip Code: 72758

Metro Area: Fayetteville-Springdale-Rogers, AR

Metro Area Type: Small

Location: Northwest Arkansas, along I-540 at the west shore of Beaver Lake

Time Zone: Central Standard Time

Pros:
Very strong economy
Local recreation, arts, and culture
Cost of living

Cons:
Traffic
Growth pressure
Crowded schools

As one local resident said, "If you can't find a job in Northwest Arkansas, you can't find one anywhere." Indeed, the isolated and once-quiet set of small Ozark Mountain towns of Fayetteville, Rogers, Springdale, and—what was that other one?—Bentonville has become one of the biggest U.S. growth stories of the past 10 years.

"Why?" you might ask. The area isn't on a coast or near a major city, and it isn't a major resort or retirement destination. And, while the University of Arkansas gives a lift to Fayetteville (especially on football weekends), that isn't the answer either. The reason is simple and lies in the smallest of the four closely grouped towns, Bentonville: The town is the world headquarters of retail giant Wal-Mart.

Wal-Mart employs 13,000 people in its complex, a large number by any measure for a retail headquarters. But this isn't the whole story, either—Wal-Mart has such influence on its supply chain and business partners that its presence attracts manufacturers, distributors, transport providers, and professional services. The area has made it onto many lists of best places to do business.

As such, the entire area has grown and prospered as a model New South town that is well integrated with its Old South roots. (The other major industries are poultry processing and trucking, which speaks to its traditional Southern economic base.) The area has the strong values, community feel, and hospitality expected in any small Southern town. And the area has a better-than-average rate of philanthropy thanks mainly to the Walton family and the Joneses (of Jones Trucking), who provide a complement of arts and cultural amenities well beyond the scale of the region. The 55,000-square-foot Walton Arts Center hosts performing arts, including a symphony, art exhibits, and arts education programs. Extending the family legacy, Alice Walton is

directing the creation of Crystal Bridges, a major $50-million art museum dedicated to American art, scheduled to open in 2009. The Jones family endowed a major family recreation complex in Springdale known as the Jones Center for Families.

Rogers, located 20 miles north of Fayetteville, is probably the most family-oriented town. Closest to Bentonville, the town as a whole has a population of about 40,000 and a married-with-children percentage of 28.5%. The chosen zip code of 72758 is on the east side toward the large reservoir called Beaver Lake. The downtown is small with a base of restaurants and local services. Downtown Rogers needs some renewal (a wall on a historic building recently collapsed), and locals gripe about it being closed evenings and weekends; but most think it has a lot of potential.

Standard of Living   The Cost of Living Index of just under 85 is a major area attraction. Meanwhile, with a recent job growth rate of 7.7% and projected job growth at a sizzling 30%, Rogers' cost-of-living profile is one of the lowest in the country for a prosperous area. Growth and land scarcity are starting to put pressure on home prices, making it increasingly hard to find family homes under $200K; but many are available in the low $200Ks. Most are new, built in the past 10 to 15 years, with lot sizes that are shrinking to a $1/5$ of an acre or less in some of the newest developments. Property tax rates run a low 0.8%, and daycare is a moderate $135 per week. The major drawback to the area is the lower household income levels. This reflects in part the number of single-earner households in the area, but wage scales are low on a national basis.

Education   Test scores show performance well above state averages. Schools are new, attractive, and well funded, but there aren't enough schools or teachers. Recently, the high school was split, putting 11th and

12th graders in one facility and 10th graders in another. Some parents complain of a little too much adherence to traditional values. Prosperity and an influx of educated people indicate a bright future for Rogers.

Lifestyle The lifestyle still reflects that of a small Southern town—except at rush hour. Although it isn't bad on a big-city scale, traffic has become a major issue as roads struggle to keep up with growth. Local arts and cultural resources are notable and continue to diversify. Outdoor recreation is plentiful in nearby mountains, rivers, and the Beaver Lake reservoir just outside of town. The Ozark Natural Science Center, sponsored by the University of Arkansas, provides free field science programs for schools and individuals. The university provides its own entertainment and arts amenities in Fayetteville.

Rapid growth is causing some bottlenecks during rush hour. According to locals, Bentonville, supposedly 5 minutes away, often takes 15 to 20 minutes. The biggest concentration of Wal-Mart and Wal-Mart–related workers is in Rogers, but employees live in all parts of the area, including southwest Missouri. Air service was once an issue but no more; the close-by NW Arkansas Regional Airport now offers direct service to most major cities.

The immediate area has gently rolling hills with farmland and some heavily wooded areas. A strong Gulf influence brings hot, humid summers with some mountain cooling, and winters are generally mild.

Health & Safety The crime risk is low, especially compared to other areas in Arkansas and the broader mid-South region. Rogers has a small hospital, and more facilities are available in Fayetteville.

Nearby Neighborhoods Fayetteville is a more liberal-minded college town, of comparable cost to Rogers but farther from the employment centers. Springdale is the least expensive, and probably least interesting, of the towns. Some live across the border in southern Missouri for tax reasons—income and sales taxes run about 2% lower.

ROGERS, AR NEIGHBORHOOD HIGHLIGHTS	
PEOPLE	
Population	21,067
15-yr Population Growth	84.40%
5-yr Population Growth	17.20%
% Married w/Children	28.5%
% Single w/Children	8.4%
No. of Households	7,740
Median Age	35.3
Avg. Household Size	2.68
Diversity Measure	35
STANDARD OF LIVING	
Median Household Income	$46,970
% Household Income > $100K	14%
Projected Future Job Growth	30%
Cost of Living Index	84.8
Buying Power Index	124
Weekly Daycare Cost	$135
Median Home Price	$157,100
"Sweet Spot" Home Price	$225,000
Home Price Ratio	3.3
Median Age of Homes	13.9
% Homes Owned	68%
Effective Property Tax Rate	0.80%
Estimated Property Tax Bill	$1,800
EDUCATION	
% High School Graduates	83%
% 4-yr Degree	20%
% Graduate or Professional Degree	7%
$ Invested per Pupil	$4,180
Student/Teacher Ratio	21.1
Primary Test Score Percentile	129.6
Secondary Test Score Percentile	151.4
% Subsidized School Lunch	23.50%
% Attending Public School	84.40%
LIFESTYLE	
Leisure Rating (Area)	3
Arts & Culture Rating (Area)	3
Climate Rating (Area)	5
Physical Setting Rating	3
Downtown Core Rating	3
% Commute < 30 Min.	82%
% Commute > 1 Hour	3%
HEALTH & SAFETY	BEST
Health Rating (Area)	8
Stress Score (Area)	2
Violent Crime Risk	63
Property Crime Risk	87

FAYETTEVILLE-SPRINGDALE-ROGERS, AR
AREA HIGHLIGHTS

PEOPLE

SIZE & DIVERSITY	AREA	U.S. AVG	FAMILY DEMOGRAPHICS	AREA	U.S. AVG
Population	353,833		% Married	65.10%	53.80%
15-yr Population Growth	69.20%	4.40%	% Single	34.90%	46.20%
Diversity Measure	25	54	% Divorced	8%	10.20%
% Religiously Observant	52%	50%	% Separated	2%	2.10%
% Catholic	6%	22%	% Married w/Children	30.60%	27.90%
% Protestant	46%	25%	% Single w/Children	8%	9.40%
% Jewish	0%	2%	% Married, No Children	35.90%	31.00%
% Other	0%	1%	% Single, No Children	25.50%	31.70%

STANDARD OF LIVING

INCOME, EMPLOYMENT & TAXES	AREA	U.S. AVG	COST OF LIVING & HOUSING	AREA	U.S. AVG
Median Household Income	$39,929	$44,684	Cost of Living Index	86.6	100
Household Income Growth	2.40%	6.10%	Buying Power Index	103	100
Unemployment Rate	2.40%	5.10%	Median Home Price	$163,900	$208,500
Recent Job Growth	7.40%	1.30%	Home Price Ratio	4.1	4.7
Projected Future Job Growth	26.60%	10.50%	Home Price Appreciation	11%	13.60%
State Income Tax Rate	7%	5.00%	% Homes Owned	69.90%	64.10%
State Sales Tax Rate	4.70%	6.00%	Median Rent	$545	$792

EDUCATION

ATTAINMENT & ACHIEVEMENT	AREA	U.S. AVG	RESOURCES & INVESTMENT	AREA	U.S. AVG
% High School Graduate	73.90%	83.90%	No. of Highly Ranked Universities	0	1
% 2-yr Graduate	5.80%	7.10%	$ Invested per Pupil	$4,671	$6,058
% 4-yr Graduate	12.90%	17.20%	Student/Teacher Ratio	16.3	15.9
% Graduate or Professional Degree	5.80%	9.90%	State University In-State Tuition	$5,135	$4,917
% Attending Public School	94.90%	84.30%			
75th Percentile State University SAT Score (Verbal)	510	477			
75th Percentile State University SAT Score (Math)	510	478			
75th Percentile State University ACT Score	22	20			

LIFESTYLE

RECREATION, ARTS & CULTURE	AREA	U.S. AVG	INFRASTRUCTURE & FACILITIES	AREA	U.S. AVG
Professional Sports Rating	2	4	No. of Public Libraries	12	28
Zoos & Aquariums Rating	1	3	Library Volumes Per Capita	2.3	2.8
Amusement Park Rating	1	3	No. of Warehouse Clubs	4	4
Professional Theater Rating	1	3	No. of Starbucks	1	5
Overall Museum Rating	6	6	Golf Course Rating	1	4
Science Museum Rating	3	4	National Park Rating	3	3
Children's Museum Rating	1	3	Sq. Mi. Inland Water	2	4

CLIMATE			COMMUTE & TRANSPORTATION		
Days Mostly Sunny	220	212	Avg. Daily Commute Time	19.6	24.7
Annual Days Precipitation	96	111	% Commute by Auto	73%	77.70%
Annual Days > 90°F	60	38	Per Capita Avg. Daily Transit Miles	4	7.9
Annual Days < 32°F	90	88	Annual Auto Insurance Premium	$1,079	$1,314
July Relative Humidity	70	69	Gas, Cost per Gallon	$2.97	$3.05

HEALTH & SAFETY

CRIME & ENVIRNOMENTAL ISSUES	AREA	U.S. AVG	HEALTHCARE & COST	AREA	U.S. AVG
Violent Crime Rate	241	517	Physicians per Capita	168.9	254.3
Change in Violent Crime	-3.20%	-7.50%	Pediatricians per Capita	10.5	16.9
Property Crime Rate	2762	3783	Hospital Beds per Capita	353.3	239.7
Change in Property Crime	-13.30%	-10.10%	No. of Teaching Hospitals	3	1.9
Air Quality Score	39	44	Healthcare Cost Index	91.7	100
Water Quality Score	66	33	Cost per Doctor Visit	$76	$74
Pollen/Allergy Score	57	61	Cost per Dentist Visit	$60	$67
Stress Score	16	49	Cost per Hospital Room	$588	$702
Cancer Mortality Rate	150.2	168.9			

Roswell, GA

Area Type: Outer suburb/exurb

Zip Code: 30075

Metro Area: Atlanta, GA

Metro Area Type: Largest

Location: 20 miles north of downtown Atlanta, 10 miles north of I-285 beltway

Time Zone: Eastern Standard Time

Pros:

Excellent homes
Strong economy
Education

Cons:

Growth and sprawl
Commute traffic
Transience of population

BEST OF THE BEST

Booming, bustling Atlanta, the South's biggest city, lies smack in the crossroads between the deep traditions of the South and the progressive beat of a modern cosmopolitan world-class city. With a number-seven rank out of 331 metropolitan areas, Atlanta was the top-rated *large* city in the 2004 *Cities Ranked & Rated*. Its financial and manufacturing center provides an alternative to the industrial North. If you live in one of its many nice suburbs outside the I-285 beltway, Atlanta reveals a small-town charm that surprises most newcomers.

And the newcomers are moving in. Atlanta is one of the most popular destinations for those looking to stay close to a big city but with affordable housing and relatively mild winters. Beyond such native industries as Coca-Cola, Delta Airlines, and UPS, Atlanta has become the regional center for offices and facilities of most of corporate America. Motivated by attractive housing and neighborhoods, professional workers are transferring in from other parts of the United States, and kindling a strong sense of community with other transferees. Guided by the strong Southern charm and hospitality of those native to the area, many jump off the "transfer" career path and simply decide to stay.

Atlanta itself sits on a high plain at the foot of the Appalachian mountain range; in fact, it is this location that gave rise to the city originally as a transportation gateway from the Deep South toward the Northeast. The downtown area, while strengthening in recent years, is plain for a large U.S. city. To the south and east it is more industrial, while to the north and west there are more residences with many large commercial/office facilities clustered along the highway corridors. The nicer suburbs start with the dignified inner suburb of Buckhead just north of downtown, which has now also become the high-end commercial and entertainment center for the area. But the "Atlanta North" area that is most ideally suited for family living starts north of the I-285 beltway. Extensive suburban communities beautifully set into the magnolias and Southern pines stretch for miles up I-75 and the "Georgia 400" (not an auto race, but a state route) with many familiar and not-so-familiar names: Dunwoody, Marietta, Alpharetta, Sandy Springs, Kennesaw. These suburbs feature exceptional housing values with well-built homes set on attractive wooded lots. Although prices have risen recently, they are less expensive for a big city than most would expect. While Atlanta has good roads, the area's increased popularity has resulted in legendary traffic problems.

Roswell is one of many fine residential communities north of I-285, and we choose it for its historic context as an 1800s textile mill town, its attractive blend of housing, and its strong family orientation: 32.4% of households are married with children.

Standard of Living Atlanta North's strong professional orientation yields high median household incomes: Roswell's is about $86K. The moderate cost of living (COL Index 127) gives a strong Buying Power Index of 154. The real story is housing: Good family homes can still be found below $200K. Choices are abundant, but the best homes are probably in the high $200Ks to mid $300Ks. The attractive wooded settings elicit feelings of wealth and seclusion, even with a smaller home. Effective property tax rates are 1.4%, and a little lower outside the city. The bottom line is that single-earner families can live quite well here.

Education Such rapid growth as experienced by Atlanta North and the Roswell area usually creates challenges to school infrastructure. Nonetheless, Fulton County schools have done a good job keeping pace, and Roswell schools, while large in enrollment, have high standards and generally test well above state averages,

ROSWELL, GA NEIGHBORHOOD HIGHLIGHTS	
PEOPLE	
Population	46,244
15-yr Population Growth	25.50%
5-yr Population Growth	-0.20%
% Married w/Children	32.4%
% Single w/Children	10.7%
No. of Households	16,542
Median Age	35.8
Avg. Household Size	2.78
Diversity Measure	27
STANDARD OF LIVING	**BEST**
Median Household Income	$85,884
% Household Income > $100K	43%
Projected Future Job Growth	11%
Cost of Living Index	127
Buying Power Index	154
Weekly Daycare Cost	$160
Median Home Price	$304,000
"Sweet Spot" Home Price	$300,000
Home Price Ratio	3.5
Median Age of Homes	15.9
% Homes Owned	80%
Effective Property Tax Rate	1.40%
Estimated Property Tax Bill	$4,200
EDUCATION	**BEST**
% High School Graduates	94%
% 4-yr Degree	38%
% Graduate or Professional Degree	19%
$ Invested per Pupil	$6,141
Student/Teacher Ratio	15.7
Primary Test Score Percentile	114.4
Secondary Test Score Percentile	101.3
% Subsidized School Lunch	10.90%
% Attending Public School	79%
LIFESTYLE	
Leisure Rating (Area)	9
Arts & Culture Rating (Area)	9
Climate Rating (Area)	7
Physical Setting Rating	6
Downtown Core Rating	3
% Commute < 30 Min.	42%
% Commute > 1 Hour	9%
HEALTH & SAFETY	
Health Rating (Area)	3
Stress Score (Area)	8
Violent Crime Risk	29
Property Crime Risk	32

and are considered excellent by locals. School renovations and construction of two new high schools will keep the area ahead of the growth curve.

Lifestyle Local community centers, parks, and pools have strong recreational programs at modest prices.

Golf and tennis are also popular in addition to the usual team sports. The historic downtown is dotted with small museums and cultural centers, such as the humorously named Kudzu Playhouse. The "artSWELL" festival is an annual highlight, and, outside of Roswell, the numerous Civil War and other historic sites are family favorites. The Chattahoochee River and Lake Lanier, a little farther away, provide ample water recreation, as do the area's Six Flags and Whitewater Great America amusement parks. The area has a notably strong community and neighborhood feel, and kids play together while parents barbeque. While there is a distinct winter, outdoor recreation and activities are possible most of the year.

It's no coincidence that "Georgia Traffic News" commands the top center of the city of Roswell's website. Traffic and commutes can be a problem; while traffic usually flows, it is heavy. Most commuters work somewhere along the I-285 perimeter, some in Buckhead or downtown. The fine "MARTA" rail system works well for downtown workers and airport trips, but it's a short drive to reach the northern terminus in the Sandy Springs–Dunwoody area.

The immediate Roswell area is gently rolling and heavily wooded. The climate is a mix of continental and subtropical, with warm, muggy summers and cool, but not bitterly cold, winters. Snow is infrequent (but can bring the city to a halt) and the area has experienced damaging ice storms.

Health & Safety The crime risk as measured by the "CAP" score is very low. Driven in part by long commutes, stress levels as measured by the Stress Score are high. There are good healthcare facilities throughout the area. Heavy traffic and summer air stagnation sometimes create air-quality issues.

Nearby Neighborhoods Most of the Atlanta North area is attractive and good for families; prospective buyers should look across a wide range of neighborhoods. Dunwoody to the south is more expensive with more singles and empty nesters but is more convenient and very attractive. Alpharetta is similar to Roswell but has pockets of much more expensive homes. Marietta, along I-75 to the west, is very large and a little less expensive, and Kennesaw to the north is still less expensive but getting far away from the commercial areas on the beltway.

ATLANTA, GA
AREA HIGHLIGHTS

PEOPLE

SIZE & DIVERSITY	AREA	U.S. AVG	FAMILY DEMOGRAPHICS	AREA	U.S. AVG
Population	4,559,736		% Married	52.80%	53.80%
15-yr Population Growth	63.80%	4.40%	% Single	47.20%	46.20%
Diversity Measure	54	54	% Divorced	9.80%	10.20%
% Religiously Observant	44%	50%	% Separated	3.60%	2.10%
% Catholic	7%	22%	% Married w/Children	28.50%	27.90%
% Protestant	35%	25%	% Single w/Children	12.10%	9.40%
% Jewish	2%	2%	% Married, No Children	27.10%	31.00%
% Other	1%	1%	% Single, No Children	32.30%	31.70%

STANDARD OF LIVING

INCOME, EMPLOYMENT & TAXES	AREA	U.S. AVG	COST OF LIVING & HOUSING	AREA	U.S. AVG
Median Household Income	$52,051	$44,684	Cost of Living Index	91.3	100
Household Income Growth	4.10%	6.10%	Buying Power Index	128	100
Unemployment Rate	4.10%	5.10%	Median Home Price	$166,500	$208,500
Recent Job Growth	-0.10%	1.30%	Home Price Ratio	3.2	4.7
Projected Future Job Growth	19.60%	10.50%	Home Price Appreciation	4.90%	13.60%
State Income Tax Rate	6%	5.00%	% Homes Owned	62.30%	64.10%
State Sales Tax Rate	6%	6.00%	Median Rent	$928	$792

EDUCATION

ATTAINMENT & ACHIEVEMENT	AREA	U.S. AVG	RESOURCES & INVESTMENT	AREA	U.S. AVG
% High School Graduate	78.70%	83.90%	No. of Highly Ranked Universities	4	1
% 2-yr Graduate	7.30%	7.10%	$ Invested per Pupil	$5,795	$6,058
% 4-yr Graduate	22.90%	17.20%	Student/Teacher Ratio	16.2	15.9
% Graduate or Professional Degree	9.50%	9.90%	State University In-State Tuition	$4,272	$4,917
% Attending Public School	91.90%	84.30%			
75th Percentile State University SAT Score (Verbal)	550	477			
75th Percentile State University SAT Score (Math)	560	478			
75th Percentile State University ACT Score	23	20			

LIFESTYLE

RECREATION, ARTS & CULTURE	AREA	U.S. AVG	INFRASTRUCTURE & FACILITIES	AREA	U.S. AVG
Professional Sports Rating	7	4	No. of Public Libraries	134	28
Zoos & Aquariums Rating	9	3	Library Volumes Per Capita	1.8	2.8
Amusement Park Rating	10	3	No. of Warehouse Clubs	10	4
Professional Theater Rating	10	3	No. of Starbucks	91	5
Overall Museum Rating	10	6	Golf Course Rating	9	4
Science Museum Rating	8	4	National Park Rating	2	3
Children's Museum Rating	9	3	Sq. Mi. Inland Water	4	4

CLIMATE			COMMUTE & TRANSPORTATION		
Days Mostly Sunny	219	212	Avg. Daily Commute Time	31.2	24.7
Annual Days Precipitation	116	111	% Commute by Auto	77%	77.70%
Annual Days > 90°F	19	38	Per Capita Avg. Daily Transit Miles	16.7	7.9
Annual Days < 32°F	59	88	Annual Auto Insurance Premium	$1,500	$1,314
July Relative Humidity	70	69	Gas, Cost per Gallon	$3.01	$3.05

HEALTH & SAFETY

CRIME & ENVIRNOMENTAL ISSUES	AREA	U.S. AVG	HEALTHCARE & COST	AREA	U.S. AVG
Violent Crime Rate	513	517	Physicians per Capita	217	254.3
Change in Violent Crime	-28.80%	-7.50%	Pediatricians per Capita	20.4	16.9
Property Crime Rate	4320	3783	Hospital Beds per Capita	249.2	239.7
Change in Property Crime	-23.40%	-10.10%	No. of Teaching Hospitals	11	1.9
Air Quality Score	32	44	Healthcare Cost Index	104.4	100
Water Quality Score	51	33	Cost per Doctor Visit	$70	$74
Pollen/Allergy Score	63	61	Cost per Dentist Visit	$66	$67
Stress Score	82	49	Cost per Hospital Room	$677	$702
Cancer Mortality Rate	166.2	168.9			

Santa Clarita, CA

Area Type: Outer suburb/exurb

Zip Code: 91354

Metro Area: Los Angeles–Long Beach, CA

Metro Area Type: Largest

Location: 22 miles north of Los Angeles along I-5

Time Zone: Pacific Standard Time

Pros:
Mild climate
Education
Nearby recreation and entertainment

Cons:
Growth and sprawl
Air quality
Cost of housing

While we balk at Santa Clarita's high home prices, cost of living, long commutes, California-style sprawl, and unpredictable employment, we applaud the high incomes, ample new housing, strong community feel, low crime, good schools, strong educational context, and strong married-with-children percentage of 44%. Taken together, it's a good place for those who can accept the lifestyle of Southern California—a lifestyle of extremes in all manner except climate.

With 46.7 square miles to its name, Santa Clarita, unlike most of its LA neighbors, has room to grow. Incorporated in 1987 to capture local tax revenues, Santa Clarita includes the formerly separate communities of Newhall, Saugus, and Valencia. The city occupies the southern tip of a broad valley that is bordered on the south by the Santa Susana and San Gabriel mountains, which isolate Santa Clarita from the rest of the county. The city boundaries extend far into the hills east of town and to the north, where the newer housing developments offer good value (for the area). This relative isolation has fostered a stronger sense of community than is found in most LA County suburbs, and the good schools, economic stability, and outdoor recreational opportunities make this one of the more attractive and family-friendly areas in southern California.

Santa Clarita sits in a valley just north of San Fernando, surrounded on all sides by low hills. I-5 and SR 14 are, for all practical purposes, the only roads in and out of the valley. The high deserts of Palmdale and Lancaster lie east; the Central Valley is north along I-5; and the enormous LA proper starts about 15 miles south with the built-up San Fernando Valley, and goes on seemingly forever. SR 126 travels west through oil fields in unincorporated Ventura County and eventually connects with Highway 101 at the coast. Most residents in Santa Clarita are connected economically, and most

certainly culturally, to the treasure-trove of the LA area, which isn't called the entertainment capital of the world for nothing.

Standard of Living Santa Clarita is a newer community compared to the county as a whole, with 50% of the homes built since 1991. As is common in California, housing costs are high and financial success here is directly tied to the ability to afford a home. Prices in Valencia for a three-bedroom, two-bath start at $500K for a smallish (1,300-square-foot) home on a small lot, with similar homes going for as high as $600K, depending on the location. Homes with a bit more room (about 1,800 square feet) start around $650K. The Home Price Ratio is a very high 6.7. Thanks to Proposition 13, property tax rates are held in check at under 1.2%, but tax bills are still high for recently purchased homes. Neighborhoods to the northeast are particularly well situated, as they border many square miles of undeveloped area, and offer a slightly better value than homes closer to the town center. The penalty for this price break is a longer commute south. Though use of public transportation is growing, nearly 80% of commuters drive alone to work, and the average commute time is 33 minutes.

Education The Santa Clarita school district is very good overall, and is rated in the top 10% of California school districts. The area population is more affluent and better educated than the county as a whole. Median household income is about $92K, and 44% of the population has a post-high-school degree. Comparable numbers for the county are $46K and 24%. Santa Clarita is home to the California Institute of the Arts, which offers undergraduate and graduate programs for professional artists in the film and music industries as well as traditional fine arts programs in theater, art, writing, and dance.

Lifestyle Santa Clarita has a lot to offer those who like outdoor activities. Nearby hills and the Los Padres National Forest offer camping, hiking, and mountain biking. The Six Flags Magic Mountain amusement park is a regional attraction, and those staying in town will also find more than a dozen parks and reserve areas, five nearby lakes, two golf courses, and hiking and bike trails along the dry Santa Clara River. The city maintains a sports complex with a gymnasium and aquatics center. Santa Clarita is, as in many communities in Southern California, somewhat reliant on Los Angeles for culture and activities: world-class museums, music, theatre, or surfing for that matter. Santa Clarita, however, can hold its own and has hosted literally thousands of location shoots for movie production companies, and extras are always in demand.

While some commercial activity is moving into the immediate area, most workers commute south, and commutes are long: 30 to 40 minutes to the San Fernando Valley and more than an hour to LA. Best of all is to completely avoid "the 5" by taking Metrolink. The seven lines in this regional rail system, with three stops in Santa Clarita, cover a lot of territory in the LA basin, most of which you'd like to avoid driving to if possible.

Santa Clarita sits in a small flat valley surrounded by the dry hills of the Coastal Range. The climate is distinctly Mediterranean with plenty of sunshine and almost no clouds or rain April through November and a cool, pleasant winter. Most of the area's 14 inches of rain fall between December and March, and outdoor activities are possible throughout the year.

Health & Safety For cities with populations over 150,000, Santa Clarita was ranked in 2002 by the FBI as the safest city in the nation with regard to violent crime, burglary, auto theft, and arson. Crime risk, as captured by the "CAP" index, is very low. Air quality is far worse than the national average, with some of the highest ozone levels. The Henry Mayo Newhall Hospital and Newhall Community Hospital are both just a few minutes from downtown.

Nearby Neighborhoods The sprawling San Fernando Valley lies a few miles to the southwest and has some less expensive homes, but these are generally smaller and in less attractive neighborhoods.

SANTA CLARITA, CA NEIGHBORHOOD HIGHLIGHTS	
PEOPLE	
Population	18,637
15-yr Population Growth	12.10%
5-yr Population Growth	4.40%
% Married w/Children	44.2%
% Single w/Children	9.9%
No. of Households	6,049
Median Age	30.5
Avg. Household Size	3.09
Diversity Measure	40
STANDARD OF LIVING	
Median Household Income	$92,439
% Household Income > $100K	38%
Projected Future Job Growth	5%
Cost of Living Index	154
Buying Power Index	134
Weekly Daycare Cost	$155
Median Home Price	$619,000
"Sweet Spot" Home Price	$650,000
Home Price Ratio	6.7
Median Age of Homes	7.2
% Homes Owned	88%
Effective Property Tax Rate	1.20%
Estimated Property Tax Bill	$7,800
EDUCATION	BEST
% High School Graduates	96%
% 4-yr Degree	31%
% Graduate or Professional Degree	13%
$ Invested per Pupil	$4,570
Student/Teacher Ratio	22.2
Primary Test Score Percentile	147.4
Secondary Test Score Percentile	104.1
% Subsidized School Lunch	2.60%
% Attending Public School	80.90%
LIFESTYLE	
Leisure Rating (Area)	10
Arts & Culture Rating (Area)	10
Climate Rating (Area)	10
Physical Setting Rating	3
Downtown Core Rating	1
% Commute < 30 Min.	37%
% Commute > 1 Hour	19%
HEALTH & SAFETY	
Health Rating (Area)	0
Stress Score (Area)	7
Violent Crime Risk	47
Property Crime Risk	52

LOS ANGELES–LONG BEACH, CA
AREA HIGHLIGHTS

PEOPLE

SIZE & DIVERSITY	AREA	U.S. AVG	FAMILY DEMOGRAPHICS	AREA	U.S. AVG
Population	9,937,739		% Married	45.60%	53.80%
15-yr Population Growth	12.10%	4.40%	% Single	54.40%	46.20%
Diversity Measure	71	54	% Divorced	9.50%	10.20%
% Religiously Observant	58%	50%	% Separated	4.40%	2.10%
% Catholic	40%	22%	% Married w/Children	24.10%	27.90%
% Protestant	11%	25%	% Single w/Children	12.30%	9.40%
% Jewish	6%	2%	% Married, No Children	22.40%	31.00%
% Other	1%	1%	% Single, No Children	40.80%	31.70%

STANDARD OF LIVING

INCOME, EMPLOYMENT & TAXES	AREA	U.S. AVG	COST OF LIVING & HOUSING	AREA	U.S. AVG
Median Household Income	$45,958	$44,684	Cost of Living Index	145.7	100
Household Income Growth	5.90%	6.10%	Buying Power Index	71	100
Unemployment Rate	5.90%	5.10%	Median Home Price	$474,800	$208,500
Recent Job Growth	2.80%	1.30%	Home Price Ratio	10.3	4.7
Projected Future Job Growth	4.80%	10.50%	Home Price Appreciation	25.60%	13.60%
State Income Tax Rate	6%	5.00%	% Homes Owned	49.40%	64.10%
State Sales Tax Rate	8.20%	6.00%	Median Rent	$1,124	$792

EDUCATION

ATTAINMENT & ACHIEVEMENT	AREA	U.S. AVG	RESOURCES & INVESTMENT	AREA	U.S. AVG
% High School Graduate	76.80%	83.90%	No. of Highly Ranked Universities	9	1
% 2-yr Graduate	11.10%	7.10%	$ Invested per Pupil	$5,519	$6,058
% 4-yr Graduate	24.10%	17.20%	Student/Teacher Ratio	22.1	15.9
% Graduate or Professional Degree	12.70%	9.90%	State University In-State Tuition	$6,586	$4,917
% Attending Public School	87.30%	84.30%			
75th Percentile State University SAT Score (Verbal)	560	477			
75th Percentile State University SAT Score (Math)	600	478			
75th Percentile State University ACT Score	23	20			

LIFESTYLE

RECREATION, ARTS & CULTURE	AREA	U.S. AVG	INFRASTRUCTURE & FACILITIES	AREA	U.S. AVG
Professional Sports Rating	10	4	No. of Public Libraries	238	28
Zoos & Aquariums Rating	10	3	Library Volumes Per Capita	2.2	2.8
Amusement Park Rating	10	3	No. of Warehouse Clubs	10	4
Professional Theater Rating	10	3	No. of Starbucks	328	5
Overall Museum Rating	10	6	Golf Course Rating	10	4
Science Museum Rating	10	4	National Park Rating	10	3
Children's Museum Rating	10	3	Sq. Mi. Inland Water	4	4

CLIMATE			COMMUTE & TRANSPORTATION		
Days Mostly Sunny	258	212	Avg. Daily Commute Time	29.4	24.7
Annual Days Precipitation	35	111	% Commute by Auto	70%	77.70%
Annual Days > 90°F	5	38	Per Capita Avg. Daily Transit Miles	18.9	7.9
Annual Days < 32°F	0	88	Annual Auto Insurance Premium	$2,356	$1,314
July Relative Humidity	71	69	Gas, Cost per Gallon	$3.00	$3.05

HEALTH & SAFETY

CRIME & ENVIRNOMENTAL ISSUES	AREA	U.S. AVG	HEALTHCARE & COST	AREA	U.S. AVG
Violent Crime Rate	854	517	Physicians per Capita	243.5	254.3
Change in Violent Crime	-16%	-7.50%	Pediatricians per Capita	18.7	16.9
Property Crime Rate	3101	3783	Hospital Beds per Capita	312.9	239.7
Change in Property Crime	-6.40%	-10.10%	No. of Teaching Hospitals	48	1.9
Air Quality Score	1	44	Healthcare Cost Index	118.8	100
Water Quality Score	52	33	Cost per Doctor Visit	$70	$74
Pollen/Allergy Score	42	61	Cost per Dentist Visit	$72	$67
Stress Score	72	49	Cost per Hospital Room	$1,301	$702
Cancer Mortality Rate	168	168.9			

Sharon, MA

Area Type: Inner suburb/suburban town

Zip Code: 02067

Metro Area: Boston, MA

Metro Area Type: Largest

Location: 24 miles south of downtown Boston

Time Zone: Eastern Standard Time

Pros:

Nature, parks, and open spaces
Education
Central location

Cons:

Low job growth
Narrow tax base
Area cost of living

It's hard to say enough about Boston as a stimulating place for families and children. The area is steeped in history, education, and arts, providing unlimited family activity. The city, shore region, and New England as a whole are both educational and fun. Most of the area's assets are well-known, from downtown Boston's Faneuil Hall Marketplace, Colonial historic sites, and Boston Common to arts amenities such as the Boston Pops and the Museum of Fine Arts. Of particular interest to children are the New England Aquarium (downtown) and the Discovery Museums in Acton to the northwest. The educational tradition and the assortment of highly ranked universities add to the strong cultural backdrop.

The manufacturing economy of this area has been trending for years toward one that is service- and financially oriented. Business consolidations continue to affect large companies in the area; Procter & Gamble/Gillette being the latest among many in the high tech, banking, and other industries. While metro area job growth is projected at a modest 5.3%, area jobs pay well, and median household incomes at over $62,000 are well above national averages. That said, cost of living and particularly housing remain well over national averages, and families coming into the Boston metro area can expect to pay more than $400K for a home.

Quiet, peaceful, and close to nature, the city of Sharon provides a welcome respite from the hustle and bustle of Boston. Located on the shores of Lake Massapoag among several state parks and a nature preserve, Sharon is the Walden Pond of Boston's South Side. Sharon is a family place: 38% of the population is married with children, one of the highest percentages in the area. A small downtown area provides an assortment of small businesses, banks, and restaurants. Lake Massapoag is a central feature, with year-round activities including boating, fishing, and ice-skating. Although residents spend a considerable amount of their free time in the area, Sharon provides easy access to many of the activities and amenities of the region, including downtown Boston, the South Shore, and Cape Cod.

Standard of Living   Although Sharon is a little more expensive than many nearby areas, its setting and calm make it easy for lots of families to make the trade-off. In fact, the area is still less expensive than many of Boston's "name" neighborhoods, such as Cambridge, Lexington, Bedford, and even family-friendly Acton. Typical family homes run in the low $500K range, from $200 to $250 per square foot, and homes are usually spacious and on a ½-acre–plus wooded lot. Homes are a typical New England mix, and vary considerably in age and style. The local Cost of Living Index is 166, high but still less than the 200-plus scores in much of the area. Local residents tend to be well educated with high incomes, many being employed in the financial services industry downtown or in the many high-tech industries to the north and west on the I-95/Route 128 beltway. With little local industry or commerce, the area has a narrow tax base. While local property tax rates (about $15.58 per $1,000, or 1.58%) remain reasonable, the area is vulnerable to residential rate and valuation increases.

Education   The population is highly educated and the local school system is strong. Over 31% of local residents possess a 4-year degree and another 31% have a graduate or professional degree. The small Sharon School District (six schools total) achieves test scores fully 20 to 30 points above state averages at all levels.

Lifestyle   Sharon has a quiet and dignified ambience; in fact, some say it's a bit *too* quiet. Parks are plentiful: Much leisure time is spent at Lake Massapoag, the

SHARON, MA NEIGHBORHOOD HIGHLIGHTS	
PEOPLE	
Population	17,483
15-yr Population Growth	6.10%
5-yr Population Growth	0.50%
% Married w/Children	37.6%
% Single w/Children	4.9%
No. of Households	5,996
Median Age	37.3
Avg. Household Size	2.91
Diversity Measure	18
STANDARD OF LIVING	BEST
Median Household Income	$99,681
% Household Income > $100K	44%
Projected Future Job Growth	9%
Cost of Living Index	166
Buying Power Index	141
Weekly Daycare Cost	$200
Median Home Price	$493,900
"Sweet Spot" Home Price	$525,000
Home Price Ratio	5
Median Age of Homes	34.6
% Homes Owned	88%
Effective Property Tax Rate	1.58%
Estimated Property Tax Bill	$8,400
EDUCATION	
% High School Graduates	97%
% 4-yr Degree	31%
% Graduate or Professional Degree	31%
$ Invested per Pupil	$6,476
Student/Teacher Ratio	11.7
Primary Test Score Percentile	127.4
Secondary Test Score Percentile	132.1
% Subsidized School Lunch	3.80%
% Attending Public School	72.60%
LIFESTYLE	
Leisure Rating (Area)	10
Arts & Culture Rating (Area)	10
Climate Rating (Area)	3
Physical Setting Rating	6
Downtown Core Rating	7
% Commute < 30 Min.	41%
% Commute > 1 Hour	17%
HEALTH & SAFETY	
Health Rating (Area)	3
Stress Score (Area)	4
Violent Crime Risk	19
Property Crime Risk	23

regionally noted Moose Hill Wildlife Sanctuary 1 mile west, Borderland State Park 3 miles south, and even the Sharon Dog Park.

Commutes are reasonable for the Boston area. Sharon is on the popular north–south Attleboro line, a 25-minute express ride or 35 minutes on a local train. The Route 128 loop is a reasonable 25- to 30-minute drive. At about $800 a month, daycare costs are a consideration for dual-earner families.

Sharon is in an area of mostly flat, deciduous woods. The climate is complex and prone to extremes of hot and cold, although the nearby ocean moderates temperatures somewhat. Snow cover and frozen lakes can be expected in winter, while summer has warm muggy periods and frequent rain.

Health & Safety Crime risk is very low, and healthcare facilities are abundant though expensive. Undoubtedly the Boston area can be high-pressure, but residents learn to manage stress factors and make the most of local resources.

Nearby Neighborhoods Most locals consider Sharon the best choice in Boston's South Side. Residents looking for more activity and less expensive housing might look to the south and northwest in Foxboro, Mansfield, Natick, or Framingham. For those employed on the southeast side, Hanover to the east is another attractive alternative.

BOSTON, MA
AREA HIGHLIGHTS

PEOPLE

SIZE & DIVERSITY	AREA	U.S. AVG	FAMILY DEMOGRAPHICS	AREA	U.S. AVG
Population	3,412,151		% Married	49.60%	53.80%
15-yr Population Growth	7.60%	4.40%	% Single	50.40%	46.20%
Diversity Measure	31	54	% Divorced	6.80%	10.20%
% Religiously Observant	68%	50%	% Separated	2.80%	2.10%
% Catholic	51%	22%	% Married w/Children	24.50%	27.90%
% Protestant	10%	25%	% Single w/Children	7.70%	9.40%
% Jewish	5%	2%	% Married, No Children	28.50%	31.00%
% Other	1%	1%	% Single, No Children	39.30%	31.70%

STANDARD OF LIVING

INCOME, EMPLOYMENT & TAXES	AREA	U.S. AVG	COST OF LIVING & HOUSING	AREA	U.S. AVG
Median Household Income	$62,504	$44,684	Cost of Living Index	132.5	100
Household Income Growth	4.20%	6.10%	Buying Power Index	106	100
Unemployment Rate	4.20%	5.10%	Median Home Price	$418,500	$208,500
Recent Job Growth	1%	1.30%	Home Price Ratio	6.7	4.7
Projected Future Job Growth	5.30%	10.50%	Home Price Appreciation	11.50%	13.60%
State Income Tax Rate	5.90%	5.00%	% Homes Owned	61%	64.10%
State Sales Tax Rate	5%	6.00%	Median Rent	$1,126	$792

EDUCATION

ATTAINMENT & ACHIEVEMENT	AREA	U.S. AVG	RESOURCES & INVESTMENT	AREA	U.S. AVG
% High School Graduate	88.20%	83.90%	No. of Highly Ranked Universities	14	1
% 2-yr Graduate	9.60%	7.10%	$ Invested per Pupil	$8,055	$6,058
% 4-yr Graduate	27.50%	17.20%	Student/Teacher Ratio	16.3	15.9
% Graduate or Professional Degree	17.30%	9.90%	State University In-State Tuition	$9,186	$4,917
% Attending Public School	85.60%	84.30%			
75th Percentile State University SAT Score (Verbal)	510	477			
75th Percentile State University SAT Score (Math)	520	478			
75th Percentile State University ACT Score	21	20			

LIFESTYLE

RECREATION, ARTS & CULTURE	AREA	U.S. AVG	INFRASTRUCTURE & FACILITIES	AREA	U.S. AVG
Professional Sports Rating	9	4	No. of Public Libraries	203	28
Zoos & Aquariums Rating	8	3	Library Volumes Per Capita	6	2.8
Amusement Park Rating	7	3	No. of Warehouse Clubs	10	4
Professional Theater Rating	10	3	No. of Starbucks	107	5
Overall Museum Rating	10	6	Golf Course Rating	9	4
Science Museum Rating	10	4	National Park Rating	2	3
Children's Museum Rating	10	3	Sq. Mi. Inland Water	7	4

CLIMATE			COMMUTE & TRANSPORTATION		
Days Mostly Sunny	205	212	Avg. Daily Commute Time	27.7	24.7
Annual Days Precipitation	128	111	% Commute by Auto	69%	77.70%
Annual Days > 90°F	12	38	Per Capita Avg. Daily Transit Miles	27.4	7.9
Annual Days < 32°F	99	88	Annual Auto Insurance Premium	$2,101	$1,314
July Relative Humidity	67	69	Gas, Cost per Gallon	$3.17	$3.05

HEALTH & SAFETY

CRIME & ENVIRNOMENTAL ISSUES	AREA	U.S. AVG	HEALTHCARE & COST	AREA	U.S. AVG
Violent Crime Rate	692	517	Physicians per Capita	383.1	254.3
Change in Violent Crime	53.70%	-7.50%	Pediatricians per Capita	30.5	16.9
Property Crime Rate	2936	3783	Hospital Beds per Capita	449.8	239.7
Change in Property Crime	11.70%	-10.10%	No. of Teaching Hospitals	36	1.9
Air Quality Score	20	44	Healthcare Cost Index	127.3	100
Water Quality Score	30	33	Cost per Doctor Visit	$65	$74
Pollen/Allergy Score	67	61	Cost per Dentist Visit	$77	$67
Stress Score	36	49	Cost per Hospital Room	$997	$702
Cancer Mortality Rate	184.1	168.9			

Shawnee, KS

Area Type: Outer suburb

Zip Code: 66216

Metro Area: Kansas City, MO-KS

Metro Area Type: Large

Location: 13 miles southwest of downtown Kansas City

Time Zone: Central Standard Time

Pros:
Strong economy
Affordable housing
Education

Cons:
Growth and sprawl
Uninteresting physical setting
Variable climate

Kansas City . . . Kansas City here I come . . . So goes the sultry 1952 blues favorite performed on the row of Vine Street jazz clubs (now a new city park) in this broad-shouldered mid-American city. Long self-sufficient and a melting pot of American cultures, the metro area regional center of Kansas City sits astride the Missouri River and the Kansas-Missouri border. The larger and more traditional city is on the Missouri side, and is big-city in every way, with a modern downtown, major-league sports, museums, arts and culture, restored architectural gems, typical city suburbs, and a stable employment base anchored by agriculture. The area has an especially strong influence from workers migrating from the Southeast, hence the characteristic barbecued ribs, blues, and jazz.

If you had crossed the river to the "KCK" (Kansas City, Kansas) side 40 years ago, you would have seen an industrial and sparsely populated landscape anchored by riverfront grain elevators, shipping terminals, and other evidence of a mostly agriculture-based commerce. But the central location, attractive business climate, and plentiful labor source predisposed the KCK area to an assortment of modern industries, including greetingcards (Hallmark), book and calendar publishing (Andrews-McMeel), and wireless communications (Sprint). The booming economy, plentiful open land, good roads, and well-managed government services have led to a series of "super-suburbs" including Overland Park, Lenexa, and Shawnee.

Shawnee is a few miles northwest of the more well-known and conspicuous Overland Park, often a recipient of a spot on national "best places" listings. The communities of Overland Park, Lenexa, Olathe, and Shawnee greatly resemble one another and are often clumped together as "Johnson County." Attractive subdivisions with reasonably priced homes, plenty of parkland, well-planned commercial districts, and good schools characterize the area; but what distinguishes Shawnee are the affordable homes and abundance of green space.

The Shawnee area, loosely defined as it is, covers parts of six or seven zip codes. The relatively small 66216 area sits west of a small older downtown area that is now in renewal. Some retail exists along the major east–west Shawnee Mission Parkway, but most of the area is newer suburbs built in the 1980s and 1990s. The area has a nice suburban lifestyle with excellent access to jobs on the KCK side and to areas in and near the Missouri city center. The married-with-children percentage is a strong 38%.

Standard of Living At 105, Shawnee's Cost of Living Index is close to the national average. When coupled with median household incomes 55% higher than the national average and a Buying Power Index of 146, the standard of living looks quite healthy. Family homes are abundant and can be found at very good prices, with some older family homes on nice lots starting in the $175K to $200K range; $225K will get you the best. As homes are likely to be 2,500 square feet or more with a basement, Shawnee is a good place for families looking for some extra space. The Home Price Ratio is an attractive 3.0. New construction near Black Swan Lake and Quivira Lake offers larger and somewhat more expensive homes on larger lots with more green space. Property taxes run about 1.1%.

Education Schools in Shawnee Mission District are top caliber. On the national scale, most Shawnee elementary schools test in the 90th percentile, many in the 99th. Middle schools test above the 80th percentile, and high-school SAT scores average 1150 or better. Kansas City itself is not a major destination for higher education, but there are three community colleges and a technical institute within 15 miles of Shawnee, and the well-regarded University of Kansas ("KU") is just 35 miles west in Lawrence (see p. 259).

Lifestyle The big-budget cultural amenities—good museums, a zoo, a metropolitan symphony orchestra, professional sports, and performing arts—are all available in Kansas City, an easy 30-minute trip. Shawnee offers community-focused sports and recreation activities, convenient shopping, and short commutes to most locations west of Kansas City. Johnson County also administers many sports programs and maintains a number of modern facilities, including two golf courses, two sports domes, an aquatic center, and two 12-field softball complexes in Shawnee.

The growth boom has resulted in some long-distance commutes with heavy traffic in the Kansas City area, but good roads and road improvements have kept commutes reasonable overall. While downtown Kansas City is half an hour away, workers who are employed on the KCK side have considerably shorter commutes. Average commute times are reasonable at about 23 minutes, and very few residents have commutes that take more than an hour.

The area around Shawnee is mainly flat with green farmland and small wooded areas. Though not as flat as stereotypical Kansas, the terrain might be described as uninteresting, particularly to the north. The climate is prairie continental: frequent winds, year-round precipitation, thunderstorms, and at least a few clouds most days of the year. There are four distinct seasons with active and variable weather at all times. That said, the bigger tornado risks for which the region is known are farther west and south, and there has never been a tornado-related fatality in Johnson County.

Health & Safety Although the Kansas City metro area crime statistics aren't very favorable, Shawnee's crime-risk rating is very low. There are two hospitals and a regional medical center within 5 miles of Shawnee.

Nearby Neighborhoods Overland Park, Lenexa, and Olathe offer similar lifestyles and housing options, although commutes from Olathe to Kansas City are longer. Prairie Village, an area of mostly 40- to 50-year-old homes east of Overland Park, features lower prices with access to the prized Shawnee Mission school district.

SHAWNEE, KS NEIGHBORHOOD HIGHLIGHTS

PEOPLE
Population	25,743
15-yr Population Growth	39.90%
5-yr Population Growth	10.10%
% Married w/Children	37.9%
% Single w/Children	9.1%
No. of Households	9,247
Median Age	34.8
Avg. Household Size	2.76
Diversity Measure	23

STANDARD OF LIVING
Median Household Income	$68,104
% Household Income > $100K	26%
Projected Future Job Growth	18%
Cost of Living Index	105
Buying Power Index	146
Weekly Daycare Cost	$140
Median Home Price	$207,100
"Sweet Spot" Home Price	$225,000
Home Price Ratio	3.0
Median Age of Homes	23.2
% Homes Owned	83%
Effective Property Tax Rate	1.1%
Estimated Property Tax Bill	$2,475

EDUCATION
% High School Graduates	95%
% 4-yr Degree	29%
% Graduate or Professional Degree	15%
$ Invested per Pupil	$5,464
Student/Teacher Ratio	16.3
Primary Test Score Percentile	111
Secondary Test Score Percentile	106.9
% Subsidized School Lunch	14%
% Attending Public School	78.60%

LIFESTYLE
Leisure Rating (Area)	8
Arts & Culture Rating (Area)	10
Climate Rating (Area)	2
Physical Setting Rating	2
Downtown Core Rating	4
% Commute < 30 Min.	75%
% Commute > 1 Hour	1%

HEALTH & SAFETY
Health Rating (Area)	3
Stress Score (Area)	9
Violent Crime Risk	33
Property Crime Risk	43

KANSAS CITY, MO-KS
AREA HIGHLIGHTS
PEOPLE

SIZE & DIVERSITY	AREA	U.S. AVG	FAMILY DEMOGRAPHICS	AREA	U.S. AVG
Population	1,863,326		% Married	57.70%	53.80%
15-yr Population Growth	20.20%	4.40%	% Single	42.30%	46.20%
Diversity Measure	36	54	% Divorced	9.70%	10.20%
% Religiously Observant	48%	50%	% Separated	2.60%	2.10%
% Catholic	15%	22%	% Married w/Children	28.80%	27.90%
% Protestant	31%	25%	% Single w/Children	9.90%	9.40%
% Jewish	1%	2%	% Married, No Children	29.80%	31.00%
% Other	0%	1%	% Single, No Children	30.90%	31.70%

STANDARD OF LIVING

INCOME, EMPLOYMENT & TAXES	AREA	U.S. AVG	COST OF LIVING & HOUSING	AREA	U.S. AVG
Median Household Income	$47,972	$44,684	Cost of Living Index	87.4	100
Household Income Growth	5.80%	6.10%	Buying Power Index	123	100
Unemployment Rate	5.80%	5.10%	Median Home Price	$157,100	$208,500
Recent Job Growth	0.30%	1.30%	Home Price Ratio	3.3	4.7
Projected Future Job Growth	13%	10.50%	Home Price Appreciation	6%	13.60%
State Income Tax Rate	7%	5.00%	% Homes Owned	66.40%	64.10%
State Sales Tax Rate	6.50%	6.00%	Median Rent	$691	$792

EDUCATION

ATTAINMENT & ACHIEVEMENT	AREA	U.S. AVG	RESOURCES & INVESTMENT	AREA	U.S. AVG
% High School Graduate	83.40%	83.90%	No. of Highly Ranked Universities	2	1
% 2-yr Graduate	7.40%	7.10%	$ Invested per Pupil	$5,790	$6,058
% 4-yr Graduate	19.90%	17.20%	Student/Teacher Ratio	15.6	15.9
% Graduate or Professional Degree	8.80%	9.90%	State University In-State Tuition	$4,737	$4,917
% Attending Public School	88.80%	84.30%			
75th Percentile State University SAT Score (Verbal)	N/A	477			
75th Percentile State University SAT Score (Math)	N/A	478			
75th Percentile State University ACT Score	21	20			

LIFESTYLE

RECREATION, ARTS & CULTURE	AREA	U.S. AVG	INFRASTRUCTURE & FACILITIES	AREA	U.S. AVG
Professional Sports Rating	6	4	No. of Public Libraries	81	28
Zoos & Aquariums Rating	7	3	Library Volumes Per Capita	6.9	2.8
Amusement Park Rating	4	3	No. of Warehouse Clubs	5	4
Professional Theater Rating	8	3	No. of Starbucks	20	5
Overall Museum Rating	9	6	Golf Course Rating	8	4
Science Museum Rating	5	4	National Park Rating	1	3
Children's Museum Rating	9	3	Sq. Mi. Inland Water	4	4

CLIMATE			COMMUTE & TRANSPORTATION		
Days Mostly Sunny	213	212	Avg. Daily Commute Time	22.9	24.7
Annual Days Precipitation	102	111	% Commute by Auto	78%	77.70%
Annual Days > 90°F	40	38	Per Capita Avg. Daily Transit Miles	7.8	7.9
Annual Days < 32°F	106	88	Annual Auto Insurance Premium	$1,585	$1,314
July Relative Humidity	69	69	Gas, Cost per Gallon	$3.02	$3.05

HEALTH & SAFETY

CRIME & ENVIRNOMENTAL ISSUES	AREA	U.S. AVG	HEALTHCARE & COST	AREA	U.S. AVG
Violent Crime Rate	751	517	Physicians per Capita	269.9	254.3
Change in Violent Crime	-13.10%	-7.50%	Pediatricians per Capita	20.8	16.9
Property Crime Rate	5413	3783	Hospital Beds per Capita	413.7	239.7
Change in Property Crime	-5.10%	-10.10%	No. of Teaching Hospitals	15	1.9
Air Quality Score	34	44	Healthcare Cost Index	96.3	100
Water Quality Score	36	33	Cost per Doctor Visit	$76	$74
Pollen/Allergy Score	74	61	Cost per Dentist Visit	$61	$67
Stress Score	89	49	Cost per Hospital Room	$1,028	$702
Cancer Mortality Rate	164	168.9			

Sheboygan, WI

Area Type: Small town

Zip Code: 53044

Metro Area: Sheboygan, WI

Metro Area Type: Smallest

Location: Eastern Wisconsin on Lake Michigan Shore, 60 miles north of Milwaukee

Time Zone: Central Standard Time

Pros:

 Clean, attractive downtown
 Nearby recreation
 Diverse economy

Cons:

 Winter climate
 Rising home prices
 Some employment concerns

"In 1845," according to Sheboygan's local Chamber of Commerce website, "Dr. Elizha Knowles wrote his wife, Olive, 'I traveled over Vermont, New York, Michigan, Indiana, and Wisconsin and have at last made up my mind to stop in Sheboygan. It is very healthy soil, good air, salubrious, no disease . . . the society here is good for a new place.' Some things never change."

Over 160 years later, Dr. Knowles's statement still applies to this small city of 115,000 residents set in an area of farmland at the Lake Michigan shore. Sheboygan is an attractive, clean, and prosperous area with excellent in-town amenities, a close-knit community, and recreational opportunities in town and in the surrounding countryside. The area is home to Kohler Manufacturing, one of the country's largest producers of bath fixtures.

The main downtown street, 8th Street, is lined with attractive small businesses and shops. The Mead Public Library is an above-average resource and an architectural highlight. Likewise, the Stefanie Weill Center for Performing Arts and its resident Sheboygan Symphony are excellent resources, especially for the size of town. Older buildings have been fixed up and put to good use. Volunteer-tended gardens and flowers beautify the downtown area. In fact, the volunteerism here is considerable even compared to other areas in Wisconsin, which is a significant statement.

Residential areas around the downtown, especially north, are spotless. City workers will knock on the door if your grass grows or your paint starts to peel, and the result is highly evident. Recreation is abundant, especially at the shore areas and on the many well-regarded golf courses. The Sheboygan area scores well on a broad assortment of measures, and has a lot of intangible qualities working in its favor, although winter weather intercedes.

Standard of Living Kohler heads up the area's employment base, which includes a number of smaller manufacturers. Some recent migration of jobs from here and the nearby manufacturing center of Manitowoc to Mexico and China have caused concern. But the economy is sufficiently diverse to avoid major shocks. Acuity (an insurance company) recently doubled its workforce. The overall cost of living is reasonable, with a COL Index just over 99. As a popular place in many "best places to live" studies, Sheboygan has seen home prices creep upward at a pace uncomfortable to some locals. Homes in the more upscale family area of Kohler just to the west run in the high $200Ks to low $300Ks, but smaller options in the north close to downtown can sell in the low $200Ks. Good incomes bring a Buying Power Index of 175 and a Home Price Ratio of 2.6. Property taxes are high at 3.1%, but services and schools are considered worth the price.

Education With more educated professionals and retirees moving in, the percentage of residents with 4-year degrees is rising, particularly in the Kohler zip code. Schools are clean and score moderately well compared to state scores, and are considered to be an area attraction. They don't differ much across different parts of town. The University of Wisconsin-Sheboygan and Lakeland College, a liberal arts school with 4,000 students, bring a college presence.

Lifestyle In-town entertainment and out-of-town recreation are abundant. Lakeshore beaches and parks are popular in the warmer months. The lakefront Blue Harbor Resort operates the Breaker Bay Water Park—one of the country's largest indoor water parks, and a major attraction, if a bit expensive for frequent use. A local YMCA, skateboard park, and "A"-level minor-league baseball team, plus plenty of local sports, keep families busy. Local golf courses receive national recog-

SHEBOYGAN, WI NEIGHBORHOOD HIGHLIGHTS	
PEOPLE	
Population	1,947
15-yr Population Growth	9.70%
5-yr Population Growth	1.20%
% Married w/Children	37.1%
% Single w/Children	4.3%
No. of Households	0,722
Median Age	37.1
Avg. Household Size	2.69
Diversity Measure	4
STANDARD OF LIVING	
Median Household Income	$74,625
% Household Income > $100K	29%
Projected Future Job Growth	8%
Cost of Living Index	99.4
Buying Power Index	175
Weekly Daycare Cost	$120
Median Home Price	$192,400
"Sweet Spot" Home Price	$300,000
Home Price Ratio	2.6
Median Age of Homes	45.3
% Homes Owned	84%
Effective Property Tax Rate	3.10%
Estimated Property Tax Bill	$9,300
EDUCATION	
% High School Graduates	98%
% 4-yr Degree	34%
% Graduate or Professional Degree	18%
$ Invested per Pupil	$7,222
Student/Teacher Ratio	14.4
Primary Test Score Percentile	100.6
Secondary Test Score Percentile	108.6
% Subsidized School Lunch	38.20%
% Attending Public School	90.10%
LIFESTYLE	
Leisure Rating (Area)	4
Arts & Culture Rating (Area)	4
Climate Rating (Area)	2
Physical Setting Rating	4
Downtown Core Rating	8
% Commute < 30 Min.	88%
% Commute > 1 Hour	4%
HEALTH & SAFETY	
Health Rating (Area)	9
Stress Score (Area)	0
Violent Crime Risk	66
Property Crime Risk	105

nition. Those wanting a change can get to Milwaukee, Green Bay, or the Fox Cities area (Appleton, Neenah, Oshkosh, and Lake Winnebago) in an hour, and to Chicago in 2 hours.

Traffic and commutes are seldom an issue; the roads are well suited to local and through traffic. Besides the usual services supported by property taxes, the area has excellent winter road-clearing services.

Sheboygan sits on a coastal plain on the west Lake Michigan Shore. The lake provides some moderating influence, but most weather arrives from the west. Summers are generally pleasant with cooling breezes. Winters can be harsh as cold air masses arrive from the west, but are less severe than nearby inland locations.

Health & Safety Crime is very low, and the area scores well on stress, allergies, and air quality. The local St. Nicholas Hospital is a teaching hospital, which is a bonus for a town of this size.

Nearby Neighborhoods All areas of the city are considered similar, but Kohler to the west is a bit younger with a higher percentage of families (37%) and a more suburban/country feel, though admittedly with higher home prices. Residential areas just to the north of the downtown core, especially near the lakeshore, work well for more of a city-neighborhood feel.

SHEBOYGAN, WI
AREA HIGHLIGHTS

PEOPLE

SIZE & DIVERSITY	AREA	U.S. AVG	FAMILY DEMOGRAPHICS	AREA	U.S. AVG
Population	113,958		% Married	63%	53.80%
15-yr Population Growth	9.70%	4.40%	% Single	37%	46.20%
Diversity Measure	17	54	% Divorced	5.50%	10.20%
% Religiously Observant	72%	50%	% Separated	1.50%	2.10%
% Catholic	27%	22%	% Married w/Children	34.90%	27.90%
% Protestant	46%	25%	% Single w/Children	5.90%	9.40%
% Jewish	0%	2%	% Married, No Children	34.50%	31.00%
% Other	0%	1%	% Single, No Children	24.70%	31.70%

STANDARD OF LIVING

INCOME, EMPLOYMENT & TAXES	AREA	U.S. AVG	COST OF LIVING & HOUSING	AREA	U.S. AVG
Median Household Income	$49,716	$44,684	Cost of Living Index	86.9	100
Household Income Growth	3.50%	6.10%	Buying Power Index	128	100
Unemployment Rate	3.50%	5.10%	Median Home Price	$129,000	$208,500
Recent Job Growth	4.80%	1.30%	Home Price Ratio	2.6	4.7
Projected Future Job Growth	9.40%	10.50%	Home Price Appreciation	9.20%	13.60%
State Income Tax Rate	6.90%	5.00%	% Homes Owned	74.90%	64.10%
State Sales Tax Rate	5.50%	6.00%	Median Rent	$543	$792

EDUCATION

ATTAINMENT & ACHIEVEMENT	AREA	U.S. AVG	RESOURCES & INVESTMENT	AREA	U.S. AVG
% High School Graduate	82.40%	83.90%	No. of Highly Ranked Universities	0	1
% 2-yr Graduate	10%	7.10%	$ Invested per Pupil	$6,817	$6,058
% 4-yr Graduate	14.10%	17.20%	Student/Teacher Ratio	16.1	15.9
% Graduate or Professional Degree	4.70%	9.90%	State University In-State Tuition	$5,862	$4,917
% Attending Public School	86.70%	84.30%			
75th Percentile State University SAT Score (Verbal)	N/A	477			
75th Percentile State University SAT Score (Math)	N/A	478			
75th Percentile State University ACT Score	26	20			

LIFESTYLE

RECREATION, ARTS & CULTURE	AREA	U.S. AVG	INFRASTRUCTURE & FACILITIES	AREA	U.S. AVG
Professional Sports Rating	2	4	No. of Public Libraries	8	28
Zoos & Aquariums Rating	1	3	Library Volumes Per Capita	4.4	2.8
Amusement Park Rating	1	3	No. of Warehouse Clubs	1	4
Professional Theater Rating	1	3	No. of Starbucks	0	5
Overall Museum Rating	5	6	Golf Course Rating	7	4
Science Museum Rating	1	4	National Park Rating	1	3
Children's Museum Rating	1	3	Sq. Mi. Inland Water	2	4

CLIMATE			COMMUTE & TRANSPORTATION		
Days Mostly Sunny	195	212	Avg. Daily Commute Time	16.9	24.7
Annual Days Precipitation	122	111	% Commute by Auto	74%	77.70%
Annual Days > 90°F	9	38	Per Capita Avg. Daily Transit Miles	7.5	7.9
Annual Days < 32°F	146	88	Annual Auto Insurance Premium	$985	$1,314
July Relative Humidity	73	69	Gas, Cost per Gallon	$3.05	$3.05

HEALTH & SAFETY

CRIME & ENVIRNOMENTAL ISSUES	AREA	U.S. AVG	HEALTHCARE & COST	AREA	U.S. AVG
Violent Crime Rate	98	517	Physicians per Capita	153.5	254.3
Change in Violent Crime	-32.40%	-7.50%	Pediatricians per Capita	10.6	16.9
Property Crime Rate	2954	3783	Hospital Beds per Capita	312.4	239.7
Change in Property Crime	-7.20%	-10.10%	No. of Teaching Hospitals	0	1.9
Air Quality Score	42	44	Healthcare Cost Index	100.7	100
Water Quality Score	20	33	Cost per Doctor Visit	$93	$74
Pollen/Allergy Score	37	61	Cost per Dentist Visit	$66	$67
Stress Score	3	49	Cost per Hospital Room	$589	$702
Cancer Mortality Rate	160.1	168.9			

Spokane, WA

Area Type: Inner suburb

Zip Code: 99223

Metro Area: Spokane, WA

Metro Area Type: Smaller

Location: 250 miles east of Seattle, 18 miles west of the Idaho border along I-90

Time Zone: Pacific Standard Time

Pros:
Attractive downtown and setting
Outdoor recreation
Arts and culture

Cons:
Harsh winters
Growth and sprawl
Crime rates and risk

Quick! Name the last three U.S. cities to host a World's Fair. If you answered New Orleans, Knoxville, and Spokane, you may be a future *Jeopardy!* champion. The earliest host of the three, Spokane had the Fair in 1974 and has perhaps made the best use of its legacy.

Through a recent annexation of areas to the east, Spokane has once again regained its title as the second-largest city in Washington. This may seem surprising given Spokane's middle-of-nowhere location far from any coast or other major geographic feature. But Spokane is the largest city between Seattle and Minneapolis. Although not a regional center on the scale of Denver or Chicago, Spokane serves the transportation, commercial, financial, healthcare, government, and entertainment needs for the "Inland Northwest"—which includes western Montana, northern Idaho, eastern Washington and Oregon, and southern Alberta and British Columbia.

Downtown Spokane is attractive and clean, with grid streets, restored older buildings, and skywalks connecting major department stores. City Hall is in a renovated Montgomery Ward department store, a fine example of the community's commitment to preservation. Downtown is a gathering place and is thought by city officials to be the largest Wi-Fi zone in the nation; the area recently won a 2004 National Civic League All-American City award. Just north of downtown lies the 50-acre World's Fair site developed on an old rail yard along the Spokane River and Spokane Falls. It's a good city park with walking and biking trails, plus a large convention center and opera house, a carousel, an IMAX theater, and an assortment of other arts and entertainment venues.

Today, the Spokane area is booming as smaller businesses develop. These firms are prospering from a good business environment, a quality labor force, trade with Canada, and an influx of residents from other areas. Recent job growth is a strong 4.4%. The largest employers are the government, the military, and the large hospitals in the area, but the small business base is building rapidly, aided by a large base of externally fueled growth. Because of climate, cost, and outdoor activities, many retirees, particularly from California, are moving in. Many live in Coeur d'Alene but seek access to retail, healthcare, and the airport in Spokane.

Most of the city is livable, but best for families is a series of neighborhoods to the south along a high bluff known as South Hill overlooking the city and river canyons farther to the south. The 99223 zip code area starts out as an older city neighborhood and grows south with an excellent mix of homes, great schools, and attractive golf courses. The married-with-children percentage of households is 29%.

Standard of Living While employment is strong in certain sectors, some basic industries and even a few tech names have had downturns. The BNSF railroad has reduced facilities as more trains are preblocked for Seattle and Portland destinations, and Agilent Technologies, long a technology industry bellwether, has been downsizing. The cost of living gets a mild coastal "shadow," but remains reasonable on a national scale with a COL Index of 101. Utility costs, aided by hydro power, are especially reasonable. Home prices exceed national averages but not to typical West Coast levels. Family homes start at about $185K with a "sweet spot" in the low to mid $300Ks. Homes are high quality and, as commonly found in the Northwest, more individual and less likely to be "spec" or tract homes. Many have basements. Property taxes are reasonable at 1.5% but sales taxes are high, and Washington has no state income tax.

Education Spokane School District encompasses the city (and all but the extreme southern edge of 99223), and the schools on the south side report better test scores than most in the northern parts of town. Ferris High School tests 5% to 10% above state averages and is noted for its extracurricular and honors programs. The elementary schools do better: Mullan Road Elementary tested 17% to 30% above state averages. Spokane is also home to Gonzaga University, Whitworth College, and a branch campus of Washington State University. Educational attainment rates show 43% of the population has either 4-year or graduate/professional degrees.

Lifestyle   Outdoor activities rank high on the list, and there's something for everyone—including hiking, camping, mountain climbing, biking, fishing, hunting, rafting, and golf. There's excellent downhill and cross-country skiing in Mount Spokane State Park 30 miles northeast. And families find plenty to do in the town's downtown core and Riverfront Park area. The Opera House and Convention Center is an outstanding facility, hosting, among other performing arts, a strong symphony orchestra with youth programs. Children's and science museums are on the upswing; thanks to a large Bill Gates Foundation challenge grant, a brand-new Mobius children's museum just opened in 2005 and a new science facility is scheduled to come on line in 2007.

Commutes are largely a non-issue, although traffic can be heavy on I-90 at times, particularly toward commercial/industrial areas east of town. Part of the key to the city's growth is its above-average air service. Southwest Airlines, among others, offers excellent discount flights.

Up on the South Hill plateau, the area is mainly flat and thickly forested with coniferous trees; deep canyons drop off to the south and west. Forests and low mountains rise to the west and north, agricultural plains to the south, with low, dry mountains and mixed terrain to the east into Idaho. The dry intermountain climate is pleasant, especially in summer, but strong northerly surges can bring cold blasts and heavy snows—fortunately, they usually don't linger long.

Health & Safety   Spokane-area violent and property crime rates are a bit higher than national averages but they're improving. Air quality is generally good, although summer stagnation can bring some unhealthy days. As a regional center, healthcare facilities are above average; Spokane is served by eight hospitals and medical centers, including a Shriner's Childrens Hospital, several smaller specialty clinics, and a well-regarded cardiology clinic.

Nearby Neighborhoods   The South Hill area offers a good variety of city and suburban living; in fact, the

SPOKANE, WA NEIGHBORHOOD HIGHLIGHTS	
PEOPLE	
Population	26,717
15-yr Population Growth	20.60%
5-yr Population Growth	4.20%
% Married w/Children	29.0%
% Single w/Children	8.9%
No. of Households	10,255
Median Age	36.7
Avg. Household Size	2.59
Diversity Measure	13
STANDARD OF LIVING	
Median Household Income	$52,403
% Household Income > $100K	17%
Projected Future Job Growth	14%
Cost of Living Index	101
Buying Power Index	116
Weekly Daycare Cost	$157
Median Home Price	$209,900
"Sweet Spot" Home Price	$340,000
Home Price Ratio	4
Median Age of Homes	22
% Homes Owned	72%
Effective Property Tax Rate	1.50%
Estimated Property Tax Bill	$5,100
EDUCATION	
% High School Graduates	95%
% 4-yr Degree	28%
% Graduate or Professional Degree	16%
$ Invested per Pupil	$5,902
Student/Teacher Ratio	20.7
Primary Test Score Percentile	119.7
Secondary Test Score Percentile	135.2
% Subsidized School Lunch	32.20%
% Attending Public School	83.40%
LIFESTYLE	
Leisure Rating (Area)	1
Arts & Culture Rating (Area)	7
Climate Rating (Area)	3
Physical Setting Rating	7
Downtown Core Rating	8
% Commute < 30 Min.	81%
% Commute > 1 Hour	2%
HEALTH & SAFETY	
Health Rating (Area)	7
Stress Score (Area)	10
Violent Crime Risk	140
Property Crime Risk	108

northern extent of the area is more of a city neighborhood and is very attractive. Less-expensive alternatives lie to the north and east of town, although some close-in areas north leave a bit to be desired. The suburbs of Dishman and Opportunity sprawl toward the east and are closer to major commercial and shopping areas but have less interesting terrain and some compromise in education.

SPOKANE, WA
AREA HIGHLIGHTS

PEOPLE

SIZE & DIVERSITY	AREA	U.S. AVG		FAMILY DEMOGRAPHICS	AREA	U.S. AVG
Population	435,644			% Married	56.90%	53.80%
15-yr Population Growth	20.60%	4.40%		% Single	43.10%	46.20%
Diversity Measure	19	54		% Divorced	10.50%	10.20%
% Religiously Observant	36%	50%		% Separated	2.40%	2.10%
% Catholic	14%	22%		% Married w/Children	29%	27.90%
% Protestant	22%	25%		% Single w/Children	10.60%	9.40%
% Jewish	0%	2%		% Married, No Children	29.40%	31.00%
% Other	0%	1%		% Single, No Children	31%	31.70%

STANDARD OF LIVING

INCOME, EMPLOYMENT & TAXES	AREA	U.S. AVG		COST OF LIVING & HOUSING	AREA	U.S. AVG
Median Household Income	$37,761	$44,684		Cost of Living Index	93	100
Household Income Growth	4.80%	6.10%		Buying Power Index	91	100
Unemployment Rate	4.80%	5.10%		Median Home Price	$158,600	$208,500
Recent Job Growth	4.40%	1.30%		Home Price Ratio	4.2	4.7
Projected Future Job Growth	13.70%	10.50%		Home Price Appreciation	12.50%	13.60%
State Income Tax Rate	0%	5.00%		% Homes Owned	66.70%	64.10%
State Sales Tax Rate	7.80%	6.00%		Median Rent	$614	$792

EDUCATION

ATTAINMENT & ACHIEVEMENT	AREA	U.S. AVG		RESOURCES & INVESTMENT	AREA	U.S. AVG
% High School Graduate	86.30%	83.90%		No. of Highly Ranked Universities	1	1
% 2-yr Graduate	15.50%	7.10%		$ Invested per Pupil	$5,879	$6,058
% 4-yr Graduate	21.30%	17.20%		Student/Teacher Ratio	20.3	15.9
% Graduate or Professional Degree	8.70%	9.90%		State University In-State Tuition	$5,286	$4,917
% Attending Public School	89.70%	84.30%				
75th Percentile State University SAT Score (Verbal)	520	477				
75th Percentile State University SAT Score (Math)	550	478				
75th Percentile State University ACT Score	23	20				

LIFESTYLE

RECREATION, ARTS & CULTURE	AREA	U.S. AVG		INFRASTRUCTURE & FACILITIES	AREA	U.S. AVG
Professional Sports Rating	3	4		No. of Public Libraries	16	28
Zoos & Aquariums Rating	1	3		Library Volumes Per Capita	2.7	2.8
Amusement Park Rating	1	3		No. of Warehouse Clubs	4	4
Professional Theater Rating	1	3		No. of Starbucks	20	5
Overall Museum Rating	5	6		Golf Course Rating	2	4
Science Museum Rating	1	4		National Park Rating	3	3
Children's Museum Rating	3	3		Sq. Mi. Inland Water	3	4

CLIMATE				COMMUTE & TRANSPORTATION		
Days Mostly Sunny	176	212		Avg. Daily Commute Time	21.2	24.7
Annual Days Precipitation	114	111		% Commute by Auto	76%	77.70%
Annual Days > 90°F	21	38		Per Capita Avg. Daily Transit Miles	5.6	7.9
Annual Days < 32°F	141	88		Annual Auto Insurance Premium	$1,599	$1,314
July Relative Humidity	63	69		Gas, Cost per Gallon	$2.97	$3.05

HEALTH & SAFETY

CRIME & ENVIRNOMENTAL ISSUES	AREA	U.S. AVG		HEALTHCARE & COST	AREA	U.S. AVG
Violent Crime Rate	382	517		Physicians per Capita	266.1	254.3
Change in Violent Crime	-30.90%	-7.50%		Pediatricians per Capita	14.2	16.9
Property Crime Rate	5543	3783		Hospital Beds per Capita	376.1	239.7
Change in Property Crime	-14%	-10.10%		No. of Teaching Hospitals	3	1.9
Air Quality Score	25	44		Healthcare Cost Index	118.7	100
Water Quality Score	38	33		Cost per Doctor Visit	$74	$74
Pollen/Allergy Score	42	61		Cost per Dentist Visit	$113	$67
Stress Score	96	49		Cost per Hospital Room	$734	$702
Cancer Mortality Rate	163.8	168.9				

St. Charles, MO

Area Type: Outer suburb/suburban town

Zip Code: 63304

Metro Area: St. Louis, MO-IL

Metro Area Type: Large

Location: Along US 40 and the Missouri River 30 miles west of downtown St. Louis

Time Zone: Central Standard Time

Pros:

Historic interest
Strong employment
Arts and culture

Cons:

Some long commutes
Hot, humid summers
High taxes

It was the "last civilized stop" for the Lewis and Clark Expedition in 1804, and the first Missouri capital from 1821 to 1826. As the second-oldest city west of the Mississippi, it has a historic downtown core filled with interesting pre-1850 residential and commercial buildings. St. Charles is a typical old river town located on a narrow peninsula between the meandering Missouri and Mississippi rivers, as they approach each other before their eventual confluence north of downtown St. Louis.

More than 200 years after that famous expedition, St. Charles continues to be on a path to progress. The business-friendly city of about 55,000 residents is 7 miles west of St. Louis–Lambert International Airport and a large assortment of enterprises in that area. Calling itself "The City That Works," St. Charles hosts a number of major employers—including Boeing, MasterCard, Coca-Cola, and a new riverboat gambling casino, plus a long, diverse list of small businesses, each employing fewer than 300 people. This area has a strong and well-educated labor force and a strategic business location: An estimated 120 million U.S. residents live within a 1-day truck drive, making it a practical center for distribution. Strong economic development forces continue to attract business; there are some 5,000 acres earmarked for commercial development in the Highway 370 corridor running north near the airport. A new convention center recently opened as well, further establishing the area as a favored business destination.

But it isn't all business. Just north, ground was recently broken on the "New Town at St. Charles," a New Urbanism exercise in residential development and community planning. New Town is a planned community of 4,300 residences and self-contained services aesthetically designed to blend old styles with new functionality around a set of canals almost European in character. Another larger phase is scheduled to follow.

Downtown St. Charles sits on the west bank of the Missouri River, surrounded by a mix of older neighborhoods. Just west, the Lindenwood University brings 8,000 liberal arts students to a 500-acre campus and adds a moderate college-town influence. Newer, more suburban settings are found to the south and west along the west bank of the Missouri. The zip code we chose to highlight in this book (63304) is located where the old US 40 crosses the Missouri River and it's a place with a significant number of married-with-children households (44%).

St. Louis, some 25 minutes away, appeared in *Cities Ranked & Rated* as a "Cultural Bargain"—a place with performing and visual arts amenities comparable to the largest cities in the United States, with a cost-of-living profile well below most such cities. Helped by corporate endowments from the likes of Anheuser-Busch and Monsanto, the area has a very good selection of museums and performing arts. Forest Park, west of downtown, is the site of the 1904 World's Fair and one of the largest urban parks in the world. The St. Louis Art Museum, St. Louis Zoo, and Missouri History Museum are among the many facilities clustered around Forest Park. There is also plenty to do along the waterfront and in the University City area—home to Washington University, the area's premier higher-education spot. And the city's reputation as a sports town is hardly exceeded anywhere, with the popular St. Louis Cardinals, Rams, and Blues plus a wide variety of other sports teams.

Standard of Living   The cost of living is reasonable for a nice part of a large U.S. metro area; the COL Index is 102. Future job growth is projected at a high 20% and stands in contrast with the relatively slow-growing metro area. The Buying Power Index is a very strong 158. Home prices are affordable, with two-story colonial-style family homes starting in the $170Ks on a

ST. CHARLES, MO NEIGHBORHOOD HIGHLIGHTS	
PEOPLE	
Population	43,760
15-yr Population Growth	50.80%
5-yr Population Growth	13%
% Married w/Children	44.0%
% Single w/Children	9.3%
No. of Households	14,406
Median Age	33
Avg. Household Size	3
Diversity Measure	9
STANDARD OF LIVING	
Median Household Income	$72,286
% Household Income > $100K	21%
Projected Future Job Growth	20%
Cost of Living Index	102
Buying Power Index	158
Weekly Daycare Cost	$171
Median Home Price	$212,000
"Sweet Spot" Home Price	$235,000
Home Price Ratio	2.9
Median Age of Homes	12.9
% Homes Owned	90%
Effective Property Tax Rate	2.20%
Estimated Property Tax Bill	$5,170
EDUCATION	
% High School Graduates	92%
% 4-yr Degree	25%
% Graduate or Professional Degree	8%
$ Invested per Pupil	$5,068
Student/Teacher Ratio	13.6
Primary Test Score Percentile	116.7
Secondary Test Score Percentile	127
% Subsidized School Lunch	7.20%
% Attending Public School	76.30%
LIFESTYLE	
Leisure Rating (Area)	6
Arts & Culture Rating (Area)	9
Climate Rating (Area)	1
Physical Setting Rating	4
Downtown Core Rating	4
% Commute < 30 Min.	45%
% Commute > 1 Hour	7%
HEALTH & SAFETY	
Health Rating (Area)	5
Stress Score (Area)	9
Violent Crime Risk	22
Property Crime Risk	35

¼ acre with trees. The "sweet spot" is $235K, and this will buy a 2,400- to 2,600-square-foot home on a ¼ to a ½ acre, some with five bedrooms. Effective property tax rates run about 2.2% with relatively high local sales, income, personal property, and utility taxes.

Education Schools in the local Frances Howell district test well above averages. Four-year educational attainment is moderate at 25%, and an additional 8% of residents have graduate-level degrees. Lindenwood University and the nearby Washington University, St. Louis University, University of Missouri–St. Louis campus, and an assortment of small colleges and vocational schools offer a diverse higher-educational environment.

Lifestyle Downtown isn't just there to look at—it's alive year-round with lots of shopping, entertainment, and history. Local offerings include a blues festival and other music performances, street fairs, and historic reenactments of Lewis and Clark and Civil War events. Other highlights include Missouri River storytelling, an Oktoberfest, and a nationally known month-long Christmas Traditions festival. There is even a St. Charles County Symphony for those who think 25 minutes to St. Louis is too far. St. Charles lies at one end of the Katy Trail, a 225-mile-long state park enjoyed by bikers and walkers throughout Missouri. For the amusements-minded, the Six Flags Over Missouri amusement park is about 20 miles south in Eureka, Missouri.

Commutes within St. Charles are easy, but reaching downtown St. Louis can take 45 minutes. If you live in St. Charles, it's best to find employment northeast toward the airport or somewhere along the Missouri River or I-270 beltway.

The St. Charles area is rolling to hilly and mainly wooded except on river plains and where used in agriculture. The continental climate is affected by Gulf moisture, especially during the summer, which brings extended periods of heat and humidity. Winters are variable and prolonged cold periods are rare.

Health & Safety St. Louis area crime is low and on a steady decline, a good sign for this relatively economically diverse area. Crime risk, as captured in the "CAP" index, is very low in St. Charles. Healthcare resources in St. Louis are strong, and the local 328-bed St. Joseph Health Center has a number of medical specialties.

Nearby Neighborhoods Lake St. Louis to the west and St. Peters to the north are also good choices. Older and more upscale areas are Richmond Heights near Washington University and the "Town and Country" area near the I-270/I-64 junction, with some attractive and more rural settings to the west. The New Town development in St. Charles is also worth a close look.

ST. LOUIS, MO-IL
AREA HIGHLIGHTS

PEOPLE

SIZE & DIVERSITY	AREA	U.S. AVG	FAMILY DEMOGRAPHICS	AREA	U.S. AVG
Population	2,667,862		% Married	54.90%	53.80%
15-yr Population Growth	10%	4.40%	% Single	45.10%	46.20%
Diversity Measure	36	54	% Divorced	8.80%	10.20%
% Religiously Observant	51%	50%	% Separated	3.10%	2.10%
% Catholic	25%	22%	% Married w/Children	28%	27.90%
% Protestant	24%	25%	% Single w/Children	11.20%	9.40%
% Jewish	2%	2%	% Married, No Children	28.90%	31.00%
% Other	1%	1%	% Single, No Children	32%	31.70%

STANDARD OF LIVING

INCOME, EMPLOYMENT & TAXES	AREA	U.S. AVG	COST OF LIVING & HOUSING	AREA	U.S. AVG
Median Household Income	$48,411	$44,684	Cost of Living Index	86.6	100
Household Income Growth	6.10%	6.10%	Buying Power Index	125	100
Unemployment Rate	6.10%	5.10%	Median Home Price	$141,900	$208,500
Recent Job Growth	1.70%	1.30%	Home Price Ratio	2.9	4.7
Projected Future Job Growth	8.20%	10.50%	Home Price Appreciation	8.40%	13.60%
State Income Tax Rate	6.90%	5.00%	% Homes Owned	66.20%	64.10%
State Sales Tax Rate	5.20%	6.00%	Median Rent	$741	$792

EDUCATION

ATTAINMENT & ACHIEVEMENT	AREA	U.S. AVG	RESOURCES & INVESTMENT	AREA	U.S. AVG
% High School Graduate	76.30%	83.90%	No. of Highly Ranked Universities	4	1
% 2-yr Graduate	7.40%	7.10%	$ Invested per Pupil	$5,908	$6,058
% 4-yr Graduate	15.50%	17.20%	Student/Teacher Ratio	16.2	15.9
% Graduate or Professional Degree	7.80%	9.90%	State University In-State Tuition	$6,622	$4,917
% Attending Public School	81.40%	84.30%			
75th Percentile State University SAT Score (Verbal)	540	477			
75th Percentile State University SAT Score (Math)	540	478			
75th Percentile State University ACT Score	23	20			

LIFESTYLE

RECREATION, ARTS & CULTURE	AREA	U.S. AVG	INFRASTRUCTURE & FACILITIES	AREA	U.S. AVG
Professional Sports Rating	8	4	No. of Public Libraries	116	28
Zoos & Aquariums Rating	9	3	Library Volumes Per Capita	4.5	2.8
Amusement Park Rating	10	3	No. of Warehouse Clubs	7	4
Professional Theater Rating	8	3	No. of Starbucks	29	5
Overall Museum Rating	9	6	Golf Course Rating	7	4
Science Museum Rating	7	4	National Park Rating	2	3
Children's Museum Rating	10	3	Sq. Mi. Inland Water	6	4

CLIMATE			COMMUTE & TRANSPORTATION		
Days Mostly Sunny	206	212	Avg. Daily Commute Time	25.5	24.7
Annual Days Precipitation	108	111	% Commute by Auto	76%	77.70%
Annual Days > 90°F	37	38	Per Capita Avg. Daily Transit Miles	13.2	7.9
Annual Days < 32°F	107	88	Annual Auto Insurance Premium	$1,577	$1,314
July Relative Humidity	70	69	Gas, Cost per Gallon	$3.10	$3.05

HEALTH & SAFETY

CRIME & ENVIRNOMENTAL ISSUES	AREA	U.S. AVG	HEALTHCARE & COST	AREA	U.S. AVG
Violent Crime Rate	476	517	Physicians per Capita	295.5	254.3
Change in Violent Crime	-36.50%	-7.50%	Pediatricians per Capita	21.9	16.9
Property Crime Rate	3902	3783	Hospital Beds per Capita	473.9	239.7
Change in Property Crime	-18.90%	-10.10%	No. of Teaching Hospitals	18	1.9
Air Quality Score	31	44	Healthcare Cost Index	103	100
Water Quality Score	45	33	Cost per Doctor Visit	$71	$74
Pollen/Allergy Score	68	61	Cost per Dentist Visit	$67	$67
Stress Score	92	49	Cost per Hospital Room	$646	$702
Cancer Mortality Rate	179.9	168.9			

Sugar Land, TX

Best OF THE BEST

Area Type: Outer suburb/exurb

Zip Code: 77479

Metro Area: Houston, TX

Metro Area Type: Large

Location: 25 miles west of downtown Houston along Southwest Freeway (US 59)

Time Zone: Central Standard Time

Pros:
Planned communities
Strong job market
Educational attainment

Cons:
Physical setting and summer climate
Long commutes
Crime risk

Texans are world-famous for doing things in a big way, and their claim to fame is apparent in the quaint-sounding (albeit, fastest-growing area in the state) Sugar Land—yes, two words. In this rapidly expanding super suburb southwest of the main beltway in Houston, a full 53.2% of households are married with children (which ties Sugar Land with Flower Mound [see p. 196] for the highest concentration of such families in an area).

And what is it exactly that Sugar Landers do in a big way? Master-planned communities. Gigantic ones. Names like River Forest, Sienna Plantation, Sugar Lakes, Cinco Ranch, Greatwood, First Colony, and Grand River are by no means mere subdivisions. They are 1,200-acre, 1,500-acre, or 2,000-acre former ranches and sugar tracts converted into complete communities, with lakes, golf courses, equestrian centers, recreation centers, captive daycare centers, shopping, and a whole lot more. The master-planned community lifestyle may not be for everyone, and "good planned communities" aren't the same thing as a "good community plan." But those looking for amazing housing values and planned community benefits will be hard-pressed to find better than the lifestyle here.

Sugar Land began over a hundred years ago as a sleepy company town of the Imperial Sugar Company, with some 500 souls surrounded by sugar cane fields. When the oil-rich, air-conditioned Houston boomed and spread mainly northwest and southwest, it became the urban planning specialist's example of how *not* to do things—haphazard construction, inadequate freeways, two airports across town from one another, and poor zoning or no zoning at all. Sugar Landers were determined not to repeat Houston's mistakes.

The master-planned communities spread mainly along US 59, with a new Sugar Land Town Square, a new City Hall, and a recreated "old town" center with

walkways, shops, and residences above the shops, surrounded by a mix of retail and mid-rise, multiunit residential communities, some of which sport the look of the old sugar-mill complex. The Imperial Sugar mill itself just closed in 2003, and the property has been recently sold to a developer. The plans for its future are still being finalized. Meanwhile, most shopping conveniences of a city have found their way to Sugar Land; it's "self-contained once you're there," according to one local resident.

The Houston area is hardly picturesque, but it is a thriving metropolis with plenty to do. For families, the Johnson Space Center, Six Flags Astroworld, and numerous museums provide weekend entertainment. Galveston and its beaches are an hour south. The oil industry, while not without its cycles and Enron debacles, is king in downtown Houston. In addition, major offices for Unocal, Schlumberger, and Baker Hughes are close to Sugar Land, not to mention the headquarters for the Imperial Holly Corporation, the old sugar company. Nonetheless, an estimated 70% of residents commute to downtown or to the satellite urban center known as the Galleria, and most of these commutes take an hour although the distances suggest something shorter.

Standard of Living   Incomes are high, and future job growth is projected at a very strong 35%. Housing is affordable, and while costs are rising overall, Sugar Land has the second-highest Buying Power Index we observed at 194. The "sweet spot" for a good family home in one of the master-planned communities is $200K to $230K, with a modest $500 annual dues—and you get a lot for the money. About the only complaint is that the homes lack basements. There are more upscale options, but even new construction still costs only $90 per square foot. Such a combination of high future job growth and reasonable housing costs is hard to find. Property tax rates are the only "gotcha" factor, running 2.2% to 3%, but modest home values and the absence of state income taxes reduce the impact.

Education Area schools are considered "exemplary" and the local Clements High School was rated one of the top 10 in Texas by *Texas Monthly* magazine. That said, the rapid growth has exceeded capacity, and while a new high school is in the works, some students have had to be bused around to balance loads. The educational context is strong, with 39% of residents possessing a 4-year degree and another 21% possessing a graduate or professional degree. The University of Houston and Rice University are well-reputed institutions of higher learning.

Lifestyle In a large master-planned community, you'll find lots of things to do and plenty of space in which to do them. Parks, recreation, golf, swimming, trails, and other activities are often self-contained. Outside of the small Rio Brazos, the landscape is fairly featureless, and many residents travel north to the Texas hill country for outdoor activities or south to the beaches at Galveston (also very interesting historically) for a weekend getaway. Affordable air service is available to almost anywhere, and standards of living make getaway trips affordable. The strong economy, high incomes, and low costs also support a lot of single-earner families. Growth is a bit of an issue, and while, in the words of one resident, "it's at its 'sweet spot' now" (no pun intended), there can be too much of a good thing, even in Texas.

Sugar Land residents accept and deal with long commutes. Most major work centers are 45 minutes to an hour away, but we expect that more jobs will eventually move out toward Sugar Land to take advantage of its low costs and good workforce.

The surrounding terrain is completely flat, green, and mainly devoid of trees. The climate is decidedly subtropical, with long, hot, wet, and humid summers. Winter and spring seasons are the most pleasant and the best time for outdoor activities.

Health & Safety The crime risk in the Houston area is moderate, and the area "CAP" score reflects a high crime risk. From our interviews with local residents we did not pick up on major concerns about crime, but we can't ignore the statistics. Healthcare facilities are excellent, with the Texas Medical Center complex along the main road toward Houston. A new local hospital is also under construction.

SUGAR LAND, TX NEIGHBORHOOD HIGHLIGHTS	
PEOPLE	
Population	69,323
15-yr Population Growth	96.40%
5-yr Population Growth	24.90%
% Married w/Children	53.2%
% Single w/Children	8.8%
No. of Households	20,557
Median Age	31.1
Avg. Household Size	3.26
Diversity Measure	57
STANDARD OF LIVING	BEST
Median Household Income	$102,248
% Household Income > $100K	47%
Projected Future Job Growth	35%
Cost of Living Index	115
Buying Power Index	194
Weekly Daycare Cost	$139
Median Home Price	$248,400
"Sweet Spot" Home Price	$220,000
Home Price Ratio	2.4
Median Age of Homes	9.4
% Homes Owned	84%
Effective Property Tax Rate	3%
Estimated Property Tax Bill	$6,600
EDUCATION	BEST
% High School Graduates	94%
% 4-yr Degree	39%
% Graduate or Professional Degree	21%
$ Invested per Pupil	$4,489
Student/Teacher Ratio	15.7
Primary Test Score Percentile	106.3
Secondary Test Score Percentile	117.3
% Subsidized School Lunch	28.60%
% Attending Public School	81%
LIFESTYLE	
Leisure Rating (Area)	9
Arts & Culture Rating (Area)	9
Climate Rating (Area)	6
Physical Setting Rating	1
Downtown Core Rating	3
% Commute < 30 Min.	38%
% Commute > 1 Hour	10%
HEALTH & SAFETY	
Health Rating (Area)	0
Stress Score (Area)	9
Violent Crime Risk	282
Property Crime Risk	152

Nearby Neighborhoods Most of Houston's family neighborhoods are outside the I-610 beltway to the northwest, west, and southwest. Katy is an older and less planned community just north of Sugar Land. North of that is the Woodlands, an area not surprisingly with more trees and a variety of housing; it's a good alternative if master-planed communities don't suit your tastes.

HOUSTON, TX
AREA HIGHLIGHTS
PEOPLE

SIZE & DIVERSITY	AREA	U.S. AVG	FAMILY DEMOGRAPHICS	AREA	U.S. AVG
Population	4,587,092		% Married	53%	53.80%
15-yr Population Growth	41.70%	4.40%	% Single	47%	46.20%
Diversity Measure	65	54	% Divorced	10%	10.20%
% Religiously Observant	50%	50%	% Separated	4.90%	2.10%
% Catholic	18%	22%	% Married w/Children	30.30%	27.90%
% Protestant	30%	25%	% Single w/Children	12.80%	9.40%
% Jewish	1%	2%	% Married, No Children	24.10%	31.00%
% Other	1%	1%	% Single, No Children	32.80%	31.70%

STANDARD OF LIVING

INCOME, EMPLOYMENT & TAXES	AREA	U.S. AVG	COST OF LIVING & HOUSING	AREA	U.S. AVG
Median Household Income	$46,848	$44,684	Cost of Living Index	86.2	100
Household Income Growth	5.70%	6.10%	Buying Power Index	122	100
Unemployment Rate	5.70%	5.10%	Median Home Price	$142,500	$208,500
Recent Job Growth	2.10%	1.30%	Home Price Ratio	3	4.7
Projected Future Job Growth	17%	10.50%	Home Price Appreciation	4.40%	13.60%
State Income Tax Rate	0%	5.00%	% Homes Owned	56.50%	64.10%
State Sales Tax Rate	8.20%	6.00%	Median Rent	$801	$792

EDUCATION

ATTAINMENT & ACHIEVEMENT	AREA	U.S. AVG	RESOURCES & INVESTMENT	AREA	U.S. AVG
% High School Graduate	76.50%	83.90%	No. of Highly Ranked Universities	2	1
% 2-yr Graduate	7.10%	7.10%	$ Invested per Pupil	$5,210	$6,058
% 4-yr Graduate	23.70%	17.20%	Student/Teacher Ratio	16.8	15.9
% Graduate or Professional Degree	10.20%	9.90%	State University In-State Tuition	$5,735	$4,917
% Attending Public School	91.40%	84.30%			
75th Percentile State University SAT Score (Verbal)	540	477			
75th Percentile State University SAT Score (Math)	570	478			
75th Percentile State University ACT Score	23	20			

LIFESTYLE

RECREATION, ARTS & CULTURE	AREA	U.S. AVG	INFRASTRUCTURE & FACILITIES	AREA	U.S. AVG
Professional Sports Rating	8	4	No. of Public Libraries	94	28
Zoos & Aquariums Rating	7	3	Library Volumes Per Capita	1.6	2.8
Amusement Park Rating	9	3	No. of Warehouse Clubs	9	4
Professional Theater Rating	10	3	No. of Starbucks	93	5
Overall Museum Rating	9	6	Golf Course Rating	9	4
Science Museum Rating	7	4	National Park Rating	4	3
Children's Museum Rating	8	3	Sq. Mi. Inland Water	6	4

CLIMATE			COMMUTE & TRANSPORTATION		
Days Mostly Sunny	203	212	Avg. Daily Commute Time	29	24.7
Annual Days Precipitation	107	111	% Commute by Auto	75%	77.70%
Annual Days > 90°F	81	38	Per Capita Avg. Daily Transit Miles	15.1	7.9
Annual Days < 32°F	24	88	Annual Auto Insurance Premium	$1,975	$1,314
July Relative Humidity	77	69	Gas, Cost per Gallon	$2.97	$3.05

HEALTH & SAFETY

CRIME & ENVIRNOMENTAL ISSUES	AREA	U.S. AVG	HEALTHCARE & COST	AREA	U.S. AVG
Violent Crime Rate	739	517	Physicians per Capita	240.1	254.3
Change in Violent Crime	-1.40%	-7.50%	Pediatricians per Capita	17.6	16.9
Property Crime Rate	4359	3783	Hospital Beds per Capita	313.3	239.7
Change in Property Crime	-2.10%	-10.10%	No. of Teaching Hospitals	19	1.9
Air Quality Score	8	44	Healthcare Cost Index	106.5	100
Water Quality Score	41	33	Cost per Doctor Visit	$78	$74
Pollen/Allergy Score	70	61	Cost per Dentist Visit	$64	$67
Stress Score	91	49	Cost per Hospital Room	$689	$702
Cancer Mortality Rate	175.9	168.9			

Tyler, TX

Area Type: Small city

Zip Code: 75791

Metro Area: Tyler, TX

Metro Area Type: Smaller

Location: 100 miles east of Dallas–Fort Worth metroplex along I-20

Time Zone: Central Standard Time

Pros:
Small-town flavor
Cost of living
Healthcare

Cons:
Growth and traffic
Some unattractive sprawl
Summer heat

"Coming to Tyler is like coming home," according to Dale Reel, former mayor of Whitehouse, Texas, a suburban town just south of Tyler. To Mr. Reel, Tyler has the right combination of size, prosperity, climate, and friendliness for any family.

Interstate 45 makes a direct north–south beeline between Dallas and Houston, slicing off a 150-mile-wide, 350-mile-high swath of the Lone Star State known as East Texas. For most folks, the image of Texas includes dry, high-plains ranchland stretching as far as the eye can see, the perfect Old West backdrop. But not so in East Texas. East Texas is more a part of the Deep South than the West. Instead of dry prairie, East Texas features stands of tall coniferous trees, hence the area nickname, the "Piney Woods" part of Texas. Many of these forests are actually tree farms on converted cotton plantations. The local lifestyles and accents also speak to the Deep South, and towns are more like old Southern towns than the modern cosmopolitan centers found in the rest of the state.

The 1920s ushered in the famous oil boom, and the oil industry is still present—especially east of Tyler. Tyler became a preferred place for those who made fortunes in the oil industry, while most field workers stayed east. That wealth supported a strong downtown and inner residential core still present today. Gradually the oil and timber industries moved south and east, giving way to a more diverse economy. Tyler has in fact become a healthcare and retail center for the region and for a territory spreading well into Louisiana and other adjacent states.

Today's Tyler consists of an attractive downtown area laid out in a grid surrounding a courthouse square (the old Courthouse was, unfortunately, replaced in the 1950s, reducing some of the downtown charm) surrounded by grid streets and a handful of attractive historic residential districts. An active downtown "Heart of Tyler" redevelopment effort has brought in some 200 new businesses, with entertainment, festivals, and newly listed entries on the National Register of Historic Places.

Interstate 20 runs north of town, fortunately confining much of the "freeway sprawl" motels and travel service to this area, while most local growth has actually moved south of town into attractive neighborhoods. The zip code we chose to include in this book, 75791, is actually the small suburban town of Whitehouse, population 12,000, about 8 miles south of downtown Tyler. Many of the medical professionals and families connected to the University of Texas at Tyler live in this area, and the married-with-children percentage of households is almost 40%.

Standard of Living Cost of living and housing is one of the undeniable attractions of the area. The Cost of Living Index is 82, the lowest on our list of best places. Good family homes start in the $160Ks, with a "sweet spot" in the low $200Ks. Those looking for a large home in the 3,500- to 4,000-square-foot range possibly with acreage (1 acre plus) will find choices in the high $200Ks. A 2,600-square-foot, four-bedroom on 31 acres was recently listed at $300K. Most homes are on wooded lots and many are secluded. Property taxes run about 1.2% and there is no state income tax. Daycare costs $105 per week ($400 to $500 per month).

Education Generally, Tyler schools are well regarded, and those in Whitehouse are particularly attractive and modern, earning four-star ratings and a 2003 to 2004 "Gold Performance Award" from the Texas Education Agency. Test scores are generally 5% to 20% above state averages. The 5,000-student University of Texas branch (University of Texas at Tyler) adds a higher-education presence, and with in-state tuition near $3,000, it's a bargain.

TYLER, TX	
NEIGHBORHOOD HIGHLIGHTS	
PEOPLE	
Population	12,002
15-yr Population Growth	23.20%
5-yr Population Growth	6.70%
% Married w/Children	39.6%
% Single w/Children	11.1%
No. of Households	4,189
Median Age	33.7
Avg. Household Size	2.86
Diversity Measure	17
STANDARD OF LIVING	
Median Household Income	$51,545
% Household Income > $100K	9%
Projected Future Job Growth	12%
Cost of Living Index	82.1
Buying Power Index	143
Weekly Daycare Cost	$105
Median Home Price	$119,700
"Sweet Spot" Home Price	$200,000
Home Price Ratio	2.3
Median Age of Homes	15.5
% Homes Owned	78%
Effective Property Tax Rate	1.20%
Estimated Property Tax Bill	$2,400
EDUCATION	
% High School Graduates	89%
% 4-yr Degree	16%
% Graduate or Professional Degree	7%
$ Invested per Pupil	$4,046
Student/Teacher Ratio	12.2
Primary Test Score Percentile	107.5
Secondary Test Score Percentile	119.8
% Subsidized School Lunch	32.80%
% Attending Public School	89.30%
LIFESTYLE	
Leisure Rating (Area)	2
Arts & Culture Rating (Area)	1
Climate Rating (Area)	7
Physical Setting Rating	3
Downtown Core Rating	4
% Commute < 30 Min.	75%
% Commute > 1 Hour	3%
HEALTH & SAFETY	
Health Rating (Area)	6
Stress Score (Area)	4
Violent Crime Risk	68
Property Crime Risk	87

Lifestyle Outdoor recreation is the "main course" for family entertainment and activity. In general, Texas has lots of man-made lakes, and the Tyler area is no exception. Lake Tyler and Lake Palestine are the closest among an assortment of state park and recreation areas. The local Caldwell Zoo is an appreciated family facility. Downtown is full of activities, especially on weekends. The area's status as one of the leading centers for the cultivation of roses and azaleas supports a local museum and garden worth visiting. New local retail establishments make it no longer necessary to frequently travel to the Dallas–Fort Worth Metroplex. Short drives take families to history-rich Palestine or Nacogdoches, and the Texas State Railroad museum and its excursion trains are notable Palestine attractions.

Commutes in and around the Tyler area are easy, although long stretches of traffic signals are starting to produce some congestion. About 90% of Whitehouse residents work in Tyler. Many people work in the healthcare profession or are employed by one of many industries like Trane, Carrier, Goodyear, or the Target Distribution Center north along I-20. Few residents commute to Dallas, and Tyler has recently become home to some entrepreneurs and contract employees with clients in the Metroplex area; it works well when the 100-mile trip must be made only occasionally.

The landscape is gently rolling with dense Southern pine forests and agricultural terrain. The climate is continental with a strong Gulf subtropical influence, which produces four seasons with a bias toward warmth. Winters are mild and outdoor activities are possible. Although summers can be hot and humid, they're generally more comfortable here than in areas closer to the Gulf and often cooler than in the Dallas area.

Health & Safety Crime rate patterns are moderate to slightly unfavorable but not atypical for the region. Local crime risk in the Whitehouse area is favorably rated in the "CAP" index. Local healthcare facilities, supporting the greater region, are better than average.

Nearby Neighborhoods Besides Whitehouse, many find attractive neighborhoods to the south and southwest of town along the US 69 corridor, and historic "Azalea District" homes near downtown are surprisingly affordable.

TYLER, TX
AREA HIGHLIGHTS

PEOPLE

SIZE & DIVERSITY	AREA	U.S. AVG	FAMILY DEMOGRAPHICS	AREA	U.S. AVG
Population	186,414		% Married	56.80%	53.80%
15-yr Population Growth	23.20%	4.40%	% Single	43.20%	46.20%
Diversity Measure	47	54	% Divorced	8.20%	10.20%
% Religiously Observant	65%	50%	% Separated	3.40%	2.10%
% Catholic	9%	22%	% Married w/Children	28.70%	27.90%
% Protestant	56%	25%	% Single w/Children	10.20%	9.40%
% Jewish	0%	2%	% Married, No Children	31.70%	31.00%
% Other	0%	1%	% Single, No Children	29.40%	31.70%

STANDARD OF LIVING

INCOME, EMPLOYMENT & TAXES	AREA	U.S. AVG	COST OF LIVING & HOUSING	AREA	U.S. AVG
Median Household Income	$39,573	$44,684	Cost of Living Index	82.1	100
Household Income Growth	3.90%	6.10%	Buying Power Index	108	100
Unemployment Rate	3.90%	5.10%	Median Home Price	$126,700	$208,500
Recent Job Growth	2.80%	1.30%	Home Price Ratio	3.2	4.7
Projected Future Job Growth	13.10%	10.50%	Home Price Appreciation	7.50%	13.60%
State Income Tax Rate	0%	5.00%	% Homes Owned	66.10%	64.10%
State Sales Tax Rate	6.30%	6.00%	Median Rent	$573	$792

EDUCATION

ATTAINMENT & ACHIEVEMENT	AREA	U.S. AVG	RESOURCES & INVESTMENT	AREA	U.S. AVG
% High School Graduate	74.40%	83.90%	No. of Highly Ranked Universities	0	1
% 2-yr Graduate	11.80%	7.10%	$ Invested per Pupil	$4,946	$6,058
% 4-yr Graduate	15.90%	17.20%	Student/Teacher Ratio	14.5	15.9
% Graduate or Professional Degree	6.90%	9.90%	State University In-State Tuition	$5,735	$4,917
% Attending Public School	90%	84.30%			
75th Percentile State University SAT Score (Verbal)	540	477			
75th Percentile State University SAT Score (Math)	570	478			
75th Percentile State University ACT Score	23	20			

LIFESTYLE

RECREATION, ARTS & CULTURE	AREA	U.S. AVG	INFRASTRUCTURE & FACILITIES	AREA	U.S. AVG
Professional Sports Rating	2	4	No. of Public Libraries	6	28
Zoos & Aquariums Rating	6	3	Library Volumes Per Capita	2.7	2.8
Amusement Park Rating	1	3	No. of Warehouse Clubs	3	4
Professional Theater Rating	1	3	No. of Starbucks	2	5
Overall Museum Rating	3	6	Golf Course Rating	2	4
Science Museum Rating	1	4	National Park Rating	1	3
Children's Museum Rating	1	3	Sq. Mi. Inland Water	2	4

CLIMATE			COMMUTE & TRANSPORTATION		
Days Mostly Sunny	217	212	Avg. Daily Commute Time	22.2	24.7
Annual Days Precipitation	97	111	% Commute by Auto	80%	77.70%
Annual Days > 90°F	87	38	Per Capita Avg. Daily Transit Miles	0	7.9
Annual Days < 32°F	1	88	Annual Auto Insurance Premium	$1,195	$1,314
July Relative Humidity	71	69	Gas, Cost per Gallon	$2.99	$3.05

HEALTH & SAFETY

CRIME & ENVIRNOMENTAL ISSUES	AREA	U.S. AVG	HEALTHCARE & COST	AREA	U.S. AVG
Violent Crime Rate	661	517	Physicians per Capita	331	254.3
Change in Violent Crime	28.60%	-7.50%	Pediatricians per Capita	16.8	16.9
Property Crime Rate	4252	3783	Hospital Beds per Capita	488.3	239.7
Change in Property Crime	-12.40%	-10.10%	No. of Teaching Hospitals	2	1.9
Air Quality Score	27	44	Healthcare Cost Index	92.9	100
Water Quality Score	87	33	Cost per Doctor Visit	$83	$74
Pollen/Allergy Score	76	61	Cost per Dentist Visit	$63	$67
Stress Score	37	49	Cost per Hospital Room	$961	$702
Cancer Mortality Rate	169.3	168.9			

Valrico, FL

Area Type: Outer suburb

Zip Code: 33594

Metro Area: Tampa–St. Petersburg–Clearwater, FL

Metro Area Type: Large

Location: 15 miles east of downtown Tampa

Time Zone: Eastern Standard Time

Pros:
Leisure activities
Winter climate
Strong economy

Cons:
Growth and traffic
Area crime rate
Hot, humid summers

When families see Valrico for the first time, "they know it's what they've been looking for," according to one local real estate agent. Valrico is a large, quiet, and attractive suburb east and a bit inland from downtown Tampa and adjacent to the more commercialized Brandon area. Families move in from other parts of the country and Florida seeking great schools and a quiet suburban life quite literally in the backyard of Tampa–St. Petersburg, one of the most livable cities in Florida. The married-with-children percentage of households is a strong 39.7%.

The complex Gulf Coast metropolitan area consisting of the cities of Tampa, St. Petersburg, and Clearwater offers a vast array of city and recreation activities in a coastal environment. Tampa sits mostly north and east of Tampa Bay, while St. Petersburg and Clearwater sit on a peninsula separating Tampa Bay from the Gulf of Mexico to the west. There are a lot of retirees in the area, but they tend toward the beaches and palm trees of St. Petersburg and Clearwater on the Gulf and Sarasota-Bradenton to the south. Tampa is more of a traditional city with more commerce and employment than other areas around the bay, and it is a more family-oriented area. The entire region is not as heavily impacted by tourists as Florida cities farther south.

Downtown Tampa is a modern city of skyscrapers and palm trees, home to such large employers as Verizon and USAA Insurance. The area is becoming a major financial center as New York and other world firms look for secondary locations to house sensitive information-processing and record-keeping activities. The area is known as being business-friendly, and has a number of high-tech and biotech firms along with some more basic industries tied to agriculture and phosphate mining. Employment is strong, especially for Florida, with a 3.5% unemployment rate, a recent job-growth rate of 3.6%, and a future job-growth rate projected at 16%.

The Tampa Bay Buccaneers (NFL), Devil Rays (baseball), and Lightning (NHL) are local major-league teams, and the Orlando Magic (NBA) is an hour away. The area has the largest performing arts center in Florida plus an assortment of museums, amusement parks, and other arts and recreational facilities.

Standard of Living   For what you get, the overall cost of living remains quite reasonable; Valrico's Cost of Living Index is 103. As in most of Florida, the strengthening economy, an influx of residents, and relatively cheap home prices over the years is bringing rather sharp home-price percentage increases, but for now good family homes are still available in the mid to high $300K range. Lot sizes are a bit smaller than in other parts of Florida at a ¼ to a ½ acre, but many are wooded and larger acreages are available with some older homes built in the 1960s and 1970s. Property taxes are normal for Florida at 2.3%, and there's no state income tax.

Education   Schools are "great," according to one resident, and locals overwhelmingly say they're one of Valrico's strengths. Most are rated grade "A" or "B" by the Florida Department of Education. Test scores typically run 5% to 20% higher than state averages. Strong parent-teacher cooperation, volunteerism, and the schools' special daily reporting systems facilitate parent-teacher communication. There isn't a dominant higher-education facility in the area, but there are a number of smaller colleges and universities nearby.

Lifestyle   About three in four homes have a swimming pool, a good starting place for recreation. And beyond the backyard, activities aren't lacking. Major Tampa attractions include a Busch Gardens just north of Tampa, the Florida Aquarium, the Museum of Science and Industry ("MOSI"), the Lowry Park Zoo, and a full set of performing arts venues all within a

30-minute drive. The area's watersports and beach recreation are hard to beat. Some go to beaches at Bradenton a few miles south. Orlando and all of its attractions are an hour away. Most shopping is done in Brandon to the northwest. The Valrico area is growing, but not as fast as the corridor to the north toward Plant City, so it still retains a quiet suburban or even country feel.

For employment, most go toward downtown Tampa or to MacDill Air Force Base, located on the small peninsula jutting southward from Tampa into Tampa Bay. Commutes take 30 to 45 minutes and can be busy at rush hour because there's really only one road, SR 60, which is now being rebuilt into an elevated freeway with bidirectional lanes. Some use bus transit and park-and-rides, as well as carpooling, which is especially common among MacDill workers.

Most of the area is flat coastal plain with grasses and some sections of pine and laurel forests inland. The climate is subtropical with long, hot summer days often interrupted by heavy late-afternoon thunderstorms. These storms and afternoon sea breezes lead to cooler evenings. The winter climate is very pleasant, and outdoor activities are possible year-round.

Health & Safety   Area crime is high, typical of bigger cities in the region, but it's not perceived as a problem in Valrico; in fact, the local crime risk, as measured by the "CAP" score, is low. Hospital and healthcare facilities are excellent, with 20 hospitals and 4 trauma centers in the area. There's a Shriner Children's Hospital, and three area hospitals were named on the *U.S. News & World Report* "Best Hospitals" list.

Nearby Neighborhoods   Largo and Seminole, to the north of Tampa, are popular areas but more oriented to retirees. The Lithia area to the south is more upscale, with still better schools and a major new 3,000-acre planned development targeted to families.

VALRICO, FL NEIGHBORHOOD HIGHLIGHTS	
PEOPLE	
Population	53,225
15-yr Population Growth	32%
5-yr Population Growth	10.20%
% Married w/Children	39.7%
% Single w/Children	8.9%
No. of Households	18,251
Median Age	35.1
Avg. Household Size	2.9
Diversity Measure	34
STANDARD OF LIVING	
Median Household Income	$66,611
% Household Income > $100K	21%
Projected Future Job Growth	16%
Cost of Living Index	103
Buying Power Index	144
Weekly Daycare Cost	$165
Median Home Price	$265,000
"Sweet Spot" Home Price	$360,000
Home Price Ratio	4
Median Age of Homes	11.9
% Homes Owned	87%
Effective Property Tax Rate	2.30%
Estimated Property Tax Bill	$8,280
EDUCATION	
% High School Graduates	90%
% 4-yr Degree	22%
% Graduate or Professional Degree	11%
$ Invested per Pupil	$5,188
Student/Teacher Ratio	18
Primary Test Score Percentile	108.4
Secondary Test Score Percentile	106.2
% Subsidized School Lunch	24.70%
% Attending Public School	79%
LIFESTYLE	
Leisure Rating (Area)	9
Arts & Culture Rating (Area)	8
Climate Rating (Area)	8
Physical Setting Rating	3
Downtown Core Rating	2
% Commute < 30 Min.	47%
% Commute > 1 Hour	8%
HEALTH & SAFETY	
Health Rating (Area)	5
Stress Score (Area)	9
Violent Crime Risk	49
Property Crime Risk	65

TAMPA–ST. PETERSBURG–CLEARWATER, FL
AREA HIGHLIGHTS

PEOPLE

SIZE & DIVERSITY	AREA	U.S. AVG	FAMILY DEMOGRAPHICS	AREA	U.S. AVG
Population	2,587,967		% Married	55.30%	53.80%
15-yr Population Growth	26.80%	4.40%	% Single	44.70%	46.20%
Diversity Measure	39	54	% Divorced	10.80%	10.20%
% Religiously Observant	38%	50%	% Separated	3.20%	2.10%
% Catholic	15%	22%	% Married w/Children	19.50%	27.90%
% Protestant	20%	25%	% Single w/Children	9.40%	9.40%
% Jewish	2%	2%	% Married, No Children	34%	31.00%
% Other	0%	1%	% Single, No Children	37%	31.70%

STANDARD OF LIVING

INCOME, EMPLOYMENT & TAXES	AREA	U.S. AVG	COST OF LIVING & HOUSING	AREA	U.S. AVG
Median Household Income	$40,833	$44,684	Cost of Living Index	94.1	100
Household Income Growth	3.50%	6.10%	Buying Power Index	97	100
Unemployment Rate	3.50%	5.10%	Median Home Price	$213,000	$208,500
Recent Job Growth	3.60%	1.30%	Home Price Ratio	5.2	4.7
Projected Future Job Growth	11.50%	10.50%	Home Price Appreciation	19.10%	13.60%
State Income Tax Rate	0%	5.00%	% Homes Owned	61.40%	64.10%
State Sales Tax Rate	6%	6.00%	Median Rent	$805	$792

EDUCATION

ATTAINMENT & ACHIEVEMENT	AREA	U.S. AVG	RESOURCES & INVESTMENT	AREA	U.S. AVG
% High School Graduate	78.20%	83.90%	No. of Highly Ranked Universities	1	1
% 2-yr Graduate	9.50%	7.10%	$ Invested per Pupil	$5,380	$6,058
% 4-yr Graduate	17.60%	17.20%	Student/Teacher Ratio	17.6	15.9
% Graduate or Professional Degree	7.80%	9.90%	State University In-State Tuition	$2,955	$4,917
% Attending Public School	89%	84.30%			
75th Percentile State University SAT Score (Verbal)	570	477			
75th Percentile State University SAT Score (Math)	590	478			
75th Percentile State University ACT Score	N/A	20			

LIFESTYLE

RECREATION, ARTS & CULTURE	AREA	U.S. AVG	INFRASTRUCTURE & FACILITIES	AREA	U.S. AVG
Professional Sports Rating	7	4	No. of Public Libraries	62	28
Zoos & Aquariums Rating	6	3	Library Volumes Per Capita	2.2	2.8
Amusement Park Rating	9	3	No. of Warehouse Clubs	7	4
Professional Theater Rating	8	3	No. of Starbucks	39	5
Overall Museum Rating	9	6	Golf Course Rating	9	4
Science Museum Rating	4	4	National Park Rating	2	3
Children's Museum Rating	7	3	Sq. Mi. Inland Water	7	4

CLIMATE			COMMUTE & TRANSPORTATION		
Days Mostly Sunny	238	212	Avg. Daily Commute Time	25.6	24.7
Annual Days Precipitation	107	111	% Commute by Auto	79%	77.70%
Annual Days > 90°F	81	38	Per Capita Avg. Daily Transit Miles	8.7	7.9
Annual Days < 32°F	4	88	Annual Auto Insurance Premium	$1,700	$1,314
July Relative Humidity	74	69	Gas, Cost per Gallon	$3.00	$3.05

HEALTH & SAFETY

CRIME & ENVIRNOMENTAL ISSUES	AREA	U.S. AVG	HEALTHCARE & COST	AREA	U.S. AVG
Violent Crime Rate	864	517	Physicians per Capita	250.1	254.3
Change in Violent Crime	54.10%	-7.50%	Pediatricians per Capita	17	16.9
Property Crime Rate	4908	3783	Hospital Beds per Capita	411.1	239.7
Change in Property Crime	4.70%	-10.10%	No. of Teaching Hospitals	11	1.9
Air Quality Score	17	44	Healthcare Cost Index	98.7	100
Water Quality Score	46	33	Cost per Doctor Visit	$80	$74
Pollen/Allergy Score	86	61	Cost per Dentist Visit	$66	$67
Stress Score	91	49	Cost per Hospital Room	$843	$702
Cancer Mortality Rate	169.7	168.9			

Vancouver-Camas, WA

Area Type: Outer suburb/suburban town

Zip Code: 98607

Metro Area: Portland-Vancouver, OR-WA

Metro Area Type: Mid-size

Location: Along the north bank of the Columbia River 19 miles east of downtown Portland

Time Zone: Pacific Standard Time

Pros:
Attractive setting
Downtown Portland
Outdoor recreation

Cons:
Rising home prices
Current employment concerns
Wet climate

The City of Roses is hard to beat. Clean and green, prosperous and attractive, modern and historic, old economy and new economy, and brimming with intellectual stimulation through its arts, architecture, and historic interest, Portland is one of our favorite urban areas in the United States.

The modern downtown core—our idea of a blueprint for the ideal 21st-century city infrastructure—has attractive high-rise commercial buildings surrounding several large city parks and squares. Nestled in are the Portland Art Museum and Performing Arts Center and several contemporary department stores. People actually do come downtown to shop, a commercial tradition that has disappeared from most other American cities. To the north along the Willamette River waterfront spreads an area of remarkably well-preserved brick city structures, anchored by the 1896 Portland Union Station rail terminal, still adorned by its "Go By Train" logo in bold neon letters atop the clock tower. Surrounding the station are blocks of seafood eateries, coffeehouses, bakeries, and other pedestrian attractions stretching west toward the large independent Powell's Books bookstore. These two areas—aside from the rain—make Portland one of the most walkable cities in the United States.

Moving away from downtown are older but mostly attractive city neighborhoods to the east and south and up the steep hills west. Most feature wooded streetscapes and nice bungalows encircling small well-kept commercial districts along old streetcar arteries. These neighborhoods have gentrified and become quite sought after—to the point of concern that they're becoming too expensive for people already residing there. Beyond these districts lie more modern suburbs, including a prosperous but somewhat cyclical belt of high-tech businesses to the south near Wilsonville. The city itself and its many suburbs have been tastefully planned, and the lush Pacific Northwest terrain creates a beautiful background.

As great as Portland is, the towns and suburbs north of the Columbia offer the best of two worlds. They're close enough to Portland to enjoy its economy and many attractions. But a favorable business and tax climate have brought even more prosperity—and a lot of families (29.7% of households are married with children)—to areas east of Vancouver, including the small renovated mill town of Camas. The area east of Vancouver has paper mills scattered along the river, but also features major high-tech and modern manufacturing facilities for the likes of Hewlett-Packard, Sharp, and Nautilus (gym equipment). The setting and residential infrastructures are attractive (though crowded in some areas), and the tax climate is favorable with no state income tax. With no Oregon sales tax, living and working in Washington while shopping in Portland works well. We also choose the Washington side of this area because of recent Oregon school funding problems. That said, those attracted to the area should also consider Portland; the Washington "advantage" is not large.

Standard of Living The job market is transitioning, with more professional and technology jobs mixing with a large manufacturing base. The job statistics reflect this, with current unemployment at a high 6.4% and recent job growth of only 1.5%. But future job growth is projected at a relatively robust 27%. Cost of living, once a bargain, has become moderately high (COL Index is 117), and income growth statistics have yet to show the benefits of the job-market transition, so there's a relatively weak Buying Power Index of 118. Economic growth and an influx from more expensive West Coast areas have driven up home prices, but good family homes remain in the low $300K range. Effective property tax rates run a moderate 1.4%.

VANCOUVER-CAMAS, WA NEIGHBORHOOD HIGHLIGHTS	
PEOPLE	
Population	20,805
15-yr Population Growth	64.80%
5-yr Population Growth	13.70%
% Married w/Children	29.7%
% Single w/Children	10.5%
No. of Households	7,252
Median Age	34.2
Avg. Household Size	2.84
Diversity Measure	15
STANDARD OF LIVING	
Median Household Income	$61,647
% Household Income > $100K	21%
Projected Future Job Growth	27%
Cost of Living Index	117
Buying Power Index	118
Weekly Daycare Cost	$175
Median Home Price	$270,000
"Sweet Spot" Home Price	$325,000
Home Price Ratio	4.4
Median Age of Homes	17.7
% Homes Owned	76%
Effective Property Tax Rate	1.40%
Estimated Property Tax Bill	$4,550
EDUCATION	
% High School Graduates	92%
% 4-yr Degree	17%
% Graduate or Professional Degree	12%
$ Invested per Pupil	$5,655
Student/Teacher Ratio	20
Primary Test Score Percentile	114.4
Secondary Test Score Percentile	79.2
% Subsidized School Lunch	21.30%
% Attending Public School	86.20%
LIFESTYLE	
Leisure Rating (Area)	8
Arts & Culture Rating (Area)	9
Climate Rating (Area)	8
Physical Setting Rating	7
Downtown Core Rating	8
% Commute < 30 Min.	66%
% Commute > 1 Hour	5%
HEALTH & SAFETY	
Health Rating (Area)	7
Stress Score (Area)	10
Violent Crime Risk	70
Property Crime Risk	95

Education Local educational attainment is, again, a mix, with 17% of the population claiming 4-year degrees plus another 12% with graduate or professional education. School test scores are very strong; the Camas Junior and Senior High School scores 10% to as much as 40% ahead of state averages. Both Washington and Oregon have good higher-educational institutions; their state university systems are especially strong and cost-effective.

Lifestyle Whether you want a day downtown or in the "great outdoors" nearby, you have many choices. National forest land stretches across much of the area north of Camas, and the Cascades are within sight to the east. The Columbia River is well-known for its water recreation, and Oregon beaches are about 1½ hours away. The Oregon Museum of Science and Industry (OMSI) is one of many museum attractions. Portland has a diverse set of cultural and spectator activities; people don't get bored easily.

Rapid growth along the Columbia River and Highway 14 corridor has brought some commute and traffic concerns, but most areas in downtown or in the eastern commercial areas can be reached in 30 minutes. Commutes within the Camas and Vancouver areas are an easy 10- to 15-minute drive.

The river valleys are flat with heavily forested hills rising in all directions, particularly west of Portland. The Cascades and Mount Hood loom on the eastern horizon. The climate is mild in all seasons but can be cloudy and wet, with clouds and/or precipitation 1 in 2 days through the year. Generally, the rains are light; and snow does occur in winter, but bitter cold does not. Summers are mild and pleasant.

Health & Safety The crime risk is moderate throughout the Portland area. Healthcare facilities and environmental quality factors are generally good, although forest product industries do leave a noticeable but harmless aroma at times.

Nearby Neighborhoods The area's abundant choices include many suburbs and smaller towns east and northeast of Vancouver. Battle Ground to the north is a bit more "country" with larger lots of land and homes. Good Portland areas include the inner neighborhoods of Irvington east and the Reed College area south, as well as the outer suburbs to the west (such as Beaverton, Tualatin, and the more upscale Lake Oswego) and Gresham to the east.

PORTLAND-VANCOUVER, OR-WA
AREA HIGHLIGHTS

PEOPLE

SIZE & DIVERSITY	AREA	U.S. AVG	FAMILY DEMOGRAPHICS	AREA	U.S. AVG
Population	2,053,787		% Married	55.70%	53.80%
15-yr Population Growth	38.40%	4.40%	% Single	44.30%	46.20%
Diversity Measure	32	54	% Divorced	11.20%	10.20%
% Religiously Observant	33%	50%	% Separated	2.90%	2.10%
% Catholic	12%	22%	% Married w/Children	27.10%	27.90%
% Protestant	19%	25%	% Single w/Children	10.10%	9.40%
% Jewish	1%	2%	% Married, No Children	29.20%	31.00%
% Other	0%	1%	% Single, No Children	33.60%	31.70%

STANDARD OF LIVING

INCOME, EMPLOYMENT & TAXES	AREA	U.S. AVG	COST OF LIVING & HOUSING	AREA	U.S. AVG
Median Household Income	$47,265	$44,684	Cost of Living Index	105.3	100
Household Income Growth	6.40%	6.10%	Buying Power Index	100	100
Unemployment Rate	6.40%	5.10%	Median Home Price	$238,000	$208,500
Recent Job Growth	1.50%	1.30%	Home Price Ratio	5	4.7
Projected Future Job Growth	23%	10.50%	Home Price Appreciation	12%	13.60%
State Income Tax Rate	9%	5.00%	% Homes Owned	64.50%	64.10%
State Sales Tax Rate	0%	6.00%	Median Rent	$717	$792

EDUCATION

ATTAINMENT & ACHIEVEMENT	AREA	U.S. AVG	RESOURCES & INVESTMENT	AREA	U.S. AVG
% High School Graduate	84.30%	83.90%	No. of Highly Ranked Universities	3	1
% 2-yr Graduate	11.20%	7.10%	$ Invested per Pupil	$6,032	$6,058
% 4-yr Graduate	22.10%	17.20%	Student/Teacher Ratio	20.1	15.9
% Graduate or Professional Degree	9.40%	9.90%	State University In-State Tuition	$5,286	$4,917
% Attending Public School	90.70%	84.30%			
75th Percentile State University SAT Score (Verbal)	520	477			
75th Percentile State University SAT Score (Math)	550	478			
75th Percentile State University ACT Score	23	20			

LIFESTYLE

RECREATION, ARTS & CULTURE	AREA	U.S. AVG	INFRASTRUCTURE & FACILITIES	AREA	U.S. AVG
Professional Sports Rating	6	4	No. of Public Libraries	65	28
Zoos & Aquariums Rating	7	3	Library Volumes Per Capita	2.5	2.8
Amusement Park Rating	8	3	No. of Warehouse Clubs	5	4
Professional Theater Rating	7	3	No. of Starbucks	120	5
Overall Museum Rating	9	6	Golf Course Rating	6	4
Science Museum Rating	7	4	National Park Rating	6	3
Children's Museum Rating	5	3	Sq. Mi. Inland Water	4	4

CLIMATE			COMMUTE & TRANSPORTATION		
Days Mostly Sunny	137	212	Avg. Daily Commute Time	24.5	24.7
Annual Days Precipitation	152	111	% Commute by Auto	73%	77.70%
Annual Days > 90°F	8	38	Per Capita Avg. Daily Transit Miles	21.9	7.9
Annual Days < 32°F	44	88	Annual Auto Insurance Premium	$1,327	$1,314
July Relative Humidity	74	69	Gas, Cost per Gallon	$2.80	$3.05

HEALTH & SAFETY

CRIME & ENVIRNOMENTAL ISSUES	AREA	U.S. AVG	HEALTHCARE & COST	AREA	U.S. AVG
Violent Crime Rate	361	517	Physicians per Capita	267.4	254.3
Change in Violent Crime	-36.20%	-7.50%	Pediatricians per Capita	18.9	16.9
Property Crime Rate	4960	3783	Hospital Beds per Capita	193.8	239.7
Change in Property Crime	-4.20%	-10.10%	No. of Teaching Hospitals	8	1.9
Air Quality Score	26	44	Healthcare Cost Index	122.4	100
Water Quality Score	53	33	Cost per Doctor Visit	$93	$74
Pollen/Allergy Score	36	61	Cost per Dentist Visit	$73	$67
Stress Score	99	49	Cost per Hospital Room	$708	$702
Cancer Mortality Rate	164.8	168.9			

Virginia Beach, VA

Area Type: Satellite city

Zip Code: 23456

Metro Area: Norfolk–Virginia Beach–Newport News, VA-NC

Metro Area Type: Large

Location: Along Atlantic coast, 15 miles east of downtown Norfolk

Time Zone: Eastern Standard Time

Pros:
Beach and water recreation
Attractive location
Relatively good climate

Cons:
Tourist impact
Growth and sprawl
No real downtown core

Whether or not the local claim—that this is the "largest resort city in the world"—is true, Virginia Beach certainly is a resort city, and definitely does *not* fall into the mold of a "typical" family city or suburb. Located along a 29-mile strip of sandy Atlantic beach, Virginia Beach has resorts and tourists and a huge assortment of the typical things that follow resorts and tourists—restaurants, amusements, souvenir shops, parks, and even a few worthwhile museums. It's a destination vacation spot for much of Virginia and the East Coast. Summers are crowded and traffic can slow to a crawl on the main road along the beach area with all of the rental cars and tour buses.

Clearly, there's plenty to do. And there are plenty of jobs—in entertainment and tourism at the coast, at the local Oceana Naval Air Station, or in the Norfolk-Hampton Roads city cluster just to the west. The question in such a place is whether or not there are adequate family-oriented places to live with good schools and quiet surroundings where families can escape the tourist hubbub. Fortunately, there are such places: When Virginia Beach and some former unincorporated areas of Princess Anne County merged, they created a well-planned set of suburbs spreading west. Indeed, these quality family neighborhoods are strategically located to take advantage of the recreation and the economic engine of the Hampton Roads area. The area defined by the easy-to-remember zip code 23456 is just south of the naval air station and inland from the shore, and is home to a large number of families: 44.5% of households are married with children.

The so-called Hampton Roads area isn't really about "roads" but a sea passage between the James River and the Chesapeake Bay. It comprises the cities of Norfolk, Hampton, Newport News, Portsmouth, Chesapeake, and Virginia Beach. The ideal harbor setting and strategic location led to major Navy and shipbuilding establishments, still the largest employers today. Defense contractors form another large economic segment, and in recent years, the economy has diversified. The downtown areas are not that interesting—and some areas are downright gritty—but they do offer the services of a big city. Not surprisingly, many of the area's attractions center on its maritime heritage; Nauticus National Maritime Center is the most popular. A strong zoo and art museum, plus more interesting sights are in "VaBeach" and in Williamsburg 25 miles up the James Peninsula.

Standard of Living   For this type of city, close to more expensive East Coast locations, the standard of living is quite attractive. Virginia Beach has been "discovered" to a degree, which has pushed costs up a bit in the past few years. But the metro area's Cost of Living Index remains at a moderate 91, and the particular neighborhood in Virginia Beach we've chosen as a best place (zip code 23456) is 102. Home prices have escalated, but most families find the price range—in the high $200Ks to low $300Ks—reasonable, especially if arriving from elsewhere. Per-square-foot costs run $130 to $150, and that gets a two-story colonial or contemporary built in the past 20 years on a reasonably sized wooded lot—not your typical beach house. Property taxes are 1.2%, the lowest in the immediate region, driven in part by a strong commercial base.

Education   Virginia Beach City Public Schools are well regarded, and all score above state averages by 5% to 20%. In part due to its military heritage, the area is not especially strong in 4-year degree attainment, for a city its size, but we expect that to change over time as more people and businesses discover the area. The area also doesn't have a lot of major colleges and universities. Old Dominion is probably the best known.

Lifestyle   The lifestyle here can be whatever a family makes of it. Outdoorsy families who love the beach and have a sense of adventure will find plenty to do at all times. Beaches are suitable for surfing, snorkeling, and swimming. Local amusement and water parks amuse the kids, but come with tourist prices. There are numerous events and festivals on the waterfront. Large shopping complexes are found along the east–west I-264 corridor, and many families only go into the Norfolk-area cities for special needs or for a change of pace. The Norfolk area isn't particularly sports oriented, but there are some minor-league teams. Nature lovers visit Fort Lending State Park on the beach, the Dismal Swamp area 30 miles southwest, or other wildlife refuges along the coast.

Traffic can be a hassle, especially at certain tourist-favored times of the year. Employment centers are scattered all over, so there's no real "rush" in any particular direction. But the heaviest commutes—20 to 30 minutes—are toward Norfolk to Navy bases and defense contractors. There is some bus service.

The area is geographically complex and dominated by water, with sections of coastal-plain woods. The climate is marine and milder than in areas just inland. Winters are pleasant but can be brisk with strong northwest winds, while Atlantic breezes temper the warm summer days. Winters may pass with no measurable snow.

Health & Safety   Crime risk is low as measured by the "CAP" score, and healthcare resources are adequate in the local area and in the Hampton Roads Cities.

Nearby Neighborhoods   Other zip codes in the VaBeach area are livable, but often have more commercial activity and tend to be more crowded. Quieter, plainer suburbs can be found in Chesapeake to the west, and families considering the area might also look north on the James Peninsula toward Williamsburg.

VIRGINIA BEACH, VA NEIGHBORHOOD HIGHLIGHTS	
PEOPLE	
Population	78,421
15-yr Population Growth	12%
5-yr Population Growth	3.50%
% Married w/Children	44.5%
% Single w/Children	11.6%
No. of Households	25,196
Median Age	30.2
Avg. Household Size	3.1
Diversity Measure	52
STANDARD OF LIVING	
Median Household Income	$63,133
% Household Income > $100K	12%
Projected Future Job Growth	14%
Cost of Living Index	102
Buying Power Index	139
Weekly Daycare Cost	$157
Median Home Price	$262,900
"Sweet Spot" Home Price	$300,000
Home Price Ratio	4.2
Median Age of Homes	14.1
% Homes Owned	75%
Effective Property Tax Rate	1.20%
Estimated Property Tax Bill	$3,600
EDUCATION	
% High School Graduates	91%
% 4-yr Degree	19%
% Graduate or Professional Degree	8%
$ Invested per Pupil	$4,834
Student/Teacher Ratio	15.6
Primary Test Score Percentile	111.9
Secondary Test Score Percentile	104.8
% Subsidized School Lunch	25.60%
% Attending Public School	85.50%
LIFESTYLE	
Leisure Rating (Area)	7
Arts & Culture Rating (Area)	7
Climate Rating (Area)	6
Physical Setting Rating	6
Downtown Core Rating	4
% Commute < 30 Min.	61%
% Commute > 1 Hour	4%
HEALTH & SAFETY	
Health Rating (Area)	2
Stress Score (Area)	4
Violent Crime Risk	38
Property Crime Risk	55

NORFOLK–VIRGINIA BEACH–NEWPORT NEWS, VA-NC
AREA HIGHLIGHTS

PEOPLE

SIZE & DIVERSITY	AREA	U.S. AVG	FAMILY DEMOGRAPHICS	AREA	U.S. AVG
Population	1,637,280		% Married	52.80%	53.80%
15-yr Population Growth	16.40%	4.40%	% Single	47.20%	46.20%
Diversity Measure	53	54	% Divorced	7.10%	10.20%
% Religiously Observant	35%	50%	% Separated	5.60%	2.10%
% Catholic	6%	22%	% Married w/Children	28.50%	27.90%
% Protestant	27%	25%	% Single w/Children	11.30%	9.40%
% Jewish	1%	2%	% Married, No Children	28.70%	31.00%
% Other	0%	1%	% Single, No Children	31.40%	31.70%

STANDARD OF LIVING

INCOME, EMPLOYMENT & TAXES	AREA	U.S. AVG	COST OF LIVING & HOUSING	AREA	U.S. AVG
Median Household Income	$49,704	$44,684	Cost of Living Index	91.1	100
Household Income Growth	4.10%	6.10%	Buying Power Index	122	100
Unemployment Rate	4.10%	5.10%	Median Home Price	$192,000	$208,500
Recent Job Growth	1.80%	1.30%	Home Price Ratio	3.9	4.7
Projected Future Job Growth	10.80%	10.50%	Home Price Appreciation	22.10%	13.60%
State Income Tax Rate	5.80%	5.00%	% Homes Owned	55.30%	64.10%
State Sales Tax Rate	4.50%	6.00%	Median Rent	$788	$792

EDUCATION

ATTAINMENT & ACHIEVEMENT	AREA	U.S. AVG	RESOURCES & INVESTMENT	AREA	U.S. AVG
% High School Graduate	77%	83.90%	No. of Highly Ranked Universities	1	1
% 2-yr Graduate	8.50%	7.10%	$ Invested per Pupil	$5,379	$6,058
% 4-yr Graduate	17.50%	17.20%	Student/Teacher Ratio	14.3	15.9
% Graduate or Professional Degree	8.20%	9.90%	State University In-State Tuition	$5,838	$4,917
% Attending Public School	89.40%	84.30%			
75th Percentile State University SAT Score (Verbal)	540	477			
75th Percentile State University SAT Score (Math)	560	478			
75th Percentile State University ACT Score	N/A	20			

LIFESTYLE

RECREATION, ARTS & CULTURE	AREA	U.S. AVG	INFRASTRUCTURE & FACILITIES	AREA	U.S. AVG
Professional Sports Rating	3	4	No. of Public Libraries	50	28
Zoos & Aquariums Rating	8	3	Library Volumes Per Capita	2.8	2.8
Amusement Park Rating	9	3	No. of Warehouse Clubs	7	4
Professional Theater Rating	6	3	No. of Starbucks	27	5
Overall Museum Rating	9	6	Golf Course Rating	5	4
Science Museum Rating	10	4	National Park Rating	5	3
Children's Museum Rating	10	3	Sq. Mi. Inland Water	8	4

CLIMATE			COMMUTE & TRANSPORTATION		
Days Mostly Sunny	212	212	Avg. Daily Commute Time	24.1	24.7
Annual Days Precipitation	115	111	% Commute by Auto	69%	77.70%
Annual Days > 90°F	30	38	Per Capita Avg. Daily Transit Miles	9.6	7.9
Annual Days < 32°F	54	88	Annual Auto Insurance Premium	$1,141	$1,314
July Relative Humidity	71	69	Gas, Cost per Gallon	$3.11	$3.05

HEALTH & SAFETY

CRIME & ENVIRNOMENTAL ISSUES	AREA	U.S. AVG	HEALTHCARE & COST	AREA	U.S. AVG
Violent Crime Rate	438	517	Physicians per Capita	250	254.3
Change in Violent Crime	-5%	-7.50%	Pediatricians per Capita	21	16.9
Property Crime Rate	3809	3783	Hospital Beds per Capita	331.7	239.7
Change in Property Crime	-14.40%	-10.10%	No. of Teaching Hospitals	11	1.9
Air Quality Score	67	44	Healthcare Cost Index	93.4	100
Water Quality Score	71	33	Cost per Doctor Visit	$76	$74
Pollen/Allergy Score	69	61	Cost per Dentist Visit	$87	$67
Stress Score	39	49	Cost per Hospital Room	$660	$702
Cancer Mortality Rate	185.9	168.9			

Waukesha, WI

Area Type: Suburban town

Zip Code: 53186

Metro Area: Milwaukee-Waukesha, WI

Metro Area Type: Mid-size

Location: 20 miles west of Milwaukee

Time Zone: Central Standard Time

Pros:

Cost of living
Community feel and resources
Attractive redevelopment

Cons:

Some employment concerns
Low educational attainment
Winter climate

Like a proverbial little sibling, Milwaukee has always lived in the shadow of Chicago. Outsiders tend not to think of the Milwaukee area as a place to live, as a place to visit, or even as a distinct place at all. Economic cycles, dependence on older manufacturing industries, the decline of national beer brands, and even less-than-stellar professional sports teams have reinforced the outsider's image of dull malaise. But as with many other Great Lakes cities, the Milwaukee experience is much different once seen from within. Almost immediately, visitors and new residents get a strong sense of community not found in many other places. They discover a strong set of amenities, cultural interest, lack of crowds and traffic, and reasonable costs, which, when taken together, present a good family package.

Waukesha is about 20 miles west of downtown Milwaukee. It has industrial and agricultural roots, and today adds a strong college-town element to its role as a mostly residential city. Schools include Carroll College, the Waukesha County Technical College, and the University of Wisconsin-Waukesha. Residents commonly work in Milwaukee, but some fan out across Milwaukee suburbs and even to Racine and Kenosha to the southeast. This is a place where one can enjoy big-city amenities (and even bigger-city amenities in Chicago, 100 miles south) with a small-town feel and prices. The married-with-children percentage of households is 29% and would be higher without the student population.

The city of Milwaukee has realized the value of its lakefront assets, and has been renovating "to become its own city again" for some time. A once-unremarkable urban core has given way to new buildings along Wisconsin Avenue and along the waterfront. The downtown area now beautifully balances its well-preserved architectural classics, like the Pabst Theater and City Hall, with its new structures. A strong immigrant heritage and endowments from early industrialists have left the city with a better-than-average set of arts and cultural amenities, including a few first-class museums, performing arts venues, and the nationally recognized Milwaukee Zoo. Lakeshore parks and boating facilities have been enhanced and host many events and festivals. The area is still oriented toward manufacturing industries, but it's gradually diversifying with companies including Harley-Davidson, Briggs & Stratton, Allen-Bradley (electrical equipment), and GE Medical Systems.

Standard of Living Waukesha housing is a mix of older homes near downtown and newer subdivisions developed on adjacent farmland. The family home "sweet spot" is in the high $200Ks but good options are available under $225K. Per-square-foot costs run about $125. Property taxes are a bit high at 1.9%, but the dollars are used to fund parks and enhanced public transit programs. Incomes are steady and would reflect higher numbers without the student influence. Although future job growth of 16% is strong for the region, there is some concern about growth in high-paying jobs.

Education Schools are adequate, but they don't test much higher than state averages. Local residents, however, speak positively of both academics and extracurricular programs. Co-op programs with local colleges offer credit to high-school students. The area is proud of marching-band appearances in the Macy's parade and the success of the Hahn brothers in 2004 Olympic gymnastics. The area has a 60,000-square-foot library recognized as one of the state's best, serving as a focus for many community activities.

Lifestyle The laid-back Waukesha lifestyle centers on the many features offered within the city. The attractive downtown area has been renovated to bring in more

WAUKESHA, WI NEIGHBORHOOD HIGHLIGHTS	
PEOPLE	
Population	34,998
15-yr Population Growth	23.80%
5-yr Population Growth	4.60%
% Married w/Children	28.6%
% Single w/Children	9.2%
No. of Households	14,232
Median Age	36.2
Avg. Household Size	2.39
Diversity Measure	30
STANDARD OF LIVING	
Median Household Income	$50,115
% Household Income > $100K	11%
Projected Future Job Growth	16%
Cost of Living Index	105
Buying Power Index	110
Weekly Daycare Cost	$183
Median Home Price	$225,100
"Sweet Spot" Home Price	$275,000
Home Price Ratio	4.5
Median Age of Homes	31.8
% Homes Owned	55%
Effective Property Tax Rate	1.90%
Estimated Property Tax Bill	$5,225
EDUCATION	
% High School Graduates	89%
% 4-yr Degree	22%
% Graduate or Professional Degree	10%
$ Invested per Pupil	$6,850
Student/Teacher Ratio	13.3
Primary Test Score Percentile	110.4
Secondary Test Score Percentile	112.3
% Subsidized School Lunch	27.80%
% Attending Public School	67.40%
LIFESTYLE	
Leisure Rating (Area)	9
Arts & Culture Rating (Area)	10
Climate Rating (Area)	2
Physical Setting Rating	3
Downtown Core Rating	4
% Commute < 30 Min.	77%
% Commute > 1 Hour	2%
HEALTH & SAFETY	
Health Rating (Area)	5
Stress Score (Area)	7
Violent Crime Risk	73
Property Crime Risk	112

activity, and today it hosts numerous events such as the summer weekend "Art Crawls." The area is loaded with parks—40 in total with over 900 acres around the city and along the riverfront. A new and second public pool and aquatic park, Horeb Park Pool, just opened with $3-per-day swimming fees. Outdoor activities—including boating, fishing, hiking, and jet-skiing—are abundant locally and in the lake areas at Oconomowoc to the northwest. The Alpine Valley Ski Resort is half an hour to the southwest. Trips downtown, visits to Chicago, and excursions to Wisconsin's attractions in the north and west round out the recreation picture.

About 30% of residents commute into Milwaukee, which takes approximately half an hour. Buses offer an effective alternative, and most commutes within the area take less than 40 minutes.

The landscape reflects its glacial influence, being mostly flat, with farmland, areas of wooded hills, and several lakes and streams. The climate is mainly continental, with warm, humid summers and variable winters. The area is far enough inland to avoid strong lake winds, but the lakes can bring cooling breezes in the summer.

Health & Safety Waukesha emphasizes health and safety, and the community's social and public safety resources get high marks from local residents. Crime risk is moderate.

Nearby Neighborhoods Similar but smaller communities surround Waukesha, including Pewaukee, New Berlin, Menomonee Falls, and North Prairie. Brookfield, just to the east, is older and a bit more upscale.

MILWAUKEE/WAUKESHA, WI
AREA HIGHLIGHTS

PEOPLE

SIZE & DIVERSITY	AREA	U.S. AVG	FAMILY DEMOGRAPHICS	AREA	U.S. AVG
Population	1,515,738		% Married	54.80%	53.80%
15-yr Population Growth	7.50%	4.40%	% Single	45.20%	46.20%
Diversity Measure	41	54	% Divorced	7.80%	10.20%
% Religiously Observant	55%	50%	% Separated	2.20%	2.10%
% Catholic	31%	22%	% Married w/Children	27.90%	27.90%
% Protestant	22%	25%	% Single w/Children	9.80%	9.40%
% Jewish	1%	2%	% Married, No Children	30%	31.00%
% Other	0%	1%	% Single, No Children	32.20%	31.70%

STANDARD OF LIVING

INCOME, EMPLOYMENT & TAXES	AREA	U.S. AVG	COST OF LIVING & HOUSING	AREA	U.S. AVG
Median Household Income	$49,680	$44,684	Cost of Living Index	97	100
Household Income Growth	4.70%	6.10%	Buying Power Index	115	100
Unemployment Rate	4.70%	5.10%	Median Home Price	$216,800	$208,500
Recent Job Growth	2.90%	1.30%	Home Price Ratio	4.4	4.7
Projected Future Job Growth	11.80%	10.50%	Home Price Appreciation	11.20%	13.60%
State Income Tax Rate	6.90%	5.00%	% Homes Owned	65.30%	64.10%
State Sales Tax Rate	5.50%	6.00%	Median Rent	$694	$792

EDUCATION

ATTAINMENT & ACHIEVEMENT	AREA	U.S. AVG	RESOURCES & INVESTMENT	AREA	U.S. AVG
% High School Graduate	84.50%	83.90%	No. of Highly Ranked Universities	2	1
% 2-yr Graduate	10.10%	7.10%	$ Invested per Pupil	$7,697	$6,058
% 4-yr Graduate	21.80%	17.20%	Student/Teacher Ratio	16.3	15.9
% Graduate or Professional Degree	8.20%	9.90%	State University In-State Tuition	$5,862	$4,917
% Attending Public School	79.20%	84.30%			
75th Percentile State University SAT Score (Verbal)	N/A	477			
75th Percentile State University SAT Score (Math)	N/A	478			
75th Percentile State University ACT Score	26	20			

LIFESTYLE

RECREATION, ARTS & CULTURE	AREA	U.S. AVG	INFRASTRUCTURE & FACILITIES	AREA	U.S. AVG
Professional Sports Rating	6	4	No. of Public Libraries	53	28
Zoos & Aquariums Rating	7	3	Library Volumes Per Capita	4	2.8
Amusement Park Rating	1	3	No. of Warehouse Clubs	5	4
Professional Theater Rating	9	3	No. of Starbucks	33	5
Overall Museum Rating	9	6	Golf Course Rating	7	4
Science Museum Rating	7	4	National Park Rating	1	3
Children's Museum Rating	7	3	Sq. Mi. Inland Water	4	4

CLIMATE			COMMUTE & TRANSPORTATION		
Days Mostly Sunny	195	212	Avg. Daily Commute Time	22.1	24.7
Annual Days Precipitation	122	111	% Commute by Auto	78%	77.70%
Annual Days > 90°F	9	38	Per Capita Avg. Daily Transit Miles	15.1	7.9
Annual Days < 32°F	146	88	Annual Auto Insurance Premium	$1,342	$1,314
July Relative Humidity	73	69	Gas, Cost per Gallon	$3.05	$3.05

HEALTH & SAFETY

CRIME & ENVIRNOMENTAL ISSUES	AREA	U.S. AVG	HEALTHCARE & COST	AREA	U.S. AVG
Violent Crime Rate	417	517	Physicians per Capita	323.5	254.3
Change in Violent Crime	-11.50%	-7.50%	Pediatricians per Capita	23.5	16.9
Property Crime Rate	3922	3783	Hospital Beds per Capita	366.3	239.7
Change in Property Crime	-8.30%	-10.10%	No. of Teaching Hospitals	14	1.9
Air Quality Score	28	44	Healthcare Cost Index	98.3	100
Water Quality Score	26	33	Cost per Doctor Visit	$78	$74
Pollen/Allergy Score	42	61	Cost per Dentist Visit	$82	$67
Stress Score	66	49	Cost per Hospital Room	$516	$702
Cancer Mortality Rate	177.5	168.9			

Wausau, WI

Area Type: Small town

Zip Code: 54403

Metro Area: Wausau, WI

Metro Area Type: Smallest

Location: North-central Wisconsin 100 miles west of Green Bay

Time Zone: Central Standard Time

Pros:
> Small-town flavor
> Recreation
> Cost of living and housing

Cons:
> Winter climate
> Isolation
> Some growth issues

"King of the Friday Night Fish Fry," Wausau is a small, clean, attractive city geographically and culturally smack in Wisconsin's center. With plenty of infrastructure, lots to do, and a "special home-town feeling," Wausau is an excellent place for families.

Located on the banks of the Wisconsin River, Wausau has a classic downtown area with mixed modern and historic buildings and some renewal efforts geared toward bringing more commercial and recreational activities into the city. The city is surrounded by livable neighborhoods, with the more modern and somewhat sprawling western suburbs and attractive in-town areas to the south and east. The married-with-children percentage of households is 27%, with a mix of older and newer families. Recreational opportunities, particularly related to water, snow, and woods, abound in the city and region, and Wausau has some notable recreational assets.

The local economy is anchored by older manufacturing industries, including paper mills, industrial equipment, and a few large financial services employers. Massachusetts-based Liberty Mutual, who bought the famous Wausau insurance company of train-station fame, is one the larger employers. Greenheck, one of the larger industrial equipment employers, is expanding, and healthcare hiring is increasing with the addition of a large new hospital on the south side. Younger families from some of the bigger cities in the region who are looking for a low cost of living and small-town life are moving here. Future job-growth projections are fairly modest at 9%, but we think it could go higher as more businesses locate in the area.

Standard of Living The cost of living is reasonable with the COL Index at a very attractive 88. Starter family homes are available for as little as $125K to $150K, and most typical family homes cost between $75 and

$100 per square foot, which is among the least expensive in the state. The "sweet spot" is in the low to mid $200Ks, and $250K will buy a very nice abode. Lots are large, usually over a ½ acre and wooded. The Home Price Ratio is an attractive 3.1, and the area is a good bet for those bringing in some wealth from other areas. Property tax rates are relatively high at 2.5%. Daycare is a very reasonable $110 per week. Employment, while growing slowly, has been dependable and will likely remain so.

Education Local schools score at to slightly above state averages, and have been going through some realignment and renewal to eliminate pockets of overcrowding. The 19-school, 9,000-student school district has just added new high schools and middle schools. The University of Wisconsin operates a small branch (UW–Marathon County) in the city, and there are a number of vocational and technical schools in the area. Four-year educational attainment is 15%, low among qualified family places and reflecting its rural small-town and blue-collar industry heritage.

Lifestyle Activities and daily life are typical for a Wisconsin small town. The Wisconsin River forms into a narrow lake as it flows through the city, and water recreation and boating are abundant. The Rib Mountain State Park offers summer hiking and night-lighted winter skiing just 10 minutes from downtown. Snowmobiling and curling are popular winter sports. The Wausau Woodchucks supply minor-league baseball, and the area hosts state school hockey tournaments at a Greenheck-funded local facility. The recently refurbished Grand Theater, supported by an IBM founder endowment, hosts a variety of local and traveling performing arts, including Broadway plays. There's also a children's theater. A new downtown park just across from the Grand hosts summer-evening activities and a weekly "concert in the park" series.

Back to the legendary fish fries we mentioned earlier, every Friday night, most Wisconsoners head to local restaurants, bowling alleys, and halls to chow down on fish and catch up with neighbors. The tradition is so strong in Wausau that, supposedly, the national seafood chain Red Lobster won't even consider coming into the area.

Commutes aren't an issue. There's some retail sprawl to the west of town, and traffic can snarl SR 52 and some Wisconsin River bridge bottlenecks. Population-growth projections are fairly high at 11% in the next 15 years, causing some local concern. Good air service for a small town is available 12 miles south at the Central Wisconsin Airport.

The city sits in a shallow river valley in a hilly and mainly wooded area of the state. Large national and state forests lie just to the north. The climate is decidedly continental with significant winter weather (about 38 days a year show below-zero temperatures) and persistent snow cover, while summers are pleasant with cool evenings and few days over 90°F.

Health & Safety   Crime risk is moderate. Stress factors are low, and the area scores well in all health categories. A brand-new large hospital has just been built south of town.

Nearby Neighborhoods   Most areas of the city offer attractive housing and are convenient to residents' employers. Homes on the east side (in zip code 54403) are a little older and more expensive with more of a city feel, while other attractive areas spread mainly to the northwest and south.

WAUSAU, WI NEIGHBORHOOD HIGHLIGHTS	
PEOPLE	
Population	24,909
15-yr Population Growth	10.70%
5-yr Population Growth	1.50%
% Married w/Children	26.8%
% Single w/Children	7.5%
No. of Households	9,764
Median Age	38.3
Avg. Household Size	2.46
Diversity Measure	19
STANDARD OF LIVING	
Median Household Income	$42,377
% Household Income > $100K	10%
Projected Future Job Growth	9%
Cost of Living Index	88.1
Buying Power Index	110
Weekly Daycare Cost	$110
Median Home Price	$131,900
"Sweet Spot" Home Price	$225,000
Home Price Ratio	3.1
Median Age of Homes	47.6
% Homes Owned	64%
Effective Property Tax Rate	2.50%
Estimated Property Tax Bill	$5,625
EDUCATION	
% High School Graduates	83%
% 4-yr Degree	15%
% Graduate or Professional Degree	9%
$ Invested per Pupil	$6,867
Student/Teacher Ratio	13.4
Primary Test Score Percentile	96.3
Secondary Test Score Percentile	103.7
% Subsidized School Lunch	36.20%
% Attending Public School	86.20%
LIFESTYLE	
Leisure Rating (Area)	1
Arts & Culture Rating (Area)	5
Climate Rating (Area)	2
Physical Setting Rating	5
Downtown Core Rating	6
% Commute < 30 Min.	85%
% Commute > 1 Hour	3%
HEALTH & SAFETY	
Health Rating (Area)	9
Stress Score (Area)	0
Violent Crime Risk	114
Property Crime Risk	179

WAUSAU, WI
AREA HIGHLIGHTS
PEOPLE

SIZE & DIVERSITY	AREA	U.S. AVG	FAMILY DEMOGRAPHICS	AREA	U.S. AVG
Population	127,733		% Married	63.30%	53.80%
15-yr Population Growth	10.70%	4.40%	% Single	36.70%	46.20%
Diversity Measure	13	54	% Divorced	5.20%	10.20%
% Religiously Observant	71%	50%	% Separated	1.30%	2.10%
% Catholic	37%	22%	% Married w/Children	35.70%	27.90%
% Protestant	34%	25%	% Single w/Children	6.50%	9.40%
% Jewish	0%	2%	% Married, No Children	32%	31.00%
% Other	0%	1%	% Single, No Children	25.80%	31.70%

STANDARD OF LIVING

INCOME, EMPLOYMENT & TAXES	AREA	U.S. AVG	COST OF LIVING & HOUSING	AREA	U.S. AVG
Median Household Income	$47,584	$44,684	Cost of Living Index	88.5	100
Household Income Growth	3.20%	6.10%	Buying Power Index	120	100
Unemployment Rate	3.20%	5.10%	Median Home Price	$130,400	$208,500
Recent Job Growth	2.70%	1.30%	Home Price Ratio	2.7	4.7
Projected Future Job Growth	9.90%	10.50%	Home Price Appreciation	7%	13.60%
State Income Tax Rate	6.90%	5.00%	% Homes Owned	75.90%	64.10%
State Sales Tax Rate	5%	6.00%	Median Rent	$546	$792

EDUCATION

ATTAINMENT & ACHIEVEMENT	AREA	U.S. AVG	RESOURCES & INVESTMENT	AREA	U.S. AVG
% High School Graduate	78.80%	83.90%	No. of Highly Ranked Universities	0	1
% 2-yr Graduate	10.40%	7.10%	$ Invested per Pupil	$6,665	$6,058
% 4-yr Graduate	10.10%	17.20%	Student/Teacher Ratio	15.2	15.9
% Graduate or Professional Degree	3.30%	9.90%	State University In-State Tuition	$5,862	$4,917
% Attending Public School	86.30%	84.30%			
75th Percentile State University SAT Score (Verbal)	N/A	477			
75th Percentile State University SAT Score (Math)	N/A	478			
75th Percentile State University ACT Score	26	20			

LIFESTYLE

RECREATION, ARTS & CULTURE	AREA	U.S. AVG	INFRASTRUCTURE & FACILITIES	AREA	U.S. AVG
Professional Sports Rating	2	4	No. of Public Libraries	8	28
Zoos & Aquariums Rating	1	3	Library Volumes Per Capita	2.7	2.8
Amusement Park Rating	1	3	No. of Warehouse Clubs	1	4
Professional Theater Rating	1	3	No. of Starbucks	1	5
Overall Museum Rating	2	6	Golf Course Rating	1	4
Science Museum Rating	1	4	National Park Rating	1	3
Children's Museum Rating	1	3	Sq. Mi. Inland Water	3	4

CLIMATE			COMMUTE & TRANSPORTATION		
Days Mostly Sunny	200	212	Avg. Daily Commute Time	18.4	24.7
Annual Days Precipitation	185	111	% Commute by Auto	69%	77.70%
Annual Days > 90°F	4	38	Per Capita Avg. Daily Transit Miles	5.3	7.9
Annual Days < 32°F	170	88	Annual Auto Insurance Premium	$975	$1,314
July Relative Humidity	72	69	Gas, Cost per Gallon	$2.95	$3.05

HEALTH & SAFETY

CRIME & ENVIRNOMENTAL ISSUES	AREA	U.S. AVG	HEALTHCARE & COST	AREA	U.S. AVG
Violent Crime Rate	155	517	Physicians per Capita	221.8	254.3
Change in Violent Crime	24.20%	-7.50%	Pediatricians per Capita	11.8	16.9
Property Crime Rate	2359	3783	Hospital Beds per Capita	491.2	239.7
Change in Property Crime	-2.60%	-10.10%	No. of Teaching Hospitals	1	1.9
Air Quality Score	41	44	Healthcare Cost Index	107.8	100
Water Quality Score	50	33	Cost per Doctor Visit	$95	$74
Pollen/Allergy Score	36	61	Cost per Dentist Visit	$53	$67
Stress Score	3	49	Cost per Hospital Room	$533	$702
Cancer Mortality Rate	158.3	168.9			

West Chester, PA

Area Type: Satellite city

Zip Code: 19382

Metro Area: Philadelphia, PA-NJ

Metro Area Type: Large

Location: 30 miles west of downtown Philadelphia

Time Zone: Eastern Standard Time

Pros:
Attractive town center
Education
Diverse economic base

Cons:
Long commute
Some traffic congestion
Hot, humid summers

Straight from West Chester's website (www.west-chester.com), "diverse . . . prosperous . . . collegiate . . . accessible" pretty much sums up this small city located in a farming area west of Philadelphia. West Chester offers a right-sized combination of stable employment, local downtown amenities, a college presence, historic interest, recreation, and convenience at an attractive cost.

West Chester has been around since Revolutionary War days as a center for agriculture and commercial activity. The historic city core has 4,000 structures listed on the National Register of Historic Places in a 1¾-square-mile area. The architecture is interesting and diverse with well-kept Victorian and Greek Revival homes, a look that's somewhat reminiscent of older San Francisco. West Chester is pretty with ample trees, and the local government will plant and care for trees on individual properties—for free. The city serves as the county seat for Chester County, and is home to the regional public school, West Chester University, and its 12,000 students. The downtown area is an active commercial and entertainment district. The married-with-children percentage of households is 30.4% and it would likely be higher without the college.

Diverse companies—including Astra-Zeneca and Wyeth in pharmaceuticals, the research firm Economy.com, and, last but not least, the studio and headquarters of TV retailer QVC, Inc.—call West Chester home. Commuting is relatively easy to Philadelphia and to the "Valley" commercial industrial areas west of Philly, such as Valley Forge and King of Prussia. Other major East Coast cities—Baltimore, Washington, DC, and New York—are accessible as well from Southeastern Pennsylvania for recreational and occasional business purposes.

About Philadelphia: Somewhat maligned over time for crime issues, urban decay, rowdy sports fans, summer heat, and better reputations up and down the coast in Washington, DC, and New York, the area has been on the comeback trail for some time. "Philly" has a rich historic and educational tradition, with such universities as the University of Pennsylvania, Villanova, Drexel, and Temple universities within its limits. Cultural amenities like the Philadelphia Museum of Art and the Philadelphia Symphony rank high on the world stage, and the Franklin Institute Science Museum is a must for families. Employment has rebounded, and there are great older and new neighborhoods to the west, north, and across the Delaware River in New Jersey, mainly along rail commute lines. East Coasters and others are increasingly finding value in the area.

Standard of Living   Although not the cheapest in the Philly area, West Chester is a reasonably priced place to live on the East Coast scale, and might be considered a "value" rather than "cheap." The Cost of Living Index is 130, and good family homes can be found in the low $400Ks with some older starter homes in the mid to high $300Ks. Lots are large and wooded and costs per square foot are under $200. The property tax rate of 1.40% is reasonable for this type of area. Future employment growth of 11% is strong for the region, and income-growth statistics are positive.

Education   The college presence and the high percentage of adults with 4-year degrees (32%) and another 21% with graduate and professional degrees provide a strong context for educational success, and the area schools don't disappoint. The West Chester Area School District has 11,600 students in 15 schools, and delivers test scores consistently 20 to 30 points above average with steady improvement in all grade ranges.

Lifestyle   West Chester provides desirable ambience of small-town life in a big-city area, and families will find plenty to do here. Sports, city parks, the local

WEST CHESTER, PA NEIGHBORHOOD HIGHLIGHTS	
PEOPLE	
Population	54,613
15-yr Population Growth	23.80%
5-yr Population Growth	7.40%
% Married w/Children	30.4%
% Single w/Children	6.6%
No. of Households	19,174
Median Age	35.4
Avg. Household Size	2.58
Diversity Measure	21
STANDARD OF LIVING	
Median Household Income	$78,418
% Household Income > $100K	32%
Projected Future Job Growth	11%
Cost of Living Index	130
Buying Power Index	134
Weekly Daycare Cost	$218
Median Home Price	$401,300
"Sweet Spot" Home Price	$425,000
Home Price Ratio	5.1
Median Age of Homes	25
% Homes Owned	68%
Effective Property Tax Rate	1.40%
Estimated Property Tax Bill	$5,950
EDUCATION	
% High School Graduates	93%
% 4-yr Degree	32%
% Graduate or Professional Degree	21%
$ Invested per Pupil	$7,564
Student/Teacher Ratio	16.7
Primary Test Score Percentile	130.5
Secondary Test Score Percentile	138.4
% Subsidized School Lunch	6.50%
% Attending Public School	78.50%
LIFESTYLE	
Leisure Rating (Area)	10
Arts & Culture Rating (Area)	10
Climate Rating (Area)	6
Physical Setting Rating	4
Downtown Core Rating	7
% Commute < 30 Min.	60%
% Commute > 1 Hour	7%
HEALTH & SAFETY	
Health Rating (Area)	2
Stress Score (Area)	7
Violent Crime Risk	82
Property Crime Risk	83

YMCA, and the West Chester Country Club provide recreation for kids and adults. When local activities or resources aren't enough, Philadelphia is easy to get to. The Delaware and New Jersey shores, Washington, DC, and the Pocono Mountains are all a couple of hours away (in different directions) and the many historic sites (such as Gettysburg) in east-central Pennsylvania are even closer.

Residents work near town or spread out in different directions for their commutes. The SEPTA (Southeastern Pennsylvania Transportation Authority) rail line goes through Exton and Paoli a few miles north, and Philly commutes take 45 minutes. Commutes to the "Valley" (Valley Forge) area, thanks to new roads, take 25 to 30 minutes. Some workers go south and east to numerous employers, even into northern Delaware.

The area is rolling and attractive with woods and farmland. Weather is variable in all seasons, and summers can get hot with still air and little ocean influence. Snow accumulation is more likely than in Philadelphia just to the east.

Health & Safety Crime risk is low to moderate. The nearby Chester County Hospital is considered to be one of the best in the greater metro area, and the availability of healthcare resources is generally better than average if a bit expensive.

Nearby Neighborhoods West Chester is one of several good suburban town choices in the area. Paoli is similar, but it doesn't have as much historic charm and lacks the college influence. Doylestown, at the end of the rail line on Philadelphia's north side, is also attractive.

PHILADELPHIA, PA/NJ
AREA HIGHLIGHTS

PEOPLE

SIZE & DIVERSITY	AREA	U.S. AVG	FAMILY DEMOGRAPHICS	AREA	U.S. AVG
Population	5,185,692		% Married	52.50%	53.80%
15-yr Population Growth	6.40%	4.40%	% Single	47.50%	46.20%
Diversity Measure	46	54	% Divorced	6.60%	10.20%
% Religiously Observant	58%	50%	% Separated	4.10%	2.10%
% Catholic	36%	22%	% Married w/Children	26.90%	27.90%
% Protestant	15%	25%	% Single w/Children	9.80%	9.40%
% Jewish	5%	2%	% Married, No Children	29.50%	31.00%
% Other	1%	1%	% Single, No Children	33.50%	31.70%

STANDARD OF LIVING

INCOME, EMPLOYMENT & TAXES	AREA	U.S. AVG	COST OF LIVING & HOUSING	AREA	U.S. AVG
Median Household Income	$54,046	$44,684	Cost of Living Index	107	100
Household Income Growth	4.80%	6.10%	Buying Power Index	113	100
Unemployment Rate	4.80%	5.10%	Median Home Price	$211,000	$208,500
Recent Job Growth	1.60%	1.30%	Home Price Ratio	3.9	4.7
Projected Future Job Growth	7.10%	10.50%	Home Price Appreciation	15.60%	13.60%
State Income Tax Rate	7.60%	5.00%	% Homes Owned	70.20%	64.10%
State Sales Tax Rate	6%	6.00%	Median Rent	$962	$792

EDUCATION

ATTAINMENT & ACHIEVEMENT	AREA	U.S. AVG	RESOURCES & INVESTMENT	AREA	U.S. AVG
% High School Graduate	82.60%	83.90%	No. of Highly Ranked Universities	8	1
% 2-yr Graduate	7.50%	7.10%	$ Invested per Pupil	$7,620	$6,058
% 4-yr Graduate	20.70%	17.20%	Student/Teacher Ratio	16.4	15.9
% Graduate or Professional Degree	11%	9.90%	State University In-State Tuition	$10,856	$4,917
% Attending Public School	78.20%	84.30%			
75th Percentile State University SAT Score (Verbal)	530	477			
75th Percentile State University SAT Score (Math)	560	478			
75th Percentile State University ACT Score	N/A	20			

LIFESTYLE

RECREATION, ARTS & CULTURE	AREA	U.S. AVG	INFRASTRUCTURE & FACILITIES	AREA	U.S. AVG
Professional Sports Rating	10	4	No. of Public Libraries	216	28
Zoos & Aquariums Rating	8	3	Library Volumes Per Capita	2.9	2.8
Amusement Park Rating	6	3	No. of Warehouse Clubs	9	4
Professional Theater Rating	10	3	No. of Starbucks	72	5
Overall Museum Rating	10	6	Golf Course Rating	10	4
Science Museum Rating	9	4	National Park Rating	3	3
Children's Museum Rating	9	3	Sq. Mi. Inland Water	5	4

CLIMATE			COMMUTE & TRANSPORTATION		
Days Mostly Sunny	205	212	Avg. Daily Commute Time	28.7	24.7
Annual Days Precipitation	116	111	% Commute by Auto	72%	77.70%
Annual Days > 90°F	19	38	Per Capita Avg. Daily Transit Miles	17.4	7.9
Annual Days < 32°F	101	88	Annual Auto Insurance Premium	$1,730	$1,314
July Relative Humidity	67	69	Gas, Cost per Gallon	$3.24	$3.05

HEALTH & SAFETY

CRIME & ENVIRNOMENTAL ISSUES	AREA	U.S. AVG	HEALTHCARE & COST	AREA	U.S. AVG
Violent Crime Rate	609	517	Physicians per Capita	384.2	254.3
Change in Violent Crime	-8.40%	-7.50%	Pediatricians per Capita	26.4	16.9
Property Crime Rate	2837	3783	Hospital Beds per Capita	414.7	239.7
Change in Property Crime	-23.60%	-10.10%	No. of Teaching Hospitals	51	1.9
Air Quality Score	24	44	Healthcare Cost Index	105.2	100
Water Quality Score	8	33	Cost per Doctor Visit	$72	$74
Pollen/Allergy Score	66	61	Cost per Dentist Visit	$86	$67
Stress Score	66	49	Cost per Hospital Room	$1,809	$702
Cancer Mortality Rate	188.6	168.9			

West Des Moines–Clive, IA

Area Type: Outer suburb

Zip Code: 50325

Metro Area: Des Moines, IA

Metro Area Type: Mid-size

Location: 9 miles west of downtown Des Moines, IA at I-35/I-80 junction

Time Zone: Central Standard Time

Pros:
> Economic stability
> Education
> Convenience

Cons:
> Growth and sprawl
> Entertainment
> High income and property taxes

Sometimes referred to as "the heartland's best-kept secret," Des Moines is a city you might expect to find in a "best places for families" book. Wholesome, traditional, safe, clean, relaxed, education-oriented, and sports-minded, the area has already established itself as a good family place. Across the entire metropolitan area, 31% of households are married with children.

Des Moines itself is a plain but attractive capital city located literally and figuratively smack in the center of the state. Aside from the state government, the city is economically driven by the insurance and financial services industries; the headquarters for 61 insurance companies and 25 banks are in this area. A diverse array of manufacturing businesses makes agricultural equipment, appliances, appliance parts, and food products. But while the manufacturing businesses have had their ups and downs, the government, financial, and insurance businesses are very steady. Downtown is modern with a few historic areas, museums, a stadium, a performing arts venue, and other new waterfront development along the Des Moines River. The Saarinen-designed Des Moines Art Center is noted for both its building design and its contents. When you're in the city, which is laid out on a grid, you're seldom more than 15 or 20 minutes from any other part of the Des Moines area.

Growth has spread mainly to the west and north, with most of the residential growth headed west into areas of attractive farmland and small wooded creek valleys near the freeway convergence west of town. West Des Moines is the largest and most established of the western suburbs, with the smaller Clive and Urbandale adjacent to the north. These areas feature well-planned subdivisions with attractive homes, good schools, excellent park and recreational facilities, and convenient commercial developments to support family life. Increasingly, they are becoming employment centers: Wells Fargo is planning a new 1-million-square-foot home office complex to employ 10,000 workers. These neighborhoods are safe, stable, and economically secure, all qualities one would expect in the best Midwestern city neighborhoods. Clive is the smallest and newest such neighborhood, and slightly upscale, with 35% married with children, but most comments in this narrative can apply to the larger neighborhood of West Des Moines as well.

Standard of Living Des Moines as a whole has an attractive cost of living profile (COL Index 87.5), and the neighborhood index as measured for the Clive portion of the area rises to 113. Homes are very attractive and reasonable, starting at about $200K for family homes and quickly reaching a "sweet spot" in the $225K to $250K range. Most homes in the area are new, set on well-planned suburban streets, with ¼- to ½-acre lots, and include basements. There's more of a country feel here than in many suburbs. Some lots are wooded but most are in areas of former farmland and most homes are of colonial style. High earners desiring expensive homes should be aware of high state income taxes and high effective property tax rates, which run about 3.5%.

Education Area schools are strong, and most test scores are 10% to 20% above state averages. Extracurricular programs, especially sports, are strong and garner a lot of community attention. Thirty-eight percent of adults have a 4-year degree and another 17% have graduate degrees, which gives this area the highest combined educational attainment percentages in Des Moines and one of the highest in the Midwest.

Lifestyle Clive and West Des Moines both have outstanding parks-and-recreation offerings. There are numerous parks of all types and resort-like aquatic centers with active family and youth programs. The older, larger, more established West Des Moines has more parks and facilities, while Clive has an outstanding "Clive Creations" recreational program with youth educational seminars, field trips, day camps, and sports programs. Valley Junction is a historic railroad town core at the southeast corner of West Des Moines, with antique shops, restaurants, and evening entertainment. Living History Farms is a 600-acre working agricultural museum and historic reenactment in Urbandale just north. Adventureland, a large amusement park, lies east of Des Moines along I-80. The popular Iowa State Fair each August is one of the largest and most traditional state fairs in the country. Downtown Des Moines offers Broadway plays at the Civic Center, outdoor movies in a waterfront amphitheater, AAA baseball, and a new hockey team, but some in the area would like to see even more diverse entertainment and restaurants.

Commutes are easy; it only takes 10 minutes to get to downtown Des Moines. Some West Des Moines and Clive residents express concern about growth becoming too rapid with too much of an annexation push by communities on the west side, but everything works so far with few of the negative effects commonly associated with uncontrolled growth and sprawl.

The surrounding terrain is flat to slightly rolling, mostly farmland with some wooded areas near creeks. The climate is continental with four seasons. Summers are warm and humid, and winters are changeable with some cold snaps. The area's humidity and storm-track location mean that there's always the potential for strong storms, but fall weather is especially pleasant.

Health & Safety Crime, stress, and health factors, in general, are favorable. Healthcare facilities are excellent. Looking like a stack of assembled children's blocks, the Blank Children's Hospital located downtown is notable.

Nearby Neighborhoods Clive and West Des Moines are comparable and both very attractive; it's hard to recommend one over the other. Clive is newer and more upscale but not by a wide margin. It's possible to go farther west for a still more rural lifestyle convenient to downtown, and Ankeny to the north is worth a look.

WEST DES MOINES-CLIVE, IA NEIGHBORHOOD HIGHLIGHTS	
PEOPLE	
Population	13,700
15-yr Population Growth	20.20%
5-yr Population Growth	5%
% Married w/Children	34.8%
% Single w/Children	8.1%
No. of Households	5,081
Median Age	33.2
Avg. Household Size	2.69
Diversity Measure	15
STANDARD OF LIVING	
Median Household Income	$82,137
% Household Income > $100K	36%
Projected Future Job Growth	12%
Cost of Living Index	113
Buying Power Index	160
Weekly Daycare Cost	$100
Median Home Price	$245,400
"Sweet Spot" Home Price	$235,000
Home Price Ratio	3
Median Age of Homes	14.3
% Homes Owned	75%
Effective Property Tax Rate	3.50%
Estimated Property Tax Bill	$8,225
EDUCATION	
% High School Graduates	98%
% 4-yr Degree	38%
% Graduate or Professional Degree	17%
$ Invested per Pupil	$5,507
Student/Teacher Ratio	15.1
Primary Test Score Percentile	109.7
Secondary Test Score Percentile	N/A
% Subsidized School Lunch	14.70%
% Attending Public School	78.50%
LIFESTYLE	
Leisure Rating (Area)	3
Arts & Culture Rating (Area)	6
Climate Rating (Area)	3
Physical Setting Rating	3
Downtown Core Rating	4
% Commute < 30 Min.	86%
% Commute > 1 Hour	1%
HEALTH & SAFETY	BEST
Health Rating (Area)	8
Stress Score (Area)	3
Violent Crime Risk	49
Property Crime Risk	85

DES MOINES, IA
AREA HIGHLIGHTS

PEOPLE

SIZE & DIVERSITY	AREA	U.S. AVG	FAMILY DEMOGRAPHICS	AREA	U.S. AVG
Population	485,335		% Married	60.60%	53.80%
15-yr Population Growth	24.80%	4.40%	% Single	39.40%	46.20%
Diversity Measure	22	54	% Divorced	8.60%	10.20%
% Religiously Observant	47%	50%	% Separated	1.90%	2.10%
% Catholic	15%	22%	% Married w/Children	30.50%	27.90%
% Protestant	32%	25%	% Single w/Children	8.60%	9.40%
% Jewish	0%	2%	% Married, No Children	31.20%	31.00%
% Other	0%	1%	% Single, No Children	29.60%	31.70%

STANDARD OF LIVING

INCOME, EMPLOYMENT & TAXES	AREA	U.S. AVG	COST OF LIVING & HOUSING	AREA	U.S. AVG
Median Household Income	$50,306	$44,684	Cost of Living Index	87.5	100
Household Income Growth	3.80%	6.10%	Buying Power Index	129	100
Unemployment Rate	3.80%	5.10%	Median Home Price	$145,100	$208,500
Recent Job Growth	3.50%	1.30%	Home Price Ratio	2.9	4.7
Projected Future Job Growth	17.10%	10.50%	Home Price Appreciation	5.90%	13.60%
State Income Tax Rate	8.80%	5.00%	% Homes Owned	71.60%	64.10%
State Sales Tax Rate	6%	6.00%	Median Rent	$657	$792

EDUCATION

ATTAINMENT & ACHIEVEMENT	AREA	U.S. AVG	RESOURCES & INVESTMENT	AREA	U.S. AVG
% High School Graduate	88%	83.90%	No. of Highly Ranked Universities	1	1
% 2-yr Graduate	10.60%	7.10%	$ Invested per Pupil	$5,807	$6,058
% 4-yr Graduate	19.30%	17.20%	Student/Teacher Ratio	15.5	15.9
% Graduate or Professional Degree	6.70%	9.90%	State University In-State Tuition	$5,396	$4,917
% Attending Public School	91%	84.30%			
75th Percentile State University SAT Score (Verbal)	530	477			
75th Percentile State University SAT Score (Math)	540	478			
75th Percentile State University ACT Score	22	20			

LIFESTYLE

RECREATION, ARTS & CULTURE	AREA	U.S. AVG	INFRASTRUCTURE & FACILITIES	AREA	U.S. AVG
Professional Sports Rating	3	4	No. of Public Libraries	35	28
Zoos & Aquariums Rating	3	3	Library Volumes Per Capita	3.3	2.8
Amusement Park Rating	1	3	No. of Warehouse Clubs	1	4
Professional Theater Rating	1	3	No. of Starbucks	6	5
Overall Museum Rating	6	6	Golf Course Rating	4	4
Science Museum Rating	6	4	National Park Rating	1	3
Children's Museum Rating	6	3	Sq. Mi. Inland Water	2	4

CLIMATE			COMMUTE & TRANSPORTATION		
Days Mostly Sunny	199	212	Avg. Daily Commute Time	19.3	24.7
Annual Days Precipitation	106	111	% Commute by Auto	75%	77.70%
Annual Days > 90°F	21	38	Per Capita Avg. Daily Transit Miles	9.4	7.9
Annual Days < 32°F	137	88	Annual Auto Insurance Premium	$885	$1,314
July Relative Humidity	69	69	Gas, Cost per Gallon	$3.09	$3.05

HEALTH & SAFETY

CRIME & ENVIRNOMENTAL ISSUES	AREA	U.S. AVG	HEALTHCARE & COST	AREA	U.S. AVG
Violent Crime Rate	253	517	Physicians per Capita	255.3	254.3
Change in Violent Crime	-18.70%	-7.50%	Pediatricians per Capita	18.1	16.9
Property Crime Rate	3962	3783	Hospital Beds per Capita	389.6	239.7
Change in Property Crime	-14.20%	-10.10%	No. of Teaching Hospitals	5	1.9
Air Quality Score	45	44	Healthcare Cost Index	106.8	100
Water Quality Score	60	33	Cost per Doctor Visit	$72	$74
Pollen/Allergy Score	40	61	Cost per Dentist Visit	$58	$67
Stress Score	25	49	Cost per Hospital Room	$752	$702
Cancer Mortality Rate	172.6	168.9			

West Lafayette, IN

Area Type: Small college town

Zip Code: 47906

Metro Area: Lafayette, IN

Metro Area Type: Smaller

Location: Northwest Indiana along I-65 between Indianapolis and Chicago

Time Zone: Eastern Standard Time

Pros:
Strong college influence
Small-town feel
Cost of living

Cons:
Growth and sprawl
Slow current job growth
Winter climate

"Two great towns, one great university" is a local's description of this area's strengths. The towns are the twin cities, Lafayette and West Lafayette, which sit across from each other along the banks of the Wabash River. And the university, of course, is Purdue University, a "Big Ten" school and one of the top schools in the Midwest. The combination results in a pleasant, full-featured Midwestern small town with a strong college accent and lots of fun things for everyone to do.

Although they share much, Lafayette and West Lafayette are quite different. Lafayette, with a population of 60,000 on the east side of the river, is a typical Midwestern small city, anchored first by agriculture, then by conventional manufacturing industries like Caterpillar, Alcoa, and A.E. Staley, and more recently by Eli Lilly and Subaru. These companies are attracted by the quality labor force and strategic location central to the Midwest. The employment base is diverse, ranging from unskilled manufacturing to high-end research. The Wabash River cuts a wooded valley through otherwise mostly flat farmland, and downtown Lafayette, situated on the east bank, is quite attractive and historic with a slightly European look at a distance. To the east and south, the area has grown rapidly with typical and fairly unattractive retail-commercial sprawl found in many other places.

Rising from the other side of the river is West Lafayette, home of Purdue and its some 30,000 undergraduate students mixed in with another 30,000 permanent residents. The campus is just west of a small town center, and attractive suburban neighborhoods spread north and west. It's a typical college town with commercial and farming elements all around, and plenty of highly skilled jobs are in this area. Purdue Research Park hosts 90 companies employing 2,500 workers. The university provides a strong intellectual influence and a

lot to do. Even with the high student population, the married-with-children household percentage is 21.2%, which helps illustrate West Lafayette's role as a family community.

Standard of Living Particularly for a college town with a strong employment base, West Lafayette has a reasonable cost-of-living profile. The Cost of Living Index is about 96, and excellent family housing can be had in the $200K to $225K range, with good starters in the $175K to $180K range. Per-square-foot costs run between $75 and $100, with a mix of colonial, ranch, and contemporary styles on moderate-sized lots (most are a ¼ to a ½ acre). Property taxes run a bit higher on the west side of the river, but are still reasonable at 1.2%. Some manufacturing job loss has weakened current job growth to 0.3%, but future job growth is projected at 10%, near national averages.

Education Schools are strong. The West Lafayette School District has a strong college-prep program and shares many of Purdue's resources. For example, the university offers free classes and workshops on a variety of academic and "fun" topics. Secondary testing scores consistently run 20% to 25% above state averages. Educational attainment is outstanding: 26% have undergraduate degrees and another 30% have graduate-level degrees, giving a very high combined percentage compared to other places.

Lifestyle The cities work effectively together on parks, recreation, and activities, as well as on other more operational city-management issues—which is especially refreshing in today's world of fragmented metropolitan regions. A pedestrian bridge connects both cities, and the waterfront area has bike trails, nature areas, and an ice-skating rink. There are six different public playgrounds and a community pool. Entertainment and performing arts are easy to find in

WEST LAFAYETTE, IN NEIGHBORHOOD HIGHLIGHTS	
PEOPLE	
Population	58,443
15-yr Population Growth	16.40%
5-yr Population Growth	2.10%
% Married w/Children	21.2%
% Single w/Children	5.8%
No. of Households	19,077
Median Age	29.6
Avg. Household Size	2.38
Diversity Measure	29
STANDARD OF LIVING	
Median Household Income	$32,031
% Household Income > $100K	12%
Projected Future Job Growth	10%
Cost of Living Index	95.8
Buying Power Index	75
Weekly Daycare Cost	$175
Median Home Price	$165,500
"Sweet Spot" Home Price	$220,000
Home Price Ratio	5.2
Median Age of Homes	25.9
% Homes Owned	43%
Effective Property Tax Rate	1.20%
Estimated Property Tax Bill	$2,640
EDUCATION	BEST
% High School Graduates	93%
% 4-yr Degree	26%
% Graduate or Professional Degree	30%
$ Invested per Pupil	$5,918
Student/Teacher Ratio	16.9
Primary Test Score Percentile	120.2
Secondary Test Score Percentile	126.3
% Subsidized School Lunch	16%
% Attending Public School	95%
LIFESTYLE	
Leisure Rating (Area)	4
Arts & Culture Rating (Area)	4
Climate Rating (Area)	7
Physical Setting Rating	3
Downtown Core Rating	4
% Commute < 30 Min.	88%
% Commute > 1 Hour	3%
HEALTH & SAFETY	
Health Rating (Area)	1
Stress Score (Area)	1
Violent Crime Risk	86
Property Crime Risk	95

town and at the university. College sports are king, and the university's health and fitness programs are available to residents. A couple of big annual festivals add interest in summer and fall. Shoppers go to Tippecanoe Mall on the southeast side or to smaller antique and specialty shops in downtown Lafayette, as well as to Chicago (2 hours away) and "Indy" (meaning Indianapolis, an hour away).

Commutes aren't a problem. The area is considered by most too distant to commute to the bigger cities in the region.

The largely agricultural landscape sits in a continental climate zone with four distinct seasons, including warm summers and variably cold winters. Lake effects can bring extensive periods of rain, snow, wind, and clouds, but the area is far enough west to escape the heaviest snows.

Health & Safety   Crime rates are favorable, stress is low, and air quality scores well. Healthcare facilities and resources are about average for this type of area.

Nearby Neighborhoods   Newer, less expensive neighborhoods can be found in southeast Lafayette, and some might look at the older areas near downtown Lafayette.

LAFAYETTE, IN
AREA HIGHLIGHTS

PEOPLE

SIZE & DIVERSITY	AREA	U.S. AVG	FAMILY DEMOGRAPHICS	AREA	U.S. AVG
Population	186,190		% Married	58.80%	53.80%
15-yr Population Growth	15.30%	4.40%	% Single	41.20%	46.20%
Diversity Measure	23	54	% Divorced	8.30%	10.20%
% Religiously Observant	37%	50%	% Separated	1.50%	2.10%
% Catholic	11%	22%	% Married w/Children	30.20%	27.90%
% Protestant	25%	25%	% Single w/Children	7.80%	9.40%
% Jewish	0%	2%	% Married, No Children	31.50%	31.00%
% Other	0%	1%	% Single, No Children	30.50%	31.70%

STANDARD OF LIVING

INCOME, EMPLOYMENT & TAXES	AREA	U.S. AVG	COST OF LIVING & HOUSING	AREA	U.S. AVG
Median Household Income	$39,844	$44,684	Cost of Living Index	80.7	100
Household Income Growth	4.10%	6.10%	Buying Power Index	110	100
Unemployment Rate	4.10%	5.10%	Median Home Price	$95,400	$208,500
Recent Job Growth	0.30%	1.30%	Home Price Ratio	2.4	4.7
Projected Future Job Growth	9.80%	10.50%	Home Price Appreciation	1.50%	13.60%
State Income Tax Rate	3.40%	5.00%	% Homes Owned	68.90%	64.10%
State Sales Tax Rate	5%	6.00%	Median Rent	$661	$792

EDUCATION

ATTAINMENT & ACHIEVEMENT	AREA	U.S. AVG	RESOURCES & INVESTMENT	AREA	U.S. AVG
% High School Graduate	83.80%	83.90%	No. of Highly Ranked Universities	0	1
% 2-yr Graduate	7.70%	7.10%	$ Invested per Pupil	$5,828	$6,058
% 4-yr Graduate	13.10%	17.20%	Student/Teacher Ratio	17.3	15.9
% Graduate or Professional Degree	9.30%	9.90%	State University In-State Tuition	$6,777	$4,917
% Attending Public School	90.20%	84.30%			
75th Percentile State University SAT Score (Verbal)	490	477			
75th Percentile State University SAT Score (Math)	500	478			
75th Percentile State University ACT Score	22	20			

LIFESTYLE

RECREATION, ARTS & CULTURE	AREA	U.S. AVG	INFRASTRUCTURE & FACILITIES	AREA	U.S. AVG
Professional Sports Rating	2	4	No. of Public Libraries	8	28
Zoos & Aquariums Rating	3	3	Library Volumes Per Capita	3.9	2.8
Amusement Park Rating	1	3	No. of Warehouse Clubs	3	4
Professional Theater Rating	1	3	No. of Starbucks	2	5
Overall Museum Rating	5	6	Golf Course Rating	2	4
Science Museum Rating	2	4	National Park Rating	1	3
Children's Museum Rating	1	3	Sq. Mi. Inland Water	5	4

CLIMATE			COMMUTE & TRANSPORTATION		
Days Mostly Sunny	191	212	Avg. Daily Commute Time	17.7	24.7
Annual Days Precipitation	122	111	% Commute by Auto	76%	77.70%
Annual Days > 90°F	15	38	Per Capita Avg. Daily Transit Miles	7.3	7.9
Annual Days < 32°F	122	88	Annual Auto Insurance Premium	$1,017	$1,314
July Relative Humidity	73	69	Gas, Cost per Gallon	$3.01	$3.05

HEALTH & SAFETY

CRIME & ENVIRNOMENTAL ISSUES	AREA	U.S. AVG	HEALTHCARE & COST	AREA	U.S. AVG
Violent Crime Rate	211	517	Physicians per Capita	185.8	254.3
Change in Violent Crime	-21.70%	-7.50%	Pediatricians per Capita	14.8	16.9
Property Crime Rate	3191	3783	Hospital Beds per Capita	438.2	239.7
Change in Property Crime	-13.40%	-10.10%	No. of Teaching Hospitals	0	1.9
Air Quality Score	51	44	Healthcare Cost Index	94.3	100
Water Quality Score	36	33	Cost per Doctor Visit	$75	$74
Pollen/Allergy Score	66	61	Cost per Dentist Visit	$64	$67
Stress Score	10	49	Cost per Hospital Room	$684	$702
Cancer Mortality Rate	170.9	168.9			

West Mobile, AL

Area Type: Outer suburb

Zip Code: 36695

Metro Area: Mobile, AL

Metro Area Type: Mid-size

Location: 15 miles west of downtown Mobile

Time Zone: Central Standard Time

Pros:
Attractive, affordable housing
Historic interest
Nearby coastline

Cons:
Summer heat and humidity
Employment, career growth
Hurricane risk

This is the Deep, Deep South. Literally and figuratively, it's harder to go any farther south in the United States than Mobile, Alabama.

Originally founded by the French in the early 1700s, Mobile still has a mix of French and Spanish influence much like its more famous New Orleans neighbor. In fact, many consider Mobile a good alternative to the "Big Easy," having much of its charm and many of its benefits without its problems of congestion, crime, and flood risk. Indeed, the Mobile Mardi Gras is the original version of the famed celebration, and the tradition is still carried on today. Beyond Mardi Gras, the rich Colonial-era traditions also carry forward the city's appearance, historic interest, and better-than-average arts and cultural amenities.

Downtown Mobile is a combination of historic charm and modest modern structures. The waterfront area is in the early stages of redevelopment. Until recently, prominent cargo port and shipping activities in the natural Mobile Bay harbor gave much of the waterfront an industrial character. A new cruise-ship port serves to boost both the economy and the visual appeal along the water. Mobile has several attractive historic districts and is expanding efforts to capitalize on them. The "LoDa"—Lower Dauphin Street—historic commercial district reflects its early days as a cotton port, while blending in today's more modern commercial structures. The Oakleigh historic residential district exhibits stately Greet revival and Victorian area structures, and the 35-mile Azalea Trail connects many of the historic areas with wooded beauty.

The employment base is diverse, but it slants toward working industries like shipping, shipbuilding, paper and paper products, agriculture, and seafood processing, with a small assortment of high-tech and research facilities and a large Coast Guard base. Recent employment statistics pose a few question marks and, at press

time, the long-term effects of Hurricane Katrina weren't clear. But the area's attractive location, its low costs, and the success story in Huntsville (see p. 277) should bring more future business. A recent upsurge in movers from other places, particularly in the South, has occurred recently. The West Mobile area, near the airport, features excellent and fairly new homes, good schools, and a high number of families with kids (42% of households are married with children).

Standard of Living   Cost of living is a major attraction; even in this relatively affluent suburb, the Cost of Living Index is just under 93. Homes cost $85 to $95 per square foot, and good single-family homes start in the mid $170Ks with excellent newer choices on large lots in the low $200Ks. The low-lying landscape doesn't allow for a lot of basements, but otherwise, features and amenities are excellent. The Home Price Ratio is a respectable 2.6. Other costs are also notably low: Property taxes are effectively 0.80%; a $1,600 tax bill on a $200K home is a decided advantage. Likewise, daycare costs are attractive at $120 per week. That being said, the state of Alabama has had some nationally noted fiscal funding issues, which you should follow if considering a move to the area.

Education   The schools here are among the best in the state, with strong college-preparatory programs and high test scores, including college entrance exams and Alabama High School Graduation Examination tests. The local Baker High School gets very strong parent reviews, and the area has notably strong private schools, including the residential secondary Alabama School of Mathematics and Science. Educational attainment is respectable, with 36% combined having 4-year or graduate degrees. The University of South Alabama, University of Mobile, and Spring Hill College are all nearby.

Lifestyle The distinctly Southern lifestyle is laid-back, genteel, and quiet with a strong base of faith and patriotism. While most of Alabama has a strong Protestant Bible Belt leaning, Mobile from its roots is also a recognized center for the Catholic Church in the South; as a resident says, "[there's] a church on every corner." Those looking for outdoor recreation look mainly south toward the Gulf, where beaches in Gulf Shores, the Mississippi Gulf Coast, and the Florida Panhandle are all available and relatively uncrowded at most times of the year. The area has excellent golf courses and a few noted wildlife viewing areas. The city offers a full assortment of arts, including the 100,000-square-foot Mobile Museum of Art in a beautiful new building, the historic Museum of Mobile, and the science-oriented Gulf Coast Explorium and IMAX center.

Growth has moved primarily westward from Mobile, but commutes downtown are still easy and usually take less than 20 minutes. Some area residents commute 45 minutes to Mississippi coastal areas, including the industrial Pascagoula and entertainment centers near Biloxi, though 2005's Hurricane Katrina caused some dislocations to these patterns. The adjacent airport has good service, particularly to other areas in the South, and some professionals servicing the South as a territory find Mobile a good central location.

The surrounding terrain is mainly flat and open or wooded coastal plain. The climate is subtropical, with hot, muggy summers but nice weather at most other times of year. The area is vulnerable to hurricanes and is low enough to have flood risk, but it's far enough inland to avoid storm surges. Most Katrina damage in 2005 was related to wind and falling trees.

Health & Safety The crime risk is high among the places listed in this book, but relatively low for a city in the Gulf region. Local "CAP" crime risk statistics reflect a moderate to low risk. Healthcare facilities are very good with five area hospitals, a university medical center, and a special USA Women's and Children's Hospital.

Nearby Neighborhoods Alternate choices include more historic or redeveloped areas in or near downtown (also quite affordable) and the more resort and retirement oriented Baldwin County communities of Fairhope and Daphne on the east side of Mobile Bay. Baldwin County schools are also considered excellent.

WEST MOBILE, AL NEIGHBORHOOD HIGHLIGHTS

PEOPLE

Population	33,531
15-yr Population Growth	5.80%
5-yr Population Growth	0.20%
% Married w/Children	42.0%
% Single w/Children	9.1%
No. of Households	12,092
Median Age	33.3
Avg. Household Size	2.74
Diversity Measure	25

STANDARD OF LIVING

Median Household Income	$58,621
% Household Income > $100K	14%
Projected Future Job Growth	9%
Cost of Living Index	92.6
Buying Power Index	135
Weekly Daycare Cost	$120
Median Home Price	$151,500
"Sweet Spot" Home Price	$220,000
Home Price Ratio	2.6
Median Age of Homes	12.2
% Homes Owned	77%
Effective Property Tax Rate	0.80%
Estimated Property Tax Bill	$1,760

EDUCATION

% High School Graduates	90%
% 4-yr Degree	23%
% Graduate or Professional Degree	13%
$ Invested per Pupil	$4,229
Student/Teacher Ratio	15.5
Primary Test Score Percentile	116.7
Secondary Test Score Percentile	101.1
% Subsidized School Lunch	36.50%
% Attending Public School	64%

LIFESTYLE

Leisure Rating (Area)	5
Arts & Culture Rating (Area)	5
Climate Rating (Area)	6
Physical Setting Rating	3
Downtown Core Rating	3
% Commute < 30 Min.	58%
% Commute > 1 Hour	6%

HEALTH & SAFETY

Health Rating (Area)	2
Stress Score (Area)	10
Violent Crime Risk	65
Property Crime Risk	92

MOBILE, AL
AREA HIGHLIGHTS
PEOPLE

SIZE & DIVERSITY	AREA	U.S. AVG	FAMILY DEMOGRAPHICS	AREA	U.S. AVG
Population	557,227		% Married	54.30%	53.80%
15-yr Population Growth	20.90%	4.40%	% Single	45.70%	46.20%
Diversity Measure	45	54	% Divorced	9.20%	10.20%
% Religiously Observant	52%	50%	% Separated	3.70%	2.10%
% Catholic	9%	22%	% Married w/Children	27%	27.90%
% Protestant	43%	25%	% Single w/Children	12.90%	9.40%
% Jewish	0%	2%	% Married, No Children	28.20%	31.00%
% Other	0%	1%	% Single, No Children	31.80%	31.70%

STANDARD OF LIVING

INCOME, EMPLOYMENT & TAXES	AREA	U.S. AVG	COST OF LIVING & HOUSING	AREA	U.S. AVG
Median Household Income	$35,679	$44,684	Cost of Living Index	83.5	100
Household Income Growth	6%	6.10%	Buying Power Index	96	100
Unemployment Rate	6%	5.10%	Median Home Price	$129,100	$208,500
Recent Job Growth	2.70%	1.30%	Home Price Ratio	3.6	4.7
Projected Future Job Growth	13.10%	10.50%	Home Price Appreciation	2.30%	13.60%
State Income Tax Rate	5%	5.00%	% Homes Owned	62.70%	64.10%
State Sales Tax Rate	9.50%	6.00%	Median Rent	$561	$792

EDUCATION

ATTAINMENT & ACHIEVEMENT	AREA	U.S. AVG	RESOURCES & INVESTMENT	AREA	U.S. AVG
% High School Graduate	72.80%	83.90%	No. of Highly Ranked Universities	0	1
% 2-yr Graduate	6.80%	7.10%	$ Invested per Pupil	$4,542	$6,058
% 4-yr Graduate	14%	17.20%	Student/Teacher Ratio	16.1	15.9
% Graduate or Professional Degree	6.20%	9.90%	State University In-State Tuition	$4,630	$4,917
% Attending Public School	83.70%	84.30%			
75th Percentile State University SAT Score (Verbal)	490	477			
75th Percentile State University SAT Score (Math)	500	478			
75th Percentile State University ACT Score	21	20			

LIFESTYLE

RECREATION, ARTS & CULTURE	AREA	U.S. AVG	INFRASTRUCTURE & FACILITIES	AREA	U.S. AVG
Professional Sports Rating	2	4	No. of Public Libraries	24	28
Zoos & Aquariums Rating	1	3	Library Volumes Per Capita	1.6	2.8
Amusement Park Rating	1	3	No. of Warehouse Clubs	3	4
Professional Theater Rating	1	3	No. of Starbucks	2	5
Overall Museum Rating	6	6	Golf Course Rating	3	4
Science Museum Rating	4	4	National Park Rating	2	3
Children's Museum Rating	3	3	Sq. Mi. Inland Water	8	4

CLIMATE			COMMUTE & TRANSPORTATION		
Days Mostly Sunny	217	212	Avg. Daily Commute Time	25.4	24.7
Annual Days Precipitation	124	111	% Commute by Auto	77%	77.70%
Annual Days > 90°F	81	38	Per Capita Avg. Daily Transit Miles	3	7.9
Annual Days < 32°F	19	88	Annual Auto Insurance Premium	$1,083	$1,314
July Relative Humidity	73	69	Gas, Cost per Gallon	$2.76	$3.05

HEALTH & SAFETY

CRIME & ENVIRNOMENTAL ISSUES	AREA	U.S. AVG	HEALTHCARE & COST	AREA	U.S. AVG
Violent Crime Rate	558	517	Physicians per Capita	240.6	254.3
Change in Violent Crime	0%	-7.50%	Pediatricians per Capita	16.4	16.9
Property Crime Rate	5749	3783	Hospital Beds per Capita	469.3	239.7
Change in Property Crime	11.50%	-10.10%	No. of Teaching Hospitals	5	1.9
Air Quality Score	21	44	Healthcare Cost Index	86.7	100
Water Quality Score	62	33	Cost per Doctor Visit	$54	$74
Pollen/Allergy Score	70	61	Cost per Dentist Visit	$51	$67
Stress Score	98	49	Cost per Hospital Room	$357	$702
Cancer Mortality Rate	186	168.9			

West Nyack, NY

Area Type: Outer suburb

Zip Code: 10994

Metro Area: New York, NY

Metro Area Type: Largest

Location: West side of Hudson Valley, 30 miles north of Manhattan

Time Zone: Eastern Standard Time

Pros:
>   Education
>   Community feel
>   Convenient to New York

Cons:
>   Cost of living and home prices
>   Long commutes
>   Low job growth

Finding an affordable place to live in the New York area is a challenge, especially when you're looking for a neighborhood that also offers fun things to do, ample resources to serve family needs, and a manageable commute to the city. Achieving a balance between these objectives is tough, but it's a challenge we've taken on more than once in this book because of the vast rich resources available for families in the New York area (see Norwood on p. 307, Livingston on p. 265, Kendall Park on p. 247, East Islip on p. 178, and Newtown on p. 298). West Nyack offers a good balance of city access with a strong set of local resources and is more of a "typical suburb" than the other places selected in the metro area.

The history of the Hudson River as a transportation route spawned numerous settlements up the valley from New York City. Most of these settlements today remain as attractive small towns situated along the rather steep bluffs of the river. The Metro North and New Jersey Transit rail lines are nearby to link residents to the city. This available train service, the area's history, a low commercial base, and relatively limited areas to build have kept these towns nice but have made them, at the same time, very expensive. Such towns as Croton-on-Hudson, Tarrytown, Ossining, and Cold Spring retain a lot of character but may be unaffordable for some families.

On the west shore, greater land availability, commercial activity, and historically more difficult commutes have made areas from the New Jersey border up to West Point and even Newburgh less expensive and more attractive to middle-class and even working-class folks. Automobiles, buses, and the Tappan Zee Bridge (connecting to rail) have improved the NYC commute, and the west shore areas have prospered as bedroom communities to the New York area with substantial local commercial activity. West Nyack is one of a group of suburbs that have evolved as attractive family places, including Tappan, Orangeburg, Nanuet, New City, and Blauvelt. A strong family presence is evidenced by the 38.5% of households in West Nyack categorized as married with children.

Standard of Living While West Nyack is a good value for the New York area, it isn't cheap. The Cost of Living Index of 172 is moderate locally but quite high by national standards. To give an idea, the COL Index in Norwood, just 10 miles south, is 191. Good family home prices settle in the low to high $500Ks, perhaps $50K to $100K less than in Bergen County. But there are more modestly sized homes available, and if a family can get by with 1,800 to 2,000 square feet, the price can drop below $500K. Most homes are on ⅓- to ½-acre lots. Property taxes are approximately $16 per $1,000 valuation, or 1.6%, which is about average for the region.

Median household incomes for the area run at a strong $117,000, reflecting the professional workforce likely commuting to New York City, but also a greater likelihood of second earners in the household. At this level, most families still prosper financially despite the high costs. The Buying Power Index is a healthy 151. West Nyack and New York jobs are stable, but not growing; New York projected job growth is only 3.9% against a relatively high current unemployment rate of 5.2%. The better news is in recent job growth of 3.6%, but there are relatively few employers in the immediate West Nyack area outside of retail and other service industries.

Education Like in many New York–area communities, locals are very positive about their schools. The Clarkstown City School District consistently turns in outstanding scores. On the 2004 New York Regents Exam, Clarkstown South Senior High School, with

WEST NYACK, NY NEIGHBORHOOD HIGHLIGHTS	
PEOPLE	
Population	6,908
15-yr Population Growth	10.60%
5-yr Population Growth	2.40%
% Married w/Children	38.5%
% Single w/Children	6.3%
No. of Households	2,242
Median Age	37.8
Avg. Household Size	3.08
Diversity Measure	31
STANDARD OF LIVING	
Median Household Income	$117,900
% Household Income > $100K	55%
Projected Future Job Growth	6%
Cost of Living Index	172
Buying Power Index	151
Weekly Daycare Cost	$275
Median Home Price	$605,700
"Sweet Spot" Home Price	$550,000
Home Price Ratio	5.1
Median Age of Homes	36.2
% Homes Owned	88%
Effective Property Tax Rate	1.60%
Estimated Property Tax Bill	$8,800
EDUCATION	BEST
% High School Graduates	93%
% 4-yr Degree	26%
% Graduate or Professional Degree	24%
$ Invested per Pupil	$10,063
Student/Teacher Ratio	12.9
Primary Test Score Percentile	119.5
Secondary Test Score Percentile	112.7
% Subsidized School Lunch	5%
% Attending Public School	69%
LIFESTYLE	
Leisure Rating (Area)	10
Arts & Culture Rating (Area)	10
Climate Rating (Area)	8
Physical Setting Rating	3
Downtown Core Rating	7
% Commute < 30 Min.	50%
% Commute > 1 Hour	16%
HEALTH & SAFETY	
Health Rating (Area)	3
Stress Score (Area)	5
Violent Crime Risk	73
Property Crime Risk	61

1,400 students, scored 96% on English, 98% to 99% on math exams versus state averages around 80%. Grade 8 Language Arts scores were 26% over state averages.

Lifestyle   West Nyack has the look and feel of a typical suburb. The Palisades Center Mall, which is the second-largest mall in the country (behind the more well-known Mall of America in the Minneapolis–St. Paul area), is a nearby destination with stores (of course), amusements, rides, concerts, and even an occasional circus. When residents are shopped out, the West Nyack area has an ample amount of outdoor space; an estimated 30% of land area is dedicated to parks. For a small-town–downtown experience, the old Village of Nyack along the Hudson offers plenty of arts and entertainment activities.

The commute, for many, is similar to that from the Norwood area in Bergen County. The Palisades Parkway provides comparatively easy access via the George Washington (GW) bridge to Manhattan. It's about 25 minutes to the GW, making a 45- to 55-minute commute overall. Some commuters cross the Hudson River by bridge or even ferry to get to Metro North—which is especially convenient if working near Grand Central Station on Manhattan's east side, but the commute still takes just over an hour. A fair number of commuters also drive or take buses into New Jersey.

The area is hilly with deciduous woods beyond the rocky Hudson River bluffs. The climate is continental with limited influence from the water to the south, and winters can be more rigorous than in other parts of the New York area.

Health & Safety   Crime risk is very low, especially attractive near a large city. With the area being upwind from most of the New York area, air quality is better than in much of the region but still doesn't score very well. Healthcare resources are adequate but predictably expensive.

Nearby Neighborhoods   Most of the west Hudson neighborhoods mentioned above have similar profiles; it's a matter of personal preference. East bank areas have more of a small-town atmosphere and are considerably more expensive.

NEW YORK, NY
AREA HIGHLIGHTS

PEOPLE

SIZE & DIVERSITY	AREA	U.S. AVG	FAMILY DEMOGRAPHICS	AREA	U.S. AVG
Population	9,440,719		% Married	45.80%	53.80%
15-yr Population Growth	10.60%	4.40%	% Single	54.20%	46.20%
Diversity Measure	72	54	% Divorced	6.60%	10.20%
% Religiously Observant	62%	50%	% Separated	5.60%	2.10%
% Catholic	39%	22%	% Married w/Children	21.70%	27.90%
% Protestant	8%	25%	% Single w/Children	11.80%	9.40%
% Jewish	13%	2%	% Married, No Children	25.80%	31.00%
% Other	2%	1%	% Single, No Children	40.70%	31.70%

STANDARD OF LIVING

INCOME, EMPLOYMENT & TAXES	AREA	U.S. AVG	COST OF LIVING & HOUSING	AREA	U.S. AVG
Median Household Income	$46,069	$44,684	Cost of Living Index	157.9	100
Household Income Growth	5.20%	6.10%	Buying Power Index	65	100
Unemployment Rate	5.20%	5.10%	Median Home Price	$506,800	$208,500
Recent Job Growth	3.60%	1.30%	Home Price Ratio	11	4.7
Projected Future Job Growth	3.90%	10.50%	Home Price Appreciation	15.60%	13.60%
State Income Tax Rate	10.50%	5.00%	% Homes Owned	46.30%	64.10%
State Sales Tax Rate	8.20%	6.00%	Median Rent	$1,042	$792

EDUCATION

ATTAINMENT & ACHIEVEMENT	AREA	U.S. AVG	RESOURCES & INVESTMENT	AREA	U.S. AVG
% High School Graduate	79.20%	83.90%	No. of Highly Ranked Universities	8	1
% 2-yr Graduate	7.30%	7.10%	$ Invested per Pupil	$8,640	$6,058
% 4-yr Graduate	21.60%	17.20%	Student/Teacher Ratio	17.3	15.9
% Graduate or Professional Degree	15.80%	9.90%	State University In-State Tuition	$5,966	$4,917
% Attending Public School	77.50%	84.30%			
75th Percentile State University SAT Score (Verbal)	520	477			
75th Percentile State University SAT Score (Math)	550	478			
75th Percentile State University ACT Score	24	20			

LIFESTYLE

RECREATION, ARTS & CULTURE	AREA	U.S. AVG	INFRASTRUCTURE & FACILITIES	AREA	U.S. AVG
Professional Sports Rating	10	4	No. of Public Libraries	279	28
Zoos & Aquariums Rating	10	3	Library Volumes Per Capita	5.1	2.8
Amusement Park Rating	6	3	No. of Warehouse Clubs	8	4
Professional Theater Rating	10	3	No. of Starbucks	213	5
Overall Museum Rating	10	6	Golf Course Rating	10	4
Science Museum Rating	10	4	National Park Rating	4	3
Children's Museum Rating	10	3	Sq. Mi. Inland Water	10	4

CLIMATE			COMMUTE & TRANSPORTATION		
Days Mostly Sunny	232	212	Avg. Daily Commute Time	38.9	24.7
Annual Days Precipitation	121	111	% Commute by Auto	42%	77.70%
Annual Days > 90°F	16	38	Per Capita Avg. Daily Transit Miles	62.9	7.9
Annual Days < 32°F	81	88	Annual Auto Insurance Premium	$2,963	$1,314
July Relative Humidity	65	69	Gas, Cost per Gallon	$3.30	$3.05

HEALTH & SAFETY

CRIME & ENVIRNOMENTAL ISSUES	AREA	U.S. AVG	HEALTHCARE & COST	AREA	U.S. AVG
Violent Crime Rate	617	517	Physicians per Capita	406.1	254.3
Change in Violent Crime	-40.50%	-7.50%	Pediatricians per Capita	30	16.9
Property Crime Rate	2154	3783	Hospital Beds per Capita	476.2	239.7
Change in Property Crime	-32.10%	-10.10%	No. of Teaching Hospitals	64	1.9
Air Quality Score	21	44	Healthcare Cost Index	177.4	100
Water Quality Score	44	33	Cost per Doctor Visit	$84	$74
Pollen/Allergy Score	63	61	Cost per Dentist Visit	$86	$67
Stress Score	50	49	Cost per Hospital Room	$1,818	$702
Cancer Mortality Rate	186.4	168.9			

Weston, FL

Area Type: Outer suburb

Zip Code: 33326

Metro Area: Fort Lauderdale, FL

Metro Area Type: Large

Location: 19 miles west of downtown Fort Lauderdale

Time Zone: Eastern Standard Time

Pros:
Local government and planning
Schools
Winter climate

Cons:
Growth pressure
Some long commutes
High and rising cost of living

Streets and sidewalks in front, canal and boats in back—this description fits most homes in the western Broward County planned community of Weston. The city of Weston covers 25 square miles, and about a third of that consists of lakes, canals, and wetlands.

Among the best places in this book, Weston has a truly unique feel and makeup. Its building plan created sweeping, curved roads and boulevards with a system of navigable, finished canals running behind developed lots. Schools, a small commercial area, and a number of common spaces were drawn directly into the plan. The innovative city government is set up as a "contract city"—meaning there are only three full-time employees. The rest is contracted out on a retainer and per-service basis, eliminating such financial burdens as pension obligations and allowing the city to better adjust services to meet needs and to adapt to growth. The city, in fact, is being studied across the country as a model for such administration. Recently, Weston annexed Bonaventure to the south, an area with a similar physical plan but with housing more attractive to retirees. Weston itself is far more family oriented, with about 31% of households categorized as married with children.

Fort Lauderdale may be described as a "typical" south Florida coastal city. Palm-tree–lined barrier island beach areas, high-rise hotels, and wealthy residential enclaves give way to an attractive downtown core, which then gives way to a less attractive mix of new and some gritty older commercial activity, airports, and lower-income residential areas to the west of the city. Farther west on the coastal plain, the area becomes more typically suburban, with malls and fairly typical housing that end abruptly at the wetlands of the Everglades. Major roads are laid out in a conventional grid, and today, most developable land areas have already been developed, giving the area a spread-out feel.

Today, Fort Lauderdale is more of a real city than a tourist attraction, although the college spring-break rush is a major annual event. The coastal area just east of downtown has a series of lagoons with plenty of boating and waterfront entertainment activities. Shadowed a bit by Miami, 30 miles south, Fort Lauderdale still has a few amenities of its own, including the Florida Panthers NHL team, a major international airport, a large science museum, and an IMAX theater complex.

Standard of Living Weston is a fairly upscale suburb, though nothing like Palm Beach, Boca Raton, and other very upscale areas closer to the water. The Cost of Living Index has risen to 148, sizably higher than our other Florida choices. Detached family homes run $400K to $450K. Attractive and spacious townhomes oriented to families are a popular choice; 1,800 square feet might sell for somewhere in the high $300Ks. Jobs are plentiful and diverse: American Express operates a large processing center; Office Depot, headquartered 45 minutes away in Delray, has facilities here; and many national companies have regional offices in the Fort Lauderdale area. Future job growth is projected at a moderate 13% and recent job trends are favorable. Property taxes are a reasonable 1.5%.

Education Weston is one of a few communities in Florida to have schools all receiving a grade "A" from the Florida Department of Education, and is the only such district in Broward County. The schools are a strong attraction; families move in from other parts of the Miami and Fort Lauderdale area just for the schools. The well-planned street and sidewalk infrastructure allows kids to ride bicycles safely to school (and, in fact, bicycles are popular for all ages).

Lifestyle The Weston lifestyle is laid-back, quiet, and oriented to the year-round outdoor climate. A large nearby Broward County regional park and YMCA with an aquatic center offer family and teen activities. A small Philharmonic Society and a few other small performing arts venues are also in Weston. Outside of Weston, a full variety of services are available in Fort Lauderdale, the Palm Beach area, Miami, and the Everglades to the west, all within an hour's reach. Beaches are 25 miles away, and Orlando is about 3 hours north.

Downtown Fort Lauderdale is a 30- to 45-minute commute, and driving to downtown Miami takes 45 minutes to an hour. Some go north about 40 minutes to the Palm Beach–Sawgrass area. At this time, there are no alternatives to commuting by car.

The natural area is a flat, marshy coastal plain with grasses and some areas of tropical forests. The Weston development is a mix of tailored canals and open wetlands immediately adjacent to the wild marshlands to the west. The climate is subtropical with long, hot summer days often marked by afternoon thunderstorms. The winter climate is dry and mild, and outdoor activities are possible year-round.

Health & Safety Typical of bigger cities in the region, crime is high, but not too high, in Weston. A Cleveland Clinic hospital and the Dan Marino Children's Hospital add to a strong hospital and healthcare picture.

Nearby Neighborhoods Coral Springs to the north is another planned community with a more diverse and generally less expensive housing base, but it tends to be oriented toward retirees and empty nesters. Pembroke Pines to the south is less planned and more expensive. Neither has the same quality of schools.

WESTON, FL NEIGHBORHOOD HIGHLIGHTS	
PEOPLE	
Population	32,679
15-yr Population Growth	39.80%
5-yr Population Growth	8.10%
% Married w/Children	30.6%
% Single w/Children	7.9%
No. of Households	11,725
Median Age	33.9
Avg. Household Size	2.79
Diversity Measure	53
STANDARD OF LIVING	
Median Household Income	$71,176
% Household Income > $100K	27%
Projected Future Job Growth	13%
Cost of Living Index	148
Buying Power Index	107
Weekly Daycare Cost	$160
Median Home Price	$243,000
"Sweet Spot" Home Price	$425,000
Home Price Ratio	3.4
Median Age of Homes	10.9
% Homes Owned	71%
Effective Property Tax Rate	1.50%
Estimated Property Tax Bill	$6,375
EDUCATION	
% High School Graduates	94%
% 4-yr Degree	27%
% Graduate or Professional Degree	16%
$ Invested per Pupil	$5,180
Student/Teacher Ratio	19.6
Primary Test Score Percentile	118.2
Secondary Test Score Percentile	106.8
% Subsidized School Lunch	11.30%
% Attending Public School	74%
LIFESTYLE	
Leisure Rating (Area)	8
Arts & Culture Rating (Area)	2
Climate Rating (Area)	8
Physical Setting Rating	4
Downtown Core Rating	5
% Commute < 30 Min.	44%
% Commute > 1 Hour	10%
HEALTH & SAFETY	
Health Rating (Area)	7
Stress Score (Area)	8
Violent Crime Risk	46
Property Crime Risk	48

FT. LAUDERDALE, FL
AREA HIGHLIGHTS

PEOPLE

SIZE & DIVERSITY	AREA	U.S. AVG	FAMILY DEMOGRAPHICS	AREA	U.S. AVG
Population	1,754,893		% Married	52.50%	53.80%
15-yr Population Growth	39.80%	4.40%	% Single	47.50%	46.20%
Diversity Measure	57	54	% Divorced	10.70%	10.20%
% Religiously Observant	46%	50%	% Separated	3.30%	2.10%
% Catholic	21%	22%	% Married w/Children	19.90%	27.90%
% Protestant	11%	25%	% Single w/Children	8.50%	9.40%
% Jewish	13%	2%	% Married, No Children	30.40%	31.00%
% Other	0%	1%	% Single, No Children	41.10%	31.70%

STANDARD OF LIVING

INCOME, EMPLOYMENT & TAXES	AREA	U.S. AVG	COST OF LIVING & HOUSING	AREA	U.S. AVG
Median Household Income	$44,799	$44,684	Cost of Living Index	112.9	100
Household Income Growth	4.20%	6.10%	Buying Power Index	89	100
Unemployment Rate	4.20%	5.10%	Median Home Price	$381,800	$208,500
Recent Job Growth	4.10%	1.30%	Home Price Ratio	8.5	4.7
Projected Future Job Growth	16.30%	10.50%	Home Price Appreciation	28.50%	13.60%
State Income Tax Rate	0%	5.00%	% Homes Owned	63%	64.10%
State Sales Tax Rate	6%	6.00%	Median Rent	$998	$792

EDUCATION

ATTAINMENT & ACHIEVEMENT	AREA	U.S. AVG	RESOURCES & INVESTMENT	AREA	U.S. AVG
% High School Graduate	81.90%	83.90%	No. of Highly Ranked Universities	0	1
% 2-yr Graduate	10%	7.10%	$ Invested per Pupil	$5,453	$6,058
% 4-yr Graduate	20.20%	17.20%	Student/Teacher Ratio	21.1	15.9
% Graduate or Professional Degree	9.70%	9.90%	State University In-State Tuition	$2,955	$4,917
% Attending Public School	86.30%	84.30%			
75th Percentile State University SAT Score (Verbal)	570	477			
75th Percentile State University SAT Score (Math)	590	478			
75th Percentile State University ACT Score	N/A	20			

LIFESTYLE

RECREATION, ARTS & CULTURE	AREA	U.S. AVG	INFRASTRUCTURE & FACILITIES	AREA	U.S. AVG
Professional Sports Rating	8	4	No. of Public Libraries	41	28
Zoos & Aquariums Rating	2	3	Library Volumes Per Capita	1.6	2.8
Amusement Park Rating	3	3	No. of Warehouse Clubs	8	4
Professional Theater Rating	3	3	No. of Starbucks	28	5
Overall Museum Rating	6	6	Golf Course Rating	8	4
Science Museum Rating	6	4	National Park Rating	5	3
Children's Museum Rating	5	3	Sq. Mi. Inland Water	3	4

CLIMATE			COMMUTE & TRANSPORTATION		
Days Mostly Sunny	248	212	Avg. Daily Commute Time	27.4	24.7
Annual Days Precipitation	129	111	% Commute by Auto	81%	77.70%
Annual Days > 90°F	30	38	Per Capita Avg. Daily Transit Miles	15.5	7.9
Annual Days < 32°F	0	88	Annual Auto Insurance Premium	$1,429	$1,314
July Relative Humidity	75	69	Gas, Cost per Gallon	$2.96	$3.05

HEALTH & SAFETY

CRIME & ENVIRNOMENTAL ISSUES	AREA	U.S. AVG	HEALTHCARE & COST	AREA	U.S. AVG
Violent Crime Rate	524	517	Physicians per Capita	223.9	254.3
Change in Violent Crime	-20.10%	-7.50%	Pediatricians per Capita	20.3	16.9
Property Crime Rate	3476	3783	Hospital Beds per Capita	422.1	239.7
Change in Property Crime	-28.40%	-10.10%	No. of Teaching Hospitals	7	1.9
Air Quality Score	8	44	Healthcare Cost Index	116.7	100
Water Quality Score	50	33	Cost per Doctor Visit	$83	$74
Pollen/Allergy Score	49	61	Cost per Dentist Visit	$78	$67
Stress Score	83	49	Cost per Hospital Room	$745	$702
Cancer Mortality Rate	163.9	168.9			

Wichita (West), KS

Area Type: Inner suburb

Zip Code: 67212

Metro Area: Wichita, KS

Metro Area Type: Smaller

Location: Southeast-central Kansas, 9 miles west of downtown Wichita

Time Zone: Central Standard Time

Pros:
> Cost of living
> Cost of housing
> Active downtown redevelopment

Cons:
> Economic cycles
> Harsh climate
> Physical setting

Once a cow town and cattle-drive railhead, Wichita boomed in the 1920s with the discovery of oil. A few oil-rich capitalists hooked up their fortunes with entrepreneurs named Stearman, Beech, and Cessna to try their hands at the new high-tech play of the day—aviation. And then, in the early stages of World War II, someone at the U.S. War Department looked at a map to find the least vulnerable place to manufacture wartime aircraft. The existing aviation base and the location near the then-center of the continental United States directed that map pin to Wichita.

On the banks of the Arkansas River in the south-central part of the state, Wichita is now the largest city in Kansas. The river meanders freely between its outer banks during dry spells and fills during the rainy season, cycles typical of such Great Plains rivers. The Wichita economy has similar cycles, and unfortunately things have been a bit dry for the past few years. The aviation-based economy has relied on business from airframe and services suppliers like Boeing, Cessna, Bombardier, and Raytheon, and the manufacture of many precision tools and parts to support this industry, and these businesses are just now recovering from a 3-year downturn. Although Wichita is far from being completely dependent on these employers, they do constitute a large percentage of the value-added manufacturing jobs, so any downturn in this sector is felt throughout the area. Business conditions in the aviation sector are expected to continue improving, however, and job opportunities are expected to grow, particularly as some 40% of the area's skilled labor force will reach retirement age in the next 5 years. The latest recent job-growth figure, 4.5%, gives reason for optimism.

Recognizing that some of its best-trained and -educated workers have moved away during the recent downturn, the city has taken steps to attract newcomers and improve its livability. Redevelopment initiatives have had positive effects on downtown, midtown, and riverfront areas. Wichita is working through some of these transitions to create an attractive, inviting community with a local economy less dependent on manufacturing and less vulnerable to the peaks and valleys of the aviation business. Yes, the area is a bit of a diamond in the rough, but the chosen neighborhood on the west side of Wichita, west of I-235 and the Arkansas River, has excellent housing values, one of the lowest cost profiles on our list, and a strong married-with-children percentage of 32.5%. Patient families will like the low cost, relatively easy lifestyle, and strong community feel.

Standard of Living Wichita has one of the lowest costs of living in the country, largely driven by the low cost of housing. The Cost of Living Index is a modest 88, and even with relatively low incomes, the Buying Power Index is a relatively high 130 and the Home Price Ratio is an enviable 2.4. The area is one of few examined with good homes below $150K. There are more qualifying four-bedroom listings below $150K than above $200K, and 90% of some 900 homes listed at press time were under $250K. Values are excellent, with the "sweet spot" between $150K and $170K. Spend $200K and you can get a 3,250-square-foot, two-story, five-bedroom, 13-year-old Tudor with a basement—for example. You get the idea. Older homes, some with larger lots, can be even better values. When shopping, be aware that in Wichita, basements can be included in square footage because the location in an area of tornado activity makes basements "popular," as one local real estate agent put it. Property taxes average about 1.1%.

Education Most of the area within the 67212 zip code attends the smallish Maize school district (with six schools), and test scores are consistently above average.

WICHITA (WEST), KS NEIGHBORHOOD HIGHLIGHTS	
PEOPLE	
Population	46,754
15-yr Population Growth	14.90%
5-yr Population Growth	2.40%
% Married w/Children	32.5%
% Single w/Children	9.0%
No. of Households	18,113
Median Age	34.4
Avg. Household Size	2.59
Diversity Measure	22
STANDARD OF LIVING	
Median Household Income	$50,871
% Household Income > $100K	10%
Projected Future Job Growth	9%
Cost of Living Index	88.4
Buying Power Index	130
Weekly Daycare Cost	$149
Median Home Price	$121,500
"Sweet Spot" Home Price	$160,000
Home Price Ratio	2.4
Median Age of Homes	19.3
% Homes Owned	69%
Effective Property Tax Rate	1.10%
Estimated Property Tax Bill	$1,760
EDUCATION	BEST
% High School Graduates	92%
% 4-yr Degree	25%
% Graduate or Professional Degree	9%
$ Invested per Pupil	$5,506
Student/Teacher Ratio	15.4
Primary Test Score Percentile	88.5
Secondary Test Score Percentile	102.8
% Subsidized School Lunch	49.70%
% Attending Public School	74.90%
LIFESTYLE	
Leisure Rating (Area)	3
Arts & Culture Rating (Area)	8
Climate Rating (Area)	6
Physical Setting Rating	2
Downtown Core Rating	2
% Commute < 30 Min.	82%
% Commute > 1 Hour	2%
HEALTH & SAFETY	
Health Rating (Area)	4
Stress Score (Area)	5
Violent Crime Risk	62
Property Crime Risk	52

The 1,600-student Maize High School typically scores 14% to 18% above state averages on the Kansas State Assessments. Wichita State University brings 14,000 students to town and adds some college-town ambience.

Lifestyle Wichita offers a good selection of art, science, and historical museums; a regional symphony orchestra; and a number of special attractions, including an aviation museum and a children's science museum. The city provides an extensive arts-and-crafts program, recreational facilities, and organized leagues for team sports and sports instruction. The well-regarded Sedgwick County Zoo is a popular family destination.

Commutes are generally easy, because the city is laid out on a grid with major north–south and east–west routes crossing in the center of town and beltways around the city. Many of the city's industrial parks are located to the north and west and are an easy 10- to 15-minute commute from the western parts of the Wichita area.

Most of the area is flat with a few hills to the north of town. The climate is Great Plains continental, and winters can be severe for the latitude, with many days below freezing but with light snowfall. Summer highs are in the mid-90s with hotter spells, but humidity is not oppressive. Spring and early summer are tornado seasons, and the threat is high for an urban area.

Health & Safety Crime rates are somewhat higher than national averages but dropping slowly. Health facilities are adequate but not abundant for a town this size, and the costs are around national averages.

Nearby Neighborhoods Most attractive family areas are west, north, and northeast of the city. A few miles to the north across 21st Street, the zip code 67205 is an area of newer, more expensive homes worth a look; these homes are excellent for the prices paid.

WICHITA, KS
AREA HIGHLIGHTS

PEOPLE

SIZE & DIVERSITY	AREA	U.S. AVG	FAMILY DEMOGRAPHICS	AREA	U.S. AVG
Population	559,399		% Married	59.90%	53.80%
15-yr Population Growth	15.30%	4.40%	% Single	40.10%	46.20%
Diversity Measure	36	54	% Divorced	8.90%	10.20%
% Religiously Observant	48%	50%	% Separated	1.80%	2.10%
% Catholic	13%	22%	% Married w/Children	31.70%	27.90%
% Protestant	34%	25%	% Single w/Children	8.50%	9.40%
% Jewish	0%	2%	% Married, No Children	30.80%	31.00%
% Other	0%	1%	% Single, No Children	27.60%	31.70%

STANDARD OF LIVING

INCOME, EMPLOYMENT & TAXES	AREA	U.S. AVG	COST OF LIVING & HOUSING	AREA	U.S. AVG
Median Household Income	$42,199	$44,684	Cost of Living Index	81.9	100
Household Income Growth	5.40%	6.10%	Buying Power Index	115	100
Unemployment Rate	5.40%	5.10%	Median Home Price	$106,300	$208,500
Recent Job Growth	4.50%	1.30%	Home Price Ratio	2.5	4.7
Projected Future Job Growth	12.10%	10.50%	Home Price Appreciation	2.30%	13.60%
State Income Tax Rate	6.30%	5.00%	% Homes Owned	68.90%	64.10%
State Sales Tax Rate	5.90%	6.00%	Median Rent	$624	$792

EDUCATION

ATTAINMENT & ACHIEVEMENT	AREA	U.S. AVG	RESOURCES & INVESTMENT	AREA	U.S. AVG
% High School Graduate	84.20%	83.90%	No. of Highly Ranked Universities	0	1
% 2-yr Graduate	7.30%	7.10%	$ Invested per Pupil	$5,477	$6,058
% 4-yr Graduate	20.10%	17.20%	Student/Teacher Ratio	16.1	15.9
% Graduate or Professional Degree	7.70%	9.90%	State University In-State Tuition	$4,737	$4,917
% Attending Public School	90.30%	84.30%			
75th Percentile State University SAT Score (Verbal)	N/A	477			
75th Percentile State University SAT Score (Math)	N/A	478			
75th Percentile State University ACT Score	21	20			

LIFESTYLE

RECREATION, ARTS & CULTURE	AREA	U.S. AVG	INFRASTRUCTURE & FACILITIES	AREA	U.S. AVG
Professional Sports Rating	3	4	No. of Public Libraries	38	28
Zoos & Aquariums Rating	5	3	Library Volumes Per Capita	3.7	2.8
Amusement Park Rating	4	3	No. of Warehouse Clubs	4	4
Professional Theater Rating	1	3	No. of Starbucks	7	5
Overall Museum Rating	8	6	Golf Course Rating	3	4
Science Museum Rating	8	4	National Park Rating	1	3
Children's Museum Rating	7	3	Sq. Mi. Inland Water	2	4

CLIMATE			COMMUTE & TRANSPORTATION		
Days Mostly Sunny	224	212	Avg. Daily Commute Time	19.1	24.7
Annual Days Precipitation	84	111	% Commute by Auto	80%	77.70%
Annual Days > 90°F	62	38	Per Capita Avg. Daily Transit Miles	4.6	7.9
Annual Days < 32°F	114	88	Annual Auto Insurance Premium	$1,023	$1,314
July Relative Humidity	66	69	Gas, Cost per Gallon	$3.08	$3.05

HEALTH & SAFETY

CRIME & ENVIRNOMENTAL ISSUES	AREA	U.S. AVG	HEALTHCARE & COST	AREA	U.S. AVG
Violent Crime Rate	471	517	Physicians per Capita	243	254.3
Change in Violent Crime	-1.60%	-7.50%	Pediatricians per Capita	12.2	16.9
Property Crime Rate	4414	3783	Hospital Beds per Capita	425.4	239.7
Change in Property Crime	-14.60%	-10.10%	No. of Teaching Hospitals	4	1.9
Air Quality Score	26	44	Healthcare Cost Index	99.7	100
Water Quality Score	41	33	Cost per Doctor Visit	$69	$74
Pollen/Allergy Score	58	61	Cost per Dentist Visit	$79	$67
Stress Score	52	49	Cost per Hospital Room	$843	$702
Cancer Mortality Rate	162.3	168.9			

Winchester, VA

Area Type: Small town

Zip Code: 22602

Metro Area: Winchester, VA

Metro Area Type: Smallest

Location: Northern Virginia, north end of Shenandoah Valley

Time Zone: Eastern Standard Time

Pros:

Historic downtown
Attractive setting
Strong economy

Cons:

Growth and sprawl
Rising home prices
Low educational attainment

The planet Courescant probably comes to mind for most Star Wars fans when watching the bustling Washington, DC, and Dulles Corridor areas south of the Potomac. People coming and going at all hours in all directions; traffic everywhere, seemingly in three dimensions; buildings; lights; nonstop commerce; nonstop activity. So where do overwhelmed families go to get away from it all? Where is the Tatooine of Northern Virginia? One answer is Winchester, located in the "outer rim," as locals say, of the DC area.

For the small but growing town of Winchester, attractively perched in the northern end of the Shenandoah Valley, being a strategic location isn't a new claim to fame. Winchester changed hands 72 times during the Civil War. Why? Not only is it a nice place in the center of a productive agricultural area, but it also offers prime access to the Shenandoah Valley and some of the best parts of Virginia, points north into Maryland and Pennsylvania, east into DC and the Potomac area, and west into the mountains. Families looking for a laid-back, rural, historic small town close to DC and within a reasonable shot of other major eastern cities find a lot to like in Winchester.

Winchester's historic and agricultural roots are still firmly planted. The downtown core is classic and could be a movie set for any Civil War or 19th-century film, with well-kept old brick commercial buildings, brick and stone streets, and period homes. A 4-block pedestrian mall anchors the center. While Winchester is proud of its past, the city is a well-kept mix of old and new. A strong sense of architecture and style leads to modern brick buildings mixed in well with the classic older buildings. The downtown area has a 125-acre Technology Zone, where technology-oriented businesses gain tax benefits. Employers are diverse, ranging from food processors like Kraft and National Fruit

Products to manufacturers like Rubbermaid and Trex (synthetic building materials). There are more jobs in a narrow tax-advantaged industrial corridor in the West Virginia panhandle just to the north.

Of course, some residents commute "over the mountain" to the DC–Northern Virginia area. Washington, DC, is a bit far away—about 80 miles—but the prosperous Dulles Airport area is 55 miles and an hour to 2 hours away, depending on the specific employment destination. For occasional excursions, Baltimore is 3 hours away and Philadelphia is about 4. Today's Winchester is becoming more crowded and more of a cosmopolitan bedroom community, which concerns many longtime residents. But for those who make the choice to commute, and, even better, for those who work in the area or are self-employed, traveling to the big cities only occasionally, Winchester is a great blend of historic country town and strategic modern-day location for professional working families. The married-with-children percentage of households is 29.9%.

Standard of Living   Winchester has been discovered, and unfortunately, that has driven real estate prices and living costs up in recent years. Family homes start in the $250K range with a "sweet spot" at $350K to $400K, expensive but still attractive compared to most DC suburbs. There's a variety of housing on all sides of town as well as in the city center. While homes are expensive, the overall cost of living has held the line (COL Index 94) and for those with "citified" incomes, this cost profile looks very attractive. Property taxes are a very reasonable 0.7%, although Virginia does tax intangible assets like investments.

Education   With only 14% of residents possessing a 4-year degree, low local educational attainment scores reflected the area's agrarian roots. But the numbers are growing more recently as the population shifts. While many new residents initially sent their kids to private schools, the city-run public school system, with notably attractive buildings, has been working hard to keep up with growth. Test scores are at and slightly above Virginia averages. Shenandoah University brings 2,500 undergraduate and graduate students to the area, and more than 20 other colleges and universities are within 125 miles.

Lifestyle The 180-acre Jim Barnett park near downtown offers full sports facilities, an outdoor and an indoor pool, playground areas, and a fishing lake. There are many historic sites, farms, old homes, and orchards open to the public, notables including the Stonewall Jackson Headquarters and the Apple Trail orchards. Cultural activities originate at the university; there is also a well-attended children's theater. The Shenandoah Valley Discovery Museum is a fun hands-on center designed for all ages. A 2-hour trip significantly expands your options of thing to do, with the DC area, King's Dominion amusement park north of Richmond, Civil War sites, historic Charlottesville to the south, state parks, and plenty of outdoor recreation south and west.

Locals do complain about growth and traffic issues, which naturally come from being so close to the rapidly growing DC area. Commutes to the DC area are possible but might not be dependable for the long term as traffic loads grow and gas prices escalate.

The immediate area is flat and mostly agricultural. Mountains protect it from all directions except the northeast, and the climate here is mild for the region, albeit with four distinct seasons.

Health & Safety The crime risk is moderate, and locals are nervous about the effects of growth and tie-in with the bigger city. Air quality is very high for the region. Healthcare is good and anchored by the 403-bed Winchester Medical Center. For more major health issues, Johns Hopkins University and University of Virginia facilities aren't far.

Nearby Neighborhoods Winchester is small enough that the choice of specific residential area matters little. Development surrounds the city. Some, especially those doing a DC commute, look to the east side (22602 zip code), which also has the highest married-with-children percentage at 31%. Excellent older homes exist down-

town. Good homes and home sites can be found in the nearby mountains, and some families looking for the small Shenandoah town lifestyle without the bedroom-community influence look to Harrisonburg 70 miles southwest.

WINCHESTER, VA NEIGHBORHOOD HIGHLIGHTS	
PEOPLE	
Population	23,537
15-yr Population Growth	45.70%
5-yr Population Growth	12.50%
% Married w/Children	29.9%
% Single w/Children	9.1%
No. of Households	8,807
Median Age	35.5
Avg. Household Size	2.66
Diversity Measure	14
STANDARD OF LIVING	
Median Household Income	$53,651
% Household Income > $100K	12%
Projected Future Job Growth	16%
Cost of Living Index	94.1
Buying Power Index	127
Weekly Daycare Cost	$135
Median Home Price	$242,800
"Sweet Spot" Home Price	$375,000
Home Price Ratio	4.5
Median Age of Homes	18.4
% Homes Owned	75%
Effective Property Tax Rate	0.70%
Estimated Property Tax Bill	$ 2,7.5
EDUCATION	
% High School Graduates	81%
% 4-yr Degree	14%
% Graduate or Professional Degree	7%
$ Invested per Pupil	$5,223
Student/Teacher Ratio	15.1
Primary Test Score Percentile	97.1
Secondary Test Score Percentile	109.4
% Subsidized School Lunch	19.30%
% Attending Public School	88%
LIFESTYLE	BEST
Leisure Rating (Area)	5
Arts & Culture Rating (Area)	5
Climate Rating (Area)	8
Physical Setting Rating	5
Downtown Core Rating	7
% Commute < 30 Min.	67%
% Commute > 1 Hour	13%
HEALTH & SAFETY	BEST
Health Rating (Area)	6
Stress Score (Area)	6
Violent Crime Risk	70
Property Crime Risk	148

WINCHESTER, VA
AREA HIGHLIGHTS

PEOPLE

SIZE & DIVERSITY	AREA	U.S. AVG		FAMILY DEMOGRAPHICS	AREA	U.S. AVG
Population	66,611			% Married	61.60%	53.80%
15-yr Population Growth	45.70%	4.40%		% Single	38.40%	46.20%
Diversity Measure	13	54		% Divorced	7.40%	10.20%
% Religiously Observant	31%	50%		% Separated	4.10%	2.10%
% Catholic	0%	22%		% Married w/Children	31.70%	27.90%
% Protestant	25%	25%		% Single w/Children	8.90%	9.40%
% Jewish	0%	2%		% Married, No Children	34%	31.00%
% Other	6%	1%		% Single, No Children	25.40%	31.70%

STANDARD OF LIVING

INCOME, EMPLOYMENT & TAXES	AREA	U.S. AVG		COST OF LIVING & HOUSING	AREA	U.S. AVG
Median Household Income	$51,686	$44,684		Cost of Living Index	91.5	100
Household Income Growth	2%	6.10%		Buying Power Index	126	100
Unemployment Rate	2%	5.10%		Median Home Price	$186,300	$208,500
Recent Job Growth	1.10%	1.30%		Home Price Ratio	3.6	4.7
Projected Future Job Growth	16.50%	10.50%		Home Price Appreciation	18.60%	13.60%
State Income Tax Rate	5.80%	5.00%		% Homes Owned	74.80%	64.10%
State Sales Tax Rate	4.50%	6.00%		Median Rent	$647	$792

EDUCATION

ATTAINMENT & ACHIEVEMENT	AREA	U.S. AVG		RESOURCES & INVESTMENT	AREA	U.S. AVG
% High School Graduate	71.70%	83.90%		No. of Highly Ranked Universities	0	1
% 2-yr Graduate	6.50%	7.10%		$ Invested per Pupil	$5,303	$6,058
% 4-yr Graduate	14.10%	17.20%		Student/Teacher Ratio	15	15.9
% Graduate or Professional Degree	4.90%	9.90%		State University In-State Tuition	$5,838	$4,917
% Attending Public School	92%	84.30%				
75th Percentile State University SAT Score (Verbal)	540	477				
75th Percentile State University SAT Score (Math)	560	478				
75th Percentile State University ACT Score	N/A	20				

LIFESTYLE

RECREATION, ARTS & CULTURE	AREA	U.S. AVG		INFRASTRUCTURE & FACILITIES	AREA	U.S. AVG
Professional Sports Rating	7	4		No. of Public Libraries	7	28
Zoos & Aquariums Rating	8	3		Library Volumes Per Capita	20.2	2.8
Amusement Park Rating	2	3		No. of Warehouse Clubs	7	4
Professional Theater Rating	8	3		No. of Starbucks	0	5
Overall Museum Rating	8	6		Golf Course Rating	8	4
Science Museum Rating	8	4		National Park Rating	4	3
Children's Museum Rating	8	3		Sq. Mi. Inland Water	8	4

CLIMATE				COMMUTE & TRANSPORTATION		
Days Mostly Sunny	206	212		Avg. Daily Commute Time	27.3	24.7
Annual Days Precipitation	118	111		% Commute by Auto	79%	77.70%
Annual Days > 90°F	33	38		Per Capita Avg. Daily Transit Miles	20.7	7.9
Annual Days < 32°F	80	88		Annual Auto Insurance Premium	$1,365	$1,314
July Relative Humidity	65	69		Gas, Cost per Gallon	$3.15	$3.05

HEALTH & SAFETY

CRIME & ENVIRNOMENTAL ISSUES	AREA	U.S. AVG		HEALTHCARE & COST	AREA	U.S. AVG
Violent Crime Rate	112	517		Physicians per Capita	120.8	254.3
Change in Violent Crime	8.10%	-7.50%		Pediatricians per Capita	1.5	16.9
Property Crime Rate	2035	3783		Hospital Beds per Capita	651.5	239.7
Change in Property Crime	-8.40%	-10.10%		No. of Teaching Hospitals	1	1.9
Air Quality Score	58	44		Healthcare Cost Index	86.3	100
Water Quality Score	55	33		Cost per Doctor Visit	$62	$74
Pollen/Allergy Score	65	61		Cost per Dentist Visit	$73	$67
Stress Score	55	49		Cost per Hospital Room	$650	$702
Cancer Mortality Rate	171.6	168.9				

Winters, CA

Area Type: Small town

Zip Code: 95694

Metro Area: Yolo County, CA

Metro Area Type: Smallest

Location: 30 miles west of Sacramento, CA, along I-505

Time Zone: Pacific Standard Time

Pros:
Small-town flavor
Attractive climate
Relatively affordable housing

Cons:
Long commutes
Schools
High home prices

On the surface, the sleepy Central Valley agricultural town of Winters may seem too small and lacking in jobs or amenities to be seriously considered as a family place. But upon closer examination, this sleepy farming community is just starting to wake up to its potential and its location, which is quite central to many of the "happening" places in Northern California.

Tucked into the east flank of California's Coast Range, Winters is one of hundreds of small agricultural towns that dot the landscape of California's 450-mile-long Central Valley. To all directions except the mountainous west are expansive fields of rice, corn, and tomatoes mixed in with neat and colorful orchards of almonds, plums, cherries, apricots, and olives, all set among miles of levee roads harnessing the Sacramento River and its tributaries. Spend a few hours in Winters (a walking tour of the entire town takes about 15 minutes) and it becomes easy to forget that you're 30 minutes from the San Francisco Bay, just over an hour from San Francisco, and 20 minutes from the state capital in Sacramento.

Besides being near San Francisco and Sacramento, Winters is also close to the rapidly expanding exurbs of Solano County, with strong job growth in Vacaville and Fairfield to the south, and it's 10 miles west of Davis, a beautiful college town and home of the University of California campus of that name. Lake Berryessa, to the west in the mountains, is a very popular camping and boating destination, and if you drive a bit farther west on the rugged SR 128, you'll soon drop down into the world-famous Napa Valley wine region. Another hour gets you to the rugged California coast south of Mendocino. You're starting to get the idea.

If it sounds like the best part of Winters is the getting out of it, then we may be overstating the case. Winters itself is a classic small town with a wide Main Street business district anchored by the Buckhorn, a famous regional restaurant and watering hole. It's peaceful and quiet, with just enough local conveniences. The quality, quantity, and accessibility of nearby cultural and recreational opportunities is part of what makes this place tick, and as more amenities come closer, we expect they'll do so in a well-planned way that doesn't spoil the local landscape or lifestyle.

Standard of Living   With a small population and few large employers in the immediate area, the city is finding it a challenge to maintain and grow some basic city services, but a recent redevelopment plan addresses these issues, and should provide for well-managed growth. High-paying jobs are found in Davis and in new technology parks in Vacaville with a broad assortment of jobs in the I-80 corridor. Recent job- and future job-growth figures are a relatively strong 2.9% and 18% respectively. New growth in "West Sac" may produce new employment opportunities.

Homes in Winters are expensive but relatively affordable on a California scale. An 1,800-square-foot home on a standard lot will cost about $450K and a 3,000-square-foot home about $600K. Median price statistics aren't very illuminating because data includes a large number of rural homes on significant acreage. We attribute the high Home Price Ratio to high median home prices influenced by the presence of higher-priced acreage homes and median income statistics diminished by the presence of agricultural workers. There are also a large number of older, smaller homes in the area; 50% of homes were built before 1970. North and west of downtown is an area of newer, larger homes on standard lots, with some homes on larger (3-plus-acre) lots available in the $800K to $900K range. So far, the area has avoided the crowded "California sprawl" look emerging along I-80, and is taking the "good growth" path of its neighbor Davis.

WINTERS, CA
NEIGHBORHOOD HIGHLIGHTS

PEOPLE

Population	9,228
15-yr Population Growth	30.60%
5-yr Population Growth	9.30%
% Married w/Children	35.3%
% Single w/Children	12.5%
No. of Households	2,965
Median Age	33.2
Avg. Household Size	3.16
Diversity Measure	70

STANDARD OF LIVING

Median Household Income	$52,850
% Household Income > $100K	13%
Projected Future Job Growth	18%
Cost of Living Index	131
Buying Power Index	93
Weekly Daycare Cost	$120
Median Home Price	$408,800
"Sweet Spot" Home Price	$500,000
Home Price Ratio	7.7
Median Age of Homes	23.4
% Homes Owned	64%
Effective Property Tax Rate	1.10%
Estimated Property Tax Bill	$5,500

EDUCATION

% High School Graduates	74%
% 4-yr Degree	15%
% Graduate or Professional Degree	8%
$ Invested per Pupil	$4,631
Student/Teacher Ratio	18.7
Primary Test Score Percentile	91.1
Secondary Test Score Percentile	96.3
% Subsidized School Lunch	46.20%
% Attending Public School	87.50%

LIFESTYLE

Leisure Rating (Area)	6
Arts & Culture Rating (Area)	3
Climate Rating (Area)	9
Physical Setting Rating	6
Downtown Core Rating	5
% Commute < 30 Min.	57%
% Commute > 1 Hour	8%

HEALTH & SAFETY

Health Rating (Area)	0
Stress Score (Area)	4
Violent Crime Risk	131
Property Crime Risk	141

Education Recently, schools in Winters have had problems meeting state standards. Most test scores, at all grade levels, are below state averages, and have not met adequate yearly progress goals established by No Child Left Behind. Some of this shortfall is attributed to the economically disadvantaged status of a percentage of students from farm-worker families, and may not be entirely reflective of the district's resources or practices.

Educational attainment also scores low; only 15% of residents have 4-year degrees and another 8% have graduate or professional degrees. Both of these issues are likely to improve as the area grows and evolves, and the nearby UC Davis casts a positive shadow.

Lifestyle If food gardening happens to be your thing, you've hit the jackpot with Winters. There are probably cheaper places to do it, but very few places where you can grow such a variety of foods. In your garden, you can grow almonds, cherries, oranges, avocados, tomatoes, corn, and just about anything else you can think of. The local climate, perfect for gardening, is good for many other year-round activities as well. Long, hot, quiet Mediterranean-style summers are characteristic of California agricultural areas. Summer average high temperatures are above 90°F with several 100-plus days. Delta breezes (usually) cool things off at night, with average summertime lows below 60°F. Most rain occurs in the cool, wet, and mostly freeze-free Mediterranean-style winter.

Entertainment and cultural activities are somewhat limited in Winters itself, but there are a city pool, summer arts and recreation programs, and a small but well-known community theater attracting visitors from the region. Beyond these resources, short drives to Davis (for entertainment and college-town amenities), Vacaville (for shopping), and Sacramento (for arts), among other areas, suffice.

Commutes vary. It's 15 minutes to Vacaville or Davis, a half-hour to Fairfield, or 40 minutes to the western reaches of Sacramento. Roads to this point are well suited to handle the load.

Health & Safety Crime rates for the Yolo County metro area are lower than national averages, show a healthy decrease, and are attractive on a California scale. That said, the "CAP"-appraised crime risk in Winters is a bit high. As with many California valley locations, there are air-quality issues, but the area's valley-west location makes it less vulnerable. Healthcare facilities in the immediate area are sparse, but they're quite good (though expensive) in Davis and Vacaville.

Nearby Neighborhoods Davis is an excellent choice, but significantly more expensive. Dixon, along I-80 to the south, offers the same location benefits and a greater home selection in California-style suburbs around a less attractive town core. Vacaville offers similar choices but is starting to get crowded. Crowding and price both escalate as you move west along I-80 toward the Bay Area.

YOLO COUNTY, CA
AREA HIGHLIGHTS

PEOPLE

SIZE & DIVERSITY	AREA	U.S. AVG	FAMILY DEMOGRAPHICS	AREA	U.S. AVG
Population	184,364		% Married	55.20%	53.80%
15-yr Population Growth	30.60%	4.40%	% Single	44.80%	46.20%
Diversity Measure	57	54	% Divorced	8.70%	10.20%
% Religiously Observant	32%	50%	% Separated	3.80%	2.10%
% Catholic	20%	22%	% Married w/Children	27.90%	27.90%
% Protestant	10%	25%	% Single w/Children	9.60%	9.40%
% Jewish	1%	2%	% Married, No Children	29.70%	31.00%
% Other	0%	1%	% Single, No Children	32.80%	31.70%

STANDARD OF LIVING

INCOME, EMPLOYMENT & TAXES	AREA	U.S. AVG	COST OF LIVING & HOUSING	AREA	U.S. AVG
Median Household Income	$45,335	$44,684	Cost of Living Index	135.2	100
Household Income Growth	5.10%	6.10%	Buying Power Index	75	100
Unemployment Rate	5.10%	5.10%	Median Home Price	$433,800	$208,500
Recent Job Growth	2.90%	1.30%	Home Price Ratio	9.6	4.7
Projected Future Job Growth	14%	10.50%	Home Price Appreciation	25.80%	13.60%
State Income Tax Rate	6%	5.00%	% Homes Owned	57.80%	64.10%
State Sales Tax Rate	7.30%	6.00%	Median Rent	$851	$792

EDUCATION

ATTAINMENT & ACHIEVEMENT	AREA	U.S. AVG	RESOURCES & INVESTMENT	AREA	U.S. AVG
% High School Graduate	74.70%	83.90%	No. of Highly Ranked Universities	0	1
% 2-yr Graduate	8.50%	7.10%	$ Invested per Pupil	$5,227	$6,058
% 4-yr Graduate	21.30%	17.20%	Student/Teacher Ratio	20	15.9
% Graduate or Professional Degree	11.10%	9.90%	State University In-State Tuition	$6,586	$4,917
% Attending Public School	92.60%	84.30%			
75th Percentile State University SAT Score (Verbal)	560	477			
75th Percentile State University SAT Score (Math)	600	478			
75th Percentile State University ACT Score	23	20			

LIFESTYLE

RECREATION, ARTS & CULTURE	AREA	U.S. AVG	INFRASTRUCTURE & FACILITIES	AREA	U.S. AVG
Professional Sports Rating	4	4	No. of Public Libraries	8	28
Zoos & Aquariums Rating	2	3	Library Volumes Per Capita	2.8	2.8
Amusement Park Rating	3	3	No. of Warehouse Clubs	1	4
Professional Theater Rating	3	3	No. of Starbucks	8	5
Overall Museum Rating	5	6	Golf Course Rating	2	4
Science Museum Rating	5	4	National Park Rating	7	3
Children's Museum Rating	3	3	Sq. Mi. Inland Water	4	4

CLIMATE			COMMUTE & TRANSPORTATION		
Days Mostly Sunny	276	212	Avg. Daily Commute Time	21.2	24.7
Annual Days Precipitation	60	111	% Commute by Auto	70%	77.70%
Annual Days > 90°F	82	38	Per Capita Avg. Daily Transit Miles	11.3	7.9
Annual Days < 32°F	25	88	Annual Auto Insurance Premium	$1,161	$1,314
July Relative Humidity	67	69	Gas, Cost per Gallon	$3.07	$3.05

HEALTH & SAFETY

CRIME & ENVIRNOMENTAL ISSUES	AREA	U.S. AVG	HEALTHCARE & COST	AREA	U.S. AVG
Violent Crime Rate	468	517	Physicians per Capita	329.4	254.3
Change in Violent Crime	-34.90%	-7.50%	Pediatricians per Capita	22.9	16.9
Property Crime Rate	3511	3783	Hospital Beds per Capita	95.2	239.7
Change in Property Crime	-3%	-10.10%	No. of Teaching Hospitals	1	1.9
Air Quality Score	43	44	Healthcare Cost Index	156.2	100
Water Quality Score	47	33	Cost per Doctor Visit	$72	$74
Pollen/Allergy Score	74	61	Cost per Dentist Visit	$81	$67
Stress Score	40	49	Cost per Hospital Room	$1,430	$702
Cancer Mortality Rate	176.9	168.9			

York, PA

Area Type: Small city

Zip Code: 17402

Metro Area: York, PA

Metro Area Type: Smaller

Location: Southeastern Pennsylvania 100 miles west of Philadelphia and 20 miles north of the Maryland border

Time Zone: Eastern Standard Time

Pros:
>Small-town flavor
>Central location
>Economic diversity

Cons:
>Lack of entertainment
>Lack of arts and culture
>Low educational attainment

Quiet, historic, and centrally located, York is a smaller city of about 45,000 in a populous, mostly rural county of almost 400,000. Parts of York look as they did 200 years ago, with older historic brick buildings of an agricultural and pre-industrial trade center mixed in among structures from the later-to-come Industrial Revolution. While there was some decay in the 1970s, today's downtown York has been revitalized, with some new buildings but a still overwhelmingly historic flavor and character.

Locationwise, York and York County are conveniently situated between Baltimore to the south and Harrisburg to the north. The south half of the county is tied economically and culturally to Baltimore, while the north half tends to look toward Harrisburg and Hershey. Gettysburg is 30 miles west, and Lancaster and the Pennsylvania Dutch country are 30 to 50 miles east, rounding out the cultural influences. Good family areas lie all around the county, but especially east and south toward the Maryland border. In the eastern sections of York, zip code 17402, 23% of households are married with children, and towns farther east have a still higher percentage.

The area's economy is diverse and a bit more working-class than other areas selected in Pennsylvania. Big manufacturers include Harley Davidson and York International, a maker of climate control systems. The area has a number of smaller manufacturers in a variety of industries, and agriculture is still important. Employment is steady and predicted to track national trends. Some residents, mainly on the south side, commute to Baltimore, 55 miles to the city center, to get a small-town lifestyle and some tax advantages over Maryland. Others commute north 25 miles to Harrisburg, the state capital. The area's proximity to the East Coast suggests a future influx of white-collar jobs and professionals moving into the area, looking to take advantage of low living costs and small-town life while still retaining access to the big cities.

Standard of Living Cost of Living in East York is moderate (COL Index 94), making the area attractive, especially among East Coast peers. Homes run about $100 per square foot, and good family homes can be bought for $200K to $220K with very nice homes available in the $250K range. Lot sizes are ample, 1/3 to 1/2 an acre, and colonial is the prevailing style of home. Property taxes vary considerably by town, township, school district, and location of industry, but they average around 1.5%. Even with relatively low median household incomes of $50K, the area is affordable.

Education Agricultural and manufacturing roots have brought relatively few degreed professionals into the area; the 4-year degree attainment rate in the metro area (including the county) is 12%, and for the eastern portions, 18%. That rate is likely to increase as white-collar professionals find the area and move in. The area has two small colleges: York College with 4,500 students and the Penn State York Campus with 1,800. Schools across the district test at about state averages, but schools to the east of the city show test results 10% to 20% above state averages.

Lifestyle The downtown area is active with theater, out-of-town performing arts acts, and restaurants. The area has a number of festivals, including the York County Fair, a hot rod convention, and an annual (no surprise) Harley get-together. The local lifestyle is laid-back and traditional, and possibly a bit too quiet for especially active families. Finding more entertainment often means trips to Baltimore, Hershey (35 miles north), or Allentown (Dorney Park, a large amusement park 100 miles northeast). Two hours away are larger Pennsylvania mountain areas, the eastern shore, Philadelphia, and Washington, DC.

Commutes vary. The Baltimore-area commute takes 45 minutes to an hour, depending on where in Baltimore and traffic. Harrisburg takes a half-hour and is a straight shot north. Local commutes are only 10 to 15 minutes maximum.

The area sits amid a rolling, mostly agricultural landscape. The climate is continental, with some shielding from harsh winter weather from the mountains to the northeast. Warm, still, and muggy spells are common in the summer.

Health & Safety For the York metro area, crime risk, stress, and allergy problems are relatively low, and crime statistics are improving. Healthcare facilities and resources are about average for this type of area, and costs are reasonable.

Nearby Neighborhoods The area is dotted with small suburbs and towns offering a family environment. Most are north toward Harrisburg or south and east. Etters to the north and the Red Lion area to the southeast are also worth a look.

YORK, PA NEIGHBORHOOD HIGHLIGHTS	
PEOPLE	
Population	45,616
15-yr Population Growth	18.30%
5-yr Population Growth	5.20%
% Married w/Children	23%
% Single w/Children	6.4%
No. of Households	18,179
Median Age	41.2
Avg. Household Size	2.36
Diversity Measure	16
STANDARD OF LIVING	
Median Household Income	$50,300
% Household Income > $100K	11%
Projected Future Job Growth	8%
Cost of Living Index	94.1
Buying Power Index	120
Weekly Daycare Cost	$160
Median Home Price	$174,700
"Sweet Spot" Home Price	$220,000
Home Price Ratio	3.5
Median Age of Homes	30.8
% Homes Owned	71%
Effective Property Tax Rate	1.50%
Estimated Property Tax Bill	$3,300
EDUCATION	
% High School Graduates	83%
% 4-yr Degree	18%
% Graduate or Professional Degree	8%
$ Invested per Pupil	$6,079
Student/Teacher Ratio	16.7
Primary Test Score Percentile	93.6
Secondary Test Score Percentile	96.9
% Subsidized School Lunch	13.30%
% Attending Public School	77.70%
LIFESTYLE	
Leisure Rating (Area)	3
Arts & Culture Rating (Area)	2
Climate Rating (Area)	3
Physical Setting Rating	4
Downtown Core Rating	4
% Commute < 30 Min.	77%
% Commute > 1 Hour	3%
HEALTH & SAFETY	
Health Rating (Area)	6
Stress Score (Area)	3
Violent Crime Risk	63
Property Crime Risk	64

YORK, PA
AREA HIGHLIGHTS
PEOPLE

SIZE & DIVERSITY	AREA	U.S. AVG	FAMILY DEMOGRAPHICS	AREA	U.S. AVG
Population	401,613		% Married	61%	53.80%
15-yr Population Growth	18.30%	4.40%	% Single	39%	46.20%
Diversity Measure	16	54	% Divorced	7.50%	10.20%
% Religiously Observant	45%	50%	% Separated	2.70%	2.10%
% Catholic	10%	22%	% Married w/Children	31%	27.90%
% Protestant	34%	25%	% Single w/Children	8.20%	9.40%
% Jewish	0%	2%	% Married, No Children	33.30%	31.00%
% Other	0%	1%	% Single, No Children	27.50%	31.70%

STANDARD OF LIVING

INCOME, EMPLOYMENT & TAXES	AREA	U.S. AVG	COST OF LIVING & HOUSING	AREA	U.S. AVG
Median Household Income	$46,867	$44,684	Cost of Living Index	87.8	100
Household Income Growth	4.20%	6.10%	Buying Power Index	119	100
Unemployment Rate	4.20%	5.10%	Median Home Price	$144,300	$208,500
Recent Job Growth	2.40%	1.30%	Home Price Ratio	3.1	4.7
Projected Future Job Growth	9.60%	10.50%	Home Price Appreciation	12.70%	13.60%
State Income Tax Rate	2.80%	5.00%	% Homes Owned	76.30%	64.10%
State Sales Tax Rate	6%	6.00%	Median Rent	$612	$792

EDUCATION

ATTAINMENT & ACHIEVEMENT	AREA	U.S. AVG	RESOURCES & INVESTMENT	AREA	U.S. AVG
% High School Graduate	77.50%	83.90%	No. of Highly Ranked Universities	2	1
% 2-yr Graduate	6.40%	7.10%	$ Invested per Pupil	$5,753	$6,058
% 4-yr Graduate	12%	17.20%	Student/Teacher Ratio	17	15.9
% Graduate or Professional Degree	4.90%	9.90%	State University In-State Tuition	$10,856	$4,917
% Attending Public School	92.10%	84.30%			
75th Percentile State University SAT Score (Verbal)	530	477			
75th Percentile State University SAT Score (Math)	560	478			
75th Percentile State University ACT Score	N/A	20			

LIFESTYLE

RECREATION, ARTS & CULTURE	AREA	U.S. AVG	INFRASTRUCTURE & FACILITIES	AREA	U.S. AVG
Professional Sports Rating	4	4	No. of Public Libraries	15	28
Zoos & Aquariums Rating	1	3	Library Volumes Per Capita	1.1	2.8
Amusement Park Rating	1	3	No. of Warehouse Clubs	3	4
Professional Theater Rating	1	3	No. of Starbucks	2	5
Overall Museum Rating	4	6	Golf Course Rating	3	4
Science Museum Rating	1	4	National Park Rating	2	3
Children's Museum Rating	1	3	Sq. Mi. Inland Water	2	4

CLIMATE			COMMUTE & TRANSPORTATION		
Days Mostly Sunny	193	212	Avg. Daily Commute Time	24	24.7
Annual Days Precipitation	125	111	% Commute by Auto	80%	77.70%
Annual Days > 90°F	24	38	Per Capita Avg. Daily Transit Miles	4.1	7.9
Annual Days < 32°F	107	88	Annual Auto Insurance Premium	$1,264	$1,314
July Relative Humidity	67	69	Gas, Cost per Gallon	$3.22	$3.05

HEALTH & SAFETY

CRIME & ENVIRNOMENTAL ISSUES	AREA	U.S. AVG	HEALTHCARE & COST	AREA	U.S. AVG
Violent Crime Rate	195	517	Physicians per Capita	188.9	254.3
Change in Violent Crime	-29.30%	-7.50%	Pediatricians per Capita	8.4	16.9
Property Crime Rate	2289	3783	Hospital Beds per Capita	216.4	239.7
Change in Property Crime	-23.20%	-10.10%	No. of Teaching Hospitals	2	1.9
Air Quality Score	20	44	Healthcare Cost Index	90.7	100
Water Quality Score	40	33	Cost per Doctor Visit	$62	$74
Pollen/Allergy Score	47	61	Cost per Dentist Visit	$56	$67
Stress Score	31	49	Cost per Hospital Room	$440	$702
Cancer Mortality Rate	168.6	168.9			

More Data

For those of you who prefer your facts all at once, the following tables compare our data by category: People, Standard of Living, Education, Lifestyle, and Health & Safety.

- Sorted alphabetically by each neighborhood's name, the first table shows selected facts for the metro area in which a neighborhood is located.
- The second table, also sorted alphabetically, shows selected neighborhood facts.

TABLE A.1 PEOPLE
Metro Area Level Data
SORTED BY NEIGHBORHOOD

ZIP CODE	NEIGHBORHOOD	METRO AREA	POPULATION	5-YEAR POPULATION GROWTH	15-YEAR POPULATION GROWTH	DIVERSITY MEASURE
79606	Abilene, TX	Abilene, TX	125,108	-1.1%	4.6%	43
87122	Albuquerque (Sandia Heights), NM	Albuquerque, NM	764,583	7.3%	31.1%	60
99516	Anchorage, AK	Anchorage, AK	272,687	4.8%	20.5%	49
54911	Appleton, WI	Appleton-Oshkosh-Neenah, WI	372,110	3.9%	18.3%	12
19810	Arden-Brandywine, DE	Wilmington-Newark, DE-MD	614,922	5.0%	20.1%	41
76002	Arlington, TX	Fort Worth–Arlington, TX	1,878,334	10.3%	38.3%	50
78732	Austin (West), TX	Austin–San Marcos, TX	1,412,271	13.6%	71.9%	54
98226	Bellingham, WA	Bellingham, WA	180,167	8.0%	41.0%	25
18018	Bethlehem, PA	Allentown-Bethlehem-Easton, PA	669,798	5.0%	12.6%	25
74012	Broken Arrow, OK	Tulsa, OK	825,091	2.8%	17.1%	43
27513	Cary, NC	Raleigh-Durham–Chapel Hill, NC	1,328,951	12.1%	57.0%	49
80104	Castle Rock, CO	Denver, CO	2,233,818	6.8%	56.9%	46
22901	Charlottesville, VA	Charlottesville, VA	165,999	6.0%	33.6%	34
01824	Chelmsford, MA	Boston, MA-NH-ME	302,059	1.0%	7.7%	25
21045	Columbia, MD	Baltimore, MD	2,639,213	3.5%	13.8%	48
65203	Columbia, MO	Columbia, MO	141,367	4.4%	25.8%	27
52241	Coralville, IA	Iowa City, IA	116,097	4.6%	20.8%	20
15108	Coraopolis–Moon Township, PA	Pittsburgh, PA	2,330,180	-1.2%	-2.3%	20
53532	DeForest, WI	Madison, WI	453,582	6.3%	23.6%	23
80220	Denver (Park Hill), CO	Denver, CO	2,233,818	6.8%	56.9%	46
83616	Eagle, ID	Boise City, ID	490,561	13.6%	66.1%	23
11730	East Islip, NY	Nassau-Suffolk, NY	2,815,129	2.3%	8.0%	39
68022	Elkhorn, NE	Omaha, NE-IA	752,597	5.0%	18.1%	30
97405	Eugene, OR	Eugene, OR	331,594	2.7%	17.2%	21
45241	Evendale, OH	Cincinnati, OH-KY-IN	1,680,102	2.7%	15.6%	28
58104	Fargo, ND	Fargo, ND	181,520	4.1%	19.2%	12
37922	Farragut, TN	Knoxville, TN	724,440	5.5%	24.8%	17
75028	Flower Mound, TX	Dallas, TX	3,886,553	11.4%	55.5%	58
95630	Folsom, CA	Sacramento, CA	1,832,338	12.7%	38.6%	53
37064	Franklin, TN	Nashville, TN	1,311,630	6.9%	38.2%	36
80526	Fort Collins–Loveland, CO	Fort Collins–Loveland, CO	268,872	6.9%	44.4%	23
32605	Gainesville, FL	Gainesville, FL	223,090	2.4%	22.8%	46
20878	Gaithersburg, MD	Washington, DC-MD-VA-WV	5,276,939	8.2%	32.3%	59
14068	Getzville, NY	Buffalo–Niagara Falls, NY	1,154,378	-1.3%	-2.9%	30
97526	Grants Pass, OR	Josephine County	79,920	5.5%	27.6%	19
54313	Green Bay, WI	Green Bay, WI	237,166	4.6%	21.9%	19
29650	Greer, SC	Greenville-Spartanburg-Anderson, SC	1,005,211	4.5%	21.1%	36
20170	Herndon, VA	Washington, DC-MD-VA-WV	5,276,939	8.2%	32.3%	59
43026	Hilliard, OH	Columbus, OH	1,615,172	5.4%	24.0%	33
37343	Hixson, TN	Chattanooga, TN-GA	477,248	2.7%	13.3%	30
78232	Hollywood Park, TX	San Antonio, TX	1,722,117	8.2%	31.1%	60
49426	Hudsonville, MI	Grand Rapids–Muskegon-Holland, MI	1,133,127	4.1%	21.3%	30
29212	Irmo, SC	Columbia, SC	565,666	5.4%	25.4%	50
84037	Kaysville, UT	Salt Lake City–Ogden, UT	1,405,136	5.4%	31.2%	30
08824	Kendall Park, NJ	Middlesex-Somerset-Hunterdon, NJ	1,231,591	5.3%	21.1%	49
60047	Lake Zurich, IL	Chicago, IL	8,541,230	3.8%	18.6%	57
55044	Lakeville, MN	Minneapolis–St. Paul, MN-WI	3,116,206	5.5%	27.1%	27
17601	Lancaster, PA	Lancaster, PA	487,332	3.5%	15.3%	21
66049	Lawrence, KS	Lawrence, KS	102,786	2.8%	25.7%	28
40503	Lexington, KY	Lexington, KY	500,869	4.7%	24.6%	26
07039	Livingston, NJ	Newark, NJ	2,079,050	2.3%	8.9%	57
84321	Logan, UT	Logan, UT	97,467	6.6%	38.9%	24
92354	Loma Linda, CA	Riverside–San Bernardino, CA	3,793,081	16.7%	47.5%	63
80027	Louisville, CO	Boulder-Longmont, CO	278,917	-4.2%	23.8%	28
35758	Madison, AL	Huntsville, AL	362,459	5.9%	23.7%	42
28105	Matthews-Stallings, NC	Charlotte-Gastonia–Rock Hill, NC-SC	1,651,894	10.5%	44.6%	44
43537	Maumee, OH	Toledo, OH	616,829	-0.2%	0.7%	33
89423	Minden-Gardnerville, NV	Douglas County	45,394	10.0%	64.3%	27
98273	Mount Vernon, WA	Mount Vernon–Anacortes, WA	111,064	7.9%	39.6%	40
98275	Mukilteo, WA	Seattle-Bellevue-Everett, WA	2,500,710	3.6%	23.6%	39

PERCENT RELIGIOUS	PERCENT CATHOLIC	PERCENT PROTESTANT	PERCENT JEWISH	PERCENT OTHER RELIGION	MARRIED	SINGLE	DIVORCED	SEPARATED	MARRIED WITH CHILDREN	SINGLE WITH CHILDREN	MARRIED NO CHILDREN	SINGLE NO CHILDREN
67%	7%	60%	0%	0%	55%	45%	7%	2%	36%	8%	28%	28%
54%	36%	17%	1%	0%	55%	45%	9%	2%	32%	13%	26%	30%
37%	9%	27%	1%	0%	55%	45%	12%	3%	34%	11%	22%	32%
70%	40%	30%	0%	0%	62%	38%	6%	1%	33%	7%	33%	27%
43%	23%	18%	2%	1%	54%	46%	8%	4%	26%	11%	30%	33%
52%	10%	40%	0%	1%	57%	43%	10%	4%	31%	11%	28%	30%
45%	18%	25%	1%	0%	53%	47%	9%	3%	28%	10%	26%	35%
29%	8%	21%	0%	0%	60%	40%	9%	2%	28%	8%	31%	32%
63%	31%	30%	1%	0%	59%	41%	7%	3%	27%	8%	34%	31%
52%	5%	46%	0%	0%	57%	43%	11%	3%	28%	10%	30%	32%
40%	7%	32%	1%	1%	52%	48%	7%	5%	25%	10%	28%	37%
39%	18%	18%	2%	0%	53%	47%	12%	3%	27%	10%	27%	36%
36%	6%	29%	1%	0%	54%	46%	7%	3%	28%	9%	29%	33%
73%	54%	11%	8%	1%	54%	46%	7%	3%	31%	9%	28%	31%
44%	21%	18%	4%	1%	53%	47%	7%	5%	28%	10%	30%	31%
41%	7%	33%	0%	1%	50%	50%	8%	2%	25%	10%	26%	39%
37%	16%	20%	1%	0%	54%	46%	7%	1%	29%	6%	28%	37%
66%	42%	23%	2%	0%	55%	45%	7%	3%	25%	8%	32%	35%
52%	28%	23%	1%	0%	54%	46%	8%	2%	28%	8%	28%	37%
39%	18%	18%	2%	0%	53%	47%	12%	3%	27%	10%	27%	36%
44%	12%	31%	0%	0%	59%	41%	10%	2%	30%	10%	30%	30%
72%	52%	8%	11%	1%	57%	43%	5%	3%	30%	7%	34%	28%
51%	24%	26%	1%	0%	60%	40%	8%	2%	32%	9%	31%	28%
25%	5%	18%	1%	0%	59%	41%	11%	3%	26%	10%	33%	31%
46%	22%	22%	1%	0%	55%	45%	9%	3%	28%	11%	27%	32%
59%	16%	43%	0%	0%	61%	39%	5%	1%	31%	6%	33%	28%
61%	3%	57%	0%	1%	57%	43%	10%	2%	26%	9%	32%	34%
52%	18%	32%	1%	1%	56%	44%	10%	4%	30%	11%	27%	32%
36%	18%	17%	1%	0%	56%	44%	11%	4%	27%	11%	31%	31%
48%	5%	42%	0%	1%	55%	45%	10%	3%	28%	10%	29%	31%
39%	13%	25%	0%	1%	57%	43%	9%	2%	25%	8%	34%	33%
34%	7%	25%	1%	0%	46%	54%	9%	3%	22%	12%	24%	42%
45%	18%	21%	3%	3%	53%	47%	7%	5%	29%	10%	28%	33%
71%	53%	16%	2%	0%	52%	48%	7%	3%	24%	10%	29%	35%
20%	3%	12%	0%	4%	60%	40%	12%	4%	23%	12%	35%	30%
73%	52%	21%	0%	0%	59%	41%	7%	2%	33%	8%	30%	30%
57%	3%	54%	0%	0%	55%	45%	8%	4%	27%	11%	30%	31%
45%	18%	21%	3%	3%	53%	47%	7%	5%	29%	10%	28%	33%
36%	13%	22%	1%	0%	55%	45%	10%	3%	28%	11%	29%	32%
53%	2%	49%	0%	0%	53%	47%	11%	3%	25%	12%	29%	34%
63%	39%	23%	1%	0%	55%	45%	9%	4%	32%	12%	27%	28%
49%	16%	32%	0%	1%	59%	41%	8%	2%	32%	10%	30%	28%
45%	4%	40%	1%	0%	51%	49%	8%	5%	29%	12%	27%	32%
70%	5%	64%	0%	0%	56%	44%	9%	2%	38%	10%	25%	27%
58%	43%	10%	5%	1%	57%	43%	6%	2%	29%	6%	34%	31%
57%	39%	14%	3%	1%	53%	47%	8%	3%	28%	10%	28%	34%
56%	26%	29%	1%	0%	56%	44%	8%	2%	31%	9%	28%	33%
48%	10%	38%	1%	0%	61%	39%	6%	3%	33%	7%	34%	26%
29%	7%	21%	0%	0%	51%	49%	7%	1%	27%	8%	28%	37%
48%	7%	40%	0%	0%	50%	50%	9%	3%	27%	10%	29%	35%
58%	39%	11%	7%	1%	54%	46%	6%	4%	28%	9%	31%	31%
85%	2%	82%	0%	1%	62%	38%	4%	1%	45%	5%	25%	25%
42%	27%	14%	1%	1%	56%	44%	10%	4%	29%	12%	28%	31%
47%	20%	21%	5%	1%	51%	49%	11%	2%	24%	9%	26%	41%
55%	5%	49%	0%	0%	60%	40%	9%	2%	31%	9%	31%	29%
50%	6%	43%	1%	1%	55%	45%	8%	5%	27%	11%	30%	32%
49%	23%	24%	1%	1%	53%	47%	9%	2%	28%	11%	28%	34%
23%	12%	10%	0%	1%	63%	37%	12%	2%	27%	9%	36%	28%
43%	18%	20%	0%	5%	59%	41%	12%	3%	24%	11%	34%	31%
33%	14%	18%	1%	0%	53%	47%	12%	3%	24%	9%	28%	39%

continues

TABLE A.1 PEOPLE (continued)
Metro Area Level Data
SORTED BY NEIGHBORHOOD

ZIP CODE	NEIGHBORHOOD	METRO AREA	POPULATION	5-YEAR POPULATION GROWTH	15-YEAR POPULATION GROWTH	DIVERSITY MEASURE
03062	Nashua, NH	Nashua, NH	199,840	4.7%	18.7%	15
06470	Newtown, CT	Danbury, CT	223,646	2.6%	9.1%	38
46060	Noblesville, IN	Indianapolis, IN	1,700,201	6.6%	30.8%	32
02760	North Attleboro, MA	Providence–Fall River–Warwick, RI-MA	1,223,610	2.9%	8.0%	27
07648	Norwood, NJ	Bergen-Passaic, NJ	1,403,425	2.2%	8.3%	52
60302	Oak Park, IL	Chicago, IL	8,541,230	3.8%	18.6%	57
98501	Olympia, WA	Olympia, WA	224,673	8.4%	39.3%	29
32073	Orange Park, FL	Jacksonville, FL	1,201,362	9.5%	35.3%	45
14534	Pittsford, NY	Rochester, NY	1,101,188	0.3%	3.7%	31
92688	Rancho Santa Margarita, CA	Orange County, CA	2,987,591	5.0%	23.9%	61
57702	Rapid City, SD	Rapid City, SD	92,631	4.6%	13.9%	26
89523	Reno, NV	Reno, NV	380,754	12.2%	49.5%	43
23233	Richmond-Tuckahoe, VA	Richmond-Petersburg, VA	1,047,366	5.4%	24.3%	49
24018	Roanoke, VA	Roanoke, VA	236,155	0.2%	6.1%	29
55902	Rochester, MN	Rochester, MN	133,283	7.2%	25.2%	20
72758	Rogers, AR	Fayetteville-Springdale-Rogers, AR	353,833	13.8%	69.2%	25
30075	Roswell, GA	Atlanta, GA	4,559,736	11.8%	63.8%	54
91354	Santa Clarita, CA	Los Angeles–Long Beach, CA	9,937,739	4.4%	12.1%	71
02067	Sharon, MA	Boston, MA-NH-ME	3,412,151	1.3%	7.6%	31
66216	Shawnee, KS	Kansas City, MO-KS	1,863,326	5.1%	20.2%	36
53044	Sheboygan, WI	Sheboygan, WI	113,958	1.2%	9.7%	17
99223	Spokane, WA	Spokane, WA	435,644	4.2%	20.6%	19
63304	St. Charles, MO	St. Louis, MO-IL	2,667,862	2.7%	10.0%	36
77479	Sugar Land, TX	Houston, TX	4,587,092	10.1%	41.7%	65
75791	Tyler, TX	Tyler, TX	186,414	6.7%	23.2%	47
33594	Valrico, FL	Tampa–St. Petersburg–Clearwater, FL	2,587,967	8.4%	26.8%	39
98607	Vancouver-Camas, WA	Portland-Vancouver, OR-WA	2,053,787	7.3%	38.4%	32
23456	Virginia Beach, VA	Norfolk–Virginia Beach–Newport News, VA-NC	1,637,280	4.6%	16.4%	53
53186	Waukesha, WI	Milwaukee-Waukesha, WI	1,515,738	1.1%	7.5%	41
54403	Wausau, WI	Wausau, WI	127,733	1.5%	10.7%	13
19382	West Chester, PA	Philadelphia, PA-NJ	5,185,692	1.8%	6.4%	46
50325	West Des Moines–Clive, IA	Des Moines, IA	485,335	6.6%	24.8%	22
47906	West Lafayette, IN	Lafayette, IN	186,190	1.8%	15.3%	23
36695	West Mobile, AL	Mobile, AL	557,227	3.4%	20.9%	45
10994	West Nyack, NY	New York, NY	9,440,719	1.4%	10.6%	72
33326	Weston, FL	Fort Lauderdale, FL	1,754,893	8.1%	39.8%	57
67212	Wichita (West), KS	Wichita, KS	559,399	2.6%	15.3%	36
22602	Winchester, VA	Winchester, VA-WV	66,611	12.5%	45.7%	13
95694	Winters, CA	Yolo, CA	184,364	9.3%	30.6%	57
17402	York, PA	York, PA	401,613	5.2%	18.3%	16

Primary sources: U.S. Decennial Census and Census American Community Survey, Glenmary Missioners

PERCENT RELIGIOUS	PERCENT CATHOLIC	PERCENT PROTESTANT	PERCENT JEWISH	PERCENT OTHER RELIGION	MARRIED	SINGLE	DIVORCED	SEPARATED	MARRIED WITH CHILDREN	SINGLE WITH CHILDREN	MARRIED NO CHILDREN	SINGLE NO CHILDREN
58%	46%	11%	2%	0%	62%	38%	8%	2%	35%	8%	30%	27%
67%	47%	15%	4%	1%	60%	40%	7%	2%	31%	6%	33%	30%
41%	12%	28%	1%	0%	58%	42%	10%	2%	30%	10%	31%	29%
63%	52%	9%	2%	0%	53%	47%	7%	2%	27%	9%	30%	34%
66%	46%	10%	7%	2%	55%	45%	6%	3%	27%	7%	33%	33%
57%	39%	14%	3%	1%	53%	47%	8%	3%	28%	10%	28%	34%
27%	9%	18%	0%	0%	53%	47%	11%	3%	31%	11%	29%	29%
43%	9%	33%	1%	0%	54%	46%	11%	4%	28%	12%	27%	33%
51%	32%	16%	2%	0%	54%	46%	7%	4%	28%	10%	29%	33%
45%	27%	14%	2%	1%	52%	48%	10%	3%	27%	9%	28%	36%
63%	28%	35%	0%	0%	65%	35%	8%	2%	31%	7%	34%	28%
28%	16%	11%	1%	0%	53%	47%	15%	3%	24%	11%	27%	38%
44%	6%	36%	2%	0%	53%	47%	7%	5%	26%	11%	30%	31%
55%	4%	50%	0%	0%	52%	48%	9%	4%	24%	9%	30%	37%
62%	22%	39%	0%	0%	62%	38%	7%	1%	33%	7%	30%	29%
52%	6%	46%	0%	0%	65%	35%	8%	2%	31%	8%	36%	26%
44%	7%	35%	2%	1%	53%	47%	10%	4%	28%	12%	27%	32%
58%	40%	11%	6%	1%	46%	54%	9%	4%	24%	12%	22%	41%
68%	51%	10%	5%	1%	50%	50%	7%	3%	25%	8%	28%	39%
48%	15%	31%	1%	0%	58%	42%	10%	3%	29%	10%	30%	31%
72%	27%	46%	0%	0%	63%	37%	5%	2%	35%	6%	34%	25%
36%	14%	22%	0%	0%	57%	43%	11%	2%	29%	11%	29%	31%
51%	25%	24%	2%	1%	55%	45%	9%	3%	28%	11%	29%	32%
50%	18%	30%	1%	1%	53%	47%	10%	5%	30%	13%	24%	33%
65%	9%	56%	0%	0%	57%	43%	8%	3%	29%	10%	32%	29%
38%	15%	20%	2%	0%	55%	45%	11%	3%	20%	9%	34%	37%
33%	12%	19%	1%	0%	56%	44%	11%	3%	27%	10%	29%	34%
35%	6%	27%	1%	0%	53%	47%	7%	6%	29%	11%	29%	31%
55%	31%	22%	1%	0%	55%	45%	8%	2%	28%	10%	30%	32%
71%	37%	34%	0%	0%	63%	37%	5%	1%	36%	6%	32%	26%
58%	36%	15%	5%	1%	52%	48%	7%	4%	27%	10%	29%	34%
47%	15%	32%	0%	0%	61%	39%	9%	2%	31%	9%	31%	30%
37%	11%	25%	0%	0%	59%	41%	8%	2%	30%	8%	31%	31%
52%	9%	43%	0%	0%	54%	46%	9%	4%	27%	13%	28%	32%
62%	39%	8%	13%	2%	46%	54%	7%	6%	22%	12%	26%	41%
46%	21%	11%	13%	0%	53%	47%	11%	3%	20%	9%	30%	41%
48%	13%	34%	0%	0%	60%	40%	9%	2%	32%	8%	31%	28%
31%	0%	25%	0%	6%	62%	38%	7%	4%	32%	9%	34%	25%
32%	20%	10%	1%	0%	55%	45%	9%	4%	28%	10%	30%	33%
45%	10%	34%	0%	0%	61%	39%	7%	3%	31%	8%	33%	28%

TABLE A.2 PEOPLE
Neighborhood Level Data
SORTED BY NEIGHBORHOOD

ZIP CODE	NEIGHBORHOOD	METRO AREA	POPULATION	5-YEAR POPULATION GROWTH
79606	Abilene, TX	Abilene, TX	17,941	4.6%
87122	Albuquerque (SandiaHeights), NM	Albuquerque, NM	13,670	23.6%
99516	Anchorage, AK	Anchorage, AK	22,712	20.5%
54911	Appleton, WI	Appleton-Oshkosh-Neenah, WI	29,754	20.5%
19810	Arden-Brandywine, DE	Wilmington-Newark, DE-MD	26,431	17.5%
76002	Arlington, TX	Fort Worth–Arlington, TX	7,832	35.7%
78732	Austin (West), TX	Austin–San Marcos, TX	4,074	50.9%
98226	Bellingham, WA	Bellingham, WA	61,037	41.0%
18018	Bethlehem, PA	Allentown-Bethlehem-Easton, PA	32,537	12.0%
74012	Broken Arrow, OK	Tulsa, OK	47,726	13.1%
27513	Cary, NC	Raleigh-Durham–Chapel Hill, NC	42,478	68.8%
80104	Castle Rock, CO	Denver, CO	40,981	294.0%
22901	Charlottesville, VA	Charlottesville, VA	34,488	30.2%
01824	Chelmsford, MA	Boston, MA-NH-ME	25,415	4.7%
21045	Columbia, MD	Baltimore, MD	40,372	42.4%
65203	Columbia, MO	Columbia, MO	47,454	25.8%
52241	Coralville, IA	Iowa City, IA	15,951	20.8%
15108	Coraopolis–Moon Township, PA	Pittsburgh, PA	36,752	-6.4%
53532	DeForest, WI	Madison, WI	12,211	23.6%
80220	Denver (Park Hill), CO	Denver, CO	36,458	19.1%
83616	Eagle, ID	Boise City, ID	16,777	61.6%
11730	East Islip, NY	Nassau-Suffolk, NY	16,663	11.6%
68022	Elkhorn, NE	Omaha, NE-IA	9,614	15.8%
97405	Eugene, OR	Eugene, OR	44,947	17.2%
45241	Evendale, OH	Cincinnati, OH-KY-IN	23,733	-6.0%
58104	Fargo, ND	Fargo, ND	16,291	25.0%
37922	Farragut, TN	Knoxville, TN	47,822	19.2%
75028	Flower Mound, TX	Dallas, TX	44,598	94.0%
95630	Folsom, CA	Sacramento, CA	57,384	29.9%
37064	Franklin, TN	Nashville, TN	43,192	81.4%
80526	Fort Collins–Loveland, CO	Fort Collins–Loveland, CO	45,333	44.4%
32605	Gainesville, FL	Gainesville, FL	23,157	22.8%
20878	Gaithersburg, MD	Washington, DC-MD-VA-WV	58,241	20.9%
14068	Getzville, NY	Buffalo–Niagara Falls, NY	9,948	-3.3%
97526	Grants Pass, OR	Josephine County	33,905	27.6%
54313	Green Bay, WI	Green Bay, WI	33,105	21.9%
29650	Greer, SC	Greenville-Spartanburg-Anderson, SC	25,133	25.3%
20170	Herndon, VA	Washington, DC-MD-VA-WV	39,503	22.6%
43026	Hilliard, OH	Columbus, OH	48,300	13.3%
37343	Hixson, TN	Chattanooga, TN-GA	37,605	8.7%
78232	Hollywood Park, TX	San Antonio, TX	36,172	26.0%
49426	Hudsonville, MI	Grand Rapids–Muskegon-Holland, MI	29,091	34.4%
29212	Irmo, SC	Columbia, SC	29,739	37.9%
84037	Kaysville, UT	Salt Lake City–Ogden, UT	27,925	39.0%
08824	Kendall Park, NJ	Middlesex-Somerset-Hunterdon, NJ	12,420	16.9%
60047	Lake Zurich, IL	Chicago, IL	41,172	34.2%
55044	Lakeville, MN	Minneapolis–St. Paul, MN-WI	37,268	37.7%
17601	Lancaster, PA	Lancaster, PA	47,226	15.3%
66049	Lawrence, KS	Lawrence, KS	21,217	25.7%
40503	Lexington, KY	Lexington, KY	27,906	18.2%
07039	Livingston, NJ	Newark, NJ	27,367	2.4%
84321	Logan, UT	Logan, UT	40,813	38.9%
92354	Loma Linda, CA	Riverside–San Bernardino, CA	20,392	35.4%
80027	Louisville, CO	Boulder-Longmont, CO	27,177	23.8%
35758	Madison, AL	Huntsville, AL	32,551	22.7%
28105	Matthews-Stallings, NC	Charlotte-Gastonia–Rock Hill, NC-SC	35,594	50.9%
43537	Maumee, OH	Toledo, OH	24,281	-2.5%
89423	Minden-Gardnerville, NV	Douglas County	9,102	64.3%
98273	Mount Vernon, WA	Mount Vernon–Anacortes, WA	27,422	39.6%

15-YEAR POPULATION GROWTH	NUMBER OF HOUSEHOLDS	MEDIAN AGE	MARRIED WITH CHILDREN	SINGLE WITH CHILDREN	AVG FAMILY SIZE	DIVERSITY MEASURE
-1.1%	7292	35	32.6%	8.8%	2.4	30
6.7%	4990	38	32.4%	6.1%	2.7	34
4.8%	7553	34	47.6%	5.9%	3.0	18
5.2%	11676	37	27.4%	8.1%	2.4	17
3.8%	10462	41	26.3%	6.2%	2.5	23
9.8%	2507	28	44.2%	8.6%	3.1	63
7.1%	1560	32	37.0%	5.8%	2.6	25
8.0%	23823	37	26.9%	9.7%	2.6	25
4.5%	13870	40	18.4%	7.4%	2.2	28
1.0%	16742	33	41.2%	9.3%	2.8	29
14.6%	16195	31	30.3%	5.6%	2.6	36
35.4%	14434	33	35.6%	8.9%	2.8	17
12.0%	14990	38	20.9%	9.2%	2.3	33
-0.1%	9370	39	29.6%	6.1%	2.7	14
7.6%	15391	34	34.2%	11.0%	2.6	56
4.4%	19536	34	24.9%	10.2%	2.4	30
4.6%	6821	32	18.5%	8.0%	2.2	26
-2.4%	14538	39	23.2%	7.5%	2.4	14
6.3%	4308	34	38.5%	8.2%	2.8	8
0.4%	15640	36	16.0%	9.9%	2.2	61
10.5%	5704	34	32.4%	10.1%	2.9	9
4.0%	5422	36	34.4%	7.3%	3.0	13
4.0%	3137	34	38.8%	9.6%	3.0	5
2.7%	18430	39	23.5%	9.6%	2.4	17
-3.6%	9539	40	31.4%	7.6%	2.4	18
4.4%	5930	32	42.8%	5.4%	2.7	8
4.7%	17267	36	36.6%	7.4%	2.8	12
22.5%	14294	30	53.2%	7.4%	3.1	24
10.5%	19004	35	29.8%	8.7%	2.6	46
16.0%	15625	35	32.3%	11.0%	2.7	28
6.9%	17297	32	32.0%	9.4%	2.6	25
2.4%	9576	39	27.2%	9.5%	2.4	30
5.5%	20291	33	37.4%	9.6%	2.9	61
-1.5%	2285	34	34.2%	8.6%	2.8	23
5.5%	13879	41	21.1%	11.3%	2.4	15
4.6%	11509	34	42.4%	8.8%	2.9	8
5.7%	9601	36	36.5%	7.9%	2.6	28
3.4%	12310	31	38.3%	9.1%	3.2	66
1.9%	18085	31	32.5%	9.7%	2.7	17
0.8%	14316	37	32.6%	9.6%	2.6	15
7.3%	14847	38	26.6%	9.5%	2.4	44
5.9%	9256	33	43.2%	5.4%	3.1	6
7.0%	11336	35	37.7%	10.7%	2.6	33
9.3%	7419	30	52.4%	8.1%	3.8	9
4.7%	3913	34	36.3%	6.3%	3.2	43
7.5%	12706	33	44.9%	4.9%	3.2	19
6.5%	11747	30	46.6%	8.7%	3.2	8
3.5%	18606	41	28.1%	6.1%	2.5	66
2.8%	8504	34	27.4%	6.9%	2.5	22
2.2%	11835	38	25.4%	7.1%	2.3	18
0.4%	9265	39	31.2%	6.7%	2.9	32
6.6%	13076	29	30.9%	6.6%	3.0	29
12.4%	7796	37	25.9%	11.2%	2.5	72
-4.2%	10392	32	33.7%	8.5%	2.6	24
5.9%	12419	33	28.2%	8.2%	2.6	36
11.0%	12975	34	35.2%	7.1%	2.7	29
-1.0%	9837	37	29.7%	9.3%	2.4	12
10.0%	3489	41	29.8%	7.9%	2.6	14
7.9%	9913	35	25.0%	11.1%	2.7	59

continues

421

TABLE A.2 PEOPLE (continued)
Neighborhood Level Data
SORTED BY NEIGHBORHOOD

ZIP CODE	NEIGHBORHOOD	METRO AREA	POPULATION	5-YEAR POPULATION GROWTH
98275	Mukilteo, WA	Seattle-Bellevue-Everett, WA	20,480	38.4%
03062	Nashua, NH	Nashua, NH	27,617	18.7%
06470	Newtown, CT	Danbury, CT	14,957	9.1%
46060	Noblesville, IN	Indianapolis, IN	55,059	112.7%
02760	North Attleboro, MA	Providence–Fall River–Warwick, RI-MA	25,517	8.3%
07648	Norwood, NJ	Bergen-Passaic, NJ	5,889	9.4%
60302	Oak Park, IL	Chicago, IL	32,145	4.4%
98501	Olympia, WA	Olympia, WA	36,073	39.3%
32073	Orange Park, FL	Jacksonville, FL	58,471	55.1%
14534	Pittsford, NY	Rochester, NY	30,053	3.0%
92688	Rancho Santa Margarita, CA	Orange County, CA	44,600	23.9%
57702	Rapid City, SD	Rapid City, SD	30,769	13.9%
89523	Reno, NV	Reno, NV	19,338	49.5%
23233	Richmond-Tuckahoe, VA	Richmond-Petersburg, VA	53,015	26.9%
24018	Roanoke, VA	Roanoke, VA	29,621	10.6%
55902	Rochester, MN	Rochester, MN	20,077	25.2%
72758	Rogers, AR	Fayetteville-Springdale-Rogers, AR	21,079	84.4%
30075	Roswell, GA	Atlanta, GA	46,241	25.5%
91354	Santa Clarita, CA	Los Angeles–Long Beach, CA	18,616	12.1%
02067	Sharon, MA	Boston, MA-NH-ME	17,485	6.1%
66216	Shawnee, KS	Kansas City, MO-KS	25,667	39.9%
53044	Sheboygan, WI	Sheboygan, WI	1,946	9.7%
99223	Spokane, WA	Spokane, WA	26,768	20.6%
63304	St. Charles, MO	St. Louis, MO-IL	43,595	50.8%
77479	Sugar Land, TX	Houston, TX	69,533	96.4%
75791	Tyler, TX	Tyler, TX	12,037	23.2%
33594	Valrico, FL	Tampa–St. Petersburg–Clearwater, FL	53,011	32.0%
98607	Vancouver-Camas, WA	Portland-Vancouver, OR-WA	20,750	64.8%
23456	Virginia Beach, VA	Norfolk–Virginia Beach–Newport News, VA-NC	78,499	12.0%
53186	Waukesha, WI	Milwaukee-Waukesha, WI	35,083	23.8%
54403	Wausau, WI	Wausau, WI	24,927	10.7%
19382	West Chester, PA	Philadelphia, PA-NJ	54,751	23.8%
50325	West Des Moines–Clive, IA	Des Moines, IA	13,669	20.2%
47906	West Lafayette, IN	Lafayette, IN	58,381	16.4%
36695	West Mobile, AL	Mobile, AL	33,531	5.8%
10994	West Nyack, NY	New York, NY	6,898	10.6%
33326	Weston, FL	Fort Lauderdale, FL	32,598	39.8%
67212	Wichita (West), KS	Wichita, KS	46,788	14.9%
22602	Winchester, VA	Winchester, VA-WV	23,660	45.7%
95694	Winters, CA	Yolo, CA	9,241	30.6%
17402	York, PA	York, PA	45,604	18.3%

Primary sources: U.S. Decennial Census and Census American Community Survey

15-YEAR POPULATION GROWTH	NUMBER OF HOUSEHOLDS	MEDIAN AGE	MARRIED WITH CHILDREN	SINGLE WITH CHILDREN	AVG FAMILY SIZE	DIVERSITY MEASURE
6.3%	7560	35	36.4%	7.6%	2.7	32
4.7%	10470	37	29.7%	5.6%	2.6	21
2.3%	5012	36	34.7%	4.9%	2.8	17
26.8%	20180	34	33.4%	8.8%	2.7	7
2.5%	9860	35	28.4%	9.4%	2.6	9
2.1%	1887	39	33.2%	5.6%	3.0	36
-0.9%	14677	37	19.3%	10.4%	2.2	47
8.4%	14996	37	23.8%	11.3%	2.4	22
16.7%	21099	36	33.4%	10.1%	2.7	35
0.0%	10883	40	36.2%	5.8%	2.7	18
5.0%	16095	29	32.6%	7.2%	2.8	48
4.6%	12346	39	29.3%	8.3%	2.5	11
12.2%	7379	34	36.3%	7.5%	2.6	30
5.4%	20817	37	31.4%	7.3%	2.5	20
2.2%	12464	41	24.7%	6.2%	2.4	10
7.2%	7941	36	27.7%	4.3%	2.5	17
17.2%	7807	36	28.5%	8.4%	2.7	35
-0.2%	16448	36	32.4%	10.7%	2.8	27
4.4%	6018	31	44.2%	9.9%	3.1	40
0.5%	5977	37	37.6%	4.9%	2.9	18
10.1%	9216	35	37.9%	9.1%	2.8	23
1.2%	724	37	37.1%	4.3%	2.7	4
4.2%	10261	37	29.0%	8.9%	2.6	13
13.0%	14405	33	44.0%	9.3%	3.0	9
24.9%	20607	31	53.2%	8.8%	3.3	57
6.7%	4173	34	39.6%	11.1%	2.9	17
10.2%	18301	35	39.7%	8.9%	2.9	34
13.7%	7278	34	29.7%	10.5%	2.8	15
3.5%	24963	31	44.5%	11.6%	3.1	52
4.6%	14183	36	28.6%	9.2%	2.4	30
1.5%	9773	39	26.8%	7.5%	2.5	19
7.4%	19192	36	30.4%	6.6%	2.6	21
5.0%	5080	34	34.8%	8.1%	2.7	15
2.1%	18497	30	21.2%	5.8%	2.4	29
0.2%	12117	34	42.0%	9.1%	2.7	25
2.4%	2231	38	38.5%	6.3%	3.1	31
8.1%	11642	34	30.6%	7.9%	2.8	53
2.4%	18019	35	32.5%	9.0%	2.6	22
12.5%	8841	36	29.9%	9.1%	2.7	14
9.3%	2910	33	35.3%	12.5%	3.2	70
5.2%	18284	41	23.0%	6.4%	2.4	16

TABLE A.3 STANDARD OF LIVING
Metro Area Level Data
SORTED BY NEIGHBORHOOD

ZIP CODE	NEIGHBORHOOD	METRO AREA	MEDIAN HOUSEHOLD INCOME	HOUSEHOLD INCOME GROWTH	UNEMPLOYMENT RATE
79606	Abilene, TX	Abilene, TX	$36,024	6%	3.1%
87122	Albuquerque (Sandia Heights), NM	Albuquerque, NM	$41,401	6%	4.4%
99516	Anchorage, AK	Anchorage, AK	$61,595	11%	4.8%
54911	Appleton, WI	Appleton-Oshkosh-Neenah, WI	$50,633	6%	3.6%
19810	Arden-Brandywine, DE	Wilmington-Newark, DE-MD	$55,626	7%	4.1%
76002	Arlington, TX	Fort Worth–Arlington, TX	$46,923	2%	5.2%
78732	Austin (West), TX	Austin–San Marcos, TX	$52,146	6%	4.2%
98226	Bellingham, WA	Bellingham, WA	$41,760	4%	4.7%
18018	Bethlehem, PA	Allentown-Bethlehem-Easton, PA	$47,005	8%	5.4%
74012	Broken Arrow, OK	Tulsa, OK	$39,941	4%	4.5%
27513	Cary, NC	Raleigh-Durham–Chapel Hill, NC	$49,562	1%	3.3%
80104	Castle Rock, CO	Denver, CO	$54,167	2%	5.0%
22901	Charlottesville, VA	Charlottesville, VA	$49,916	10%	2.0%
01824	Chelmsford, MA	Boston, MA-NH-ME	$65,906	11%	3.3%
21045	Columbia, MD	Baltimore, MD	$56,986	11%	4.6%
65203	Columbia, MO	Columbia, MO	$40,813	9%	2.4%
52241	Coralville, IA	Iowa City, IA	$40,344	1%	3.9%
15108	Coraopolis–Moon Township, PA	Pittsburgh, PA	$40,992	9%	5.2%
53532	DeForest, WI	Madison, WI	$52,663	7%	2.2%
80220	Denver (Park Hill), CO	Denver, CO	$54,167	2%	5.0%
83616	Eagle, ID	Boise City, ID	$45,313	6%	4.5%
11730	East Islip, NY	Nassau-Suffolk, NY	$74,969	9%	3.6%
68022	Elkhorn, NE	Omaha, NE-IA	$47,673	6%	3.9%
97405	Eugene, OR	Eugene, OR	$38,082	3%	6.5%
45241	Evendale, OH	Cincinnati, OH-KY-IN	$47,700	6%	5.0%
58104	Fargo, ND	Fargo, ND	$43,342	14%	2.0%
37922	Farragut, TN	Knoxville, TN	$40,316	9%	3.5%
75028	Flower Mound, TX	Dallas, TX	$50,996	2%	5.6%
95630	Folsom, CA	Sacramento, CA	$53,610	14%	4.7%
37064	Franklin, TN	Nashville, TN	$50,251	10%	3.9%
80526	Fort Collins–Loveland, CO	Fort Collins–Loveland, CO	$49,178	1%	4.7%
32605	Gainesville, FL	Gainesville, FL	$33,574	7%	2.0%
20878	Gaithersburg, MD	Washington, DC-MD-VA-WV	$69,558	9%	3.1%
14068	Getzville, NY	Buffalo–Niagara Falls, NY	$41,251	7%	5.7%
97526	Grants Pass, OR	Josephine County	$32,281	3%	7.5%
54313	Green Bay, WI	Green Bay, WI	$49,635	7%	3.8%
29650	Greer, SC	Greenville-Spartanburg-Anderson, SC	$38,857	1%	5.8%
20170	Herndon, VA	Washington, DC-MD-VA-WV	$69,558	9%	3.1%
43026	Hilliard, OH	Columbus, OH	$49,029	8%	5.0%
37343	Hixson, TN	Chattanooga, TN-GA	$37,688	0%	3.6%
78232	Hollywood Park, TX	San Antonio, TX	$41,050	5%	4.7%
49426	Hudsonville, MI	Grand Rapids–Muskegon-Holland, MI	$46,084	0%	6.2%
29212	Irmo, SC	Columbia, SC	$43,177	3%	4.2%
84037	Kaysville, UT	Salt Lake City–Ogden, UT	$49,037	1%	4.3%
08824	Kendall Park, NJ	Middlesex-Somerset-Hunterdon, NJ	$76,726	14%	3.3%
60047	Lake Zurich, IL	Chicago, IL	$55,785	6%	5.8%
55044	Lakeville, MN	Minneapolis–St. Paul, MN-WI	$60,762	11%	3.7%
17601	Lancaster, PA	Lancaster, PA	$50,197	10%	3.4%
66049	Lawrence, KS	Lawrence, KS	$40,026	7%	4.3%
40503	Lexington, KY	Lexington, KY	$39,520	0%	3.2%
07039	Livingston, NJ	Newark, NJ	$60,902	6%	4.3%
84321	Logan, UT	Logan, UT	$40,843	3%	3.0%
92354	Loma Linda, CA	Riverside–San Bernardino, CA	$47,554	12%	5.0%
80027	Louisville, CO	Boulder-Longmont, CO	$60,645	8%	4.4%
35758	Madison, AL	Huntsville, AL	$48,552	12%	4.0%
28105	Matthews-Stallings, NC	Charlotte-Gastonia–Rock Hill, NC-SC	$45,823	-2%	5.3%
43537	Maumee, OH	Toledo, OH	$40,828	3%	6.7%
89423	Minden-Gardnerville, NV	Douglas County	$51,942	0%	3.4%
98273	Mount Vernon, WA	Mount Vernon–Anacortes, WA	$44,319	5%	6.1%

RECENT JOB GROWTH	FUTURE JOB GROWTH	INCOME TAX RATE	SALES TAX RATE	COST OF LIVING INDEX	BUYING POWER INDEX	MEDIAN HOME PRICE	HOME PRICE RATIO	HOME PRICE APPRECIATION	PERCENT HOMES OWNED	MEDIAN RENT
2.2%	5.6%	0.0%	8.3%	80.4	100	$114,500	3.2	10%	59%	$522
2.7%	17.9%	7.1%	5.7%	90.5	102	$171,700	4.1	9%	64%	$699
4.3%	14.3%	0.0%	0.0%	114.1	121	$219,700	3.6	12%	45%	$916
2.0%	14.4%	6.9%	5.0%	86.5	131	$129,600	2.6	6%	75%	$563
1.2%	9.8%	8.2%	0.0%	95.2	131	$176,300	3.2	15%	67%	$802
1.2%	18.1%	0.0%	7.7%	83.3	126	$124,600	2.7	11%	61%	$732
1.4%	21.8%	0.0%	7.9%	91.1	128	$166,800	3.2	2%	58%	$912
5.6%	22.2%	0.0%	6.5%	96.1	97	$203,500	4.9	19%	60%	$693
2.2%	5.9%	3.8%	6.0%	98.2	107	$249,100	5.3	13%	73%	$671
2.5%	10.3%	7.0%	7.4%	82.5	108	$117,400	2.9	2%	63%	$640
1.0%	20.7%	7.0%	4.0%	100.1	111	$185,200	3.7	5%	64%	$779
3.4%	14.7%	5.0%	7.0%	112.2	108	$248,400	4.6	4%	61%	$973
1.2%	13.5%	5.8%	3.5%	110.5	101	$301,500	6.0	17%	66%	$744
0.9%	5.1%	6.0%	5.0%	113.4	130	$239,100	3.6	10%	70%	$1,161
2.3%	13.0%	7.5%	5.1%	107.3	119	$264,700	4.6	21%	68%	$847
-0.5%	15.5%	6.0%	4.2%	91.3	100	$153,700	3.8	7%	61%	$557
-2.4%	9.2%	7.9%	5.0%	88.6	102	$131,800	3.3	6%	66%	$648
2.8%	5.2%	4.6%	6.0%	87.9	104	$118,500	2.9	6%	70%	$639
2.6%	11.5%	6.9%	5.5%	94.9	124	$220,100	4.2	11%	63%	$746
3.4%	14.7%	5.0%	7.0%	112.2	108	$248,400	4.6	4%	61%	$973
3.4%	26.9%	8.2%	5.0%	86.5	117	$161,800	3.6	7%	68%	$654
0.7%	7.3%	7.1%	4.0%	149.9	112	$467,700	6.2	16%	73%	$1,225
1.3%	14.5%	6.7%	6.0%	88.5	121	$137,300	2.9	5%	67%	$650
1.8%	10.9%	9.0%	0.0%	95.4	89	$192,400	5.1	15%	66%	$687
0.0%	11.6%	7.0%	5.5%	87.8	122	$148,500	3.1	5%	65%	$698
3.3%	14.3%	3.9%	5.0%	84.5	115	$132,600	3.1	9%	72%	$524
2.3%	17.5%	0.0%	8.3%	82.1	110	$143,400	3.6	7%	65%	$553
1.3%	20.0%	0.0%	8.2%	91.2	125	$149,100	2.9	3%	60%	$862
1.2%	22.4%	6.0%	7.7%	136.1	88	$377,400	7.0	26%	58%	$971
2.3%	18.0%	0.0%	8.2%	87.9	128	$159,700	3.2	6%	66%	$697
0.8%	22.6%	5.0%	3.0%	103	107	$197,500	4.0	5%	54%	$750
4.0%	12.8%	0.0%	6.0%	84.8	89	$188,800	5.6	18%	57%	$614
2.6%	13.6%	9.4%	11.5%	116	134	$429,200	6.2	22%	65%	$1,162
-0.5%	2.0%	7.1%	8.0%	87.3	106	$97,500	2.4	7%	65%	$648
2.9%	13.1%	9.0%	0.0%	91.1	79	$138,300	4.3	13%	67%	$597
4.2%	13.2%	6.9%	5.0%	85.1	131	$159,200	3.2	7%	72%	$587
3.7%	13.8%	7.0%	5.0%	84.8	103	$121,500	3.1	4%	69%	$562
2.6%	13.6%	9.4%	11.5%	116	134	$429,200	6.2	22%	65%	$1,162
-0.9%	12.8%	6.8%	5.7%	91.9	119	$155,900	3.2	5%	64%	$675
1.5%	11.0%	0.1%	7.7%	83.2	101	$130,500	3.5	6%	64%	$569
2.2%	17.5%	0.0%	6.3%	77.9	118	$134,000	3.3	5%	61%	$716
2.1%	15.4%	5.4%	6.0%	89.2	116	$139,000	3.0	5%	73%	$658
6.3%	14.7%	6.9%	4.9%	86.4	112	$133,700	3.1	5%	66%	$625
2.3%	18.4%	7.0%	6.0%	90.4	121	$169,900	3.5	5%	65%	$747
2.6%	14.3%	2.5%	6.0%	118.7	145	$394,100	5.1	16%	72%	$1,210
1.5%	9.0%	3.0%	8.0%	113.8	110	$265,000	4.8	11%	66%	$903
2.7%	14.3%	7.9%	7.0%	102.3	133	$237,700	3.9	9%	71%	$928
2.7%	10.2%	2.8%	6.0%	92.3	122	$162,900	3.2	10%	72%	$643
4.9%	11.9%	6.4%	6.0%	90.9	99	$149,500	3.7	7%	62%	$626
4.3%	13.0%	7.9%	6.0%	87	102	$144,800	3.7	5%	57%	$571
1.3%	5.7%	2.5%	6.0%	129.7	105	$414,400	6.8	13%	67%	$1,020
4.8%	25.4%	7.0%	6.2%	90.7	101	$148,200	3.6	6%	72%	$577
3.6%	22.1%	6.0%	7.3%	122.4	87	$367,600	7.7	29%	54%	$752
1.9%	15.9%	5.0%	3.3%	113.8	119	$346,200	5.7	5%	51%	$1,022
0.5%	14.2%	5.0%	9.2%	93.1	117	$166,700	3.4	5%	67%	$523
3.1%	18.1%	7.0%	6.0%	90.8	113	$145,900	3.2	4%	68%	$719
-2.2%	6.1%	7.2%	6.0%	88.8	103	$118,600	2.9	4%	67%	$571
1.8%	19.3%	0.0%	6.8%	144.1	81	$466,300	9.0	31%	61%	$863
5.7%	18.5%	0.0%	7.8%	96.5	103	$170,100	3.8	14%	67%	$767

continues

ZIP CODE	NEIGHBORHOOD	METRO AREA	MEDIAN HOUSEHOLD INCOME	HOUSEHOLD INCOME GROWTH	UNEMPLOYMENT RATE
	TABLE A.3 STANDARD OF LIVING (continued)				
	Metro Area Level Data				
	SORTED BY NEIGHBORHOOD				
98275	Mukilteo, WA	Seattle-Bellevue-Everett, WA	$54,298	3%	5.0%
03062	Nashua, NH	Nashua, NH	$59,203	11%	3.5%
06470	Newtown, CT	Danbury, CT	$71,368	12%	3.6%
46060	Noblesville, IN	Indianapolis, IN	$48,830	2%	4.8%
02760	North Attleboro, MA	Providence–Fall River–Warwick, RI-MA	$50,205	18%	4.3%
07648	Norwood, NJ	Bergen-Passaic, NJ	$63,392	6%	4.0%
60302	Oak Park, IL	Chicago, IL	$55,785	6%	5.8%
98501	Olympia, WA	Olympia, WA	$48,608	3%	4.7%
32073	Orange Park, FL	Jacksonville, FL	$46,394	7%	4.3%
14534	Pittsford, NY	Rochester, NY	$45,985	4%	5.0%
92688	Rancho Santa Margarita, CA	Orange County, CA	$64,416	10%	2.9%
57702	Rapid City, SD	Rapid City, SD	$42,112	12%	3.3%
89523	Reno, NV	Reno, NV	$47,402	3%	3.0%
23233	Richmond-Tuckahoe, VA	Richmond-Petersburg, VA	$54,197	12%	3.8%
24018	Roanoke, VA	Roanoke, VA	$44,698	11%	2.7%
55902	Rochester, MN	Rochester, MN	$57,338	12%	3.0%
72758	Rogers, AR	Fayetteville-Springdale-Rogers, AR	$39,929	6%	2.4%
30075	Roswell, GA	Atlanta, GA	$52,051	-1%	4.1%
91354	Santa Clarita, CA	Los Angeles–Long Beach, CA	$45,958	9%	5.9%
02067	Sharon, MA	Boston, MA-NH-ME	$62,504	17%	4.2%
66216	Shawnee, KS	Kansas City, MO-KS	$47,972	1%	5.8%
53044	Sheboygan, WI	Sheboygan, WI	$49,716	8%	3.5%
99223	Spokane, WA	Spokane, WA	$37,761	1%	4.8%
63304	St. Charles, MO	St. Louis, MO-IL	$48,411	7%	6.1%
77479	Sugar Land, TX	Houston, TX	$46,848	4%	5.7%
75791	Tyler, TX	Tyler, TX	$39,573	7%	3.9%
33594	Valrico, FL	Tampa–St. Petersburg–Clearwater, FL	$40,833	8%	3.5%
98607	Vancouver-Camas, WA	Portland-Vancouver, OR-WA	$47,265	0%	6.4%
23456	Virginia Beach, VA	Norfolk–Virginia Beach–Newport News, VA-NC	$49,704	15%	4.1%
53186	Waukesha, WI	Milwaukee-Waukesha, WI	$49,680	5%	4.7%
54403	Wausau, WI	Wausau, WI	$47,584	5%	3.2%
19382	West Chester, PA	Philadelphia, PA-NJ	$54,046	9%	4.8%
50325	West Des Moines–Clive, IA	Des Moines, IA	$50,306	8%	3.8%
47906	West Lafayette, IN	Lafayette, IN	$39,844	2%	4.1%
36695	West Mobile, AL	Mobile, AL	$35,679	0%	6.0%
10994	West Nyack, NY	New York, NY	$46,069	9%	5.2%
33326	Weston, FL	Fort Lauderdale, FL	$44,799	7%	4.2%
67212	Wichita (West), KS	Wichita, KS	$42,199	-1%	5.4%
22602	Winchester, VA	Winchester, VA-WV	$51,686	10%	2.0%
95694	Winters, CA	Yolo, CA	$45,335	11%	5.1%
17402	York, PA	York, PA	$46,867	4%	4.2%

Primary sources: U.S. Census, Bureau of Labor Statistics, National Association of Realtors

RECENT JOB GROWTH	FUTURE JOB GROWTH	INCOME TAX RATE	SALES TAX RATE	COST OF LIVING INDEX	BUYING POWER INDEX	MEDIAN HOME PRICE	HOME PRICE RATIO	HOME PRICE APPRECIATION	PERCENT HOMES OWNED	MEDIAN RENT
4.4%	12.8%	0.0%	8.2%	117.1	104	$310,300	5.7	12%	60%	$834
1.0%	10.0%	0.0%	0.0%	108.3	122	$228,400	3.9	12%	74%	$776
1.1%	5.2%	4.5%	6.0%	113.8	140	$203,400	2.9	14%	73%	$916
-1.7%	14.2%	4.1%	5.0%	83.4	131	$124,600	2.6	3%	70%	$655
-0.3%	3.0%	7.4%	6.9%	105.4	107	$291,600	5.8	16%	63%	$788
1.9%	4.9%	2.5%	6.0%	144.3	98	$407,400	6.4	16%	67%	$1,132
1.5%	9.0%	3.0%	8.0%	113.8	110	$265,000	4.8	11%	66%	$903
4.6%	16.2%	0.0%	6.5%	98.6	110	$193,100	4.0	14%	66%	$747
3.6%	17.7%	0.0%	6.0%	90.6	115	$200,800	4.3	15%	61%	$732
-1.0%	5.1%	7.1%	6.8%	88.4	116	$110,700	2.4	4%	68%	$687
1.8%	13.3%	6.0%	7.2%	167.5	86	$696,100	10.8	6%	58%	$1,317
1.7%	11.5%	0.0%	6.0%	89.6	105	$140,800	3.3	9%	57%	$609
4.3%	12.3%	0.0%	6.8%	106.8	99	$357,400	7.5	32%	56%	$852
2.3%	12.6%	5.8%	4.4%	90.3	134	$198,400	3.7	14%	67%	$810
1.9%	6.1%	5.8%	3.5%	95	105	$209,600	4.7	9%	67%	$586
3.6%	11.7%	8.0%	7.0%	97.3	132	$151,500	2.6	6%	75%	$745
7.4%	26.6%	7.0%	4.7%	86.6	103	$163,900	4.1	11%	70%	$545
-0.1%	19.6%	6.0%	6.0%	91.3	128	$166,500	3.2	5%	62%	$928
2.8%	4.8%	6.0%	8.2%	145.7	71	$474,800	10.3	26%	49%	$1,124
1.0%	5.3%	5.9%	5.0%	132.5	106	$418,500	6.7	11%	61%	$1,126
0.3%	13.0%	7.0%	6.5%	87.4	123	$157,100	3.3	6%	66%	$691
4.8%	9.4%	6.9%	5.5%	86.9	128	$129,000	2.6	9%	75%	$543
4.4%	13.7%	0.0%	7.8%	93	91	$158,600	4.2	12%	67%	$614
1.7%	8.2%	6.9%	5.2%	86.6	125	$141,900	2.9	8%	66%	$741
2.1%	17.0%	0.0%	8.2%	86.2	122	$142,500	3.0	4%	56%	$801
2.8%	13.1%	0.0%	6.3%	82.1	108	$126,700	3.2	7%	66%	$573
3.6%	11.5%	0.0%	6.0%	94.1	97	$213,000	5.2	19%	61%	$805
1.5%	23.0%	9.0%	0.0%	105.3	100	$238,000	5.0	12%	65%	$717
1.8%	10.8%	5.8%	4.5%	91.1	122	$192,000	3.9	22%	55%	$788
2.9%	11.8%	6.9%	5.5%	97	115	$216,800	4.4	11%	65%	$694
2.7%	9.9%	6.9%	5.0%	88.5	120	$130,400	2.7	7%	76%	$546
1.6%	7.1%	7.6%	6.0%	107	113	$211,000	3.9	16%	70%	$962
3.5%	17.1%	8.8%	6.0%	87.5	129	$145,100	2.9	6%	72%	$657
0.3%	9.8%	3.4%	5.0%	80.7	110	$95,400	2.4	2%	69%	$661
2.7%	13.1%	5.0%	9.5%	83.5	96	$129,100	3.6	2%	63%	$561
3.6%	3.9%	10.5%	8.2%	157.9	65	$506,800	11.0	16%	46%	$1,042
4.1%	16.3%	0.0%	6.0%	112.9	89	$381,800	8.5	29%	63%	$998
4.5%	12.1%	6.3%	5.9%	81.9	115	$106,300	2.5	2%	69%	$624
1.1%	16.5%	5.8%	4.5%	91.5	126	$186,300	3.6	19%	75%	$647
2.9%	14.0%	6.0%	7.3%	135.2	75	$433,800	9.6	26%	58%	$851
2.4%	9.6%	2.8%	6.0%	87.8	119	$144,300	3.1	13%	76%	$612

TABLE A.4 STANDARD OF LIVING
Neighborhood Level Data
SORTED BY NEIGHBORHOOD

ZIP CODE	NEIGHBORHOOD	METRO AREA	MEDIAN HOUSEHOLD INCOME	PERCENT OF HOUSEHOLDS W/INCOME > $100K	FUTURE JOB GROWTH	COST OF LIVING INDEX
79606	Abilene, TX	Abilene, TX	$49,378	11%	7%	84
87122	Albuquerque (Sandia Heights), NM	Albuquerque, NM	$98,844	46%	15%	130.9
99516	Anchorage, AK	Anchorage, AK	$107,470	48%	13%	134
54911	Appleton, WI	Appleton-Oshkosh-Neenah, WI	$45,629	8%	17%	90.2
19810	Arden-Brandywine, DE	Wilmington-Newark, DE-MD	$72,168	28%	10%	117.5
76002	Arlington, TX	Fort Worth–Arlington, TX	$70,857	13%	20%	93.1
78732	Austin (West), TX	Austin–San Marcos, TX	$109,908	55%	21%	125.2
98226	Bellingham, WA	Bellingham, WA	$46,034	11%	21%	109.4
18018	Bethlehem, PA	Allentown-Bethlehem-Easton, PA	$42,391	7%	5%	92.5
74012	Broken Arrow, OK	Tulsa, OK	$54,060	12%	9%	87.5
27513	Cary, NC	Raleigh-Durham–Chapel Hill, NC	$73,117	31%	21%	112.8
80104	Castle Rock, CO	Denver, CO	$78,438	34%	52%	133.4
22901	Charlottesville, VA	Charlottesville, VA	$53,863	18%	12%	110.8
01824	Chelmsford, MA	Boston, MA-NH-ME	$82,209	32%	6%	147.5
21045	Columbia, MD	Baltimore, MD	$76,424	27%	25%	114.7
65203	Columbia, MO	Columbia, MO	$46,474	15%	20%	96.2
52241	Coralville, IA	Iowa City, IA	$38,226	11%	10%	96.9
15108	Coraopolis–Moon Township, PA	Pittsburgh, PA	$54,621	15%	1%	100.3
53532	DeForest, WI	Madison, WI	$64,523	15%	13%	103.8
80220	Denver (Park Hill), CO	Denver, CO	$45,465	19%	5%	137.3
83616	Eagle, ID	Boise City, ID	$68,359	24%	22%	110.4
11730	East Islip, NY	Nassau-Suffolk, NY	$78,859	29%	7%	150.9
68022	Elkhorn, NE	Omaha, NE-IA	$75,816	25%	13%	99.2
97405	Eugene, OR	Eugene, OR	$46,158	16%	11%	107.4
45241	Evendale, OH	Cincinnati, OH-KY-IN	$66,560	27%	4%	106.6
58104	Fargo, ND	Fargo, ND	$69,218	23%	19%	101.7
37922	Farragut, TN	Knoxville, TN	$82,326	33%	13%	102.9
75028	Flower Mound, TX	Dallas, TX	$93,617	42%	26%	108.3
95630	Folsom, CA	Sacramento, CA	$83,829	30%	13%	151.2
37064	Franklin, TN	Nashville, TN	$65,177	22%	30%	108.2
80526	Fort Collins–Loveland, CO	Fort Collins–Loveland, CO	$52,204	15%	25%	114.3
32605	Gainesville, FL	Gainesville, FL	$55,734	17%	12%	90.5
20878	Gaithersburg, MD	Washington, DC-MD-VA-WV	$97,790	40%	9%	112.8
14068	Getzville, NY	Buffalo–Niagara Falls, NY	$73,486	28%	2%	107.8
97526	Grants Pass, OR	Josephine County	$33,346	6%	13%	97.2
54313	Green Bay, WI	Green Bay, WI	$68,000	17%	16%	102
29650	Greer, SC	Greenville-Spartanburg-Anderson, SC	$58,797	24%	15%	99.8
20170	Herndon, VA	Washington, DC-MD-VA-WV	$91,379	39%	16%	135.3
43026	Hilliard, OH	Columbus, OH	$66,433	19%	9%	103.4
37343	Hixson, TN	Chattanooga, TN-GA	$49,902	13%	7%	90.1
78232	Hollywood Park, TX	San Antonio, TX	$67,498	26%	19%	92.3
49426	Hudsonville, MI	Grand Rapids–Muskegon-Holland, MI	$60,415	15%	18%	103.9
29212	Irmo, SC	Columbia, SC	$63,487	20%	22%	96.7
84037	Kaysville, UT	Salt Lake City–Ogden, UT	$62,789	17%	25%	107.1
08824	Kendall Park, NJ	Middlesex-Somerset-Hunterdon, NJ	$101,760	42%	6%	136.6
60047	Lake Zurich, IL	Chicago, IL	$106,694	51%	18%	155.8
55044	Lakeville, MN	Minneapolis–St. Paul, MN-WI	$86,314	31%	29%	132
17601	Lancaster, PA	Lancaster, PA	$60,084	18%	10%	87.9
66049	Lawrence, KS	Lawrence, KS	$54,299	17%	12%	102.5
40503	Lexington, KY	Lexington, KY	$46,017	12%	10%	93
07039	Livingston, NJ	Newark, NJ	$105,769	50%	0%	164.4
84321	Logan, UT	Logan, UT	$32,874	6%	25%	92.1
92354	Loma Linda, CA	Riverside–San Bernardino, CA	$43,764	11%	18%	122.8
80027	Louisville, CO	Boulder-Longmont, CO	$78,989	30%	13%	144.7
35758	Madison, AL	Huntsville, AL	$70,126	22%	14%	96
28105	Matthews-Stallings, NC	Charlotte-Gastonia–Rock Hill, NC-SC	$63,789	23%	18%	104.6
43537	Maumee, OH	Toledo, OH	$52,383	15%	4%	101
89423	Minden-Gardnerville, NV	Douglas County	$58,214	14%	19%	120.3
98273	Mount Vernon, WA	Mount Vernon–Anacortes, WA	$42,147	9%	18%	105

BUYING POWER INDEX	WEEKLY DAYCARE COST	MEDIAN HOME PRICE	"SWEET SPOT" HOME PRICE	HOME PRICE RATIO	HOME PRICE APPRECIATION 2004–2005	PERCENT HOMES OWNED	MEDIAN HOME AGE	EFFECTIVE PROPERTY TAX RATE	APPROXIMATE PROPERTY TAX BILL
132	$110	$129,200	$160,000	2.6	10%	59%	35	2.2%	$3,520
169	$144	$332,800	$350,000	3.4	9%	83%	38	1.0%	$3,500
179	$200	$340,000	$400,000	3.2	12%	89%	34	1.4%	$5,600
113	$143	$131,400	$200,000	2.9	6%	60%	37	2.2%	$4,400
137	$203	$324,400	$325,000	4.5	15%	79%	41	0.8%	$2,600
170	$128	$150,600	$180,000	2.1	4%	89%	28	3.1%	$5,580
196	$145	$295,900	$240,000	2.7	2%	87%	32	3.0%	$7,200
94	$125	$320,100	$375,000	7.0	19%	65%	37	1.2%	$4,500
103	$107	$154,300	$220,000	3.6	13%	57%	40	1.2%	$2,640
138	$122	$124,000	$190,000	2.3	2%	74%	33	1.0%	$1,900
145	$159	$242,300	$230,000	3.3	5%	63%	31	1.0%	$2,300
132	$140	$240,000	$260,000	3.1	-6%	79%	33	0.8%	$2,002
109	$140	$304,300	$375,000	5.6	19%	54%	38	2.1%	$7,875
125	$240	$399,200	$450,000	4.9	10%	84%	39	1.2%	$5,400
149	$219	$350,800	$400,000	4.6	21%	68%	34	1.4%	$5,400
108	$155	$177,600	$200,000	3.8	7%	57%	34	1.0%	$2,000
88	$150	$171,600	$275,000	4.5	6%	47%	32	1.6%	$4,400
122	$172	$160,900	$260,000	2.9	6%	69%	39	2.5%	$6,500
139	$120	$221,600	$325,000	3.4	11%	76%	34	2.5%	$8,125
74	$181	$275,000	$350,000	6.0	-3%	56%	36	0.5%	$1,750
139	$95	$264,100	$350,000	3.9	7%	82%	34	1.8%	$6,300
117	$215	$476,000	$500,000	6.0	16%	85%	36	2.0%	$10,000
171	$130	$187,900	$190,000	2.5	5%	88%	34	2.5%	$4,750
96	$125	$255,600	$300,000	5.5	15%	66%	39	1.8%	$5,400
140	$174	$220,500	$280,000	3.3	5%	74%	40	1.3%	$3,640
152	$130	$215,900	$225,000	3.1	9%	64%	32	2.0%	$4,500
179	$125	$224,900	$225,000	2.7	7%	84%	36	0.8%	$1,688
193	$141	$211,700	$225,000	2.3	3%	88%	30	2.8%	$6,300
124	$184	$500,000	$525,000	6.0	20%	73%	35	1.2%	$6,300
135	$154	$243,600	$325,000	3.7	6%	74%	35	1.8%	$5,850
102	$155	$245,500	$225,000	4.7	5%	65%	32	1.0%	$2,250
138	$124	$183,400	$240,000	3.3	18%	70%	39	3.0%	$7,200
194	$241	$353,400	$550,000	3.6	21%	68%	33	1.2%	$6,600
153	$139	$201,600	$240,000	2.7	7%	77%	34	2.6%	$6,240
77	$85	$190,000	$300,000	5.7	13%	62%	41	1.4%	$4,200
149	$130	$204,500	$220,000	3.0	7%	83%	34	1.8%	$3,960
132	$80	$184,900	$190,000	3.1	4%	67%	36	1.0%	$1,900
151	$216	$489,700	$525,000	5.4	19%	71%	31	1.0%	$5,250
144	$174	$205,700	$225,000	3.1	5%	69%	31	1.5%	$3,375
124	$132	$145,400	$190,000	2.9	6%	74%	37	1.0%	$1,900
164	$104	$173,500	$210,000	2.6	5%	64%	38	2.5%	$5,250
130	$160	$197,300	$235,000	3.3	5%	89%	33	0.8%	$1,763
147	$110	$174,800	$190,000	2.8	5%	73%	35	1.0%	$1,900
131	$85	$209,100	$250,000	3.3	4%	85%	30	1.3%	$3,250
167	$215	$408,300	$500,000	4.0	16%	88%	34	1.8%	$9,000
153	$190	$411,000	$425,000	3.9	-2%	92%	33	1.7%	$7,225
146	$202	$310,100	$325,000	3.6	9%	89%	30	1.0%	$3,250
153	$162	$139,200	$220,000	2.3	10%	72%	40	1.5%	$3,300
119	$147	$212,100	$210,000	3.9	7%	59%	34	1.3%	$2,730
111	$140	$156,000	$225,000	3.4	5%	67%	38	1.4%	$3,150
144	$257	$514,400	$550,000	4.9	16%	93%	39	1.2%	$6,600
80	$105	$156,000	$200,000	4.7	6%	45%	29	1.1%	$2,200
80	$145	$363,000	$425,000	8.3	18%	39%	37	1.1%	$4,675
122	$145	$297,500	$350,000	3.8	6%	65%	32	1.0%	$3,500
163	$106	$171,400	$190,000	2.4	5%	65%	33	0.6%	$1,140
136	$152	$205,200	$220,000	3.2	4%	72%	34	1.2%	$2,640
116	$150	$170,000	$190,000	3.2	4%	66%	37	1.8%	$3,325
108	$65	$461,600	$450,000	7.9	31%	82%	41	1.0%	$4,500
90	$132	$235,400	$350,000	5.6	14%	57%	34	1.4%	$4,900

continues

TABLE A.4 STANDARD OF LIVING (continued)
Neighborhood Level Data
SORTED BY NEIGHBORHOOD

ZIP CODE	NEIGHBORHOOD	METRO AREA	MEDIAN HOUSEHOLD INCOME	PERCENT OF HOUSEHOLDS W/INCOME > $100K	FUTURE JOB GROWTH	COST OF LIVING INDEX
98275	Mukilteo, WA	Seattle-Bellevue-Everett, WA	$69,166	26%	25%	141.1
03062	Nashua, NH	Nashua, NH	$73,176	23%	9%	119
06470	Newtown, CT	Danbury, CT	$102,105	44%	4%	165.2
46060	Noblesville, IN	Indianapolis, IN	$62,555	20%	29%	97.7
02760	North Attleboro, MA	Providence–Fall River–Warwick, RI-MA	$69,585	18%	6%	134
07648	Norwood, NJ	Bergen-Passaic, NJ	$98,779	47%	5%	190.7
60302	Oak Park, IL	Chicago, IL	$60,390	27%	5%	139.2
98501	Olympia, WA	Olympia, WA	$48,871	13%	21%	108.4
32073	Orange Park, FL	Jacksonville, FL	$59,002	17%	26%	97.7
14534	Pittsford, NY	Rochester, NY	$90,809	43%	4%	112.5
92688	Rancho Santa Margarita, CA	Orange County, CA	$81,230	30%	13%	155.9
57702	Rapid City, SD	Rapid City, SD	$53,255	12%	14%	97.8
89523	Reno, NV	Reno, NV	$61,263	17%	12%	116.5
23233	Richmond-Tuckahoe, VA	Richmond-Petersburg, VA	$76,143	29%	12%	109.6
24018	Roanoke, VA	Roanoke, VA	$61,822	19%	3%	94.6
55902	Rochester, MN	Rochester, MN	$67,373	28%	12%	116.1
72758	Rogers, AR	Fayetteville-Springdale-Rogers, AR	$46,970	14%	30%	84.8
30075	Roswell, GA	Atlanta, GA	$87,206	43%	11%	126.6
91354	Santa Clarita, CA	Los Angeles–Long Beach, CA	$92,439	38%	5%	153.9
02067	Sharon, MA	Boston, MA-NH-ME	$104,568	44%	9%	165.6
66216	Shawnee, KS	Kansas City, MO-KS	$68,124	26%	18%	104.7
53044	Sheboygan, WI	Sheboygan, WI	$77,541	29%	8%	99.4
99223	Spokane, WA	Spokane, WA	$52,403	17%	14%	101.4
63304	St. Charles, MO	St. Louis, MO-IL	$71,851	21%	20%	101.7
77479	Sugar Land, TX	Houston, TX	$99,555	47%	35%	114.7
75791	Tyler, TX	Tyler, TX	$52,501	9%	12%	82.1
33594	Valrico, FL	Tampa–St. Petersburg–Clearwater, FL	$66,177	21%	16%	103.2
98607	Vancouver-Camas, WA	Portland-Vancouver, OR-WA	$61,647	21%	27%	117.2
23456	Virginia Beach, VA	Norfolk–Virginia Beach–Newport News, VA-NC	$63,133	12%	14%	101.7
53186	Waukesha, WI	Milwaukee-Waukesha, WI	$51,496	11%	16%	104.6
54403	Wausau, WI	Wausau, WI	$43,146	10%	9%	88.1
19382	West Chester, PA	Philadelphia, PA-NJ	$77,454	32%	11%	129.7
50325	West Des Moines–Clive, IA	Des Moines, IA	$80,455	36%	12%	112.7
47906	West Lafayette, IN	Lafayette, IN	$32,205	12%	10%	95.8
36695	West Mobile, AL	Mobile, AL	$55,849	14%	9%	92.6
10994	West Nyack, NY	New York, NY	$116,191	55%	6%	172.1
33326	Weston, FL	Fort Lauderdale, FL	$71,176	27%	13%	148.2
67212	Wichita (West), KS	Wichita, KS	$51,388	10%	9%	88.4
22602	Winchester, VA	Winchester, VA-WV	$53,346	12%	16%	94.1
95694	Winters, CA	Yolo, CA	$54,530	13%	18%	131
17402	York, PA	York, PA	$50,300	11%	8%	94.1

Primary sources: U.S. Census, Bureau of Labor Statistics, National Association of Realtors

BUYING POWER INDEX	WEEKLY DAYCARE COST	MEDIAN HOME PRICE	"SWEET SPOT" HOME PRICE	HOME PRICE RATIO	HOME PRICE APPRECIATION 2004–2005	PERCENT HOMES OWNED	MEDIAN HOME AGE	EFFECTIVE PROPERTY TAX RATE	APPROXIMATE PROPERTY TAX BILL
110	$188	$358,800	$400,000	5.2	6%	66%	34	1.4%	$5,600
138	$210	$291,500	$340,000	4.0	12%	72%	37	2.0%	$6,800
138	$200	$499,200	$475,000	4.9	14%	89%	36	1.9%	$9,025
143	$170	$176,800	$200,000	2.8	3%	75%	34	2.0%	$4,000
116	$198	$413,700	$400,000	5.9	16%	66%	35	0.9%	$3,720
116	$265	$631,000	$625,000	6.4	16%	84%	39	1.6%	$10,000
97	$155	$399,200	$500,000	6.6	12%	53%	37	3.0%	$15,000
101	$140	$203,500	$350,000	4.2	4%	59%	37	1.5%	$5,250
135	$156	$234,200	$280,000	4.0	15%	69%	36	1.8%	$5,040
181	$174	$221,000	$220,000	2.4	4%	89%	40	3.2%	$7,040
117	$200	$523,800	$650,000	6.4	-6%	73%	29	2.0%	$13,000
122	$80	$181,400	$190,000	3.4	9%	69%	39	2.0%	$3,800
118	$132	$465,500	$450,000	7.6	32%	60%	34	1.3%	$5,850
155	$140	$289,500	$300,000	3.8	14%	70%	37	1.4%	$4,200
146	$112	$219,000	$200,000	3.5	19%	76%	41	1.2%	$2,400
130	$148	$239,500	$275,000	3.6	6%	72%	36	1.3%	$3,575
124	$135	$157,100	$225,000	3.3	11%	67%	36	0.8%	$1,800
154	$160	$304,000	$300,000	3.5	5%	80%	36	1.4%	$4,200
134	$155	$619,000	$650,000	6.7	13%	89%	31	1.2%	$7,800
141	$200	$493,900	$525,000	4.7	12%	89%	37	1.6%	$8,400
146	$140	$207,100	$225,000	3.0	6%	82%	35	1.1%	$2,475
175	$120	$192,400	$300,000	2.5	9%	86%	37	3.1%	$9,300
116	$157	$209,900	$340,000	4.0	12%	71%	37	1.5%	$5,100
158	$171	$212,000	$235,000	3.0	8%	90%	33	2.2%	$5,170
194	$139	$248,400	$220,000	2.5	4%	86%	31	3.0%	$6,600
143	$105	$119,700	$200,000	2.3	7%	78%	34	1.2%	$2,400
144	$165	$265,000	$360,000	4.0	19%	85%	35	2.3%	$8,280
118	$175	$270,000	$325,000	4.4	5%	78%	34	1.4%	$4,550
139	$157	$262,900	$300,000	4.2	22%	74%	30	1.2%	$3,600
110	$183	$225,100	$275,000	4.4	11%	54%	36	1.9%	$5,225
110	$110	$131,900	$225,000	3.1	7%	63%	38	2.5%	$5,625
134	$218	$401,300	$425,000	5.2	15%	70%	36	1.4%	$5,950
160	$100	$245,400	$235,000	3.1	6%	74%	34	3.5%	$8,225
75	$175	$165,500	$220,000	5.1	2%	42%	30	1.2%	$2,640
135	$120	$151,500	$220,000	2.7	2%	75%	33	0.8%	$1,760
151	$275	$605,700	$550,000	5.2	16%	90%	38	1.6%	$8,800
107	$160	$420,000	$425,000	5.9	35%	71%	34	1.5%	$6,375
130	$149	$121,500	$160,000	2.4	2%	68%	34	1.1%	$1,760
127	$135	$242,800	$375,000	4.6	19%	76%	36	0.7%	$2,738
93	$120	$408,800	$500,000	7.5	25%	65%	33	1.1%	$5,500
120	$160	$174,700	$220,000	3.5	13%	72%	41	1.5%	$3,300

			HIGH SCHOOL GRADUATE	2-YEAR COLLEGE DEGREE	4-YEAR COLLEGE DEGREE
TABLE A.5 EDUCATION					
Metro Area Level Data					
SORTED BY NEIGHBORHOOD					
ZIP CODE	**NEIGHBORHOOD**	**METRO AREA**			
79606	Abilene, TX	Abilene, TX	76%	6%	21%
87122	Albuquerque (Sandia Heights), NM	Albuquerque, NM	81%	8%	20%
99516	Anchorage, AK	Anchorage, AK	92%	13%	29%
54911	Appleton, WI	Appleton-Oshkosh-Neenah, WI	83%	9%	13%
19810	Arden-Brandywine, DE	Wilmington-Newark, DE-MD	81%	8%	19%
76002	Arlington, TX	Fort Worth–Arlington, TX	80%	9%	23%
78732	Austin (West), TX	Austin–San Marcos, TX	81%	7%	27%
98226	Bellingham, WA	Bellingham, WA	85%	9%	22%
18018	Bethlehem, PA	Allentown-Bethlehem-Easton, PA	79%	8%	14%
74012	Broken Arrow, OK	Tulsa, OK	79%	8%	17%
27513	Cary, NC	Raleigh-Durham–Chapel Hill, NC	80%	10%	23%
80104	Castle Rock, CO	Denver, CO	87%	10%	29%
22901	Charlottesville, VA	Charlottesville, VA	74%	7%	20%
01824	Chelmsford, MA	Boston, MA-NH-ME	86%	11%	24%
21045	Columbia, MD	Baltimore, MD	81%	7%	21%
65203	Columbia, MO	Columbia, MO	85%	7%	23%
52241	Coralville, IA	Iowa City, IA	91%	12%	28%
15108	Coraopolis–Moon Township, PA	Pittsburgh, PA	79%	7%	13%
53532	DeForest, WI	Madison, WI	90%	13%	26%
80220	Denver (Park Hill), CO	Denver, CO	87%	10%	29%
83616	Eagle, ID	Boise City, ID	81%	11%	21%
11730	East Islip, NY	Nassau-Suffolk, NY	87%	10%	22%
68022	Elkhorn, NE	Omaha, NE-IA	87%	10%	19%
97405	Eugene, OR	Eugene, OR	81%	10%	18%
45241	Evendale, OH	Cincinnati, OH-KY-IN	76%	7%	15%
58104	Fargo, ND	Fargo, ND	83%	15%	20%
37922	Farragut, TN	Knoxville, TN	72%	6%	15%
75028	Flower Mound, TX	Dallas, TX	79%	8%	25%
95630	Folsom, CA	Sacramento, CA	85%	15%	24%
37064	Franklin, TN	Nashville, TN	75%	6%	18%
80526	Fort Collins–Loveland, CO	Fort Collins–Loveland, CO	89%	11%	26%
32605	Gainesville, FL	Gainesville, FL	84%	11%	22%
20878	Gaithersburg, MD	Washington, DC-MD-VA-WV	84%	7%	26%
14068	Getzville, NY	Buffalo–Niagara Falls, NY	81%	12%	15%
97526	Grants Pass, OR	Josephine County	79%	9%	14%
54313	Green Bay, WI	Green Bay, WI	84%	11%	15%
29650	Greer, SC	Greenville-Spartanburg-Anderson, SC	70%	9%	15%
20170	Herndon, VA	Washington, DC-MD-VA-WV	84%	7%	26%
43026	Hilliard, OH	Columbus, OH	82%	7%	19%
37343	Hixson, TN	Chattanooga, TN-GA	68%	7%	15%
78232	Hollywood Park, TX	San Antonio, TX	75%	8%	18%
49426	Hudsonville, MI	Grand Rapids–Muskegon-Holland, MI	81%	11%	15%
29212	Irmo, SC	Columbia, SC	80%	11%	21%
84037	Kaysville, UT	Salt Lake City–Ogden, UT	88%	12%	26%
08824	Kendall Park, NJ	Middlesex-Somerset-Hunterdon, NJ	87%	8%	27%
60047	Lake Zurich, IL	Chicago, IL	83%	8%	23%
55044	Lakeville, MN	Minneapolis–St. Paul, MN-WI	88%	11%	23%
17601	Lancaster, PA	Lancaster, PA	74%	5%	13%
66049	Lawrence, KS	Lawrence, KS	89%	6%	26%
40503	Lexington, KY	Lexington, KY	78%	7%	23%
07039	Livingston, NJ	Newark, NJ	85%	7%	26%
84321	Logan, UT	Logan, UT	91%	8%	28%
92354	Loma Linda, CA	Riverside–San Bernardino, CA	76%	12%	15%
80027	Louisville, CO	Boulder-Longmont, CO	94%	8%	37%
35758	Madison, AL	Huntsville, AL	78%	9%	24%
28105	Matthews-Stallings, NC	Charlotte-Gastonia–Rock Hill, NC-SC	75%	10%	19%
43537	Maumee, OH	Toledo, OH	81%	9%	15%
89423	Minden-Gardnerville, NV	Douglas County	89%	12%	23%
98273	Mount Vernon, WA	Mount Vernon–Anacortes, WA	83%	12%	20%

GRADUATE/ PROF DEGREE	ATTENDING PUBLIC SCHOOL	EXPENDITURES PER PUPIL	STUDENT/ TEACHER RATIO	STATE UNIVERSITY SAT (VERBAL)	STATE UNIVERSITY SAT (MATH)	STATE UNIVERSITY COMBINED ACT	STATE UNIVERSITY TUITION
6%	97.0%	$5,370	13.3	540	570	23	$5,735
14%	88.3%	$4,869	16.1	470	460	19	$3,738
13%	93.0%	$6,669	22.5	440	440	18	$3,517
4%	83.4%	$6,418	15.7	N/A	N/A	26	$5,862
10%	78.5%	$7,214	17.6	540	560	24	$6,954
8%	93.3%	$4,983	15.9	540	570	23	$5,735
12%	94.3%	$5,243	14.8	540	570	23	$5,735
9%	91.2%	$5,593	19.7	520	550	23	$5,286
7%	85.1%	$6,369	17.8	530	560		$10,856
7%	91.3%	$4,635	17	N/A	N/A	23	$4,515
12%	91.6%	$5,390	15.5	530	570	23	$4,282
13%	90.6%	$5,796	19.3	530	550	23	$4,341
14%	86.8%	$6,316	12.7	540	560		$5,838
13%	88.3%	$7,033	15.4	510	520	21	$9,186
13%	83.7%	$6,846	16.8	560	590		$7,410
15%	92.8%	$5,234	14.5	540	540	23	$6,622
17%	89.5%	$5,599	17.2	530	540	22	$5,396
6%	86.3%	$6,954	17.3	530	560		$10,856
13%	91.6%	$7,553	13.9	N/A	N/A	26	$5,862
13%	90.6%	$5,796	19.3	530	550	23	$4,341
8%	93.4%	$4,582	19.1	450	425	18	$3,520
16%	87.9%	$11,562	14.5	520	550	24	$5,966
7%	85.0%	$5,382	15.7	510	530	22	$5,268
9%	93.7%	$5,941	20.7	490	500		$5,490
8%	80.1%	$5,950	17.6	520	550	23	$7,542
5%	92.6%	$5,194	16.5	N/A	N/A	20	$4,828
7%	92.5%	$5,334	14.6	500	500	21	$4,748
10%	92.3%	$5,162	15.2	540	570	23	$5,735
9%	91.8%	$5,233	21.6	560	600	23	$6,586
8%	87.3%	$5,306	15.1	500	500	21	$4,748
15%	92.2%	$5,460	18.8	530	550	23	$4,341
20%	90.3%	$5,183	17.7	570	590		$2,955
17%	86.9%	$7,203	15.7	560	590		$7,410
9%	84.5%	$8,605	14.5	520	550	24	$5,966
4%	91.2%	$5,949	19.21	490	500		$5,490
5%	84.7%	$6,626	15.5	N/A	N/A	26	$5,862
7%	91.1%	$5,108	16.4	510	520	22	$6,416
17%	86.9%	$7,203	15.7	540	560		$5,838
9%	89.7%	$6,272	17.6	520	550	23	$7,542
6%	85.0%	$5,075	14.1	500	500	21	$4,748
10%	91.8%	$5,639	15.2	540	570	23	$5,735
6%	85.9%	$6,324	18.5	490	515	22	$6,999
11%	92.8%	$5,817	16.2	510	520	22	$6,416
11%	95.9%	$3,863	22.9	N/A	N/A	21	$4,000
14%	86.7%	$9,491	14.4	530	550		$8,564
12%	84.6%	$6,567	17.6	N/A	N/A	25	$7,944
8%	89.0%	$6,266	17.6	540	560	23	$8,230
5%	81.0%	$6,075	16.6	530	560		$10,856
18%	96.2%	$5,900	14.4	N/A	N/A	21	$4,737
15%	87.1%	$5,478	19.1	510	510	22	$5,240
13%	85.4%	$10,159	14.5	530	550		$8,564
11%	95.0%	$3,655	20.6	N/A	N/A	21	$4,000
8%	93.7%	$5,048	22.4	560	600	23	$6,586
23%	86.7%	$4,981	18.4	530	550	23	$4,341
9%	89.9%	$5,171	15.9	490	500	21	$4,630
8%	89.6%	$5,252	16.6	530	570	23	$4,282
6%	82.4%	$6,275	15.7	520	550	23	$7,542
9%	91.4%	$5,728	18	450	450	18	$3,270
7%	91.4%	$5,324	19.5	520	550	23	$5,286

continues

TABLE A.5 EDUCATION (continued)
Metro Area Level Data
SORTED BY NEIGHBORHOOD

ZIP CODE	NEIGHBORHOOD	METRO AREA	HIGH SCHOOL GRADUATE	2-YEAR COLLEGE DEGREE	4-YEAR COLLEGE DEGREE
98275	Mukilteo, WA	Seattle-Bellevue-Everett, WA	89%	12%	30%
03062	Nashua, NH	Nashua, NH	88%	12%	28%
06470	Newtown, CT	Danbury, CT	91%	8%	31%
46060	Noblesville, IN	Indianapolis, IN	82%	8%	16%
02760	North Attleboro, MA	Providence–Fall River–Warwick, RI-MA	78%	9%	21%
07648	Norwood, NJ	Bergen-Passaic, NJ	83%	7%	25%
60302	Oak Park, IL	Chicago, IL	83%	8%	23%
98501	Olympia, WA	Olympia, WA	88%	14%	22%
32073	Orange Park, FL	Jacksonville, FL	79%	10%	17%
14534	Pittsford, NY	Rochester, NY	82%	12%	17%
92688	Rancho Santa Margarita, CA	Orange County, CA	87%	14%	31%
57702	Rapid City, SD	Rapid City, SD	83%	8%	17%
89523	Reno, NV	Reno, NV	82%	11%	21%
23233	Richmond-Tuckahoe, VA	Richmond-Petersburg, VA	75%	7%	18%
24018	Roanoke, VA	Roanoke, VA	73%	9%	15%
55902	Rochester, MN	Rochester, MN	89%	15%	21%
72758	Rogers, AR	Fayetteville-Springdale-Rogers, AR	74%	6%	13%
30075	Roswell, GA	Atlanta, GA	79%	7%	23%
91354	Santa Clarita, CA	Los Angeles–Long Beach, CA	77%	11%	24%
02067	Sharon, MA	Boston, MA-NH-ME	88%	10%	28%
66216	Shawnee, KS	Kansas City, MO-KS	83%	7%	20%
53044	Sheboygan, WI	Sheboygan, WI	82%	10%	14%
99223	Spokane, WA	Spokane, WA	86%	15%	21%
63304	St. Charles, MO	St. Louis, MO-IL	76%	7%	15%
77479	Sugar Land, TX	Houston, TX	77%	7%	24%
75791	Tyler, TX	Tyler, TX	74%	12%	16%
33594	Valrico, FL	Tampa–St. Petersburg–Clearwater, FL	78%	10%	18%
98607	Vancouver-Camas, WA	Portland-Vancouver, OR-WA	84%	11%	22%
23456	Virginia Beach, VA	Norfolk–Virginia Beach–Newport News, VA-NC	77%	9%	17%
53186	Waukesha, WI	Milwaukee-Waukesha, WI	85%	10%	22%
54403	Wausau, WI	Wausau, WI	79%	10%	10%
19382	West Chester, PA	Philadelphia, PA-NJ	83%	8%	21%
50325	West Des Moines–Clive, IA	Des Moines, IA	88%	11%	19%
47906	West Lafayette, IN	Lafayette, IN	84%	8%	13%
36695	West Mobile, AL	Mobile, AL	73%	7%	14%
10994	West Nyack, NY	New York, NY	79%	7%	22%
33326	Weston, FL	Fort Lauderdale, FL	82%	10%	20%
67212	Wichita (West), KS	Wichita, KS	84%	7%	20%
22602	Winchester, VA	Winchester, VA-WV	72%	7%	14%
95694	Winters, CA	Yolo, CA	75%	9%	21%
17402	York, PA	York, PA	78%	6%	12%

Primary sources: U.S. Census, National Center for Education Statistics

GRADUATE/ PROF DEGREE	ATTENDING PUBLIC SCHOOL	EXPENDITURES PER PUPIL	STUDENT/ TEACHER RATIO	STATE UNIVERSITY SAT (VERBAL)	STATE UNIVERSITY SAT (MATH)	STATE UNIVERSITY COMBINED ACT	STATE UNIVERSITY TUITION
11%	89.1%	$5,838	20.4	520	550	23	$5,286
12%	84.6%	$7,291	15	510	520		$9,226
19%	89.2%	$8,149	13.9	530	550		$7,490
9%	87.5%	$6,249	18	490	500	22	$6,777
11%	85.0%	$7,469	12.6	510	520	21	$9,186
13%	82.8%	$10,178	14.5	530	550		$8,564
12%	84.6%	$6,567	17.6	N/A	N/A	25	$7,944
12%	95.1%	$6,035	19.5	520	550	23	$5,286
7%	87.1%	$4,985	19.2	570	590		$2,955
10%	90.2%	$8,436	13.7	520	550	24	$5,966
14%	88.9%	$5,119	22.9	560	600	23	$6,586
5%	92.6%	$4,715	16.2	N/A	N/A	20	$4,802
8%	93.0%	$5,235	19.5	450	450	18	$3,270
9%	93.5%	$5,653	14.7	540	560		$5,838
7%	95.2%	$6,060	13.9	540	560		$5,838
11%	86.1%	$5,629	16.9	540	560	23	$8,230
6%	94.9%	$4,671	16.3	510	510	22	$5,135
9%	92.4%	$5,795	16.2	550	560	23	$4,272
13%	88.0%	$5,519	22.1	560	600	23	$6,586
17%	87.3%	$8,055	16.3	510	520	21	$9,186
9%	89.4%	$5,790	15.6	N/A	N/A	21	$4,737
5%	85.9%	$6,817	16.1	N/A	N/A	26	$5,862
9%	90.8%	$5,879	20.3	520	550	23	$5,286
8%	81.4%	$5,908	16.2	540	540	23	$6,622
10%	92.7%	$5,210	16.8	540	570	23	$5,735
7%	92.7%	$4,946	14.5	540	570	23	$5,735
8%	89.9%	$5,380	17.6	570	590		$2,955
9%	90.9%	$6,032	20.1	520	550	23	$5,286
8%	90.3%	$5,379	14.3	540	560		$5,838
8%	80.7%	$7,697	16.3	N/A	N/A	26	$5,862
3%	86.0%	$6,665	15.2	N/A	N/A	26	$5,862
11%	78.9%	$7,620	16.4	530	560		$10,856
7%	92.0%	$5,807	15.5	530	540	22	$5,396
9%	90.4%	$5,828	17.3	490	500	22	$6,777
6%	83.8%	$4,542	16.1	490	500	21	$4,630
16%	80.3%	$8,640	17.3	520	550	24	$5,966
10%	86.6%	$5,453	21.1	570	590		$2,955
8%	89.0%	$5,477	16.1	N/A	N/A	21	$4,737
5%	85.1%	$5,303	14.9556	540	560		$5,838
11%	92.9%	$5,227	20	560	600	23	$6,586
5%	92.2%	$5,753	17	530	560		$10,856

TABLE A.6 EDUCATION
Neighborhood Level Data
SORTED BY NEIGHBORHOOD

ZIP CODE	NEIGHBORHOOD	METRO AREA	HIGH SCHOOL GRADUATE	4-YEAR COLLEGE DEGREE
79606	Abilene, TX	Abilene, TX	94%	23%
87122	Albuquerque (Sandia Heights), NM	Albuquerque, NM	98%	30%
99516	Anchorage, AK	Anchorage, AK	97%	31%
54911	Appleton, WI	Appleton-Oshkosh-Neenah, WI	87%	21%
19810	Arden-Brandywine, DE	Wilmington-Newark, DE-MD	93%	27%
76002	Arlington, TX	Fort Worth–Arlington, TX	90%	23%
78732	Austin (West), TX	Austin–San Marcos, TX	96%	47%
98226	Bellingham, WA	Bellingham, WA	90%	21%
18018	Bethlehem, PA	Allentown-Bethlehem-Easton, PA	82%	15%
74012	Broken Arrow, OK	Tulsa, OK	90%	23%
27513	Cary, NC	Raleigh-Durham–Chapel Hill, NC	96%	39%
80104	Castle Rock, CO	Denver, CO	95%	32%
22901	Charlottesville, VA	Charlottesville, VA	91%	26%
01824	Chelmsford, MA	Boston, MA-NH-ME	93%	27%
21045	Columbia, MD	Baltimore, MD	94%	30%
65203	Columbia, MO	Columbia, MO	93%	29%
52241	Coralville, IA	Iowa City, IA	96%	30%
15108	Coraopolis–Moon Township, PA	Pittsburgh, PA	89%	22%
53532	DeForest, WI	Madison, WI	92%	20%
80220	Denver (Park Hill), CO	Denver, CO	87%	27%
83616	Eagle, ID	Boise City, ID	94%	27%
11730	East Islip, NY	Nassau-Suffolk, NY	91%	16%
68022	Elkhorn, NE	Omaha, NE-IA	95%	24%
97405	Eugene, OR	Eugene, OR	94%	27%
45241	Evendale, OH	Cincinnati, OH-KY-IN	91%	27%
58104	Fargo, ND	Fargo, ND	96%	33%
37922	Farragut, TN	Knoxville, TN	96%	34%
75028	Flower Mound, TX	Dallas, TX	98%	39%
95630	Folsom, CA	Sacramento, CA	89%	26%
80526	Fort Collins–Loveland, CO	Fort Collins–Loveland, CO	96%	30%
37064	Franklin, TN	Nashville, TN	86%	26%
32605	Gainesville, FL	Gainesville, FL	94%	24%
20878	Gaithersburg, MD	Washington, DC-MD-VA-WV	94%	34%
14068	Getzville, NY	Buffalo–Niagara Falls, NY	89%	23%
97526	Grants Pass, OR	Josephine County	84%	10%
54313	Green Bay, WI	Green Bay, WI	93%	22%
29650	Greer, SC	Greenville-Spartanburg-Anderson, SC	89%	29%
20170	Herndon, VA	Washington, DC-MD-VA-WV	85%	30%
43026	Hilliard, OH	Columbus, OH	93%	31%
37343	Hixson, TN	Chattanooga, TN-GA	87%	19%
78232	Hollywood Park, TX	San Antonio, TX	96%	30%
49426	Hudsonville, MI	Grand Rapids–Muskegon-Holland, MI	90%	19%
29212	Irmo, SC	Columbia, SC	95%	31%
84037	Kaysville, UT	Salt Lake City–Ogden, UT	95%	27%
08824	Kendall Park, NJ	Middlesex-Somerset-Hunterdon, NJ	94%	28%
60047	Lake Zurich, IL	Chicago, IL	95%	33%
55044	Lakeville, MN	Minneapolis–St. Paul, MN-WI	96%	30%
17601	Lancaster, PA	Lancaster, PA	89%	24%
66049	Lawrence, KS	Lawrence, KS	96%	31%
40503	Lexington, KY	Lexington, KY	93%	22%
07039	Livingston, NJ	Newark, NJ	94%	31%
84321	Logan, UT	Logan, UT	89%	22%
92354	Loma Linda, CA	Riverside–San Bernardino, CA	87%	23%
80027	Louisville, CO	Boulder-Longmont, CO	97%	40%
35758	Madison, AL	Huntsville, AL	94%	34%
28105	Matthews-Stallings, NC	Charlotte-Gastonia–Rock Hill, NC-SC	93%	29%
43537	Maumee, OH	Toledo, OH	93%	23%
89423	Minden-Gardnerville, NV	Douglas County	93%	15%
98273	Mount Vernon, WA	Mount Vernon–Anacortes, WA	79%	14%
98275	Mukilteo, WA	Seattle-Bellevue-Everett, WA	96%	29%
03062	Nashua, NH	Nashua, NH	91%	24%

GRADUATE/ PROF. DEGREE	COMBINED 4-YR + GRADUATE	EXPENDITURES PER PUPIL	STUDENT/ TEACHER RATIO	PRIMARY TEST SCORES	SECONDARY TEST SCORES	SCHOOL LUNCH PERCENTAGE
13%	36%	4298	15.2	110	107	18.1%
35%	65%	4590	23.4		90	7.5%
20%	50%	6598	18.2	143		6.4%
8%	30%	6305	17.5	102	110	24.4%
18%	45%	7185	16.2	105	107	27.4%
5%	28%	4274	17	103	106	28.8%
18%	65%	4716	16.8	119	101	3.1%
11%	32%	5415	21.7	120	135	32.2%
9%	25%	6435	16.2	89	87	36.8%
8%	31%	4256	17.6	118		30.0%
24%	63%	4847	16.5	110	113	28.6%
14%	46%	4905	15.4	113	137	4.8%
28%	54%	6640	13.2	99	101	26.6%
18%	45%	6545		90	72	3.9%
26%	56%	7188	15.8	138	145	22.5%
27%	56%	5146	14.3	100	117	18.4%
22%	51%	5646	18.8	109		21.2%
10%	32%	7992	15.5	111	124	6.6%
6%	26%	6911	15.4	107	103	11.2%
22%	49%	5665	18.8	66	52	55.3%
12%	39%	3834	18.7	119	98	10.7%
13%	29%	10935	18.2	108	109	5.7%
10%	34%	4674	15.4	99	100	8.7%
21%	48%	6026	21	123	108	29.8%
17%	44%	7236	15.8	114	113	28.2%
12%	45%	5024	24.3	133	112	3.8%
21%	55%	4793		131		
12%	51%	4720	15.4	110	104	4.4%
12%	38%	4695	21	173	145	8.6%
20%	51%	4722	19.3	121	135	15.6%
11%	37%	5339		129		
29%	53%	4932	17.8	100	91	47.8%
30%	64%	8201	18.3	121	123	13.1%
21%	44%	8845	14.3	128	110	
5%	15%	5459	20.6	107	95	47.6%
7%	29%	5972	17.5	97	104	11.8%
14%	43%	4724	16.1	101	112	18.0%
18%	48%	7116	17.2	108	107	23.5%
13%	44%	5130	17.5	113	118	9.7%
9%	28%	4802		123	102	
19%	49%	5286	16.3	109	103	20.7%
8%	27%	4613	20.7	121	107	12.8%
17%	49%	5497	14.8	107	91	33.6%
11%	38%	3624	22.2	107	102	26.5%
17%	44%	8415	14.5	116	106	5.0%
17%	50%	5249	16.9	77	64	15.2%
9%	39%	5218	14.9	111	105	10.1%
13%	37%	6640	17.9	94	78	11.4%
24%	56%	5823	15.8	111	107	14.0%
19%	41%	5856	20.4	99	121	25.6%
27%	58%	11466	14.6	115	109	0.8%
12%	33%	3745	18.9	139	87	42.4%
21%	43%	4452	20.2	78	101	54.6%
24%	63%	5124	19.2	126	120	4.8%
17%	51%		17.9	151	111	17.6%
12%	41%	4996	18.6	104	89	20.4%
10%	33%	6281	16.6	109	108	13.8%
7%	23%	5855	19.1	129	131	19.0%
7%	21%	5270	20.6	112	113	36.6%
13%	42%	5484	20.7	84	97	62.3%
14%	38%	5556	19.3	102	125	12.6%

continues

TABLE A.6 EDUCATION (continued)
Neighborhood Level Data
SORTED BY NEIGHBORHOOD

ZIP CODE	NEIGHBORHOOD	METRO AREA	HIGH SCHOOL GRADUATE	4-YEAR COLLEGE DEGREE
06470	Newtown, CT	Danbury, CT	93%	31%
46060	Noblesville, IN	Indianapolis, IN	90%	27%
02760	North Attleboro, MA	Providence–Fall River–Warwick, RI-MA	88%	23%
07648	Norwood, NJ	Bergen-Passaic, NJ	91%	29%
60302	Oak Park, IL	Chicago, IL	95%	32%
98501	Olympia, WA	Olympia, WA	93%	23%
32073	Orange Park, FL	Jacksonville, FL	92%	19%
14534	Pittsford, NY	Rochester, NY	96%	32%
92688	Rancho Santa Margarita, CA	Orange County, CA	95%	31%
57702	Rapid City, SD	Rapid City, SD	93%	24%
89523	Reno, NV	Reno, NV	95%	26%
23233	Richmond-Tuckahoe, VA	Richmond-Petersburg, VA	96%	37%
24018	Roanoke, VA	Roanoke, VA	94%	27%
55902	Rochester, MN	Rochester, MN	94%	26%
72758	Rogers, AR	Fayetteville-Springdale-Rogers, AR	83%	19%
30075	Roswell, GA	Atlanta, GA	94%	38%
91354	Santa Clarita, CA	Los Angeles–Long Beach, CA	96%	31%
02067	Sharon, MA	Boston, MA-NH-ME	97%	31%
66216	Shawnee, KS	Kansas City, MO-KS	95%	28%
53044	Sheboygan, WI	Sheboygan, WI	98%	35%
99223	Spokane, WA	Spokane, WA	95%	27%
63304	St. Charles, MO	St. Louis, MO-IL	92%	25%
77479	Sugar Land, TX	Houston, TX	94%	38%
75791	Tyler, TX	Tyler, TX	89%	16%
33594	Valrico, FL	Tampa–St. Petersburg–Clearwater, FL	90%	22%
98607	Vancouver-Camas, WA	Portland-Vancouver, OR-WA	92%	18%
23456	Virginia Beach, VA	Norfolk–Virginia Beach–Newport News, VA-NC	91%	20%
53186	Waukesha, WI	Milwaukee-Waukesha, WI	89%	22%
54403	Wausau, WI	Wausau, WI	83%	15%
19382	West Chester, PA	Philadelphia, PA-NJ	93%	32%
50325	West Des Moines–Clive, IA	Des Moines, IA	98%	39%
47906	West Lafayette, IN	Lafayette, IN	93%	25%
36695	West Mobile, AL	Mobile, AL	90%	23%
10994	West Nyack, NY	New York, NY	93%	26%
33326	Weston, FL	Fort Lauderdale, FL	94%	26%
67212	Wichita (West), KS	Wichita, KS	92%	24%
22602	Winchester, VA	Winchester, VA-WV	81%	14%
95694	Winters, CA	Yolo, CA	74%	14%
17402	York, PA	York, PA	83%	18%

Primary sources: U.S. Census, National Center for Education Statistics

GRADUATE/ PROF. DEGREE	COMBINED 4-YR + GRADUATE	EXPENDITURES PER PUPIL	STUDENT/ TEACHER RATIO	PRIMARY TEST SCORES	SECONDARY TEST SCORES	SCHOOL LUNCH PERCENTAGE
20%	51%	7539	15.7	119	118	17.7%
11%	38%	5237	17	126	123	21.1%
10%	33%	4853		112	97	8.0%
14%	43%	8456	14.8	111	115	1.0%
31%	63%	7037	15.4	117	127	7.2%
13%	36%	5671	21.1	111	104	13.6%
11%	29%	4458	19	109	105	25.4%
31%	63%	9397	16.7	126	122	1.5%
12%	43%	4660	20.3	175	95	5.4%
12%	36%	4363	17.9	95	139	
13%	38%	4896	21	123	123	13.9%
21%	58%	5306	18.4	123	112	6.1%
15%	42%	5790	15	115	109	9.8%
26%	52%	6102	20.3	106	93	13.5%
7%	26%	4180	23.4	130	151	23.5%
19%	57%	6141	16	114	101	10.9%
13%	44%	4570	22.6	147	104	2.6%
31%	62%	6476		127	132	3.8%
15%	43%	5464	16.5	89	103	49.7%
18%	53%	7222	13.8	101	109	38.2%
16%	44%	5902	22.4	114	79	21.3%
8%	33%	5068	14.1	124	211	25.2%
21%	59%	4489	17.4	106	117	28.6%
7%	23%	4046	16.5	108	120	32.8%
11%	33%	5188	19.3	108	106	24.7%
12%	29%	5655	21.3	113	110	23.4%
8%	27%	4834	18.2	112	105	25.6%
10%	33%	6850	14.9	110	112	27.8%
9%	23%	6867	14.6	96	104	36.2%
21%	53%	7564	18.2	131	138	6.5%
17%	56%	5507	18.3	110		14.7%
30%	55%	5918	18.2	120	126	16.0%
13%	35%	4229	16.5	117	101	36.5%
24%	50%	10063	12.9	119	113	5.0%
16%	42%	5180	22.2	118	107	11.3%
9%	33%	5506	16.1	116		11.4%
7%	21%	5223	15.4	97	109	19.3%
8%	23%	4631	19.4	91	96	46.2%
8%	26%	6079	18.1	94	97	13.3%

TABLE A.7 LIFESTYLE
Metro Area Level Data
SORTED BY NEIGHBORHOOD

ZIP CODE	NEIGHBORHOOD	METRO AREA	PROFESSIONAL SPORTS	ZOO/ AQUARIUM RATING	AMUSEMENT PARK RATING	PROFESSIONAL THEATER	OVERALL MUSEUM RATING	SCIENCE MUSEUM RATING	CHILDREN'S MUSEUM RATING	PUBLIC LIBRARIES	LIBRARY VOLUMES
79606	Abilene, TX	Abilene, TX	2	3	1	1	3	1	4	3	1.9
87122	Albuquerque (Sandia Heights), NM	Albuquerque, NM	3	6	5	1	7	9	8	33	2.7
99516	Anchorage, AK	Anchorage, AK	3	3	1	10	5	6	7	6	2.4
54911	Appleton, WI	Appleton-Oshkosh-Neenah, WI	4	1	1	1	7	4	1	18	3.6
19810	Arden-Brandywine, DE	Wilmington-Newark, DE-MD	8	4	4	8	7	4	2	23	2.3
76002	Arlington, TX	Fort Worth–Arlington, TX	8	7	9	9	7	7	10	51	2.2
78732	Austin (West), TX	Austin–San Marcos, TX	3	1	1	1	8	7	6	44	2.4
98226	Bellingham, WA	Bellingham, WA	2	1	1	1	5	3	5	11	3.3
18018	Bethlehem, PA	Allentown-Bethlehem-Easton, PA	5	1	7	6	9	6	2	22	2.2
74012	Broken Arrow, OK	Tulsa, OK	3	6	1	5	6	5	7	40	2.6
27513	Cary, NC	Raleigh-Durham–Chapel Hill, NC	5	4	1	6	8	7	6	41	2.2
80104	Castle Rock, CO	Denver, CO	9	7	7	10	9	7	7	63	2.6
22901	Charlottesville, VA	Charlottesville, VA	2	1	1	1	6	2	6	9	3.0
01824	Chelmsford, MA	Boston, MA-NH-ME	8	3	5	8	6	3	3	12	2.8
21045	Columbia, MD	Baltimore, MD	9	10	5	10	10	9	9	82	3.6
65203	Columbia, MO	Columbia, MO	2	1	1	1	4	4	1	4	2.7
52241	Coralville, IA	Iowa City, IA	2	1	1	1	5	3	1	5	3.6
15108	Coraopolis– Moon Township, PA	Pittsburgh, PA	7	8	6	10	9	9	5	128	2.7
53532	DeForest, WI	Madison, WI	2	6	1	1	7	2	5	26	3.8
80220	Denver (Park Hill) , CO	Denver, CO	9	7	7	10	9	7	7	63	2.6
83616	Eagle, ID	Boise City, ID	3	1	1	1	5	5	1	15	2.2
11730	East Islip, NY	Nassau-Suffolk, NY	10	7	6	9	10	10	7	126	6.3
68022	Elkhorn, NE	Omaha, NE-IA	3	8	1	8	7	5	7	33	2.8
97405	Eugene, OR	Eugene, OR	2	1	1	1	6	6	1	8	2.6
45241	Evendale, OH	Cincinnati, OH-KY-IN	6	7	9	8	9	7	10	83	4.6
58104	Fargo, ND	Fargo, ND	2	1	1	1	5	1	3	17	2.5
37922	Farragut, TN	Knoxville, TN	2	5	8	1	8	7	8	35	2.1
75028	Flower Mound, TX	Dallas, TX	9	6	5	10	9	8	8	101	2.2
95630	Folsom, CA	Sacramento, CA	6	5	9	9	8	7	2	42	1.6
37064	Franklin, TN	Nashville, TN	7	5	1	1	9	5	1	44	1.8
80526	Fort Collins–Loveland, CO	Fort Collins–Loveland, CO	4	1	1	1	6	7	1	7	3.0
32605	Gainesville, FL	Gainesville, FL	2	2	1	6	5	4	6	11	3.7
20878	Gaithersburg, MD	Washington, DC-MD-VA-WV	9	10	2	10	10	10	10	153	3.0
14068	Getzville, NY	Buffalo–Niagara Falls, NY	6	5	1	10	8	5	2	64	2.7
97526	Grants Pass, OR	Josephine County	1	1	1	1	2	1	1	4	2.3
54313	Green Bay, WI	Green Bay, WI	6	1	1	1	5	1	3	9	1.9
29650	Greer, SC	Greenville-Spartanburg-Anderson, SC	3	3	1	1	8	7	1	37	2.4
20170	Herndon, VA	Washington, DC-MD-VA-WV	9	10	2	10	10	10	10	153	3.0
43026	Hilliard, OH	Columbus, OH	5	7	4	1	9	9	8	57	4.2
37343	Hixson, TN	Chattanooga, TN-GA	2	8	5	1	7	1	6	14	3.4
78232	Hollywood Park, TX	San Antonio, TX	6	7	9	1	9	8	6	32	1.4
49426	Hudsonville, MI	Grand Rapids–Muskegon-Holland, MI	3	5	7	1	8	7	7	62	3.5
29212	Irmo, SC	Columbia, SC	3	7	1	1	7	6	5	19	3.1
84037	Kaysville, UT	Salt Lake City–Ogden, UT	6	7	3	9	8	7	7	34	2.6
08824	Kendall Park, NJ	Middlesex-Somerset-Hunterdon, NJ	10	4	5	9	8	7	3	56	3.9
60047	Lake Zurich, IL	Chicago, IL	9	10	10	10	10	10	10	291	3.8
55044	Lakeville, MN	Minneapolis–St. Paul, MN-WI	7	9	10	10	10	9	8	132	3.5
17601	Lancaster, PA	Lancaster, PA	4	1	3	1	7	3	4	17	1.6
66049	Lawrence, KS	Lawrence, KS	2	1	1	1	5	4	1	3	3.2
40503	Lexington, KY	Lexington, KY	3	1	1	1	8	5	7	12	2.1
07039	Livingston, NJ	Newark, NJ	10	8	7	10	9	9	9	114	3.8
84321	Logan, UT	Logan, UT	4	4	1	3	4	5	4	7	3.1
92354	Loma Linda, CA	Riverside–San Bernardino, CA	9	5	7	5	9	10	8	78	1.3
80027	Louisville, CO	Boulder-Longmont, CO	8	2	2	3	6	5	4	9	3.8
35758	Madison, AL	Huntsville, AL	2	1	2	1	5	5	1	16	1.6
28105	Matthews-Stallings, NC	Charlotte-Gastonia–Rock Hill, NC-SC	5	2	5	1	8	8	4	50	2.2
43537	Maumee, OH	Toledo, OH	6	7	1	1	6	5	1	39	5.5

WAREHOUSE CLUBS	STARBUCKS	GOLF COURSE RATING	NATIONAL PARK RATING	INLAND WATER AREA	DAYS MOSTLY SUNNY	DAYS PRECIP.	DAYS >90°F	DAYS <32°F	JULY RELATIVE HUMIDITY	AVERAGE DAILY COMMUTE	COMMUTE BY AUTO	DAILY TRANSIT MILES	AUTO INSURANCE	GAS COST PER GALLON
3	1	2	1	2	246	65	89	56	59	16.4	75%	5.3	926	$2.96
4	15	3	5	1	283	59	61	123	43	22.9	72%	8.9	1255	$3.06
5	0	1	9	4	131	113	12	192	71	19.5	70%	13.1	1059	$2.65
1	2	4	1	10	192	120	7	163	73	18.1	77%	9.0	775	$3.04
3	4	7	2	6	201	123	18	102	70	24.9	77%	16.9	1198	$3.23
5	25	7	1	4	234	79	92	41	67	26.8	79%	5.5	1020	$2.98
4	32	4	1	4	231	82	101	23	67	25.5	73%	18.1	1012	$2.92
3	8	1	10	5	136	160	3	32	74	20.8	73%	14.4	979	$3.08
4	0	5	3	2	206	133	16	127	71	23.6	79%	8.0	988	$3.22
4	4	5	1	7	228	90	70	85	52	21.5	77%	6.5	1120	$2.97
5	17	6	1	2	220	112	25	82	71	24.9	75%	4.9	834	$3.14
5	70	7	3	3	246	88	32	163	53	26.5	73%	24.3	1480	$3.02
3	3	1	4	2	218	125	19	94	69	22.8	67%	5.7	792	$3.25
5	1	5	2	4	197	137	15	120	68	26.9	82%	5.0	1308	$3.15
9	23	8	3	9	205	112	31	100	67	29.8	73%	17.2	1100	$3.30
3	0	2	1	2	191	109	39	108	69	17.8	67%	5.0	836	$3.06
1	0	2	1	2	194	107	16	157	73	17.7	67%	13.8	656	$3.07
4	29	9	2	4	161	152	7	124	68	25.3	75%	21.4	1116	$3.10
3	7	3	1	4	190	117	12	164	73	19.9	70%	16.4	780	$3.07
5	70	7	3	3	246	88	32	163	53	26.5	73%	24.3	1480	$3.02
3	9	2	2	2	214	91	43	124	57	20.2	77%	3.4	709	$2.95
9	56	10	4	9	219	125	10	85	68	33	73%	32.4	1558	$3.32
4	6	5	2	4	220	99	38	138	68	19.4	76%	6.1	1007	$3.26
3	6	2	8	4	158	137	15	54	72	19.9	74%	15.5	867	$2.91
7	21	8	1	3	177	131	28	98	70	24.6	76%	12.0	873	$3.00
3	0	2	1	2	199	102	12	181	71	16.2	63%	5.0	647	$3.04
4	3	5	8	8	202	128	19	71	71	23.2	79%	3.9	834	$3.17
8	87	8	1	7	233	79	88	39	67	27.9	76%	16.2	1499	$3.00
8	67	6	10	9	265	57	77	17	66	26.1	76%	9.5	1322	$3.03
6	16	5	2	4	210	119	37	75	71	25.8	74%	5.4	1085	$3.11
4	7	2	10	4	246	88	32	163	53	21.4	72%	4.9	1035	$3.04
3	6	1	1	5	242	116	104	2	74	21.1	70%	9.0	1019	$2.99
10	155	10	4	8	207	111	37	75	64	32.8	66%	24.4	1140	$3.31
5	12	6	1	2	159	168	2	137	73	21.1	76%	8.9	1385	$3.37
1	2	2	7	7	196	125	54	90	67	20	73%	0.0	870	$3.06
3	1	2	1	2	192	120	7	163	73	17.5	79%	9.8	753	$2.93
5	0	5	1	2	221	119	29	68	70	22.5	78%	1.9	894	$3.11
10	155	10	4	8	207	111	37	75	64	32.8	66%	24.4	1140	$3.31
5	25	8	1	3	181	136	15	122	70	23.2	79%	9.0	1059	$2.99
3	0	3	2	4	213	121	49	75	72	23.7	76%	5.0	1046	$3.06
5	20	5	2	2	227	81	111	22	67	24.5	73%	20.9	1030	$2.90
5	3	7	1	3	163	144	11	149	73	20.7	82%	4.8	1030	$3.00
4	2	3	3	5	223	111	64	60	73	23.5	75%	4.6	856	$3.20
7	11	5	8	10	232	88	58	134	54	22.4	74%	19.5	930	$2.87
6	10	9	3	6	216	128	17	88	67	31.3	79%	24.9	1457	$3.17
10	197	10	2	3	197	123	21	119	67	31.5	70%	26.5	1090	$3.04
7	41	9	3	10	200	113	15	158	69	23.7	73%	10.9	1144	$2.84
4	1	3	1	3	193	125	24	107	67	21.7	73%	7.1	994	$3.22
1	1	1	1	3	205	96	45	123	68	19.4	74%	0.0	758	$3.10
3	2	4	1	2	197	130	16	97	70	21.2	72%	3.9	879	$2.90
4	19	10	4	7	207	129	20	87	65	30.8	75%	24.9	1633	$3.16
4	2	2	8	10	232	92	58	134	54	16.8	65%	3.2	820	$2.89
9	59	10	10	7	268	35	20	0	69	31.1	72%	6.7	1378	$3.03
1	9	3	7	3	246	88	32	163	53	22.4	69%	0.0	1040	$3.03
3	0	2	2	2	207	121	38	65	73	21.9	81%	3.0	823	$3.14
7	20	7	2	3	214	111	31	71	69	26.1	78%	3.9	844	$3.17
1	0	5	2	2	181	136	13	145	72	20.5	80%	7.4	1062	$2.98

continues

TABLE A.7 LIFESTYLE (continued)
Metro Area Level Data
SORTED BY NEIGHBORHOOD

ZIP CODE	NEIGHBORHOOD	METRO AREA	PROFESSIONAL SPORTS	ZOO/AQUARIUM RATING	AMUSEMENT PARK RATING	PROFESSIONAL THEATER	OVERALL MUSEUM RATING	SCIENCE MUSEUM RATING	CHILDREN'S MUSEUM RATING	PUBLIC LIBRARIES	LIBRARY VOLUMES
89423	Minden-Gardnerville, NV	Douglas County	1	1	2	1	4	4	2	2	2.5
98273	Mount Vernon, WA	Mount Vernon–Anacortes, WA	5	5	5	6	6	7	7	6	2.4
98275	Mukilteo, WA	Seattle-Bellevue-Everett, WA	8	8	8	10	9	9	10	89	2.9
03062	Nashua, NH	Nashua, NH	8	3	5	8	4	3	3	15	3.5
06470	Newtown, CT	Danbury, CT	10	4	5	8	5	7	3	13	4.0
46060	Noblesville, IN	Indianapolis, IN	7	7	1	8	9	8	10	69	3.5
02760	North Attleboro, MA	Providence–Fall River–Warwick, RI-MA	5	6	3	10	10	7	5	80	3.3
07648	Norwood, NJ	Bergen-Passaic, NJ	10	7	5	8	8	7	9	84	4.2
60302	Oak Park, IL	Chicago, IL	9	10	10	10	10	10	10	291	3.8
98501	Olympia, WA	Olympia, WA	7	3	3	3	7	3	5	27	2.7
32073	Orange Park, FL	Jacksonville, FL	6	8	1	1	8	5	1	27	2.7
14534	Pittsford, NY	Rochester, NY	3	5	6	6	9	7	7	78	4.0
92688	Rancho Santa Margarita, CA	Orange County, CA	10	5	10	5	8	7	5	53	1.9
57702	Rapid City, SD	Rapid City, SD	2	5	1	1	6	7	1	4	1.7
89523	Reno, NV	Reno, NV	2	1	5	1	5	5	4	13	2.3
23233	Richmond-Tuckahoe, VA	Richmond-Petersburg, VA	3	1	8	8	9	7	7	51	3.1
24018	Roanoke, VA	Roanoke, VA	3	1	1	1	5	5	1	17	4.0
55902	Rochester, MN	Rochester, MN	2	1	1	1	3	1	1	2	0.7
72758	Rogers, AR	Fayetteville-Springdale-Rogers, AR	2	1	1	1	6	3	1	12	2.3
30075	Roswell, GA	Atlanta, GA	7	9	10	10	10	8	9	134	1.8
91354	Santa Clarita, CA	Los Angeles–Long Beach, CA	10	10	10	10	10	10	10	238	2.2
02067	Sharon, MA	Boston, MA-NH-ME	9	8	7	10	10	10	10	203	6.0
66216	Shawnee, KS	Kansas City, MO-KS	6	7	4	8	9	5	9	81	6.9
53044	Sheboygan, WI	Sheboygan, WI	2	1	1	1	5	1	1	8	4.4
99223	Spokane, WA	Spokane, WA	3	1	1	1	5	1	3	16	2.7
63304	St Charles, MO	St. Louis, MO-IL	8	9	10	8	9	7	10	116	4.5
77479	Sugar Land, TX	Houston, TX	8	7	9	10	9	7	8	94	1.6
75791	Tyler, TX	Tyler, TX	2	6	1	1	3	1	1	6	2.7
33594	Valrico, FL	Tampa–St. Petersburg–Clearwater, FL	7	6	9	8	9	4	7	62	2.2
98607	Vancouver-Camas, WA	Portland-Vancouver, OR-WA	6	7	8	7	9	7	5	65	2.5
23456	Virginia Beach, VA	Norfolk-Virginia Beach-Newport News, VA-NC	3	8	9	6	9	10	10	50	2.8
53186	Waukesha, WI	Milwaukee-Waukesha, WI	6	7	1	9	9	7	7	53	4.0
54403	Wausau, WI	Wausau, WI	2	1	1	1	2	1	1	8	2.7
19382	West Chester, PA	Philadelphia, PA-NJ	10	8	6	10	10	9	9	216	2.9
50325	West Des Moines–Clive, IA	Des Moines, IA	3	3	1	1	6	6	6	35	3.3
47906	West Lafayette, IN	Lafayette, IN	2	3	1	1	5	2	1	8	3.9
36695	West Mobile, AL	Mobile, AL	2	1	1	1	6	4	3	24	1.6
10994	West Nyack, NY	New York, NY	10	10	6	10	10	10	10	279	5.1
33326	Weston, FL	Fort Lauderdale, FL	8	2	3	3	6	6	5	41	1.6
67212	Wichita (West), KS	Wichita, KS	3	5	4	1	8	8	7	38	3.7
22602	Winchester, VA	Winchester, VA-WV	7	8	2	8	8	8	8	7	20.2
95694	Winters, CA	Yolo, CA	4	2	3	3	5	5	3	8	2.8
17402	York, PA	York, PA	4	1	1	1	4	1	1	15	1.1

Primary sources: Sperling's BestPlaces, assorted trade associations, U.S. National Climatic Data Center

WAREHOUSE CLUBS	STARBUCKS	GOLF COURSE RATING	NATIONAL PARK RATING	INLAND WATER AREA	DAYS MOSTLY SUNNY	DAYS PRECIP.	DAYS > 90°F	DAYS < 32°F	JULY RELATIVE HUMIDITY	AVERAGE DAILY COMMUTE	COMMUTE BY AUTO	DAILY TRANSIT MILES	AUTO INSURANCE	GAS COST PER GALLON
2	1	2	7	10	255	51	50	189	50	23.5	79%	0.0	1100	$3.05
6	5	5	10	5	136	152	3	32	74	25.1	77%	2.1	1345	$3.01
8	191	7	10	8	136	160	3	32	74	27.3	72%	39.4	1615	$2.91
4	1	5	2	4	197	147	2	147	68	25.5	82%	1.0	906	$3.06
4	4	8	3	6	188	128	20	137	68	25.1	81%	5.7	1215	$3.10
6	30	7	1	2	191	122	15	122	73	23.9	80%	6.3	871	$3.00
4	9	5	1	7	205	134	8	123	68	22.6	78%	12.2	1213	$3.22
6	19	9	3	6	207	129	20	87	65	28.6	73%	24.9	1467	$3.15
10	197	10	2	3	197	123	21	119	67	31.5	70%	26.5	1090	$3.04
3	7	3	7	6	137	163	6	89	71	24.4	74%	23.5	985	$2.87
6	17	6	2	10	226	116	82	12	75	26.6	74%	8.6	1063	$3.00
8	9	7	1	4	170	182	11	135	73	21.1	76%	6.7	1358	$3.21
8	105	8	10	4	258	40	5	0	71	27.2	78%	8.2	1093	$2.97
3	0	2	10	2	205	96	32	169	71	17.3	70%	3.9	646	$3.05
3	11	2	8	10	255	49	52	189	50	19.2	70%	14.6	1140	$3.06
7	13	5	2	6	210	113	41	85	72	24.3	72%	7.5	848	$3.12
1	0	2	5	2	217	121	20	92	65	20.6	76%	6.7	800	$3.12
3	0	9	3	2	200	113	15	158	69	16.3	74%	7.5	951	$2.80
4	0	1	3	2	220	96	60	90	70	19.6	73%	4.0	830	$2.97
10	80	9	2	4	219	116	19	59	70	31.2	77%	16.7	1154	$3.01
10	281	10	10	4	258	35	5	0	71	29.4	70%	18.9	1812	$3.00
10	91	9	2	7	205	128	12	99	67	27.7	69%	27.4	1616	$3.17
5	19	8	1	4	213	102	40	106	69	22.9	78%	7.8	1219	$3.02
1	0	7	1	2	195	122	9	146	73	16.9	74%	7.5	758	$3.05
4	12	2	3	3	176	114	21	141	63	21.2	76%	5.6	1230	$2.97
7	21	7	2	6	206	108	37	107	70	25.5	76%	13.2	1213	$3.10
9	77	9	4	6	203	107	81	24	77	29	75%	15.1	1519	$2.97
3	1	2	1	2	217	97	87	1	71	22.2	80%	0.0	919	$2.99
7	28	9	2	7	238	107	81	4	74	25.6	79%	8.7	1308	$3.00
5	103	6	6	4	137	152	8	44	74	24.5	73%	21.9	1021	$2.80
7	16	5	5	8	212	115	30	54	71	24.1	69%	9.6	878	$3.11
5	21	7	1	4	195	122	9	146	73	22.1	78%	15.1	1032	$3.05
1	1	1	1	3	200	185	4	170	72	18.4	69%	5.3	750	$2.95
9	52	10	3	5	205	116	19	101	67	28.7	72%	17.4	1331	$3.24
1	2	4	1	2	199	106	21	137	69	19.3	75%	9.4	681	$3.09
3	1	2	1	5	191	122	15	122	73	17.7	76%	7.3	782	$3.01
3	1	3	2	8	217	124	81	19	73	25.4	77%	3.0	833	$2.76
8	182	10	4	10	232	121	16	81	65	38.9	42%	62.9	2279	$3.30
8	22	8	5	3	248	129	30	0	75	27.4	81%	15.5	1099	$2.96
4	2	3	1	2	224	84	62	114	66	19.1	80%	4.6	787	$3.08
7	3	8	4	8	206	118	33	80	65	27.3	79%	20.7	1050	$3.15
1	5	2	7	4	276	60	82	25	67	21.2	70%	11.3	893	$3.07
3	1	3	2	2	193	125	24	107	67	24	80%	4.1	972	$3.22

TABLE A.8 LIFESTYLE
Neighborhood Level Data

SORTED BY NEIGHBORHOOD

ZIP CODE	NEIGHBORHOOD	METRO AREA	LEISURE RATING	ARTS RATING
79606	Abilene, TX	Abilene, TX	3	6
87122	Albuquerque (Sandia Heights), NM	Albuquerque, NM	7	8
99516	Anchorage, AK	Anchorage, AK	7	7
54911	Appleton, WI	Appleton-Oshkosh-Neenah, WI	5	2
19810	Arden-Brandywine, DE	Wilmington-Newark, DE-MD	4	4
76002	Arlington, TX	Fort Worth–Arlington, TX	8	6
78732	Austin (West), TX	Austin–San Marcos, TX	5	8
98226	Bellingham, WA	Bellingham, WA	6	2
18018	Bethlehem, PA	Allentown-Bethlehem-Easton, PA	8	6
74012	Broken Arrow, OK	Tulsa, OK	4	7
27513	Cary, NC	Raleigh-Durham–Chapel Hill, NC	4	8
80104	Castle Rock, CO	Denver, CO	9	10
22901	Charlottesville, VA	Charlottesville, VA	3	6
01824	Chelmsford, MA	Boston, MA-NH-ME	8	6
21045	Columbia, MD	Baltimore, MD	9	9
65203	Columbia, MO	Columbia, MO	3	7
52241	Coralville, IA	Iowa City, IA	1	6
15108	Coraopolis–Moon Township, PA	Pittsburgh, PA	9	10
53532	DeForest, WI	Madison, WI	4	9
80220	Denver (Park Hill), CO	Denver, CO	9	10
83616	Eagle, ID	Boise City, ID	6	7
11730	East Islip, NY	Nassau-Suffolk, NY	10	9
68022	Elkhorn, NE	Omaha, NE-IA	5	8
97405	Eugene, OR	Eugene, OR	8	6
45241	Evendale, OH	Cincinnati, OH-KY-IN	8	10
58104	Fargo, ND	Fargo, ND	2	6
37922	Farragut, TN	Knoxville, TN	6	7
75028	Flower Mound, TX	Dallas, TX	9	9
95630	Folsom, CA	Sacramento, CA	9	7
37064	Franklin, TN	Nashville, TN	7	7
80526	Fort Collins–Loveland, CO	Fort Collins–Loveland, CO	9	6
32605	Gainesville, FL	Gainesville, FL	3	8
20878	Gaithersburg, MD	Washington, DC-MD-VA-WV	10	10
14068	Getzville, NY	Buffalo–Niagara Falls, NY	8	10
97526	Grants Pass, OR	Josephine County	5	2
54313	Green Bay, WI	Green Bay, WI	5	5
29650	Greer, SC	Greenville-Spartanburg-Anderson, SC	6	8
20170	Herndon, VA	Washington, DC-MD-VA-WV	10	10
43026	Hilliard, OH	Columbus, OH	5	9
37343	Hixson, TN	Chattanooga, TN-GA	4	4
78232	Hollywood Park, TX	San Antonio, TX	7	4
49426	Hudsonville, MI	Grand Rapids–Muskegon-Holland, MI	6	7
29212	Irmo, SC	Columbia, SC	1	7
84037	Kaysville, UT	Salt Lake City–Ogden, UT	9	9
08824	Kendall Park, NJ	Middlesex-Somerset-Hunterdon, NJ	9	10
60047	Lake Zurich, IL	Chicago, IL	10	10
55044	Lakeville, MN	Minneapolis–St. Paul, MN-WI	9	10
17601	Lancaster, PA	Lancaster, PA	6	0
66049	Lawrence, KS	Lawrence, KS	0	6
40503	Lexington, KY	Lexington, KY	2	8
07039	Livingston, NJ	Newark, NJ	9	9
84321	Logan, UT	Logan, UT	7	2
92354	Loma Linda, CA	Riverside–San Bernardino, CA	9	7
80027	Louisville, CO	Boulder-Longmont, CO	9	6
35758	Madison, AL	Huntsville, AL	1	5
28105	Matthews-Stallings, NC	Charlotte-Gastonia–Rock Hill, NC-SC	7	7
43537	Maumee, OH	Toledo, OH	5	9
89423	Minden-Gardnerville, NV	Douglas County	9	2
98273	Mount Vernon, WA	Mount Vernon–Anacortes, WA	5	4
98275	Mukilteo, WA	Seattle-Bellevue-Everett, WA	7	2
03062	Nashua, NH	Nashua, NH	6	2

CLIMATE RATING	PHYSICAL SETTING SCORE	DOWNTOWN CORE SCORE	PERCENT OF COMMUTES < 30 MIN	PERCENT OF COMMUTES > 1 HOUR
9	2	6	89%	3%
9	8	7	72%	4%
1	10	5	79%	4%
2	5	6	86%	2%
5	5	3	69%	5%
9	2	2	44%	10%
9	5	6	41%	2%
8	9	7	78%	4%
3	3	6	81%	5%
8	1	3	73%	2%
6	5	5	70%	3%
5	8	6	47%	8%
7	7	10	85%	2%
1	5	6	60%	7%
4	4	7	54%	12%
4	4	6	84%	3%
3	3	5	83%	3%
3	4	6	71%	5%
2	4	9	64%	7%
5	5	9	66%	4%
6	8	6	66%	2%
8	6	6	56%	17%
2	4	5	69%	2%
6	7	9	82%	3%
3	4	3	75%	2%
4	1	4	88%	3%
4	5	5	68%	4%
9	3	4	42%	7%
9	3	5	54%	7%
2	4	6	59%	3%
5	9	10	80%	5%
8	5	8	82%	4%
4	6	8	47%	14%
1	3	2	78%	2%
5	7	7	78%	3%
2	5	6	87%	3%
5	4	4	77%	4%
4	3	6	57%	9%
4	3	3	69%	4%
2	5	6	71%	3%
10	3	3	67%	3%
1	3	5	74%	2%
2	5	5	66%	4%
4	7	7	59%	5%
6	4	4	49%	20%
3	3	8	43%	12%
1	4	8	60%	4%
3	3	2	79%	4%
3	2	5	70%	4%
4	4	5	82%	3%
5	3	3	56%	16%
3	8	6	87%	3%
10	3	1	75%	8%
6	9	6	70%	5%
2	6	6	84%	1%
4	4	6	51%	5%
4	2	4	82%	3%
8	10	5	68%	8%
7	9	5	70%	8%
8	9	8	57%	12%
0	5	5	61%	10%

continues

TABLE A.8 LIFESTYLE (continued)
Neighborhood Level Data
SORTED BY NEIGHBORHOOD

ZIP CODE	NEIGHBORHOOD	METRO AREA	LEISURE RATING	ARTS RATING
06470	Newtown, CT	Danbury, CT	8	6
46060	Noblesville, IN	Indianapolis, IN	8	9
02760	North Attleboro, MA	Providence–Fall River–Warwick, RI-MA	9	8
07648	Norwood, NJ	Bergen-Passaic, NJ	10	7
60302	Oak Park, IL	Chicago, IL	10	10
98501	Olympia, WA	Olympia, WA	8	3
32073	Orange Park, FL	Jacksonville, FL	3	2
14534	Pittsford, NY	Rochester, NY	8	8
92688	Rancho Santa Margarita, CA	Orange County, CA	10	5
57702	Rapid City, SD	Rapid City, SD	5	0
89523	Reno, NV	Reno, NV	7	5
23233	Richmond-Tuckahoe, VA	Richmond-Petersburg, VA	5	9
24018	Roanoke, VA	Roanoke, VA	3	8
55902	Rochester, MN	Rochester, MN	7	10
72758	Rogers, AR	Fayetteville-Springdale-Rogers, AR	3	3
30075	Roswell, GA	Atlanta, GA	9	9
91354	Santa Clarita, CA	Los Angeles–Long Beach, CA	10	10
02067	Sharon, MA	Boston, MA-NH-ME	10	10
66216	Shawnee, KS	Kansas City, MO-KS	8	10
53044	Sheboygan, WI	Sheboygan, WI	4	4
99223	Spokane, WA	Spokane, WA	1	7
63304	St Charles, MO	St. Louis, MO-IL	6	9
77479	Sugar Land, TX	Houston, TX	9	9
75791	Tyler, TX	Tyler, TX	2	1
33594	Valrico, FL	Tampa–St. Petersburg–Clearwater, FL	9	8
98607	Vancouver-Camas, WA	Portland-Vancouver, OR-WA	8	9
23456	Virginia Beach, VA	Norfolk–Virginia Beach–Newport News, VA-NC	7	7
53186	Waukesha, WI	Milwaukee-Waukesha, WI	9	10
54403	Wausau, WI	Wausau, WI	1	5
19382	West Chester, PA	Philadelphia, PA-NJ	10	10
50325	West Des Moines–Clive, IA	Des Moines, IA	3	6
47906	West Lafayette, IN	Lafayette, IN	4	4
36695	West Mobile, AL	Mobile, AL	5	5
10994	West Nyack, NY	New York, NY	10	10
33326	Weston, FL	Fort Lauderdale, FL	8	2
67212	Wichita (West), KS	Wichita, KS	3	8
22602	Winchester, VA	Winchester, VA-WV	5	5
95694	Winters, CA	Yolo, CA	6	3
17402	York, PA	York, PA	3	2

Primary sources: Sperling's BestPlaces, assorted trade associations, U.S. National Climatic Data Center

CLIMATE RATING	PHYSICAL SETTING SCORE	DOWNTOWN CORE SCORE	PERCENT OF COMMUTES < 30 MIN	PERCENT OF COMMUTES > 1 HOUR
6	6	7	52%	13%
5	2	8	53%	5%
3	3	5	60%	12%
5	5	6	43%	15%
3	3	8	39%	8%
5	8	8	77%	5%
5	4	5	51%	6%
1	3	7	79%	3%
10	4	2	47%	10%
1	6	7	84%	3%
8	7	6	88%	2%
4	5	5	69%	4%
8	7	10	82%	3%
1	4	4	89%	2%
5	3	3	82%	3%
7	6	3	42%	9%
10	3	1	37%	19%
3	6	7	41%	17%
2	2	4	75%	1%
2	4	8	88%	4%
3	7	8	81%	2%
0	4	4	45%	7%
6	1	3	38%	10%
7	3	4	75%	3%
8	3	2	47%	8%
8	7	8	66%	5%
6	6	4	61%	4%
2	3	4	77%	2%
2	5	6	85%	3%
6	4	7	60%	7%
3	3	4	86%	1%
7	3	4	88%	3%
6	3	3	58%	6%
8	3	7	50%	16%
8	4	5	44%	10%
6	2	2	82%	2%
8	5	7	67%	13%
9	6	5	57%	8%
3	4	4	77%	3%

TABLE A.9 HEALTH AND SAFETY
Metro Area Level Data
SORTED BY NEIGHBORHOOD

ZIP CODE	NEIGHBORHOOD	METRO AREA	VIOLENT CRIME RATE	CHANGE IN VIOLENT CRIME	PROPERTY CRIME RATE	CHANGE IN PROPERTY CRIME	AIR-QUALITY SCORE
79606	Abilene, TX	Abilene, TX	372	-20%	4213	-2%	44
87122	Albuquerque (SandiaHeights), NM	Albuquerque, NM	815	-23%	4903	-34%	23
99516	Anchorage, AK	Anchorage, AK	679	6%	4548	-1%	27
54911	Appleton, WI	Appleton-Oshkosh-Neenah, WI	93	0%	1952	-25%	47
19810	Arden-Brandywine, DE	Wilmington-Newark, DE-MD	606	129%	3323	-16%	33
76002	Arlington, TX	Fort Worth–Arlington, TX	437	-16%	4840	3%	20
78732	Austin (West), TX	Austin–San Marcos, TX	354	-11%	4382	-2%	28
98226	Bellingham, WA	Bellingham, WA	240	-19%	4936	-6%	33
18018	Bethlehem, PA	Allentown-Bethlehem-Easton, PA	250	-2%	2538	-19%	39
74012	Broken Arrow, OK	Tulsa, OK	634	-11%	4496	2%	26
27513	Cary, NC	Raleigh-Durham–Chapel Hill, NC	369	-34%	3522	-32%	37
80104	CastleRock, CO	Denver, CO	391	2%	4367	4%	26
22901	Charlottesville, VA	Charlottesville, VA	275	-36%	2253	-30%	66
01824	Chelmsford, MA	Boston, MA-NH-ME	327	-33%	1872	-17%	12
21045	Columbia, MD	Baltimore, MD	883	-17%	3818	-26%	37
65203	Columbia, MO	Columbia, MO	351	-2%	3272	-23%	44
52241	Coralville, IA	Iowa City, IA	394	-28%	2653	-20%	49
15108	Coraopolis–MoonTownship, PA	Pittsburgh, PA	360	16%	2408	0%	29
53532	DeForest, WI	Madison, WI	222	-29%	2932	-15%	25
80220	Denver (ParkHill), CO	Denver, CO	391	2%	4367	4%	26
83616	Eagle, ID	Boise City, ID	287	-7%	3458	-15%	28
11730	EastIslip, NY	Nassau-Suffolk, NY	197	18%	1845	-20%	14
68022	Elkhorn, NE	Omaha, NE-IA	447	-44%	4809	2%	39
97405	Eugene, OR	Eugene, OR	263	-32%	5022	-18%	15
45241	Evendale, OH	Cincinnati, OH-KY-IN	383	9%	4135	3%	38
58104	Fargo, ND	Fargo, ND	100	-29%	2481	-16%	42
37922	Farragut, TN	Knoxville, TN	514	-18%	3974	-6%	45
75028	FlowerMound, TX	Dallas, TX	653	-10%	5208	0%	19
95630	Folsom, CA	Sacramento, CA	505	-14%	4226	-10%	23
37064	Franklin, TN	Nashville, TN	845	-14%	4480	-24%	42
80526	Fort Collins–Loveland, CO	Fort Collins–Loveland, CO	261	-12%	3441	-5%	34
32605	Gainesville, FL	Gainesville, FL	857	-31%	4396	-47%	37
20878	Gaithersburg, MD	Washington, DC-MD-VA-WV	548	4%	3572	-10%	41
14068	Getzville, NY	Buffalo–Niagara Falls, NY	448	-4%	2958	-15%	15
97526	Grants Pass, OR	Josephine County	54	-53%	1196	-41%	35
54313	Green Bay, WI	Green Bay, WI	199	37%	2566	-27%	33
29650	Greer, SC	Greenville-Spartanburg-Anderson, SC	606	-27%	3682	-18%	34
20170	Herndon, VA	Washington, DC-MD-VA-WV	548	4%	3572	-10%	41
43026	Hilliard, OH	Columbus, OH	465	-6%	5210	-11%	35
37343	Hixson, TN	Chattanooga, TN-GA	599	-24%	4616	3%	44
78232	Hollywood Park, TX	SanAntonio, TX	485	13%	5716	0%	16
49426	Hudsonville, MI	Grand Rapids–Muskegon-Holland, MI	453	-3%	3154	-14%	31
29212	Irmo, SC	Columbia, SC	859	1%	4784	-11%	26
84037	Kaysville, UT	Salt Lake City–Ogden, UT	363	-4%	5577	-4%	23
08824	Kendall Park, NJ	Middlesex-Somerset-Hunterdon, NJ	195	-9%	2020	-18%	33
60047	Lake Zurich, IL	Chicago, IL	631	-41%	3452	-24%	16
55044	Lakeville, MN	Minneapolis–St. Paul, MN-WI	327	-18%	3453	-20%	35
17601	Lancaster, PA	Lancaster, PA	230	12%	2362	-14%	20
66049	Lawrence, KS	Lawrence, KS	412	26%	4925	6%	40
40503	Lexington, KY	Lexington, KY	361	-19%	4064	-5%	52
07039	Livingston, NJ	Newark, NJ	450	-33%	2824	-21%	33
84321	Logan, UT	Logan, UT	63	60%	1804	102%	48
92354	Loma Linda, CA	Riverside–San Bernardino, CA	544	-16%	3691	-3%	12
80027	Louisville, CO	Boulder-Longmont, CO	302	7%	3285	-25%	35
35758	Madison, AL	Huntsville, AL	354	-22%	3955	-1%	36
28105	Matthews-Stallings, NC	Charlotte-Gastonia–Rock Hill, NC-SC	740	-22%	5137	-10%	35
43537	Maumee, OH	Toledo, OH	540	-1%	5103	-6%	37
89423	Minden-Gardnerville, NV	Douglas County	168	35%	2412	8%	60
98273	Mount Vernon, WA	Mount Vernon-Anacortes, WA	86	109%	1832	21%	43
98275	Mukilteo, WA	Seattle-Bellevue-Everett,WA	410	-6%	5049	-13%	11

WATER-QUALITY SCORE	POLLEN/ALLERGY SCORE	STRESS SCORE	CANCER MORTALITY PER CAPITA	PHYSICIANS PER CAPITA	PEDIATRICIANS PER CAPITA	HOSPITAL BEDS PER CAPITA	TEACHING HOSPITALS	HEALTHCARE COST INDEX	COST PER DOCTOR VISIT	COST PER DENTAL VISIT	HOSPITAL COST PER DAY
100	78	7	151.3	218	13	495	0	93	$70	$55	$625
49	74	86	153.6	245	26	301	4	107	$99	$97	$724
49	57	97	170.2	283	25	270	1	159	$106	$104	$985
31	30	9	160	198	14	318	3	102	$82	$66	$438
21	45	65	187.7	212	33	346	5	111	$67	$83	$785
91	87	87	173	147	15	227	4	100	$73	$59	$658
82	76	56	154	185	20	212	3	106	$77	$69	$622
60	48	83	153.2	218	15	122	0	119	$78	$81	$624
46	59	20	174.9	238	16	441	6	103	$62	$75	$887
62	72	74	172	209	20	328	6	99	$100	$59	$670
86	65	45	161.2	290	50	352	6	105	$86	$80	$515
88	85	70	152.8	228	26	251	18	126	$96	$77	$979
74	63	38	159.1	479	80	543	1	99	$86	$70	$634
44	44	46	184.6	98	12	401	0	125	$98	$87	$997
50	65	71	194.7	294	39	494	18	96	$79	$73	$750
60	55	18	154.4	473	58	859	2	94	$74	$56	$750
73	46	18	156.7	594	108	861	2	92	$73	$55	$712
50	73	61	185.2	263	27	535	18	93	$65	$61	$781
48	34	23	155.1	337	45	359	3	105	$75	$72	$612
88	85	70	152.8	228	26	251	18	126	$96	$77	$979
24	45	53	148.9	203	13	236	3	112	$76	$68	$714
60	62	4	190.4	359	49	473	20	164	$79	$76	$1,639
58	50	29	176	237	34	513	7	98	$80	$59	$610
60	64	98	160.2	215	16	206	0	122	$82	$72	$723
32	60	86	191	229	43	286	10	95	$65	$66	$682
47	30	0	158.1	241	16	319	2	98	$79	$62	$693
62	61	59	164.4	256	23	409	1	89	$71	$55	$621
82	87	94	166.4	179	20	264	17	108	$72	$72	$789
46	74	78	179.4	191	20	211	7	150	$74	$87	$2,249
77	68	82	162.8	251	32	432	5	82	$69	$52	$335
100	78	21	133.3	192	12	189	1	108	$75	$62	$994
45	68	61	175.6	469	79	587	2	90	$71	$75	$788
51	69	43	176.8	273	36	242	20	111	$92	$70	$531
65	57	28	190.8	225	30	674	10	105	$61	$90	$826
65	58	85	175.2	149	8	252	0	113	$75	$70	$708
24	28	27	162.3	212	19	419	2	101	$86	$87	$729
49	56	66	161.7	192	20	312	3	96	$79	$60	$636
51	69	43	176.8	273	36	242	20	111	$92	$70	$531
44	57	65	180.7	220	31	318	10	97	$67	$62	$632
61	64	62	171.7	225	26	600	3	88	$85	$49	$746
74	94	79	164.1	228	28	349	9	88	$70	$63	$692
36	49	53	164.8	180	20	284	6	96	$69	$67	$510
56	65	50	166.7	243	26	465	2	93	$71	$83	$533
65	60	64	132.5	193	27	261	8	90	$72	$77	$631
25	62	5	194.3	261	38	299	7	117	$66	$83	$4,440
38	58	77	183.4	220	28	327	57	115	$88	$67	$1,437
27	47	35	163.2	202	23	272	16	130	$87	$97	$1,442
20	53	3	160.7	169	9	238	2	93	$62	$72	$790
45	74	7	141.5	173	8	177	0	92	$69	$59	$649
61	62	51	169.3	292	39	568	4	98	$69	$70	$674
21	63	42	187	266	37	476	16	119	$69	$83	$3,360
47	60	64	135.2	146	14	186	0	90	$60	$56	$678
49	51	68	164.2	120	13	202	9	127	$70	$82	$1,484
100	83	48	136.5	297	24	183	1	118	$75	$73	$987
9	67	36	162	235	19	439	1	90	$59	$53	$731
65	68	73	163.9	184	18	261	5	101	$90	$71	$614
22	53	84	179.8	241	29	528	7	100	$73	$51	$679
30	63	80	175.2	145	2	0	0	121	$70	$89	$990
52	48	91	165.7	233	14	259	0	118	$78	$85	$683
56	48	98	170.3	265	26	191	9	126	$84	$93	$702

continues

			VIOLENT CRIME RATE	CHANGE IN VIOLENT CRIME	PROPERTY CRIME RATE	CHANGE IN PROPERTY CRIME	AIR-QUALITY SCORE
TABLE A.9 HEALTH AND SAFETY (continued) Metro Area Level Data							
SORTED BY NEIGHBORHOOD							
ZIP CODE	NEIGHBORHOOD	METRO AREA					
03062	Nashua, NH	Nashua, NH	127	38%	2028	-12%	28
06470	Newtown, CT	Danbury, CT	107	-15%	1592	-25%	30
46060	Noblesville, IN	Indianapolis, IN	548	-21%	3938	-1%	37
02760	North Attleboro, MA	Providence-Fall River-Warwick, RI-MA	362	16%	2854	-12%	40
07648	Norwood, NJ	Bergen-Passaic, NJ	243	-7%	2057	-17%	24
60302	Oak Park, IL	Chicago, IL	631	-41%	3452	-24%	16
98501	Olympia, WA	Olympia, WA	263	9%	3385	-14%	40
32073	Orange Park, FL	Jacksonville, FL	755	-21%	4564	-19%	25
14534	Pittsford, NY	Rochester, NY	293	4%	3377	-7%	43
92688	Rancho Santa Margarita, CA	Orange County, CA	277	-21%	2464	-9%	2
57702	Rapid City, SD	Rapid City, SD	345	-2%	3806	-31%	45
89523	Reno, NV	Reno, NV	517	16%	4518	2%	33
23233	Richmond-Tuckahoe, VA	Richmond-Petersburg, VA	411	-19%	3922	-15%	59
24018	Roanoke, VA	Roanoke, VA	340	0%	2835	-12%	66
55902	Rochester, MN	Rochester, MN	196	-26%	2372	-9%	44
72758	Rogers, AR	Fayetteville-Springdale-Rogers, AR	241	-3%	2762	-13%	39
30075	Roswell, GA	Atlanta, GA	513	-29%	4320	-23%	32
91354	Santa Clarita, CA	Los Angeles–Long Beach, CA	854	-16%	3101	-6%	1
02067	Sharon, MA	Boston, MA-NH-ME	692	54%	2936	12%	20
66216	Shawnee, KS	Kansas City, MO-KS	751	-13%	5413	-5%	34
53044	Sheboygan, WI	Sheboygan, WI	98	-32%	2954	-7%	42
99223	Spokane, WA	Spokane, WA	382	-31%	5543	-14%	25
63304	St Charles, MO	St. Louis, MO-IL	476	-37%	3902	-19%	31
77479	Sugar Land, TX	Houston, TX	739	-1%	4359	-2%	8
75791	Tyler, TX	Tyler, TX	661	29%	4252	-12%	27
33594	Valrico, FL	Tampa–St. Petersburg–Clearwater, FL	864	54%	4908	5%	17
98607	Vancouver-Camas, WA	Portland-Vancouver, OR-WA	361	-36%	4960	-4%	26
23456	Virginia Beach, VA	Norfolk–Virginia Beach–Newport News, VA-NC	438	-5%	3809	-14%	67
53186	Waukesha, WI	Milwaukee-Waukesha, WI	417	-12%	3922	-8%	28
54403	Wausau, WI	Wausau, WI	155	24%	2359	-3%	41
19382	West Chester, PA	Philadelphia, PA-NJ	609	-8%	2837	-24%	24
50325	West Des Moines–Clive, IA	Des Moines, IA	253	-19%	3962	-14%	45
47906	West Lafayette, IN	Lafayette, IN	211	-22%	3191	-13%	51
36695	West Mobile, AL	Mobile, AL	558	0%	5749	12%	21
10994	West Nyack, NY	New York, NY	617	-41%	2154	-32%	21
33326	Weston, FL	Fort Lauderdale, FL	524	-20%	3476	-28%	8
67212	Wichita (West), KS	Wichita, KS	471	-2%	4414	-15%	26
22602	Winchester, VA	Winchester, VA-WV	112	8%	2035	-8%	58
95694	Winters, CA	Yolo, CA	468	-35%	3511	-3%	43
17402	York, PA	York, PA	195	-29%	2289	-23%	20

Primary sources: Federal Bureau of Investigation, National Centers for Disease Control, U.S. Environmental Protection Agency, American Medical Association

WATER-QUALITY SCORE	POLLEN/ ALLERGY SCORE	STRESS SCORE	CANCER MORTALITY PER CAPITA	PHYSICIANS PER CAPITA	PEDIATRICIANS PER CAPITA	HOSPITAL BEDS PER CAPITA	TEACHING HOSPITALS	HEALTHCARE COST INDEX	COST PER DOCTOR VISIT	COST PER DENTAL VISIT	HOSPITAL COST PER DAY
60	52	31	190.1	177	22	251	1	112	$82	$78	$1,013
39	55	7	177.1	250	28	180	1	149	$78	$90	$1,248
15	73	75	178.2	244	33	374	9	99	$76	$62	$625
50	61	38	188	246	34	353	9	135	$100	$76	$1,023
34	62	13	188.5	327	45	381	4	145	$66	$80	$3,408
38	58	77	183.4	220	28	327	57	115	$88	$67	$1,437
50	47	90	167.7	215	13	200	1	127	$74	$95	$1,107
27	65	91	188.9	224	24	274	6	88	$56	$59	$561
54	67	43	171.5	231	36	469	7	102	$67	$83	$1,322
65	45	31	166.3	232	25	269	7	120	$91	$77	$1,549
42	52	5	158.9	288	13	406	1	92	$62	$65	$697
40	63	72	180.7	239	16	306	1	117	$69	$89	$963
80	66	50	177.8	241	30	576	4	90	$77	$68	$598
85	53	33	157	329	20	747	2	94	$76	$53	$480
20	46	1	151.5	1083	91	963	2	113	$98	$66	$991
66	57	16	150.2	156	11	353	3	92	$76	$60	$588
51	63	82	166.2	188	23	249	11	104	$70	$66	$677
52	42	72	168	203	23	313	48	119	$70	$72	$1,301
30	67	36	184.1	377	52	450	36	127	$65	$77	$997
36	74	89	164	215	29	414	15	96	$76	$61	$1,028
20	37	3	160.1	151	12	312	0	101	$93	$66	$589
38	42	96	163.8	243	15	376	3	119	$74	$113	$734
45	68	92	179.9	225	30	474	18	103	$71	$67	$646
41	70	91	175.9	186	25	313	19	106	$78	$64	$689
87	76	37	169.3	318	17	488	2	93	$83	$63	$961
46	86	91	169.7	223	21	411	11	99	$80	$66	$843
53	36	99	164.8	228	22	194	8	122	$93	$73	$708
71	69	39	185.9	217	26	332	11	93	$76	$87	$660
26	42	66	177.5	259	30	366	14	98	$78	$82	$516
50	36	3	158.3	210	12	491	1	108	$95	$53	$533
8	66	66	188.6	291	35	415	51	105	$72	$86	$1,809
60	40	25	172.6	223	23	390	5	107	$72	$58	$752
36	66	10	170.9	180	17	438	0	94	$75	$64	$684
62	70	98	186	195	24	469	5	87	$54	$51	$357
44	63	50	186.4	281	45	476	64	177	$84	$86	$1,818
50	49	83	163.9	212	22	422	7	117	$83	$78	$745
41	58	52	162.3	190	16	425	4	100	$69	$79	$843
55	65	55	171.6	121	2	652	1	86	$62	$73	$650
47	74	40	176.9	252	30	95	1	156	$72	$81	$1,430
40	47	31	168.6	162	9	216	2	91	$62	$56	$440

TABLE A.10 HEALTH AND SAFETY
Neighborhood Level Data

SORTED BY NEIGHBORHOOD

ZIP CODE	NEIGHBORHOOD	METRO AREA
79606	Abilene, TX	Abilene, TX
87122	Albuquerque (Sandia Heights), NM	Albuquerque, NM
99516	Anchorage, AK	Anchorage, AK
54911	Appleton, WI	Appleton-Oshkosh-Neenah, WI
19810	Arden-Brandywine, DE	Wilmington-Newark, DE-MD
76002	Arlington, TX	Fort Worth–Arlington, TX
78732	Austin (West), TX	Austin–San Marcos, TX
98226	Bellingham, WA	Bellingham, WA
18018	Bethlehem, PA	Allentown-Bethlehem-Easton, PA
74012	Broken Arrow, OK	Tulsa, OK
27513	Cary, NC	Raleigh-Durham–Chapel Hill, NC
80104	Castle Rock, CO	Denver, CO
22901	Charlottesville, VA	Charlottesville, VA
01824	Chelmsford, MA	Boston, MA-NH-ME
21045	Columbia, MD	Baltimore, MD
65203	Columbia, MO	Columbia, MO
52241	Coralville, IA	Iowa City, IA
15108	Coraopolis–Moon Township, PA	Pittsburgh, PA
53532	DeForest, WI	Madison, WI
80220	Denver (Park Hill), CO	Denver, CO
83616	Eagle, ID	Boise City, ID
11730	East Islip, NY	Nassau-Suffolk, NY
68022	Elkhorn, NE	Omaha, NE-IA
97405	Eugene, OR	Eugene, OR
45241	Evendale, OH	Cincinnati, OH-KY-IN
58104	Fargo, ND	Fargo, ND
37922	Farragut, TN	Knoxville, TN
75028	Flower Mound, TX	Dallas, TX
95630	Folsom, CA	Sacramento, CA
37064	Franklin, TN	Nashville, TN
80526	Fort Collins–Loveland, CO	Fort Collins–Loveland, CO
32605	Gainesville, FL	Gainesville, FL
20878	Gaithersburg, MD	Washington, DC-MD-VA-WV
14068	Getzville, NY	Buffalo–Niagara Falls, NY
97526	Grants Pass, OR	Josephine County
54313	Green Bay, WI	Green Bay, WI
29650	Greer, SC	Greenville-Spartanburg-Anderson, SC
20170	Herndon, VA	Washington, DC-MD-VA-WV
43026	Hilliard, OH	Columbus, OH
37343	Hixson, TN	Chattanooga, TN-GA
78232	Hollywood Park, TX	San Antonio, TX
49426	Hudsonville, MI	Grand Rapids–Muskegon-Holland, MI
29212	Irmo, SC	Columbia, SC
84037	Kaysville, UT	Salt Lake City–Ogden, UT
08824	Kendall Park, NJ	Middlesex-Somerset-Hunterdon, NJ
60047	Lake Zurich, IL	Chicago, IL
55044	Lakeville, MN	Minneapolis–St. Paul, MN-WI
17601	Lancaster, PA	Lancaster, PA
66049	Lawrence, KS	Lawrence, KS
40503	Lexington, KY	Lexington, KY
07039	Livingston, NJ	Newark, NJ
84321	Logan, UT	Logan, UT
92354	Loma Linda, CA	Riverside–San Bernardino, CA
80027	Louisville, CO	Boulder-Longmont, CO
35758	Madison, AL	Huntsville, AL
28105	Matthews-Stallings, NC	Charlotte-Gastonia–Rock Hill, NC-SC
43537	Maumee, OH	Toledo, OH
89423	Minden-Gardnerville, NV	Douglas County
98273	Mount Vernon, WA	Mount Vernon–Anacortes, WA
98275	Mukilteo, WA	Seattle-Bellevue-Everett, WA
03062	Nashua, NH	Nashua, NH
06470	Newtown, CT	Danbury, CT

HEALTH RATING	STRESS SCORE	CAP INDEX VIOLENT CRIME RISK	CAP INDEX PROPERTY CRIME RISK
6	7	80	89
3	86	36	44
2	97	50	57
8	9	50	78
6	65	31	31
1	87	39	41
2	56	63	56
7	83	100	152
6	20	149	139
3	74	37	45
8	45	83	82
5	70	22	30
10	38	88	87
5	46	115	76
4	71	38	34
7	18	72	74
10	18	109	103
5	61	32	50
10	23	31	71
5	70	178	100
5	53	82	112
4	4	102	57
7	29	17	32
5	98	100	117
1	86	106	54
9	0	37	51
8	59	34	55
1	94	48	70
0	78	34	33
7	82	66	94
7	21	81	102
7	61	205	189
3	43	58	48
5	28	42	48
3	85	117	161
8	27	43	78
7	66	75	93
3	43	83	77
3	65	30	37
8	62	33	64
0	79	63	46
4	53	37	76
10	50	35	42
2	64	36	61
2	5	25	32
1	77	29	31
4	35	24	35
3	3	85	88
4	7	88	75
8	51	109	86
2	42	38	41
5	64	80	97
1	68	279	233
8	48	36	47
4	36	88	55
4	73	26	41
4	84	72	71
2	80	40	58
5	91	94	114
5	98	49	64
3	31	29	33
3	7	20	23

continues

TABLE A.10 HEALTH AND SAFETY (continued)
Neighborhood Level Data

SORTED BY NEIGHBORHOOD

ZIP CODE	NEIGHBORHOOD	METRO AREA
46060	Noblesville, IN	Indianapolis, IN
02760	North Attleboro, MA	Providence–Fall River–Warwick, RI-MA
07648	Norwood, NJ	Bergen-Passaic, NJ
60302	Oak Park, IL	Chicago, IL
98501	Olympia, WA	Olympia, WA
32073	Orange Park, FL	Jacksonville, FL
14534	Pittsford, NY	Rochester, NY
92688	Rancho Santa Margarita, CA	Orange County, CA
57702	Rapid City, SD	Rapid City, SD
89523	Reno, NV	Reno, NV
23233	Richmond-Tuckahoe, VA	Richmond-Petersburg, VA
24018	Roanoke, VA	Roanoke, VA
55902	Rochester, MN	Rochester, MN
72758	Rogers, AR	Fayetteville-Springdale-Rogers, AR
30075	Roswell, GA	Atlanta, GA
91354	Santa Clarita, CA	Los Angeles–Long Beach, CA
02067	Sharon, MA	Boston, MA-NH-ME
66216	Shawnee, KS	Kansas City, MO-KS
53044	Sheboygan, WI	Sheboygan, WI
99223	Spokane, WA	Spokane, WA
63304	St Charles, MO	St. Louis, MO-IL
77479	Sugar Land, TX	Houston, TX
75791	Tyler, TX	Tyler, TX
33594	Valrico, FL	Tampa–St. Petersburg–Clearwater, FL
98607	Vancouver-Camas, WA	Portland-Vancouver, OR-WA
23456	Virginia Beach, VA	Norfolk–Virginia Beach–Newport News, VA-NC
53186	Waukesha, WI	Milwaukee-Waukesha, WI
54403	Wausau, WI	Wausau, WI
19382	West Chester, PA	Philadelphia, PA-NJ
50325	West Des Moines–Clive, IA	Des Moines, IA
47906	West Lafayette, IN	Lafayette, IN
36695	West Mobile, AL	Mobile, AL
10994	West Nyack, NY	New York, NY
33326	Weston, FL	Fort Lauderdale, FL
67212	Wichita (West), KS	Wichita, KS
22602	Winchester, VA	Winchester, VA-WV
95694	Winters, CA	Yolo, CA
17402	York, PA	York, PA

Primary sources: Federal Bureau of Investigation, National Centers for Disease Control, U.S. Environmental Protection Agency

HEALTH RATING	STRESS SCORE	CAP INDEX VIOLENT CRIME RISK	CAP INDEX PROPERTY CRIME RISK
1	75	29	57
2	38	38	54
3	13	39	49
1	77	531	143
6	90	97	125
1	91	49	63
4	43	22	34
4	31	23	30
7	5	64	102
3	72	168	158
8	50	31	31
10	33	52	57
10	1	77	117
8	16	63	87
3	82	29	32
0	72	47	52
3	36	19	23
3	89	33	43
9	3	66	105
7	96	140	108
5	92	22	35
0	91	282	152
6	37	68	87
5	91	49	65
7	99	70	95
2	39	38	55
5	66	73	112
9	3	114	179
2	66	82	83
8	25	49	85
1	10	86	95
2	98	65	92
3	50	73	61
7	83	46	48
4	52	62	52
6	55	70	148
0	40	131	141
6	31	63	64

Best Places by Name

Index

Best Places by Region

Best Places by State

Best Places by Neighborhood Type

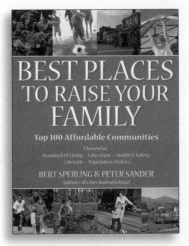

Visit Sperling's BestPlaces at **www.bestplaces.net** and join to receive your FREE membership today.

Photo: ©Brett Patterson

"I've spent much of my life learning about cities and towns, but there's always more to know. That's why I'm inviting you to share your insights with me and others on our Web site, **www.bestplaces.net**. You'll receive a free membership to the BestPlaces community, where you can read about cities and towns all over the United States and conduct your own research using our latest data. I hope I'll be reading your comments soon!"

—BERT SPERLING, bestselling author of *Cities Ranked & Rated*

Sperling's BestPlaces is your best resource for:

- Information on hundreds of metro areas
- City and neighborhood profiles
- Cost of living indices and Salary Calculator
- Details on 130,000 public and private schools
- Reading and posting members' comments
- A "Find Your Best Place" online quiz

Don't miss BestPlaces in print:

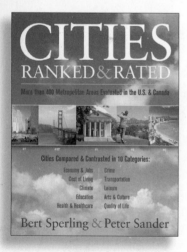

Cities Ranked & Rated
The latest facts and figures on 400 best places to live in North America.

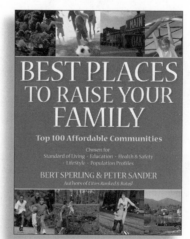

Best Places to Raise Your Family
Data and expert insights on 100 top places to raise a family in the United States today.

WILEY
Now you know.
wiley.com